Charles R. Gallagher, David I. Kertzer,
Alberto Melloni (Eds.)

Pius XI and America

CHRISTIANITY AND HISTORY

Series of the John XXIII Foundation
for Religious Studies in Bologna

edited by

† Prof. Dr. Dr. h.c. mult. Giuseppe Alberigo
Prof. Dr. Alberto Melloni

(Fondazione per le scienze religiose Giovanni XXIII, Bologna)

Volume 11

LIT

Pius XI and America

Proceedings of the
Brown University Conference
(Providence, October 2010)

edited by

Charles R. Gallagher,
David I. Kertzer,
Alberto Melloni

LIT

Cover Picture: Pius XI by Teresa Valdaliso Casanova

Realizzato con il contributo del PRIN 2008 "I nodi storici degli Anni 20-30 negli archivi vaticani: ordine internazionale, democrazie e totalitarismi nella chiesa di Pio XI".

Bibliographic information published by the Deutsche Nationalbibliothek
The Deutsche Nationalbibliothek lists this publication in the Deutsche Nationalbibliografie; detailed bibliographic data are available in the Internet at http://dnb.d-nb.de.

ISBN 978-3-643-90146-0

A catalogue record for this book is available from the British Library

©LIT VERLAG GmbH & Co. KG Wien,
Zweigniederlassung Zürich 2012
Klosbachstr. 107
CH-8032 Zürich
Tel. +41 (0) 44-251 75 05
Fax +41 (0) 44-251 75 06
e-Mail: zuerich@lit-verlag.ch
http://www.lit-verlag.ch

LIT VERLAG Dr. W. Hopf
Berlin 2012
Fresnostr. 2
D-48159 Münster
Tel. +49 (0) 2 51-620 320
Fax +49 (0) 2 51-23 19 72
e-Mail: lit@lit-verlag.de
http://www.lit-verlag.de

Distribution:
In Germany: LIT Verlag Fresnostr. 2, D-48159 Münster
Tel. +49 (0) 2 51-620 32 22, Fax +49 (0) 2 51-922 60 99, e-mail: vertrieb@lit-verlag.de

In Austria: Medienlogistik Pichler-ÖBZ, e-mail: mlo@medien-logistik.at
In Switzerland: B + M Buch- und Medienvertrieb, e-mail: order@buch-medien.ch
In the UK: Global Book Marketing, e-mail: mo@centralbooks.com
In North America: International Specialized Book Services, e-mail: orders@isbs.com

Contents

Vatican Transnationalism

Pius XI and the Racial Laws

ROMANO PRODI

Foreword

1. The Two Europes

The object of research of the scholars gathered here for this congress, and in the newly created network linking Bologna, Münster, and Rome, is Europe between the two World Wars, the Europe of Pius XI and his diplomacy, and the Europe of the generations shaped by the ferocity of totalitarian regimes. It is vital to know the historical events and great policy directions of that Europe since it was in the total reversal of those directions that the other Europe was born, the one that, from the Second World War to the fall of the Berlin Wall, has fortunately gone in the opposite direction.

During the period between 1918 and 1938, the twenty years between the two World Wars, Europe saw the logic of rearmament as a means of emerging from an economic crisis and experienced the tragic development of nationalisms. This convergence of rearmament and nationalism saw nations as protagonists, and often cultures and ideologies as well, each becoming armed identities facing off against one another.

This giant convergence led to a conflict which no politician and no politics was able to govern. Evidently, neither totalitarianisms nor democracies understood where Europe was headed; neither France nor Great Britain had a political class capable of interpreting the climate. There was a lack of common intentions, which are the force that allows politics to fight against degenerative processes. Europe was kept prisoner by a framework which, from the end of World War One to the crisis of 1929, laid the foundations for those policies of public and military spending which in Germany and Italy became the tools par excellence of the formation of an ill-conceived and violent consensus.

The Europe that emerged from the rubble of that world, the Europe we would like to see today as an active participant on the international scene,

---

* Opening lecture given in Münster and Brown as forewords to the Pius XI research.

as an important force for internal development, as a promoter of research in which ethical and political themes are not at all marginal or less – the Europe that emerged from the Second World War moved in a direction opposite to that of the continent between the Wars. When Adenauer, De Gasperi and Schumann spoke together in German, without the aid of translators, they had a clear plan for Europe, even if it was not yet formalised or complete. Their aim was to avoid War at all cost, to build peace. All three men had strong religious roots. Was it a coincidence? Maybe. But all three found in religion harmony of the fundamental principles of peace and human coexistence.

Paradoxically, even the division of Europe and the Soviet threat strengthened this common intent rather than making it waver: the memory of the War, of the tragedy of the Thirties, of the dictatorships, was so alive in the European soul that it pushed that generation, which had witnessed its own impotence, to find in collaboration, economic development, and peace the strength to tie the continent together. They formed a political class which interpreted and guided a profound impulse that originated from below. It was so deep that even the Cold War and the division of Germany became unifying factors rather than disaggregating agents.

After the Second World War this plan experienced some interruptions, prey to hesitations and nationalistic insurgencies, but overall continued to progress, overcoming obstacles, until finally leading to the creation of the Euro. The adoption of a continental currency was an historic miracle without precedents. Never before in the history of humankind had a state voluntarily renounced one of its fundamental pillars, a national currency. We must, however, recognize that as the War progressively became a distant memory, and particularly after the fall of the Berlin Wall, the great spirit of concord and convergence has receded and been increasingly replaced by an idea of Europe as a sum of conveniences to be negotiated through repeated compromises until the latest compromise was reached: the Lisbon Treaty. It is certainly better than nothing (woe if it had not been ratified), but it is also the suspension of a project conceived in the hopes of a better future. Just a few years ago, during the Commission over which I presided, the Euro and the expansion of the European Union signified a continuation of that great historical design which represented a response to each and every one of the great political and cultural pressures that had destroyed Europe between 1918 and 1938. Today, the distance from that project has increased, making the writing of a new European project more difficult.

Paradoxically, the fact that Europe is perceived by everyone, by the populace and by special interests, as something to be taken for granted, almost a bureaucratic fact of life from which there is no turning back, does not help. We know that the great economic interests that are always at the base of dictatorial pressures are less dangerous today, as they are regulated and weakened in a larger European space (it is not an accident that the founding fathers came from these industries, from steel and coal). The elimination of the custom-houses, the establishment of common economic rules, and the Euro itself, do not allow nationalisms to be the driving force of European politics anymore. And this is also the reason why we are witnessing the recovery of populist forces on a national scale and the radicalisation of local «ethnicisms» which support localized racisms that have become part of the foundation of populism.

What damages Europe today is the triumph of the short political period, working in concert with a very short electoral cycle. Indeed, there are many political leaders who understand what the general interest is, but they prefer, when dealing with the European, national, regional, or municipal electoral deadlines, the path of populism and localism. In some countries such a tendency has developed in a traditional way, such as the conservative party in Great Britain, in others it takes on new shapes such as LePenism, the Northern League, and so on: all this creates an insurmountable obstacle to the construction of unified European policy.

These tendencies introduce in the European market and in political opinions a factor which, in the Europe of the interwar period, the Europe of dictatorships and of catastrophe, was dangerously decisive: the element of fear. Today the catalysts of fear are globalisation and the enormous upheavals of migration, and not, as commonly thought terrorism. Terrorism can be controlled by introducing rational security measures. Immigration by contrast enters the sphere of the irrational, of fears about daily life and the future.

It is a delicate issue since we know that after the First World War it was in soil nourished by the fears of veterans and fears of the economic crisis that anti-Semitism grew and the logic that led to the Holocaust was set on its course. As far as the question of comparing that experience with anti-Semitism and the current fear of the immigrant, as well as the conscience expressed by the Church then and now, I do not know what the answer is and I leave it to you to study these issues. I would simply like to point out that every time Europe stands at an important crossroads, the Church has a great and extraordinary responsibility.

2. The Catholic Formation

I briefly mentioned Adenauer, Schumann, and De Gasperi, members of a generation that grew up during the pontificate of Pius XI and in an atmosphere in which not even the Church understood that the deal offered by totalitarian regimes – anticommunism in exchange for dictatorships – was a tragic deception. Moreover, I have mentioned the fact that a type of faith and a religious sensibility gives dictatorships something in common with the Church, even though, when dictators give concreteness to their idea of Europe, they do not expect (and they do not receive) ecclesiastic approval.

This is an important point I need to highlight since – I say this as a former student of the Università Cattolica of Milan – I was educated in time to participate in a school that formed consciousnesses prepared to respond to situations and choices with a great sense of responsibility despite personal risk. We were trained to respond with a mature mentality that was one of the key points of our Catholic upbringing.

At the same time, however, a conscience without a political outlet remains private: if we had not had an idea of Europe, sooner or later the appearance of other interests would have made us regress. Moreover, the objective of avoiding the tragedies of war over time becomes impossible if suitable political instruments are not built.

The strength of the generation which came out of the war was the result of its association of a solid spiritual structure with a political idea which allowed – for the first time since the fall of the Roman Empire – three generations to be born who have not known war. The recomposition of all our nations in a single European project has worked: this is something we cannot deny. We have had the historical counterproof in Yugoslavia, where a leader's death and the collapse of a system have brought civil war, something which has not happened in any member State of the European Union.

Thus, we may criticize the present impasse, but the situation is today infinitely better than what it might have been. This does not, however, diminish the need for leaders who try to combine the interest of their country with that of Europe as a whole. I remember Helmut Kohl saying, «many of my citizens are against the Euro, but I want the Euro because, after the fall of the Berlin wall, it must be clear that we do not want another German Europe but a European Germany». This is leadership. During my first Government I myself launched a provocative message by proposing a tax for Europe, in order to render explicit the fact that if Italy had not had the capacity to enter into the Euro zone paying the necessary price, it would have remained a slave of historic vices and imbalances.

What seems clear today is that every country looks at Europe so as to maximise its own gain: a legitimate objective only when compatible with the progress of Europe as such.

It is in this context that religious experience can reveal itself as a useful resource of general utility: the particularly universalist sensibility of Christianity, which places nationalisms and identity politics in their proper light, can help everyone to lay down common rules for a life in which all can live in freedom and reciprocal responsibility.

3. The Value of Historical Knowledge

All this is a simple introduction to the work that you are engaged in by studying the diplomatic formations of Pius XII and the phases of government of Pius XI. From my point of view as a European politician, I see it as a useful call to the challenge which lies before us and that we still have not faced. That is to say, the teaching of European history to Europeans: a history which is still taught today from an old perspective both in its analyses and its judgments.

The lack of a common vision on a political and cultural level does not expose Europe to the risk of fascist involutions but to the risk of irrelevance: an irrelevance which, on a symbolic level, has become evident when, during the celebrations for the fall of the Berlin wall, President Obama was not in Berlin but in China. This did not happen as a consequence of a political clash between Europe and the United States but because of the Babel of European positions which deprived the American President of a single interlocutor with whom to discuss and confront the past. As a matter of fact, today's Europe does not have a common vision such as the one carried by the previous generation, the one which spoke in German of a European future, fully aware that there are moments in history which occur only once.

That vision, which has generated today's world, is in need of new foundations: an effort to construct a common economic policy, a common foreign policy, and an end to the necessity of unanimity in fundamental decisions regarding our future, along with the possibility of leaving the Union for those who do not accept its objectives and prevent the others from carrying out common projects.

Being together can be easy or difficult no matter what the number of the states. Having been President of the EU when it had 15 and 25 members, I may say that the difficulties remain the same whether the members are 15 or 25. I say this fully aware that my speech is characterised by a basic naïveté, a willing historical naïveté which lies in thinking that today's Europe still has a shared goal, an authentic common sensibility. In reality, fears dominate.

In order that countries not be consumed by fear they all must make a choice: either to stay within the Union aware that it is an entity which must evolve and grow, or to withdraw from the European Union itself. You cannot be a member of the Union only to serve as a constraining force.

If the «no» vote in the Irish referendum does not produce any effect on the Irish people, it is clear that the next vote will be an irresponsible one. However, if the referendum asked: «Do you want to move ahead together with the entirety of Europe or do you want to leave this federal pact?». I do believe that eventually, in order not to lose the great advantages of the Union, even the most difficult choices must be faced. I also believe that, as happened just after the First World War when democracies without any overarching plan surrendered to dictatorships, without any plan we will finally surrender to fear today, too.

4. Looking for what Unifies

I was born in 1939. During my adolescence, reconstruction, hope, everything was called Europe. For a Catholic boy, the expectation of an enduring European peace overlapped with the trust in the brotherhood of nations, leading to a spontaneous sense of hope which was at the same time all-encompassing and never questioned.

Indeed, thanks to that strength and that shared trust, even communism appeared to my generation as an external and extraneous fact. When confronted with communism, some of us chose a pure and exclusive form of anticommunism. On a political level, though, not even anticommunism succeeded in definitively dividing Europe: the fact that after the fall of the communist regimes Europe felt that its natural harmony had been restored can be thus explained.

The simple and radically anti-communist option was justified and seemed almost obvious during the period of the Cold War. However, it is a typical Italian paradox that the «strongest» and «purest» anticommunism affirmed itself only after the definitive death of communism. But maybe it is not a paradox since the «strongest» and «purest» anticommunism is also based on the idea that fear is a unifying element.

Nonetheless, as was said by the Nunzio in Italy, Mgr. Giuseppe Bertello (eyewitness to the genocide in Rwanda before coming to Rome), he who sows fears soon loses the ability to control them.

Obviously, besides its ideological aspects, the market of fear is today fuelled by other factors that I have mentioned earlier and that are channelled through a system of mass media which is the only system that has not been Europeanized. The media are still national. There are of course the great world networks, but they are all American. Debate and information in Europe are still confined by national borders and dominated by national questions. Only rarely does one look to the horizons which unify and generate hope. The attempts made towards European information networks have failed, probably due to linguistic reasons. The Middle Ages were unified by the possibility of preaching in Latin; the first Europeanism, as I said at the beginning, was constituted while speaking German at a window. Sooner or later English will eventually come to be the new European Latin, but this has not happened yet and information remains weighed down by a fragmented representation which leaves more space for incomprehension and fear.

In this context the Churches have a great opportunity to provide an ethically unifying boost, to encourage aspirations toward peace in a pluralistic society in which the capacity to mediate – which is the heart of politics – is valued within a broader vision and a far longer time span. The Catholic Church in particular has a specific vocation which derives from the fact that some of its children have been the protagonists of that season of convergence which gave this continent a lasting peace, never known before.

In doing so, the European episcopate has succeeded in different ways. Think of the way in which John Paul II sustained the process of unification and enlargement, managing to read in the bloodless collapse of the communist regimes something which involved his entire Church. Think of the German episcopate which has maintained an open dialogue with the other Germany and has supported the choices of chancellor Kohl, taking a long term view whose symbol has been Cardinal Lehmann. I remember with gratitude the continuous and enriching collaboration of the German Episcopal Conference during all the years of my Presidency at the European Commission, aimed at strengthening the ethical and spiritual principles of the Union. In addition I would cite the effort of Cardinal Martini to create an ecumenical structure of European bishops, and the positive role played in this by Cardinals Daneels and Lustiger.

Of course, not everyone wanted to share this project based on dialogue and mediation. I encountered significant difficulties during my government activities when the President of the Italian Episcopal Conference, Cardinal Camillo Ruini, forcing the concept of non-negotiability of principles, hampered with great political ability all possibility of mediation on certain themes concerning which wise mediation is absolutely necessary for a civil society and for the complete application of the principles themselves. I am also personally convinced that dialogue renders the message of the Gospel more fruitful.

The Churches know more than others that the crux, the future of politics is a wise cultural mediation: the ability to find dynamic points of equilibrium which, without compromising and confusing principles, values, and convictions, looks at a pluralistic society as a gift. Thus, everyone, being a part of his own conscious and joyful, observing and modest religious family, should understand that his place is as a member of a pluralistic society that attempts to adapt itself in different ways and in different shapes according to necessity, in this way making the pursuit of the common good easier.

If this development comes from internal resources, fine: otherwise it will come from elsewhere, because Europe must go ahead and it will go ahead. I do not hope that the necessary stimulus will come from a serious crisis, but I feel I can say that if there is not a push to go ahead, then a crisis could become the propelling impulse to start a political project capable of catalysing economic, intellectual, and spiritual energies, a project strongly centred on a pluralism that arouses people's emotion and hope so as to oppose those projects that play on fears and emphasize identities that divide people.

In the years between the two Wars nationalism was nourished by the illusion of Europe's centrality: the economic and military power of the United States was largely undervalued. The great European project of the second half of the twentieth century is instead based on the understanding that the complexity of the world itself – today increased by the definitive emergence of China, by the transfer of the centre of power to the Pacific area, and by the impossibility of keeping African living conditions subhuman for generations – needs a unifying message.

Today Europe does not have the centrality it once had, but, above all, it lacks a unifying message to propose, except for a banally populist one. Populism diminishes Europe's authority in the eyes of the world and makes it irrelevant even in those areas (such as, for example, the Middle East) which are nearby. But this critical situation can open new opportunities, thus demonstrating that we need to change our mentality and to be able to pay a serious price in terms of recognition of the other. The Church can teach us this new mentality by using a positive pedagogical method, which knows when to say no and how to guide a society in tumultuous transformation. Today we are no longer the centre of the world. Therefore, we must be able to think of words of peace and we must be able to say words of peace at the right time, because to everything there is a season and also a time that is too late.

5. Conclusion

Here are some contributions to your discussion that I hope will show you how much one expects from research such as yours, which concerns a starting point in the process of European unification and whose consequences reach us, and which I hope will find the support it deserves from those who direct the research policies of the Union today.

For a long time, the European system as well as the great national agencies have had few instruments to invest in these fields of research as they were worried that financing something in which the word «religious» appeared could lead to forms of direct or indirect discrimination and would endanger the impartiality of the institutions of the Union. Initiatives like this one can help the decision-making bodies to better distinguish between the level of dialogue with the religious communities as such – with their lists of issues and their well established modes of practice – and the level of historical knowledge of the life and relationships of those communities in the broader European context. The formation of a generation of scholars studying these facts and processes constitutes an opportunity in which Europe must invest.

CHARLES R. GALLAGHER

Introduction

In our discussions on «Pius XI, the Americas, and the Vatican», we are fortunate enough to have under our consideration, papers which both provide us with exciting new information, but also, I believe, will compel historians not only to reassess various issues of papal diplomacy and culture in the 1930's, but also to place the new information into the general matrix of how we write about the pontificate of Pope Pius XI. I believe that all of our papers will not only force changes in the way historians view the topical episodes offered by our authors, but also will create shifts in how the larger history of papal policy during this era is written in the future.

When this conference was called about a year ago, I was teaching at a diplomatic training school in Switzerland. Surrounded by practitioners of diplomacy who were mainly invigorated by present and future concerns, when I explained that our conference was on the topic, «Pius XI and America», many of my colleagues expressed some skepticism that Pope Pius XI had much at all, if anything at all, to do with America. For them, Pius XI was merely the Pope who stood firm against the rise of totalitarianism and exercised a fighting spirit doing so – and he was often contrasted with his successor. To my friends in Geneva, connecting Pius XI, a Pope who had never even visited the United States, to causal events bearing on the United States, seemed shaky at best.

But our papers today have proved my Genevois diplomatic colleagues wrong. In fact, all our presenters have provided excellent discovery and analysis of what diplomats usually should know all along – that surface events and press reports hardly tell the entire story. We are grateful to the Holy See for opening its archives in 2006 so that our panelists, armed with excellent professional historical skills, might be allowed to uncover a history which is not only papal, but political, cultural, economic, and global. A recounting, in part, of «Pius XI in America».

In this regard, the paper by Lucia Ceci casts bright new light on the role of the United States and the Vatican in arguably the first «modern» invasion of the Fascist era. Ceci has highlighted what seems to be the first attempt since the World War I era to engage the Holy See and the United States in a joint effort for peace. As Domenico Tardini's statements indicate, the legacy of Wilson's dismissal of the Holy See as a bargaining power after World War I still loomed large in the eyes of the Vatican. But by 1935, Pius XI was willing at least to have conversations about working jointly with the United States to settle the Ethiopian crisis in favor of peace. In its larger context, I think the demarche by the Holy See showed two immediate effects, namely that FDR had not changed his mind from the original calculus of the Wilson years – that is, to spurn Vatican peace efforts placing the Holy See on equal footing as a moral personality.

And secondly, there was a new development – the Holy See now would access the President directly not necessarily through its own Apostolic Delegate exclusively, but through the offices of the National Catholic Welfare Conference and its president. (A situation which would last through the early Cold War).

Ceci's paper is provocative in many ways. First, she shows that Vatican initiatives to seek joint US-Vatican arbitration of the Ethiopian War started *at the Vatican*, and were not designed in concert. She shows, as well, that economic pressures were certainly driving Vatican concerns for peace.

But the largest question, I think, is raised by Ceci's opening observations and closing remarks. One of the biggest questions that this new research has opened up is precisely its connection to the Vatican policy of «absolute impartiality» – as distinct from neutrality – and how this delicately calibrated policy shaped the behind-the-scenes moves with the US, and more importantly, the public stand of the Pope Pius XI (in what could be construed as *silence*) in the face of, as Ceci states: «Italian aggression on a sovereign state, conducted through the use of chemical weapons banned by international treaties, and which caused, among military and civilians, more than 300,000 Ethiopian deaths».

One small thread which is common to all papers on this topic is the mention of the place of Father Charles E. Coughlin, the Radio Priest of Detroit. In our second paper, Father Gerald P. Fogarty looks at the international dimensions of the Coughlin phenomenon and points out the challenges and struggles for church leaders inside the Vatican as they attempted to come to terms with the new medium of radio. Among other things, what Fogarty shows in his paper, is that Coughlin was an international problem for the Holy See long before he entered his «anti-Semitic phase» in November of 1938. This is all new and ground-breaking work, since the standard biographies of Coughlin have tended to concentrate on his domestic policies and activities. The paper is important not only because Coughlin was the first priest to «use his pulpit» for political discourses, but also (I would argue) because Coughlin was the first Catholic to generate enough power to capture a national audience and, more importantly, *shape* the country's political conversation. This was a point of deep pride among many American Catholics – who themselves were the product of decades of Catholic «Americanization».

Although focused on its early phases, Fogarty's paper shows for the first time that Vatican officials were concerned with Coughlin's use of the radio and his political and doctrinal positions as early as 1934 – and at the highest levels. What is a real contribution here is that Fogarty shows that the Holy See deferred to Coughlin, or was perhaps fearful of Coughlin precisely because he had attained such a huge following – and that this attitude prevailed not only around the Dome of St. Peter's but in America as well. This is important because the same level of fears, inertia, and trepidation would cause paralysis on the Coughlin issue later in 1938, once his anti-Semitic phase was engaged. In other words, the first instincts of both Coughlin's local and Vatican handlers were shaped as early as 1934 – and prevailed for another eight years.

If radio technology played a role in spreading Coughlin's brand of Catholicism, the technology of the Airplane helped to speed Cardinal Pacelli around the US during his extended visit to the US in 1936. The conversations between Pacelli and Franklin Roosevelt are some of the most elusive and important of the 1930's. They are elusive because a complete transcription of the 1936 conversations between the President and the future Pontiff of World War II has yet to be found. D'Alessio investigates with clarity why the original meeting was postponed – but the larger question might be why Pacelli was sent in the first place? Was the cross-country itinerary a long thought out junket or a spontaneous reaction to plans not well thought-out?

What *is* new are revelations about Francis Cardinal Spellman's assiduous work to get full ambassadorial relations started between the United States and the Holy See. Spellman's recommendations for how the relationship should move forward, his end-runs around the Apostolic Delegate, and collusion with Joseph P. Kennedy all show a prelate who was fixated with the visit of Pacelli moving the question of full diplomatic relations forward. For example, I find it out of character for Spellman, who had worked in the Holy See's diplomatic corps, to suggest that a

US-Vatican position be «sub-compartmentalized» into an existing ambassadorship (that to the Kingdom of Italy).

Moreover, it does not seem that the ASV contains a copy of the memorandum from Spellman sent to Roosevelt, and it is unclear whether this memo exists at the FDRL. D'Alessio has provided a bird's-eye view of the complexities and mechanics at play regarding the famous Pacelli visit in 1936. There was clear unity of opinion on issues of peace and refugee work. One question which emerges, is: if Roosevelt was presenting such a cheery face to American Catholics during and after Pacelli's visit, why did he wait until 1940 to create the position Myron Taylor would hold?

Giulia D'Alessio's paper gives us an inside view of the mechanics present at the creation of the Myron Taylor representation – the US-Vatican nexus was to be a parallel endeavor for peace. But parallel lines never intersect, and our next paper points out, in 1937, the United States government took an aloof posture in dealing with some off-the-cuff remarks by George Cardinal Mundelein.

Monsignor Robert Trisco has written a study of the incident where Hitler was described by the American Cardinal as an «Austrian paperhanger, and a poor one at that». Trisco's paper provides a fascinating look at diplomatic crisis management inside the Vatican. For the first time, we see both the gravity and the scope of the episode. We see that the comments in Chicago had clear ramifications for both principals and their policies. Trisco provides a comprehensive and captivating account of all that went on in deliberating over next steps – all of it new, and all of it important.

That the issue was brought for consultation before the Sacred Congregation for Extraordinary Ecclesiastical Affairs is new information, and suggests the gravity of the matter. Trisco's chronicling of the inner ideas and impressions of the Cardinals of the Congregation attests to the disparate views of the case. That the Pope weighed-in on the final decision is also new.

The back and forth between Pacelli and Deigo von Bergen is a key battle, but it was played out within the backdrop of many larger tussles. These larger issues compel us to ask what this sort of diplomatic brinkmanship was really all about. Was the Mundelein affair really a battle over the ongoing Morality Trials, which, if analyzed minutely, Pope Pius XI may have minutely conceded (in terms of the morality of some)? Was it a battle over the papal encyclical on Germany *Mit Brennender Sorge*? Was it a battle over the status of the Concordat? And was the Concordat, as shaky as it was, ever in jeopardy of being pulled?

Or was this an internal struggle over who would control the political statements coming out from the walls of the Vatican. It is clear that Cardinal Pacelli takes center stage here. It is Pacelli who is tasked with gathering both evidence and recommendations. While Pacelli emerges as the second-highest creator of policy, we must ask where this episode stands with regard to the larger questions? At every turn, Pacelli's primary concern was the reaction of the German side. This observation brings up other issues about both Pacelli and Pius XI – when Pius XI indicated that if there was any *harshness in Pacelli's writing*, – it set the tone for how Pius XI operated in terms of his view of righteousness, the Allies, and America.

Pius XI, the United States and the Vatican

MARISA PATULLI TRYTHALL

Pius XI and American Pragmatism*

«Decretum de Episcopalibus conventibus in Fœderatis Americæ Statibus mos novissime inductus fuerat...»[1]. So begins the decree, deliberated by

---

ACRONIMS: ASV = Archivum Secretum Vaticanum; ARA = American Relief Administration; CIC = Codex Iuris Canonici; CNEWA: Catholic Near East Welfare Association; EAWP = Edmund Aloysius Walsh Papers; GUSCRCC = Georgetown University Special Collections Research Center; NCWC = National Catholic Welfare Council; SCEO = Sacra Congregatio pro Ecclesia Orientali; WWI = WWI.

* «The inextricably American character of the pragmatism of such figures as C.S. Peirce and William James lies in its often understated affirmation of America as a uniquely religious country with a God-given mission and populated by God-fearing citizens». M.G. HAMNER, *American Pragmatism: A Religious Genealogy*, Front Cover. «Pragmatism is perhaps America's most distinctive contribution to philosophy. Developed by Peirce, Dewey, and James in the late nineteenth and early twentieth centuries, pragmatism holds that both the meaning and the truth of any idea is a function of its practical outcome. The pragmatists rejected all forms of absolutism and insisted that all principles be regarded as working hypotheses that must bear fruit in lived experience. [...] The phrase «American Pragmatism» has a double meaning since both the school of philosophy and the average American seems more interested in getting things done and the result of action rather than abstract theories which do not inspire action. [...] The original tenet of pragmatism according to Charles Sanders Peirce: "Think about what the truth of statements means in terms of action, or what the consequences of truth are". William James' view of pragmatism: "If something is true it is useful, and if it isn't useful, then talking about its truth doesn't make sense"». J. McDERMOTT, Distinguished Professor of Philosophy and Humanities, Texas A&M University, 2006, http://www.philosophytalk.org/pastShows/Pragmatism.html – Stanford University.

[1] The decree, written in Latin by the Sacred Consistorial Congregation (AES, POS. 172 P.O., Fasc. 14, 1010) is translated thusly in *Never Look Back: The Career and Concerns of John J. Burke*, ed. by J.B. SHEERIN, 67-680: «A decree on Episcopal Gatherings in the United States. In the United States of America, the custom has recently arisen that all diocesan ordinaries assemble, even from outlying provinces, to treat some matters which seemed to require assembled deliberation. Furthermore, in order to settle other matters which may occur during the year they have determined to establish a certain committee of bishops called the NCWC. But now, because circumstances have changed, some bishops in their own name and that of others have decided that the

the Sacred Consistorial Congregation (Sacra Congregazione Concistoria-le) during their meeting of February 23, 1922[2], which called for the disso-lution of the National Catholic Welfare Council[3]. This decree was one of the very first acts of *internal* politics, but with a character of international

---

procedure and this establishment is no longer needful or useful; so they have asked the Holy See that steps be taken. When, therefore, by direction of the Holy Father, Pope Pius XI, this matter was taken up in the full committee of the Sacred Consistorial Con-gregation, on February 23 of this year, the eminent Fathers decided that the rule of the common law be wholly re-established, and therefore, such general gatherings be not held anymore, except for reasons reviewed and approved by the Holy See in each case, in keeping with Canon 281 of the Code. Likewise, the eminent Fathers have cited that the office and activity of the above NCWC committee should cease, and what is laid down about conferences and provincial councils in Chapter VII of Book II of the Code and in the decree of the Congregation of July 25, 1916, be observed. The Holy Father sustained and confirmed this decision and ordered that it be made known through the Apostolic Delegate to all the Ordinaries of the United States of America. Given at Rome, in the Office of the Consistorial Congregation, February 25, 1922. C. Cardinal De Lai, Bishop of Sabina, Secretary; A. Sincero, Assessor».

[2] The Sacred Consistorial Congregation met on February 23, 1922, and the decree, ap-proved by the newly appointed Pope, Pius XI, and signed by Cardinal Gaetano De Lai (1853-1928), Secretary of the Congregation and by the Assessor of the Congregation, Aloisius (Luigi) Sincero (1870-1936), the future Secretary of the Congregation for the Oriental Churches, was published on February 25, 1922.

[3] The United States' entry into WWI (April 6, 1917) motivated the clergy of the Ameri-can Catholic Church – concerned about possible exclusion from the national war effort and desiring to demonstrate both Catholic national loyalty and organizational capac-ity – to form the «National Catholic War Council». Founded in 1917 at the Catholic University of America (CUA) in Washington DC, the Council gave voice to the needs of the soldiers at the front, organized Catholic funded aid programs in war zones and helped assure the Americanization of new immigrants. Following the war, it also backed the development of the Program for the Social Reconstruction of American Society. The organization descended from the plenary meetings held by American bishops in Baltimore in 1852, 1866 and 1884 and was led by American bishops who directed the various internal committees. The contribution of the NCWC was recog-nized by the US War Department in August of 1918 and, as an official aid agency of the government, it participated in the United War Work Campaign of 1918. The NCWC received 36 million dollars of government funds to be applied towards war aid. Most of these funds were managed by the Knights of Columbus and by units of the NCWC posted abroad. The Committee on Special War Activities (CSWA) was organized by the NCWC to administer these funds. The head of the Committee was John J. Burke, CSP (a Paulist Father), who functioned as a liaison with the government committee for Training Activities and the Morale Division of the US War Department. A year fol-lowing the armistice of November 1918, the NCWC was converted into a permanent organization. The American bishops voted to create the National Catholic Welfare Council on September 24, 1919, and, three months later, this organization took over the preceding organization maintaining its headquarters in Washington, DC.

significance, approved by Pope Pius XI shortly after his election to the throne of Saint Peter[4]. The text made direct reference to several grievances which had been brought against the NCWC and brought to the attention of the Vatican: perplexities as to both the enormous size of the organization and, above all, as to a presumed tendency toward «Gallicanism»: the notion that national customs might trump Roman (Catholic Church) regulations[5]. It was objected that, given the renewed cultural climate following WWI, the presence of such a large, complex organization, originally formed to give visibility to the Catholic Americans' contribution to WWI and subsequently transformed by the American bishops into a sort of permanent assembly of a supra-diocesan nature[6], was neither necessary or advisable.

---

[4] Pius XI, born Ambrogio Damiano Achille Ratti (May 31, 1857 – February 10, 1939), was elected on February 6, 1922.

[5] Professor J. McGREEVY (University of Notre Dame, IN) defines *Gallicanism* in his *Catholicism and American Freedom*, New York 2003, 26.

[6] The text of Canon 281, inserted in the Code of Canon Law in 1917, in Book II (The People of God), Section II (Particular Churches and Their Groupings), Title VII (Supreme Power), Chapter VII (Plenary and Provincial Councils) reads thusly: «Ordinarii plurium provinciarum ecclesiasticarum in Concilium plenarium convenire possunt, petita tamen venia a Romano Pontifice, qui suum Legatum designat ad Concilium convocandum eique praesidendum». («Several Ordinaries of ecclesiastical provinces *can convene* a plenary Council, *having come with a petition to the Roman Pontiff, who will designate his Legate to convoke and preside over the Council»* – [author's emphasis]). *The 1917 Pio-Benedictine Code of Canon Law*, San Francisco 2001, 118. It is clear from these few lines that the faculty of convening a Council as contemplated by Canon 281 is only a possibility. It is something out of the ordinary which is subordinated to the presentation of a petition to the Pope (i.e. an extraordinary appeal to the Supreme Pontiff), who, in turn, designates a Legate who will convoke the Council, for and on behalf of the Pope himself, and who will preside over it. It is, therefore, evident that the reasons for convoking such a Council, as described in the petition, have the character of an unusual exception to the normal practice, so much so as to require that a Papal delegate preside over the Council in his place. As we will read later, the NCWC's defense was principally centered on the fact that Benedict XV had favorably accepted the creation of a Catholic agency to interconnect with the American Government (the National Catholic *War* Council [author's emphasis]) during the war years. This favorable acceptance was interpreted by the National Catholic *Welfare* Council (author's emphasis) as approval and ratification of the actions which then led to the creation of this new organization, overlooking, however, the fact that the National Catholic War Council had been formed to confront truly exceptional conditions and tasks – among others, bringing aid to the distraught populations caught in World War I (of particular importance to Benedict XV). Apart from whatever might have been Cardinal O'Connell's motivations in bringing his reservations with regard to the new NCWC before the Holy See, his criticism, in the light of the dictates of the Code of Canon Law, were correct

These perplexities had been forcefully expressed to the Vatican by Cardinal William O'Connell of Boston[7] who protested against both the new, post-war form of the NCWC and the expansion of its area of intervention which, according to him, was a menace to the independence of the bishops themselves. In truth, of course, Cardinal O'Connell had already given proof of his own curial astuteness, as well as of American pragmatism, when he, according to one observer, intentionally selected relatively slow transport to journey to Italy for the conclave called to select the successor to Pope Benedict XV in 1922. By arriving too late to participate in the conclave, he underlined both the insufficient amount of time allowed for Cardinals, living at a distance from Rome, to reach Rome after being informed of the Pope's death and the increased importance of the American participation in the conclave. Nor was Cardinal O'Connell's protest made in vain: Pius XI prolonged the intervening period by a week, thereby facilitating the presence of Cardinals coming from distant geographical locations in the future: «Pius Says Conclave Must Wait for US; Pope Tells Cardinal O'Connell America Is Too Important to Be Ignored as in Past. Audience Lasts An Hour. Pontiff Says This Government's Respect for Religion Merits All That Religion Can Give It»[8].

This is the «New York Times» (NYT) headline announcing Pius XI's decision to extend the interim waiting period. Cardinal O'Connell was received in a papal audience, while Cardinal Dennis Joseph Dougherty[9]

---

and well-founded (as, for that matter, was the decision of the Prefect of the Sacred Consistorial Congregation, Cardinal De Lai). Cardinal O'Connell maintained that the reasons motivating this second Catholic organization – with an identical acronym but with completely different functions – were implausible. Furthermore, there was no urgent or extraordinary condition which warranted such an organization. In fact, the two organizations, at that moment, co-existed. It is informative to note that Canon 281 was reformulated in the CIC of 1983: «§1. A plenary council for all the particular Churches of the same Bishops' Conference *is to be celebrated* as often as the Bishops' Conference, *with the approval of the Apostolic See, considers it necessary or advantageous*». In his commentary on Canon 439 (ex 281), Eloy Tejero makes specific reference to the case of Church assemblies within the United States of America. *Exegetical Commentary on the Code of Canon Law*, Vol. II/1, Chicago 2004, 961-967.

[7] William Henry O'Connell (December 8, 1859 – April 22, 1944), Archbishop of Boston from 1907 to 1944.

[8] Rome, February 28 (Associated Press): «New York Times», March 1, 1922.

[9] For a detailed report of the relations between Cardinal O'Connell, Cardinal Dougherty and the NCWC see G.P. Fogarty, *The Vatican and the American Hierarchy: From 1870 to 1965*, Stuttgart 1982, 214-236.

from Philadelphia, whose arrival was also delayed, was given the news of the Vatican's decree disbanding the NCWC.

The brief NYT article continues supplying us with an interesting insight into what was said and done by Cardinal O'Connell, the Vatican and the NCWC at this point. The headline already reveals a certain nationalistic rhetoric and the article continues dispensing words of «do-goodery» which, as we will see, had little to do with the actual state of affairs:

«Cardinal O'Connell then told the Holy Father of the relations between the Catholics and Protestants in America and how both co-operate in the social and economic life. He said that no enmity existed between the members of the two faiths and that when a good and noble work was to be done both united for the common good. The Pontiff, hearing the Boston Cardinal's words, seemed deeply moved. He said: "I like that. It is a great advantage. It makes for peace and harmony everywhere: America is truly wonderful and full of hope and promise. My prayer is that the Catholics of America will continue to be united in the bonds of brotherly affection. Let the hierarchy stand together for all that is best in human life"».

The situation, however, was not as idyllic as described in the NYT article or, for that matter, by Cardinal O'Connell: neither with regard to the relations between the Catholics and the Protestants nor, in particular, with regard to the relations within the hierarchy of the American Catholic Church itself – as the Vatican's almost simultaneous decree disbanding the NCWC testified.

Let us concentrate our attention on this latter issue, and on the reactions addressed to Pius XI by the American bishops who were opposed to the dissolution of the NCWC, by first taking a step backwards to examine a letter sent by the Paulist[10] Father John J. Burke, General Secretary of the NCWC, to Mgr. Francesco Borgongini Duca, Pro-Secretary of the Congregation of Extraordinary Ecclesiastical Affairs, to explain the scope and actions of the

---

[10] The Paulist Fathers, or Missionary Society of Saint Paul the Apostle, or Congregation of St. Paul, were founded in New York City in 1858 by Servants of God: Fr. Isaac Thomas Hecker, Fr. George Deshon, Fr. Augustine Hewit, and Fr. Francis A. Baker – all of whom had converted to Catholicism and subsequently left the Congregation of the Most Holy Redeemer (Redemptorists). Being the first community of priests to arise in the United States, it had a markedly American character, particularly in the area of organization and administration, but also with regard to its utilization of all means of communication to spread the Gospel. The first goal of the Paulists, in fact, was the evangelization of North America – developed above all in the United States with some presence in Canada.

NCWC. The letter, dated February 18, 1922[11], and accompanied by various publications of the NCWC, confirms the fact that there was already a certain attention in Rome towards the activities of the NCWC – an attention which went beyond the accusations raised by Cardinal O'Connell:

«Dear and Most Reverend Archbishop:
The National Catholic Welfare Council of the United States, organized in answer to a letter of the late Benedict Fifteenth, is composed of the entire Hierarchy of the United States, who work through an Administrative Committee of Bishops, elected by them.
Under the direction of this Committee are several departments which include in their province every field of Catholic activity. The National Catholic Welfare Council is, therefore, the united Catholic body – bishops, priests, laymen – working together as one, united for the welfare of the Catholic Church in the United States.
Under separate cover we are mailing you a number of pamphlets which will inform Your Grace of the organization and the work so far accomplished of the departments of the National Catholic Welfare Council. Before the establishment of this Council, there was no definite and united Catholic influence in our public life. The Council has both added to the prestige of our Holy Church and has aroused a spirit of zeal and co-operation among our Catholic people which was never equaled. The Council is the united Catholic people of the United States, working together and directed by their appointed ecclesiastical leaders on a general programme of religious, social and educational activities.
Your interest in our country and in the part which opportunity permits it to take in advancing the welfare of our Holy Church leads us to send you this literature, which we trust will be of service to you in evaluating this great movement in our Catholic American life.
Asking Your blessing and with sentiments of deepest esteem, I remain,
Your obedient servant in Christ,
John J. Burke, C.S.P., General Secretary».

Thus is the description of the NCWC as supplied by one of its founders. It is interesting to compare this description by Fr. Burke with the following undated and unsigned report, written in English and intended for the Pope's personal consideration:

«Ad Usum Summi Pontificis
In my opinion, the central and original idea of the National Catholic Welfare Council is good. There is need of a national organization to protect the Church and public morality from anti-Catholic and anti-Christian legislation. This can best be done by an association that is empowered to speak with the collective voice of the Catholics of the United States.

---

[11] AES, POS. 172 P.O., Fasc. 14, Nord America, Prot. 1068, 55.

However the powers and scope of such an organization should be carefully defined by supreme authority. Moreover great care should be exercised in the means employed to accomplish the ends of the organization and in the persons chosen to put those means into effect. The present National Welfare Council has undertaken work which it should never have touched and it has employed persons unfit for this work. Thus, for instance, it has founded a National Training School for Social Workers, an entirely unnecessary institution in view of the fact that good training schools for social workers already existed. It has also begun to institute correspondence courses for educational purposes, an affair that should be left to our colleges. Then too, it has not been wise in the choice of its employees. Thus the chief layman in the educational department was educated not in Catholic but in secular schools. As a consequence he sent out last year a letter which directly contradicted the syllabus of Pius IX. Again, the lady in charge of the National Training School for Social Workers has uttered entirely wrong ideas about the norm of morality.

In view of all conditions I most respectfully suggest:

1. That the American Hierarchy be represented in Washington by an association which will act for them, under their direction, in time of crises;

2. That the scope of this association and the means to be employed in attaining an object be clearly defined by competent authority, care being taken to safeguard the liberty of each Bishop in his own diocese;

3. That no document be issued without previous censorship and approval by a directive council of Bishops chosen by the Hierarchy;

4. A) That in defining the scope of the association special stress be laid on non-interference with societies – such as the Knights of Columbus – and works already existing; B) That work peculiar to colleges be left to colleges and not undertaken by the association»[12].

It can be presumed that this text was written by Cardinal O'Connell and was brought to the attention of the Pope and of the Consistorial Congregation by Cardinal Rafael Merry del Val y Zulueta, a long time friend of Cardinal O'Connell. This analysis is, to the aforementioned NYT article, much like the distorted image from a deformed mirror to the image it reflects. One can not avoid noticing, immediately, that the author is a person who is considered reliable, so much so that he offers his own opinion as a relevant factor in the decision to be taken. Above all, however, one notices that the analysis made by the author is aimed at protecting his own specific interests from any possible external interference (talk about *Gallicanism* or *Americanism*!).

Another step in the correspondence which follows the issuance of the decree and precedes the response of the Administrative Committee of the NCWC contains, considering the situation, a similar surprise. On March

---

[12] *Ibidem*, 53-54.

31, 1922, Mgr. Francesco Borgongini Duca responded to Father Burke's letter in the following manner:

> «Illustrious Sir,
> In acknowledgement of the fine letter written by Your Most Reverend Eminence on February 18ᵗʰ of this year, I hasten to inform you that I always receive the pamphlets published by the NCWC with real gratitude and that I read them with great interest.
> I am happy to take this occasion to send you my highest congratulations for the actions carried out under the direction of NCWC's Episcopal Committee and I fervently pray for the prosperous success of all the initiatives undertaken for the good of the Church in that noble America»[13].

Finally, on April 6, 1922, while meeting in Cleveland, the seven members of NCWC's Administrative Committee[14] telegrammed the Pope imploring suspension of the decree and its non-publication in the *Acta Apostolicae Sedis*:

> «His Holiness, Pope Pius XI,
> The Vatican,
> Rome, Italy.
> We, the Administrative Committee of Bishops, elected by the United States Hierarchy, which is the National Catholic Welfare Council, have met today.
> We receive with supreme reverence the decree of the Consistorial Congregation dated February 25, regarding National Catholic Welfare Council. Legal and business obligations make it imperative to continue work. It is necessary to carry on important religious and charitable works begun publicly under approbation of the late Pontiff, Benedict XV. Officially obligated to United States Government to carry on immigration and Russian relief work. Sudden suspension of all these now would cause grave public scandal.
> We therefore reverently and earnestly implore a suspension of the decree and its non-publication in Acta and permission to continue work until full report of these obligations and of character and extent of work be sent to the Holy See.
> Secular newspaper reports of condemnation have already caused consternation among Catholics, and renewed at once attack of Masonic sect on Holy See and on the Church, and encouraged endeavor in Federal Congress to push through at once legislation that would imperil our Catholic School System.

---

[13] AES, POS. 172 P.O., Fasc. 14, Nord America, Prot. 1068, 56.

[14] The Administrative Committee was composed of: Edward J. Hanna, Archbishop of St. Francisco; Peter J. Muldoon, Bishop of Rockford; Augustin Dowling, Archbishop of St. Paul; Joseph Schrembs, Bishop of Cleveland; William T. Russell, Bishop of Charleston; Edmund F. Gibbons, Bishop of Albany and Louis S. Walsh, Bishop of Portland.

We humbly implore an early reply so we may know how to act. We implore it the more earnestly because the present critical situation: certain most harmful consequences which we foresee and the necessity of immediately allaying distress of Catholic body seem to us to make it most desirable. Begging the special blessing of Your Holiness on us, your devoted servants, and requesting that the reply be sent to Bishop Schrembs, Cleveland, Ohio, where we are in session»[15].

On April 8, Bishop Schrembs of Cleveland, received a telegram of response from the Secretary of State, Pietro Cardinal Gasparri: «Decree will not be published in Acta. Fuller information will shortly be given by Apostolic Delegate [Archbishop John Bonzano, ndr]»[16]. The telegram to the Pope, however, was only the first act of the organic, detailed response which the Administrative Committee carried out in order to save the NCWC from disbandment. On April 25, 1922, there was a meeting in Washington of the Board of Trustees of the Catholic University of America[17]. Two different documents emerged from this meeting: one was a petition in Latin which was addressed to the Pope on April 26[18] (signed by the Board of Trustees) and the second was a letter which was sent to all of the Archbishops and bishops of the United States on April 29, 1922. In this latter letter[19], the recipients were requested to give formal adhesion

---

[15] AES, America, POS. 172 P.O., Fasc. 14, *National Catholic Welfare Council*, 57r-57v.

[16] *Ibidem*, 57v.

[17] Three members of the Board of Trustees were also members of NCWC's Administrative Committee [Archbishop Dowling, Bishop Muldoon and Archbishop Hanna] and nine others were members of the NCWC: John J. Glennon, Archbishop of St. Louis; Henry K. Moeller, Bishop of Cincinnati; George W. Mundelein, Archbishop of Chicago; John W. Shaw, Archbishop of New Orleans; Patrick J. Hayes, Archbishop of New York; Michael J. Curley, Archbishop of Baltimore; Thomas F. Lillis, Bishop of Kansas City; John J. Nilan, Bishop of Hartford, and Thomas J. Shahan, Bishop of Germanopolis and Rector of the American Catholic University. The foundation of the Catholic University (1887) was decided in Baltimore in 1884, during the third plenary meeting of the American bishops, and was authorized by Pope Leo XIII.

[18] AES, America, POS. 172 P.O., Fasc. 14, *National Catholic Welfare Council*, 49v-50r-50v; 57v-58r.

[19] «Your Lordship: Wishing to keep you fully informed of the action which we, as your Administrative Committee, have taken with regard to the decree of the Consistorial Congregation, dated February 25, we send you the enclosed cablegram and letter. We have personally interviewed His Eminence, the Apostolic Delegate, and acquainted him with the action we had taken; but no further word from the Holy Father has as yet reached him. After a meeting of the Board of Trustees of the Catholic University, the Archbishops and bishops present drew up and signed a petition to the Holy Father, which we herewith enclose and to which we earnestly hope you will give your signature. We feel that it is most important for the welfare of the Church that we show una-

to the petition against the disbandment of the NCWC (signed by the Administrative Committee) by signing an accompanying card, preprinted in Latin, and returning it in the stamped and addressed envelope which was provided. This material was then sent to Rome as additional support of the petition[20].

The bishops' response to the NCWC's appeal was nearly unanimous: 11 Archbishops, 63 bishops and 7 Auxiliary or titular bishops – for a total of 73 out of the 107 Episcopal seats in the United States – signed and returned their card. Additionally, it was further observed that 6 bishops were away from their seats, 3 bishops had not yet taken control of their assigned seats and several others were invalids, thereby reducing the number of possible responses to 85. Missing from the appeal were, most certainly, Cardinal O'Connell, Cardinal Dougherty and Archbishop James Keane of Dubuque.

The text of the lengthy report[21] attached to the petition, underwritten by the American bishops and sent to the Pope, however, was much more articulate than the brief card in Latin which had been sent to the bishops. The bishops were, in fact, asked only for their adhesion to the request for suspension of the dissolution of the NCWC, in a show of support for the NCWC's Administrative Committee. Fortified by the almost total adhesion to the request for suspension of the decree, the Committee met in Washington and drafted a long letter to the Pope. Several interesting points emerged in this document among which was the marked conflict of the NCWC hierarchy with Cardinals Dougherty and O'Connell. The letter, however, reveals much more than that: under the well calibrated, apparently meek and submissive words used to address the newly elected Pope, there is a clear show of strength – reinforced, as it was, by the quasi-unanimous support expressed by the American clergy.

It will be helpful at this point, in outlining the conflicting points of view presented to the Vatican, to cite Cardinal O'Connell's note of May 10, 1922, to Cardinal Gaetano De Lai. The Cardinal, referring to the NCWC Administrative Committee's telegram of April 6 quoted previously, cau-

---

nimity of judgment in the matter of these petitions at the present time. We respectfully request you, "if you agree with our judgment", to send the separate enclosed memorial with your signature to Bishop Muldoon of Rockford, as soon as possible. We enclose an addressed and stamped envelope for that purpose. Fraternally yours, [signed by the Administrative Committee members]». AES, America, POS. 172 P.O., Fasc. 14, *National Catholic Welfare Council*, 57.

[20] AES, America, POS. 172 P.O., Fasc. 16.

[21] AES, America, POS. 172 P.O., Fasc. 15, 1-99.

tions the Secretary of the Consistory not to be intimidated by these concerted actions of the NCWC[22].

> «I hope and remain certain that Your Eminence and the other Roman authori-
> ties will not allow yourselves to be intimidated by this "bluff". The fact is that
> the telegram they sent to Card. Gasparri is nothing else than an attempt at in-
> timidation – by asserting certain phrases which are a long way from the truth.
> They speak in that telegram of the "consternation of America". The people
> feel no disturbance at all at the consequence of the decree, do not know that
> such a decree exists, and do not care at all. The consternation is found among
> those who have to render an account of the immense sums they have thrown
> away on huge salaries and futile and useless works».

In addition to the mobilization mounted by the Administrative Committee of the NCWC (which felt itself to be the primary target of the reservations expressed by the Consistorial decree) and the Secretary of the
NCWC (the Paulist Fr. Burke), one must add the direct action carried
out in Rome by the Bishop of Cleveland, Mgr. Joseph Schrembs. Bishop
Schrembs, in Rome on an *ad limina* visit, took the occasion to request a
special audience with Pius XI to plead the NCWC's cause[23].

Another point of reference in the literature connected with the NCWC
is the biography of Fr. John J. Burke, authored by the Paulist Fr. John
B. Sheerin[24] in 1975. Here the description of this historical period of the
NCWC is rather colorful and the tone of emphatic Apologia adopted by
Fr. Sheerin remains consonant, notwithstanding the difference of histori-
cal period, with the 99 page report which was presented to the Pope in
June of 1922 and which was published by the NCWC in what was literally
and metaphorically a «White book» (conserved in the Vatican Archives).
The following are a few quotes taken from Sheerin's book:

a. The inquisitorial research regarding who had caused the decree:
«The decree, at this time, prompted some amateur detective work and
much speculation as to who was the culprit and "who got Rome into this
mess"?»[25]. With consequent insinuations toward Cardinals O'Connell[26]

---

[22] G.P. FOGARTY, *The Vatican...*, 222-223, 21n, quotes AABo, May 10, 1922.

[23] Documentation regarding Schrembs' actions in Rome exist in the Secret Archives of
the Vatican as well as in NCWC publications.

[24] J.B. SHEERIN, *Never Look Back: The Career and Concerns of John J. Burke*, Mahwah,
NJ, 1975.

[25] *Ibidem*, 71.

[26] D.J. SLAWSON, in his book, *Ambition and Arrogance: Cardinal William O'Connell of
Boston and the American Catholic Church*, IX, depicts O'Connell thusly: «In 1913, the
bishops of New England began an eleven-year, on-again-off-again drive for the remov-

and Dougherty and their friends and correspondents in the Roman Curia, Cardinals De Lai and Merry Del Val.

b. Exhibition of force and national pride: «In the NCWC archives is a carbon copy of a letter from an unidentified correspondent (perhaps W.T. Russell) addressed "Dear Archbishop" and lamenting "Italian ecclesiastical politics" while asserting he would prefer persecution from honest but prejudiced Americans rather than Italian domination»[27]. Reinforced by: «Then in an handwritten note (May 10), Burke informed Muldoon confidentially that he had succeeded in having President Harding send word to the Vatican, through the American ambassador, that he would be much displeased and disappointed if the NCWC were suppressed. "No one knows of this except Senator McCormack and he and I have pledged secrecy". (And no one in the NCWC office except Iona McNulty, Burke's secretary, was aware of it)»[28]. The text proceeds with the clarification that Burke pressed Bishop Schrembs (who, as mentioned earlier, was in Rome at the time) not to accept a mere *tolerari potest* as a result of his entreaty to the Pope, but rather to insist on obtaining a special letter of approval of the NCWC's actions from the Holy See.

---

al from office of their metropolitan Archbishop, Cardinal William Henry O'Connell of Boston. Their reasons were several and longstanding [...] some clergy and laypeople in the United States sought to accommodate their church to American circumstances and viewed the American Catholic church as the model for the future worldwide. After Pope Leo XIII condemned a theological distortion of this "Americanism", O'Connell portrayed himself as the Vatican's man in the ecclesiastical province of New England, reputed to be rife with adherents of the Americanist movement. His branding of others as opponents of Rome was the means he used to lift himself onto the archiepiscopal seat of Boston. Potent Vatican allies (Cardinal Merry del Val, candidate for the papal throne during the Consistory which elected Pius XI, ndr) whose friendship he had cultivated during his years in Rome, helped in this grasp of power. His rise in this fashion marked him as the first of a new breed of American prelate: one who advanced through Vatican connections. His ascendancy through Roman, rather than American, channels alienated him from the bishops of the province and from many prelates in the American hierarchy. Deepening this estrangement were his attempts to bring Roman discipline to New England and the revelation of scandals touching his administration in Boston. [...] The height of the drive for O'Connell's ouster coincided with a new movement to give national expression to American Catholicism. The bishops of the country had recently organized themselves as the National Catholic Welfare Council, an assembly intended to introduce collaborative leadership in the church. Never friendly to the idea, O'Connell viewed the council as a rival to his authority and power as a cardinal. It was too collegial and too tied to the Sulpician Fathers, who had been quiet, but ardent, promoters of the Americanist movement». Preface, IX.

[27] J.B. SHEERIN, *Never Look Back...*, 71.

[28] *Ibidem*, 72.

c. A certain crude naïveté in recounting personal meetings with members of the Vatican Curia and, even, with Pope Pius XI: «He [Schrembs, ndr] was thrilled to hear the Pope say, "Do you think I am a man who can be believed? If so, I tell you as the Holy Father that I did not know what the decree meant... I promise you on my word as the pontiff that I have been deceived and that I shall carry out justice for the Bishops of the United States"...»[29].

And from the meeting with Cardinal Sincero: «June 1 Ryan went with Schrembs to the Consistorial Congregation: had an hour with Cardinal Sincero, the big gun of the Congregation. Schrembs was simply wonderful, inexpressibly so, explaining the copies of the relatio he was giving Sincero, the nature of the NCWC, etc. [...] Sincero deprecated the decree and said it would be retracted. Here was Sincero, the assessor, saying this and that NCWC would rise stronger than ever. "My name is Sincero and I am now sincere in this promise, not only in word but in fact". Ryan exults, "Isn't it glorious! They feel they have been sold by Boston and Philadelphia and they are now going to the other extreme"»[30].

It is pertinent to note that, throughout this period, everything written by the representatives of the NCWC was translated into Italian. This not only avoided incomprehension, it also had a political relevance: the translations wcrc assigned to Filippo Bernardini, professor of Canon Law at the Catholic University, advisor to the Apostolic Delegate Bonzano and, above all, nephew of the Secretary of State of the Holy See, Pietro Cardinal Gasparri. We can therefore compare and verify both the correct wording

---

[29] *Ibidem*, 73.

[30] *Ibidem*, 75. There is some confusion with regard to the possible identity of this *Ryan*. Fr. Sheerin suggests two identities for Mgr. Schrembs' companion: Dr. *James A.* Ryan, head of the education department of NCWC (*ibidem*, 70) and *James H.* Ryan, later rector of Catholic University (*ibidem*, 73). Another historian, Emmett Curran, in his review of *The Catholic University of America: a Centennial History,* by Joseph C. Nuesse, mentions both a Fr. *John A.* Ryan, and a *John Hugh* Ryan, the latter identified as the Rector of Catholic University and successor of Thomas J. Shahan. It should be noted, however, that the successor of Shahan as Rector of Catholic University in 1928 was, in fact, *James Hugh Ryan*. It is also certain that Mgr. *John A.* Ryan, who obtained his Doctorate in Theology from the Catholic University in 1906, was extremely active during this same period in Washington and at the Catholic University where he taught from 1915 to 1939. Therefore the companion of Mgr. Schrembs, if we can trust Fr. Sheerin's second annotation, was James Hugh Ryan, at that time Instructor in Philosophy, who later became Rector in 1928. (He was raised to the rank of Domestic Prelate in 1927, of Protonotary Apostolic in 1929 and became Archbishop of Omaha on August 4, 1945).

of the concepts and their correspondence with the individual contributions prior to the NCWC's final report. The first example is the letter from the Bishop of Duluth, John T. McNicholas, addressed to Cardinal De Lai and the members of the Consistorial. In addition to a summary of the activity of the NCWC, McNicholas outlines the cultural differences between America and the Roman Church:

«I have often thought that the NCWC must seem a complicated, unclear and unnecessary thing, to Your Eminence and to the members of the Sacred Consistorial Congregation. I confess that, upon leaving Rome four years ago and returning to the United States, I found a great change. The War had multiplied the number of activities to a supreme degree. The number of organizations had grown considerably. Now it might seem unnecessary to create new organizations in the Church, when we already have the divine organization of the priesthood and the episcopacy. However I believe our condition before the law and the United States government is exceptional. Here we have a legal incorporation for each parish and diocese... The formation of these corporations is legally perpetual and it exempts us from practically all estate and inheritance taxes... without these corporations we would have to pay a large amount in taxes each year, additionally our property would not be secure in the eyes of the law and we would have many serious difficulties... it seemed useful to the Bishops of the United States to form a legal corporation of all the Bishops, as exists for every diocese»[31].

Going farther to say:

«I have often thought, and I frequently spoke with S.E. Mons. Cerretti about this, that it would be useful to have the Holy See incorporated in the United States, that is, to have the Holy See designated as a legal entity before the law of the United States. That would be very simple. It would give the Holy See the right to own property and, if bequests or wills are made to the Holy See, no taxes would need be paid. Additionally if the Holy See were incorporated in this way, it could appeal to the United States Catholics to remember the needs of the Holy See in their wills»[32].

In defense of the choice of the bishops of the NCWC:

«The incorporation of the Bishops of the United States under the name *National Catholic Welfare Council* is intended only to give the body of the Bishops a position before the law. The name given to a corporation often depends upon the type of work it carries out or the law under which it is formed. Many parishes,

---

[31] AES, America, POS. 172 P.O., Fasc. 16, 9-11.
[32] Bonaventura Cerretti (1872-1933) was auditor to the apostolic delegation in the United States from 1906 to 1914. He was named Cardinal by Pius XI in 1925.

for example, are incorporated as literary societies. The reason for this is that the law for literary corporations is more lenient than the law for religious organizations and allows for greater benefits and exemptions. Almost every Dominican parish in the United States is incorporated as a literary society.

One could ask what is the reason for which the Bishops desire to have a national organization. The principal reason is that all of our enemies are organized nationally. The masons have a national organization. The secular schools have a national organization. Your Eminence is aware that we have a dual government in the United States, that of the State and that of the Nation. Each national organization has a certain influence before the national government and, without a national organization, it is practically impossible to exercise even the slightest influence... If we are a national organization and if through this organization we unify our people, legislation hostile to the Church can not be passed. We are twenty million and we can always balance our enemies if we remain united. Your Eminence knows the uproar made by the paltry few Methodists in Rome. In the United States we have seven or eight million of these people. They possess great wealth, influence and union. They hate the Catholic Church. They are nationally organized and exercise great influence in Washington. The Episcopalians, the Anglicans and other sects refer to themselves as Catholics and no one disturbs them for this pseudonym as Catholics, but all of these hate us because we add Roman to the name Catholic... To deprive the Church of any form of organization is to do exactly what our enemies so warmly desire».

Comparing the American bishops and the representatives of the Vatican Curia:

«May I say with the most profound sense of deference, that the condemnation of the NCWC by the Sacred Consistorial Congregation was, according to the judgment of nine-tenths of the Bishops, the most grave blow which the Church has ever received in America? The Bishops found it difficult to believe their eyes when the telegraphed news arrived. There were three things which seemed almost impossible to them:

1. That the Holy See had the slightest doubt of their loyalty. Our Bishops are not acquainted with the Curial style, nor do they possess knowledge of the language. [...]

2. That the decree of condemnation intimated a suspicion of schism. Whatever may be the peculiarities of our Bishops – be that a lack of communication, of making reports or a deficiency in that marvelous prudence which characterizes the Italian Bishops and those of many other European countries, they nevertheless would die with joy for the unity of the Church and for the union with the Holy See.

3. That the condemnation should come at the suggestion of a few Bishops. It is well known that almost eighty Bishops addressed their supplications to

the Holy Father, asking him to consider the responsibilities that the Holy See would bear should the Bishops be deprived of a national organization»[33].

Then concluding with the final blow:

«Confidential. Most Reverend Eminence: perhaps I should not take the liberty to write the following, but I do so saying it in the greatest confidence. May God preserve the Church from a scandal in Boston. [...] Sincerely I confide for the good of religion that the Holy See not believe the information which comes from Boston... Some openly say that there is little evidence of faith there. [...] We all know that Philadelphia is a zealous, holy, apostolic and tireless Prelate. [...] but it is generally said that he can not work with others, that he is not a man of counsel. He has a strong character and is irremovable in his decisions. I do not write Your Eminence in a spirit of censure, but solely with the desire that you know the facts and how the facts are considered by the majority of the Bishops»[34].

Amen! One may say.

We are now ready to read the letter which Bishop Schrembs sent to Pope Pius XI on June 6, 1922, following receipt of the report created in Washington, during the Catholic University meeting:

«Most Holy Father –
Permit me to hand to your Holiness through the kindness of Mgr. Pizzardo, the original letter which was sent to all the Bishops of the United States, to inform them of the action taken by the Administrative Council of the NCWC in regard to the Consistorial decree of Feb. 25, as well as the recursus of the trustees of the Catholic University at Washington, on April 26, which recursus was at once forwarded to Your Holiness by the Archbishops. [...] The enclosed eighty individual signatures are the answer of the overwhelming majority of the Bishops of the United States. I am also taking the liberty of presenting to Your Holiness a volume of official letters and Press-Clippings, evidencing the practically unanimous cooperation of the Hierarchy of the United States in the various activities of the NCWC during the past two years.
His Grace, the Archbishop of Cincinnati and Your Holiness' humble servant, had a conference with His Eminence, Cardinal De Lai, on last Friday morning. It pains us grievously to say that His Eminence's own answer to all our pleadings and arguments was invariably: "C'est inutile de discuter cette question. C'est bien votre opinion, je la respecte, mais j'ai mes convictions. Il faut que les évêques des Etats Unis retournent à l'imperium juris". This attitude of His Eminence has filled our hearts with deep sorrow and dismay. To forbid the annual meetings of our Hierarchy, while other countries such as England,

---

[33] AES, America, POS. 172 P.O., Fasc. 16, 10.
[34] *Ibidem.*

Ireland, Germany, Australia and now France are holding them without let or hindrance from the Holy See, but even with its approval, singles us out from among the Bishops of the world, and brands us as suspects and dangerous to the welfare of the Church. If the episcopate of other countries can meet annually to discuss ways and means to promote the educational, social and religious interests of their countries and to safeguard the civic and religious rights of their peoples, why not the Bishops of the United States? The "imperium juris" is not touched by our meetings, and we have never contemplated interfering with the individuals' rights or the autonomous action of any bishop or diocese. I make bold to say, Most Holy Father, that no body of Bishops in the world today is more loyal, more zealous, more energetic, more generous to the Holy See, or more awake to the interests of the Church, than the Bishops of our Country.

We come before Your Holiness to plead our cause against those of our own who, we know not for what personal reasons, have misled the Sacred Consistorial Congregation as to the real conditions of our country and the beneficent activities of the NCWC, which was called into being by Pope Benedict XV and repeatedly merited his commendation and his blessing.

Without the liberty of frequent mutual counsel and united organized action, we must fall an easy prey to our many mighty and thoroughly organized enemies.

Most Holy Father, in the name of the great majority of the Bishops of the United States, I kneel before Your Holiness, to plead for the welfare, yea for the very life of the Church in the United States. Forgive me, Holy Father, if I seem importunate, but as the days wear on, the uncertainty of the issue is lying heavily upon us, and is a real menace to activities which are urgent and which can prosper only in the bright light of the wholehearted approval and the blessing of the Holy See.

With the expression of sentiments of affectionate loyalty and filial devotion, I beg to remain Your Holiness most humble and devoted servant in Christ. [...] (Signed)»[35].

The defensive line of the NCWC was concentrated, essentially, in three points: 1. The adhesion of the majority of American bishops; 2. The menace presented by the hardened enemies of Catholicism in the United States; 3. The misinformation which had been given by someone as to the real scope of the work carried out by NCWC and which had caused an unjust censure by the beloved Mother Church. This was further colored in Schrembs' letter by the accusation of Rome's negative singling out of the United States and by the description of a Prince of the Church (Cardinal De Lai) as inflexible in his attitude and deaf to the pleadings of the «sons».

Let us examine at close range the final broadside which the NCWC launched in its defense: the report developed on April 25, 1922, at the

---

[35] AES, America, POS. 172 P.O., Fasc. 16, 12-14.

Catholic University of America, Washington DC, and assembled in a «White Book» of 99 pages (Italian and English)[36] conserved in the Vatican Secret Archives.

The report bears the signature of the seven members of the Administrative Committee, but we know that Bishop Schrembs went to New York on April 25 in order to embark for Rome and that the report was, in reality, the work of only one member of the Committee[37], Peter J. Muldoon, the Bishop of Rockford, assisted by Fr. Burke and by Fr. John F. Fenlon, a Sulpician[38]. Here the words have lost the candor of McNicholas and Schrembs' letters and show clearly that the writers feel both that they are absolutely in the right and that the Vatican's decision in this matter could have serious consequences – and not just for the members of the NCWC or for American Catholics. From the beginning the tone is understated but relentlessly critical and even, one might say, suggests a tinge of blackmail:

> «Most Holy Father:
> While the whole Catholic world was still celebrating with intense joy the election of a Pontiff preeminently gifted in mind and heart for his supreme office, while the church of America, with a joy even more intense, was welcoming a Father who has a most sympathetic understanding of her situation and needs, suddenly, like a lighting bolt from a sunny sky, came a decree from the Holy See which filled us with astonishment and grief. Upon the whole Hierarchy of our country it seems to put the stigma of a suspected loyalty and of incompetence. [...] Upon us particularly, the seven bishops of the Administrative Committee of the National Catholic Welfare Council, has the displeasure of our Father descended. We are dismissed peremptorily on the eleventh day of a new pontificate, without warning, without a hearing; without a word of commendation, without even a word of benevolence. Our work is declared no longer necessary or useful. [...] Holy Father, that an accusation like this could be entertained for a moment, fills us with shame; [...] Apparently, the danger was believed to be imminent; and we ourselves were adjudged so manifestly guilty that no defense was possible and no hearing necessary. [...]
> We who know well the paternal kindness of the Popes towards their children in every nation and who have ourselves long experienced their cordial affection towards the Church of America and their confidence in the American Hierarchy, are certain that a decree so severe could only have been issued upon representations which seemed to admit no doubt. [...] We confess, Holy

---

[36] AES, America, POS. 172 P.O., Fasc. 15, 1-99.

[37] J.B. SHEERIN, *Never Look Back...*, 70.

[38] A few years later, in 1937, Pius XI, through Cardinal Bisleti, Prefect of the Congregation of Seminaries and Universities, would sanction the non-conformity of the Sulpician Seminary's program for the academic degrees in Theology and Philosophy. J. NUESSE, *The Catholic University of America: a Centennial History...*

Father, that we are entirely ignorant of the identity or number of the bishops, who have made representations to the Holy See, and of their brethren for whom they spoke. Not even one is known to us, or, apparently to anyone of the very many American bishops who have revealed their mind to their brethren.

We believe ourselves fully justified, however, Holy Father, in saying that these prelates were not commissioned to speak in the name of any considerable number of American bishops, and that the information which they gave about the work of the NCWC must have been entirely misleading. It was well known to us that a few bishops entertained misconceptions of this work, chiefly because they were not informed about its real character. This did not surprise us. We had been chosen by the Hierarchy to look after the things that concerned the welfare of the whole country, almost a continent in extent, and were expressly selected to represent all its different sections. [...]

To speak in defense of our loyalty would be indeed to us a great humiliation. Conscious of the filial love and obedience which we have ever cherished to the Pontiffs whom God has given us, and which we cherish today towards Your Holiness, we leave our vindication in the hands of the Apostolic Delegate. We are confident of the judgment which will be rendered, and we humbly petition Your Holiness, therefore, to clear our names of the stigma which all believe has been placed upon us. In our own country, we are sure, no such suspicion of our loyalty is entertained or will ever be really believed; we beg this for the honor of the American Episcopate in other lands, where false ideas about us are too easily believed, with grave injury to the harmony and good will which should unite Catholics of all nations. As loyal bishops, therefore, Holy Father, we are perfectly ready to obey this decree to the fullest extent; but our very loyalty to the Holy See, as well as our loyalty to our consciences and to the interests committed to us by the Hierarchy, oblige us first to point out the consequences which, in our well-weighed judgment, are sure to result.

First of all, Holy Father, we are profoundly convinced that this decree, if it stands, will gravely affect the prestige of the Holy See in this country. [...] One remarkable fact will show the universal fear that this decree will injure the prestige of the Holy See. Although the decree is in the hands of a hundred and ten bishops [...] its true nature has not yet been revealed to the public. Furthermore, the few who have spoken of it in the press have beclouded its real nature and have thought it necessary to take very special pains to shield the Holy See from any responsibility for the act. Never before have American Catholics felt constrained to conceal an act of the Holy See. Why this extraordinary precaution? Why should everyone feel fear and shame lest a decree of the Holy See become known? Simply, Holy Father – we say it with sorrow, but with no doubt of the truth – because it is the instinctive judgment of all that the publication of this decree would be an injury to the prestige of the Holy See and a scandal to religion. [...]

Our people and the public will inevitably learn, Holy Father, that this decree suppressing the NCWC was granted on the ex parte and hostile statements of a few Bishops, and that no opportunity for defense or explanation was given to the great body of American bishops, and particularly to the seven bishops best qualified to speak for the work of the NCWC. It will be regrettable if the decree be interpreted, as we fear it will be, so as to lessen the deep reverence all have for the habitual fairness, justice and wisdom of the Holy See and for the deliberateness which characterizes judgments in the Eternal City; and to lead many to believe that the Holy See is out of sympathy with the American Hierarchy and with American way of action. This would be all the more deplorable now, since Your Holiness has won the hearts of all our Catholic people»[39].

The report by Fr. Burke, Bishop Muldoon and Fr. Fenlon, however, does not stop at the presumed disastrous consequences of the decree disbanding the NCWC, instead it uses a rhetorical expedient of great efficiency, particularly at that time: the dangers to the Church posed by Protestantism and the Masonry.

«The effect of the decree upon our non-Catholic American brethren would, we fear, be particularly unfortunate. Protestantism as a positive religion has lost its hold upon the majority; multitudes of them admire the Catholic Church, the American Hierarchy and the great dignity and power of the Papal office. The chief obstacle to the conversion of many is their belief that the Papacy is a spiritual autocracy which leaves no liberty of action to Catholics, not even to the Hierarchy, and consequently that devotion to the Pope is incompatible with the true American spirit. [...] No other earthly force opposing the spread of Catholicism in this country is so powerful as this idea. [...] Masonry here, which years ago did not appear very antagonistic to the Church, is more and more showing the spirit which it has in many European countries. Now the effect of this decree on non-Catholics, we feel certain, would be to confirm their fear of Catholicism and to intensify suspicion and hatred of the Papacy. The strong act of the Consistorial Congregation by which, in the eyes of the country, a great Hierarchy would be humiliated and a nation-wide organization, known to be doing immense good for the nation, annihilated, could but strengthen the prejudices of non-Catholics».

The report then turns to the possible international implications should the NCWC be disbanded. The first practical point it considers, the NC-WC's participation in the *American Relief Administration's* (ARA) famine relief program in Russia, was, in fact, definitely a «sore point» with the Vatican – perhaps even more so than the NCWC seems to have understood. The facts, as presented in this petition, are misleading and would seem to suggest that the American Catholics had, in some mysterious way, been «left out» of the project. In fact, at that moment, the ARA had already been distributing food in Russia for 7 months without any participation from the NCWC. This because the NCWC, though included in this

---

[39] AES, America, POS. 172 P.O., Fasc. 15, 1-99.

program from the very beginning, had still not selected a representative to manage the use of its contributions in Russia – notwithstanding repeated solicitations by the ARA to do so:

«The NCWC secured, after much effort, representation on the American Relief Administration. The Protestant body had been recognized by being asked to appoint a representative. No official Catholic representative was appointed until the NCWC acted. Moreover, a most important point is that owing to the coming resignation of Secretary Hoover from the Russian relief a new plan is to be inaugurated. This plan, as yet not made public, is to have a national committee representative of the Catholic, Protestant and Jewish national organizations to take charge of the administration of this work. Advances have already been made to the NCWC. If it must go out of existence, this exceptional opportunity of Catholic influence will be lost, and doubtless many others of a like character in the future».

The report concludes with a final reference to Latin America and, once more, to the proselytizing zeal of the Protestants:

«The NCWC is the body consulted by the President of the United States on legislation and other matters which affect the Philippines, Porto Rico, Hayti and Santo Domingo, all Catholic countries now occupied by American troops and administered by American officials. The same protection that is granted by the United States Military and Naval Forces in these countries to Protestant missionary and welfare workers is granted to us, and puts us in a position to counteract their proselytizing efforts. The influence of the United States grows every day more powerful in all countries of Latin America. [...] The feeling is growing rapidly here that the Catholic Church of the United States, if properly organized, and recognized by our Government, can be of immense service to the Holy See in all Latin American countries. Without the Welfare Council, on the other hand, it is evident that the religious bodies which will have influence with our Government in its relations with Latin America are those Protestant missionary organizations which every year send to these Catholic countries thousands of missionaries and millions of dollars. [...] The financial support which American Protestant missions receive, particularly from business men, almost passes belief. These missionaries have often in the past determined the policy of our Department of State. Would not the extinction of the NCWC, now when the United States is gaining in power and influence all over the globe, tend to make the Federal Council of Churches supreme in Washington and be a serious blow to Catholicism in many countries?».

The Protestants, useful as a provocation in pleading the cause, were then, after all, not quite the welcome companions with whom to share the ministry to the poor. Not only that, the danger of their competition was so great and imminent that even the slightest change to the equilibrium established by the NCWC was inadvisable. On one hand America, according to this detailed description, is seen as a rich frontier land in which rules, valid for the rest of the world, become ineffective in front of the arrogance of the competitors with whom the Catholics must contend. On the other hand, America and its government – the rules of the game itself – become the aspired goal in order to increase the Church's size and competitive capacity, both on the national level and, given the increasing world importance of the United States, on the international level.

This detailed message from the NCWC, corroborated by the testimony of so many bishops, was understood by the Pope. The analysis of the NCWC made by Cardinal O'Connell was not incorrect, however, this was Americanism, though not in a theological formulation, but in its simplest, every day application: pragmatism. Nevertheless, one can't easily trade 81 bishops spread over the entire national territory for two Princes of the Church – particularly when one of these Princes, Bishop O'Connell, was not, strictly speaking, a Saint. Certainly under his guidance the Boston Diocese had almost tripled in parishioners, churches, schools and offerings, but one city alone does not make the Union!

The beginning of a pontificate is, without doubt, a reason of great joy for the newly elected Pope, but also of concern. Not by chance he dons his papal cassock for the first time within the celebrated «Room of Tears», the sacristy of the *Cappella Sistina*. It was clear immediately that the pontificate of Pius XI would not be an easy one. Postwar Europe still bore the debilitating signs of its devastating human losses and both the winners and the losers toiled with difficulty to find a social and economic balance. As for Italy, the social turbulence was leading inexorably towards a dictatorship. In the Vatican, one breathed a closed, local – almost country – air: the Pope was a «Prisoner in the Vatican» and the specter of Pius IX – and of the «Roman Question» – troubled the thoughts of the Curia.

In the early days of Pius XI's pontificate, then, America aggressively entered the Vatican scene, bringing new considerations and above all, new balances which would permanently change the relationship of the Roman Curia with the American clergy. The time of Leo XIII and of his condemnation of «Americanism» had passed, as also had his words of mediation to Cardinal James Gibbons[40]:

«Our daily experience obliges US to confess that We have found your people, through your influence, endowed with a perfect docility of mind and alacrity

---

[40] C.R. MORRIS, *American Catholic: The Saints and Sinners Who Built America's Most Powerful Church*, New York 1997, 112.

of disposition. Therefore, while the changes and the tendencies of nearly all the nations which were Catholic for many centuries give cause for sorrow, the state of your churches, in this flourishing youthfulness, cheers Our heart and fills it with delight».

In the meantime there had been a World War ending favorably for the Allies thanks to the United States' weaponry and their massive contribution of both human and economic resources. Four Empires had disappeared and a Socialist Revolution had occurred on Europe's doorstep.

The Vatican, however, had not been inactive. Pope Benedict XV had worked intensely for the reestablishment of peace, to aid prisoners of war, and to succor the Christian populations which had been so brutally affected by the events which ended the four-century rule of the Ottoman Empire. He had, in fact, created a specific Congregation to take particular care of the Churches found in the land of the Church's origin: the Sacred Congregation for the Eastern Churches (Sacra Congregatio pro Ecclesia Orientali [SCEO]), with its Motu Proprio, *Dei Providentis*, on May 1, 1917[41]. To give a strong sign of brotherhood and of special papal concern, he himself had assumed the role of Prefect for the new Congregation.

Pope Pius XI, therefore, was also Prefect of the SCEO and in this role he inherited yet another unresolved matter from Benedict XV – a matter which has been mentioned briefly and is intricately interconnected with the «American Question» presented by the NCWC: the Papal Relief Mission to Russia. Even the «red danger» represented by Bolshevik Russia was tinted in some way by the «Stars and Stripes» creating further complications for the new Pope.

The serious internal disorder and disruption within Czarist Russia had been further aggravated by the Revolution and, subsequently, by one of the droughts which periodically afflicted Russia. The meager harvest and even the seeds for planting were completely consumed, leaving the country faced with the most serious famine in memory. On July 13, 1921, the Russian writer, Maxim Gorky, published an appeal: «To All Honest People», asking

---

[41] The SCEO was the result of a long process of rapprochement and increasing interest for the Eastern Churches which culminated in the Apostolic Constitution Romani Pontificis [January 6, 1862], which instituted a special section, *«pro Negotiis Ritus Orientalis»* within the Sacred Congregation for the Propagation of the Faith (S. Congregatio de Propaganda Fide – SCEO). This Congregation had one Prefect (a Cardinal), but the two sections had their own Secretary, Officials and Consultants. Pope Benedict XV (1914-1922) created the SCEO as an autonomous Congregation, because the affairs of the Eastern Church did not seem considered *«quasi quædam accessio»* by the Sacred Congregation for the Propagation of the Faith.

help for the famished Russian population. In response, the Congress of the
United States voted an appropriation of $20,000,000 for use by the Ameri-
can Relief Administration (ARA)[42] in aiding Russia. On August 20, 1921,
at Riga, an agreement was signed between the ARA, represented by Walter
Lyman Brown, and the Soviet government, represented by Maxim Litvinov.
The Riga Agreement detailed all of the stringent stipulations regarding the
operation of the American aid program in Russia.

President Warren Gamaliel Harding (1865-1923) further strengthened
the ARA's role by stipulating, at the behest of Herbert Hoover, that the
State Department would issue passports for relief work in Russia only to
Americans who were officially in the service of the ARA[43]. Hence, the ARA
had the final say as to who went to Russia and how the American funds
were used. As a consequence, therefore, the funds gathered from American
Catholics for use in Russia could only be administered by an American who
was an official member of the ARA's Russian Relief Program. The ARA's
Russian relief program was joined by 8 American charities[44] of which the

---

[42] The American Relief Administration (ARA) was a relief organization, established by
President Woodrow Wilson in 1919 and headed by Herbert Hoover (later Secretary of
Commerce under President Harding and subsequently US President). The ARA was
charged with feeding Europeans in the wake of WWI's destruction. The ARA's purpose is precisely outlined in the 1921-22 edition of the «Year Book of the Churches»:
«Purpose: receives and distributes relief for children of Austria, Poland and Russia.
Conducting medical and general relief in Russia on behalf of cooperating organizations». Year Book of the Churches: 1921-22, Federal Council of the Churches of Christ
in America, Washington 1922, 307.

[43] B.M. WEISSMAN, Herbert Hoover and Famine Relief to Soviet Russia, 1921-1923, Stanford 1974, 55.

[44] The European Relief Council Agreement was signed in Washington on August 24,
1921. Participants included The American Relief Administration, American Friends
Service Committee, American Red Cross, Federal Council of the Churches of Christ
in America, Jewish Joint Distribution Committee, Knights of Columbus, Young Men's
Christian Association, Young Women's Christian Association, The National Catholic
Welfare Council. «It was decided that inasmuch as the whole problem was apparently
beyond the resources of private charity, the work of the Associations represented at
this meeting would in its initial stages be directed in priority toward children and in
medical supplies». Point C of this agreement signed by the 8 groups adhering to the
ARA on August 24, 1921, reads: «The Director of the American Relief Administration
in Russia shall appoint on his staff at headquarters, one or more representatives (to be
mutually agreed) of any of the organization members of the European Relief Council.
In turn, the member organizations who may be represented in Russia agree to furnish
such representatives. The object of this arrangement is to secure complete coöpera-
tion and coördination among the different organizations». H.H. FISHER, The Famine in

NCWC represented the Catholic branch[45]. Pope Benedict XV had been immediately active on behalf of Russian famine relief beginning in the summer of 1921 and had hoped that a Papal Relief Mission – under the aegis of the ARA – would begin in October of 1921 (the month after the ARA had begun its distribution work in Russia). According to Mgr. d'Herbigny, in fact, Pope Benedict XV continued to ask about this mission up until the day he died[46]. In effect the Papal Relief Mission to Russia *could* have operated independently in Russia (in fact, it had already done so, in collaboration with the Italian Red Cross and at the wish of Pope Benedict XV, but, due to constant pilfering from the trains in Russia, it had little effect). There was also another international aid organization, the International Committee for Russian Relief (ICRR), which had been formed in July of 1921 and which had been in close contact with the Vatican, but the Vatican, in order to have access to the funds gathered from American Catholics for Famine Relief and access to the food resources, expertise and considerable distribution facilities offered by the ARA, clearly preferred to work through the American Relief Administration.

Let us return, then, to the point of intersection between the Vatican's decree disbanding the NCWC (February 23, 1922), the announcement of the famine in Russia (July of 1921), the Riga Agreement between Russia and the ARA (August 20, 1921), the NCWC's membership in the ARA Russian relief program (August 24, 1921), the beginning of ARA's food distribution in Russia (September 1921), Pope Benedict XV's intense interest in this mission, his death and subsequently Pope Pius XI's election (February 6, 1922), and, above all, to the point that, notwithstanding the profound interest expressed by the Holy See (which viewed this mission as an opportunity to win back the East), the Papal Relief Mission to Russia was still inoperative because the NCWC had not known how, been able,

---

Soviet Russia, 1919-1923: The Operations of the American Relief Administration, New York 1927, 511.

[45] «The National Catholic Welfare Council was one of the original members of the European Relief Council, but did not establish its own organization in Russia, affiliated with the ARA, until March 1922. An appeal from Vatican for funds for Russian relief received such a generous response that the Catholic Mission was able to carry out a mass feeding program which reached 157,507 persons (daily, ndr) in the districts of Crimea, Orenbourg, Moscow, Rostov/Don and Krasnodar. In addition to this feeding, which was conducted without distinction as to race, religion or politics, the Mission imported and distributed $250,000 worth of textiles and medicines». H.H. FISHER, *The Famine in Soviet Russia...*, 463.

[46] M. D'HERBIGNY, SJ, *L'aiuto pontificio ai bambini affamati della Russia*, in «Orientalia Christiana», 4 (1925)/1, 25.

or wanted to chose a representative to direct it, thereby frustrating the Vatican's wish to undertake this important mission within Russia. Here we begin to see more clearly how all of these events, now on the desk of the new Pope Pius XI, intersected.

During those months in which the Vatican awaited the action of the NCWC, even before the death of Benedict XV, however, other American Catholics had tried to prod the NCWC to give a positive response to Rome. One of the most concerned, of course, was Colonel William Nafew Haskell, the director of the ARA's Aid Mission in Russia. Frustrated when his repeated requests for the appointment of an NCWC representative were not answered by Fr. Burke, Haskell took the immediate route and contacted Fr. Edmund Aloysius Walsh[47] directly to ask him to lead the American Catholics' portion of the mission in Russia. Fr. Walsh, in turn, contacted the Jesuit Superior General Włodzimierz Ledóchowski.

Well before John Burke's letter to Mgr. Borgoncini-Duca and before the Consistorial's decree, then, Fr. Włodzimierz Ledóchowski, had written to Mgr. Giuseppe Pizzardo, Substitute Secretary of State. The urgent tone of his letter and his clear excitement about undertaking the Russian Mission testify to the importance he ascribes to it:

«Illustrious and Most Reverend Mgr.,
I beg forgiveness if in moments of such activity I disturb Your Excellence with the present matter. However the affair it concerns is so urgent and important that I can not defer it to a time which is more comfortable.
Fr. Edmund Walsh of our Company, American, excellent cleric, of great talents, who is presently in France, writes me that Colonel William Haskell, head of the American Commission which has been constituted with 20 million dollars of aid for the famine in Russia, asks him to join the expedition immediately.
According to the convention stipulated between the United States and the Soviets, every religious society in the United States has the right to send a representative to the Commission to take care of their co-religionists in Russia. All of the sects have already sent their representative; only the Catholic Church, which relatively speaking is the largest and most powerful both in America and in Russia, still has not.

---

[47] Edmund Aloysius Walsh, SJ, (1885-1956): Founder (in 1919) and Regent of Georgetown University's School of Foreign Service, second generation American, son of Irish immigrants. When Colonel Haskell contacted Fr. Walsh, he was in Paray-le-Monial, France, completing his Tertianship at the Jesuit community there. Walsh entered the Company of Jesus in 1902 along with Joseph Farrell (brother of Winifred A. Farrell, Colonel Haskell's wife). He was ordained in 1916 by James Cardinal Gibbons.

His Eminence, Cardinal O'Connell, with whom I have spoken recently, is of the opinion that we should take advantage of this favorable occasion and send Fr. Walsh as soon as possible.

An additional reason suggests the choice of said Father. Colonel Haskell, now a fervent Catholic, was led to the religion by the same Fr. Walsh, in whom he (Haskell) has the greatest faith.

It is understood that the expenses of the trip and the living expenses would be taken over by the American Commission.

If the Holy See would permit that the Father accepts the invitation, I would call him to Rome by telegram in order to give him the necessary instructions and I would send him directly to Russia.

There the Father would appear only as a Catholic priest, completely concealing that he belongs to the Company of Jesus. This, I believe, can be easily affected. In all the rest he would be under the protection of the United States government.

Awaiting your revered response». (Signed)[48]

Fr. Walsh left Paray-le-Monial on February 22, 1922, bound for Rome[49], where he arrived the evening of February 26. The following day, Walsh had a long conversation with Father Ledóchowski. The diary he kept throughout this period will help us follow the events closely:

«Long conference P. Led. 3-5 P.M. Has full plans for future – reestablishment of Society in Russia and *union* of orient churches. Frail, delicate man, quick to see a situation or an argument, not too formal; ready to change a plan or opinion if good reason shown.

Tuesday Feb. 28 – Tuesday March 1: Continual Conferences with P. Led., P. D'Herbigny and Mgsr. Ropp, Archbishop of most of Russia, Metropolitan of Mohilev. Old, gray-bearded gentleman, long white beard with signs of aristocracy. Later found he is *Baron* Ropp. Was arrested and imprisoned for long time by Soviet Government – released on representation of Holy See. Has written and labored much for union. Was living at Machiavelli St. – a convent of German or Polish sisters. He talked long on religious situation and hopes for future. Question of *rite* the all important question. He is a *biritualist* and is endeavoring to make this solution prevail in Rome. Consumed many cigarettes during 2 conferences».

On March 1, 1922, Fr. Walsh went to the Vatican accompanied by Fr. Ledóchowski to meet Cardinal Gasparri and Mgr. Pizzardo. «S.S. videtur omnia velle committere P. Led. et Soc. – et omnia approbare quæ ille statuat. [...] Interim multum perdo tempus nam the Cable from USA. – NCWC said "for 3 months"».

---

[48] AES, Pont. Comm. Pro Russia, Sc. 73, Fasc. 332, 14.

[49] EAWP, Diaries, 2:125, GUSCRC.

Walsh's brief reference to NCWC is rather clear: after a long wait, Fr. Burke had, at long last, made a temporary appointment of Walsh as representative of the NCWC in the ARA relief campaign «for 3 months». The Holy See, in the meantime, had totally committed the mission to the counsel and conduct of the Company of Jesus: «*Alius verbis, S.S. se vertit totaliter ad Soc. Responsabilitas enormis*»[50].

On the same date, March 1, 1922, Fr. Ledóchowski wrote Mgr. Pizzardo to send him the Curriculum Vitae of some of the Jesuits destined for Russia. He also specifies his plans for Walsh:

«I don't think it will be necessary to prepare Father Walsh's curriculum vitae. If His Eminence the Cardinal Secretary of State approves Cardinal O'Connell's proposal that means that Fr. Walsh is the representative of the Catholic Church on the American Commission and, at the same time, he is one of the Holy See's Delegates. In any case, I would like that Fr. Walsh is the Superior of the Company's group – first because he has already given proof of his exceptional organizational talent and secondly because I hope that his close relationship with the head of the American Commission [Col. Haskell, ndr] could be of great service not only to our Fathers, but also to others. [...] I believe we are on the right path. The Holy See will organize a splendid charitable action for the Russian poor and, without any further publicity, this in itself will be a forceful way of demonstrating to the Russian people that its health is in union with the Church of Peter. I believe that the Catholic world will understand that this is a splendid crusade of charity to save, perhaps, all the East and that one could obtain with a good organization, to which we are ready to contribute with our small efforts, very ample means to this end. It will be useful to point out that the Delegates from the Holy See all belong to diverse nationalities. In closing I would observe that a few things need to be decided now – for example should the Delegates have beards or not»[51].

The Superior General wrote Mgr. Pizzardo again on the morning of March 8, 1922, relaying a request from Fr. Walsh, who was about to leave for Russia: to present his respects to Mgr. Pizzardo and the Cardinal Secretary of State and to request a brief meeting with the Holy Father to receive his benediction.

«This will be of grand consolation to him, but will also be useful for his work. Additionally he would like to have a recommendation from the Holy See which could be prepared in the way indicated by the card which I attach. It is desirable that the recommendation is written on the Holy See's official

---

[50] *Ibidem.*
[51] AES, Pont. Comm. Pro Russia, Sc. 73, Fasc. 335, 44-46.

stationery and provided with seals, things to which the Russians give great importance»[52].

Thanks to Edmund Walsh's diary, we know that he received all that was requested in Fr. Ledóchowski's letter on that very day. Wednesday, March 8, 1922, at 8:30 A.M. Walsh went to the Vatican with d'Herbigny. There they met Mgr. Pizzardo who took them to the Secretary of State where Walsh received an Apostolic Letter[53]: «Le Saint Siège autorise Mr. l'abbé Edmond Walsh [sic] à s'occuper de préparer l'organisation des secours pontificaux pour la Russie. Il bénit tous les efforts qu'il fera pour mieux montrer aux Russes l'amour du Saint-Père à leur égard, et prie Dieu de récompenser tous ceux qui l'aideront»[54].

Father Walsh's private audience with the Holy Father was arranged for the same morning:

«Hour 10:30 made arrangements for private audience with Pius XI, at 1 P.M. Spent intervening time in going through Vatican Library, Vatican Museum, Sistine Chapel, etc. At 1 was at Vat. second floor – ushered through many crimson chambers – Many Swiss guards – papal Chamberlains etc. Spent last 10 min. before small study of Pius XI talking with Englishman papal chamberlain, father of a S.J. Scholastic, English province. About 1.15 ushered to private study – simply furnished, large desk, pictures of previous popes on wall. Pius XI – presented the usual 3 genuflections – advanced to the door, took me up by hands. Somewhat shorter than pictures – face rounder – plumper than pictures. Democratic, stood with arms folded leaning against desk»[55].

According to Walsh's diary, the conversation with Pius XI was conducted in Latin. The Holy Father expressed gratitude to Walsh for accepting to lead the papal aid program in Russia. He recommended great prudence and cautioned Walsh not to act in a way which might compromise the image of the Holy See in the eyes of the Russians, but also: «*Dixit se multum mihi confidere*». The Pope gave Walsh a special crucifix for himself and one for William N. Haskell, whom Pius XI praised. The Pope also praised the generous charity of the Americans and blessed Walsh and assured him the comfort of his prayers in a mission of such danger. «*"Good bye" dixit accentus Italiano quando discessi*».

---

[52] *Ibidem*, 48-49.
[53] EAWP, Diaries, 2:125, GUSCRC, ad diem.
[54] AES, Pont. Comm. Pro Russia, Sc. 73, Fasc. 332, 15.
[55] EAWP, Diaries, 2:125, GUSCRC, ad diem.

This brief summary of the meeting between Edmund Walsh and Pius XI gives us some idea of the practical characters of both men. The meeting was, in fact, a harbinger of things to come: Pius XI would use this American Jesuit several times again – in diplomatic missions of equal delicacy and risk.

Walsh spent the following day preparing for his departure for Russia: «Long final conversation evening with Vladimir [Ledóchowski] who stressed importance of mission at this time when entire world is regarding Russia, "120,000,000 people with no shepherd". Gave me reliquary with relics St. Ign., Fr. Xav., Holy Cross, etc.».

Walsh began his trip on Friday, March 10, and arrived in Moscow on March 23, 1922: «Met at station by Mr. Morgan – hence to Col. Haskell for supper. Mrs. Haskell present. First impression of Moscow – Dirt – filth run down – decay – wind – people in rags – no signs of business – everybody with pack on back with morsel of food – Terrorism of Tcheka».

At the same time, the Vatican continued to prepare the details of the papal mission. Ledóchowski wrote to Secretary of State Gasparri on March 19, 1922:

«In fulfillment of Your Eminence's order, I send a few suggestions for the organization of the Pontifical expedition in Russia. After the approval or modification of these plans, it will not be difficult to compose the instructions for the Missionaries of which Your Eminence spoke and which appear not only convenient but also necessary, a few other points need to be established, for example, how the Missionaries must be dressed, whether they should have beards or not, and other similar points[56]. Beyond the instructions, I think it would be helpful if at least one Father of each group came to Rome to meet one another and thus assure greater unity of action and mutual cooperation, upon which the success of the Mission depends.
As for our Company, I want to assure Your Eminence that while, as I said yesterday, I believe that Fr. Walsh is particularly adapted to organize the center, having given proof of his grand organizational talent both in his founding of the first commercial/consular school in Washington and through his work during the war, nonetheless, we will be equally content should the center be assigned to others because our single desire is to serve the great cause well according to the will of the Holy See and to help others. [...] As for the posts which will be assigned to our Fathers – now and in the future, we desire, in as far as possible, that these are the most difficult and dangerous places where

---

[56] Fr. Ledóchowski's insistent reference to the external aspect of the missionaries sent to Russia was due to the terms of the agreement signed on March 12, 1922 by the Holy See and the unofficial representative of the Soviets in Rome, Vatslav Vatslavovich Vorovsky (1871-1923). These terms specified that the representatives of the Holy See were required to wear civilian clothes. AES, IV, Russia, Fasc. 40, POS. 659.

one can work all the better for the greater glory of God and in order to pay the particular debt of gratitude[57] which our Company has towards Russia».

Already on March 26, 1922, Walsh was able to make a first, informative report[58] which he sent to Rome by way of Mrs. Haskell:

«Dear Father Hanselman[59]:
After a long and varied trip I arrived in Moscow on the evening of Wednesday, March 23. From Rome to Riga there was not anything special [...] but at Riga there appeared the first signs of the new world over the Lithuanian border. I met another four Americans traveling to carry information to Col. Haskell [...] The sleeping compartments are primitive – to speak euphemistically – and one needs to pay a bit of attention. The trains are running not on coal, but simply on burning wood: delays are long and frequent. [...] During the journey, one observed enormous companies of peasants walking toward the west, each one inevitably with a sack of flour and other provisions on his shoulders. The same is true in Moscow. [...] The ruble is practically without value. I have changed dollars at the rate of 2 million rubles for a dollar. The cost for a ride in a car is 30,000 rubles, a pair of good shoes costs 10 million rubles. A complete suit, ordinary, costs 25 million rubles, etc. Knowing that a talented man can receive a salary of 2 Million a month, you will understand what it means to live here. [...] The famine is at its highest point and all the forces of the American Relief Administration are working with utmost intensity. We have 180 Americans with about 50,000 Russian employees scattered everywhere. By the end of this month the Americans will be sustaining 3,500,000 children and more adults. When the harvest comes, when one hopes the danger will have passed, the total number of people maintained will be 10,000,000. The funds at our disposition are 52,000,000 dollars. There is not so much a need of funds as of the means to facilitate distribution. The ships which have arrived form a large flotilla of 147 boats which arrive at Riga, Reval, Danzica and in the ports of the Black Sea like Odessa.
Among the ways of helping those that suffer is the "food remittance system". A person, for example, in New York, London, Paris, Rome or elsewhere, can go to an office of the ARA and deposit 10 dollars, or any multiple thereof, for a certain quantity of food for a specific person whom the donor knows in any

---

[57] This refers, evidently, to the permanence and survival of the Company of Jesus in Russia (and in Slesia) at the time of its disbandment, which occurred under Pope Pius VI, but was decided with the edict *Dominus ac Redemptor* issued by Pope Clement XIV in 1773.

[58] AES, Pont. Comm. Pro Russia, Sc. 72, Fasc. 325, 3-5.

[59] Father Joseph F. Hanselman [1856-1923], 14° President of Holy Cross College [Worcester, MA] – then part of the Maryland Province (also Edmund Walsh's Province), was nominated American Assistant to the General of the Society of Jesus. This office made him the principal counselor for the personnel and projects of the American Jesuits. Fr. Hanselman had been Provincial of the Maryland Province from 1906 to 1912, during Walsh's first years in the Order, and certainly knew him well.

Russian village or city. Here in Moscow the ARA will take care of a large number of packages of victuals which will serve to maintain a man for two months or a family of four persons for about a month. The package contains a certain quantity of nutritious food chosen with great care (flour, milk, rice, sugar, cooking fat). [...] These packages will be made here; they will then be sent to the person for whom they are destined under our supervision, it will be consigned and a receipt will be sent to the donor. If, after 90 days, the person is not found, the money is returned to the donor.

This is simply a small action promoted in the area devastated by famine; the others consist in large kitchens where all are always welcome to get what they need. But the "Food Remittance" permits us to pay attention to individuals and to take care of them, in addition to the general aid which they receive by means of the kitchens and hospitals organized in all of the famine regions.

It is, of course, impossible for us to know, or for you or others in distant countries to be acquainted with, who is in need of these food packages and it is for this reason that the various organizations – Jewish, Lutheran, YMCA, Baptist, etc. – have their representative in Moscow to pay attention to the most terrible cases and take care of the packages for these persons. In this way, for example, the representative's organization places 50,000 dollars at disposition: this gives him the right to 5,000 packages of provisions, enough to maintain 5,000 persons for two months... He will make his rounds, compile a list, return to Moscow and send the packages immediately to the persons that he wishes to aid. Naturally he will give aid to his own, although one could distribute to anyone.

This method has been amply used by the Jews to aid their own. In this moment the Jewish representative is seated in front of me preparing the addresses for his victuals. And I remind you that these victuals are placed in packages, transported and consigned with receipt, all with the means of the ARA organization.

This will be a good way for us to begin. I will do this within a few days for the famine regions, preparing the lists and obtaining the victuals to send them. I will pay attention to ours, that is to say, to the clergy, convents, schools, etc. and I will succeed perhaps in sustaining entire communities or also villages. But to accomplish this, funds are needed immediately. If Francesco [Father Ledóchowski] wants us to do this, he should send me the money by telegram, and in the largest amount possible, for example, 20,000 dollars to begin with. [...] The money can be sent by marine cable in the following way [...].
I am fine. Commend me to Francesco[60]. (Signed E.A. Walsh)».

---

[60] Walsh mentions the name, Francesco, twice in this report. This was the code name Walsh used to indicate the Superior General of the Jesuits, Wlodzimierz Ledóchowski. Prudently, Walsh maintained a «low profile» with regard to his Jesuit identity, particularly because the Superior General of the Jesuits, Fr. Ledóchowski, was from a noble Polish family (cause enough for ill feelings among the Russians) and the son of a General in the Polish Army. Throughout his assignment in Russia, Walsh used this code name (or the variants thereof: François or Francis) for Fr. Ledóchowski.

Walsh left Moscow on April 25, 1922, and arrived in Rome on May 2. In the meantime, thanks to a letter from the Superior General of the Jesuits to the Secretary of State on April 29, we know the course which the mission in Russia was taking:

«Yesterday I had another long chat with Miss [sic] Haskell and, everything considered, I think it is best to have Fr. Walsh come to Rome and arrange everything with him. Miss Haskell assures me that, by sending a telegram immediately, he could be in Rome within two weeks. However I have now received a letter from Fr. Walsh written in Moscow on April 20 informing me that he will arrive here on the 4 or 5 of May for six days. I think, therefore, that it would be prudent to await his arrival and, for the moment, not to make any commitments even though this slightly delays the dispatch of the Holy See's aid.

If I am not mistaken, there are serious difficulties, which I will explain in person, with sending our delegates along with the grain bought in Romania. I think the first project of Your Eminence would be much better. That is to say, that, for awhile, the Fathers profit from the food distribution organization already existent [i.e. ARA] and only later take the grain from Romania.

Miss Haskell is extremely grateful for the good reception which she received from Your Eminence and for the audience with the Holy Father.

Permit me to ask whether the two Spanish Fathers of which Your Eminence spoke should come immediately or if they should be sent later; as far as we are concerned, there is no difficulty in immediately placing them at the disposition of the Holy See»[61].

On May 3 Walsh was already in conference with the Superior General:

«Conference at once with Vladimir L. who sent various documents at once to Vatican. Fortunate I came this moment as plans and policy undetermined. Found plans almost ready to send 12 agents to distribute relief for Papacy, but am dissatisfied with conditions. Without any knowledge on my part they have agreed in writing with Vorovsky (Soviet Representative at Rome) to do certain things which I consider dangerous to ultimate control of relief. Moreover they have agreed that agents should enter by Novorossysk, not by northern ports and confine activities to South. Vlad. expressed suspicions of a certain Mr. Brown who had managed to get some say about the relief – who wanted to plant agents in German zones of influence and buy grain from Roumania. Vlad. has insisted on his elimination; suspects politics. I have advised moving very slowly as present religious persecutions do not seem fully appreciated.

Thursday May 4. Saw Mgr. Pizzardo who showed me agreement signed between Vat. (Gasparri) and Soviets (Vorovsky). Found it ambiguous, not strong enough for guaranteeing control. One paragraph (5) seemed to give ultimate

---

[61] AES, Pont. Comm. Pro Russia, Sc. 73, Fasc. 332, 17.

control to local Soviet authorities. Explained all to Pizzardo and ARA difficulties. Drew up 5 articles to be added by way of interpretation. He promised to take same with him to Genoa tomorrow and have them agreed to. Left satisfied.

Friday May 5, 1922 – Conference with Card. Gasparri – 7.30-9 P.M. at Vatican. [...] Gave whole situation to him and finally ventured to say time had come for protest from Pope. Old gentleman said nothing but rose from the lounge where he sits during audiences and went to his desk, brought back 2 large printed sheets and said "Read". To my joy found first was "a Memorandum" addressed to Powers at Genoa demanding etc. (cfr. Document). No. 2 was a detailed list of the religious persecutions, some of which were stigmatized as «unknown in history of civilized nations». At end of this No. 2 it said "This protest is based on authentic information given by reliable people recently come from Russia". He referred to documents I brought from Shepherd CPLK [Archbishop Jan Cieplak, Bishop of Ohrid, ndr] but said to protect him in R[ussia] they put it that way. He added "We are sending Mgr. Pizzardo to Genoa tomorrow and he will hand these 2 documents to diplomats with whom Holy See has relations". We spoke of Relief and I outlined my plans; he regretted possible withdrawal of Americans and ended by proposing an appeal to President of US to continue Relief from Pope and letter to Hoover on same. It was decided that I should carry these letters personally to Washington at once and make further arrangements for cooperation. $200,000 now available, much more to come. He told me to draw up draft of the 2 letters, to be signed by Pope and himself and wrote a few words on his card to Vlodimir saying he wished EAW to be set aside for this work – in Europe and in America. Left 9 P.M. He could not bear to look at famine pictures».

These few lines in Edmund Walsh's diary provide us with an open window on events, such as the Genoa Conference of 1922, which have marked world history. It was here that, for the first time, a Russian Commissar of Foreign Affairs intervened in an international conference, in this case, it was the renowned Georgy Vasilyevich Chicherin[62].

«Saturday May 6. Audience with Pius XI, 11.30-12.10. As before he was kind, democratic, cordial. Listened to all details. Asked of Shepherd CLPK. Looked at all pictures of famine followed my explanation of map of Russia and my plans. Thanked me again. Knew of my trip to America and said he would add personal note to Mr. Hoover, whom He knew at Warsaw. I spoke to him about life in Russia and my scruples about Breviary. He confirmed all faculties given and said "Charity supplies all" then added, "*I communicate to you all faculties and powers which I can communicate*". He did not add

---

[62] The Genoa Conference took place from April 10 to May 19, 1922. It was a concerted attempt by the representatives of 34 countries, including Soviet Russia, to reconstruct European finance and commerce.

for Russia – hence strictly speaking they are not limited geographically. Sent benediction to all in Russia, promised to send help, blessed my efforts. Gave me another crucifix and sent me away after 40 minutes.

At 5 P.M. returned to Vatican for Conference with some of "agents" – evident that some will never do for work in Russia – timid – unused to work with men».

In this second personal audience, Walsh had confirmation of Pius XI's open and cordial character and, something which impressed him, expressed again his opinion of the Pope as «democratic» – a characteristic of the Pope which was, evidently, unexpected by Walsh and by which he was pleasantly surprised. We can imagine that, most likely, Walsh had been prepared to confront a very formal atmosphere characterized by calm, cordial words spoken from a regal distance.

In the following days, Walsh's diary records the news of the reactions to Vatican diplomacy at the Genoa Conference. The press reported at length on the meeting between Chicherin and the archbishop of Genoa, Mgr. Giosuè Signori, and on their toast, made during the reception hosted by the King of Italy on the Royal Battleship, «Dante Alighieri», which provoked a great international furor. A few days later, Mgr. Pizzardo presented his aforementioned Memorandum in three points to the delegates of the countries attending the conference[63].

«Sunday May 7 – Saturday May 13 – Preparing draft of a letter to Pres. Harding and Hoover. Read draft to Gasparri – about Tuesday. Papers now quoting «Memorandum» as delivered at Genoa. Other papers – French – Belgian – scandalized at idea of Pope having anything to do with Soviets – they speak of a concordat with horror. Osservatore Romano publishes denial saying it was only an agreement about sending agents to distribute relief. Hear many disgusting rumor about astonishment that Archbishop of Genoa had anything to do with Soviet delegate at banquet given by King at Genoa. French papers particularly bitter, probably inspired by anti clerical influences that would like

---

[63] The three points of the Vatican Memorandum were, briefly: liberty of worship and conscience; liberty of private and public worship; restoration of the property which had been confiscated from all religious confessions. The Vatican requested that countries in attendance at the Conference should not sign agreements with the Soviets if the Soviets had not guaranteed liberty of worship and religion and interrupted religious persecutions. Great Britain did not acknowledge the Memorandum and Chicherin did not accept to discuss it because, as he affirmed, there was no religious persecution in Russia. He did, however, consent to the Vatican's request to send a pontifical relief mission to Russia. For more information: G.M. CROCE, *Santa Sede e Russia Sovietica alla Conferenza di Genova*, in «Cristianesimo nella Storia», 23 (2002)/2, 345-365.

to see rupture of recent relations between Rome and France (cfr. Documents – papers)».

Mgr. Pizzardo's return from Genoa reserved some surprises for Walsh, offering him a first hand example of the vaunted, centuries-old diplomatic capacity of the Vatican:

«Saturday May 13 – Mgr. Pizzardo returns from Genoa – met him on 4 floor outside gallery of Vatican – made date for 4 P.M., his apartments. Conference at 4 P.M. showed that he has been impressed by Chicherin at Genoa. Expressed confidence in Chicherin, despite my warning about liars and hypocrites. Astonished me by explaining he had not asked them to sign the added articles of the agreement which I had given him; said he did not think it necessary after the 2 hours talk with Chicherin!! What can it mean? In view of what I know about their tactics in Russia with ARA their word is worth nil. M. Pizz. even went so far as to say that I must not insist too much on question of control of goods – that was second (the first he admitted with ARA), first thing for Papal Relief was good will of present authorities in order to work for souls later. This is a complete change of attitude he had before he went to Genoa. Told me too he found diplomats very unwilling to bring in question of religious guarantees. On return to [Jesuit] Curia, told V. my impressions of surprise and disappointment. He understood and agreed that he believed they were on false track, especially in regard to buying at least some grain or supplies in *Roumania* which M. Pizzardo said *must* be done. M. Pizz. also said not to bind Holy See too much to Americans. He said I could use at once in America $100,000.
Said if crisis arose rather to sacrifice few trainloads of food rather than lose good will of Soviets! Cannot understand this and pointed out to Vlad. how difficult that would make my mission. We would lose confidence of world and get no more money! Vlad. agrees with me – says situation grave and imposes silence on me. World would think Vat. is compromising with Soviets. He promised to see Pizz. and Gasp.
Sunday – May 14. Preparing for departure from R. for America. Monday – All letters – to President – Hoover etc. ready at 6 P.M. Brought to my room personally by Vlad. who brought them from Vat. He was encouraged and said he believed they were now on right track – he had conference with Gasp. and Pizz. They have agreed to publish Memorandum and the other letter (No. 2) in Osservatore Romano for Tuesday evening. Hope they will publish the document no. 2 which I have *never seen mentioned* – the second one I read in Card. Gasparri's study Friday evening May 5. Chicherin had answered in papers by quoting laws guaranteeing religions freedom. I gave to D'Herbigny copy of *Russian decree* prohibiting religious instruction even in *homes*. This shows facts, not *theories* (emphasis in original)».

On May 15, Walsh left Rome for the United States. On May 21st he embarked on the «Berengaria» which docked in New York on May 27 at

5 P.M. During the trip Walsh used his diary to record an extensive analysis of the Russian revolution and of the men who had realized it. But let us move our attention to the papal letter which he was carrying for Herbert Hoover.

The letter was composed of two parts: a Memorandum (in English) directed to Hoover in his function as Chairman of the American Relief Administration (in which reference was made to the letter for President Harding) and a personal letter (in French) from Pius XI, who had met Hoover when he was the apostolic nuncio in Poland:

«Memorandum:
[...] Under separate cover His Holiness, Pope Pius XI, has addressed a letter to President Harding concerning the possibility of a continuance of Russian relief. The admirable part now being played in combating the famine by the American Relief Administration under your direction has touched His Holiness deeply and He is encouraged to hope that you will find it possible to second His plea with the President, knowing as He does not only actual conditions as they exist in Europe today but also your own compassionate sympathy for the distressed peoples of Europe.
To the voice of the Vicar of Christ thus raised in anxious solicitude for the famine stricken millions of that demoralized land may I add the following considerations for your own attention?
1. Should the decision to withdraw the ARA sometime in September or October still seem necessary, the Holy See will undertake to enlarge its relief programme to embrace as much of the stricken regions as is possible with the necessarily limited resources at our disposal. The Holy Father is now preparing a communication to the entire Christian world in which He rallies all Christendom to a crusade of charity for Russia. Should you decide to withdraw the ARA shortly, would it not be possible for your efficient organization still to assist by continuing to purchase supplies in America and shipping them to Russian ports, where the Papal Relief Administration would undertake to receive and distribute them in the same manner adopted by the ARA in Russia? No discrimination would be made but food would be distributed to all who stood in need for help. The only requirement for assistance would be hunger and want, now, alas so widespread in Russia. Expenses would be guaranteed up to delivery at Russian ports where Papal control would begin. The excellent system of control and distribution already set up by your organization would supply a model and a working basis for the later organization in which American personnel would largely figure. The programme would include child feeding, – limited adult feeding and the distribution of food packages in certain districts hereafter to be determined.
2. Should it be found possible, – as we pray God may so ordain –, for you to continue Russian relief for another year, the Holy See will so arrange contributions through American Catholics that the Catholic representative with the ARA at Moscow will be enabled to supplement your work by reaching spots where the ARA has not found it possible to set up stations. Funds for a substan-

tial program will be placed at his disposal from the Catholics of America and from such other sources as may wish to contribute, so that by means of Food Remittances, Eurelcon sales and new kitchens where necessary, help can be brought to those regions newly threatened, as for example, the Caucasus and the Crimea. In either case, dear Mr. Hoover, whether the ARA withdraws or continues its noble work, the common good will be immensely served if you can further the efficient distribution of Catholic funds in either of the manners herein described. In order to provide for such discussion of details as may assure a speedy and definite decision we have asked the Catholic representative on the ARA staff at Moscow, Professor Edmund A. Walsh, to proceed at once to Washington as our personal representative and delegate»[64].

The personal letter from the Pope opened by recalling the relief aid which Hoover had brought to Poland:

«Nous avons encore présentes à l'esprit les belles heures que Nous avons passées avec Votre Excellence à Varsovie, tandis que défilaient devant Nous, en acte de reconnaissant hommage, les émouvantes phalanges des petits enfants Polonais que la sollicitude et la générosité de Votre Excellence et du peuple Américain avaient sauvés d'une mort certaine. Aussi bien, ayant adressé à cette même date un pressant appel au Président de la grande République Américaine, en faveur des pauvres petits enfants Russes, en proie à la faim et à la maladie. Nous ne pouvons Nous refuser le plaisir de manifester à Votre Excellence combien Nous avons à cœur que soit maintenue et poursuivie l'œuvre destinée à les soulager. Connaissant fort bien vos généreux sentiments, ainsi que le rôle si admirable et si efficace que sous votre sage direction l'American Relief Administration joue présentement pour combattre la famine en Russie, Nous vous prions de seconder Notre appel au Président pour ce peuple malheureux. Votre Excellence aura peut être déjà appris que Nous enverrons prochainement en Russie des agents spéciaux chargés de distribuer des secours à cet infortuné pays. Et Nous sommes persuadés que votre coopération et vos conseils leur seront très utiles. C'est pourquoi Nous chargeons le Professeur Edmond Walsh de se rendre immédiatement à Washington pour vous mettre au courant de Nos intentions et pour s'entendre avec vous. Dans la confiance que vous voudrez bien le favoriser dans toute la mesure possible, Nous prions le Seigneur de répandre sur vous l'abondance de Ses faveurs. Rome, le 15 Mai 1922»[65].

Before Walsh's arrival, the Vatican's Secretary of State telegraphed the Apostolic Delegate in Washington DC, Mgr. Giovanni Bonzano, to inform him that Walsh was arriving with two letters from the Pope: «Holy See sends 12 agents Russia distribution aid to famished. Holy Father has

---

[64] AES, Pont. Comm. Pro Russia, Sc. 73, Fasc. 334, 70-71.
[65] *Ibidem*, 72.

encharged Jesuit Walsh to present papal letters President Harding and Mr. Hoover. Request you counsel him, help him, telegraphing me practical way. Father Walsh will request sums for eventual purchases. Inform me of this and await my orders. Card. Gasparri»[66].

Following are Walsh's diary annotations of the meetings with the Apostolic Delegate, Fr. John Burke, President Harding, Herbert Hoover, Cardinal O'Connell, Archbishop Hayes and Archbishop Curley:

«Monday May 29 – To Mgr. Bonzano at 9 A.M. He had code message instructing him to prepare meeting with President, give me money needed, and report progress. An explaining mission, he despatched Mgr. Floersch [John A., ndr (1886-1968)] to arrange meeting with President H. [...]
Went to N.C.W.C. 1312 Massachusetts Ave. to see Burke – not in town – in tomorrow. [...] Monday May 30 – Washington – [...] To see Fr. Burke in A.M. and got [that?] strange story of NCWC. This makes mission doubly hard. No organization to mobilize funds and danger of loss of official representation on ARA. Expressed belief that Pius XI did not really know, also hazarded guess that one Congregation in Rome did not know what other, e.g. Sec. of State, was doing – as all my dealings have been with Sec. of State Pizzardo. Recalled to Fr. Burke my showing slips I use for fund remittances in Russia – "NCWC" on them. Pope thanked me for efforts! He could not have known entire situation. This explains long silence of Fr. Burke regarding re-appointment and extension of 3 months appointment. Meeting with President tomorrow 11:30.
Wednesday May 31 – To White House at 11:30. [...] Did not get in until about 12:25. President cordial and courteous. Explained I came direct from Moscow and ARA work. He questioned me as to situation – listened attentively – on spoliation of Churches and anti religious programme, he said "No nation can exist without religion". Asked no. of Catholics in Russia [...] Gave him Pope's letter after little conversation. He opened it – saw French – immediately said "I regret I am not a linguist" and rang for secretary – "Take it to State Department and have translated at once". Then I informed him that I would be returning shortly, if any answer was to be sent by that way. He said "If any answer at once, you may expect it through Mr. Hoover». Shook hands – ended at 12,50. [...] In evening, finally found his [Hoover, ndr] private telephone no. (W831) (2300 S. St.) through Nelson Shepherd. Called him up – got him on "phone explained was leaving soon" – He answered "Come here to breakfast tomorrow at 7 A.M.".
Thursday, June 1. At Hoover's, 2300 S. St. at 6.55A.M. Explained Catholic programme – at last they were convinced that funds would be properly administered and outlined plan – Rather taciturn – few words – positive in attitude against P.C.Φ.C.P. until they show reasonable regard for outsiders. Particularly emphatic against confiscation of Church property. Without saying so, seemed to welcome proposals of cooperation; said he was not yet fully

---

[66] AES, Pont. Comm. Pro Russia, Sc. 73, Fasc. 332, 18.

decided about continuing unless P.C.Ф.C.P. did more themselves. Believed time not ripe for general appeal "would not get 2 millions". Listened much during breakfast, smoked several cigars and related experiences. Gave letter of Pope – left 8:15 – in his auto – went to Commerce with him and he said to chauffer "Take Fr. Walsh wherever he wants to go". It was understood that I would see him again for details after he had considered letter.

To see Fr. Burke – more details about NCWC. Told me he had cable from Vladimir – "Reappoint Walsh – delay unfavorable". [...]

Monday June 5 – Boston – Home – A.M. to see Cardinal O'C [O'Connell, ndr], Boston, explained forthcoming appeal for funds – very intimate conversation about work and type of cooperation from R [Rome, ndr] – What kind of helpers? P – B – (?) – Other – picturesque – language – expressed full accord with cooperation. "Tell G. [Gasparri, ndr] I'm with him"! – Left for N.Y. midnight.

Tuesday June 6 – N.Y. To "America" for dinner. Saw article in defence of stand of H. Father on Russia, written by Reville. Saw Archbishop Hayes [Patrick Hayes, Arch. of NY, ndr], Madison Ave. promised full cooperation, but expressed great embarrassment about decree re NCWC. Washington by midnight.

Wednesday June 7. Conference Mr. Hoover 12 noon. Agreed to plan of cooperation – NCWC to act as liaison between Catholic Mission and ARA. I buy food and distribute by our own personnel, no objection to Europeans, but preferred Americans. No objection to my bringing back assistant. How much money? $100,000 in hand – more in sight. Called stenographer – send cable to Haskell "Can you allocate $100,000 food at once to Walsh – similar amount to follow. Districts between Rostow and Ekaterinadar".

June 7- 17 – Boston – N.Y. – Washington – GU – Saw Arch. Curley – promised cooperation but again expressed regret NCWC affair. June 17 Sailed from N.Y. with S.J. Gallagher».

Now that we have had a panoramic vision of Walsh's trip to America, and his meetings with several of the central characters up to this moment, let us read how the Apostolic Delegate, Giovanni Bonzano, interpreted his meetings with Walsh in a long, detailed letter to Cardinal Gasparri on June 16, 1922[67]:

«The Rev. Edmund Walsh, SJ, left yesterday for New York where he will embark tomorrow to return to Rome. He will arrive at the same time as this letter, if not before, to inform Your Most Reverend Eminence concerning his actions.

Father Walsh presented himself to the Delegation as soon as he arrived in Washington, at the end of last month. He told me the intent of his journey and let me read copies of the letters to President Harding and Mr. Hoover relative to the continuation of the relief aid for Russia, and he asked me to

---

[67] AES, Pont. Comm. Pro Russia, Sc. 73, Fasc. 334, 51-53.

obtain an audience with the President in order that he might present him the Pope's signed letter. [...] On May 31 the President received Fr. Walsh who presented him the letter. He accepted it with pleasure, but since the letter was in French, he said that he would send it to the Department of State for translation and that he would reply to the Holy Father in good time, implying then he would have left the matter to Mr. Hoover, the Director of the Relief Aid work. Fr. Walsh also consigned the pontifical letter to Mr. Hoover and had a conversation concerning the conditions in Russia, the wishes of the Holy Father and the necessity to continue the aid to the famished. Mr. Hoover, however, responded that he could not yet make a decision, the which depended upon confidential information, and that he awaited his Secretary who had been dispatched specifically to gather precise news of the situation in Russia. In the meantime he implied that the Relief Aid would continue until January indeed until September 1, on the condition that the Soviet Government renews its guarantee to protect the American personnel and the freedom of distribution of the aid. From other, unofficial sources, however, it was learned that very probably the aid work would be continued.

Mr. Hoover was not only pleased with the cooperation of the Holy See in this humanitarian work, but himself suggested the regions to aid, that is, the provinces of the Caucasus and of the Crimea, at the moment the most needy, and he immediately offered part of the food resources now deposited in Russia – for the sum of one hundred thousand dollars, to the Holy See. Since Mr. Hoover would have had to immediately order new food shipments to replace those given to the Holy See, Fr. Walsh asked me immediately for the aforementioned sum, as I mentioned to Your Eminence in my encoded message N. 42, not having all of this money at my disposition. Following the response which was given me by Your Eminence with the coded message N. 41, Father Walsh concluded that the payment of this sum was not urgent and that it would be possible to defer it until his arrival in Rome where he will personally give the necessary explanations.

The other day the Secretary of President Harding told Fr. Walsh by telephone not to await the President's reply to the Holy Father, since that had already been sent with the usual intermediary. What was intended by the usual intermediary is not clear. Up to now the few letters exchanged between this Administration and the Holy See have passed through the Apostolic Delegation and I would not be surprised, as it was said to Fr. Walsh, that he had not understood well and that the Secretary, instead of saying that the letter had been sent, could have said that it will be sent. That does not exclude the possibility that the President's letter could have been sent by mail or by an intermediary of the American Embassy in Rome».

This first taste of the meticulous, bureaucratically irreproachable way which Mgr. Bonzano utilized to write his reports to the Holy See already hints at a prejudicial view towards Walsh. His recital of the facts concerning the details of the payment for the ARA food supply would seem to imply something negative about Walsh's behavior. In the next paragraph he then suggests that Walsh simply had not understood his conversation with the President's Secretary, that – we are to assume – Walsh was incapable of distinguishing between two very different English verb tenses! The Apostolic Delegate's letter concerning the «Jesuit Walsh» then continues and reveals even more clearly his lack of sympathy for Walsh:

> «Allow me to add a few words with regard to Fr. Walsh. Some people accuse this young Jesuit[68], who does not lack in intelligence or ability, of being ambitious. I don't know how correct this is, but to me he appeared quite imprudent and without experience. While at first he insisted on the necessity of immediately making payment of the one hundred thousand dollars, for which I had to telegraph Your Eminence, he then no longer insisted on this necessity; and I wouldn't be surprised if he agreed that the sum should be paid at the moment the food is delivered to the Pontifical Delegates. Father Walsh asked me for five or six thousand dollars for his and his companion's trip and other expenses; but seeing my reluctance to give him such a large sum, which seemed unjustified to me, he was satisfied with a thousand dollars and, perhaps, would have accepted even less».

At this point these insinuations against Walsh are already sufficiently grave, but the Prelate adds something more to the weight of his words:

> «He told me that no one in Russia knows of his identity as a Priest, but shortly thereafter informed the American newspapers of his trip there, with information which might not please the Soviets and would impede his reentry in Russia. When he read in the paper that Mons. Cieplak[69] had been imprisoned, even Fr. Walsh became worried that his indiscretions might have caused that arrest. Perhaps these are things of little importance; nevertheless I thought it good to bring them to Your Eminence's attention because it seems to me that they might be useful in the future».

This final accusation – which, had there been any truth in it, most certainly would have had serious repercussions on both Walsh and the Mission – should be immediately clarified. First, as part of his activities in America in support of the Papal Relief Mission, Walsh was preparing a publicity campaign to raise funds for this mission. He was, therefore, in

---

[68] Edmund A. Walsh, born in 1885, at this time was 37 years old. Not having an ecclesiastical career behind him, he must have seemed like a rank beginner to Mgr. Bonzano, born 1867, 55 years old, and, as a Prelate of the Curia, an experienced hand at Vatican politics – as this letter so well demonstrates.

[69] Jan Cieplak (1857-1926), born of Polish nobility, became Auxiliary Bishop of the Archdiocese of Mohilev in 1908, titular archbishop of Achrida in 1919. He died in the United States during a pastoral visit in 1926.

contact with the press and, in such matters, Walsh was particularly astute[70] – though Mgr. Bonzano is implying the contrary. Secondly, at this time Mgr. Jan Cieplak's position as an important intermediary with the Roman Catholic Church was well known in Russia – particularly following the deportation of his superior, Eduard von der Ropp, Archbishop of Mohilev, by the Bolsheviks in 1919. Additionally Mgr. Cieplak had already come under police surveillance during Czarist Russia – for suspicion of Polish nationalism. Cieplak was arrested twice before the famous Soviet trial which was to occur in the following year, 1923, in which he, his Vicar, Mgr. Konstantin Budkevich, various other priests and lay persons, as well as the Exarch of the Byzantine-Russian Catholic Church, Leonid Feodorov, were prosecuted and condemned. Furthermore it is appropriate here to recall that, during the proceedings of this Russian «show trial», Walsh succeeded in securing the admittance of an American journalist, helped the journalist send his articles out of Russia (avoiding censorship) and, by alerting the world to the true nature of Soviet communism and creating an international furor, was instrumental in saving Mgr. Cieplak from execution. Cieplak's Vicar, Mgr. Konstantin Budkevich, however, was executed by the Soviets shortly after the trial ended.

Returning to Fr. Walsh's trip to America, let us read his official report (the original text, written in French, is printed in the footnotes) submitted to the Vatican on June 29, 1922[71]: *Résumé du rapport du P. Walsh après son voyage en Amérique (28 mai – 17 Juin 1922) – À Son Eminence le Cardinal Secrétaire d'Etat*. The report is divided into six points. The first point concerns his meeting with President Harding and is essentially identical with what we read in his diary and in the report written by Mgr. Bonzano, except for a few small observations concerning Harding:

«He led me to the door very cordially, in marked contrast with the Presbyterian reserve of President Wilson...[72]. In effect, a few days later I received a telephone call from the White House by the President's Secretary. She advised me that the President would respond through the normal channels. Three days later a note appeared in the press, announcing that the President would be

---

[70] This is well demonstrated by the fund raising campaign Walsh organized five years later as the first President of the Catholic Near East Welfare Association in 1927. Thanks to his innovative methods, he collected a staggering $1,000,000 from American Catholics wishing to support CNEWA's work for the Eastern Churches.

[71] AES, Pont. Comm. Pro Russia, Sc. 73, Fasc. 332, 19-23.

[72] President Harding was a Baptist.

disposed to continue the aid, even beyond the deadline which had been fixed earlier of September 1. The newspaper clipping is attached herewith»[73].

The second point is dedicated to his meeting with Herbert Hoover. It too is substantially the same as we have read except for a detailed account of the present state of relations between the United States and the Soviet Union – upon which, in fact, depended the continuation of the relief aid offered by the ARA. Walsh recounts the practical matters he discussed with Hoover in this manner:

«As for the requested cooperation, it was readily accorded for as long as the ARA was active. In this way the pontifical mission can purchase its food and provisions from the A.R.A. and distribute them through its own personnel, the contact being assured through Prof. Walsh who remains a member of the American Commission (as the appointed representative of the NCWC, ndr).
He asked me how much money I could put out immediately in Russia for the two places where the necessity was greatest, Rostov and Jekatérinodar – places which he himself had foreseen, independently of us, and which are the same that the Holy See designated. Following the instructions given me by Mgr. Pizzardo who, on the eve of my departure (May 14), had authorized me to commit myself for one hundred thousand dollars in America, I responded to Mr. Hoover that I could make acquisitions for one hundred thousand dollars immediately. Mr. Hoover picked up his telephone at once, "Cable Moscow and order Colonel Haskell to reserve one hundred thousand dollars of food for Fr. Walsh and the Catholic program". In effect, the money never enters Russia, only the food; the price is paid in America. Therefore he asked me to settle the payment with the central office in New York»[74].

---

[73] «Il me reconduisit à la porte, très cordialement, en opposition marqué avec la froideur presbytérienne du Président Wilson [...] En effet, quelques jours plus tard, je reçus un message téléphonique, adressé de la Maison Blanche par le Secrétaire du Président. Il m'avisait que le Président ferait venir sa réponse par la filière ordinaire. Trois jours plus tard, une note parut dans la presse, annonçant que le Président se montrait disposé à continuer les secours, même au delà du délai précédemment fixé du I Septembre. La coupure est ci-jointe».

[74] «Quant à la coopération demandée, elle fut accordée volentiers pour tout le temps que l'ARA restera en action. Ainsi la mission pontificale pourra acheter, sur place de l'ARA les vivres et autres denrées, et les distribuer par son propre personnel, la liaison étant assurée par le Prof. Walsh qui reste membre de la Commission américaine. Il me demanda combien de fonds je pourrais lancer aussitôt en Russie pour les deux endroits où les nécessités sont très graves, Rostov et Jekatérinodar – endroits qu'il avait prévus lui-même, indépendamment de nous, et qui sont ceux-là mêmes que le Saint Siège a désignés. Suivant les instructions données par Mgr. Pizzardo qui m'avait autorisé la veille de mon départ (14 Mai) à m'engager à la somme de cent mille dollars en Améri-que, je répondis à M. Hoover que je pouvais acheter aussitôt cent mille dollars. M. Hoover prit aussitôt son téléphone, "Câblez à Moscou et ordonnez au Colonel Haskell

In this detailed report, we already note a mild discord with Mgr. Bonzano's report – a discord which, after a few more lines, becomes increasingly strident:

«After this first meeting, I met Mr. Hoover two more times in order to arrange details. He approved of my intention to bring an assistant from America, an American secretary (Louis Gallagher, SJ, ndr). Immediately after the first meeting, I prepared a dispatch to assure the Holy See of my arrival and the presentation of the letters, which found a favorable reception without, as yet, a definitive response. Mgr. Bonzano, to whom I gave this dispatch to be coded, judging that it was better to await a definitive response, did not send the cablegram. This is the reason why the Holy See remained without news during the first period»[75].

In the third point of Walsh's report, the versions enter into clear collision. The facts are established and yet, notably, the integrity of Mgr. Bonzano's actions, notwithstanding Walsh's frustration that, because of Bonzano's hesitation, he missed concluding a good bargain (*une très belle occasion*) for the Holy See, remain unremarked by Walsh[76]:

---

de réserver cent mille dollars de vivres pour le P. Walsh et le programme catholique". L'argent n'entre en effet, jamais en Russie, mais seulement les vivres; leur prix reste consigné en Amérique. Il m'invita donc à régler les chèques avec le bureau central à New York».

[75] «Après cette première entrevue, je revis M. Hoover deux autres fois pour arranger les détails. Il approuva mon intention d'emmener un aide d'Amérique, un secrétaire américain [Louis Gallagher, SJ, ndr]. Aussitôt après les premiers entretiens j'ai préparé une dépêche pou assurer le Saint Siège sur mon arrivée et sur la présentation des lettres, qui avaient trouvé un accueil favorable sans réponse encore définitive. Mgr. Bonzano, à qui je remis cette dépêche pour être chiffrée, jugeant qu'il valait mieux attendre une réponse définitive, n'envoya pas ce câblogramme. C'est pourquoi le Saint Siège est resté sans nouvelles pendant une première période».

[76] It is evident that Walsh's concerns at this moment corresponded to a mentality which was diametrically opposed to that of the Apostolic Delegate, or of the Secretary of State. Mgr. Bonzano's judgment of Walsh as young and inexperienced made sense from his point of view. Walsh paid attention to details – like paying the bills immediately, saving money through a good deal, organizing a publicity campaign – none of which were matters of importance to the Apostolic Delegate who, instead, formulated and altered his convictions on the basis of the instructions he received from Rome. Most likely Walsh assumed that his attention to details would be appreciated, instead, in the eyes of the Apostolic Delegate, Walsh was seen as a *parvenu*, or, worse, even as a profiteer or a thoughtless publicity seeker; a *petit bourgeois* social climber (ambitious!), someone who had entered the palace by grace received, an army private who had been given a captain's uniform. These distorted suspicions of Walsh corresponded, in fact, to a deeply rooted European prejudice which was associated with all Americans and mitigated only by slight differences of perception accorded to the

«Here I must confess my embarrassment when, the following day, following the instructions of the Holy See, I met with Mgr. Bonzano to settle the deposit of one hundred thousand dollars. We wrote a dispatch in which the Apostolic Delegate explained that he only had fifty thousand dollars and asked that the remainder be sent. But the response from Rome a few days later was not affirmative. Nevertheless, although the deposit was not made, the American authorities consented to anticipate the supplies, in spite of the irregularity, since the Catholic credit justified this trust. It is necessary, therefore, that the one hundred thousand dollars are immediately paid to the American administration in New York by Mgr. Bonzano. For this reason, I had to renounce an excellent occasion to buy at Coblenz all of the American surplus reserves which were sold at a good price, saving the Holy See thousands of dollars. Mgr. Bonzano, in fact, as a result of the response that came from Rome, did not feel authorized to give me even five thousand dollars»[77].

The fourth point dealt with the National Catholic Welfare Council. Reviewing Walsh's diary annotations made while he was in the United States, it becomes clear that practically all those with whom he spoke expressed their sorrow regarding the NCWC problem. It was, understandably, on everyone's mind and the decree – and the events which had led up to that decree – had clearly impacted the American Catholics' participation in the ARA and, consequently, the Papal Relief Mission to Russia. It is surprising, then, that the Apostolic Delegate did not express an opinion on so vital a point. Certainly he was well aware of the situation (as representative of the Holy See in America and as a permanent resident in Washington DC where both the NCWC and the Catholic American University were located). Furthermore, the possible effects of such a disbandment would inevitably effect the aid mission to Russia, putting not only the

---

American's wealth, social class and, for clergymen particularly, place of education: Rome, Europe or only in America.

[77] «Ici je dois avouer mon grand embarrasse quand, le lendemain, suivant les instructions du Saint Siège, je me présentai chez Mgr. Bonzano pour régler ce dépôt de cent mille dollars. Nous avons composé une dépêche où le Délégué Apostolique expliquait qu'il n'avait que cinquante mille dollars et priait qu'en expédiât le reste. Mais les réponses venues de Rome quelques jours plus tard n'étaient pas affirmatives. Pourtant, quoique le dépôt ne fût pas fait, les autorités américaines consentirent à avancer les vivres, malgré l'irrégularité, parce que le crédit catholique justifiait cette confiance. Il faut donc que les cent mille dollars soient immédiatement versés à l'administration américaine à New York par Mgr. Bonzano. Pour cette raison, j'ai du renoncer à une très belle occasion d'acheter à Coblence tout le surplus des réserves américaines qui se vendaient à très bon prix, en épargnant au Saint Siège des milliers de dollars. Mgr. Bonzano, en effet, par suite de la réponse venue de Rome, ne se crut même pas autorisé à me remettre cinq mille dollars».

nomination of Walsh (or of anyone else) as representative of the Holy See
and of the American Catholics in doubt (as Walsh noted in his diary), but
placing the Mission itself in doubt, since the Catholic organization on the
ARA would cease to exist:

> «The mission was made very difficult by the recent decree suppressing the
> National Catholic Welfare Council. My position in Russia, which serves as a
> liaison between the Catholics and the United States government, is due solely
> to this Catholic organization. Naturally, I was asked, also by the White House,
> if the NCWC continued to exist and if, consequently, I still had the right to
> present myself in Russia as a member of that organization. Fortunately I was
> able to settle this matter in a satisfactory manner, but my embarrassment was
> great»[78].

The fifth point does not directly relate to our discussion, but the sixth
point most certainly does: it discusses the meeting between Fr. Walsh and
Cardinal O'Connell of Boston (the outspoken critic of the NCWC and a
strong supporter of Fr. Walsh for the position Walsh now held in the Papal
Relief Mission). It then mentions the discomfort caused to the Archbishops of New York and Baltimore by the decree disbanding the NCWC and
faithfully transmits their convictions to Cardinal Gasparri:

> «In addition, I judged it opportune to visit the Archbishops of Boston, His
> Eminence the Cardinal O'Connell; of New York, Mgr. Hayes; and of Bal-
> timore, Mgr. Curley in order to stimulate their interest in favor of the Holy
> See's appeal for Russia, and prepare the ground for the alms collectors. His
> Eminence, the Cardinal of Boston, welcomed me warmly and committed him-
> self to do all which was possible to aid the Holy See in its effort for the Rus-
> sians, he appointed me to carry these special promises to His Eminence, the
> Cardinal Gasparri. The Archbishops of New York and Baltimore gave me the
> same welcome and also promised their support. They added that they were
> extremely embarrassed by the decree suppressing the National Welfare Coun-
> cil because they counted heavily on this organization to unify efforts within a
> country as large as America»[79].

---

[78] «La mission fut rendue très difficile par le récent décret supprimant le National Welfare Council. Ma position en Russie est due uniquement à cette organisation catholique
qui servait de liaison entre les catholiques et le gouvernement d'Amérique. Naturel-
lement, on me démenait, même au Capitole, si le National Welfare Council existait
encore et si, par suite, j'aurais encore le droit de me représenter en Russie comme
membre de dette organisation. Heureusement j'ai pu régler ces points de façon satis-
faisante, mais mon embarras était très grand».

[79] «En outre, j'ai jugé opportun de visiter les archevêques de Boston, Son Em. le Card.
O'Connell; de New York, Mgr. Hayes; et de Baltimore, Mgr. Curley pour éveiller
leur intérêt en faveur de l'appel du S. Siège pour les Russes et préparer le terrain aux

The report concludes with Walsh's enthusiastic summary of what, to-day, would be termed a publicity barrage, a promotional campaign intend-ed to create expectation for a product's appearance on the market. Here, however, the product to be publicized was the Pope, or even Catholicism itself, which finds its highest expression in the Pope. Walsh, as the evi-dence shows, was neither a small pawn with great ambitions nor even less a profiteer, but rather an American organizational mind, innovative and, above all, in the *avant garde* in such matters as «marketing»:

> «Fr. Walsh also prepared a complete documentation with photographs and articles to excite interest when the Holy See's appeal is published, with a large poster portraying St. Peter as the protector of the Russian people. All of this will be published when the Holy See's appeal is made public in America. The ground has been partially prepared by the articles, conferences and newspaper interviews given by Fr. Walsh. The document is awaited, and it is thought that, with a bit of organization, the response obtained could be magnificent. Rome, on the Feast Day of Saints Peter and Paul, June 29, 1922»[80].

At this point in narrating the intertwining concerns of the Vatican and of the American Catholics during the first months of Pius XI's pontificate, we have come full circle and returned to the pivotal point – and the point of friction - between the Vatican and America: the NCWC. The new Pope had a clear idea as to the doubts expressed regarding the conduct of the NCWC and knew well the objectives he wished to pursue. He had devel-oped his own strategy both as to how to overcome the impasse created by the NCWC's internal diatribes and as to how to jump-start the Papal Re-

---

collecteurs d'Aumônes. Son Em. le Card. de Boston m'accueillit chaleureusement et s'engagea à faire son possible pour aider le S. Siège dans son effort pour les Russes, il me chargea de porter ces promesses spécialement à Son Em. le Cardinal Gasparri. Les archevêques de New York et Baltimore me firent le même accueil promirent aussi leur appui. Ils ajout airent qu'ils se trouvaient extrêmement embarrassées par le décret supprimant le National Welfare Council parce qu'ils comptaient beaucoup sur cette organisation pour unifier les efforts dans un pays aussi étendu que l'Amérique».

[80] «Le P. Walsh prépara de même toute une documentation par photographie et articles pour exciter l'intérêt quand paraîtra l'appel du S. Siège, avec de grande affiche où le Saint-Père est représenté comme protecteur du peuple russe. Tout cela paraîtra dès que l'appel du Saint Siège sera rendu public en Amérique. Le terrain est partiellement préparé maintenant par les articles, les conférences et entretiens donnés par le P. Walsh dans les journaux. On attend le document, et l'on pense qu'avec un peu d'organisa-tion la réponse obtenue pourrait être magnifique. Rome, en la fête des Saints Apôtres Pierre et Paul, 29 Juin 1922».

lief Mission to Russia while utilizing the human and economic resources which America offered to the fullest. It would seem likely, then, that the decree of the Consistorial Congregation[81] took into consideration several interrelated concerns connected with the suspected «Americanism» (or Gallicanism) of the NCWC – a glaring example of which had been provided by the NCWC's omission of immediately appointing a representative to the ARA's Russian relief program, notwithstanding the Vatican's wishes (one of Pope Benedict XV's last wishes, in fact) that the Papal Relief Mission to Russia should act under the aegis of the NCWC's participation in the ARA program[82].

This omission revealed, at best, a surprising lack of coordination within the NCWC or, at worst, a paralyzing conflict of opinions which was only resolved in February of 1922 by direct interventions from the hierarchy above: Colonel Haskell for the ARA and Fr. Ledóchowski and the Secretary of State for the Vatican. In effect Walsh's first three month appointment as the American Catholics' representative to the ARA program was granted directly by the Vatican Secretary of State acting upon the proposal of Cardinal O'Connell[83] and only after the decree disbanding the NCWC had been issued! Even the subsequent three month renewal of Walsh's NCWC appointment, granted in June by NCWC Secretary, Fr. John Burke while Walsh was visiting the States, was directly «advised» in a telegram from Fr. Ledóchowski. The paralysis revealed in the NCWC non-appointment – in contrast to the laudatory reports the organization had sent to Rome regarding its utility and capacity, inevitably exposed Fr. Walsh to the discontent of the heads of the NCWC – not only because Walsh's nomination by the Secretary of State could be viewed as an offense to the authority of the NCWC and as an acknowledgement of their own failure to do so, but also because Walsh's nomination had been ardently championed by fellow Bostonian, Cardinal O'Connell – precisely the man whose complaints had played such a fundamental role in bringing the wrath of the Vatican down on the NCWC!

---

[81] Or simply, as Fr. Sheerin ironically suggests, «Cardinal De Lai's decision», J.B. SHEERIN, *Never Look Back...*, 70-80.

[82] The Vatican nurtured great hopes for what might result from the mission in Russia. In retrospect, one might say completely unrealistic hopes. Nevertheless the importance which the Vatican attached to this mission should not be underestimated. The almost simultaneous timing of the decree disbanding the NCWC and Walsh's summons to Rome by Ledóchowski can hardly be explained as happenstance.

[83] AES, Pont. Comm. Pro Russia, Sc. 73, Fasc. 335, 44-46.

Naturally, the idea of making enemies and creating malcontent among the ecclesiastic hierarchy of a vast, wealthy and emerging country was not among the objectives either of the Pope or of the Roman Curia. Already in June the scent of certain victory for the NCWC was in the air: «June 9. The battle goes on merrily with victory appearing in the future. [...] Rome does not like to be pushed, to be made to fight, and we have carried the fight to her, and put the issue up to her»[84].

The final decision was issued by the Consistorial Congregation on June 22, 1922, after being informed by Secretary of State Gasparri that «His Holiness wishes the NCWC to continue and will not support the decree of suppression»[85]. It was a subtle operation of mediation. The NCWC was allowed to continue its existence, but regulations were suggested concerning the organization of the bishops' meeting and limits were established upon the extent of their decisional power. Minutes of the meetings were to be sent to the Holy See for review by Church authorities and it was affirmed that this organization «is not to be identified with the Catholic hierarchy itself in the United States». Additionally every effort was made to guarantee that the NCWC could not interfere with the Catholic hierarchy in any way.

So closed a painful chapter in the life of the NCWC[86]. As far as the Vatican and Pius XI were concerned, they had achieved the goals of re-affirming the primacy of Rome and of removing the obstacle that had prevented the Papal Relief Mission from beginning its work in Russia under the ARA's organization and protection. Fr. Walsh, who was returning from the United States when the news was announced, was informed upon arrival in Rome. The survival of the NCWC, of course, had been essential to the Mission's existence.

Shortly thereafter Walsh left for Moscow to take up his post with the Papal Relief Mission to Russia. This was Walsh's first, longest and most formative papal mission. The working relationships he developed here – and the trust his services earned him within the Vatican hierarchy – would serve him throughout his following missions. The direct experience and observations which he gathered in Russia would also determine much of his subsequent thought and work. In effect, the Russian mission would become a watershed event in his life. And it would use his organizational

---

[84] James Ryan quoted in: J.B. SHEERIN, *Never Look Back...*, 76.

[85] *Ibidem*, 79.

[86] Subsequently the NCWC, at the suggestion of the Consistorial Congregation, changed its name to the National Catholic Welfare Conference.

and diplomatic capacities to the fullest both as Director General for the Papal Relief Mission to Russia – charged with organizing the distribution of the food and medical supplies contributed by Catholic charities to the Russian population – and as acting Representative of the Holy See in Russia – designated to deal with the Soviet Government regarding Roman Catholic interests in Russia. It was, essentially, two missions in one. At its height, the papal relief effort would have 701 feeding points (public kitchens, orphanages, hospitals, refugee camps) with the capacity to feed from 125,000 to 158,000 people daily – the great majority of whom were children – in five geographical areas: Crimea (Eupatoria and Djankoy), Moscow, Krasnodar, Rostov and Orenbourg[87].

Walsh completed his work with the Russian Mission in November of 1923. When he returned to Georgetown University and to his work in the United States, however, he did not leave his concern for Russia – or his inventive, organizational side – behind. Well aware of the countless difficulties facing the Church in Russia, he created a new project: «Project for the Adoption of Russian Churches by American Dioceses» and proposed it to the Pope. The project was accepted enthusiastically and on January 8, 1924, the text of Walsh's proposal, printed under the letterhead of the Secretary of State to His Holiness, Cardinal Gasparri and accompanied by a letter from the Cardinal recommending support for this proposal, was sent to the Apostolic Delegate to the United States, now Mgr. Pietro Fumasoni-Biondi, and to the American Church Hierarchy.

> «Professor Edmund Walsh, former General Director of the Papal Relief Mission to Russia, having completed his assignment, returns now to his pious home in America. It is, therefore, the Holy See's wish that he, being present there, should be able to ascertain the clergy's opinion regarding the maintenance of the Catholic churches in Russia which are going through grave trials and tribulations and are menaced by constant persecution – also of a material nature.
> The Holy See also wishes that Prof. Walsh ascertain the clergy's opinion in regard to a project to provide further aid to Russia, in particular to the Catholic Church in Russia which is presently in grave danger of persecution. To this end, he has authorized me to submit a concrete project (which has already been presented to the Holy See) to the opinion of Your Excellency and of the members of the American Catholic Hierarchy.
> Please help and support this in as far as it seem wise and opportune»[88].

---

[87] M. PATULLI TRYTHALL, *The Little Known Side of Fr. Edmund Walsh: His Mission to Russia in the Service of the Holy See*, in «Studi sull'Oriente Cristiano», 14 (2010)/1, 169-177.

[88] ASV, SDS, 1925, R. 181, F. 1, 2-3.

Walsh's innovative idea was simple yet full of moral and political significance:

«The recent visit of an Anglican Bishop to Moscow and his interview with the Patriarch Tychon brings to the foreground again and emphasizes the needs of the various Catholic Churches in Russia.

This Anglican Bishop (Bishop Bury) is the same prelate who succeeded in persuading the Greek Patriarch of Costantinople to recognize the validity of Anglican orders and it is rumored that the purpose of his interview with Tychon was to induce the head of the Russian Church to do the same. If such recognition of the validity of Anglican orders should be granted by the Orthodox Church, it is supposed that Great Britain would assume a sort of protectorate over the Russian Church, an act which would consolidate Canterbury and Moscow against the Vatican.

Such a religious «entente» would have important political results also, as the Bolsheviks would hesitate before persecuting the orthodox faith if the Russian Church had come under a quasi protectorate of England. This possibility is a further argument for the immediate execution of a plan already known to the Holy See and warmly approved by the Holy Father.

To save the remaining Catholic churches in Russia from extermination, it is proposed to ask the American dioceses to "adopt" the Catholic churches in Russia, which are on the verge of being completely destroyed by the Bolsheviks. Having "nationalized" the property and declared the vessels of the altar confiscated, the Government is now instituting a system of taxation which will slowly crush the already impoverished priests and parishes. To meet this immediate danger it is proposed to ask the diocese of New York to «adopt» the eleven churches in the city of Petrograd; the diocese of Boston will be asked to "adopt" the three churches of Moscow; the diocese of Brooklyn will be asked to "adopt" the churches of Odessa, – etc. etc. These American dioceses will be asked to contribute each year a certain sum of money to save the faith in these Russian cities by saving the Churches from confiscation by the Bolsheviks. The sum needed will not be large and P. Walsh feels confident that it will be contributed at once as the Catholics of America have been particularly outraged by the religious persecutions in Russia. It will suffice to let it be known that the Holy Father desires it, and the sums will be assured.

But the most important result will be in the moral sphere, – in the manifestation of that solidarity of Catholicism which the Bolsheviks fear and respect. Being masters in propaganda themselves, they have openly said that the "black international", i.e. the Catholic Church, is the greatest enemy of the "Red International" and to its programme of de-Christianizing Russia and then the entire world.

Thus, when it becomes known that the diocese of New York has a particular interest in the Petrograd churches, the Bolsheviks will think twice before applying any more oppression to the Petrograd churches, as this would excite a strong protest from the people of New York. So, *mutatis mutandis*, each Catholic Church in Russia would have a quasi protector in America, and as the Soviets are particularly anxious at this time to conciliate public opinion in America in order to achieve political recognition, it is believed that this

"adoption" plan will have very practical and valuable results in protecting religion in Russia and opposing an obstacle to the atheistic programme of Bolshevism.
The plan has been heartily approved by His Holiness.
Respectfully submitted (Edmund A. Walsh)»[89].

On November 25, 1924, Cardinal Gasparri sent a Christmas letter to Fr. Walsh:

«With real pleasure I take advantage of the approaching Christmas Holidays and the new year, to send to Your Most Reverend the assurances of my constant remembrance and the expression of my most fervid wishes for all that is good and prosperous in the Lord.
I am delighted to express these wishes also in the name and at the behest of the Holy Father, to whom I had indicated my intention to write you this present letter. The Holy Father, who always remembers with a thankful spirit your zealous activities on behalf of the Papal Relief Mission to Russia, sends you from his heart – through my services and as a sign of fatherly benevolence, a special Apostolic Benediction.
Profiting from the occasion, I would like to ask you to let me know, as soon as is possible for you, at what point is the project for the adoption of the Churches in Russia and what are the hopes for the future.
The news which arrives from Russia concerning the condition of the Church and of the Catholic clergy is, unfortunately, always bad and the Apostolic Delegate to China has recently written to the Sacred *Congregation* for the *Propagation of the Faith* that the "Siberian priests, eight or ten in number, are in very grave condition; so that a worthy way to assist their distress would be to provide for them through American charity". If you could provide these priests with the required aid, you would accomplish a real act of charity and would acquire new gratitude from the Holy See and the Holy Father.
Awaiting to receive your good news soon»[90].

From the words and tone of this letter, one can measure the personal respect which Walsh had earned from both Cardinal Gasparri and Pope Pius XI and see that Walsh had become, for them, an important point of reference in the United States – particularly for what concerned fund raising and Russian matters. This in spite of the fact that Walsh did not occupy a significant position in the American Church hierarchy! Such recognition was to have two consequences for Walsh's future collaborations with the Vatican.

---

[89] *Ibidem*, 13.
[90] *Ibidem*, 5.

The first is that Walsh would, indeed, carry out a number of assignments at the direct bidding of Pius XI. In 1926, after Fr. Walsh had written
Pius XI criticizing the confusion caused by the multiplicity of charitable
projects vying for the American Catholics' attention, Pius XI established
the Catholic Near East Welfare Association (CNEWA) and placed Fr.
Walsh in charge as President. Almost immediately, in January of 1927,
Walsh mounted a fund raising campaign which gathered more than one
million dollars. He used a number of innovative «marketing» methods
to encourage contributions and attract this considerable sum – the size of
which surprised the entire hierarchy of the Church on both sides of the
Atlantic and, of course, brought further luster to Walsh's reputation. During Walsh's administration – which lasted until the summer of 1931, the
CNEWA carried out relief projects in a variety of areas (in accordance
with the Pope's wishes that the association should function as a sort of
Catholic Red Cross agency) and also supported other humanitarian and
educational projects.

In the Spring of 1929, Walsh acted as the Pope's personal representative during the peace conference held between the President of Mexico,
Emilio Portes Gil, and the Mexican representatives of the Catholic Church,
Archbishop Leopoldo Ruiz y Flores and Bishop Pascual Díaz y Barreto, SJ
During Walsh's visit to Rome in the previous summer, Pope Pius XI had
drilled Walsh thoroughly on the demands that must be fulfilled in order
for the *Arreglos* to be signed by the Church. In his final report to the Vatican, Walsh lists these and explains in detail how each point was satisfied
either in the written declarations or through verbal agreements. Though he
did not participate directly in the conference discussions, Walsh played
a significant role in several other capacities – preparing the text of the
agreement, carrying out liaison work with Rome and, above all, personally contacting the radical members of the Mexican Church hierarchy and
explaining the Vatican's reason for concluding a peace settlement. The
conference resulted in an agreement, the *Arreglos,* which re-established
peace between Church and State (in the degree to which such was possible) and brought an end to the Cristero Revolution after three years of
strife[91].

---

[91] It also put a strain on the relationship with the NCWC and with the Apostolic Delegate
Fumasoni Biondi. The NCWC, through Fr. Burke's efforts and with the support of
Fumasoni Biondi, had been very active in the earlier stages of this process, but, having
lost the confidence of the Vatican, was not asked to take part in the final conference.
Walsh, on the other hand, had been sworn to secrecy by the Vatican and never spoke or
wrote publicly about the details of this mission.

Two years later, in the Spring of 1931, at the request of both Pius XI in his role as the Prefect of the Sacred Congregation for the Oriental Church-es and the Superior General of the Society of Jesus, Fr. Ledóchowski, Walsh went to Iraq to ascertain the possibility of establishing a Catholic secondary school there. The result was the founding of Baghdad College (later flanked by Al-Hikma University) which was sponsored and staffed by American Jesuits[92]. In their audience of April 30, 1931, Pius XI au-thorized the use of the reserve funds of CNEWA (Walsh, as the outgoing President of CNEWA was, of course, well aware of its financial reserves) in order to finance this project[93].

The second consequence of this special recognition from the Vatican – when granted to a person who was not a significant member of the Church hierarchy (i.e. an «upstart») – was the resentment it created within that same hierarchy – both the Roman Curia and the American Church hierar-chy. We have already encountered an early example of this while discuss-ing the Apostolic Delegate Mgr. Bonzano's critical analysis of Walsh as young, imprudent and inexperienced in 1922 and we can compare that with the analysis of Walsh made by Bonzano's successor as Apostolic Delegate to the United States, Mgr. Pietro Fumasoni Biondi in 1930[94].

> «This good father is the negation of any cooperation whatsoever. Although he lives in Washington, he has never informed me of what he does or what he writes to Rome: he sent me the minutes of the Commission Assembly only once – and this only at my request. He does not have the slightest idea of what an Apostolic Delegate is and it is impossible to make him understand given his age, his habits and his education»[95].

---

[92] For further information see: M. Patulli Trythall, *Edmund Aloysius Walsh: La Missio Iraquensis, Il contributo dei Gesuiti Statunitensi al sistema educativo iracheno*, in Supplement, «Studi sull'Oriente Cristiano», 14 (2010)/2, I-XI/1-445.

[93] *Ibidem*, 306-307.

[94] Mgr. Pietro Fumasoni Biondi (1872-1960): Apostolic Delegate and Titular Bishop of Doclea, from 1916; Secretary of the Sacred Congregation for the Propagation of the Faith in 1921; Apostolic Delegate to United States from December 1922; was made Cardinal by Pius XI during the Consistory of 1933, before being appointed Prefect of the Sacred Congregation for the Propagation of the Faith, a post he covered until his death.

[95] E. Walsh, Archivio PIO, Roma. It should be recalled that, in addition to his Presidency of the CNEWA, Walsh was the Regent of Georgetown University's School of Foreign Service (SFS), that he taught courses at the SFS regularly, that he gave over 1,500 public lectures on Soviet Russia throughout the United States, that he wrote many books and articles on that and other subjects and was a well known public figure. It

In less than eight years, the «young Jesuit», Walsh, had become too old – «given his age» – a rapid decline to be sure! Unfortunately, this estimation of Walsh by the Apostolic Delegate, who was also a key member of the Sacred Congregation for the Propagation of the Faith, was to present a serious problem for Walsh – who needed the Apostolic Delegate's approval for his CNEWA projects. In fact, the origins of the CNEWA lay with a number of associations, fund raising groups, Prelates, etc. (the variety and number of which had originally motivated Walsh's criticism to Pius XI) all of whom had formerly been grouped under the aegis of the powerful Sacred Congregation for the Propagation of the Faith. When these smaller organizations were, essentially, taken over – to the chagrin and, in some cases, resentment of their directors – and fused into one organism, CNEWA, they were placed at the service of the Sacred Congregation for the Oriental Churches – a «piece» of the Sacred Congregation for the Propagation of the Faith which had been «cut out» and made into a separate Congregation by Pope Benedict XV. With Pius XI's creation of CNEWA, then, Walsh inadvertently, but inevitably got in the way of a few of the «big guns» of the Sacred Congregation for the Propagation of the Faith: the Bavarian Mgr. Clemens August Count von Galen, O.S.B., (whose organization, Catholica Unio, had been absorbed by CNEWA) and Count von Galen's long time friend, the Apostolic Delegate to Germany, future Secretary of State to Pius XI and future Pope Pius XII, Cardinal Eugenio Pacelli.

At this point, we can summarize, then, that from the beginning of Pius XI's Pontificate and for the following ten years i.e. during approximately the first half of Pius XI's pontificate, Walsh was utilized as a resource by Pope Pius XI on an annual basis. In many cases Walsh was asked to carry out a role which today we would define as *Intelligence.* This was certainly partially his function in Russia, in Mexico and in Iraq. Often his work was carried out without official acknowledgement with others taking the merit for his accomplishments. Then, however, there is an interruption of his services for Pius XI: on Feb. 7, 1930, neo-Cardinal Eugenio Pacelli became Secretary of State replacing the aging Gasparri. Shortly thereafter Walsh was informed that he would be removed as President of CNEWA (there was an interim year while matters were prepared for the change). When Walsh returned from his Papal Mission to Iraq in 1931 – the results of which satisfied the requests of the Iraqi Catholics, led to the founding

---

is not surprising, therefore, that Walsh had little spare time to visit with the Apostolic Delegate.

of two important Jesuit educational institutions (Baghdad College and Al-Hikma University) and had the complete approval of Pius XI, but which had irritated the members of the Congregation for the Oriental Churches – powerful members of the Roman Curia[96], Walsh was informed categorically he was to have nothing more to do with the project. Without advancing any hypothesis, we can safely say that the wind had changed.

In 1939, with the death of Pius XI, Cardinal Eugenio Pacelli became Pope Pius XII. It would take a World War, the complete defeat of Germany and the confirmation of the United States as the dominant force on the international scene before the Vatican of Pacelli would call on Walsh's services once again. In the meantime Walsh had served his country in many different capacities during the war years and, following the war, had been Consultant to Judge Robert H. Jackson, US Chief of Counsel during the Nuremberg Trials.

Walsh uses only one adjective, in the first line of his letter to Judge Jackson, dated December 29, 1947, which, however, confirms his surprise over the Vatican's reawakened interest in his services for international assignments after many years of neglect: *unexpected*. Walsh had been called, in fact, to carry out the function of Consultor for the Company of Jesus at the Jochi/Sophia University in devastated, postwar Japan.

«My Dear Justice Jackson:
By an unexpected assignment (from Church authorities, Rome) I now find myself here in the Far East over the winter and am having a first hand view of the effects of total war in Japan. [...] The devastation reminds one of the destruction we saw in 1945-6 in Germany, but with a notable difference: – the flimsy wooden structure, so common in Japan burned down to the very ground, hence there is not that heaped-up rubble which we saw in all sides in Nurnberg and elsewhere. There is much more reconstruction in progress than we saw in Germany. The Japanese people are showing an amazing activity and are putting up thousands of small (wooden) homes and shops. We can do things here we would not have dared to do in Germany»[97].

---

[96] Though the Congregation originally requested the Company of Jesus to establish a secondary school in Iraq, they changed opinions (for reasons of hierarchical politics) and expressly limited Walsh's mandate to establishing a dormitory for young Catholic students attending Iraqi state schools. Walsh, however, in response to the Iraqi Catholics' pleas, returned from Iraq with plans for a secondary school in Baghdad, to be staffed by American Jesuits. These plans were then approved by Pius XI who was, in effect, the Prefect of the Congregation for the Oriental Churches. M. PATULLI TRYTHALL, *Edmund Aloysius Walsh...*, 225-312.

[97] Robert H. Jackson Papers, General Correspondence, Walsh, Edmund A., Box 21, F6, Manuscript Division, Library of Congress, Washington, DC.

To close this discussion regarding the relation of Pius XI with America – as exemplified by the confrontation with the National Catholic Welfare Council during the early months of his pontificate and by the confidence Pius XI placed in the American Jesuit, Fr. Edmund Walsh, from 1921 to 1931 – and in more general terms, the relation between Europeans and Americans during this period, let us return to the Vatican of 1923 and read two reports regarding Fr. Edmund Walsh in Russia:

«Opinion regarding Prof. Walsh expressed by the Bolshevik representative in Warsaw during a conversation held at the residence of the Bolshevik legation with a Russian woman who had converted to Catholicism. "The gentleman pleases everyone a great deal. The impression he makes, as far as I know, is optimum". Warsaw, October 7, 1923 – the attached sheet is the original text written by the converted Russian woman, which contains the opinion of the Bolshevik representative; the words written in small letters are by Archbishop Mons. Ropp and refer to whom and where the aforementioned opinion of Prof. Walsh was expressed»[98].

The second testimony reveals a great deal more about the actual state of relations between Fr. Walsh and Soviet authorities after a year of his presence in Moscow. The narrator is Cavalier Giovanni Belardo[99], the scene is the Russian Delegation in Corso d'Italia, Rome. The protagonists are Dr. Marco Sceftel of the Russian Red Cross and Mr. Straoujan, Secretary Chief of the Russian Delegation – at that moment recalled to his country and preparing to leave for the Ministry of Foreign Affairs in Moscow. The date is September 30, 1923[100].

«Called several times by telephone "for urgent reasons" by Dr. Marco Sceftel, [...] I went this very day, at 5:30 P.M. to the seat of the Russian Delegation [...] It struck me immediately that, contrary to usual custom, the Doctor invited me to enter the studio of the Secretary Chief of the Delegation. I asked if Mr. Straoujan had already left. "No" – Dr. Sceftel responded – "not yet, he went out for a walk". The conversation with regard to the question of the medicines began and Doctor Sceftel frequently repeated that the relations of Mr. Chicherin and the Moscow authorities with Prof. Walsh "are very grave, much worse than can be believed". Then he said that he was authorized by Mr. Jordanski to say that, "if the Holy See did not act to recall Prof. Walsh, the Government will take it upon themselves to invite him to leave Moscow". I answered immediately that this would be "another inopportune gesture on

---

[98] AES, Pont. Comm. Pro Russia, Sc. 73, Fasc. 332, 30.
[99] Cavalier Giovanni Belardo, Writer, *Extraordinary Ecclesiastical Affairs of the Secretary of State, Annuario Pontificio* (Pontifical Yearbook), 1923, 667.
[100] AES, Pont. Comm. Pro Russia, Sc. 73, Fasc. 334, 10-14.

the part of the Soviets". "It's worth it" Dr. Sceftel interrupted "because things are at that point by now". I continued: "And if the Holy See might think in the future to substitute Prof. Walsh, would such an act completely exclude the possibility of sending another person?". At this moment Mr. Straoujan entered. Dr. Sceftel immediately repeated what he had already said to me concerning Prof. Walsh. Straoujan limited himself to approving in monosyllables or with a rare phrase, for example: "Walsh has done much harm". Although admitting that Prof. Walsh had a strong, American character, I said that it was absolutely impossible that he had done harm with the intention of doing harm and that one must take into account the difficult moments he has had to endure in Moscow, particularly during the period of the Cieplak trial... At this, Straoujan jumped up furiously, shouting in fits: "That's the point, for the trial!... It's Walsh that should have been executed. Walsh instead of the poor Budkevich!... We did so much with Vorovski to save them all[101]... It was he who condemned Budkevich!!!... Budkevich was his victim!... With all of his intrigues from America and by Americans!"».

At this point Cavalier Belardo inserts a note, note 1, which reads thusly:

«This appears to be a clear allusion to the continual relations of Fr. Walsh with various American journalists[102] in Moscow and, in particular, with Mc-Cullagh, correspondent for the "New York Herald" during the Cieplak trial. Fr. Walsh gave McCullagh a permanent ticket to attend the trial. (Walsh had been given 3 permanent tickets by Chicherin); then McCullagh was expelled from Moscow. [...] During the trial, McCullagh, with his hat pulled down over his eyes and his collar raised, would go secretly to Walsh's office entering by a hidden door. They remained there together until the following morning in order to draft the precise account and impressions of the trial».

Returning to the scene in the Russian delegation:

«"I didn't want to say it to Mons. Pizzardo, but I say it to you!... Walsh should have been executed". This fit by Mr. Straoujan, even if calculated, was violent; several times staff members of the Delegation opened the door to see what was happening; several times they announced a visit, the arrival of an urgent telegram. All in vain. Straoujan continued to shout and to rudely respond to all who approached him. Outwardly, this fit and the words of Straoujan seemed exaggerated to me, Dr. Sceftel only smiled and explained to me that

---

[101] Vorovski, however, was not saved. On May 10, 1923, while he was in Lausanne, Switzerland, attending a conference, he was shot by a young Swiss, born in Russia, who had served in the White Russian Army, «La Vanguardia», *Noticias de todo el Mundo*, Viernes, 11 mayo 1923.

[102] At ARA's insistence, the Riga agreement permitted American journalists to enter Russia in order to report on conditions there. H.H. FISHER, *The Famine Relief in Soviet Russia...*, 143.

"poor Mr. Straoujan, he and Vorovski did so much at the time of the trial and yet they suffered greatly because of Walsh"».

In closing, a last piece of «friendly» advice: «This is the situation: there is a person and a thing, if the thing is important to the Holy See, send away the person; if the person is important, renounce the thing».

The following day, October 1, 1923[103], Mgr. Pizzardo, Substitute Secretary of State, felt obliged to send a polite word to the official Representative in Rome of the Soviet Russian Republic, Mr. Nicolas Jordanski. If one is to believe the notation in blue pencil written on the carbon copy, this letter was not sent. Its contents and tone, however, are instructive and germane to much of what we have discussed earlier:

«Excellency,
First, with regard to Prof. Walsh, I can tell you confidentially that I have just written him to recommend that he moderate his behavior in his relationship with Soviet authorities. Permit me to say that this somewhat rude way of acting can be explained by the fact that Prof. Walsh is American, having very progressive ideas regarding religious liberty, and being accustomed to seeing the American Bishops perfectly free in the exercise of their sacred ministry and concluding agreements with the civil power with little difficulty. It could be that he is not taking into account the tradition of civil power in Russia nor the difficulties of the present regime»[104].

Superficially this letter would seem to concern only Fr. Walsh. Looking at it more closely, however, it offers us a remarkable insight into the Vatican's opinion of Americans and – particularly in Pizzardo's description of the complete freedom of action to which the American bishops were accustomed – it would seem to sum up the general conviction of the Vatican with regard to «Americanism» and its dislike of accommodating itself to authority (most particularly that of Rome), the same «Americanism» which had, in fact, led the Consistorial Congregation to emit its de-

---

[103] AES, Pont. Comm. Pro Russia, 23-24.
[104] «Excellence, [...] Et d'abord, en ce qui concerne le Prof. Walsh, je puis vous dire confidentiellement que je viens de lui écrire pour lui recommander d'adoucir sa manière d'agir dans ses rapports avec les autorités Soviétiques.Mais permettez-moi de Vous dire que cette manière d'agir un peu rude pourrait s'expliquer par le fait que le Prof. Walsh est américain, ayant des idées très progressistes en fait de liberté religieuse, et étant habitué à voir les évêques Américains parfaitement libres dans l'exercice de leur ministère sacré, et conclure sans trop de difficultés les conventions avec le pouvoir civil. Peut être aussi ne se rend-il pas parfaitement compte des traditions du pouvoir civil en Russie et des difficultés du régime actuel».

cree disbanding the NCWC in the preceding year. Beyond that, however, the conciliatory tone which Pizzardo adopts provides a revealing portrait of Vatican diplomacy. Here, an official spokesman for the Roman Catholic Church, while addressing an official spokesman of the Soviet government which had, only five months earlier, placed the Catholic Church hierarchy of Russia on trial, condemned all of them and put one to death – events which the Vatican's representative to Russia, Fr. Edmund Walsh, had experienced at first hand – nonetheless, in his condescending defense of Walsh, makes appeal to a community of shared values, to a common European sensibility and historical perspective, saying, essentially: «We are Europeans and he is American. What can you expect?».

Considered in this light, rather than *Pius XI and American Pragmatism*, perhaps this paper should be entitled: *America and the Vatican: Two Pragmatisms in Action.*

LUCIA CECI

The First Steps of «Parallel Diplomacy»: The Vatican and the US in the Italo-Ethiopian War (1935-1936)

1. The Silence of the Pope during the Italian War of Aggression

The war in Ethiopia represents the first, profound international crisis which involved Italy after the Lateran Agreements. Six years after the historical signing of the pact in the Lateran palace on the part of Benito Mussolini and the Cardinal Secretary of State, Pietro Gasparri, it became necessary to acknowledge the limits to the independence of the Holy See in international politics caused by the re-structuring of relations with the Italian government and the advantages obtained with the Concordat.

Vatican papers confirm the absolute opposition of Pius XI to the Italian war of conquest[1]. In the confidential meeting held with members of the Holy See and with diplomats, Pope Achille Ratti disapproved the aggression in Ethiopia for a variety of reasons. He, along with many other critics, believed that the conflict would expand to Europe. He also knew that a war of aggression against a sovereign state that was a member of the League of Nations would have led to a closer relationship of Mussolini with Hitler. Finally, the «Pope of missions» was highly worried about the inevitable consequences which a conflict between Italy and other colonial powers would have on the organizational development relative to the spreading of the faith.

However, the stronger and more explicit condemnation of the war of conquest, stated by Pius XI in Castelgandolfo on August 27, 1935[2], initi-

---

[1] For a general reconstruction of events, refer to L. CECI, *Il papa non deve parlare. Chiesa, fascismo e guerra d'Etiopia*, Roma-Bari 2010.

[2] AES, Italia, IV periodo, POS. 967, vol. III, ff. 9r-11r, «Testo – ripreso stenograficamente – del discorso del S. Padre alle infermiere cattoliche il 27 agosto 1935 (a foglio 3° vi sono in lapis le correzioni di cui molte furono poi approvate dallo stesso S. Padre)». The official version of the speech, modified and «sweetened», was published in the «Osservatore Romano» on August 29, 1935. A synoptic edition in two versions can be found in L. CECI, *La guerra di Etiopia fuori dall'Italia: le posizioni dei vescovi*

ated a very difficult crisis with the government of Rome. The reaction of Italian diplomats – acting on the personal commission of Mussolini – was aggressive and aimed to influence any future public positions assumed by the Pope with regard to the conflict by threatening to jeopardize the positive relations between the State and the Church which had existed after the Lateran Agreements. And the Pope acquiesced to this blackmail attempt, a decision which was shared by his closest collaborators[3].

In order to more clearly understand the extent to which Pius XI had accepted Mussolini's order for silence with respect to the Fascist war of conquest, a specific event should be noted; this event was reconstructed on the basis of Italian and Vatican papers. In December 1935 – when the extension of the conflict to Europe was avoided and the Italian Catholic community participated, in a united manner, in the «Gold for the Fatherland» initiative by means of public gestures that were clearly promulgated by the media – Pius XI would have wanted to express himself publically in favor of peace in his consistorial address of December 16 or in his Christmas speech. The level of prudence on the part of the Pope, however, reached such a level that he actually asked permission from Mussolini. On December 13, in fact, the Vatican Secretary of State, Eugenio Pacelli, told the Italian ambassador to the Holy See, Mgr. Bonifacio Pignatti, that the Holy Father would have liked to declare, in some manner, his hope for peace during his address and prayed that the head of state would provide him with such an opportunity[4].

Diplomatic courtesy certainly limited vehemence in communications, but the response of the Italian ambassador to the Secretary of State was truly threatening: any call for a truce on the part of the Pope would have been considered to be an unfriendly act with respect to the Fascist Government and the country[5]. Pacelli understood the message and, without needing to speak to the Pope about this matter, reassured the ambassador:

---

cattolici europei, L'Impero fascista. Italia ed Etiopia (1935-1941), a cura di R. BOTTONI, Bologna 2008, 117-143. This event also emerged from the publication of the diary of Mgr. Tardini (C.F. CASULA, *Domenico Tardini (1888-1961). L'azione della Santa Sede nella crisi fra le due guerre*, Roma 1988, 384-386).

[3] Cfr. L. CECI, *Il papa non deve parlare...*, 43-54.

[4] AES, Stati Ecclesiastici, IV periodo, POS. 430b, Fasc. 362, f. 152r, 13 December 1935.

[5] Bonifacio Pignatti Morano di Custoza to Mussolini, December 14, 1935, in *I Documenti diplomatici italiani*, ottava serie, 1935-1939, II, Istituto Poligrafico e Zecca dello Stato, Roma 1991, 836-837.

«In this case, nothing will come of it»[6]. The following day, Father Pietro Tacchi Venturi met with Mussolini. He was supposed to be the messenger of a final attempt at persuasion on the part of the Pope with respect to the Laval-Hoare plan. But first of all – as Pius XI had told him that morning – the Jesuit had to reassure the Duce about the speech of December 16. «Il Santo Padre – father Tacchi Venturi told Mussolini – edotto della conversazione dell'Ambasciatore col Cardinale Segretario di Stato, non avrebbe nel prossimo Concistoro neppur nominato il conflitto italo-etiopico, contenendosi di fronte ad esso *tamquam non esset*»[7]. Staying true to his word, Pius XI – during his consistorial address of December 16 and during his Christmas speech – did not make specific references to the Italo-Ethiopian war.

At the beginning of the same month of December – 90 days from the initiation of military operations in Ethiopia, initiated on October 3, 1935 without a formal declaration of war – monsignor Domenico Tardini, undersectretary of the Congregation for Extraordinary Ecclesiastical Affairs, asked himself the following question within his notes on the Italo-Ethiopian conflict:

> «Dunque deve parlare il Papa? sì o no? Io farei una distinzione. *In pubblico*, per ora, no. Ma *in segreto sì*, subito, chiarissimamente, a tutti. Parlare e agire. [...] Anche perché si vedrà che, se la S. Sede non ha parlato in pubblico, è stato solo per non intralciare con le frasi la sua azione pacificatrice. Parlando, si risparmiava forse le critiche, ma paralizzava certamente la sua opera di bene»[8].

Tardini therefore forcefully questioned the decision of silence of the Pope given that the public rallying of the clergy, as well as the bishops and many Italian cardinals, created an image of total alignment of Catholicism, including its leadership, with the war of conquest of Mussolini's government.

The strong support offered by Catholics to the regime during the Italo-Ethiopian conflict is a fact which stands out in Italian political history as

---

[6] *Ibidem*, 837.

[7] AES, Italia, IV periodo, POS. 967, vol. II, ff. 260r-262v, P. Tacchi Venturi to Pio XI, «Relazione dell'udienza avuta con S.E. Mussolini nel pomeriggio di sabato 14 dicembre 1935, alle ore 17,30, a Palazzo di Venezia».

[8] *Previsioni e giudizi di Mons. Tardini sul conflitto tra l'Italia e l'Etiopia*, in AES, Italia, IV periodo, POS. 967, vol. I bis, ff. 1r-71r. The document is fully published in L. CECI, *«Il Fascismo manda l'Italia in rovina». Le note inedite di monsignor Domenico Tardini (23 settembre-13 dicembre 1935)*, in «Rivista storica italiana», 120 (2008), 313-367, these lines, written in December 3, 1935, in 342-344.

few others have in the past. During numerous public statements of position, bishops expressed their most fervid support for the initiatives of the
government in Ethiopia. Other prelates blessed the troops and ships which
were departing for eastern Africa. The national chair of *Azione Cattolica*
adopted a policy of open support for the war. Significantly political declarations with respect to the government came from various branches of
Gioventù cattolica. The group of priests of «Italia e Fede», which played
a central role in directing provincial clergy, reiterated its support for the
imperialist and autartic goals of the Duce. The missionary and devotional
press, as well as Catholic cinema and theater, contributed towards spreading colonial enthusiasm amongst the population as well as an image of the
war as a Catholic missionary crusade within a heretical country.

The image of the Italian Catholic community aligned with the policies
of the regime in Ethiopia – amplified by Fascist propaganda – echoed
throughout the world press. It was reported to all European governments
by the diplomats stationed in Italy or in the Holy See. It was noted in
reports of the League of Nations and was highlighted by anti-fascists, although the top leaders of the Vatican were also perfectly aware of this fact
and in some cases were embarassed.

The support for government propaganda, often public, flat and thick
with rhetoric, was undoubtedly the highly dominant element, but a more
in-depth analysis reveals that several stages occurred. A diversified position, composed of moments of caution, silence and approval, characterized the phase of political/diplomatic negotiations. A massive response
was incurred following the general mobilization of October 2, 1935. However, the entry into force of sanctions on Italy on the part of the League
of Nations as a result of the aggression on Ethiopia (November 18, 1935)
generated nearly unanimous support for the African war on the part of
Catholics.

This support reached its peak in the mobilization for the «Gold for the
Fatherland» initiative which culminated in the *Giornata della fede* (December 18, 1935) and was publicly expressed at the time of the proclamation of the Empire (May 9, 1936); it gradually lost force as the «crusade»
for defense of Christianity threatened in the war in Spain superceded the
Ethiopian war as the major international focus[9].

In any case, and starting with the anti-sanctions movement – which
attempted to bend the general image of the war from one of conquest in
Ethiopia to one of defending Italy from the group aggression of plutocratic

---

[9] Cfr. L. Ceci, *Il papa non deve parlare...*, 67-108.

democracies – the support of Catholics for the war was absolute. To many, this appeared to be a great opportunity to express the loyalty of Catholics towards a nation that had been reconciled, through the Lateran Agreements, with the Church of Rome and towards the Duce of fascism, who appeared to be the catalyst of this reconciliation.

The triumph of Imperial rhetoric, and its tone and slogans perhaps does not allow one to fully understand to what extent the clichés uttered in this period by the episcopacy were caused by the excessive and plethoric language of the time and how, on the other hand, they were profoundly introjected. It should, in any case, be noted that the connection between Italian Catholicism and Fascism was not merely tactical and the result of mutual manipulation but more intimate and profound. The cult of authority, a mistrust of civil liberties, the need for discipline, diffidence with respect to all forms of debate constituted the pillars for harmony between these two communities, strengthened by the perception of the existence of common enemies such as the Masons, Anglicanism, liberalism, and communism[10].

Nor can it be concluded that, in these areas, Italian bishops were in debt with respect to the totalitarian pursuits of the regime. None of the bishops holding office in 1935 were born after 1900; the entire national episcopacy had therefore completed its education before the rise of Mussolini. The educational process and selection of Italian bishops was, on the other hand, affected by the cultural impoverishment and general atmosphere of fear generated by the anti-modernist repression of Pius X. Although the ecclesiastical climate had, under Benedict XV, changed with respect to that of his predecessor, the continuity of «level» management was guaranteed by the uninterrupted permanence, within the Curia, of certain individuals that were most aligned to the policies of Pope Sarto; these individuals held managerial positions, for many years, in key bodies that decided on issues relating to bishops: above all, Cardinal Gaetano De Lai, head of the Consistorial until 1930, and Cardinal Rafael Merry del Val, who remained the secretary of the Holy office until 1930[11].

The most widespread and theatrical moment of exaltation of Italian Catholicism coincided with the «Gold for the Fatherland» initiative. In that spectacular event of propaganda and mobilization against the «unfair

---

[10] Cfr. G. MICCOLI, *Tra mito della cristianità e secolarizzazione. Studi sul rapporto chiesa-società nell'età contemporanea*, Casale Monferrato 1985, 126.

[11] Cfr. G. BATTELLI, *Santa Sede e vescovi nello Stato unitario. Dal secondo Ottocento ai primi anni della Repubblica*, in G. CHITTOLINI, G. MICCOLI (a cura di), *Storia d'Italia, Annali 9, La Chiesa e il potere politico dal Medioevo all'età contemporanea*, Torino 1986, 809-854.

sanctions» decreed by the League of Nations[12], bishops and cardinals of all of Italy provided the nation at war and provincial party secretaries with episcopal necklaces, rings, precious objects and family memories. And they called upon all believers, even the humblest, to do the same. The Archbishop of Monreale even reached the point of requiring its priests to melt down the votive offerings donated by devout believers to sanctuaries for graces received, generating protests even in Venezuela. In the province of Grosseto, a parish priest requested permission to melt the bells of the Church for the fatherland and the Duce. Sermons, pastorals, and diocesan letters all contributed towards infusing the collective imagination with a missionary interpretation of the war of conquest, stating that the Fascist empire would open the doors to the spreading of Roman Catholicism in Africa[13].

The bellicose and clerical/imperial enthusiasms of Italian Catholics did not conflict with the public position of the Holy See. Following the diplomatic incident which occurred between the Vatican and Mussolini's government at the end of August 1935 – as a result of the condemnation pronounced by Pius XI on August 27 – there were no further public condemnations of Italy's war of aggression on the part of the Pope. This silence was essentially interpreted by the episcopacy as a form of support for the colonial policies of the regime. Italian bishops maintained an attitude of general consensus with respect to the policy assumed by the Holy See[14]. As a result, and although they were not capable, for reasons of a lack of culture, of discussing and debating the commonplaces inherent in fascist propaganda, it was unthinkable for them to assume positions which they deemed to be in contrast with those of the Pope himself.

Given that he did not publicly intervene in a direction that differed with respect to that of high-level clergy, the Pope led the episcopacy, as well as priests, believers and the national and international opinion to believe that the Holy See fundamentally approved of the war in Africa as well as the attitude assumed by the Italian Catholic community. This, in fact, seemed to be confirmed by the positions assumed by the «Osservatore Romano» which, for the entire duration of the conflict, legitimized the imperial exploits of Fascist Italy, although it avoided the most heated speeches of the

---

[12] Cfr. P. Terhoeven, *Oro alla patria. Donne, guerra e propaganda nella giornata della Fede fascista*, Bologna 2006.

[13] L. Ceci, *Il papa non deve parlare...*, 94-107.

[14] Cfr. G. Martina, *I Cattolici di fronte al fascismo*, in «Rassegna di teologia», 18 (1976), 175-194.

episcopacy and allowed the *Acta diurna* column of Guido Gonella to serve as an area where the press campaign of the government was occasionally lightly questioned.

The pro-Empire and pro-Fascist declarations of Italian Catholics generated reactions across the world. Dozens of letters and telegrams from individual believers, Catholic associations, Protestant associations and Catholic parties were sent to the Vatican from various countries around the world in order to dissociate themselves from the colonialist and bellicose declarations of Italian bishops[15]. In addition to these letters, the British government protested with the Vatican for the anti-British excesses which were expressed in many speeches of the Italian episcopacy and which were broadly advertised in the press[16].

The papal nuncio in Paris, Mgr. Luigi Maglione received the protests of the emperor of Ethiopia for the speech made by the Archbishop of Brindisi in which the latter stated, according to that reported in newspapers, believers were called upon to donate gold to the fatherland «in order to bring civilization to those areas thus far dominated by slavery and barbarity»[17]. As the nuncio noted to Pacelli, the attempt to dissociate the Holy See from the initiatives of Italian bishops received the following response: «In Ethiopia, where Catholic doctrine is known, these views of Italian bishops are traced back to the Holy See, thereby generating an aversion to Catholicism and hostility toward missions»[18].

No less embarassing for the Holy See was that which was reported by Nazi newspapers in Germany: the multiple declarations of the high-level Italian clergy – unthinkable without the consent of the Vatican – demonstrated that the Holy See had allowed the national clergy to fully support the Fascist war which however, due to political reasons, could not be expressed by the Pope[19].

---

[15] L. CECI, *Il papa non deve parlare...*, 144-160.

[16] AES, Italia, IV periodo, POS. 967, vol. V, ff. 180r-181r, H. Montgomery to A. Ottaviani, November 26, 1935, and f. without number between f. 186v and f. 187r, November 29, 1935.

[17] AES, Italia, IV periodo, POS. 967, vol. V, f. 189r, L. Maglione to E. Pacelli, November 28, 1935.

[18] *Ibidem.*

[19] AES, Italia, IV periodo, POS. 967, vol. III, f. 91r, «Rassegna stampa del 2 novembre 1935».

2. The Secretariat of State, the Nuncios and the Jesuit

Hence the questioning of the silence of the Pope in the notes of Mgr. Tardini, who considered the clergy and the Italian bishops to be «tumultuosi,
esaltati, guerrafondai, squilibrati». Hence also the concern over the effect
of pro-Italian and pro-Imperial attitudes on the part of the episcopacy on
the international image of the Holy See, which was accused of collaborat-
ing with Fascism[20].

The decision taken by top Vatican leaders was, in any case, to maintain
a public policy of silence, *tamquam non esset*, and to concentrate on diplomatic channels and on confidential negotiations. At the international level,
the most significant action areas were the nunciature of Paris – which was
crucial for probing the attitudes of Mgr. Laval in order to construct a form
of French mediation between Italy and Great Britain – as well as that of
Bern, where it was necessary to intercept the policies of the League of
Nations as soon as possible, and the nunciatures of Latin American countries, due to their importance for Italian foreign policy after the second
half of the 1920's. Mgr. Arthur Hinsley, the Archbishop of Westminster
and Catholic primate of England and Wales, was instead the key person
for the British side; this was significant for the Holy See – not in terms of
diplomatic relations, with respect to which it was sidelined – but for the
influence which the public opinion of that country, which was strongly
against the war, had on international relations[21].

Just three days from the start of military operations, the Secretariat
of State implemented the *desiderata* of the Duce in relation to the involvement of nuncios and apostolic delegates; these orders required the
latter to act within government circles of various countries in order to
promote the Italian perspective. This policy was promoted by Mussolini
as of the month of September during his meetings with Tacchi Venturi.
These meetings, between the Jesuit and the Duce, were frequent during
the months of the crisis and the war: 10 meetings in 19 weeks, ie. on average one meeting every 10/12 days. The modalities were always the same:
Tacchi Venturi went to the Vatican and was dictated the essential points of
the message from the Pope, then reported the latter's thoughts to the Duce
while occasionally adding a few personal thoughts into the conversation;
he would then note the response of Mussolini and, on the basis of the time

---

[20] *Ibidem.*
[21] L. Ceci, *Il papa non deve parlare...*, 144-160.

and urgency, either returned to the Vatican during the days immediately following.

Pius XI entrusted Tacchi Venturi with different messages for Mussolini. Before the start of the war, the Pope sent a very strong message to the Duce, although late in coming. He asked him to renounce the invasion in Ethiopia, even stating that the war would have placed Italy in a state of «mortal sin»[22]; this appeal brought the definition of unjust war to its logically extreme conclusion, and it is not easy to find traces of this position in the Papal teachings of the nineteenth and twentieth centuries. In other cases, the Jesuit provided Mussolini with proposals of French negotiations which were received in the Secretariat of State through the papal nuncio in Paris, Mgr. Luigi Maglione, who was in contact with Pierre Laval, as well as through the French ambassador to the Holy See, François Charles-Roux.

But after having discussed the specific issues during the course of these meetings, Mussolini never failed to touch upon all those issues which most worried the Holy See beyond the Tiber. Once he mentioned the gigantic plot being implemented against Italy by the Third International as well as by liberals to overthrow the regime and to threaten the Church[23], while another time he communicated to the Pope that the true enemy of the government were the Masons who could not forgive and forget all the lodges which had been destroyed in Italy as well as the pact wit the Church[24]; in another case, he threatened to join forces with Hitler[25].

The nuncios, pressed by the Secretariat of State, sent detailed reports to Rome on the policies adopted by local governments with respect to the Italo-Ethiopian crisis as well as the changes in public opinion with respect to the position of the Pope. In Venezuela, the initiative of the Archbishop of Monreale, Mgr. Eugenio Filippi, generated quite a stir and much indignation when he proposed to melt the votive offerings of the *duomo* in order to donate the gold bars to the Italian government; the press in Venezuela insinuated that the Holy See had approved[26]. In order to cor-

---

[22] AES, Italia, IV periodo, POS. 967, vol. I, 165*r*, «Contatti con Mussolini per tramite del P. Tacchi-Venturi, «Appunti dettati dal S. Padre al P. T. il 24 settembre 1935».

[23] AES, Italia, IV periodo, POS. 967, vol. II, 260*r*-262*v*, P. Tacchi Venturi, «Relazione dell'udienza avuta con S.E. Mussolini nel pomeriggio di sabato 14 dicembre 1935 alle ore 17,30 a Palazzo Venezia».

[24] AES, Italia, IV periodo, POS. 967, vol. II, 343*r*-346*r*, P. Tacchi Venturi, «Relazione dell'Udienza avuta con sua eccellenza il Capo del Governo il 3 gennaio 1936».

[25] AES, Italia, IV periodo, POS. 967, vol. II, 80*r*-*v*, P. Tacchi Venturi, «Udienza col Capo del Governo», October 24, 1935.

[26] *La campaña del arzobispo Filippi*, in «El Heraldo», November 21, 1935.

rect the Vatican position, the diligent nuncio, Fernando Cento, had several thousand copies of a booklet titled *Por los fueros de la Verdad. La Santa Sede y el conflicto italo-etiope*[27] printed and then distributed them for free throughout the country[28].

In some cases, the actions implemented by the Holy See through its delegates around the world demonstrated full alignment with the Italian government. In December 1935, the government in Rome protested with the Secretariat of State since the apostolic delegate of Ottawa, Mgr. Andrea Cassulo, had not received instructions to stay in contact with the local royal consul and had not implemented the desired activities in the Holy See[29]. On behalf of the Secretariat of State, Mgr. Giuseppe Pizzardo, on December 26, 1935, wrote to Cassulo in order to support the Italian position within Canadian circles by describing the Italo-Ethiopian issue as an epochal conflict which was orchestrated by forces hostile to Fascism (communism, freemasonry) that, by attacking Catholic Italy, intended to strike against the Church and the Holy See[30].

Following such a strong call from the Secretariat of State, poor Cassulo was forced to implement the Vatican directives. Canadian public opinion – he wrote to Pizzardo on January 2, 1936 – was against the war and had approved the sanctions against Italy by hoping that these would prevent the loss of human life. The apostolic delegate stated that he had, in any case, well understood the position of the Holy See and would have done his best in order to «make others understand it as well»[31]. He would therefore respond to the consul general of Italy that the position of the Holy See was well known, just as the feelings with respect to the nation were well known; the nation is, and intends to maintain, a good relationship with the Church. Some time later, Pizzardo thanked him for «such clear-sightedness»[32].

---

[27] *Por los fueros de la Verdad. La Santa Sede y el conflicto italo-etiope*, Caracas 1935.

[28] AES, Italia, IV periodo, POS. 967, vol. V, 34r, F. Cento to E. Pacelli, December 12, 1935.

[29] AES, Italia, IV periodo, POS. 967, vol. V, 128r, «Appunto riservatissimo», December 1935.

[30] AES, Italia, IV periodo, POS. 967, vol. V, 129r-131r, G. Pizzardo to A. Cassulo, December 26, 1935.

[31] AES, Italia, IV periodo, POS. 967, vol. V, 132r-134r, A. Cassulo to G. Pizzardo, January 2, 1936.

[32] AES, Italia, IV periodo, POS. 967, vol. V, 135r, G. Pizzardo to A. Cassulo, February 25, 1936.

Although these were some of the areas of intervention requested of the nuncios, the key area of diplomatic activity was implemented by the top leaders of the Vatican. For several weeks, the Secretariat of State was involved in a highly confidential attempt at mediation between France and Italy; this seemed to be essential after the start of the crisis in Anglo-Italian relations. The negotiations continued throughout October and November with regular three-way meetings between the Vatican, Palazzo Venezia and Quai d'Orsay, in which the Duce communicated through Tacchi Venturi, Maglione, and Charles-Roux.

In this period, Vatican efforts were directed towards the United States.

3. The Ethiopian War in the US

The Italian expansion into Ethiopia caused a very strong reaction in the United States. In the «Little Italies» of the entire country, explosions of enthusiasm greeted the news that Italy had invaded Ethiopia in search of an empire in Africa. On November 10, 1935, in Philadelphia, 200,000 Italo-Americans marched along Broad Street in order to protest against the imposition of sanctions against Italy on the part of the League of Nations. Nor was there any lack of volunteers for the Italian Army in the Ethiopian conflict. In all Italo-American communities across the US, funds were collected for the Italian Red Cross and the Fascist Day of Faith was celebrated, including the collective donation of wedding rings to the Italian government in exchange for steel rings[33]. For example, more than 700,000 dollars were paid to the Italian Red Cross in New York; in Philadelphia, 33 thousand came only from the Committee of Friends of Italy, while 40 thousand were donated in San Francisco and 37,132 dollars in Providence. Italian consuls in black shirts distributed tens of thousands of iron wedding rings in exchange for a donation of the gold wedding ring to Italy. In Providence, for example, the Italian vice consul, Vincenzo Verderosa, distributed more than seven hundred iron wedding rings while

---

[33] For information on Italo-American lobbying on the issue of legislation relating to US neutrality during the war in Ethiopia, refer to S. LUCONI, *La «diplomazia parallela». Il regime fascista e la mobilitazione politica degli italo-americani*, Milano 2000, 85-111.

rigorously dressed in a black shirt. Four hundred more were delivered within a month[34].

Ethiopia also had support in the US. The war had, as mentioned above, a global dimension[35]. African Americans in various cities created committees and associations in defence of Ethiopia and of *Negus* Haile Sellassie. As demonstrated by Nadia Venturini and Joseph Harris, the reaction of African Americans to the war in Ethiopia was the symbol of a growing racial pride and an important step in political growth[36]. The city of New York lived through moments of tension between Italo-Americans and the black community, starting from the neighborhood of Harlem. Protesters also marched in the streets against the Italian invasion in San Francisco and Chicago[37].

In other words, American public opinion exerted different types of pressure on the position to be taken with respect to Mussolini. However, and for the entire duration of the conflict, Roosevelt assumed a very cautious position. On October 5, 1935, the American president had issued a statement in which he recognized a state of war between Italy and Ethiopia[38]. This statement led to an immediate embargo on the supply of arms and munitions to Italy and Ethiopia, in accordance with a resolution of Congress that was approved on August 31, 1935, and which prohibited the exporting of weapons to any belligerent country fighting in a conflict which did not involve the United States. The resolution of Congress did not provide any margin for discretion to the President once the hostilities were acknowledged.

At the same time, and in the absence of a formal declaration of war from Italy to Ethiopia, the immediate acknowledgement of a state of war on the part of Roosevelt could have appeared to be a forced gesture in order to prevent the sale of armaments to Italy. Subsequently, and after noting the difficulty in putting together a majority in Congress, Roosevelt allowed his plans for a bill (*Pittman-McReynolds Bill*) to be derailed; by means of this bill, he would have been able to limit the volume of US

---

[34] *Hundreds Given Tokens by Italians at Meeting Here*, in «Providence Journal», April 20, 1936; *Italy Gives 400 Steel Rings Here, ibidem*, May 25, 1936.

[35] N. Labanca, *L'Impero del fascismo. Lo stato degli studi*, in *L'Impero fascista...*, 35-61.

[36] N. Venturini, *Neri e italiani a Harlem. Gli anni Trenta e la guerra d'Etiopia*, Roma 1990, e J.E. Harris, *African-American Reactions to War in Ethiopia, 1936-1941*, Baton Rouge 1994.

[37] J.P. Diggins, *L'America, Mussolini e il fascismo* (1972), Roma-Bari 1982, 375 ss.

[38] Proclamation no. 2141, in *The Public Papers and Addresses of Franklin D. Roosevelt*, vol. IV, *The Court Disapproves*, New York 1938, 412-416.

exports of oil and other products which were not part of the embargo. Presidential elections were imminent and Roosevelt did not want to risk losing the vote of Italo-Americans which lived in the United States nor did he want to alienate the support of US exporters[39]. From the perspective of international politics, finally, he hoped to be able to use Mussolini in order to restrain Hitler[40].

4. Confidential Negotiations and Unofficial Contacts between Rome and Washington

The idea of initiating unofficial talks with the American presidency took form in the Vatican a few days after the invasion of Ethiopia. Pius XI had abandoned the idea of condemning the Fascist war of aggression after the condemnation of his speech to the Catholic nurses on August 27, 1935, which had been followed by appeals and threats from the Italian government during the course of which Mussolini himself had intervened[41]. Given this position of silence which was officially held by Pius XI on the conflict, an image was immediately created of substantial Vatican support for the regime's policy of conquest: if the Pope did not speak out and allowed bishops, cardinals and Catholic intellectuals to publicly uphold the heroic mission of faith and civilization of Italy in Africa, this implied that he essentially approved of the war and allowed the high-level clergy to state that which he could not due to the supranational nature of the Holy See.

After putting aside the prospects of a public condemnation of the war on the part of the Pope, the Secretariat of State concentrated on diplomatic actions and confidential negotiations, attempting on the one hand to distinguish its position from that of Italy and, on the other hand, not create conflict with the government in Rome. The intent was to avoid that the war extended to Europe and to halt the embargo as soon as possible.

This was the environment in which confidential negotiations between Rome and Washington initiated. The opportunity for communication with

[39] G.G. MIGONE, *Gli Stati Uniti e il fascismo. Alle origini dell'egemonia americana in Italia*, Milano 1980, 350-361.

[40] D.F. SCHMITZ, *Speaking the Same Language: The US Response to the Italo-Ethiopian War and the Origins of American Appeasement*, in *Appeasement in Europe. A Reassessment of US Policies*, D.F. SCHMITZ, R.D. CHALLENER (eds.), Westport 1990, 75-102.

[41] Cfr. L. CECI, *Santa Sede e guerra di Etiopia: a proposito di un discorso di Pio XI*, in «Studi storici», 14 (2003), 511-525.

the American president was reported in the first days of October to Pius XI by Bernardino Nogara, the engineer and financer who held the important post of delegate to the Special Administration of the Holy See, a body created after the Lateran Agreements in order to manage Vatican finances and known as «La Speciale»[42]. The idea of Nogara, which was theoretically conceived by the Pope, was to take some steps with the Roosevelt administration in order to urge an American mediation between Italy and Ethiopia due to the influence of the US on Great Britain[43]. Mgr. Nogara, who previously was the director of a branch of Banca Commerciale in Istanbul, probably took action due to worries of a financial nature. As of 1870, the Holy See and the Vatican depended on income which was almost exclusively generated from financial flows associated with Peter's Pence and various forms of stock and bond investments which were managed indirectly by Nogara through a shrewd, and not entirely transparent, monopoly.

In addition to representing the major source of income for Peter's Pence, the United States were the country where the financial investments of Pius XI were – in terms of stocks and purchases of gold – definitely considerable. More generally, and halfway through the 1930's, the finances of the Vatican were more closely linked to the Italian economy and government following important operations which were managed after the 1929 crisis (and after the Lateran Agreements) by Mgr. Nogara himself. These led to the acquisition of significant amounts of stock in companies associated with IRI, including Breda, Officine Reggiane, Compagnia Nazionale Aereonautica, all of which produced arms for the Italian government[44].

On October 12, the US ambassador in Italy, Breckinridge Long, known for his pro-Fascist positions, wanted Pius XI to know «Roosevelt's desire to directly contact the Holy Father for the preservation of peace». The communication channel which was selected by the ambassador was relatively unusual for the protocols of Vatican diplomacy: the prince Domenico Orsini went to speak, along with his American wife Laura Schwarz, with the Superior-General of the Jesuits, Wlodozmierz Ledóchowski, who relayed the information to the Secretariat of State through the prelate that had the clos-

---

[42] J. POLLARD, *Money and the rise of the modern papacy: financing the Vatican, 1850-1950*, Cambridge 2005, 145 ss.

[43] An initial sketch of this project was found by Renzo De Felice within the diary of Mgr. Nogara himself. Cfr. R. DE FELICE, *La Santa Sede e il conflitto Italo-Etiopico nel diario di Bernardino Nogara*, in «Storia contemporanea», 8 (1974), 823-834.

[44] J. POLLARD, *Money and the rise of the modern papacy...*, 178.

est access to Pius XI, Father Tacchi Venturi[45]. This leads one to suppose that the idea of a contact between the Pope and the US President was not actually a desire of Roosevelt but of ambassador Long. The Secretariat of State wrote, in any case, to the apostolic delegate for the United States, Amleto Giovanni Cicognani, on October 18, and managed to contact the president within a few days through Father John J. Burke, Secretary of the National Catholic Welfare Conference and a confidant of Roosevelt.

According to reports made by Cicognani to the Secretariat of State, the meeting which Fr. Burke had in Washington with the president at the end of October was, however, disappointing. The two had spoken for an hour. Roosevelt had avoided taking a direct position and was rather evasive: on the one hand, he had recognized the legitimacy of Italian ambitions, and on the other hand, he had condemned the war as a tool to meet these ambitions. He had expressed his high level of admiration for the beneficial influence of the Pope on all nations but was not willing to support the proposal for collaboration of the Holy See. Finally, and although he was suspicious of the imperialist plans of Mussolini, given that he was very «influenced by British arguments and a Protestant mentality», Roosevelt had confirmed to Fr. Burke that the United States would not have supported the application of sanctions and would have maintained a position of total neutrality:

«Padre Burke ha conferito col Presidente giovedì.
Presidente, pur dicendosi bene disposto verso Italia scopo pace et riconoscendo necessità espansione Italia, disapprova e deplora fortemente che Italia abbia mosso guerra per quello che, secondo lui, doveva comporsi per via diplomatica: chiama ciò crimine nazionale et violazione trattati.
Per tale motivo dice di non vedere al presente come possa fare passo che a suo parere sembrerebbe sostenere violazione principî etici et trattati internazionali.
Presidente nel corso del colloquio durato un'ora ha sempre cercato di evitare di dare risposta chiara definitiva circa sua posizione sulla questione, si è mostrato sospettoso piani imperialistici di Mussolini e molto influenzato da tesi inglese e mentalità protestante; non sembra disposto dare cooperazione.
Ma esprime altissima ammirazione per influenza benefica Santo Padre presso tutte le Nazioni.
Ha dichiarato, pur volendo mantenere assoluta neutralità, che non intende associarsi applicazione sanzioni.
Ha promesso P. Burke che lo chiamerà di nuovo»[46].

---

[45] AES, Italia, IV periodo, POS. 967, vol. II, foll. 11r e v, W. Ledóchowski to P. Tacchi Venturi, October 12, 1935.

[46] AES, Italia, IV periodo, POS. 967, vol. II, fol. 76r, A.G. Cicognani to the Secretary of State, October 27, 1935.

The idea of diplomatic actions with the US presidency re-emerged in the first days of December. On December 3, 1935, Mgr. Nogara wrote to Pius XI of a conversation which he had the day before with Count Giuseppe Volpi, Chairman of Confindustria and of the Committee for Economic Defence against Sanctions and who was «in almost daily contact with the head of the government»[47]. Nogara had prepared a note in which he summarized his impressions relative to his conversation with Volpi. The note of Nogara fully reflected the Fascist point of view and began with a very strong statement: «Il Duce desidera la pace». The conflict was also defined, from the title, not as «Italo-Ethiopian» but as «Anglo-Italian». The strongly anti-British perspective with which Nogara illustrated the primary issues of the time to the Pope led to the conclusion that the only way out was to direct diplomatic actions towards the US presidency:

> «L'attitudine dell'Inghilterra e della Società delle Nazioni, rimorchiata dalla prima, non è giustizia politica, né sociale, né economica, ma l'espressione di un insano egoismo, che la storia giudicherà.
> Se ne conclude che la pazzia maggiore sta dalla parte dell'Inghilterra, e non si vuole credere che questa, a mente fredda, possa lanciarsi in tale avventura, e si spera perciò in un compromesso.
> Roosevelt potrebbe assumersi il compito di mediatore in questa vertenza per evitare la guerra. In questo senso si dirige il lavoro diplomatico.
> Il Papa può molto con la sua autorità morale»[48].

What was more problematic, on the other hand, was the assessment of Tardini who considered the attitudes of US leaders to be reluctant with respect to the Holy See and therefore not very disposed to align themselves with pacifying actions taken by the Vatican. The proposal, according to the undersecretary of Extraordinary Ecclesiastical Affairs, should be structured differently: it was necessary to tell Roosevelt that American mediation could be «decisive» and add that the Holy See was ready to use its influence in order to facilitate the implementation of the initiative. Tardini wrote in a few notes dated December 6, 1935:

> «L'intervento di Roosevelt può senza dubbio essere assai utile perché gli Stati Uniti possono molto sull'Inghilterra e sull'Italia. Ma occorre tener presente: 1. – che la mentalità delle alte sfere negli Stati Uniti è, in genere, poco favorevole alla Santa Sede. È vero che alcuni segni fanno comprendere che in America

---

[47] AES, Italia, IV periodo, POS. 967, vol. II, fol. 182r, B. Nogara to Pio XI, December 3, 1935.
[48] AES, Italia, IV periodo, POS. 967, vol. II, foll. 183r-185r, B. Nogara, «Nota sul conflitto anglo-italiano», December 3, 1935.

si comincia ad apprezzare di più la Santa Sede. Ma non sembra si sia ancora al punto che gli Stati Uniti si adattino a fiancheggiare un'azione pacificatrice della S. Sede. Sarebbe, forse, meglio invertire le parti. Dire a Roosevelt che l'opera pacificatrice degli Stati Uniti può essere decisiva, che gli Stati Uniti posso essere arbitri della situazione e che la S. Sede, dal canto suo, è pronta ad usare la sua influenza per facilitare il felice compimento di questa iniziativa. 2. – La mentalità di Roosevelt – come quella del fu Wilson – non è finora capace di comprendere l'Italia. Egli già ha definito l'attività di Mussolini come un crimine nazionale e internazionale. Ora, se Roosevelt diventasse mediatore con una mentalità puramente inglese o societaria, più che risolvere, aggraverebbe la situazione. Sarebbe, perciò, necessario che qualcuno facesse capire a Roosevelt che al popolo italiano bisogna dar qualche cosa; che è sommamente pericoloso inasprire 40.000.000 di persone; che le sanzioni non solo tendono a impedire la guerra, ma tendono a danneggiare ed affamare il popolo italiano perché, per esempio, quando si impedisce qualsiasi esportazione non si fa che ridurre un popolo alla miseria. E solamente quando Roosevelt fosse persuaso di ottenere qualche cosa per l'Italia, il suo intervento di mediatore potrebbe avere qualche speranza di successo»[49].

In the Secretariat of State, a framework for negotiations was drafted to present to Roosevelt; Italian conditions were re-proposed and the American president was asked to play a mediating role which could be decisive:

«Se la Società delle Nazioni è entrata già nella controversia quale giudice, sentenziando che l'Italia è venuta meno agli impegni presi ed applicando in pena le sanzioni, è però sommamente da desiderarsi che eserciti altresì la sua opera pacificatrice (solennemente sancita nel patto stesso) facilitando la via ad una soluzione, che giovi a ridare ai popoli la desiderata tranquillità e a dissipare il timore di più gravi complicazioni.
Per giungere a un tale risultato nessun intervento può essere più opportuno e più prezioso di quello degli Stati Uniti, la cui opera pacificatrice potrebbe essere decisiva per il bene di tutta l'umanità.
Sarebbe questa una nuova ed altissima benemerenza civile della nobile Nazione degli Stati Uniti.
Il prestigio di cui è meritamente circondato il Signor Presidente Roosevelt, non solo negli Stati Uniti, ma anche in Europa, potrebbe contribuire non poco al felice esito di una così provvida iniziativa»[50].

These notes, which would be encoded, were accompanied by a deciphering code for Mgr. Fietta who reported the various correspondences. For example: Roosevelt: «dottore»; Mussolini: «paziente»; Italy:

---

[49] AES, Italia, IV periodo, POS. 967, vol. II, foll. 215r-216v, D. Tardini, Notes, December 6, 1935.
[50] AES, Italia, IV periodo, POS. 967, vol. II, foll. 217r-219r, Notes, December 7, 1935.

«ospedale»; United States: «giudici»; England: «società»; France: «tri-
bunale»; League of Nations: «congregazioni»; public opinion: «parenti»;
propaganda: «dichiarazioni»[51]. The project was delivered on December 7,
1935, from Mgr. Giuseppe Pizzardo to Mgr. Giuseppe Fietta, who at the
time was the papal nuncio in the Dominican Republic and who on December 21 would have passed through Washington. However the definitive failure, on December 18, of the Laval-Hoare plan – which attempted
to reach a settlement for the Italo-Ethiopian conflict by accepting certain
Italian requests – and the great victories of general Pietro Badoglio as of
January 1936, made the Vatican proposal soon outdated.

In another area of diplomacy, a Vatican action within US circles was
entrusted to Pacelli on November 22, 1935, also by the Italian ambassador within the Holy See[52]. Mgr. Pignatti had spoken with the Secretary of
State of the actions implemented within the US by Father Coughlin who
had implemented an intense campaign of pro-Italian propaganda in those
weeks. Initially close to Roosevelt and then a strong opponent, Charles
Coughlin broadcasted a radio show that was very widespread, with about
one third of the nation tuning in to listen; during the Italo-Ethiopian conflict, he constantly supported Fascist imperialism and heated critique of the
general national policy[53]. The interest for Coughlin was part of a broader
attempt of Fascism to mobilize US Catholics in support of Italy, as previously reported to Mussolini in the first ten days of November by the Italian ambassador in Washington, Augusto Rosso. After having discussed
the use of the Italo-American electorate as a lobby to push the US to assume pro-Italian positions in the conflict, Mgr. Rosso recommended using
«the reaction of Catholic circles against the pro-British propaganda of the
Protestant churches», and received approval from the head of the government[54]. But, according to Pacelli, Father Coughlin had already «spoken
out strongly against England and the sanctions» and «did not need to be
incited further»[55]. After returning to the Secretariat of State on December

---

[51] AES, Italia, IV periodo, POS. 967, vol. II, fol. 220r, «Fietta».
[52] AES, Stati Ecclesiastici, IV periodo, POS. 430b, fasc. 362, «Udienza del 22 novembre
1935».
[53] Cfr. P.V. CANNISTRARO, T.P. KOVALEFF, *Father Coughlin and Mussolini: Impossible Allies*, in «Journal of Church and State», 13 (1971)/3, 427-443, and D. WARREN, *Radio
Priest: Charles Coughlin. The Father of Hate Radio*, New York 1996.
[54] A. Rosso to B. Mussolini, Washington, DC, November 9, 1935, in *I documenti diplomatici italiani*, VIII serie, vol. II, Roma 1991, p. 571.
[55] AES, Stati Ecclesiastici, IV periodo, POS. 430b, fasc. 362, «Udienza del 22 novembre
1935».

6, 1935, the Italian ambassador declared himself to be very satisfied with
the actions taken against the sanctions within the US on the part of the
Detroit priest[56]. About one month later, even Mussolini was enthusiastic
about the initiatives of the Irish priest who had decided to counter the offensive with methods that were «very American and completely effective
for the Americans»[57].

Gaetano Salvemini considered Roosevelt to be rather compliant with
respect to the proclamation of Empire by Mussolini (May 9, 1936), an
attitude which aimed to attain the support of Italo-Americans in the presidential elections of 1936[58]. In reality, and despite the pressures of Mgr.
Long on Washington to accept what was now a fact, the United States did
not recognize the annexation of Ethiopia. The Vatican was, on the other
hand, the second nation to recognize the *de facto* situation of the Empire.
The first government was Hitler's Germany. There were, in other words,
still some differences between the US and the Vatican on how to manage
the power politics of Mussolini, although they shared the same goal of sta-
bilizing the European situation. The hardening of ecclesiastical positions
with respect to national socialism and the increasing tensions between the
Holy See and the Third Reich led Vatican leaders to assume a softer stance
with respect to the Italian Government. This approach appeared opportune
to Vatican leaders due to certain developments in Europe: above all, the
Spanish Civil War. Pacelli and Roosevelt probably also discussed this in
Hyde Park, on November 5, 1936.

---

[56] AES, Stati Ecclesiastici, IV periodo, POS. 430b, fasc. 362, foll. 145r-146r, «Udienza
del 6 dicembre 1935».

[57] AES, Italia, IV periodo, POS. 967, vol. II, foll. 343r-346r, P. Tacchi Venturi, «Relazione dell'Udienza avuta con sua eccellenza in Capo del Governo il 3 gennaio 1936 alle
ore 17».

[58] G. SALVEMINI, *Preludio alla seconda guerra mondiale*, a cura di A. TORRE, Milano
1967, 633.

GERALD P. FOGARTY

The Case of Charles Coughlin:
The View from Rome

In the early 1930s, the Catholic Church almost everywhere was under siege – in Germany Mexico, Spain, and even Italy. The United States, formerly regarded with suspicion by the Vatican, seemed to be a lone beacon of hope, a place where the Church was flourishing. Yet, all was not paradise in the land across the Atlantic. Father Charles Coughlin presented a constant problem for Catholic leaders, but his case also revealed the problem as Church officials, whether Cardinal Eugenio Pacelli, the Vatican Secretary of State, or the American bishops grappled with the need to distance themselves from the radio priest without appearing to violate his freedom of speech. The situation was even more critical after the anti-Catholicism that broke out during the presidential campaign of 1928, when the fear of a Catholic in the White House, Alfred E. Smith, the Democratic candidate, stemmed in part from the perception that the Church would limit his freedom of thought and speech[1].

Coughlin had been born in Hamilton, Ontario in 1891. Ordained in 1916 in Toronto, he taught at the Basilian order's Assumption College in Windsor, Ontario, just across the river from Detroit, where he began helping out at various parishes. In 1923, he formally became a Detroit diocesan priest under Bishop Michael Gallagher. In 1926, he was assigned to found a new parish in Royal Oak, outside of Detroit. The Ku Klux Klan had burned a cross on the lawn of the simple frame church he had built there, named the Shrine of the Little Flower. He soon undertook a more ambitious project, a church of stone and carved marble with a towering cross that no one could burn. To pay off his debt, Coughlin turned to the radio. He originally stuck strictly to religious topics and aroused no controversy and many of his programs were aimed at instructing children. By 1930, he had a contract with the Columbia Broadcasting System (CBS),

---

[1] For a general overview, see my *American Hierarchy from 1870 to 1965*, Stuttgart 1982; Collegeville, MN, 1985, 243-246.

but his excursions into the economic crisis, the plight of the poor, and the failure of politicians to act led CBS to rescind its contract in the spring of 1931. Coughlin then created his own network[2].

As the first American religious figure to use the radio as his pulpit, Coughlin began as a supporter of Roosevelt, – «Roosevelt or Ruin» was his cry during the presidential campaign of 1932 – but gradually turned against him[3]. In June, 1933, ten senators and thirty five congressmen signed a petition to Roosevelt urging him to appoint Coughlin to the London economic summit meeting, for the priest represented the common person and was a student of international affairs[4]. For more than a year, Coughlin praised Roosevelt for moving toward silver as the American medium of exchange – and condemning Al Smith for adhering to the gold standard. His speeches in New York, where he did not have the actual approval of the archdiocese, drew a crowd of 7000 to the Hippodrome theater to hear him support Roosevelt and condemn the president's opponents. By the end of 1933, he continued to draw praise from Mgr. John A. Ryan, professor of economics at the Catholic University of America and director of Social Action Department of the National Catholic Welfare Conference (NCWC), the bishops' conference, although this may well have been a prudent decision on Ryan's part not to give his real opinion in a newspaper interview[5]. But even before Coughlin broke with Roosevelt, the Vatican expressed concern.

In March, 1934, Archbishop Giuseppe Pizzardo, undersecretary of State, wrote Archbishop Amleto Cicognani, the Apostolic Delegate to the American hierarchy, of the Holy See's growing concern about Coughlin. In his radio discourses, Pizzardo continued, the priest was frequently inaccurate in regard to Catholic social teaching and used expressions that came close to being Communistic. The Vatican was aware of Coughlin's great influence, but considered his excursions onto the economic plane to be dangerous. Pius XI wanted Cicognani to conduct an investigation[6]. The archival evidence is lacking, but it is probable that complaints about

---

[2] L. Woodcock Tentler, *Seasons of Grace: A History of the Catholic Archdiocese of Detroit*, Detroit 1990, 322-323.

[3] For Coughlin's career until 1937 under Bishop Gallagher, see E. Boyea, *The Reverend Charles Coughlin and the Church: the Gallagher Years, 1930-1937*, in «The Catholic Historical Review» 81 (1995), 211-225.

[4] «The New York Times», June 15, 1933, 5.

[5] *Ibidem*, Nov. 28, 1933, 1; Dec. 5, 1933, 7; Jan. 17, 1934, 14.

[6] AES, America, POS. 238, Fasc. 66, 3: Monsignor Secretary [Pizzardo] to Cicognani, March 5, 1934.

Coughlin had come from a place like New York, where the priest had not exercised the courtesy of at least asking the archbishop's permission to speak in the archdiocese.

Cicognani did not respond until June, at which time he also alluded to two telegrams, which are no longer available. As early as December 18, 1933, he reported, he met with Bishop Gallagher and succeeded in having Coughlin no longer speak from his church before benediction every Sunday, since that venue would confuse the faithful and other listeners into thinking he was speaking for the Church. He noted that Coughlin supported the silver standard, but that Catholics were divided on this, with bankers and industrialists opposing it and farmers and workers preferring it. Cicognani then consulted Ryan, Raymond A. McGowan, Ryan's assistant, and John Burke, Secretary General of the NCWC. McGowan reported that Coughlin had attacked the socialist, Norman Thomas, but his citations of papal encyclicals were highly selective. The unanimous advice of the American bishops and their advisers, which Cicognani passed on to Rome, was that it would be imprudent for Rome to curtail Coughlin's activity, since he had such a large following. As an example, he cited the case of a priest in Brooklyn who wrote a letter to a newspaper disagreeing with Coughlin and received 1500 letters of protest within one week, principally from women. Roosevelt, continued Cicognani, was growing more concerned about Coughlin, who had turned on Roosevelt for accepting a combination of gold and silver as the basis for the dollar. Late in April, Roosevelt met with Burke of the NCWC to express his concern about the priest. Coughlin also opposed the Wagner act providing for collective bargaining between management and labor unions on the grounds that, in his mind, it violated the teaching of Pius XI's *Quadragesimo Anno* – Coughlin was not a supporter of labor unions. Ryan, however, rejected Coughlin's opinion on the Catholic Hour radio show. The previous November, Cicognani noted, the bishops at their annual meeting discussed whether it was opportune for them to issue a declaration dissociating themselves and the Church from Coughlin's speeches, but reached no decision. Roosevelt formally asked Cicognani, through Burke, if there were not someway the Church could intervene. The delegate informed Pizzardo that he merely thanked the president for his letter[7].

Pizzardo informed Cicognani that the Pope had approved the «wise suggestion, i.e. that the Holy See, and therefore the Apostolic Delegation, should remain aloof from the Coughlin question, at least under the actual

---

[7] *Ibidem*, 6-9: Cicognani to Pizzardo, June 4, 1934.

conditions and circumstances, and that if anything is to be done, it should be done by the episcopate...»[8]. The bishops and even more so the Holy See had to walk the thin line between distancing themselves from Coughlin, who continued to have Gallagher's support, and not appearing to violate freedom of speech and alienating Coughlin's following.

Over the next year, the Holy See continued to wrestle with the problem. But Coughlin was becoming more extreme, moving away from his treatment of social justice to a virtually exclusive concentration on his monetary theories. He had also founded his own political party, the National Union of Social Justice. In December, 1934, Cardinal William O'Connell, Archbishop of Boston, declared that «no priest has the right to speak for the whole Church». This was actually the third time the Cardinal had attacked the radio priest. On December 9, Coughlin responded during his weekly speech. He first of all pointed out that O'Connell had no authority outside his archdiocese and that Coughlin spoke not only with the approval of his own Bishop, Michael Gallagher, but at «the command of my highest ecclesiastical superior, His Holiness Pope Pius XI». He charged that for forty years the Cardinal had «been more notorious for his silence on social justice than for any contribution which he may have given either in practice or in doctrine toward the decentralization of wealth and toward the elimination of those glaring injustices which permitted the plutocrats to wax fat at the expense of the poor»[9]. The «New York Herald Tribune» report of Coughlin's attack on the Cardinal was sent to the Secretariat of State[10].

By May, 1935, other prelates were privately expressing their concern about Coughlin. Cardinal Dennis Dougherty of Philadelphia thought the priest was «aided and abetted by his Most Reverend Ordinary, Bishop Gallagher» and was «now quite beyond control». He was, continued the Cardinal, «a hero in the minds of the proletariat and especially those members of that rabble, who are of Jewish extraction or belong to the Socialists or Communists»[11]. It was ironic that Dougherty thought Coughlin appealed to Jews, since the priest would soon emerge as one of the nation's greatest anti-Semites.

---

[8] *Ibidem*, 14: Pizzardo to Cicognani, June 23, 1934.
[9] «The New York Times», Dec. 10, 1934, 3.
[10] AES, America, POS. 238, Fasc. 66, 17-18.
[11] Archives of the Archdiocese of Philadelphia, Dougherty to Bernardini, Philadelphia, May 7, 1935 (copy), quoted in G.P. FOGARTY, *Vatican...*, 243.

In June 1935, Pizzardo sent Cicognani galleys of an article planned for «L'Osservatore Romano», stating that Coughlin did not speak for the Church, but the delegate urged Pacelli not to publish it. For one thing, he emphasized, no one thought Coughlin spoke as an «official, authorized interpreter of the teaching of the Church or hierarchy». O'Connell and several bishops had made this clear, as had some of the leading Catholic journals. Gallagher continued to give Coughlin public support and, in a radio talk, stated that, just as a Bishop in one diocese could grant an *imprimatur* for a book, allowing it to be read in other dioceses, so permission for a priest to speak on the radio meant he could be listened to in other dioceses. A writer in the «American Ecclesiastical Review», however argued that Coughlin was then engaging in politics, contrary to the legislation of the Third Plenary Council of Baltimore in 1884. Gallagher denied this in his diocesan paper and countered that the priest was simply presenting the teaching of Leo XIII and Pius XI. Since the Associated Press had earlier reported that the Vatican would take no action against Coughlin, Cicognani thought the publication of the proposed article in the «Osservatore Romano» would reverse that earlier neutral position and appear to make the statement the definitive and official position of the Vatican[12].

In early August, Cicognani again wrote the Vatican, this time a handwritten letter to Pizzardo. The delegate said he knew Pizzardo and Gallagher were friends and that the latter had good qualities. He found, nevertheless, that Gallagher could not discuss Coughlin and would not change his mind. Cicognani sent a copy of his letter to Giuseppe Bruno, Secretary of the Congregation of the Council, the branch of the Vatican charged with implementing the reform decrees of the Council of Trent and subsequent local councils and renamed the Congregation for the Clergy in 1967[13]. The letter does not make it clear whether Cicognani thought perhaps Pizzardo could influence Gallagher or whether the delegate suspected Gallagher was using his friendship with the Vatican official to keep higher authorities from speaking against the radio priest. Pizzardo did respond that the previous year Gallagher had requested a papal blessing, presumably for Coughlin[14]. Sometime around that period, moreover, a memo in English, probably written by Mgr. Joseph Hurley, an American working in the Secretariat of State, was submitted to Pacelli. It pointed out that Coughlin reached 20,000,000 – other estimates went as high as 40,000,000 – each

---

[12] AES, America, POS. 238, Fasc. 66, 51-58: Cicognani to Pacelli, July 9, 1935.

[13] *Ibidem*, 69-70: Cicognani to Pizzardo, Aug. 5, 1935.

[14] *Ibidem*, 79: Pizzardo to Cicognani, Sept. 17, 1935.

week, a greater audience than that of all the other priests in the country. The writer noted that Coughlin had lost sight of his original social justice principles and now focused exclusively on his monetary theories. He had, moreover, broadened his attack to include not only Roosevelt, but also Al Smith, Senator Robert Bulkley of Ohio, Senator Robert Wagner of New York, and Secretary of the Treasury Henry Morgenthau. The memo recommended that the bishops issue a clear statement of Catholic social teachings that would be an «unmistakable dissent» from Coughlin and thus avoid «a frontal assault»[15].

One other item in the Vatican archives indicates that perhaps something was afoot there about reining in Coughlin. A document summarized the case and then posed three questions. Was it appropriate for a priest speaking on the radio to use polemical language against the President? Was it appropriate for such a priest to speak in the name of the Church and present his own conclusions as Catholic doctrine? A third question was whether it was appropriate for a Bishop to give support to Coughlin and thus give the impression that he enjoys hierarchical support for his positions[16]?

Early in 1936, Cicognani asked Archbishop John T. McNicholas, O.P., of Cincinnati, Gallagher's metropolitan, about the possibility of having the administrative board of the NCWC issue a statement on Coughlin. McNicholas suggested to Archbishop Edward Mooney, chairman of the administrative board and Bishop of Rochester, a statement something like:

> «Father Coughlin's discourses on a variety of subjects over a period of several years show the liberty of opinion permitted in the Catholic Church and among Catholic priests. One may not agree with Father Coughlin, but Catholics recognize his right as a citizen, as an individual and as a student of social questions, to express his opinion. Father Coughlin, naturally, is not speaking for the Catholic Church of the United States, nor for the American Hierarchy. As his own Bishop has publicly stated, he is speaking with his approval, etc.».

McNicholas was trying to defend the Holy See against bearing the full brunt of censoring Coughlin, but «it has seemed to me that if Father Coughlin is to be censured, a formula must be found by which an American Bishop, or Bishops, can do it. This will not be easy». If either an individual Bishop or the administrative board should ban Coughlin's

---

[15] *Ibidem*, 80: Memorandum.
[16] *Ibidem*, 77-78.

broadcasts, he argued, the people would protest. If, however, Coughlin «should transgress in the domain or [*sic*] faith or morals», he would not hesitate to disapprove his preaching for Cincinnati. To illustrate the difficulty of finding an appropriate statement, he recalled that he had chided Gallagher for allowing Coughlin «to violate charity in denouncing people by name», but the Bishop replied: «Well, St. John the Baptist denounced Herod and his wife because of their adulterous union»[17]!

Mooney was faced with the dilemma that had long confronted the American Church before the public. If authorities silenced Coughlin, they would be charged with denying him freedom of speech. If they said nothing, they would be accused of agreeing with what he said. Mooney summed up this problem for McNicholas – and perhaps presaged what he would face when he became Coughlin's ordinary. Cicognani's suggestion, he wrote, «does, indeed, raise a delicate question». He went on to say:

> «It is unwise, perhaps, for me to start with the thought (or "hunch["]), but I am wondering whether, when all concerned, including the Delegate, see the only kind of statement they feel can be made, they will not all conclude that it is not worth making. After all, there are just two authorities who can, with clear right, step in to this affair, his own Bishop and the Holy See. His own Bishop has spoken – and how! Evidently the Holy See does not care to speak – and in this, as in so many other things, it is probably very wise. Where then do we come in and how? Of course, if there is any transgression of faith or morals, then, as you say, anyone of us can step to the front, but, short of that, what can we say that will not result in greater confusion? If supreme authority wishes to exercise some indirect control, could that not better be done by bringing pressure to bear on the Ordinary than through the medium of a necessarily vague statement of a group whose competence is not clear enough to defy a challenge – perhaps on the part of the proper Ordinary who is something of a challenger? I very much fear that any statement which stops short of condemnation – and it must do that – will almost inevitably be taken as some sort of approbation»[18].

Mooney did not point out the inconsistency that, in 1922, the Holy See had ordered the National Catholic Welfare Council to disband and tolerated its continuation with several restrictions, such as the change of the name «Council» to «Conference». Now, the Holy See wished it to take a

---

[17] Archives of the Archdiocese of Cincinnati, McNicholas, Cincinnati, Feb. 28, 1936 (copy), quoted in G.P. FOGARTY, *Vatican...*, 244

[18] Archives of the Archdiocese of Cincinnati, Mooney to McNicholas, Rochester, Mar. 5, 1936, quoted in G.P. FOGARTY, *Vatican...*, 245.

stand against Coughlin when it had no canonical authority. The result was the NCWC made no statement.

In 1936, Coughlin announced that his National Union of Social Justice was entering the presidential race with William Lemke, representative from North Dakota, running as president. In a major address kicking off the campaign, Coughlin ripped his Roman collar off and called Roosevelt a «traitor» and «liar». Mgr. Egidio Vagnozzi, then an assistant to Cicognani, reported to Rome of the negative reaction such an attack on a head of State caused the American population[19]. In the meantime, Bishop Gallagher was on his way to Rome amid speculation that he was to discuss the Coughlin situation. Hurley drew up his own opinion for Pacelli on what he thought should be done. He explained the dilemma of the American bishops:

> «It is the humble opinion of the undersigned that a way should be found to dissociate American Catholics and the Church from the above mentioned injurious words against the President. It may be that Monsignor Gallagher, as Father Coughlin's ordinary, could be induced to make a formal declaration to the Press stating that he regretted the attack because contrary to Catholic teaching on the respect due to constituted authority. If this humble suggestion should find favor, it must also be borne in mind that Monsignor Gallagher should be required to guard the secret of instructions given him. In the past he has divulged to Father Coughlin and to others matters which he should have kept to himself».

He further recommended that it would be advisable to have the delegate come to Rome at the same time as Gallagher[20]. As it happened, Cicognani was already in Rome and had an audience with the Pope on July 4[21]. In the meantime, Pacelli recorded on July 30 that the Pope would be seeing Gallagher the following day and would definitely discuss Coughlin. The Pope, the Cardinal continued, had instructed Hurley, who was about to return to the United States on vacation, to convey to Coughlin orally the Pope's concern about his attacks on Roosevelt[22].

Hurley had in fact seen the Pope just before Pacelli. He recorded that Pius XI had instructed him to tell Coughlin that «it is the desire of His Holiness that he (Coughlin) be prudent and priestly in all his utterances and that he refrain from doing or saying anything which might dimin-

---

[19] AES, America, POS. 238, Fasc. 67, 27-32, Vagnozzi to Pizzardo, July 20, 1934.

[20] *Ibidem*, 42-43: Joseph Hurley, July 22, 1936 – appunto.

[21] «The New York Times», July 5, 1936, N. 1.

[22] AES, America, POS. 238, Fasc. 66, 17: Pacelli, notes of audience on July 30, 1936.

ish respect for constituted authority». On September 5, Hurley quietly paid Coughlin a visit in Detroit to convey the Pope's message. Coughlin «received it with deep respect and veneration», Hurley wrote, but asked for further explanation. Hurley thought the message was clear, but communicated the information to Cicognani with the request of forwarding it to Pacelli. Since Hurley's mission was not public, however, Coughlin continued his activity as though he had never received any formal or informal instructions from the Pope[23].

Meanwhile, Vagnozzi consulted several Church leaders and learned a lesson about American Catholic history. In New York, he had met Cardinal Dougherty of Philadelphia and Cardinal Patrick Hayes of New York. Dougherty thought that if the Holy See ordered Gallagher to put an end to Coughlin's political activities, his followers might well react. Any orders the Holy See did give would have to be explicit and detailed, so that Gallagher and Coughlin could not find a way out of them. Hayes informed Vagnozzi of the action of his predecessor, Archbishop Michael A. Corrigan, who gained the excommunication of Father Edward McGlynn in 1887 – Vagnozzi erroneously identified the priest as «McGinley» – only to face protests in the streets of more than 75,000 people. He did think, however, that the Holy See could order Gallagher to stop supporting Coughlin and giving him approval and state that Coughlin was acting as a citizen and not as a priest who spoke in any way in the name of the Church or as her representative – while not prohibiting him from speaking[24].

The difficulty was that neither Gallagher nor Coughlin could really be trusted. Early in September, «L'Osservatore Romano» published an article, possibly written earlier by Hurley, rebuking Coughlin for his attacks on Roosevelt and stating that Gallagher erred in saying Coughlin had the Vatican's approval for his statements. Upon his return to the United States, however, Gallagher asserted that the article represented not the mind of the Holy See but only of the editors and that he had not discussed Coughlin with the Pope. He argued furthermore that the failure of the Holy See expressly to condemn Coughlin meant that it approved of his statements, so, as Coughlin's Bishop, Gallagher continued to give him support. Cicognani now requested «instructions and particulars» so that he could authoritatively declare that the Holy See had explicitly reproved Gallagher for Coughlin's remarks about Roosevelt and that Gallagher

---

[23] *Ibidem*, fasc. 72, 42 Hurley, appunto. C.R. GALLAGHER, SJ, *Vatican Secret Diplomacy: Joseph P. Hurley and Pope Pius XII*, New Haven 2008, 52-53.

[24] AES, America, POS. 238, Fasc. 67, 44-45: Vagnozzi to Pizzardo, July 31, 1936.

knew that the article in «L'Osservatore Romano» reflected the thought of the Vatican[25].

As Cicognani sought to wend his way through Coughlin's wiles, he also had to contend with opposition from another source. Spellman knew of Roosevelt's strong dismay at Coughlin's attacks. Perhaps to ingratiate himself with the President, he first wrote Cicognani and then paid him a personal visit. When the delegate said he could do nothing more, Spellman recorded that «he could at least rebuke Gallagher or demand that he keep Coughlin in Detroit». He thought the delegate «weak and frightened and I am sure that he is suspicious and cautious»[26]. Spellman churlishly did not tell the delegate that Pacelli was coming to the country, a visit that, as will be seen, had Coughlin as a backdrop, but perhaps not as a focus.

In the meantime, Roosevelt sought to counter what he thought was Coughlin's growing power. In October, he arranged for Mgr. Ryan to go on the radio to challenge Coughlin's interpretation of papal encyclicals and attacks on Roosevelt[27]. This won for Ryan Coughlin's charge that he was «Right Reverend New Dealer» and Archbishop Curley's attack in his newspaper on both Coughlin and Ryan, Coughlin for his extreme views and Ryan for going on the radio without the permission of Curley, under whose jurisdiction Washington then fell[28].

Pacelli's visit to the United States was the first ever of such a high ranking official of the Vatican as the Secretary of State. Ostensibly, he came as the private house guest of Genevieve Garvin Brady, a papal duchess and widow of Nicholas Brady, a wealthy financier. She and her husband had been major benefactors of the Maryland-New York Province of the Jesuits and of Cardinal Mundelein. She had also built the Ospedale del Bambino Gesù on the Janiculum Hill in Rome. The visit was quite a coup on her part, but Spellman soon took charge of it and made several «suggestions» to Enrico Galeazzi, Pacelli's confidant and travelling companion, much to her chagrin with the result that she ultimately left him out of her will. In his official pronouncement on the purpose of his visit, Pacelli denied to journalists that he came to do anything about Coughlin, although Spellman had met with Roosevelt and discussed both the forthcoming visit and Coughlin shortly before the Cardinal's arrival. Whether or not Spellman

---

[25] *Ibidem*, 58: Cicognani to Pacelli, Sept. 9, 1936 telegram. On Hurley being the author of the article, see C.R. GALLAGHER, *Vatican Secret Diplomacy...*, 55, but by Sept. 5, Hurley was already in the United States.

[26] Spellman Diary, Sept. 25, 27, 1936, quoted in FOGARTY, *Vatican...*, 345-346.

[27] «The New York Times», Oct. 9, 1936, 1; Oct. 12, 18.

[28] G.P. FOGARTY, *Vatican...*, 247.

was acting on Pacelli's private instructions, he succeeded in alienating not only Mrs. Brady but Cicognani and Cardinal Hayes as well. He was firmly convinced that either Cicognani or Hayes had found a memorandum that he had made before Pacelli's ship had docked and that this became the basis for Mrs. Brady's attacks on him[29].

Although the available evidence indicates that Pacelli had followed Cicognani's advice to leave the Coughlin case to the American bishops, one of the purposes of the visit was to meet Roosevelt. With the Coughlin issue in the background, however, there were numerous protests, apparently from Coughlin's followers, against the Cardinal being photographed with Roosevelt[30]. In fact, there were no photographs of the two together, and the meeting of the two took place only at the end of Pacelli's trip. In the meantime, Archbishop John G. Murray of St. Paul chartered a plane to fly the Cardinal across the country as far as Los Angeles with stops in between. Spellman was Pacelli's constant companion. On October 30, Pacelli was in Cincinnati, where he probably discussed the Coughlin case with McNicholas, Gallagher's metropolitan, but supposedly refused to see Bishop Gallagher or Bishop Joseph Schrembs of Cleveland, who sought an audience on Coughlin's behalf. Spellman, who was garrulous in his diary about every stop along the way, said nothing of this episode, evidence for which depends solely on the later testimony of Coughlin who argued that the Cardinal had him taken off the radio, a fact that does not bear up under-scrutiny – Coughlin was still on the radio more than three years later[31]. Despite Coughlin's third-party efforts, Roosevelt was overwhelmingly elected to a second term. Two days later, Roosevelt hosted Pacelli for lunch at his mother's home in Hyde Park, New York.

Arranging for a meeting between the president and the Cardinal Secretary of State took some negotiations. As soon as Cicognani learned of Pacelli's coming, he enlisted the assistance of John Burke of the NCWC to arrange a meeting with the president at the White House. Burke had just about completed arrangements when Pacelli called Cicognani to say that Spellman had worked through Joseph Kennedy to have the meeting at Hyde Park. The delegate was quite angry that he, the papal representative, had been by-passed by the Cardinal and an auxiliary Bishop. For

---

[29] *Ibidem*, 347; ASV, DAUS, V. 194 Pacelli Visit, 185-189: Spellman to Cicognani, Inisfada, Oct. 9, 1936; 191: Cicognani to Spellman, Oct. 12, 1936; 192: Spellman to Cicognani, Inisfada, n.d.
[30] *Ibidem*, 70-72: Cicognani to Pacelli, Oct. 9, 1936.
[31] G.P. FOGARTY, *Vatican...*, 247-248.

that matter, Burke was furious that the Cardinal had ignored the bishops' conference. It was one of several issues that would create tension between Cicognani and Spellman[32].

At the meeting, which lasted two hours, Spellman and Joseph Kennedy were also presented with the Cardinal and the President, but no one took notes of what was discussed, nor were there any photographs. In light of Spellman's as well as Cicognani's efforts since 1933 to establish diplomatic relations between the Holy See and the United States, this, rather than the Coughlin case as such, was the principal topic of conversation. After the meeting, Spellman's correspondence with Roosevelt focused only on diplomatic relations[33]. Diplomatic relations between the United States and the Holy See and the Coughlin case were not mutually exclusive, since, as will be seen, Roosevelt used the later appointment of Myron C. Taylor as his personal representative to the Pope to voice his continued concern about Coughlin.

In the meantime, the Coughlin case continued to fester in 1936. With the defeat of his third party in 1936 and, therefore, his failure to throw the presidential election into the House of Representatives, he announced that he was leaving the radio. In January, 1937, however, Bishop Gallagher died, and Coughlin resumed his broadcasts saying this was the late Bishop's dying wish. In the summer, the Holy See announced that Detroit was elevated to an archdiocese with Edward Mooney as the first archbishop. Mooney had been Apostolic Delegate to India and then Japan before returning to the United States as Bishop of Rochester. He had also been elected the chairman of the administrative board of the NCWC. Despite his skill and experience, he would face a formidable problem in the radio priest.

Hardly had Mooney assumed office than Coughlin opened a new offensive. Mooney appointed a diocesan censor, Mgr. William Murphy – he later appointed a second censor – for Coughlin's radio addresses and articles in «Social Justice», the journal he had founded in 1936. On the basis of the censor's decision, Mooney refused to give his *imprimatur* to three articles in «Social Justice» entitled *Can Christians Join the CIO?*[34]. But Coughlin was not to be put off. In August, he sent Pacelli copies of his «Social Justice» articles, which, he claimed, had further factual information of the danger of the CIO. A Vatican official, probably Hurley, sum-

---

[32] *Ibidem*, 248.
[33] *Ibidem*, 248-251.
[34] L.W. TENTLER, *Seasons of Grace...*, 332 and 555.

marized the articles against John L. Lewis and the CIO and recommended that Mooney be told of the receipt of the articles and that Pacelli was grateful[35]. In September, Pacellli wrote Mooney to use «prudence» in thanking Coughlin for the articles[36]. Mooney decided to say nothing to Coughlin.

Before Mooney could even think of conveying any thanks to Coughlin for the articles, the priest became even more provocative. He had not yet begun his broadcasting season, but he gave an interview in which he charged Roosevelt for «personal stupidity» in his nomination of Hugo Black, a former member of the Ku Klux Klan, for the Supreme Court. Coughlin had also stated that a Catholic could no more become a member of the CIO, which he claimed was dominated by Communists, than become a Moslem. Mooney challenged both statements in his newspaper, «The Michigan Catholic». He did not deny that some Communists were in the CIO, but argued that the presence of «conscientious Catholics» in the CIO prevented Communist domination[37].

By this time, Coughlin or his close associates had organized a campaign of sending telegrams to the Vatican to protest Mooney's demand that Coughlin submit the texts for his radio addresses and other writings to diocesan censorship[38]. Having already publicly disagreed with Coughlin in regard to Roosevelt's appointment of Black and Catholic membership in the CIO, Mooney now wrote Pacelli that he had not communicated the Cardinal's gratitude to Coughlin for sending the Vatican his three articles because his two censors had advised him to deny the *imprimatur*. Not only did he fear the articles would stir up negative feelings among the working class toward the Church, but they also misquoted papal encyclicals and claimed papal approval for Coughlin's monetary theories. He therefore asked Pacelli to have the articles examined to see if his diocesan censors were incorrect[39]. At the bottom of an Italian summary of this letter, is a notation that Hurley wanted instructions in regard to a response[40]. While the Pope continued to be bombarded with telegrams from Coughlin's follow-

---

[35] AES, America, POS. 238, Fasc. 67, 70-71: Coughlin to Pacelli, Royal Oak, MI, Aug. 5 and 13, 1937; 72: pro-memoria.

[36] *Ibidem*, 74 Pacelli to Mooney, Sept. 7, 1937 (copy).

[37] «The New York Times», Oct. 8, 1937, p. 18.

[38] AES, America, POS. 238, Fasc. 68, 1: list of telegrams.

[39] *Ibidem*, Mooney to Pacelli, Oct. 13, 1937 (copy).

[40] *Ibidem*, 4.

ers, the clippings from the «Detroit News» about the Coughlin-Mooney dispute also flowed into the Secretariat of State[41].

With Mooney's refusal to give his *imprimatur* to the articles in «Social Justice» and his criticism of Coughlin for the priest's position on Roosevelt and the Black nomination and on Catholic membership in the CIO, Coughlin announced that he was cancelling his twenty-six broadcasts over thirty-five stations. Mooney stressed that Coughlin's decision to cancel his broadcasts was totally his own[42].

But Coughlin had yet two more ploys. First, he or his associates prepared postcards to be sent to Cicognani to protest the priest's «with-drawl [sic]» from the radio. Second, Coughlin sold «Social Justice» to a Protestant businessman. As the priest's lawyer said, the journal was not Catholic, so Mooney had no authority over it. On October 29, Mooney reported this to Cicognani[43]. On November 5, Cicognani had Mooney's letter translated into Italian and forwarded it and other material to Pacelli as part of his own lengthy report on the case. The delegate recounted Coughlin's retirement from the radio late in 1936 and his return in early 1937, supposedly at the will of the late Bishop Gallagher. On August 2, the day Mooney was installed as the first Archbishop of Detroit, Coughlin began his campaign against the CIO in «Social Justice». Mooney then appointed a censor for Coughlin's radio addresses and writings in his journal. Coughlin agreed, but then made his assault on Roosevelt. The delegate praised Mooney's tact, especially in view of Gallagher's public support of Coughlin before his followers. Despite Coughlin's promise of obedience to his archbishop, however, he veered away from that course and intentionally complicated the situation by playing to the simplicity of his followers and the prejudice of Protestants. To Catholics, Coughlin claimed merely to present papal teaching. To Protestants, he claimed to be exercising freedom of speech. Now there was the «committee of one million», which engaged in a campaign to appeal to the Holy See to have Coughlin return to the radio. That appeal was construed as a potential victory for Coughlin, as he showed himself to be loyal to the Pope, so the delegate urged that the Holy See sustain Mooney[44].

---

[41] *Ibidem*, 36-37: summary of Coughlin-Mooney case, in «Detroit News», Oct. 4-7, 1937; Oct 11, 1937; «Detroit News» reports Coughlin cancelled his radio program.

[42] «The New York Times», Oct. 10, 1937, 1.

[43] AES, IV periodo, America, POS. 238, Fasc. 69, 17-25: Mooney to Cicognani, Detroit, Oct. 29, 1937 (Italian translation).

[44] *Ibidem*, 3-9: Cicognani to Pacelli, Nov. 5, 1937.

In Rome, Hurley had the task of preparing a lengthy response to Cicognani's letter. He recounted his involvement with Coughlin beginning in the summer of 1936 through the most recent events. In particular, Hurley supported Mooney's request for a published statement in support of his actions. Coughlin had already brought the issue to the attention of the Holy See by sending his articles to Pacelli. That he had misquoted *Quadragesimo Anno* and attacked Roosevelt by name went beyond the instructions Hurley himself had been charged to give to Coughlin in the summer of 1936. Coughlin had, moreover, created the present situation by comparing Catholic membership in the CIO with membership in Islam. Hurley was convinced that the moment had come to end Coughlin's influence, especially since he condemned his opponents by misquoting encyclicals. Reflecting his deep support for Roosevelt, he stated that such a condemnation would be pleasing to the president. Finally, he noted, in 1936, the Holy See remained silent about Coughlin because of the need for prudence in an election year, but that concern no longer applied[45]. On November 20, Pius XI instructed Cicognani to issue a statement that «corrections made by the Archbishop of Detroit to the remarks of Father Charles E. Coughlin on Oct. 5 were just and timely». The delegate added to these instructions that «every Bishop has not only the right but the duty to supervise Catholic teaching in his diocese». A priest who felt «aggrieved» could appeal to the Holy See, «but in loyalty to the church, he also had the duty of using his influence to keep the matter from being made the occasion of public agitation and thus possibly creating confusion in the minds of many Catholics»[46].

On December 1, Cicognani thanked Pacelli for the statement on his own behalf and that of Mooney. He reported also that the three articles about the CIO had been submitted to two censors and to Father Francis Haas of the Catholic University of America. All upheld Mooney's refusal of the *imprimatur*. They said Coughlin had misquoted *Quadragesimo Anno* and misunderstood the Pope's speaking in favor of trade unions as an endorsement of the American Federation of Labor. Coughlin, the delegate continued, tried to show himself a loyal son of the Church, but he stressed that he only «seemed» to accept the refusal of the *imprimatur*, but

---

[45] *Ibidem*, fasc. 68, 42-44: Hurley, Appunto, n.d., but apparently after Cicognani's letter of Nov. 5, 1937.

[46] «The New York Times», Nov. 21, 1937, 19.

«he simply seemed and for a short time»[47]. Coughlin had written Cicognani that he deplored the agitation and called upon his followers to cease their campaign to have him return to the air[48]. For some reason, Cicognani failed to mention at this time that Coughlin had visited him twice, on November 26 and 30.

Two weeks later, Cicognani added more information. The continued attacks on Roosevelt and the CIO in «Social Justice», he wrote, annulled the statement of the Holy See. Coughlin had personally been to see him and was making Murphy, Mooney's censor, his scapegoat; he claimed Murphy did not understand encyclicals and suggested the appointment of three of his assistant priests in his parish as censors. A short time later, Coughlin announced that he was returning to radio early in 1938 and would also be an «editorial counsel or adviser» to «Social Justice». Mooney was caught off guard. He gave Coughlin permission rather than provoke a public battle[49].

Early in January, Pius XI told Pacelli to assure Mooney that he stood behind him and should continue to act as he had done. To Cicognani, however, Pacelli wrote that the Pope wanted to be kept informed, and, despite the Holy See's declaration and Coughlin's promise, he remained suspicious about the priest's ultimate intentions[50]. Cicognani replied that so far Coughlin's discourses conformed to the promises he had made to Mooney and the delegate that he had no objections to Mooney's censorship. But he himself would continue to monitor Coughlin[51]. Mooney himself thanked Pacelli for the Holy See's intervention and said Coughlin's first broadcast pledged his loyalty to ecclesiastical authority and disavowed his followers who opposed it[52]. But storm clouds were gathering. Unfortunately, the Vatican archives contain nothing for this period of the Coughlin affair.

Until the summer of 1938, Coughlin was non-controversial in both his radio broadcasts and articles in «Social Justice». The journal focused principally on maintaining American neutrality in the increasing likelihood of war in Europe. In the process, it heaped blame on Great Britain for being too bellicose, but excused what was happening in Germany and

---

[47] AES, IV periodo, America, POS. 238, Fasc. 69, 45-51: Cicognani to Pacelli, Dec. 1, 1937.

[48] *Ibidem*, 52: Coughlin to Cicognani, n.d.

[49] *Ibidem*, Fasc. 70, 2-7: Cicognani to Pacelli, Dec. 15, 1937.; Tentler, p. 334-335.

[50] AES, IV periodo, America, POS. 238, Fasc. 70, 13-14: Pacelli note, Jan. 3, 1938; 15: Pacelli minute of audience, Jan. 4, 1938; 16: Pacelli to Cicognani, Jan. 7, 1939 (draft).

[51] *Ibidem*, 18: Cicognani to Pacelli, Jan. 31, 1938.

[52] *Ibidem*, 19: Mooney to Pacelli, Jan. 27, 1938.

Italy. The journal then became decidedly anti-Semitic. In Coughlin's own column, «Social Justice» serially published the «Protocols of the Elders of Zion», the fabricated account of a Jewish plot to take over business and banking. Although Coughlin admitted they were fiction, he stood by the basic truth of the allegations that some Jews, antireligious ones, were seeking to undermine Christianity. In his broadcast on November 20, less than two weeks after *Kristallnacht*, he went beyond the pale. As the «The New York Times» summarized it, he argued «that the Jewish people had risen to influence in radio, journalism and finance, which tended to give the Nazi actions tremendous publicity and that the Jews had leadership in communism, which Nazi Germany believed it must fight in self-protection». But then, in a passage that Mooney said was typical of his apparently denying what he had first said, Coughlin was quoted as stating «I say to the good Jews of America, be not indulgent with the irreligious, atheistic Jews and Gentiles who promote the cause of persecution in the land of the Communists the same ones who promote the cause of atheism in America». He went on to assert that Communists in Russia, Mexico, and Spain had killed far more Christians in comparison to the number of Jews slain by the Nazis[53]. The New York radio station carrying Coughlin's program issued a strong and unprecedented rejoinder and subsequently refused to air later programs.

But Coughlin's was not the only American Catholic response to the *Kristallnacht*. On November 16, 1938, four days before Coughlin's offensive program, The Catholic University of America sponsored a radio broadcast consisting of a series of speeches by leading Catholic clerics and laity. Introduced by Father Maurice Sheehy, professor of religious education at the university, the speakers were Archbishop John J. Mitty of San Francisco, Bishops John Mark Gannon of Erie, and Peter L. Ireton of Richmond and Mgr. Joseph Corrigan, Rector of the University. Joining them to represent the laity was former Governor Alfred Smith. All supported Roosevelt's condemnation of the persecution of the Jews in Germany[54].

Mooney had disavowed many of Coughlin's ideas in his newspaper, «The Michigan Catholic», but he apparently thought he lacked canonical authority to rein in the priest any further without perhaps alienating many Catholics. Late in December, he did ask Cicognani to procure a letter from the Pope repudiating Coughlin's broadcasts and his publica-

---

[53] «The New York Times», Nov. 21, 1938, 7.
[54] «The New York Times», Nov. 17, 1938, 1.

tion of the «Protocols». Mooney may have intended to use such a letter in private negotiations with Coughlin and would make it public, only if the priest still disobeyed. But Pius XI, then on the eve of his death, was reluctant or unable to get involved. Cicognani recommended to Coughlin through Mooney that, in the name of the Holy See, the priest was to follow «the suggestions and directions» of Mooney «in a spirit of priestly docility»[55]. More outspoken was Cardinal George Mundelein of Chicago, who had just returned from Rome. In an address, read for him over the radio by Bernard Sheil, his auxiliary Bishop, he stated that «as an American citizen, Father Coughlin has the right to express his personal views on current events, but he is not authorized to speak for the Catholic Church nor does he represent the doctrine or sentiments of the church»[56]. From Rome, Hurley told Mooney the Chicago Cardinal's action was «a shining example of bad tactics in handling Charlie»[57].

Despite Hurley's animadversions, Mooney did take an unprecedented action. Just before Christmas, 1938, the Reverend George Buttrick, president of the Federal Council Churches, the umbrella group for many main-line Protestant denominations, approached Michael Ready, General Secretary of the NCWC, with a draft statement from other Protestant groups condemning the persecution of Jews in Germany and the atrocities against them. Ready originally offered to sign the statement in his own name, but Mooney made a few emendations and signed it as chairman of the administrative board of the NCWC. Although on other occasions before the advent of ecumenism, the NCWC and Federal Council would simultaneously issue identical, but separate statements, Mooney joined Buttrick, Bishop Henry St. George Tucker, presiding Bishop of the Protestant Episcopal Church, and leaders of the Presbyterian Church in the United States and the Southern Baptist Convention in publicly condemning the Nazi actions against Jews and Christians[58]. Although the statement said nothing of Coughlin, its signing by Mooney, Coughlin's ordinary, was a formal condemnation of the priest's anti-Semitism. Since Mooney himself had been an Apostolic Delegate, it seems probable that he would have consulted Cicognani, but there is nothing in the Vatican archives to indicate that there was any written consultation, although there are numer-

---

[55] L.W. TENTLER, *Seasons of Grace...*, 337-338.
[56] «The New York Times», Dec. 12, 1938, 1, 3.
[57] C.R. GALLAGHER, *Vatican Secret Diplomacy...*, 59.
[58] «The New York Times», Dec. 24, 1938, 6.

ous newspaper clippings about the statement. Mooney could, of course, have spoken with Cicognani on the telephone.

During this same period, Mooney had also written Hurley at the Vatican, still hoping to have the Pope to make a statement. Hurley put the situation into a broader context. Coughlin had become the darling not only of the Nazis, but also of the Italian Fascists, especially Roberto Farinacci, editor of «Il Regime fascista». There was danger of reprisals against the Vatican and the Church in Italy if the Pope spoke out in what was still regarded as an American problem. The Fascists, moreover, saw some people in the Vatican as being pro-Semitic[59].

But Pius XI's pontificate was drawing to a close. On February 10, 1939, he died. On March 2, the Cardinals chose Eugenio Pacelli to succeed him. By September, the Second World War had broken out. The United States and the Holy See now partially realized what Pacelli and Roosevelt probably discussed at Hyde Park in 1936. On December 24, 1939, Roosevelt announced that he was sending Myron C. Taylor as his «Personal Representative to Pope Pius XII». He was given the personal title of «Extraordinary Ambassador», since the United States did not have diplomatic relations with the Holy See. On February 27, 1940, Taylor presented his credentials to the Pope in ceremonies usually reserved for a regular ambassador. Among his assignments, in bold capital letters was «COUGHLIN». Roosevelt then had added that the anti-Semitism in Baltimore, Brooklyn, and Detroit, which «is said to be encouraged by the church», would therefore «automatically stir up anti-Catholic feeling and that makes a general mess»[60]. He was most probably alluding to the Christian Front, inspired by Coughlin and responsible for a terrorist plot to take over the New York Post Office, the Federal Reserve, and blow up bridges into New York. The group was anti-Semitic and composed primarily of Catholics. In January, 1940, the FBI captured the eighteen members of the group with a sizable arsenal of rifles, cordite, and ammunition. Coughlin originally disavowed any association with the group, only to reverse himself a week later[61].

On March 8, Taylor, accompanied by Hurley, had his first audience with Cardinal Luigi Maglione, the Secretary of State. Taylor brought up the Catholic anti-Semitism in Brooklyn, Baltimore, and Detroit. Maglione

---

[59] C.R. GALLAGHER, *Vatican Secret Diplomacy...*, 60-67.
[60] Quoted in FOGARTY, *Vatican...*, 263-264.
[61] C.R. GALLAGHER, *Vatican Secret Diplomacy...*, 68. See «The New York Times», Jan. 15, 1940, 1, 3; *ibidem*, Jan. 22, 1940, 1.

noted the work of Pius XI in behalf of the Jews and suggested that Taylor draw up a memorandum for Cicognani. Taylor then referred to Coughlin and his «violent speeches». Hurley's diary account of this meeting makes it clear that Roosevelt wanted the Holy See to issue a statement against Coughlin and, perhaps, the Christian Front. Maglione promised that he would study the matter. That summer, Hurley submitted a note about Coughlin to Giovanni Battista Montini, then the substitute Secretary of State for ecclesiastical affairs. Hurley, who shared much of the anti-Semitism widespread in his era, made no mention of the Jews, but urged that the Vatican reprimand Coughlin for his «bitter criticism» of American policy[62].

Coughlin's anti-Semitism may have made him a hero in Nazi Germany and Fascist Italy, but radio stations began to cancel his program. The diocesan censors also grew more diligent. In February, 1940, they refused to give approval to an openly anti-Semitic text, so Coughlin responded with a «silent broadcast» of music. As more stations cancelled their contracts with him, he had to cancel his 1940-1941 season. «Social Justice», however, remained. Technically, Coughlin had left the journal, and a group of his parishioners took it over. Mooney, however, knew that Coughlin remained its major influence. What brought the journal to its definitive end was a threat by the Government to charge it with sedition for continuing to write against American involvement in the war. By that time, Mooney had threatened Coughlin with suspension from his priestly faculties. Coughlin, who again admitted he was in charge of «Social Justice» asked not to be suspended if he was going to go to civil trial, for this would prejudice his case. Mooney agreed. This ended Coughlin's «political» activity[63].

Coughlin had been a thorn in the hierarchy's side for a decade. Part of his problem was his paranoia and suspicion of conspiracies against the Church and nation – something he shared with Gallagher[64]. Like so many people who are convinced that they see things hidden from others, Coughlin thought nothing of going over the head of his superior, Mooney, to appeal to the public, such as his decision to return to the radio and to «Social Justice» in 1938. This trait also led him to take phrases of encyclicals out of context. In short, he was so convinced that he was correct that he would

---

[62] C.R. GALLAGHER, *Vatican Secret Diplomacy...*, 69-70. Hurley's official note on the meeting of Taylor with Maglione is in *Actes et Documents du Saint Siège relatifs à la Seconde Guerre Mondiale*, ed. by P. BLET, A. MARTINI, and B. SCHNEIDER, 11 vols., Vatican 1970, I, 381-382.

[63] L.W. TENTLER, *Seasons of Grace...*, 341-342.

[64] *Ibidem*, 320.

use any means, even dissimulation or selective use of Church documents, to get his ideas across.

But the hierarchy was virtually helpless in curbing the radio priest. Many Catholics then and now think that, since the Church is hierarchical, a Cardinal can discipline a priest in another diocese. But, until 1937, Coughlin had the complete support of Bishop Gallagher, who was the only one, other than the Pope, with canonical authority over him. Mooney, who was not sympathetic, found himself largely stymied in the face of what Coughlin had mastered – manipulation of public opinion. On the advice of Cicognani in 1934, the Holy See likewise stayed out of direct confrontation for fear of repeating what had happened with McGlynn in 1887; it did, of course, attempt other means of toning Coughlin down, especially after his attacks on Roosevelt. Moreover, with the recent defeat of Al Smith, the Holy See was extremely cautious about intervening in an American domestic issue, even one so pressing as anti-Semitism. The American Church and the Holy See were at a loss about how to control a priest who so skillfully used the new medium of the radio. Yet, Mooney was not inactive. He signed the joint statement with Protestant leaders condemning the Nazi persecution of Jews and Christians. Mooney therefore went on public record against anti-Semitism at the same time Coughlin was preaching the opposite. Many previous historians missed Mooney's public ecumenical gesture, which, for some reason, was not carried on the front page of the «The New York Times» and did not appear at all in «The Washington Post».

GIULIA D'ALESSIO

The United States and the Vatican (1936-1939): From Eugenio Pacelli's Visit to the US to Myron Taylor's Mission to the Holy See

As results from the title, this paper will focus on the final four years of Pius XI's pontificate, a decisive period for the development of diplomatic relations between the Holy See and the United States: the protagonists were, on one hand, President Franklyn Delano Roosevelt, and on the other Pope Achille Ratti and Eugenio Pacelli, who, during those events, fully demonstrated his great diplomatic skills.

We will examine the period which starts with Pacelli's 1936 visit to America and ends with Myron Taylor's appointment as President Roosevelt's representative to the Holy See, just a few months after the election of Pope Pius XII and shortly after the start of World War II.

If these are crucial years, several documents from theVatican Secret Archives show that the process of rapprochement between the US and the Holy See had begun to significantly develop during the initial phase of the first Roosevelt Presidency.

We will not analyze all the complicated events that, at the end of the nineteenth century, lead to the breaking of official relations between the White House and the Holy See. It is well known that it was the result of misunderstandings and problems of both an ideological and political order: the fundamental principles of the US Constitution, which provided a clear separation between State and religious confessions, contrasted with the possibility of maintaining official contacts with an institution that had at his top a religious leader. It seems of paramount importance to stress that the advent of F.D. Roosevelt at the White House marked a decisive change of perspective. The starting point was represented by the convergence of views on issues relating to economic and social policy, as witnessed by the high consideration Roosevelt had of *Quadragesimo Anno* («*Quadragesimo Anno* is as radical as I am, is one of the greatest documents of modern times»[1],

---

[1] F.D. ROOSEVELT, *Detroit Speech*, October 2, 1932, in G.Q. FLYNN, *American Catholics and the Roosevelt Presidency, 1932-1936*, Lexington 1968, 17.

the President said during a 1932 speech in Detroit) and the appreciation accorded to the New Deal policies shown by Pius XI.

We can find the evidence of these first diplomatic and political contacts in several documents in the Vatican Secret Archives (ASV). It seems interesting, in this context, bringing to light the words written by Amleto Cicognani (just appointed new Apostolic Delegate to the US) in June 1933, after his first meeting with Roosevelt.

We see how the Delegate stressed the importance of the kind welcome given to him at the White House: never before had an Apostolic Delegate been granted a meeting there.

The symbolic relevance of this event is highlighted by Cicognani, who, reporting his meeting with Roosevelt, describes a President deeply concerned with the promotion of that diplomatic and political process that had as its goal a rapprochement between the Holy See and the United States. According to a document kept in the ASV, during the meeting the President said: «Of course, I wouldn't say this publicly, but I hope the day will soon come when I will be able to welcome you as an Ambassador»[2].

The detailed report of the meeting with Roosevelt is the subject of a letter, dated June 15, 1933[3], sent by the Apostolic Delegate to Pacelli. The passage in which Cicognani underlines the high esteem demonstrated by Roosevelt for Pius XI and the enthusiasm of the President when he talked about the contents of *Quadragesimo Anno* is particularly significant:

> «Dopo un mio accenno alla stampa cattolica che sta seguendo col più grande interesse gli sforzi che egli fa per un riassetto economico e di pace, il Presidente ha mostrato di sapere che anche l'Osservatore Romano ha avuto parole di lode per lui. Con vero entusiasmo ha parlato del Santo Padre, lodando la larghezza delle Sue vedute, la perfetta comprensione dei bisogni dei popoli e l'opportunità e la bellezza delle Sue Encicliche. Applicando queste alla condizione sociale ed economica del Paese, assicurava che dette Encicliche avrebbero grande influenza sul pensiero sociale ed economico degli Stati Uniti, se meglio conosciute, come constatò personalmente in un discorso tenuto a Detroit per la campagna elettorale: citando in quella occasione la Quadragesimo Anno con lettura di qualche brano suscitò la meraviglia di tutti e fu applauditissimo».

It's worth noting that The Holy See had been positively impressed by Roosevelt's policy of condemnation of religious persecution carried out

---

[2] ASV, Delegazione Apostolica Stati Uniti, Titolo V, POS. 153 (see Doc. 1 in the Documentary Appendix).

[3] AES, America, IV periodo, XXX P.O., Fasc. 53.

by the US President, as highlighted by «L'Osservatore Romano» just a month before the meeting between the Apostolic Delegate and the US President took place:

> «I giornali informano che i delegati degli Stati Uniti alla conferenza economi-ca mondiale riceveranno istruzioni di non far nessun accordo con quei governi i quali non diano assicurazione che "tutti i conflitti di natura religiosa nei loro paesi cesseranno", secondo una risoluzione presentata alla Camera dei Rappresentanti. Il Governo del Signor Roosevelt si stacca così nettamente ed altrettanto onorevolmente dalla linea seguitasi qui dai suoi predecessori. I quali, in verità, lungi dall'avere sì alta e nobile sensibilità civile, rimasero di fronte a simili fatti indifferenti o furono più o meno consenzienti. Spagna e Messico informino. Non dubitiamo che l'annunziato provvedimento avrà una provvida ripercussione in tutti gli uomini di buona volontà»[4].

«L'Osservatore Romano», in another article, dated April 1, 1934[5], un-derlines the positive attitude Roosevelt had towards a policy of collabora-tion with the Church, which was based on the recognition of some basic common goals to be attained, particularly, in social policy. The article reports the following Roosevelt statements:

> «Siamo d'accordo nel chiedere uno sforzo collettivo sulle grandi linee del piano sociale, sforzo collettivo che è in pieno accordo con gli insegnamenti sociali del cristianesimo... Cercando una maggiore prosperità materiale... dob-biamo cercare... una prosperità costruita sui valori spirituali e sociali... Verso questa nuova definizione della prosperità, la religione e i governi, sia pure nel-la loro sfera d'azione, possono lavorare concordi. Il governo può ben chiedere che la religione esponga nel suo insegnamento gli ideali di giustizia sociale, mentre contemporaneamente il governo garantisce le sue libertà. Essa pur non potendo essere sospettata di qualsiasi interferenza nel governo, può tuttavia con i suoi insegnamenti porre i suoi milioni di fedeli in condizione e nel diritto di chiedere al governo di propria scelta il mantenimento e il progresso di una vita più feconda... La religione... ha oggi la maggior influenza nel modo per trionfare dell'avidità e per diffondere questa nuova filosofia del governo. La Chiesa e lo Stato sono giustamente uniti in uno scopo comune. Con l'aiuto di Dio, siamo sulla strada che conduce a questa meta».

I think these examples help to show how Pacelli's US journey, held between October and November 1936, represents part, albeit important,

---

[4] *Un intervento degli Stati Uniti contro le persecuzioni antireligiose*, in «L'Osservatore Romano», May 13, 1933.

[5] *I valori religiosi del cristianesimo esaltati dal presidente Roosevelt, ibidem*, April 1, 1934.

of a dialogue which had been initiated in previous years. The first news of the arrival of Pacelli in New York, reported by «L'Osservatore Romano», do not reveal the diplomatic nature the visit would assume. The Vatican newspaper, in fact, on October 10, 1936 wrote that the Cardinal wanted to spend his holiday period in the US[6]. In a subsequent article, dated October 19-20, 1936[7], we read: «Il Cardinale... mette quindi bene in chiaro che la sua visita non ha carattere ufficiale né tanto meno di missione in rapporto al suo alto ufficio vaticano».

The attitude of the US press was different. For example, «Time Magazine», on the same date of October 19, 1936[8], wondered what the real reason was behind Pacelli's visit. The magazine was skeptical about the Vatican statement, which stressed that the trip had no official motivations: «To the U.S. press these explanations of the advent of the most potent catholic prelate ever to take a ship for New York were decidedly inadequate».

In the same article, «Time Magazine» puts forward various hypotheses about the real aims of the trip: the attempt to promote the development of diplomatic relations between the US and the Holy See, the desire to seek the support of the US Government in the Church's battle against communism, or the need to take action against the «radio priest» Charles Coughlin.

Probably, behind Pacelli's decision to visit the US, there were both these and other aims: they should be analyzed one by one. Here I would like to dwell only on a specific aspect of the Cardinal's stay, linked to what many suggested to be one of the main reasons which lead the Secretary of State to cross the Ocean.

We cannot ignore that Pacelli visited the United States in full pre-election period (before the presidential elections of November 1936). During his tour, in addition to the most important members of the Hierarchy and the different components of the Catholic community, he had the opportunity to meet many of the most respected American political authorities. Among them, the catholic Joseph Kennedy represented one of the most important promoters and creators of the dialogue between the Holy See and the White House.

Following the logical thread of my speech, it's not worth recalling in detail all the stages and important moments of the Cardinal's trip. Thus I

---

[6] *Il Cardinale Pacelli a Nuova York* , in «L'Osservatore Romano», October 10, 1936.

[7] *Le visite dell'Em.mo Cardinale Pacelli ai Cardinali e agli istituti cattolici negli Stati Uniti, ibidem*, October 19-20, 1936.

[8] *Pulse taker*, in «Time Magazine», October 19, 1936.

will focus on the context of the most important meeting in terms of politics, the one held between President Roosevelt and Pacelli.

It is well known that the meeting took place on November 5, 1936, even if Pacelli, at first, had decided to meet the President in early October, at the initial stage of his journey.

But why was the meeting postponed?

The date change was caused by a problem of political nature: many objections and protests against such a meeting were voiced by both Catholics and non-Catholics. Part of the Catholics did not want the Vatican Secretary of State to meet Roosevelt because they considered the President a «socialist». Many people, both Catholics and of other denominations, criticized Pacelli's decision to meet only the democratic candidate. Others, however, were against this meeting because this would represent an interference on the part of the Catholic Church in American politics, particularly in the pre-election weeks.

Among the documents kept at the Secret Vatican Archives, we find several letters from Cicognani to Pacelli in which the Apostolic Delegate refers to the protests, advising the Cardinal to wait until the elections before meeting Roosevelt.

On October 9, 1936[9], Cicognani writes the Cardinal:

«Mi permetto di inviare a Vostra Eminenza due lettere, che mi sono giunte insieme ad un altro centinaio, le quali esprimono più o meno lo stesso pensiero. La lotta elettorale si fa ogni giorno più acuta, e i partiti tentano ogni via per sfruttare qualunque cosa o occasione in proprio vantaggio e combattersi a vicenda con ogni acredine; così sarà sino al 3 novembre p. v., giorno dell'elezione presidenziale. Probabilmente qualche giornale ha diffuso la notizia che Vostra Eminenza avrebbe fatto visita al Presidente Roosevelt sabato 10 corrente, e che per l'occasione sarebbero state prese fotografie di Vostra Eminenza insieme al Presidente. La stampa naturalmente non mancherà di pubblicare le notizie più fantastiche e sensazionali, ed è facile prevedere che una visita di Vostra Eminenza al Presidente, prima delle elezioni, susciterà senza dubbio grande scalpore, coi più svariati e opposti commenti. Vostra Eminenza giudicherà se, qualora l'Eminenza Vostra decidesse lasciare gli Stati Uniti nel novembre, non sia più opportuno rimandare la visita al Presidente dopo le elezioni. Vostra Eminenza sa bene come, in questo periodo acuto di passioni politiche, è di supremo interesse religioso, come vari Vescovi mi vanno ripetendo, non solo tenere estranea la Chiesa Cattolica a questo affare delle elezioni, ma anche di confermare con fatto e nelle stesse apparenze, e cioè far "realizzare" al pubblico, che la Chiesa è al di fuori e al di sopra dei partiti

---

[9]   ASV, Del. Ap. Stati Uniti Tit. V Pos. 194 Visita negli US del Card. Eugenio Pacelli, Segr. di Stato di Sua Santità (36-37-39) (see Doc. 2 in the Documentary Appendix)

politici. Ma è proprio superfluo scrivere ciò all'Eminenza Vostra, e non faccio che riportare le voci che sento in questi giorni».

The day after, in another letter to Pacelli[10], Cicognani writes:

«Continua, al mio indirizzo, la pioggia di lettere di protesta, contro la presunta notizia, apparsa in un giornale di Baltimore, che Vostra Eminenza poserà per una fotografia insieme al Presidente Roosevelt. Sono altresì pervenuti a questa Delegazione Apostolica innumerevoli telegrammi, coi quali si chiede che la Santa Sede si astenga dall'intervenire nelle attività politiche di Padre Coughlin...».

The italian historian Ennio di Nolfo, in this regard, recently wrote:

«La visita, che avveniva alla vigilia della seconda elezione di Roosevelt, diede luogo alle ovvie speculazioni e in particolare fece supporre che fosse dettata dal progetto di offrire un certo appoggio al presidente presso l'elettorato cattolico»[11].

This assumption is probably not entirely unfounded: as we have seen, previous years had shown there was a significant harmony between many positions of the President and those of the Church.

It is also known that Roosevelt held in high esteem Catholic public opinion, which in fact played a relevant role in his re-election.

Pacelli's US visit, especially (but not only) in the opinion of the Vatican press, was undoubtedly a great success from a religious perspective. Less clear, however, are the diplomatic and political results of both the Cardinal's journey and particularly of the meeting held between him and President Roosevelt.

US newspapers tried to reconstruct its contents, assuming the two may have talked about the Communist issue (the Spanish Civil War had just started) or about that of Nazi-fascism, or about the more specific «Coughlin issue».

Others speculated that they may have discussed the possibility of resuming diplomatic relations. This is underlined by Gerald P. Fogarty: «Newspapers speculated at the time that the topic of discussion between

---

[10] ASV, Del. Ap. Stati Uniti, Tit. V, POS. 194 Visita negli USA del Card. Eugenio Pacelli, Segr. di Stato di Sua Santità (36-37-39).
[11] E. Di Nolfo, *Dear Pope, Vaticano e Stati Uniti. La corrispondenza segreta di Roosevelt e Truman con Papa Pacelli*, Roma 2003.

the President and the Cardinal was the establishment of diplomatic relations between the Holy See and the United States»[12].

The fact that the meeting took place at FDR's mother's house in Hyde
Park, makes it clear that the President wanted to avoid excessive publicity
of this event: therefore all the media speculation on the course of events
remain mere hypotheses.

However, the diplomatic work behind the idea of a possible rapprochement with the Holy See was certainly accelerated, although the time for
a formalization of the relationship was not ripe yet. Citing the diary of
Spellman, Fogarty recalls:

> «A few weeks after the Roosevelt – Pacelli meeting, Spellman recorded that
> a friend "told me that the President wanted me to represent the Church in
> Washington. It was, of course impossibile or impractical"»[13].

All this is confirmed by an exchange of letters (kept at the ASV) between
Pacelli and Spellman which took place between 1937 and 1938: these letters
show that the will of both Roosevelt and the Vatican (and in particular of the
Cardinal Secretary of State and his primary referent in the US) was to come
to diplomatic relations between the two States, while the difficulties that
hindered the implementation of the project were still evident.

The correspondence begins with a letter, dated September 21, 1937[14],
in which Spellman reported his meeting with James Roosevelt, son and
secretary of the President. It is significant that the meeting had taken place
at the initiative of Joseph Kennedy. During the meeting, James Roosevelt,
though highlighting the difficulties for achieving the diplomatic goal,
also related the good attitude of the President on the matter, and therefore
asked Spellman to write a memorandum about the grounds that, according
to the Holy See, might support rapprochement. Spellman then asks the
Secretary of State Pacelli advice in order to better draft this memorandum.
Spellman also reports that everything would have been facilitated if the
Vatican had accepted that the US ambassador to the Kingdom of Italy
would also be appointed as representative to the Holy See. This would
overcome the problems related to the Senate vote on financing the creation of a specific embassy. Here again he asked Pacelli his opinion about

---

[12] G.P. FOGARTY, *The Vatican and the American Hierarchy from 1870 to 1965*, Stuttgart
1982, 248.

[13] *Ibidem.*

[14] AES, America, IV P.O. 237 (1) Fasc. 65 (see Doc. 3 in the Documentary Appendix).

it. Spellman stressed that the enthusiasm of the President was not bound to any pressure from the Vatican.

In his reply of November 26, 1937[15], Pacelli reported that Pius XI had praised the work of Spellman. The Cardinal attached a comprehensive memorandum[16] on the evolution of the system of diplomatic relations of the Church and the importance of the Concordat policy.

He also declared that it would be impossible to accept the ambassador to the Kingdom of Italy as the US representative at the Vatican: «La situazione speciale della... Santa Sede nei riguardi dell'Italia esige, anche per evitare confusioni, che vi siano due distinti Corpi Diplomatici».

On January 8, 1938[17], Spellman announced to the Cardinal that he has sent his own memorandum[18] (which was based on the one received from the Vatican Secretary of State) to Roosevelt. He expresses cautious optimism about the outcome of the diplomatic process.

In another letter, dated January 26, 1938[19], Spellman wrote to Pacelli that Roosevelt had appreciated the memorandum. The President, reiterating that he had failed to obtain the consent of the Senate for financing an embassy to the Holy See, this time proposed a different solution: the appointment of a minister instead of an ambassador.

His idea is broadly accepted by Pacelli, as stated in a letter of February 26, 1938[20], although preference is given to the appointment of an ambassador.

I dwell on this correspondence because it expresses very well the climate in which a dialogue between the two countries was developing and the attitude of the main protagonists which were working for that diplomatic project. I think it is important to highlight the mediating role played by Spellman and the great attention paid to the issue by Pacelli, as demonstrated by the drafting of the dense memorandum that would have been sent to the future Archbishop of New York.

Other ASV documents relating to my research topic are not accessible. The documents relating to the «Fifth Period» are obviously not available, but also part of the last phase of the Fourth period documents about the U.S. are currently not available. Therefore, to complete the reconstruction of the process which lead to the appointment of a United States repre-

---

[15] *Ibidem* (see Doc. 4 in the Documentary Appendix).
[16] *Ibidem* (see Doc. 5 in the Documentary Appendix).
[17] *Ibidem* (see Doc. 6 in the Documentary Appendix).
[18] *Ibidem* (see Doc. 7 in the Documentary Appendix).
[19] *Ibidem* (see Doc. 8 in the Documentary Appendix).
[20] *Ibidem* (see Doc. 9 in the Documentary Appendix).

sentative at the Vatican I have restorted to other sources, especially the American ones, like the Foreign Relations of the United States (FRUS) collection, F.D. Roosevelt Library papers, «Time Magazine» articles.

As mentioned, Cardinal Pacelli played a decisive role in the issue of restoring diplomatic relations. Therefore the fact that the diplomatic process arrives at its own partial completion during the first year of Pius XII's pontificate is not surprising. Of course, besides this, the historical moment in which the event occurred is fundamental: the appointment of Roosevelt's special representative to the Holy See took place only three months after the outbreak of World War II. I will try to reconstruct how and why F.D. Roosevelt came to that decision.

The United States very much welcomed Pope Pacelli's election and understandably. A series of «Time Magazine» articles about the new Pope were published in the March 13, 1939 issue.

One of the first articles, entitled *Habemus Papam*, chronicles the election of Pacelli. The drama of the time in which it took place is strongly emphasized: «Last week, when its Princes met in Rome to choose a new Pope, the Church's war against heresy, the totalitarian heresy of Left and Right, had reached a critical point».

The magazine describes the figure of Pacelli and underlines his intelligence and diplomatic skills. It recalls the great attention and the favor with which democratic States welcomed the advent of the new Pope:

> «For the first time since the 18th century's enlightment, believers in individual liberty found themselves taking the same side as the Roman Catholic Church, the champion of the individual soul, and facing a common enemy».

The second article, *Name*, particularly emphasizes the role played by Pius XII in supporting a peace policy. A symbolic element is located in the last name of the new Pope: «In Italian the first four letters of the name Pacelli spell peace. The world hoped last week after that name was converted to Pius XII, that the first acts of its owner might help bring it».

The last article, *Thy servant, Franklin*, focuses on Roosevelt's reaction to the Pope's election, and stresses their friendship , begun in the days of Pacelli's 1936 visit to the US. It states that Pius XII is the «First Pope in history to have personal knowledge of the U.S.» and recalls the message sent by Roosevelt to the new Pope:

> «To Eugenio Pacelli , newly His Holiness Pope Pius XII, the President cabled "It is with true happiness that I learned of your election as Supreme Pontiff. Recalling with pleasure our meeting on the occasion of your recent visit to the

United States, I wish to take this occasion to send you a personal message of felicitation and good wishes. Roosevelt"».

The relationship between the President and the Pope had become of the utmost cordiality. As Harold H. Tittman recalls, «Roosevelt si riferì spesso a Pacelli, specialmente dopo la sua salita al soglio pontificio, come al "suo vecchio e buon amico" con un tocco personale e familiare insolito per gli statisti che avevano a che fare con il Papa»[21].

On the occasion of the Papal Coronation, Roosevelt was represented by Joseph Kennedy. Sending the important diplomat (and promoter of rapprochement policy between the United States and Holy See) to the Vatican was a further demonstration of the special consideration that Roosevelt had for the new Pope. It is also important to underline that Pius XII, immediately after his Coronation, appointed Spellman (another great protagonist in the dialogue between the United States and the Holy See) Archbishop of New York.

The plan for a permanent reopening communication began to see the light in the Summer of 1939, when the outbreak of World War II was close at hand, and the process continued until the end of the year. This was also the result of the action of a pressure group inside the Roosevelt administration lead by the Secretary of State Cordell Hull and his vice Sumner Wells.

Of course there were still problems in completing the project. The possible opening of relations with the Vatican contrasted with the fundamental US Constitution principle of the separation of Church and State: Roosevelt intended to send a special envoy to the Pope, but he had difficulties accepting a papal envoy with the rank of ambassador (nuncio) in Washington. Roosevelt's opponents also feared that behind the President's project there was an electoral maneuver to capture the Catholic vote in the following year's elections.

In this context the proposal of persuasive reasons to re-establish direct communications between the two States was indispensable. But what were those reasons?

First of all, the Holy See was a privileged observation point on Mussolini's policy and indirectly on his Nazi ally. Then there was the idea of a strong link between the US and the Holy See to promote world peace. But there was another aspect of great importance: in the Summer and Au-

---

[21] H.H. TITTMANN JR., *Il Vaticano di Pio XII. Uno sguardo dall'interno*, ed. by H. TITT-MANN III, Milano 2005.

tumn 1939 the humanitarian issue assumed great relevance. Roosevelt and Pacelli wanted to create a link between the two States to assist people oppressed by dictatorships, refugees and those persecuted.

The final phase of this diplomatic process can be traced reading the correspondence between the major figures of American and Vatican politics.

We will try to summarize.

The starting point was represented by a letter, sent on July 24, 1939 by a New York Jewish Congressman, Emanuel Cellar, to Cordell Hull[22]. He expresses concern about the critical global situation and called for the opening of official communications with the Holy See. He praises Pius XII and his actions in favor of policies of peace and his closeness to the people oppressed by the war.

Sumner Wells, after reading Cellar's letter and having agreed with Corder Hull, wrote to Roosevelt on August 1, 1939[23]. In his letter he says:

«My dear Mr. President: Some weeks ago the Secretary and I were speaking of the advantage which might be gained by this Government if we had direct diplomatic relations with the Vatican. I think it is unquestionable that the Vatican has many sources of information, particularly with regard to what is actually going on in Germany, Italy, and Spain, which we do not possess, and it seemed to us that the question of whether it would be desirable for our Government to obtain access to this information was of considerable importance».

On October 2, 1939, President Roosevelt sent a memorandum to the Secretary of State[24], in which he spoke of the problem of European War refugees, in relation to a possible restart of official communications with the Holy See. For the first time he proposes to send a personal representative to the Vatican.

It should be noted that the name of Myron Taylor (Roosevelt's future representative to the Holy See) is mentioned in the memorandum because he was a member of the Board of refugees. In the last part of this memorandum we read:

«It is my thought... that while there is no particular reason for haste, we might give consideration to sending at a later date a special Minister or Ambassador

---

[22] In Diplomatic Files: Correspondence with the Vatican 1939. From: F.D. Roosevelt Library & Digital Archives – http://www.fdrlibrary.marist.edu.

[23] *Ibidem.*

[24] FRUS, 1939, vol. II.

on Special Mission to the Vatican, in order that we could have a direct system of communication covering the subject of European Catholic refugees. I am inclined to think that, this is not only a practical idea but that it also puts the whole refugee problem on a broad religious basis, thereby making it possible to gain the kind of world-wide support that a mere Jewish relief set-up would not evoke».

In the Autumn of 1939, after several meetings between Roosevelt and Spellman took place, and after talks between the Archbishop of New York with the Secretary of State Luigi Maglione and with Cicognani[25], the idea of sending a personal representative of Roosevelt to the Vatican had already taken shape.

For the delicate task, Roosevelt chose Myron Taylor, a successful entrepreneur in charge of the United Steel Corporation. It's worth highlighting a few aspects of his personality. He was a Protestant and not a Catholic: this could have been both a limit but also a guarantee given to the Congress in order to balance the relations between the US and a State lead by the Head of the Catholic Church. It should however be noted that, although a Protestant, in front of Pius XII he «knelt asking his blessing»[26].

Taylor was not unknown to Pacelli: in fact, the Cardinal had met him during his 1936 visit to the US. Taylor's candidature was particularly appropriate to emphasize the humanitarian nature of the mission. In fact, «era stato rappresentante del Presidente al comitato intergovernativo per i rifugiati politici, costituito nel 1938 per facilitare l'emigrazione nel mondo libero dei rifugiati, molti dei quali ebrei, dalla Germania e dai Paesi occupati»[27].

The diplomatic mission was announced to Pius XII and to Taylor by Roosevelt with two letters dated December 23, 1939[28].

On the same date the Secretary of State, Hull, informed William Phillips, the American ambassador to Italy, of Roosevelt's decision. The ambassador's answer came the next day.

The President's long letter to the Pope is full of references to the dramatic international situation and to the role that the religious dimension could have played in alleviating people's suffering. The President then

---

[25] Until now remembered, see J. NICHOLSON, *Usa e Santa Sede. La lunga strada*, in «30 Giorni», October 2002; G.P. FOGARTY, *The Vatican and the American Hierarchy from 1870 to 1965...*

[26] A. SPINOSA, *Pio XII. Un papa nelle tenebre*, Milano 2004.

[27] H.H. TITTMANN, *Il Vaticano di Pio XII. Uno sguardo dall'interno...*

[28] FRUS, 1939, vol. II.

called for a strengthening of cooperation between religious and political authorities to achieve the common goal of peace:

«In this present moment, no spiritual leader, no civil leader can move forward on a specific plan to terminate destruction and build anew. Yet the time for that will surely come. It is, therefore, my thought, that though no given action or given time may now be prophesied, it is well that we encourage a closer association between those in every part of the world – those in religion and those in government – who have a common purpose. [...] I am, therefore, suggesting to Your Holiness that it would give me great satisfaction to send to you my personal representative in order that our parallel endeavors for peace and the alleviation of suffering may be assisted».

In the letter sent by Roosevelt to Taylor, the President gives him the status of «my personal representative with the rank of ambassador to His Holiness, Pope Pius XII» and asks him «to serve as the channel of communication for any views I may wish to exchange with the Pope».

Particularly interesting is Phillips letter of response to Cordell Hull, dated December 24, 1939[29], in which we read: «The Pope today [...] told the Sacred College of Cardinals that he was deeply gratified by the appointment of Myron Taylor to the Vatican».

He then refers the following words by the Pope:

«This is Christmas news which could not be more welcome since it represents on the part of the eminent Head of a great and powerful nation a worthy and promising contribution to our desires for a just and honorable peace and for a more effective work toward alleviating the sufferings of the victims of the war. Hence we are anxious to express here and now our felicitations and our spirit for this generous act to Roosevelt».

On that same Christmas Eve Spellman expresses all his enthusiasm, as a Catholic and especially as an American, for Roosevelt's initiative[30]:

«As an American, living and working and willing to die for the welfare of my Country and my Countrymen, all of them, I'm very happy that President Roosevelt has harmonized the voice of Pope Pius XII with his own clarion call for peace among nations and peoples. It's opportune that, on the vigil of the anniversary of the birth of Prince of Peace, the President of United States, should take this action for peace. President Roosevelt is our leader, the leader of a free people determined on peace for ourselves, desirous of peace for

---

[29] *Ibidem.*
[30] In Diplomatic Files: Correspondence with the Vatican 1939. From: F.D. Roosevelt Library & Digital Archives – http://www.fdrlibrary.marist.edu.

others. We are a people who believe in, who practice and defend freedom of religion, freedom in the dissemination of truth, freedom of assembly, freedom of trade. It is timely that our President, intrepid enunciator of these principles and champion of them, should join with other forces for peace, for charitable and humanitarian influences. Such an influence is the Catholic Church. As an American, I rejoice in this action of President Roosevelt».

Myron Taylor arrived in Rome in February 1940. Pacelli had crossed the sea that separates New York from Rome and Italy on an ocean liner, the Count of Savoy, in 1936. Four years later, the same journey in reverse had been made on another liner, the Rex, by Taylor.

Pius XII, on January 7, 1940[31], in response to Roosevelt's letter of December 23, 1939, wrote: «We have been deeply moved by the noble thought contained in your note, in which the spirit of Christmas and the desire to see it applied to the great human problems have found such eloquent expression».

The Pope describes the President's letter as a «courageous document, inspired by a far-seeing statemanship and a profound human sympathy».

«Far seeing statemanship»: the Pope had recognized, in the words of Roosevelt, the reference to the path that the Holy See and the United States could have taken together in a future in which the world was reconciled. The US President, in fact, had outlined the possibility of an alliance of ideals, which could have been established even in times of peace:

«When the tier shall come for the restablishment of world peace on a surer foundation, it is of the most importance to humanity and to religion that common ideals shall have united expression. Furthermore when that happy day shall dawn, great problems of practical import will face us all... common ideals for parallel action»[32].

On August 22, 1940 Pacelli writes to the President, and the words of this letter are the expression of the close relationship that had arisen between the Holy See and Washington and of the very high consideration Pius XII had of Roosevelt. In a significant passage we read:

«In our unceasing search for that peace which will be no longer... we feel a distinct sense of comfort in the thought that We shall not be without the powerful support of the President of the United States. It is therefore with heartfelt goodwill that We again assure Your Excellency of Our prayers for

---

[31] *Ibidem.*
[32] FRUS, 1939, vol. II.

Your continued health and happiness and for the prosperity and the progress of the American people»[33].

DOCUMENTARY APPENDIX

DOC. 1
Vatican Secret Archives (ASV) – Del. Ap. Stati Uniti Tit. V Pos. 153
June 12, 1933 (Visit of del Apostolic Delegate Cicognani to President Roosevelt)

The ceremony of reception
On all other occasions when an Apostolic Delegate went to see the President of the United States, the President received him in what is known as the Executive Offices – a small building separate from the White House.

On this occasion, the reception took place not in the Executive Offices but in the White House itself. Moreover , the President had seen to it that no newspaper reporters were present, and no photographers.

When the Apostolic Delegate arrived, he was ushered into the large reception room. Later, one of the President's aides – Colonel Watson of the United States Army – came to escort the Delegate to the President.

The President was standing in another room with another of his aides - Captain Vernue of the United States Navy- at his left. Thus standing, the President received the Delegate. The President then asked the Delegate to be seated with him.

I mention the manner of the reception because it was unusual, significant, and I think a manner used only for the special representative of the government.

The President greeted the Apostolic Delegate by saying, «Of course, I wouldn't say this publicly, but I hope the day will soon come when I will be able to welcome you as an Ambassador». The Delegate said in answer that the United States once had an official representative to the Papal States: the President again said he hoped the United States would have one again.

DOC. 2
ASV Del. Ap. Stati Uniti Tit. V Pos. 194 Visita negli USA del Card. Eugenio Pacelli, Segr. di Stato di Sua Santità (36-37-39)
October 9, 1936 (Letter from Cicognani to Pacelli)
Eminenza Reverendissima,
Ho l'onore di rimettere qui acclusa la corrispondenza personale di Vostra Eminenza Reverendissima. Al tempo stesso mi permetto di inviare a Vostra Emi-

---

[33] In Diplomatic Files: Correspondence with the Vatican 1939. From: F.D. Roosevelt Library & Digital Archives – http://www.fdrlibrary.marist.edu.

nenza due lettere, che mi sono giunte insieme ad un altro centinaio, le quali esprimono più o meno lo stesso pensiero. La lotta elettorale si fa ogni giorno più acuta,
e i partiti tentano ogni via per sfruttare qualunque cosa o occasione in proprio
vantaggio e combattersi a vicenda con ogni acredine; così sarà sino al 3 novembre
p. v., giorno dell'elezione presidenziale.

Probabilmente qualche giornale ha diffuso la notizia che Vostra Eminenza
avrebbe fatto visita al Presidente Roosevelt sabato 10 corrente, e che per l'occasione sarebbero state prese fotografie di Vostra Eminenza insieme al Presidente.
La stampa naturalmente non mancherà di pubblicare le notizie più fantastiche e
sensazionali, ed è facile prevedere che una visita di Vostra Eminenza al Presidente, prima delle elezioni, susciterà senza dubbio grande scalpore, coi più svariati e
opposti commenti.

Vostra Eminenza giudicherà se, qualora l'Eminenza Vostra decidesse lasciare
gli Stati Uniti nel novembre, non sia più opportuno rimandare la visita al Presidente dopo l'elezione.

Vostra Eminenza sa bene come, in questo periodo acuto di passioni politiche,
è di supremo interesse religioso, come vari Vescovi mi vanno ripetendo, non solo
tenere estranea la Chiesa Cattolica a questo affare delle elezioni, ma anche di
confermare con fatto e nelle stesse apparenze, e cioè far «realizzare» al pubblico,
che la Chiesa è al di fuori e al di sopra dei partiti politici. Ma è proprio superfluo
scrivere ciò all'Eminenza Vostra, e non faccio che riportare le voci che sento in
questi giorni.

Anticipo l'onore e il piacere della venuta di Vostra Eminenza a Washington;
sarei per tanto profondamente grato all'Eminenza Vostra se, dopo averne fissato
la data, si degnerà incaricare qualcuno del suo seguito a darmene notizia.

[...]

Doc. 3
AES America IV P.O. 237 (1)Fasc. 65
September 21, 1937 (Lettera from Spellman to Pacelli)

Eminenza Reverendissima,

Alla richiesta del Signore Joseph Kennedy, ho avuto un colloquio con figlio
del Presidente Roosevelt, il Signore Giacomo Roosevelt che Vostra Eminenza
ha conosciuto a Roma ed in America. Il Signore Roosevelt è il Segretario ufficiale del Presidente. Abbiamo parlato intorno ad un possibile riconoscimento
della Santa Sede da parte del governo degli Stati Uniti e l'entrata in relazioni
diplomatiche. Il Signore Roosevelt cominciava dicendo che già si sapeva bene
tutte le ragioni contro un tal riconoscimento e tutte le difficoltà e tutte le persone
che si opporrebbero ma che lui voleva che io gli enumerasse tutti i motivi che si
potrebbero adoperare in favore di questo atto, motivi per convincere il pubblico
Americano che questo riconoscimento sarebbe una cosa buona e practica dal punto di vista del governo degli Stati Uniti.

Io ho fatto il mio meglio per portare ragioni dal punto di vista iuridico e dal punto di vista storico ed ho citato tutti i vantaggi che credevo potrebbero accrescere al governo degli Stati Uniti, alla Santa Sede e al mondo in genere. Dicevo che in molte cose le idee e gli scopi del governo e della chiesa erano identiche.

Credo che ho fatto progresso e sono sicuro che già tutto quello che io ho detto è stato raccontato al Presidente.

Il Signore Roosevelt mi ha chiesto di preparare una pro-memoria per presentare al Presidente ma siccome è una grande responsabilità vorrei avere un aiuto in questa materia, se è creduto opportuno di fornirmi con un tal documento. Anche se potessi sapere le cose sulle quali il Vaticano si sentirebbe obbligato insistere nell'evento di un accordo, sarebbe forse utile.

Oltre delle cose essenziali, si potrebbe indicare altre cose che pure non essendo assolutamente necessarie, sarebbero nondimeno molto desiderabili.

Sarebbe anche utile se potessi avere qualche indicazione intorno alle modalità colle quali, le relazioni eventuali potrebbero essere iniziati.

Ho l'impressione che sarebbe una cosa molto difficile ottenere che un eventuale nunzio sia riconosciuto come il decano del corpo diplomatico. Sembra pure che un eventuale accordo potrebbe essere facilitato se il Vaticano fosse disposto di consentire che l'Ambasciatore Americano alla Real Corte d'Italia potesse essere screditato anche alla Santa Sede, perché così facendo, si potrebbe evitare l'opposizione di quelli nel Senato che potessero essere oppositori ad una speciale appropriazione di fondi per mantenere un'Ambasciata.

Non mi permetto di essere troppo ottimista ma sono contento che è un passo nella giusta direzione e un passo preso dal Presidente verso la Santa Sede dal suo iniziativo non provocato da nessun richiesta dalla parte della Santa Sede.

Doc. 4
AES America IV P.O. 237 (1)Fasc. 65
November 26, 1937 (Letter from Pacelli to Spellman)

Eccellenza Reverendissima,

mentre mi trovavo a Rorschach per un breve riposo ho ricevuto l'importante lettera di Vostra Eccellenza Rev.ma in data del 21 Settembre u.s.

Appena ritornato a Roma ne ho riferito al Santo Padre il Quale compiacendosi della costante sollecitudine di Vostra Eccellenza per l'onore della Chiesa ed il bene delle anime, mi ha incaricato di redigere il Pro-Memoria a cui Ella fa accenno. Ora ho il piacere di inviarlo qui accluso, affinchè Vostra Eccellenza lo esamini e [[*decida*]] veda se è adeguato. Se così fosse potrà farlo giungere a destinazione come Ella crederà più opportuno.

Circa gli schieramenti che Ella mi chiedeva riguardo alla Decananza del Nunzio Apostolico, Le significo che la Santa Sede [[*ha sempre richiesto che il Suo Rappresentante sia anche Decano del Corpo Diplomatico, come si verifica attualmente eccetto che nell'Olanda, per specialissime ragioni*]] esige che il Suo

Rappresentante sia riconosciuto Decano dei diplomatici dello stesso grado, come Ella potrà rilevare... dal qui unito opuscolo che Le rimetto in via riservata affinchè Vostra Eccellenza vi possa ricavare quanto Le può servire per favorire tale prerogativa dei Nunzi. Riguardo poi alla questione se il Rappresentante Diplomatico accreditato presso il Governo Italiano se possa essere altresì accreditato presso la Santa Sede, Le faccio presente che la situazione speciale della [[*del Vaticano*]] Santa Sede nei riguardi dell'Italia esige, anche per evitare confusioni, che vi siano due distinti Corpi Diplomatici.

Non credo che vi siano altre questioni pregiudiziali sulle quali la Santa Sede ritenga di dover insistere per stabilire le relazioni diplomatiche.

La procedura per giungere praticamente allo stabilimento delle relazioni è semplice, basterà che il Governo esprima un desiderio perché tutto possa facilmente prepararsi.

Doc. 5
AES, America IV P.O. 237 (1)Fasc. 65
November 26, 1937 (Pro-memoria sent by Pacelli to Spellman)

La Chiesa Cattolica, società perfetta, ordinata da Dio al conseguimento di un fine supremo, la felicità eterna del genere umano, guidata da una legittima autorità che con potere sovrano la governa e la dirige al suo fine, gode in virtù della sua stessa natura (del) la personalità giuridica pubblica.

Tale posizione della Chiesa Cattolica è un fatto giuridico mondiale non solo in virtù della dottrina cattolica e della prescrizione di una lunga serie ininterrotta di secoli, ma ancora in virtù del riconoscimento avuto da tutto il mondo civile non meno in teoria che nella pratica, ossia nei cercati Accordi con la Santa Sede sopra materie miste, nella stipulazione di Trattati e Concordati, le quali cose tutte costituiscono la prova autentica che gli stessi Capi e Rappresentanti delle nazioni civili hanno ritenuta la Chiesa come società pubblica e giuridica di sua natura.

Se dunque la Chiesa è persona di diritto pubblico ed il Romano Pontefice che la impersona ha «de iure» una posizione giuridica nell'ordinamento internazionale, si deve necessariamente ammettere che al Sommo Pontefice compete il diritto di comunicare liberamente con tutti i Governi che vogliano avere rapporti con la Santa Sede, vale a dire che la Santa Sede ha il diritto di legazione attivo e passivo. [[*È risaputo come un tale diritto fu veramente dedotto nella pratica fin dai primi secoli del Cristianesimo*]]. È risaputo come un tale diritto fu veramente dedotto nella pratica.

Gli storici infatti dividono generalmente in tre periodi lo svolgimento delle Legazioni Pontificie:

1) – dal secolo V al secolo XI – In questo primo periodo abbiamo gli Apocrisari Pontifici presso la corte di Costantinopoli, i quali avevano per compito di tutelare l'unità della fede tra L'Oriente e l'Occidente e stabilire buone relazioni fra l'Imperatore, ormai fisso a Bisanzio, e il Pontefice Romano, a cui era ricono-

sciuto nella legislazione di Giustiniano, un primato in tutta la Chiesa. Contemporaneamente si sviluppa l'istituto dei Vicarii apostolici, prima nell'Illirico, poi nelle Gallie, nella Spagna e per tutta l'Europa, i quali avevano come compito di rappresentare l'autorità pontificia nelle varie regioni specialmente nei riguardi della locale gerarchia ecclesiastica.

2) – dal secolo XI al secolo XV – Finiti con la lotta delle immagini (secolo VIII) gli Apocrisari e assai incerte le relazioni con l'Oriente si diffondono invece i Vicari Apostolici nell'Occidente, con carattere stabile, e si moltiplicano gli inviati straordinari da Roma, e particolarmente al momento della riforma ecclesiastica di Gregorio VII. Gli uni e gli altri si chiamano oramai Legati Pontifici: quelli permanenti vanno mutando la natura del loro incarico che di personale diventa locale, e sorgono così i *Legati nati* o Primati (sec. XIII) in una data regione; e quelli inviati per missioni transeunti (Legati missi) acquistano sempre maggiore autorità. Simultaneamente da Roma partivano o dipendevano altri rappresentanti, detti *nuncii*, con incarichi diversi (*nuncii collectores*, *nuncii oratores*: questi ultimi avevano funzioni diplomatiche presso i vari sovrani, ma transeunti).

3) – dall'inizio del secolo XVI al presente – Al principio di questa epoca i Romani Pontefici seguendo l'uso introdotto dalle altre corti e attribuendo ai propri nuncii facoltà generali e permanenti sia di carattere ecclesiastico che diplomatico, inviano i loro rappresentanti presso i vari Sovrani d'Italia e d'Europa; e nella seconda metà del secolo XVI sono istituite e perfezionate le Nunziature propriamente dette, le cui funzioni non riguardano tanto le relazioni dello Stato Pontificio col le varie Nazioni, ma piuttosto (e decisamente dopo la pace di Westfalia) le relazioni del Romano Pontefice, come capo della Chiesa, con gli altri Stati.

In questi ultimi tempi nei quali notiamo un intenso sviluppo del Diritto Internazionale, abbiamo un maggior numero di Rappresentanti Pontifici presso singoli Stati ed altrettanti Agenti Diplomatici accreditati presso la Santa Sede, tanto che, oggi, risalgono a 43 le rappresentanze della Santa Sede con carattere diplomatico ad a 28 quelle senza carattere diplomatico [[*Queste ultime sono stabilite ordinariamente presso Stati a maggioranza non cattolica e tuttavia, sia pure in via ufficiosa, svolgono sovente importantissime mansioni presso i rispettivi Governi*]].

È ancora infatti da rilevarsi come le relazioni diplomatiche fra Sante Sede e Governo non soltanto sono domandate dalla dottrina cattolica e sono state riconosciute da tutto il mondo civile, ma esse sono ormai diventate un postulato necessario dell'odierna coscienza politica, una attività indispensabile del moderno Diritto Internazionale.

Se noi esaminiamo le attuali concezioni politiche, dobbiamo constatare come esse hanno ormai ripudiato quei principii che lo Stato liberale era venuto forgiando nel secolo scorso, per esempio quelli che facevano considerare la Chiesa come una associazione privata retta dal Diritto Comune, la religione un problema della coscienza individuale, lo Stato un'organizzazione agnostica in materia di religione.

Al tempo stesso assistiamo ad un evoluzione veramente fondamentale del Diritto Internazionale.

Anzitutto è per opera di eminenti internazionalisti che il Diritto Naturale viene richiamato al suo posto di fondamento del Diritto positivo.

Si è constatato, infatti, come il punto centrale di tutte le dottrine ispirate al positivismo fu precisamente il problema della ricerca di una norma che costituisca la base dell'obbligatorietà del diritto. Abbattuta la base fondamentale del Diritto Naturale, le multiformi dottrine positivistiche si sono date faticosamente alla ricerca di un principio che di quella facesse le funzioni. Si sono avuti così tentativi numerosi e sempre rinnovatisi, ma i conclusione nulla s'è potuto trovare da sostituire al principio fondamentale del Diritto Naturale: «Pacta sunt servanda».

Per questa esigenza, dunque, si... un [[principio]] elemento superiore alla volontà degli Stati e capace quindi di imporsi ad essa, torna ad affermarsi nella dottrina internazionalistica la legge naturale alla stregua della quale commisurare tutte le norme giuridiche internazionali all'effetto di determinarne l'efficacia e il valore obbligatorio.

Senza contare poi che sono completamente ripudiati i vecchi preconcetti che facevano degli Stati gli unici subietti del Diritto Internazionale e che, in questo campo, il medesimo Diritto, di fronte ai nuovi fenomeni verificatisi specie nel dopoguerra, ha già di fatto allargato le sue concezioni, è necessariamente da constatarsi come la dottrina internazionalistica vada sempre più orientandosi verso quei principi umani che fanno del mondo intero un solo corpo che risente del bene e del male delle sue singole parti.

Ed è pure per opera di eminenti internazionalisti che oggi viene affermato il bisogno della morale nelle relazioni internazionali. La moderna dottrina va sempre più affermando che la morale costituisce una delle più importanti fonti materiali del Diritto Internazionale.

Si dichiara anzi che il progresso di questo ultimo, come il temperamento umano delle sue norme, sono legati alla sua sempre più ampia ricezione dei principi morali.

Appena abbiamo voluto accennare ad alcuni punti di orientamento del moderno diritto internazionale e giudichi ora ognuno se, le finalità assegnate dai nuovi principi alla Comunità Internazionale siano conseguibili senza l'opera di quella potenza spirituale che, per essere la custode, la tutrice, l'interprete dell'ordine morale ne è, al tempo stesso, per divino mandato, l'inculcatrice diretta e feconda in tutto il mondo.

È necessario dunque concludere che la Chiesa deve essere presente nell'ordinamento Internazionale mediante i suoi Rappresentanti i quali svolgono un'attività che è di sommo interesse per la consecuzione del fine della Chiesa, mentre, d'altra parte, l'opera loro viene pure giudicata attiva e rilevante per la stessa consecuzione del fine della Comunità Internazionale.

Di questa coscienza politica moderna e di questi nuovi orientamenti hanno dato prova i Governi dei più grandi Stati civili, anche quelli non a maggioranza cattolica, stipulando Concordati, cioè vere Convenzioni di Diritto Internazionale, con la Santa Sede.

È veramente imponente questo evolversi del Diritto Concordatario nelle mani delle Supreme Potestà della Chiesa e degli Stati e che tanto interessamento suscita negli studiosi del Diritto Internazionale.

Omettendo di enumerare i solenni Accordi prebellici come quelli con l'Inghilterra, con varie Repubbliche dell'America Meridionale, con la Svizzera, ci limitiamo ad un accenno delle Convenzioni più recenti:

Concordato con la Lettonia 1922
Concordato con la Baviera 1924
Concordato con la Polonia 1925
Concordato con la Francia 1926
Concordato con la Lituania 1927
[[*Concordato*]] ... con la Cecoslovacchia 1927
Concordato con la Romania 1927
Concordato con l'Italia 1929
Concordato con la Prussia 1929
Concordato con il Baden 1929
Concordato con la Germania 1933
Concordato con l'Austria 1933
[[*Convenzione*]]... con l'Equatore 1937.

Non è chi non veda la grandissima importanza di questa imponente mole di Legislazione Concordataria che chiama alla più fondamentale e feconda collaborazione la Chiesa e gli Stati e stabilisce una reciproca corrente d'interessi, di comprensioni, di servigi, di benefici.

La qual corrente funziona attraverso l'opera di quegli organi che si denominano «Rappresentanze Diplomatiche».

Per quanto riguarda il compito dei Rappresentanti Pontifici, l'opera loro è espressamente determinata dal Codice di Diritto Canonico il quale al Can. 267 prescrive: «Legati qui mittuntur cum titulo Nuntii aut Internuntii». «Fovent , secundum normas a S.Sede recepita, relationes inter Sedem Apostolicam et civilia Gubernia apud quae legatione stabili funguntur».

Basta questo enunciato per misurare la straordinaria portata del compito assegnato ai Rappresentanti della Santa Sede.

La storia del resto ci dichiara i profondi benefici effetti di queste Missioni Diplomatiche.

Mediante l'opera dei Rappresentanti Diplomatici si stabiliscono armoniche regolamentazioni sulle diverse materie che interessano non meno la vita della Nazione che quella della Chiesa, viene favorita la concordia tra le due supreme Potestà, si stabilisce una collaborazione leale, tra il Sommo Pontefice ed i Supremi Gerarchi dei singoli Governi che ridonda a favore non meno del benessere temporale che di quello eterno dei popoli. In una parola: i Rappresentati diplomatici della Santa Sede, favorendo le relazioni tra Santa Sede e Governi, danno la possibilità agli stessi Governi di poter agire in un'atmosfera di pace, di ordine, di civiltà, di moralità; e ciò non tanto per il compito che i Governi sono chiamati a compiere all'interno, quanto per lo svolgimento delle loro relazioni internazionali, e non è troppo dire che in certe situazioni critiche specialmente di indole internazionale, gli Stati che non sono rappresentati presso la Santa Sede risentono di un gravissimo disagio davanti a problemi di prima importanza e di palpitante attualità.

E a tal proposito non sarà inutile ricordare la testimonianza del primo Imperatore che inaugurò la concordia tra il Sacerdozio e l'Impero e le relazioni tra la Chiesa e lo Stato, il grande Costantino, che in un suo Rescritto ad Anulino Proconsole in Africa diceva da molte prove constatare: «Religionem illam, in qua summa Divinae Majestatis reverentia custoditur, spretam quidem maxime reipublicae importasse discrimina, eandem vero rite susceptamet custoditam et Nomini Romano maximam prosperitatem et cunctis mortalibus rebus, divina id tribuente beneficentiam, praecipuam felicitatem contulisse». (Eus. Hist. Eccles. 1. X.)

Né sono mancati eminenti uomini di governo nei tempi nostri che, rilevando la nuova coscienza politica moderna, della quale abbiamo detto più sopra, hanno dichiarato ed inculcato la grande importanza delle relazioni diplomatiche con la Santa Sede.

Affrettandosi la Francia nel 1921 a chiudere l'infausta parentesi della rottura delle relazioni diplomatiche con la Santa Sede, il Governo Francese così si esprimeva per bocca del suo Ministro degli Esteri Sig. Millerand:

«Il governo della Repubblica giudica venuto il momento di riannodare con Governo Pontificio le sue relazioni tradizionali. Il Governo Francese deve essere presente là ove si dibattono questioni che interessano la Francia. Questa non potrebbe restare più a lungo assente dal Governo Spirituale, presso il quale la più parte degli Stati hanno avuto cura di farsi rappresentare».

Il Capo del Governo Italiano <*Sig. Mussolini*> [add. in the draft] nel discorso pronunziato alla Camera dei Deputati il 13 Maggio 1929, prendendo in mano «L'Annuario Pontificio» ed agitandolo dal suo tavolo così dichiarava: «Quasi tutti gli Stati, Signori, meno l'Italia, hanno Rappresentanti presso la Santa Sede. Vi consiglio di procurarvi l'Annuario Pontificio del 1929, perché vi troverete l'elenco di tutti i diplomatici accreditati presso la Santa Sede, e avrete anche un'idea della potentissima organizzazione cattolica in tutto il mondo».

Doc. 6
AES, America IV P.O. 237 (1)Fasc. 65
January 8, 1938 (Letter from Spellman to Pacelli)

Eminenza Reverendissima,

Sono gratissimo a Vostra Eminenza per la lettera molto importante e utile che Vostra Eminenza ha avuto la bontà di scrivermi in gentile risposta alla mia lettera del 21 settembre 1937 intorno alla possibilità di stabilire relazioni diplomatiche fra la Santa Sede ed il governo degli Stati Uniti.

Le indicazioni e gli schiarimenti che Vostra Eminenza colla massima chiarezza e gentilezza degnava offrirmi saranno di prezioso aiuto nelle discussioni che avrò col Presidente Roosevelt intorno a questa materia.

Accludo una pro-memoria che avevo preparato e che ho già presentato al Presidente ed ho fatto il mio meglio per prepararmi nel miglior modo possibile per poter rispondere alle questioni sollevate nella mia lettera alle quali Vostra Eminenza mi ha fornito le adeguate risposte.

Non mi permetto essere troppo ottimista ma ritengo che nonostante le gravi difficoltà di molti generi, la possibilità di un esito favorevole non è esclusa.

Doc. 7
AES, America IV P.O. 237 (1)Fasc. 65
Pro-memoria sent by Spellman to Roosevelt

Diplomatic relations between the United States of America and the Holy See would be to the advantage of both parties because both have identical desires in regard to world peace and the welfare of humanity. The association would lead to the realization of this common purpose.

Both governments desire and are striving for social reforms for the betterment of all people, and especially the working classes, and both desire and are striving to accomplish these reform *without revolution.*

Friendly consular relations between the United States and the Papal States began on December 15, 1784, when the Papal nuncio in Paris wrote to the American Commissioners that this Government had agreed to open the ports of Civita Vecchia on the Mediterranean and Ancona on the Adriatic to the vessels of the new Republic, and in June, 1797, John B. Sartori was commissioned First Consul to represent the United States. Consular representation continued until 1870 when Rome became the capital of the Kingdom of Italy, and David M. Armstrong, at that time accredited to the Holy See, remained as First Consul to the United Kingdom.

On June 1, 1847, Nicholas Browne, then Consul at Rome, in a dispatch to Secretary Buchanan, stated that the Holy Father, Pope Pius IX, had expressed to him the desire that diplomatic relations might be established between the two Governments. President Polk agreed and advocated this measure in his message to Congress on December 7, 1847.

Following the Presidential recommendation, items appeared in the Deficiency Appropriation Bill of that Session providing for «an outfit and the salary of a charge» at the Court of Rome. There was opposition to the House of Representatives led by Congressman L. C. Levin of Pennsylvania of the «Native American Party».

In the Senate, Senator Badger of North Carolina accused President Polk and his party of making overtures for the votes of Catholics, but on the whole the opposition was based on the opinion that the Consulate already in existence was adequate to care for the political and commercial needs of the situation.

The new mission was created by the President «with the advice of consent of the Senate» on April 1st, 1848, and Jacob L. Martin, Secretary of the American Legation at Paris, was appointed chargè d'affaires.

He was received by Pope Pius IX and presented his credentials on August 1, 1848. Mr. Martin died that same year and was succeeded by Lewis Cass, Jr., who remained until 1858. Mr. Cass was raised to the rank of Minister Resident in 1854.

In 1867 the American Mission in Rome came to an official end, through the refusal of Congress to continue the appropriation for the Mission. The pretext for this action was based on an erroneous charge that the American Protestant Church had been ordered outside of the walls of Rome, but the real reason was a combination of religious prejudices, partisan opposition to the President, and a sympathetic feeling among many Americans for the aspirations of the Italians for national unity.

Legally, the action of the Congress, wrote Secretary of State Seward, left the mission «still existing but without compensation».

The American Mission was withdrawn some three years before 1870 when Rome became the capital of Italy. But even after the Pope was deprived of his de facto temporal sovereignty, diplomatic relations were maintained by the Holy See with various governments, and also with those whose people were not in the majority Catholic. These diplomatic relations were continued and increased in number all during the period from September 20, 1870 to February 11, 1929, when Italy made a Treaty of Peace with the Holy See, recognized her sovereignty, and stipulated a Concordat with her.

Now, with the exception of the United States, Russia, Japan, and Mexico, the great nations of the world maintain diplomatic relations with the Vatican.

[...]

The compiler of this memorandum is one of the three hundred thirty million Catholics in the world, and one of one hundred thirty million American citizens. He is one of twenty million individuals who are both American and Catholic. He hopes that the majority of understanding and broadminded Americans not of his religious belief would not oppose the resumption of diplomatic relations with the Holy See.

He believes that all Catholics, of whatever nationality, would be gratified and grateful to the United States Government if such recognition were accorded. He knows that twenty million American Catholics would be overjoyed and deeply appreciative of such consideration extended to the head of their Church.

DOC. 8
AES, America IV P.O. 237 (1)Fasc. 65
January 26, 1938 (letter from Spellman to Pacelli)

Eminenza Reverendissima,

Il Presidente Roosevelt è rimasto contento della pro-memoria che gli ho presentato e delle quale ho già mandato una copia a Vostra Eminenza. Mi pare pure che le risposte colle quali Vostra Eminenza degnava fornirmi come schiarimenti delle due difficoltà suscitate nella prima discussione erano considerate ragionevoli ed adequati.

Sono persuaso che il Presidente vuole dare recognizione diplomatica alla Santa Sede, ma che lui non è sicuro che può convincere il Congresso di fornire i fondi per la manutenzione del posto, e non vuole fare la prova se non è sicuro di riuscire. E, difatto, è la verità che l'annunzio di questo progetto anti-Cattolico ed anti-Roosevelt. Il Presidente non vuole andare contro una tale campagna se non è sicuro di raggiungere la sua meta, perché se non riesce, è meglio non provare.

Mi ha domandato, se, nel caso che sia possibile di riuscire, se la nomina di un ministro invece di un ambasciatore sarebbe gradita alla Santa Sede. Io gli ho risposto che, benché l'Inghilterra è rappresentata da un solo Ministro, sarebbe molto più dignitoso per gli Stati Uniti d'avere un Ambasciatore. Prego Vostra Eminenza d'avere la bontà di farmi sapere se ho risposto bene.

Ho concluso la conversazione dicendo che non sarà mai un'occasione più opportuna che adesso per prendere questo passo, e che non posso immaginare altro Presidente meglio disposto di lui o più capace di lui per concludere questo affare.

DOC. 9
AES, America IV P.O. 237 (1)Fasc. 65
February 26, 1938 (Letter from Spellman to Pacelli)

Eccellenza Rev.ma,

Ho ricevuto la pregiata lettera dell'Eccellenza Vostra Rev.ma in data 26 dello scorso gennaio e La ringrazio delle notizie inviatemi.

Come Ella ha opportunamente fatto notare a S. E. il Presidente Roosevelt, per quanto sarebbe più dignitoso per gli Stati Uniti avere qui un vero e proprio ambasciatore, pure la Santa Sede non porrebbe difficoltà ove si preferisse dare al Rappresentante suddetto la sola qualifica di Ministro.

ROBERT TRISCO

The Holy See and Cardinal Mundelein's Insult of Hitler (1937)

On May 18, 1937, the archbishop of Chicago, Cardinal George William Mundelein, addressed the priests of the archdiocese assembled at a quarterly clergy conference at Quigley Preparatory Seminary. He sternly denounced the Nazi persecution of the Church in Germany, indignantly asserting that the German Government was «giving out through its crooked minister of propaganda [Joseph Goebbels] stories of wholesale immorality in religious institutions». He insisted that it would be «not only unwise but cowardly as well» to «take the thing lying down and not fight back». He noted that the «immediate issue which brought up resumption of the [immorality] trials[1] was the struggle over the school question». The Cardinal reviewed the suppression of confessional schools in several regions and the enactment of a law that destroyed the remaining Catholic youth organizations, and he exposed the fraudulent procedures of the school elections. He recalled the frequent pastoral letters protesting against the school campaigns and finally «the Papal Encyclical on Palm Sunday [March 14, *Mit brennender Sorge*[2]], constituting the most drastic challenge yet presented to the Nazis». Thus, he concluded, the truce was broken. «The government threw all the immorality trials into the courts simultaneously and mobilized its tremendous propaganda machine to give them the maximum

---

[1] The trials had been started in 1935 but then halted before the Olympic Games. On April 6, 1937, Hitler personally ordered the resumption of the trials, which were brought to a climax in May with publicity in the press, radio, pamphlets, and fly sheets. They were trials of priests and lay brothers in religious orders who were indicted for sexual offenses. H.G. HOCKERTS, *Die Sittlichkeitsprozesse gegen katholische Ordensangehörige und Priester, 1936/1937: Eine Studie zur nationalsozialistischen Herrschaftstechnik und zum Kirchenkampf*, Veröffentlichungen der Kommission für Zeitgeschichte bei der Katholischen Akademie in Bayern, Reihe B: Forschungen, Band 6, Mainz 1971, 112.

[2] *The Papal Encyclicals, 1903-1939*, ed. by C. CARLEN, I.H.M, N.p.: A Consortium Book; McGrath Publishing Company, n.d., 525-535. Actually, it was dated Passion Sunday but read from the pulpits of the Catholic churches in Germany on Palm Sunday.

publicity». He drew the lesson that if American Catholics were to show no interest in this struggle they might some day face a similar crisis alone. He then delivered the sentence that was to be quoted so widely: «Perhaps you will ask how is it that a nation of 60,000,000 people, intelligent people, will submit in fear and servitude to an alien, an Austrian paperhanger, and a poor one at that I am told, and a few associates like Goebbels and Goering who dictate every move of the people's lives». He described the Government's oppressive control of the lives of ordinary people and begged his hearers to show open sympathy to the German Catholics and to «pray for the Church in Germany and the German people», to whom American Catholics owed much for building up the Church in the United States[3].

This was not the first time that the Cardinal publicly expressed his anxiety about the Church in Germany. Addressing the Holy Name Society on January 5, 1936, he asserted, «Even in the days of the Kulturkampf, Germany was far better off than today. Then the Catholics had a voice. [...] Today [...] there is no voice, the Church is slowly being strangled, the Superiors of almost every Religious Community are in jail, the youth of the land is being weaned away from the faith of their fathers...». The Cardinal regarded such calamities as «signs and portents» and concluded that Catholic men, if organized like his audience, could prevent such harm being done in the United States[4].

---

[3] Manuscript in the Archdiocese of Chicago's Joseph Cardinal Bernardin Archives and Records Center [hereafter «AAC»], Chancery Correspondence, No. 136, 1937, Record Number EXEC G0500/38; better: Box 43845.06, Folder 14, No. 136. In the archival copy instead of «an Austrian paperhanger and a poor one at that» an adverb is inserted thus: «a darn poor one at that». Also Allegato II al Rapporto N. 230/37, Secret Vatican Archives (hereafter «ASV»), Sacra Congregazione degli Affari Ecclesiastici Straordinari (hereafter «AES»), America, Anno 1937-1938, POS. 247 P.O., Fasc. 87, fols. 28^r-33^r (including «a darn poor one»). Italian translation printed as «Il Allegato al Rapporto No. 230/37», Num. X in the Sommario of the Ponenza, «Germania: Situazione religiosa e politica, discorso dell'E.mo Cardinale Mundelein», prepared for the Sacra Congregazione degli Affari Ecclesiastici Straordinari, June, 1937, in AES, Rapporti delle Sessioni, 1937, Vol. 92, numero 1376, stampa 1971, 41-42. Published in «The New World», Chicago, May 21, 1937, 1 (with a misprint of «6,000,000» for 60,000,000 and other typographical errors). Reprinted in T.M. KEEFE, *The Mundelein Affair: A Reappraisal*, in «Records of the American Catholic Historical Society of Philadelphia», 89 (1978), 79-82; see J. NEUHÄSLER, *Kreuz und Hackenkreuz: Der Kampf des Nationalsozialismus gegen die katolische Kirche und der Kirchliche Widerstand*, Munich 1946, 13, 288-292; and E.R. KANTOWICZ, *Corporation Sole: Cardinal Mundelein and Chicago Catholicism*, Indiana 1983, 224-227.

[4] AAC, Chancery Correspondence Collection, 1936, Record Number EXEC/G0500/34 (better: Box 43845.06), Folder 14, No. 131. Moreover, it should be noted that Munde-

It may seem surprising that the Cardinal mentioned Pius XI's encyclical, issued two months before, in only one sentence. The Pope had treated at length «the painful trials of the Church [in Germany] and the increasing vexations» afflicting those who remained loyal to the faith. In particular, he deplored the campaign against the confessional schools, which were guaranteed by the Concordat of 1933. He expressed his gratitude «to religious and nuns» as well as his sympathy for so many who, as a result of administrative measures hostile to Religious, had been wrenched from the work of their vocation. The pontiff merely alluded to the immorality trials, saying, «If some have fallen and shown themselves unworthy of their vocation, their fault, which the Church punishes, in no way detracts from the merit of the immense majority who, in voluntary abnegation and poverty, have tried to serve their God and their country». (The immorality trials were not prohibited by the Concordat). The aged and infirm Pope set an example of defiance, proclaiming that although he had desired nothing more than «the restoration of a true peace between Church and State» in Germany, if through no fault of his, such peace was not to come, «the Church of God will defend her rights and her freedom»[5]. The reading of this encyclical in the churches has been called «the strongest protest ever issued in Germany against Hitler's regime throughout the entire Nazi period»[6] and «one of the greatest condemnations of a national regime ever pronounced by the Vatican»[7]. On April 12 the German ambassador to the Holy See, Diego von Bergen, presented to the Cardinal Secretary of State, Eugenio Pacelli, his government's formal protest against the encyclical. Eighteen days later Pacelli replied in detail to the German complaints[8].

---

lein's archdiocesan weekly, *The New World*, carried frequent reports and editorials on the religious situation and the state of the Church in Germany and on the Nazi policies and aggression.

[5] Pars. 1, 31, 37, and 43, C. CARLEN, *The Papal Encyclicals...*, 525, 532, 533, and 534.

[6] W.M. HARRIGAN, *Pius XI and Nazi Germany, 1937-1939*, in «Catholic Historical Review», 51 (1966), 461.

[7] A. RHODES, *The Vatican in the Age of the Dictators, 1922-1945*, London 1973, 204. For brief accounts of the Nazis' reaction to the encyclical see J.S. CONWAY, *The Nazi Persecution of the Churches, 1933-45*, New York 1968, 166-167, A. RHODES, *The Vatican in the Age of the Dictators...*, 205-209, and R.J. EVANS, *The Third Reich in Power, 1933-1939*, New York 2005, 243-245.

[8] *Der notenwechsel zwischen dem Heiligen Stuhl und der deutschen Reichsregierung*, Band II: *1937-1945, Veröffentlichungen der Komission für Zeitgeschichte, Reihe A. Quellen*, Band 10, ed. by D. ALBRECHT, Mainz 1969, Nos. 1 and 2, 1-5 and 5-15; *Documents on German Foreign Policy, 1918-1945: From the Archives of the German Foreign Ministry*, Washington, DC, 1949 (hereafter «DGFP»), No. 646, pp. 951-954, and No. 649, pp. 956-966. Reprinted in AES, America, 1937-1938, POS.

This exchange of notes foreshadowed the exchange that would be provoked by Mundelein's speech.

In some way that is not clear, intelligence regarding the speech was obtained by a newspaper reporter; perhaps it was conveyed to him by one or more of the priests present at the conference. Then to prevent misquotations the Chancery Office released the authentic text. In any case an account was promptly published and repeated in countless newspapers throughout the United States; editorials and cartoons, all favorable to Mundelein, were multiplied[9]. News of the speech was also widely circulated in the European press and thus quickly reached the Vatican.

Already on May 21 Pacelli sent a cablegram in cipher to the Apostolic Delegate in Washington, Archbishop Amleto Cicognani, saying that the newspapers reported the «courageous speech of the Cardinal Archbishop of Chicago regarding the religious situation in Germany, against which

---

247 P.O., Fasc. 90, fol. 6ᵛ, pagine stampate 1-20. W.M. HARRIGAN, *Pius XI and Nazi Germany...*, 461-463.

[9] The papers of the Apostolic Delegation in Washington for the 1930s, which are preserved in the Secret Vatican Archives, in the section «V – Affari Esteri» under the Posiz[ione] 166b entitled «Germania: Dissenso del Cardinal George Mundelein contro il governo di Hitler (1937-1938, s.d.)», include numerous clippings from secular papers. The records of the Sacra Congregazione degli Affari Ecclesiastici Straordinari, Anno 1937-1938, POS. 247 P.O., Fasc. 88, contain clippings from seven secular newspapers and one Catholic daily, and Fasc. 89 contains «Comments in the Press of the United States and Canada on the Speeches of His Eminence Cardinal George Mundelein» «from the National Catholic Welfare Conference» (fol. 3), consisting of a «List of [thirty-two] Newspapers in the United States Carrying Favorable Editorial Comment» dated May 21 to June 10 (fol. 4), long editorials from the *Philadelphia Inquirer,* May 22 (fol. 5) and the *Boise Statesman*, May 24 (fol. 5v), a «List of [forty-six] Newspapers Supporting Cardinal Mundelein's Speech to the Extent of Emphasizing American Principles of Free Speech» dated May 21 to June 2 (fol. 69r), a «List of [sixty-five] Newspapers Carrying Editorial Criticism of Chancellor Hitler and Only Incidental and Non-Committal Comment on Cardinal Mundelein» (fols. 17r, 18r), a «List of [five] Newspapers Carrying Editorial Comment Unfavorable to Cardinal Mundelein's Speech», dated May 22 to June 3, with the full editorial of the *New York Herald-Tribune*, «The Dictatorial Jitters», that merely characterizes the Cardinal's insult of Hitler as certainly «not discreet» and adds that one is strongly inclined «to waive the question of discretion on the Cardinal's part», May 31 (fol. 19); a «List of [six] Magazine Editorials, Feature Articles, Signed Articles, etc.», May 29 to June 19; a list of ten papers that carried other signed and feature articles, May 22 to June 12; a list of four papers that carried cartoons, May 21 to June 8; a «list of [four] Jewish and [two] Protestant Papers Carrying Editorial Comment on Cardinal Mundelein's Speech, May 28 to June 4 (fol. 31), and a «List of [eleven] Canadian Newspapers Carrying Editorial Comment on Cardinal Mundelein's Speech» (fol. 33).

the German Embassy» was said to have protested. The Secretary of State asked him to collect information on the matter and to report in detail[10]. Cicognani replied the same day that the «declaration» of the Cardinal Archbishop had had the vastest favorable publicity in the American press and the approval of groups of Protestants and Jews. He also wrote that the German embassy in Washington had presented the case to the Department of State but without protesting formally; hence, the American authorities had thought it best not to reply. He promised to send a report as soon as possible[11]. Still on May 21 the Apostolic Delegate wrote a confidential letter to Mundelein, quoting from the cablegram of the Secretariat of State the reference to his «coraggioso discorso» and saying that he was asked «to submit a report on the reaction in this country to the Cardinal's words». He asked Mundelein to send him two copies of the address and to let him know what reaction there had been to the address «in the form of personal messages directed to» the Cardinal[12].

Mundelein replied promptly, saying, «When I prepared my talk of last Tuesday, I had not the slightest idea or intention that it should be given to the press or such publicity»[13]. He wrote that he was accustomed to give a talk at the end of the quarterly conference of the clergy and always prepared it in advance, and he continued:

«This time, being provoked by the daily repetitions in the press of the so-called morality trials in Germany. [...]. I just hurriedly wrote what was on my mind and gave it to the priests just as I wrote it. The newspapers got wind of it, and the Chancery on its own responsibility, gave it out verbatim as I had written it. I cannot explain it on any grounds other than it was all providential. Had I prepared it for the press, I would have left out the personal allusions, and yet it was just that that hit home».

The Cardinal added somewhat disingenuously that «it would have remained just a local incident» if the Nazi Government, «the fools», «because of the fancied insults had not plastered it over the press of the world.

---

[10] ASV, Arch. Deleg. Stati Uniti, POS. 166b, fol. 13r, Cifr. 79.

[11] *Ibidem*, fol. 14r, Cifr. 154.

[12] *Ibidem*, fol. 15r (carbon copy).

[13] In spite of Mundelein's disavowal, Kantowicz wrote that «it seems likely that Mundelein intended it [the speech] for the public» and added, «Since Mundelein was usually capable of imposing secrecy on the clergy when he wanted to, it seems that he desired wide publication of his remarks» (p. 226). The Holy See, however, took the Cardinal at his word, perhaps not only because it was not proper to doubt a Cardinal's word but also because it served the Holy See's interests.

[...] They themselves brought to the notice of the poor persecuted Catholics of Germany the news that they were not entirely deserted by their Catholic brethren here». Since then, he wrote, he had declined to utter one word. As a result he had received «a great mass of mail, telegrams and telephone messages». Fully nine out of every ten messages were congratulatory and endorsed his attitude; they were «about equally divided in number» between Catholics and Protestants, and «of course the Jews» were «one hundred per cent» for him. He thought that the priests were moved by the fact that at last someone had «come out and endorsed the Holy Father's encyclical *Mit brennender Sorge*». The Episcopal and Methodist bishops of Chicago had both publicly endorsed his position, and even the Lutherans «said no word to the contrary, just begged for more time for study of the situation». He admitted that he did not know what effect his speech might have in Germany, but he felt that in the United States it had «definitely taken the sting out of these numberless charges from Germany of immorality among the clergy and Religious». He concluded, «Should harm result from my impetuosity, then I must be prepared to carry all the blame; should some permanent good come from it all, then all the credit most go to the Holy Ghost, and I offer it as a birthday gift to our Holy Father»[14]. (Pius XI's eightieth birthday was May 31).

When Cicognani acknowledged receipt of this letter, he promised to report to the Secretariat of State at greater length than in his cablegram of May 21 «on the very favorable reaction in this country» to Mundelein's words. Congratulating the Cardinal again for his «courageous address», the Apostolic Delegate wrote, «It has accomplished much good in this country, and let us hope and pray that it may be productive of some good results also in Germany. No government, no matter how strong it may be within its own boundaries, can long afford to continue policies which create distrust and arouse indignation and justified criticism among large foreign groups»[15].

The next day, May 27, Cicognani sent Pacelli a report on Mundelein's speech and enclosed both the Cardinal's reply and the text of his speech. He unquestioningly accepted the Cardinal's statement that the speech was not intended for the public but rather only for the archdiocesan priests. «But by a fortunate indiscretion of the archiepiscopal Curia, the text went

---

[14] ASV, Arch. Deleg. Stati Uniti, POS. 166b, fols.16r, 17r. An Italian translation printed as «I Allegato al Rapporto 230/37» in the Sommario, June, 1937, in AES, Rapporti delle Sessioni, 1937, Vol. 92, numero 1376, stampa 1971, 42-43.

[15] May 26, 1937, carbon copy, ASV, Arch. Deleg. Stati Uniti, POS. 166b, fol. 18r.

into the hands of the journalists; whence the great publicity». Cicognani added that many of the principal newspapers of the United States had reported the speech on the first page with headlines in big block capital letters, and not a few editorials expressed the applause of the American press for the Cardinal's position. Cicognani continued, «in Berlin it was announced that the German Embassy in Washington had presented a vigorous diplomatic protest to the Department of State in regard to the speech in question. Instead, from what the newspapers have reported, the counselor of the Embassy, Dr. Hans Thomsen, went to the Department of State to make simply an "informal representation", to which the Government of Washington did not think it [necessary] to reply»[16].

Meanwhile Pacelli was growing impatient to receive the text of Mundelein's speech with all the opportune pieces of information, as he urged Cicognani by cable on May 30. The Delegate replied immediately that the report had been sent the day before on the steamship *Rex*[17]. On June 7 Pacelli thanked Cicognani for the report and asked him to inform Pacelli by telegraph authentically and not only according to newspaper reports in regard to the steps taken by the counselor of the German embassy at the Department of State. The Cardinal Secretary of State desired confirmation of the negative outcome of that *démarche*[18]. In reply Cicognani fully confirmed the account given in his report of May 27. He wrote that James Clement Dunn of the Department of State had declared to Mgr. Michael J. Ready, the General Secretary of the National Catholic Welfare Conference, that the counselor of the German embassy, Hans Thomsen, went to visit Dunn on May 20 in a sort of private way; he mentioned Mundelein's speech and began to discuss the religious situation in Germany, asserting that the Church was trying to re-establish the Center Party; therefore the Catholics had to be suppressed for the purpose of unifying Germany. The counselor appeared to be upset by Cardinal Mundelein's speech, but he made no formal protest; therefore, he did not receive any response. Dunn added that in Berlin it had been stated in print that the German Embassy had presented an official protest; that was false, and if it had happened,

---

[16] Prot. No. 230/37, carbon copy, *ibidem,* fols. 19r, 20r, 23r; printed as Num. X in the Sommario, June, 1937, AES, Rapporti delle Sessioni, 1937, Vol. 92, numero 1376, stampa 1971, 41-42; an Italian translation of Mundelein's letter to Cicognani of May 24, fols. 21r, 22r, 23r. It was only on June 18 that Pacelli acknowledged receipt of this report: No. 2312/37, fol. 42r. «Memorandum of Michael J. Ready on Mundelein Affair», carbon copy, *ibidem*, fols. 35r, 36r, 37r.

[17] *Ibidem*, ciphers 86 and 158, fol. 24r.

[18] *Ibidem*, cipher 89, fol. 34.

the American Government would have declared the protest baseless and would not have received it. The Secretary of State, Cordell Hull, declared that he did not intend to receive any protest from the German Embassy. With this the incident was considered closed by both sides[19].

On the next day, June 11, the Apostolic Delegate sent Pacelli the memorandum that Mgr. Ready had written about the conversation he had had at midday on the tenth with James Dunn, the chief of the Division of Western European Affairs in the Department of State. Cicognani explained that he could not reply immediately to Pacelli's telegram of June 7, because Ready was absent from Washington the morning of the tenth, and Cicognani could not make use of anybody else for this purpose. He added that the local press of every shade was continuing to publish reports that the relations between Germany and the Holy See were as strained as ever, and Mundelein's speech was always brought up, noting that the Vatican had not censured the Cardinal for his attack on Hitler. The general sentiment, Cicognani said, deplored the persecutions unleashed against the Catholics and every spiritual force. It was understood that the «Cardinal Mundelein speech» and «immorality of the clergy» were malicious pretexts for carrying out whatever they wanted[20].

The reason for Pacelli's eagerness to have the precise text of Mundelein's speech and the Apostolic Delegate's report was that on the morning of May 24 the German Ambassador to the Holy See, Diego von Bergen, asked to be received by the Cardinal Secretary of State. He first spoke in a private way about the attempts that had been made for his recall and

---

[19] June 10, 1937, cipher 160, *ibidem*, fol. 38r. Cicognani's report, based on Ready's memorandum, was corroborated by the dispatch of the German Ambassador to the United States, Hans Heinrich Dieckhoff, to the German Foreign Ministry sent by telegraph on May 21. He wrote, «Immediately after the publication of Mundelein's statements concerning the Fuehrer, I made serious representations, on my own initiative through Thomsen, to the Chief of the Western European Division. [...]. I purposely refrained from making a formal protest to the United States Government, [...] because Cardinal Mundelein, [...] according to the interpretation prevalent here, holds an office that has absolutely no connection with the United States Government and is not dependent on it, and because the Cardinal is therefore regarded by the United States Government merely as a private person. In his *démarche* Thomsen pointed out, in particular, how seriously such offensive utterances of prominent Americans are to be judged, and how much German-American relations would be disturbed thereby». DGFP, No. 654, 969-970.

[20] Prot. 268/37, carbon copy, ASV, Arch. Deleg. Stati Uniti, POS. 166b, fols. 39r, 40r; original in AES, America, 1937-1938, POS. 247 P.O., Fasc. 87, fol. 56r-v. Pacelli acknowledged receipt of this report by Western Union on June 20, ASV, Arch. Deleg. Stati Uniti, POS. 166b, fol. 41r.

added that in the coming days he would go to Berlin on a normal leave of absence. The age limits for an ambassador were about to expire for him. Then speaking officially, he handed the Cardinal a sheet of paper with the letterhead of the embassy but without date or signature, in which the case of Mundelein's speech was set forth[21].

Pacelli replied with a statement and a counter-question. First, he said that he was not accustomed to express an opinion on speeches of which, as in the present case, he did not have an absolutely accurate text, and even if he had such a text, he would not be in a position to take a stance until he had a clear, definitive, and satisfactory answer to the following question: «What has the German Government done and what does it intend to do in the future against the malicious slander and defamation, against the disgraceful calumnies that day by day occur in German newspapers and magazines and in the speeches of prominent personages against the Church, church institutions, Pope, Cardinals, bishops, priests, etc.?». Pacelli said he wished to lighten the ambassador's task by answering the first part of the question himself: «The German Government, in spite of all the remonstrances, has done nothing against all that. On the contrary, it is itself responsible for it, since state and party authorities and particularly the Propaganda Ministry organize and direct a great part of this journalistic and oratorical activity, and as for the other part they at least encourage and promote it with all means». Only the German Government, he said, could answer the question about the future. To be sure that his reply would be transmitted to the Government exactly, the Cardinal offered, and the Ambassador accepted, to give him his words in writing, and he did so that same day[22]. Bergen indeed forwarded Pacelli's reply to the German Foreign Ministry by telegraph the next day, noting that it contained several phrases and expressions not used in the oral reply, such as «malicious» slander and «disgraceful» calumnies. Bergen attributed the sharper tone to the impression made by his «unequivocal criticism of Mundelein's utterances». He reported that he had reiterated to Pacelli the suggestion that he had made so frequently during the past few years, that is, «to make the general charges specific and to instruct the nuncio, as the competent authority in such instances, to bring any cases involving grievances of

---

[21] June 20, 1937, AES, America, 1937-1938, POS. 247 P.O., Fasc. 88, Relazione, pp. 7-8; Sommario, Num. III, pp. 18-19 (original German and Italian translation); Aide Mémoire des Botschafters v. Bergen an Kardinalstaatssekretär Pacelli, Albrecht, No. 4, 20-21.

[22] AES, America, 1937-1938, POS. 247 P.O., Fasc. 88, Relazione, p. 8; Sommario, Num. IV, pp. 20-21.

the Vatican to the attention of the Government of the Reich, for without knowledge of alleged acts neither investigation nor remedy was possible». Bergen added that he «was not aware of a single instance where any leading personage in Germany ever used insulting or offensive language against the person of the Pope, against the Cardinal Secretary of State, against other members of the College of Cardinals, etc». The Ambassador also warned «that a further exacerbation of the already severe tension in the relations between the Vatican and Germany was fraught with the gravest danger». Bergen then suggested a text for a reply to Pacelli's note. He also suggested the he «be instructed to transmit the reply to the Cardinal Secretary of State in the form of a note soon after the celebration of the Pope's birthday on May 31»[23].

Bergen had intended to postpone his vacation trip, but he was asked by the German Foreign Ministry to leave for Germany at once. Hence, he told Pacelli that he had to discuss official business in Berlin. He replied to his superiors, «The fiction of my absence on official business is therefore maintained»[24]. Accordingly, it was not the ambassador but rather the chargé d'affaires, Fritz Menshausen, who presented the German protest to Cardinal Pacelli.

The very next day, May 27, the Minister of Foreign Affairs, Freiherr (Baron) Konstantin von Neurath, «who would remain as the last practicing Catholic in the government»[25], telegraphed the German Embassy that «without regard to the date of the Pope's birthday and immediately after the departure of the Ambassador», the chargé d'affaires should transmit to the Cardinal Secretary of State a note the text of which was attached. It said that Cardinal Mundelein had «referred to the German Chief of State, members of the Reich government, and certain occurrences in the domain of church affairs in Germany in outrageously insulting terms... The German Government thought it a foregone conclusion that the Holy See would dissociate itself from the utterances of the Cardinal, which had become known all over the world; that it would correct them and express its regrets». Instead to the very great surprise and profound astonishment of the German Government, the Holy See turned aside the German Ambassador's representations «without a reply, using as a pretext some general, unsubstantiated, and incorrect but all the more injurious remarks to the

---

[23] DGFP, No. 655, 970-972.
[24] May 26, 1937, DGFP, No. 657, 973.
[25] H. WOLF, *Pope and Devil: The Vatican's Archives and the Third Reich*, Cambridge, MA, 2010, 157.

effect that at the most the Cardinal had retaliated in kind». The German Government, therefore, charged that the Holy See was «permitting those indescribable public attacks against the person of the German Chief of State on the part of one of its highest prelates to stand uncorrected» and was «thereby actually endorsing them in the eyes of the world». The note concluded that as long as the Holy See failed to remedy its «incomprehensible conduct in this matter», it «eliminated the conditions necessary for a normal state of relations between the German Government and the Curia», and the full responsibility for this development rested solely with the Curia[26]. The chargé, Fritz Menshausen, presented this note to Cardinal Pacelli on May 29[27].

On that same day the Reich Minister of Propaganda, Joseph Goebbels, delivered in the Deutschlandhalle in Berlin a violent speech, broadcast by radio throughout the country, in reply to Cardinal Mundelein. First, he dilated on the immorality trials of an enormous number of members of the Catholic clergy who had been sentenced to long terms of imprisonment and forced labor. He deplored a moral decadence never before recorded in the whole cultural history of mankind. The criminal sexual aberrations of the Catholic clergy, he asserted, were apt to threaten most seriously the physical and spiritual health of the German youth, and he promised that since the Church had showed itself too weak to root out this sexual plague, the state would do so. Then with mendacity mixed with hypocrisy Goebbels said that the Government of the Reich had truly intended not to speak in public about these things and to let the facts speak for themselves, but now he was forced to break the silence, because a clear reply was necessary to a Catholic Cardinal in America, Mundelein, who had insulted the Fuehrer in an indescribable way and said that «the dishonest minister of propaganda in Germany» organized these trials solely for the purpose of harming the persecuted Catholic Church. He vigorously repudiated this accusation as a National Socialist and as a father of four children. He alleged that Mundelein's attack against the National Socialist state was inspired by persons in Germany who were directly hit by the trials. In sum, Goebbels slandered the Catholic Church as if it were defending thousands

---

[26] DGFP, No. 658, 973-974.

[27] Albrecht, No. 6, 23-24; German original and Italian translation in AES, America, 1937-1938, POS. 247 P.O., Fasc. 88, Sommario, Num. V, pp. 22-25; also in AES, Rapporti delle Sessioni, 1937, Vol. 92, numero 1376, stampa 1971, and AVS, Arch. Deleg. Stati Uniti, POS. 166b, printed texts, pp. 1-2 (German), 3-4 (Italian translation). The note was published by the German Government on June 1, without previous notice to the Holy See, by means of the semiofficial agency DNB.

of priests and religious men who were sexually abusing and corrupting children[28].

The apostolic nuncio in Austria, Gaetano Cicognani (Amleto's brother), promptly sent Pacelli a report on the attitude of the press in that country toward Goebbels' speech. He wrote that all the Catholic newspapers considered it the prelude to a religious struggle that the German Government wished to wage against the Church in grand style[29].

Eleven days later the apostolic nuncio in Germany, Cesare Orsenigo, reported to Pacelli that the position of the Holy See on the incident provoked by Mundelein's speech found there full understanding on the part of the Catholics. The publicity of the trials appeared, he wrote, at least in some newspapers to give signs of weariness. He thought that the determined campaign conducted by Catholics abroad to frustrate all the anti-Catholic mines hidden under the tinsel of the chase after immorality and political Catholicism was causing serious concern to the Government even though it kept repeating that for it foreign countries counted for nothing[30].

The «Kulturkampf Newsletter» for June 15, after reviewing recent events that it considered to be various phases of a process that appeared «to show a conversion of the struggle conducted by the dictatorship against the Catholic Church with the obvious objective of depriving the German people entirely of Christianity», continued:

«The Berlin ultimatum was quite unacceptable to the Vatican. The Holy See can hardly disavow the expressions of opinion of Cardinal Mundelein against the policy of the Reich Government with regard to the Church, for they were in harmony with the condemnation by the Vatican of that policy. As for the

---

[28] AES, Germania, 1937-1938, POS. 720, fasc. 326, fol. 42; AES, Rapporti delle Sessioni, 1937, Vol. 92, numero 1376, stampa 1971, and AES, America, 1937-1938, POS. 247 P.O., Fasc. 88, Sommario, Num. VI: Traduzione italiana dei brani più importanti del discorso del Ministro della Propaganda del Reich, Dr. Goebbels, from *Völkischer Beobachter*, Edizione A – Edizione di Berlino, Sabato, 29 maggio 1937, pp. 26-34. Extract in English in *The Persecution of the Catholic Church in the Third Reich: Facts and Documents Translated from the German*, New York 1940, 305, with the full English translation of an «Open Letter» to Goebbels written under the pseudonym «Michael Germanicus» and secretly distributed and reprinted on an immense scale in Germany during the summer of 1937, pp. 322-325.

[29] G. Cicognani to Pacelli, Vienna, June 1, 1937, AES, Germania, 1937-1938, POS. 720, Fasc. 328, fol. 50; printed in AES, Rapporti delle Sessioni, 1937, Vol. 92, numero 1376, stampa 1971, Sommario, Num. IX, 40.

[30] Berlin, June 12, 1937, AES, America, 1937-1938, POS. 247 P.O., Fasc. 88, and Rapporti delle Sessioni, 1937, Vol. 92, numero 1376, stampa 1971, Sommario, Num. XI, 49-50.

actual form of these expressions, obviously the remarks of a citizen of free America are not liable to censorship. As regards the German Government's insistence, therefore, on a censure of Cardinal Mundelein's action, no compromise can be envisioned. The fact is of decisive importance that the German Government now believes it possible to undertake the risks of an open attack upon the Church and to intensify its campaign of suppression without mercy or stint. As far as authoritative circles in Germany are concerned, the Concordat is already dissolved, and any *modus vivendi*, based upon the principles expressed in the Concordat, would be merely a bond with which they have no need to cripple themselves.

Nevertheless, there does exist reason for considering that, at the moment, no further important events will follow. Following upon Goebbels' speech and the threatening note, an "interpretation" was published which represented a certain regression. In well-informed quarters it is stated that the Italian Government had intervened with the advice not to let things go too far. For this reason, it is possible that the Reich Government will temporarily assume a waiting attitude, while the Vatican likewise exercises reserve and has postponed publication of the White Book on the German attack on the Church, a work which has been completed in all details and is ready for publication.

However, all this refers only to "official" relationships. But the attack on the Church is being continued on the most drastic lines, both in the daily activities of Government departments and in Nazi Party propaganda. In this relation, the question as to whether the papal nuncio should remain in Berlin, and whether the present German Ambassador to the Vatican – who has reached retiring age – should be succeeded only by a *chargé d'affaires*, is comparatively a minor one. Recent events have at any rate left no room for doubt that the Kulturkampf is an official undertaking of the German Government in its entirety. The old legend, that it originated from the "radical wing" of the Nazi Party, has been dispersed by the rulers themselves»[31].

Meanwhile Pacelli was drafting a note in reply to the German Embassy's note of May 29 regarding Cardinal Mundelein's statement. He said that the Holy See could not take a position immediately after the Ambassador's *démarche* of May 24, because it was based only on newswires from New York; there was no complete text of the speech, nor were the circumstances of its delivery or its being made public stated precisely. Since the ambassador's *aide-mémoire* contained no request for an intervention on the part of the Holy See, the reproach contained in the note of May 29 of having evaded an officially presented request lacked a foundation. Pacelli also pointed out that before making the *démarche* of May 24, the Government of the Reich, according to press reports, had had recourse to the Gov-

---

[31] Newsletter 58, in *Confronting the Nazi War on Christianity: The* Kulturkampf *Newsletters, 1936-1939*, ed. by R. BONNEY, Vol. 4, Oxford 2009, 193-195. The writer was well informed.

ernment of the United States. When the American Government gave no response, the Reich did not modify its relations with the United States, but it was saying that the Holy See, by not responding to the Ambassador's remonstrances, had eliminated prerequisites for a normal framework of the relations between the German Government and the Curia. Pacelli criticized this application of a double standard as unusual. He observed that the part of Mundelein's speech to which the German Government took the strongest exception was not in the political-religious field but contained statements and observations of another kind made by an American citizen who was using the rights guaranteed by the constitution of his country of the free expression of opinion in the area of publicly known facts. The Holy See had ascertained that the speaker made these remarks on the supposition that his speech was not to be publicized. He certainly did not intend the incomplete publication that resulted from an indiscretion. Pacelli stated that his reply to the Ambassador did not contain a refusal to concern himself with this case; on the contrary, the Holy See made a great effort to engage in a discussion that could improve the long-troubled relations. Then the Cardinal Secretary showed how those relations, which according to the preamble to the Concordat should be amicable, were for years strained by the fact that the head of the Catholic Church, ecclesiastical institutions and officials, and religious convictions and practices were exposed to the vilest invectives and disparagements and by the fact that an intervention on the part of the State authorities against this abuse could never be obtained. Pacelli then went on to list instances of such contempt and to call for reciprocity in safeguarding the honor of the German and Church authorities. Without leaving the Holy See time for its immediately opened investigations, the German Government staged a defensive campaign against Cardinal Mundelein's remarks that by the sharpness of its tone and the unruliness of its literary genre served neither Germany's well understood interests nor the normal further development of diplomatic steps. Borrowing a reflection of Mundelein, Pacelli noted that the extremeness of this defense gave the incident that otherwise would have remained limited to local effects, a world-wide echo that surprised the speaker himself. The American Cardinal's merits for having helped the German people in the difficult postwar period now recalled did not let broad foreign circles understand what interest the German Government could have in denying to such a personage previously counted as a benefactor of its people all good faith and truthfulness with such a base press campaign that shrank from no coarseness. If the press campaign struck an echo in America that was not beneficial to Germany's interests, the Holy

See was not responsible for that development. Pacelli proceeded to affirm that certain parts of Mundelein's remarks that dealt with making political capital out of certain morality trials were in substance irrefutable. He lamented the different treatment of accused ecclesiastics and members of the Nazi party and State organizations with show trials for the former and secret proceedings for the latter. Returning to Mundelein, Pacelli emphasized that the Cardinal of Chicago assumed full personal responsibility for what he had said. Pacelli explained, «As a Bishop he is admittedly under the authority of the Holy See, but he is no functionary of the Holy See like a nuncio or Apostolic Delegate». Developing this distinction, Pacelli said that the Holy See itself and its official representatives scrupulously observed the boundary between factual and personal controversies. In agreement with these principles Mundelein stated that he would have omitted certain personal remarks if he had intended the speech for the public. As an American citizen he claimed for himself, especially in opposition to the excesses of the German propaganda against the Church and to the harsh criticisms of other political groups against the institutions of his country, the right on his side to make critical evaluations and to point out to his fellow citizens the peculiarities of differently constructed State systems. In conclusion Pacelli reasserted that the Holy See had not refused and would not refuse to discuss this case but insisted that it not be torn out of the factual and psychological circumstances that characterized it. He said that a diplomatic discussion of the case had sense and a prospect of success only if the whole series of causes out of which the present conflict situation had evolved would be examined in calm and objectivity. In that frank exchange of views a way could be found to eliminate the complex of causes that were at the origin of the present tension[32].

This draft was printed and sent out to the other Cardinals who were members of the Sacred Congregation for Extraordinary Ecclesiastical Affairs with Pacelli's covering *Relazione*, in which he cited letters from several German bishops and reviewed the sequence of events beginning with Mundelein's speech of May 18 and ending with a summary of Mgr. Ready's memorandum[33]. All the documents to which he referred were printed in the attached *Sommario*. The Cardinals of the congregation were

---

[32] AES, America, 1937-1938, POS. 247 P.O., Fasc. 88, Sommario, Num XII, German text, pp. 51-57, Italian translation, pp. 58-64. Also in AES, Rapporti delle Sessioni, 1937, Vol. 92, numero 11376, stampa 1971, Num. XII of the Sommario, 51-64, and Arch. Deleg. Stati Uniti, POS. 166b, printed texts, 5-12 (German) and 13-30 (Italian).

[33] AES, America, 1937-1938, POS. 247 P.O., Fasc. 88, Relazione, 3-11.

asked to answer the following question: What position is advisable for the Holy See to hold after the note of the embassy of Germany of May 29, 1937[34]? The secretary of the Sacred Congregation, Archbishop Giuseppe Pizzardo, notified the Cardinals on June 17 that a plenary session of the Congregation would be held on Sunday, June 20, in the Pontifical Palace at Castelgandolfo in the presence of the Holy Father to examine the attached reports. This letter was sent to fifteen Cardinals other than Pacelli; they were all Italians, and the majority of them had been nuncios or Apostolic Delegates[35]. The opinions of nine Cardinals besides Pacelli who attended the plenary session have been preserved in one form or another. Ten Cardinals besides Pacelli attended the meeting. The Subdean of the Sacred College, Donato Sbarretti, who was also Secretary of the Supreme Sacred Congregation of the Holy Office, was absent, as well as Enrico Gasparri, Prefect of the Supreme Tribunal of the Apostolic Signature, Angelo Maria Dolci, Archpriest of the Patriarchal Liberian Basilica (St. Mary Major), and Nicola Canali. Francesco Marchetti-Selvaggiani, Vicar General of His Holiness for the City of Rome, who had been auditor of the Apostolic Delegation in Washington, internuncio in Venezuela, and the first nuncio to the new Republic of Austria, was also absent, but he had expressed his opinion in a private conversation with a *minutante* of the Sacred Congregation and of Section I of the Secretariat of State, Luigi Valentini, who then wrote a memorandum. The Cardinal thought that the form of publishing the encyclical *Mit brennender Sorge* in Germany was less appropriate («meno conveniente») since it dealt with a government with which the Holy See had diplomatic relations. He deplored that in a moment when the German Reich was trying to acquire world-wide trust, it was publicly declared by the Holy See to have broken faith («fedifrago»). Convinced that one could not clash with the Government of the Reich, Marchetti-Selvaggiani proposed that in a most confidential manner the Holy See suggest to Cardinal Mundelein that he, as if of his own spontaneous initiative, declare that with his words he did not intend to arouse such a squabble, that he did not have the least intention of offending the Reich Government, that if in improvising his remarks he let some less fitting words slip out, it was contrary to his intention. Otherwise, Marchetti-Selvaggiani feared, the storm would be unloaded on the Holy See with grave

---

[34] *Ibidem*, Relazione, 11.
[35] N. 2225/37, mimeographed, AES, America, 1937-1938, POS. 247 P.O., Fasc. 88, fol. 11r.

harm to the German Catholics[36]. Obviously he was advocating appeasement, and in relation to the other Cardinals he was singing *extra chorum*. He «had studied with Pacelli and was considered one of the most skilled diplomats in the Curia»[37]. According to Bishop Alois Hudal, the rector of the German Church of Santa Maria dell'Anima in Rome, the Cardinal believed an «open battle against the NS to be inopportune because of its repercussions in Italy, whose Fascist Party was becoming ever more dangerously dependent on Berlin»[38].

At the plenary session of the Sacred Congregation on June 20 the Cardinals presumably spoke in order of seniority. The first would have been the Cardinal Bishop Gennaro Granito Pignatelli di Belmonte, Dean of the Sacred College and Prefect of the Sacred Ceremonial Congregation, who had been nuncio in Belgium and had taken part in several papal missions to England and other countries and was now eighty-six years old[39]. After expressing his satisfaction with Pius XI's encyclical, which had raised spirits in Germany, he replied to the question in the *Relazione* that the draft of a reply was suitable («degno») and thorough («esauriente»). After it would be presented it to the German embassy, he recommended that it be published in the «Acta Apostolicae Sedis» and translated into various languages because that would upset the Nazi schemes[40].

Next the Cardinal priest Camillo Laurenti, Prefect of the Sacred Congregation of Rites, said that from the study of the lucid and careful report and from the attached documents two things appeared clearly: (1) the gravity of the religious situation in Germany and (2) the need for a firm position in regard to religion and a prudent position in regard to the political question. After praising Pius XI's encyclical, which defended the rights of God and the Church and enlightened and comforted the German Catholics, he said that Cardinal Mundelein's speech was certainly inspired by a most noble purpose and had produced great good in the United States, exposing before the Catholics and also the Protestants the disgraceful campaign against the Church in Germany. Laurenti thought, however, that perhaps some expressions seemed to be less felicitous, having too personal a target. Still even from that some advantages might follow, the first being that the harm that would result to the prestige of Germany abroad from the reli-

---

[36] June 5, 1937, *ibidem*, fol. 54r.

[37] H. WOLF, *Pope and Devil...*, 262.

[38] A.C. HUDAL, *Römische Tagebücher: Lebensbeichte eines alten Bischofs*, Graz-Stuttgart 1976, 121.

[39] *Dizionario Biografico degli Italiani*, Vol. 58 (2002), 543-545.

[40] AES, Rapporti delle Sessioni, 1937, Vol. 92, No. 1376, 2 (typewritten).

gious persecution being waged against the Church would be better understood by the Government, if it wished to understand. The great advantage,
in Laurenti's opinion, was precisely this discussion between the Holy See
and the German Government to which Mundelein's speech gave rise. The
notes presented by the German embassy on the subject provided the occasion for the beautiful reply prepared by the Secretariat of State, which
clarified so many points and took an opportune position. Laurenti thought
it was a dignified, clear, cogent reply that, seizing the opportunity from
this case, accepted the discussion, framing it in all the circumstances and
opening the way to sincere diplomatic negotiations, which could lead to
some good results. If, through the bad faith of others, that did not happen,
the good will of the Holy See was safe. Laurenti assented to the prepared
reply but noted that in its sober and dignified style here and there some
words appeared that were somewhat forceful («vibrante»), at least in the
Italian version, that could be slightly softened. In conclusion he said that
the position of the Holy See was always firm[41].

Cardinal Lorenzo Lauri, the Major Penitentiary and Camerlengo of the
Sacred College, who had been nuncio in Peru and Poland, quoted the German Government's note, which asserted that «the premise for a normalization of relations was removed», and he replied that the Holy See had
nothing to change in its noble, prudent position of protest against errors,
of exhortation to the faithful who remained unshakable in their faith and
closely united with their bishops, and of encouragement of the Catholics
who did not fear the persecutions. Lauri believed that the Apostolic Nun-
tiature in Germany should be maintained in every circumstance, because
the Catholics saw in it the presence of the Holy Father and the person most
qualified to transmit information to Rome and to transmit the directives
of the Holy See. In regard to Mundelein's speech Lauri observed that the
note of the German Government threatened consequences if nothing were
done. He distinguished two aspects: (1) The doctrinal part of the speech
was sound, and the Holy See was solidly with him; the Fuehrer could not
demand that the Holy See renounce its defense of him. (2) The personal
criticisms were a matter for Mundelein to handle. Bishops, he asserted,
were not representatives of the Holy See; only when they acted as such
was the Holy See responsible. Concluding his remarks, Lauri approved
the reply, in which a complete diplomatic discussion was requested on the
occasion of the Mundelein case. That would demonstrate that the Holy
See had not failed to use the means of clarifying the situation. But good

---

[41] *Ibidem.*

will on the Government's part was necessary. The Holy See was not the cause of the commotion; the responsibility fell on the German Government, which had aroused the Catholics to defend themselves[42].

Next, Cardinal Raffaello Carlo Rossi, Secretary of the Sacred Consistorial Congregation, had the floor. He thought that the German Government wanted to break diplomatic relations while blaming the Holy See and that Mundelein's speech – or, rather, the lack of reproof and, perhaps, of reparation, on the part of the Holy See – offered a pretext. Rossi argued that the Holy See had no reason to reprove or, in relation to the German Government, to repair. Nevertheless, he believed that the Holy See had to respond and could not maintain a silence that would lend itself to wrong interpretations. On the other hand, he considered it necessary once again to remind that Government that it had reason to reprove itself precisely for what it was reproving others. Therefore, Rossi concluded that it was fitting to transmit the proposed reply as it was composed, although he modestly observed that he would omit the allusions to the United States Government at the end of the third and ninth paragraphs. He asked himself what effect this note would produce; perhaps not a good one, he averred; still he believed that silence would produce a worse effect. If nothing else, it would enter into the documentation that one day could demonstrate to the world the patient forbearance and the constant rectitude of the Holy See[43]. One would have to call Rossi's judgment of the situation realistic.

The Prefect of the Sacred Congregation of the Council, Cardinal Giulio Serafini, began his comments by vigorously deploring all that the German Government was carrying out against the Catholic Religion and in a special way against its bishops, clergy, and institutions. He thanked God for having inspired the Pope, who was listening, to write the great encyclical that had brought so much light and comfort to the Catholics of that sorely tried nation, and he applauded the German episcopate, which with apostolic courage and perfect union of mind and heart with the Holy See was waging the good battle of the Lord. Finally, he praised the Secretariat of State for its diligent, prompt, and prudent work in this case. His reply to the *dubbio* was that his first impression was that the Holy See should pay no heed to the German note of May 29, but since the Secretary of State had not refused in principle (wisely and prudently, in Serafini's opinion) to take into consideration the remonstrances of the German Government, especially the official note, which maintained that the Holy See wished

---

[42] *Ibidem*, 3-4.
[43] AES, America, 1937-1938, POS. 247 P.O., Fasc. 90, fols. 27r-v, 28r.

to put aside a reply as if it were short of arguments or did not know what to answer, Serafini thought that in the present state of affairs a reply of the Holy See was highly opportune. He considered the draft suitable to confirm publicly with the proviso, on the example of Germany, to publish with this reply its first reply, that the oral reply did not contain a refusal to be concerned with the present case. The drafted reply also seemed to Serafini to be suitable because it offered a favorable occasion to put things in their true light and at the same time to request explanations of so many other things that had happened contrary to the Concordat. The drafted reply was well suited to bring the German Government back to safeguard the principle of reciprocity of respect for the Head of the Catholic Church and ecclesiastical authorities, because it was precisely the need for honor that the German Government claimed for itself as an essential premise for a sincere reciprocity. Furthermore, the reply to the German note could avoid the danger that failure to respond could furnish a pretext for asserting that the Holy See was the first not to desire and will a normal order of diplomatic relations with the German Government, as was insinuated in the note of May 29. Serafini was all the more convinced of the opportuneness of the reply on the part of the Holy See insofar as the note drafted by the Secretariat of State took no account of what was asserted in the German note, namely, that the Holy See should have distanced itself from the remarks of Cardinal Mundelein and corrected them and expressed its regret, as had always been the proper international custom. Hence, Serafini concluded that the Holy See should reply to the German note of May 29 and do so with the note drafted by the Secretariat of State, which summed up so well the explanation of the case and offered sure and solid elements for normalizing the situation, that is, for restoring good and friendly relations between the German State and the Holy See[44]. Thus Serafini fully supported Pacelli.

The next speaker, Cardinal Pietro Fumasoni-Biondi, Prefect of the Sacred Congregation *de Propaganda Fide*, had been Apostolic Delegate in the United States from 1922 to 1933 and knew Mundelein well. From a careful reading of the *Sommario* he was convinced that the Reich Government wanted to break official relations with the Holy See and was striving to have it believed that breaking relations was a consequence of the action of the Holy See itself. For that reason he found very appropriate the detailed reply prepared by the Secretariat of State to the German note of

---

[44] AES, IV periodo, Rapporti delle Sessioni, 1937, Vol. 92, numero 1376, no folio number (handwritten on stationery of his Congregation).

May 29. He said that Mundelein's speech had not been intended for publication, but when it came to the knowledge of the public, especially after the publicity given it by the Reich Government, it roused the applause not only of the American Catholics and bishops of German descent but of the most important Catholic journals of the country and of the greatest newspapers such as the «New York Sun» (May 22), and even of Protestants and Jews, as was reported by the Bulletin of the National Catholic Welfare Conference News Service. Referring to Mundelein's letter to Cicognani, Fumasoni-Biondi said that if the Cardinal had prepared his speech for the press, he would have left out the personal allusions to the Fuehrer, which were those that got on the nerves of the German Government. If those expressions, which were, Fumasoni-Biondi averred, of an absolutely nonpolitical-religious nature, pronounced by an American citizen making use of the freedom guaranteed him by the Constitution, raised questions, such questions should be cleared up, if need be, between Berlin and Washington and not between Berlin and the Holy See. He commended the draft for pointing out that a Bishop, while subject to the authority of the Holy See as a Bishop, was not a functionary of it as were the nuncios and Apostolic Delegates. Therefore, he approved the draft, which was so well reasoned and set forth with such grace that it should not push the Reich Government to retaliation and even to the breaking of diplomatic relations. Considering the ill will of the Reich Government, Fumasoni-Biondi saw the great opportuneness of having all the documents ready and collecting them in a white book that at the proper moment could quickly be made known to the world against further injuries to the Catholic religion[45]. This was a practical suggestion.

The longest *voto* was that presented by Cardinal Federico Tedeschini, who had been nuncio in Spain from 1922 to 1935. He dwelt on the triple consequences of the note of the German embassy: (1) those openly begun, namely, the rupture or at least the interruption of normal diplomatic relations between the German Government and the Curia, for which the Curia itself would be made fully responsible; (2) the consequences that were already concomitant with the present deplorable state of affairs in Germany, namely, to suppress religious instruction and, where it had already been suppressed, to justify the suppression, to snatch the Catholic youth away from the Church, and to force it to be educated by the State, and *«that State»*; and to destroy all trust between the Church and the faithful

---

[45] *Ibidem*, no folio number (handwritten on stationery of his Congregation).

and between parents and churchmen; (3) the consequences that were in the aims of the Reich Ministry of Propaganda and were known confidentially, namely, to forbid all Catholic publications, to impose previous censorship on diocesan bulletins, to establish the placet for pastoral letters and even for encyclicals, and to appeal to a popular vote to decide whether religious houses should continue to exist; this, united to the preceding measures, would be equivalent to suppressing the Catholics so that, as Goebbels expressed it «in his infernal speech», the Germans would no longer appear as Catholics or anything else, but above and before all as Germans and children of the German conception which was the enemy of Catholicism[46]. Tedeschini predicted that if the Holy See would not yield to the orders of this haughty government, the Church would be harassed with all the forces of perfidy and Government propaganda of this new Julian the Apostate and pushed to take a step backwards far worse than under Luther, for then it was a retrogression from Catholicism to simple Christianity, while now it would be to the denial of Christ. Nevertheless, with or without the Mundelein speech as also with or without the note of that tyrannical («prepotente») government, this was the aim of the German Government, which, perhaps without being aware of it, was laying all the foundations, all the principles, and all the precedents that would inevitably lead to the denial of all religion and the establishment of Bolshevism. Leaving aside these intentions of the German Government, Tedeschini said he would restrict himself to its note, or its ultimatum, and asserted that in spite of the threats and the seen or unforeseen or unforeseeable consequences, the Holy See should not yield or be frightened or fall at the feet of the government. Rather it should continue in the firm and prudent position in which it placed itself from the first moment, that is, May 24, with the wise and suitable response of the Cardinal Secretary of State; it should by no means play the game of the Government and by making any comment whatsoever on the brave («valoroso») Cardinal Mundelein approve all the iniquities committed by that Government against the Church.

Tedeschini noted that the German Government with its two notes of May 24 and 29 had done nothing but show the excessive haste that inflated and spread the incident beyond all measure and demonstrate that it was

---

[46] Cf. «Sanzioni governative che verrebbero prese se la Santa Sede non volesse cedere nel caso Mundelein», AES, America, 1937-1938, POS. 247 P.O., Fasc. 88, fol. 9ʳ, Numero di Protocollo 2326. «Sanktionen für den Fall Mundelein», which according to circles in the Reichspropagandaministerium, were to be implemented in case Rome would not yield. Typewritten half-page, *ibidem*, no folio number.

seeking every means and every pretext to reach as quickly as possible and with a pretense of legality the goal that it had in view for years and for years was pursuing and that after the publication of the providential and inspired encyclical of March 14 it wanted to attain all the more rapidly and avidly because it was incited by the spirit of revenge. Indeed, how could it have reasonably expected a reply to the note of May 24, in any case imprecise, vague, and only narrative, after only five days for an incident that happened in America and that did not have for the Church more importance than that of one of the innumerable little sermons that a Bishop preaches to his priests? Perhaps Tedeschini was disingenuous, since Mundelein's little talk obviously had exceptional importance. In any case, he continued, asking how to find the lesser proportion between the confidential and paternal address delivered *in camera caritatis* by Cardinal Mundelein without the least intention of going beyond the walls of that hall on the one hand and on the other the enormous publicity that the Government gave it, thereby creating new harm to the Church, an irreparable discredit to the politics and prestige of the German people. He was convinced that this maneuver responded to a predetermined object, seeing that in so many other cases the Government had allowed the Church and its head to be insulted and had itself insulted them without ever deigning to give satisfaction or even a reply, while now, for such a trifling motive, not imputable to the Holy See, it came to say after only five days that normal relations lacked a basis.

Tedeschini contended that the German Government, feeling offended by Mundelein's speech, had three ways to obtain satisfaction: (1) the way of the American Government, (2) the way of the Holy See, and (3) the way of the accused himself. It went down the first road and came back empty-handed. It jumped over the third, which was the most logical but would have had the same result. It lurched headfirst into the second way, taking revenge on the innocent and deluding itself that it could have two advantages: to shorten the course that it had set itself for years against the German Church and to come out justified in its persecution and justified in addition by the Church itself, guilty of weakness and foolishness («dabbenaggine»). That the American Government had done well to feign ignorance («a fare l'indiano») was not a matter of discussion. That the German Government would have done well to turn to Cardinal Mundelein himself Tedeschini judged to be evident, because it was a question that concerned him as a Cardinal since he had defended the Church but also as a free American citizen; these conditions he assumed to be privileges that the Holy See would not think of taking away and the Cardinal would not understand how they could be renounced. But the German Government would not do this, because the Cardinal would reply in the American fashion, surely giving some other lessons. The Cardinal, Tedeschini repeated, was not a functionary of the Secretariat of State; he was a dignitary who spoke on his own behalf, who spoke in defense of the Church, who spoke according to the customs, the laws, and the character of the Americans. He urged the Government to address Mundelein, who would not refuse to give an account. But what Tedeschini found inadmissible was that the German Government had recourse to the Holy See and did so in such an overbearing and leonine manner. He went on to denounce the Government for its double standards and its demand that the Holy See disown and silence a man who rose up as a defender against the injuries, and disown him because according to American usage normally never disapproved of by anyone, he privately criticized the real objects of the persecution, of the incongruities of such persecution, and of the anomaly that the German nation presented, even on the persons who were leading it to such excesses. Any step that the Holy See would take in the direction desired by the German Government, Tedeschini asserted, would be equivalent to its moral suicide. It would show that the Holy See had no idea of its rights, which had been repeatedly and incredibly trampled upon, or of its divinely imposed duties to defend the patrimony of the faith against all. The consequence would be, he predicted, that the German Government would make a laughing stock of the Holy See that justified its executioner and condemned itself; another consequence would be that no one would dare to stand up to protest in favor of the Church and against the persecutors.

On the other hand, Tedeschini professed not to see how the German Government could complain about Mundelein's words, first because they were caused by the Government itself, and then because in those times no Government could aspire to be immune to honest and serene criticism. Looking concretely at Mundelein's expressions regarding the head of the German Government and State, Tedeschini claimed (presumably with tongue in cheek) not to see anything really offensive. That Hitler was Austrian and had been a paperhanger was an honor for him because he rose to be head of the Government. Tedeschini admitted that Mundelein's comment that a nation of 60,000,000 inhabitants, an intelligent people, was following with slavish fear a *condottiero* who was leading it astray could and did damage Germany's prestige, but it was said out of love for that people and out of a desire for its good and reputation, all the more so inasmuch as the speaker was of German descent and a proven benefactor of that people in the most tragic period of its history. Tedeschini went on in this line of thought, excusing and even justifying Mundelein, which would hardly have been useful in a diplomatic reply to the German Government's note. He insisted that the only course that the Government could and should follow was to ask Mundelein the reason for his speech. With rhetorical flourishes Tedeschini warned against suffocating the protest against the injuries done to the Mystical Body of Christ and silencing the apostolic voices through the signature of the August Pontiff through that of the Secretary of State, no matter what sacrifice it might cost. He commended the Holy See and the Secretariat of State for having conducted themselves as good soldiers and apostles of Christ, and said that the draft of a reply deserved not only approval but also praise and applause as a diplomatically, historically, and religiously effective and sober composition. He remarked that the Holy See had done well to recall that it personally never made personal or political assertions, thus separating its own style and responsibility from those that might be the American style, which, moreover, had so many and notorious justifications that no one would dare to disapprove of it. Tedeschini also agreed that the Holy See should show itself to be ready for the diplomatic discussion hypocritically desired by the Government, but a discussion that would serenely examine the whole complex of causes that led to the present conflict without glossing over the Government's persecutions and injustices and putting a gag on public criticism and the protests of good men. Tedeschini concluded, saying that he would assent to the draft except the reference to the American Government and, in general, expressions that could have some slight revision of details[47]. His analysis of the German Government's motives and designs was, if prolix, certainly correct.

In contrast to his verbosity the next speaker, Cardinal Enrico Sibilia, who had been Apostolic Delegate and then internuncio in Chile and, following Marchetti-Selvaggiani, nuncio in Austria, simply recommended the dignified firmness and strength proper to the Holy See in the position it should hold, and the temperate, suave, and gentle («dolce») form characteristic of papal diplomacy. He did not think a reply was necessary, but if it were made necessary he would have it much more strengthened in substance and well drawn up in form. He observed that the responsibility belonged exclusively to the German Government[48].

---

[47] AES, IV periodo, Rapporti delle Sessioni, 1937, No. 92, fascicolo inserito, 1-10.

[48] Apparently a summary of his remarks written for the minutes of the meeting, *ibidem*, 5. Alois Hudal called him an elderly Cardinal who had grown up in the service of the Curia (p. 269).

Cardinal Francesco Marmaggi, who had been nuncio in Poland, admitted that what he would have liked to say had already been said by his eminent colleagues, and said better than he could have said it. That admission did not deter him from underlining, in his words, some points that seemed to merit particular attention. He considered the question in three regards. First, from that of the «Hitlerian Government» he declared a reply to the note of the German embassy to be necessary; it should be elevated, serene, firm, and conciliatory in the sense of precluding further explanations. He recognized that the design of the reply satisfied these criteria admirably and followed this tactic. He thought that such calm was required all the more insofar as the adversary had lost his temper, and understandably. Hitler had conceived the dream of the pagan unification of Germany and had pursued it with the schemes in the single school and state education of the young. Then came the papal encyclical, which he called not only the strongest challenge to Nazism but its tombstone as doctrine. Learned Germany could give in opposition only foolish statements and spiteful actions; therefore, in its present position were seen vengeance, reprisal, violence, which he thought of their nature should be exhausted quickly. The reaction was to try to deprive the Church and particularly the clergy of its reputation and trust through the trials for currency crimes[49] and immorality, and then perhaps also the (Catholic) statesmen. In Marmaggi's opinion the violence had eclipsed the *Kulturkampf* and could only recall the conflicts that devastated Germany for more than a century after Luther's Reformation. Secondly, he pointed out, the Holy See had given an incomparable comfort and brilliant guidance to the German episcopate, clergy, and people. Besides this, it had providentially laid the basis of a united front for all upright and right-thinking persons and for bringing the Protestants closer to the Catholic Church. He urged continued assistance to the persecuted Catholics in this singular terrible trial, all the more so because, according to estimations, in half of the German nation the Christian faith was in immediate danger. The Church should also protect itself, ur-

---

[49] Confronted with the problem of currency exchange during the depression of the 1930s, the German Government had issued complicated regulations regarding sending funds abroad. Many male and female religious orders had mother houses or supported missions in other countries «or had simply incurred debts abroad. They felt honor-bound to meet their financial obligations, and there is no question that at times they did not abide by the currency regulations. [...] Nazi propaganda equated currency smuggling with monasticism, although secular clergy were also involved» as well as religious women. E.C. HELMREICH, *The German Churches under Hitler: Background, Struggle, and Epilogue*, Detroit 1979, 278.

gently and severely, against a multiplication of cases of immorality, which at least in part had played into the hands of the Government against the Church. Thirdly, Marmaggi deemed it important to arouse the interest and stimulate the activity and diligence of the nuncios and representatives especially in friendly or neutral states in opposition to Germany, so that the opinion of the respective bishops, governments, diplomatic corps, press, and public might have the true and right understanding of this conflict[50]. Marmaggi at least contributed some practical advice to the discussion.

The last speaker, Cardinal Luigi Maglione, who had been nuncio first in Switzerland and then in France and at this time was President of the Cardinalitial Commission for the Administration of the Property of the Holy See, merely proposed some modifications of the draft[51].

Cardinal Pacelli then gave some information that had arrived after the *ponenza* had been printed. In particular he read Cicognani's report of June 11 and mentioned recent events in Germany. At this point the Pope spoke, saying that his Secretary of State could not be praised enough and that if there was any harshness in his writings, the Pope had wanted it[52]. He added that through the constant habit of the past to have contacts with the élites of the German intellectual world, they knew that these élites were more pessimistic than the Pope in judging their government; they were simply disorientated, humiliated, and did not believe that Germans could go so low. Pacelli then spoke again about affairs in Germany. As far as the note under consideration was concerned, he promised that all the modifications suggested by the Cardinals would be introduced and expressed his sincere gratitude for them. He said that the Holy See had the right to publish the note, and Pius XI added, «right that begins to become a duty». Pacelli continued, saying that a representative of the Austrian Legation in Berlin had asked someone in the German ministry what would happen if the Holy See did not reply or did not give satisfaction; the answer was that he did not believe that Germany would push matters to break relations[53].

---

[50] AES, IV periodo, Rapporti delle Sessioni, 1937, Vol. 92, numero 1376, no folio number.

[51] AES, 1937-1938, POS. 247 P.O., Fasc. 90, fol. 26r.

[52] It had been rumored that there was a difference of opinions between the Pope and the Secretary of State, but Pius's praise of Pacelli contradicted such rumors. A. MARTINI, SJ, *Pio XII e Hitler*, in «La Civiltà Cattolica», 116 (1965)/1, 345.

[53] AES, IV periodo, Rapporti delle Sessioni, 1937, Vol. 92, fascicolo inserito, 5-6. The deletions, substitutions, and corrections in Pacelli's handwriting are given with the pagination (51-57) of No. XII of the Sommario, *ibidem.*

At the end of the session the Holy Father thanked the divine goodness and then those who were the instrument of that goodness. After having followed attentively the things written, read, and said, he saw the goodness of the Lord in making him note the marvelous agreement of the Sacred College, of those present who represented it, which was the constant norm of making the interests of the Church and of souls [prevail] and of doing it with due firmness and authority. In second place the Pope observed with great joy, satisfaction, and consolation their opinion in what the Holy See should do (not what it could do) in such difficult conditions in history for the spouse and body of Christ. Pius XI welcomed their filial comforting desire which was a shove to the old father that he not fail to do what the harsh hardness of the conditions required. That was what in those times more than ever he had renewed the intention to do, even in view of the approaching end of his pontificate, so that the King, the Head of that divine body, might not find him too far below the Pope's duty and Christ's expectations. As they had done with their enlightened counsel and proposals, he counted on their prayers that would accompany him in the days that still awaited him according to God's will, but that could not be but few. On that somber note he gave them the apostolic blessing[54].

On June 25 Pacelli handed the final version of the note, dated June 24, to the German chargé d'affaires, Fritz Menshausen[55]. The two Vatican notes were not made public, and the Holy See continued to attempt to carry on diplomatic relations with the German Government through the nuncio in Berlin, Cesare Orsenigo, who continued to lodge complaints with the Foreign Ministry but received no or only evasive replies. The Government did not consider the relations to be normal, because it had not received satisfaction from the Vatican.

A few days previously the ambassador of Italy to the Holy See, Count Bonifacio Pignatti Morando di Custoza, had passed on to Pacelli a summary of a report of his colleague Bernardo Attolico, the Italian ambassador to Germany, who asserted that the Cardinal of Chicago had caused «a very acute phase» in the relations between Germany and the Holy See by insulting Hitler. Claiming that up to now the Third Reich had wished to avoid a break, the ambassador predicted that after the statements interpreted or at least presented as offensive not only to the Fuehrer but also to the whole German people, the government would push its investiga-

---

[54] AES, Rapporti delle Sessioni, 1937, Vol. 92, fascicolo inserito, 7-8.
[55] German text in Albrecht, No. 7, 24-30; English translation in DGFP, No. 660, 976-981.

tions of the religious orders to the extreme and would find a way to shut some down; the program of unifying schools would be quickly brought to completion, and thus the Concordat would be emptied of all its essential contents. Attolico deemed it certain that any further reaction on the part of the German clergy would bring about not only a complete rupture but even open strife in the streets and churches. The Vatican would not be able to rely on the youth of the Catholic families who were all swept away while inside Germany. The Ambassador went on to repeat the German Governement's complaints about Pacelli's conduct regarding its protest and said that the Government did not think it proper to publish the Vatican response lest it further poison the situation[56]. Three days later Pignatti forwarded Attolico's report saying that he had learned from confidential sources that the Government and party circles displayed great optimism over the conflict. The Catholics in the Government and party were not taking up the question because they were afraid of being accused of militant Catholicism; only some of them deplored the conduct of many pastors who insisted on carrying on anti-Nazi politics. Always sympathetic with Hitler, Attolico thought that the Cancellor's good disposition should be supported by a less rigid attitude on the Vatican's part[57].

Meanwhile Cardinal Mundelein continued to warn and forearm American Catholics against the danger of developments similar to those in Germany. Speaking at a retreat for the clergy on June 20, 1937, he recalled the supreme effort being made in countries where violent changes had placed a new kind of government in the saddle, whether «communist or so-called fascist», to take the youth away from the control of the Church and have them regimented by the State. Even more significant he declared was «the forcible attempt at taking over by the State of Catholic schools, converting them into non-sectarian schools» over which the Church had no influence. That was, in his opinion, precisely the crux of the situation in Germany. The Nazis' «unprecedented zeal in punishing more offenders in religious garb – who in most cases have already been punished by the Church – is

---

[56] Pignatti forwards Attolico's report, June 21, 1937, AES, Germania, POS. 720 P.O., fasc. 329, fols. 15r-16r, as cited in G. BESIER, *The Holy See and Hitler's Germany*, translated by W.R. Ward, New York 2007, 168; E. FATTORINI, *Pio XI, Hitler e Mussolini: La solitudine di un papa*, Turin 2007, 150, and P. GODMAN, *Hitler and the Vatican: inside the Secret Archives that Reveal the New Story of the Nazis and the Church*, New York 2004, 153; cf. G. BESIER, *Die Kirchen und das Dritte Reich: Spaltungen und Abwehrkämpfe, 1934-1937*, Berlin 2001, 799 ff.

[57] Pignatti forwards Attolico's report, June 30, 1937, AES, Germania, POS. 720 P.O., Fasc. 329, fols. 17r, 18r, 19r. 150.

not a sudden burst of virtue on the part of these politicians whose skirts are none too clean themselves [...] but it is a smokescreen to cover their steal [*sic*] of the children from their church and religious influence». He devoted the rest of his address to the priests' obligation to foster Catholic schools in the archdiocese[58]. It is notable that he did not denounce Hitler or any other Nazi leader by name.

It might seem strange that in all the correspondence generated by Mundelein's speech of May 18 there was no exchange of letters between him and Pacelli on the subject[59]. The Cardinal in Chicago did, however, receive some information about attitudes of Roman ecclesiastics. The Reverend Peter A. Schaetz of St. Alphonsus Church in Brooklyn, an old friend from the Cardinal's years in that diocese, wrote to him from Rome. He first reported on his recent sojourn in Germany, where, he said, the Cardinal's courageous stand was a godsend to the leaders of the Church. Everywhere he went he heard, «The Cardinal of Chicago has done the Catholics of Germany a great act of charity». In Rome Father Schaetz «had several opportunities to be present when prelates of importance were at dinner». Mundelein's «remarks always formed the topic of conversation», and all agreed that he had spoken in time»[60].

More specific and detailed about one prelate of importance was the long letter that Bishop James E. Walsh, Superior General of the Maryknoll Missioners since the previous year, wrote to Mundelein late in June. He had been in Rome when the Cardinal's «comment on the Nazi regime was reported in the papers of the world», and he had «chanced to witness a little reaction» that he was now passing on. He had conversed with Cardinal Fumasoni-Biondi at some length and had found him jubilant. He quoted the Cardinal as calling Mundelein's speech «the best thing that ever happened», and the Roman curialist continued:

«If I were in America, I would urge Cardinal Mundelein to continue. If the Nazi government could be made to feel the disapproval of the strong German element in America, it might have a great effect. It is perhaps the one hope, as the Nazis have proved impervious to all reason. They will not let any breath of fresh air get in from outside, unless it comes in some unusual form they cannot ignore. Meanwhile our own hands are rather tied here as we are "half-

---

[58] AAC, Chancery Correspondence Collection, Box 43845.06, Folder 14, No. 140.

[59] Pacelli did write to Mundelein on June 5, 1937, to thank him for his letter of May 3 and the «doppia offerta» that accompanied it for the Pope's birthday, but he did not allude to the famous speech. AAC, Personal Correspondence, Box 5, Folder 43.

[60] Schätz to Mundelein, Rome, June 15, 1937, handwritten, AAC, Personal Correspondence, Box 5, Folder 44.

friends" with Germany, on account of their cooperation against Communism in Spain. Of course, such criticism may incense them a bit. But we feel that there is nothing to lose, as the situation is so bad already that it can scarcely get any worse. And there is always the hope that it may wake them up to see the light».

Walsh asked Fumasoni-Biondi for permission to cable «this word of encouragement» to Mundelein in view of the possible adverse criticism that the Chicago Cardinal might be subjected to in some quarters, but «Fumasoni-Biondi demurred at that saying the question pertained officially to the Secretary of State, and that he was only giving his personal opinion in a matter that did not directly concern him». Later in the conversation, however, Walsh returned to his request and «was led to feel that Fumasoni-Biondi would not object to such a confidential reference to his reaction» as Walsh gave Mundelein in his letter. It was Walsh's «strong impression» that Fumasoni-Biondi's opinion was shared generally by ecclesiastical circles in Rome. He also believed that the Holy See was even more worried about Germany than about Spain. At the end of his letter Walsh complimented Mundelein, saying that it was inspiring «to see somebody not afraid to fight for the Church»[61].

The tinderbox of tense relations between the Holy See and Germany was ignited by Pius XI himself when he received in the general audience at Castelgandolfo on July 17 a group of pilgrims from Chicago who had traveled to Rome after attending the French National Eucharistic Congress in Lisieux. Addressing them, the Pope said he was pleased «to recall the greatness of their city and also – why not say it – of their magnificent («magnifico») Cardinal Archbishop, so solicitous and zealous in the defense of the rights of God and of the Church and for the salvation of souls»[62]. The German Ambassador, Diego von Bergen, who had returned to Rome, reported Pius XI's remarks to the German Foreign Ministry on July 20[63], and the next day August von Mackensen replied from Berlin that the Pope's address was «in striking contrast with the need, asserted in the note of June 24 from the Vatican on the Mundelein case, for a frank and objective exchange of views, and for the elimination of speeches which

---

[61] Walsh to Mundelein, Maryknoll, New York, June 28, 1937, typewritten, AAC, Personal Correspondence, Box 5, Folder 45. No reply of Mundelein exists in AAC.

[62] «L'Osservatore Romano», Vol. 77 (Monday-Tuesday, July 19-20, 1937), *Nostre Informazioni*, 1. Pacelli was the Pope's personal legate to the congress and dedicated the Basilica of St. Thérèse. See Bonney, Newsletter 62, July 26, 1937.

[63] DGFP, No. 665, 989.

disturb discussion». With irony Mackensen said that the Foreign Ministry had to consider the Pope's discourse as an authoritative interpretation of the methods by which the Curia was striving for a normalization of the situation. He wrote that an equivocal reaction from Berlin was inevitable, and he asked Bergen to impress this upon the Cardinal Secretary of State at the earliest opportunity[64]. The ambassador replied that «the improvised discourses of Pius XI, often delivered emotionally and with utter disregard for political considerations», had already been a nightmare for the previous Secretary of State, Cardinal Pietro Gasparri, and that Pacelli had not «succeeded in persuading the aging, self-willed, and irascible Pope to exercise greater caution and reserve in his discourses». Bergen was «convinced that the content and form of the welcoming words of the Pope to the pilgrims from Chicago [had] caused unpleasant surprise in the Secretariat of State». He came to this conclusion from the fact, which he had learned confidentially, that publication in «L'Osservatore Romano» was postponed for two days and occurred only after a consultation with the Pope and after a slight change in the text; actually, Pius XI did not call Mundelein «solicitous and zealous» in the defense of the rights of God and of the Church but rather «courageous»[65]. The change hardly placated the German Government.

Bergen went on to relate his first call on Pacelli after his return to Rome, on July 16, the day before the papal audience. He said that Pacelli had received him «with decided friendliness» and had assured him that normal and friendly relations with Germany would be restored as soon as possible; this applied particularly to the Cardinal, «who had spent thirteen years in Germany and had always shown the greatest sympathy for the German people»[66]. Pacelli stated that he would be prepared at any time for a discussion with outstanding personages such as the Foreign Minister (Baron Konstantin von Neurath) and Minister President Hermann Goering. Bergen replied that he hoped the time would come when such a meeting could be arranged, but, as he wrote to Berlin, he personally considered it impossible at the present time in view of the serious controversy caused by the encyclical *Mit brennender Sorge* and other events and in view of the extreme tension. Bergen obtained another interview with Pacelli af-

---

[64] Berlin, July 21, 1937, DGFP, No. 666, 990.
[65] This is the word reported by NC Radio and recorded in the «New World», No. 30 (July 23, 1937), 1.
[66] G.O. Kent, *Pope Pius XII and Germany: Some Aspects of German-Vatican Relations, 1933-1943*, in «American Historical Review», 70 (1964), 63.

ter he received the telegram of July 21. According to the ambassador, the subject of the Pope's praise of Mundelein was «obviously very much embarrassing» to the Secretary of State, who replied that he had not been present at that audience and that he had learned of the Pope's statement only from the «Osservatore Romano». He said that the Pope, when receiving pilgrims, often praised their Bishop; thus, in the present case too, he had wanted to show his recognition of the fact that Mundelein, «sollecito e zelante», was defending the rights of the Church. Pius XI had not wished to discuss Mundelein's controversial speech, but the Cardinal had the reputation of being an excellent priest and spiritual leader. Pacelli said that the Pope's address had been interpreted by a part of the foreign press in a way different from that intended, for in reality Pius XI was referring neither to Germany nor to Mundelein's speech. In the last analysis, however, only the Pope himself could give an interpretation of his remarks[67]. On the very next day Bergen was notified by the Foreign Ministry that it had been informed by the Ministry of Justice that upon instructions from the Führer and Chancellor, until further notice, no more trials would be held in the immorality proceedings against Catholic priests[68].

---

[67] Rome, July 23, 1937, DGFP, No. 667, pp. 990-992. Also on July 23 Alexander Kirk, Counselor of the American Embassy in Rome, wrote for the Ambassador, William Phillips, to the Secretary of State, Cordell Hull, about the incident. He said that although no reference was made either in «L'Osservatore Romano» or in the Italian press to German comment in regard thereto, it was understood from foreign press sources that the German Government was angered at the Pope's reference to the anti-Nazi declarations of Cardinal Mundelein and might dispatch a further protest to the Vatican. Kirk added that the recall of the German «representative» to the Holy See had been previously scheduled as he was due for retirement, but no successor to Bergen had yet been appointed. Kirk reported the opinion «expressed in Vatican circles» that there was little hope for improvement of relations with Germany as long as persecutions of the Catholic clergy continued in that country and as long as violations of the Concordat continued. National Archives (II) at College Park, Maryland, RG 84, Records of the Foreign Service Posts of the Department of State, General Records, 1937: 840.4 – Germany, Box 26, bound volume, on spine: 1937, American Embassy Rome, Correspondence. Phillips File No. 821-840.4. Volume XXIV, carbon copy.

[68] Secretary Ernst von Weizsäcker to Bergen, Berlin, July 24, 1937, DGFP, No. 670, p. 995. Tornielli believes that this change of direction, as well as the sending of Bergen back to his post at the Vatican and the order of Rudolf Hess, Hitler's deputy in the leadership of the Nazi Party, to those in charge to refrain from any action against the Church, was due to the Fuehrer's intention to concentrate all his attention on the foreign policy of the Reich and the project of the *Anschluss* of Austria and the annexation of part of Czechoslovakia, A. TORNIELLI, *Pio XII: Eugenio Pacelli, un uomo sul trono di Pietro*, Milan 2007, 229.

In August Archbishop Pizzardo at Cardinal Pacelli's behest sent Orsenigo the German text and the Italian translation both of the note sent by the Cardinal Secretary of State to the chargé d'affaires of Germany and of the Cardinal's reply to the same official. He also supplied twenty-five copies of these documents and asked the nuncio to forward them to all the ordinaries of Germany. The purpose was to show the injustice of the accusations against the Holy See that the German press was continuing to spread in regard to the widely known speech of the Cardinal Archbishop of Chicago[69]. Acknowledging his receipt of the copy of the Cardinal Secretary's note, Orsenigo told Pizzardo that it had served him well in a recent conversation with the Ministry of Foreign Affairs[70].

The Nazis' ire against Mundelein did not abate. The journal of the Sturm Abteilung, «Der S.A. Mann», published an article attacking the Chicago Cardinal under the title *Mundelein wird unkeusch*. In September Pacelli sent a copy of this periodical to Cicognani and observed, «The insults contained in that article seem so grave that they could be grounds for a criminal charge on the part of the Cardinal. In any case Your Excellency and His Eminence will see whether such is the case»[71]. Cicognani then forwarded the copy to Mundelein and in his covering letter quoted Pacelli's comment. The delegate added that he was leaving it to the Cardinal's prudent judgment «to decide whether any attention should be paid to the article»[72]. It was only in January that Cicognani could answer Pacelli's question, since he had to wait more than three months for Mundelein to reply. He then wrote that the Most Eminent Archbishop did not intend to take any step to refute the vulgar accusations contained in the article

---

[69] Pizzardo to Orsenigo, No. 3125/37, August 7, 1937, typewritten carbon copy, AES, America, 1937-1938, POS. 247 P.O., fasc. 90, fol. 47r; draft of same, fol. 48r. In an undated draft of a letter to Orsenigo the Cardinal Secretary of State complained that the German press, even the most authorized, was continuing to take advantage of Mundelein's speech to accuse the Holy See of hostility to the Government of the Reich. Therefore, he thought it useful to send the nuncio a copy of the note that by order of the Holy Father he had sent to the German chargé d'affaires in reply to his note on the subject. *Ibidem*, fol 50.

[70] Orsenigo to Pizzardo, No. 21317, Berlin, August 20, 1937, AES, America, 1937-1938, POS. 247 P.O., fasc. 90, fol. 51ʳ. The nuncio also asked Pizzardo to thank Pacelli for what had been sent him, and he said that he had distributed the copies to the ordinaries.

[71] No. 3677/37, September 18, 1937, ASV, Arch. Deleg. Stati Uniti, POS. 166b, fol. 62r, and AES, America, 1937-1938, POS. 247 P.O., fol. 55r, carbon copy.

[72] No. 83/37, October 2, 1937, carbon copy, ASV, Arch. Deleg. Stati Uniti, POS. 166b, fol. 63r.

and still less to institute a lawsuit against the journal[73]. Pacelli replied to Cicognani that although no one in Rome put faith in the injurious assertions in the slanderous article, the Secretariat of State in transmitting the article intended only to bring it to the knowledge of the one concerned so that he could act in the way that seemed best to him. Pacelli added that he now learned from Mundelein's letter to the delegate that the Cardinal did not intend to do anything, preferring to treat those vulgar publications with disdain[74]. It is not clear whether Pacelli was pleased with Mundelein's reaction.

Officials of the German Government continued to be angry over the Holy See's failure to give it satisfaction in the Mundelein affair, and relations remained tense. Finally, in October, the Foreign Ministry decided that it did not seem «opportune to take up the Mundelein case again». Rather, it considered it to be advisable to find a new form for its relations with the Curia. Meanwhile it viewed the state of indecision in its relations with the Curia caused by the Mundelein case best suited to serve the needs of its further action[75].

During the summer vacation of the Curia, after *Ferragosto,* Pizzardo went to Montecatini Terme, where the Italian ambassador to Germany, Bernardo Attolico, had twice sought him out for a conversation. The ambassador feared that serious measures against the Church were being prepared for the forthcoming NSDAP congress in Nuremberg. He thought it would be useful for the Holy See to re-examine the Mundelein affair, which remained the heaviest blow against Germany, having touched the «Idol». The Holy See still had the appearance of standing firmly with Mundelein. Pizzardo replied that the Cardinal was not a functionary or dependent of the Holy See and the Holy See was not responsible for what he did. Attolico answered that all that was not understood in Germany and that it was necessary to clarify the matter again. Attolico could not do anything for the Church, since he had been told that the question was out-

---

[73] No. 52/38, January 23, 1938, AES, America, 1937-1938, POS. 247 P.O., fasc. 90, fol. 57r-v; also Arch. Deleg. Stati Uniti, POS. 166b, fols. 66r, 67r. Cicognani thanked Mundelein for his letter of January 19 and promised to forward the information it contained to the Cardinal Secretary of State. No. 83/37, January 24, 1938, carbon copy, ASV, Arch. Deleg. Stati Uniti, POS. 166b, fol. 71r.

[74] Pacelli to Cicognani, No. 577/38, February 15, 1938, ASV, Arch. Deleg. Stati Uniti, POS. 166b, fol. 74r-v; draft in AES, America, 1937-1938, POS. 247 P.O., fol. 60r-v, and an earlier draft, fol. 61r.

[75] August von Mackensen of the Foreign Ministry to the Reich and Prussian Ministry for Ecclesiastical Affairs, Berlin, October 7, 1937, DGFP, No. 683, p. 1007.

side his ordinary competence, but he suggested that something could be attempted through the head of the Italian Government (Benito Mussolini), who would go to Germany on September 24 or 25. But the ground had to be prepared. Attolico also said that von Bergen would soon cease to be the German ambassador to the Holy See. Pizzardo reported their conversation to Pacelli, who, two days later, August 27, in his daily audience read Pizzardo's letter to the Pope and noted the Pope's reaction on the same sheet of paper. Pius XI replied that nothing should be done or conceded in the question of Cardinal Mundelein beyond what was set forth to the German ambassador in the very courteous note of June 24. «The Church», Pacelli quoted him as exclaiming, «does not bow before idols, which, on the contrary, should be smashed [infranti]»[76].

In conclusion, it may be suggested that by his powerful speech Mundelein on the one hand comforted and encouraged the Catholics of Germany[77] and convincingly reminded Americans that Catholics were not supporters of National Socialism but on the other hand caused the Holy See much trouble and aggravated its already tense relations with the German Government. Nevertheless, the Secretary of State, the Sacred Congregation for Extraordinary Ecclesiastical Affairs, and Pius XI himself astutely used the formal protest to reiterate the Church's own serious grievances and claims based on the Concordat. One might ask whether it would have been advisable to publish the Cardinal Secretary's note of June 24, as Cardinals Granito Pignatelli and Serafini had recommended. The text was not disclosed even to the German hierarchy until August. Perhaps Pacelli feared that publication would only intensify the antagonism, and surely he was wise in trying to put the contretemps behind the contending parties; the incident, in fact, became a dead issue by October, though the Nazis' resentment lingered on. It is doubtful whether Mundelein was ever apprised of the diplomatic controversy he had provoked, though it is possible that when he was in Rome in the autumn of 1938 or again a few months later when he took part in the conclave in which Pacelli was elected Pope, one or another of his Cardinalitial friends might have revealed to him some of

---

[76] Pizzardo to Pacelli, August 25, 1937, handwritten on note paper with a paragraph in Pacelli's hand on fol. 53r, AES, America, 1937, POS. 247 P.O., Fasc. 90, fols 52r-v, 53r-v. Cf. C.M. Martini, *Pio XII e Hitler...*, 346.

[77] However, a special court in Bochum, Westphalia, sentenced a local newsagent to one year's imprisonment for having duplicated Mundelein's speech (presumably in a German translation) and distributed copies by enclosing one in each journal or periodical he sold. Bonney, Newsletter 107, November 19, 1938, citing the Essen *National-Zeitung* of November 11.

the secret proceedings. He would have been chagrined to learn that Cardinal Marchetti-Selvaggini had proposed that Mundelein apologize, but he would have been gratified by the support of his other colleagues in the Sacred College and of the fearless Pope.

American Catholicism, Culture, and the Pontificate of Pius XI

John F. Pollard

American Catholics and the Financing of the Vatican in the Great Depression: Peter's Pence Payments (1935-1938)

In 1915, in an exasperated letter of response to Cardinal Secretary of State Gasparri's request that he seek funding from American bishops to help save Italy's Catholic daily press from bankruptcy, Archbishop Giovanni Bonzano, Apostolic Delegate in Washington, retorted, «Italians think that the American Catholic (bishops) are made of money»[1]. He was right, they did, especially in the Vatican, and they seemed to have had good reason for doing so because during the First World War American Catholics had become the major contributors to Peter's Pence, and more generally the Vatican's chief financial support. Whereas in 1864 the Church in the US contributed only 826,400 scudi (0.08%) of the Holy See's income in Peter's Pence and in 1870 Fr 96,587 (1.52%)[2], by 1917, Pope Benedict XV told Baron Carlo Monti, his confidant and secret envoy to the Italian Government, «the bulk of the offerings (Peter's Pence) come from the United States and then from Germany»[3], and this remained the situation throughout the 1920s and 1930s.

We have known for some time of the crucial importance of the generosity of American Catholics to the financing of the Vatican[4], based on scattered and fragmentary evidence of the dimensions of the US Catholic contribution to the Vatican finances in this period, but precise details of the size of the offerings of individual US dioceses have not hitherto

---

[1] Archivio Segreto del Vaticano (henceforth ASV), Apostolic Delegation to the United States (DAUS), b. (busta), 70, Prestito a favour dell'Unione Editoriale Romana (1915-16), letter of 21 Dec. 1915.

[2] C. CROCELLA, *Augusta miseria: aspetti delle finanze pontificie nell'età del capitalismo*, Milano 1982, 126-127

[3] *La Conciliazione Ufficiosa: diario del barone Carlo Monti incaricato d'affari del governo italiano presso la Santa Sede, 1914-1922*, ed. by A. SCOTTA, 2 vols., Vatican City 1997, II: 3 (3 Jan. 1917).

[4] J.F. POLLARD, *Money and the Rise of the Modern Papacy: Financing the Vatican, 1850-1950*, Cambridge 2005, especially chaps. 5 and 6.

been available, short of examining the archives of each and every one of them. Now, due to the opening of the archives for the pontificate of Pius XI (1922-1939) in the Archivio Segreto Vaticano in September 2006, we have exact figures for the Peter's Pence contributions of ninety of the one hundred and thirteen American dioceses in the period 1936-1938, which are to be found in the *Obolo* (Peter's Pence) files of the Secretariat of State[5].

By analysing the nature and contents of the *Obolo* files, we can identify the biggest contributors among American dioceses by size of donation and also *per capita*, highlighting some interesting discrepancies between the two. It is also possible to reassess the importance of the American Church, and American financial institutions, in the Vatican's «economy» in the late 1930s. In this process, the material reveals much about the relationship between the Holy See, the American hierarchy and American Catholics more generally, between 1934 and 1939 (as well as casting light upon the ways in which bishops sought to obtain papal titles of nobility for Catholic lay people), and the attitude of the men in the Vatican towards American Catholicism.

1. The *Obolo* Files

The *Obolo* files for this period cover not only the US dioceses, but dioceses in Canada, Europe, Latin America and Oceania. There are only a few files on missionary dioceses in either Africa or Asia, for obvious reasons. In the case of the US, there are files on ninety of the one hundred and thirteen dioceses existing at that time[6]. Taking account of boundary changes and the erection of new bishoprics and archdioceses, the files range geographically from dioceses on the East coast to the West, the Mid-West to the deep South, rural and urban, rich and poor, and include most of the major archiepiscopal sees, and the larger episcopal ones, from Chicago, the second largest diocese in terms of Catholic population, 1.25 million souls, to Savannah with just under 19,000[7]. Some ecclesiastical provinces are better represented than others; for example, whereas five out of the eight dioceses within the metropolitan jurisdiction of the archbishop

---

[5] ASV, Segreteria di Stato, 1936-1939, *Obolo* (henceforth, SdS, *Obolo*).
[6] For a list of the American dioceses, see *The Official Catholic Directory, Anno Domini 1991*, New York 1999.
[7] *Official Catholic Directory*, 1934, pp. 17-59.

Dubuque have *Obolo* files here, only three out of the eight in that of the Archbishop of Chicago are to be found, only three out of the ten dioceses of the province of Santa Fe – Santa Fe itself, Denver, Colorado and San Antonio, Texas – and only three out of the nine dioceses of the Minneapolis-St. Paul province. No diocese has files here for every one of the four years from 1935 to 1938, though five (Providence, Springfield, MA, Indianapolis, Newark and Rochester) have files for three successive years: twenty-seven dioceses have two files and the rest one. Twenty-three dioceses are not represented by files at all[8].

Not all of the files deal solely with Peter's Pence contributions. In fact, what emerges from these files is that American Catholics (and Catholics throughout the world) were contributing in a number of different ways to the financing of the universal Church. As well as Peter's Pence, the files contain references to extraordinary collections for Spain and Spanish refugees which were common throughout the Catholic world after the outbreak of the Spanish Civil War in 1936, collections *Pro Sommo Pontefice* (for the Supreme Pontiff, which was not always the same as Peter's Pence) – the clearest example being Albany and «mass stipends» – a tactful way of helping to ameliorate the poverty of some priests in Europe. In May 1938, Cardinal George Mundelein, Archbishop of Chicago, said that the Pope was at liberty to distribute these stipends where he thought most useful[9], and in fact many were destined for Germany. Despite the fact that American Catholics were already major contributors to Catholic missions world-wide through their own missionary societies – especially the American Board of Catholic Missions – sometimes special donations were made for the missions with the *Obolo*[10]. There are also some references to other personal gifts of bishops, clergy and lay people in the files[11], and contributions to the Pope's «charitable funds» – the only reference to the New York diocese is precisely one of these in which, in 1938, archbishop

---

[8] Richmond (VA), Hartford, Detroit, Toledo (OH), Fort Wayne (IN), Superior (WI), Syracuse, Trenton, Portland (OR), Reno (NV), Wichita (KS), Bismarck (ND), St. Cloud (MN), Sioux Falls (SD) and Galveston, Des Moines, Salt Lake City; Lansing (MI) and Camden (NJ), both erected in 1937; Owensboro (KY) and Saginaw (MI), created in 1938, and the apostolic vicariates of Alaska and Hawaii.

[9] See for example, ASV, SdS, Obolo, 1937, 444, Chicago.

[10] *Ibidem*, 1936, 181, Spellman-Missions, in which Cardinal Pacelli thanked Bishop Spellman for a gift of $1,000 for the missions in a letter of November 20, 1936, written by Mgr. Joseph Hurley who was working in the Secretariat of State.

[11] *Ibidem*, 1937, 480, Louisville (KY).

Cardinal Hayes gave the Pope $10,000, plus a thousand more for masses[12]. Occasionally they report contributions to the restoration of St. Peter's Basilica (Fabbrica di San Pietro)[13]. In May 1938, Cardinal Mundelein, made a special offering of $80,000 to the Pope, «one (thousand dollars) for every year of his life», to celebrate the Pope's 80th birthday that year[14].

Each file usually consists of four items:

1. A letter from the individual contributing Bishop to the Apostolic Delegate in Washington (Archbishop Amleto Cicognani from 1933 to 1958);

2. A pro-forma letter from the Apostolic Delegate to the Secretariat of State;

3. A «thank-you» letter to the Bishop from either Cardinal Pacelli, papal Secretary of State since 1930, or Mgr. Domenico Tardini, papal undersecretary of State since 1935 or Mgr. Giambattista Montini, *Sostituto* for the Secretary of State since 1937;

4. Another pro-forma letter from the Apostolic Delegate, this time to the Amministrazione per i Beni della Santa Sede (the main Vatican office responsible for administering the finances and property of the Holy See – henceforth ABSS) indicating the destination of the money.

The *pro forma* letter from the Apostolic Delegate, as well as indicating the amount contributed by each diocese and whether this was less, more or equal to that for the previous year, made comments upon the size of the offering and in certain cases explained the financial condition of a diocese where appropriate. For example, the Apostolic Delegate commented on the contribution of the Bishop of Mobile on October 1, 1936: «The donation has much more value because it comes from a diocese of the South of the United States whose financial conditions are poor»[15], and again, in 1938, he wrote of the Bishop of El Paso's offering of $588, «quite good given the poverty of the diocese; an increase of $88 on last year»[16]. In fact, Cicognani almost always commented on the individual dioceses' annual «performance», as with that from Springfield (MA) about whose 1936 Peter's Pence collection he said, «Good; an increase of $500»[17], and Providence, 1937, where he commented, «$15,000 (Excellent; an increase of

---

[12] *Ibidem*, 1938, 666, New York.
[13] *Ibidem*, 1937, 480, Louisville.
[14] *Ibidem*, 1938, 444, Chicago.
[15] ASV, SdS, Obolo, 1936, 371, Mobile.
[16] *Ibidem*, 1938, 622, El Paso.
[17] *Ibidem*, 1936, 473, Springfield, MA.

$2,353 on the previous year)»[18]. On the other hand, he could be critical, saying this of the contribution from the Bishop of the San Francisco in July, 1937, «Modest: the same as the previous year»[19], and of that of the Bishop of Lafayette (LA) in 1938, «$653.62 (Mediocre; a diminution of $135.38 on last year)»[20].

Usually, the file contains the original letter from the contributing Bishop, normally in English, but sometimes in Italian, Latin or even occasionally in French. The bishops' letters are very revealing of the state of the economy in the various parts of the United States in these years. In November, 1937, for example, Cardinal O'Connell of Boston writing to Pacelli informed him of «the continued unemployment and the advance of the cost of living...»[21] and Cardinal Mundelein of Chicago, through the mouth of his auxiliary, Mgr. William O'Brien, told the Pope in private audience that «America is passing through a very difficult period of economic and social depression»[22]. In their replies, Pacelli and Tardini never failed to acknowledge this state of affairs.

The bishops' letters also demonstrate that Pius XI was held in enormous affection, respect and even awe by American Catholics, confirming the effectiveness of the «personality cult» that had built up around the Pope since the reign of Pius IX. In 1937, Cardinal O'Connell wrote that, «Notwithstanding continued unemployment and the advance of the cost of living, our good people have not failed to give testimony, by their generosity, of the love and esteem for our beloved Pontiff»[23]. The cynics might say that O'Connell was just toadying to Rome, but when O'Connell's counterpart in Chicago, George Mundelein wrote that the people of his diocese, «Thank the Almighty for having listened to our prayers and rescued our Holy Father from the worries of his long and painful illness» (Pius had spent a large part of the winter of 1936 and Spring of 1937 in bed, due to diabetes and cardiacal problems), he was undoubtedly being sincere»[24]. On the other hand, bishops could be a little over the top in their comments, thus the Bishop of Ogdensburg, NY, in the letter accom-

---

[18] *Ibidem*, 1937, 757, Providence.
[19] *Ibidem*, 1937, 654, San Francisco.
[20] *Ibidem*, 1938, 177, Layfayetteville (sic); oddly enough, given the small size of the offering, the «thank you» letter was signed by Cardinal Pacelli. Maybe it was a charitable gesture, intended to encourage the efforts of the literally poor Bishop?
[21] *Ibidem*, 1937, 843, Chicago.
[22] *Ibidem*, 1937, 472, Detroit.
[23] *Ibidem*, 1937, 843, Boston.
[24] *Ibidem*, 1937, 444, Chicago.

panying his Peter's Pence offering for 1938 described Pius XI as «the Great White Father of Christendom»[25].

A «thank you» letter signed by either Pacelli, for Cardinals and big donations, or Tardini or Montini, for other bishops and smaller donations, is also invariably included in the files. Whereas the «thank you» letters sent to the bishops of other countries, Germany, for example, were almost always in Latin and pro-forma[26], this was not the case with the US; though, as we shall see, the form of words in these letters was drawn from a limited range. Some were quite short: in one to the Bishop of La Crosse (WI), in November, 1936, Tardini talked of the Bishop giving «of his own insufficiency in order to lighten the burden which the solicitude of the Church places upon the shoulders... of the Pope»[27], and in more than one letter he uses the phrase «the offering of the poor to the Father of the Poor»[28].

Occasionally the letters are extremely long and fulsome, as in the case of Pacelli's letter of thanks for a particularly large offering ($100,000) made by Cardinal Dougherty of Philadelphia in August 1936:

> «His Holiness is profoundly moved by this most generous evidence of the filial attachment to the Vicar of Christ and devotion to the Holy See... His Holiness well realises how many sacrifices must have been made by Your Eminence, your devoted clergy and your worthy people, in this time of economic depression and destitution, in order to place this sum in his hands»[29].

Normally, the thank you letters – especially those in English – were not written by either Pacelli, Tardini or Montini, rather by a subordinate and in the case of Philadelphia there is a note written in Italian on the file, «Cody: prepare a very ample letter» («very ample» underlined)[30]. John Cody, later Cardinal Archbishop of Chicago, 1964-1982, had been educated in Rome with the Apostolic Delegate and was a monsignor in the archdiocese of St. Louis in 1936[31]. Mgr. Joseph Hurley, another American working in the Secretariat of State, who interpreted for Pius XI during audiences with

---

[25] *Ibidem*, 1938, 137, Ogdensburg (NY); strictly speaking, the letter was from the Chancellor of the diocese.

[26] See, for example, 395, Nunziatura Apostolica, Germania.

[27] See, for example, *ibidem*, 1936, 269, La Crosse (WI).

[28] See, for example, *ibidem*, 269, Cheyenne (WY), October 22, 1936 Latin pro forma for drafts – amended.

[29] *Ibidem*, 1936, 321, Filadelfia.

[30] *Ibidem*.

[31] *Annuario Pontificio*, Vatican City 1939, 706.

English-speaking visitors and translated his speeches and radio messages into English, was also sometimes called upon to perform this role[32].

Finally, a pro-form letter from the Secretariat of State to the Amministrazione dei Beni della Santa Sede, informing it of the sum involved and where it had been deposited, is included in these files. This latter document was largely an accounting formality for it is clear that by no means all of the money from American collections of Peter's Pence was sent directly to the Vatican: much was kept on account at Riggs' bank in Washington, the Apostolic Delegation paying quarterly instalments of $60,000 to the ABSS[33]. Riggs National Bank, to give it its full title, was *the* bank specialising in providing financial services to the diplomatic corps in the American capital[34]. It is now clear that Bernardino Nogara, the director of the Amministrazione Speciale della Santa Sede, the office established to administer and invest the $90 million financial payment from Italy which was part of the overall settlement of disputes between the Holy See and the Italian State in 1929 (the Lateran Pacts), used Riggs Bank for various financial transactions on behalf of the Vatican[35].

In terms of the relative size of individual diocesan contributions to Peter's Pence, the *Obolo* files provide few surprises. By and large, the biggest contributors were rich, metropolitan archdioceses and dioceses with the largest population in the North East. Thus by far the largest contribution to Peter's Pence recorded in the four years covered by the files was provided by Philadelphia with $100,000, as has already been noted, but this seems to have been exceptional and may have included other forms of giving; the 1935 Peter's Pence contribution from Philadelphia was only $36,000[36]. Boston, with $36,500 in 1937, was marginally larger than that of Philadelphia[37], then came Newark ($34,198 in 1936)[38], Brooklyn ($30,000)[39],

---

[32] For example, ASV, SdS, Obolo, 1938, Layfayetteville (sic); for the career of Mgr. Hurley, see C. GALLAGHER, SJ, *Vatican Secret Diplomacy: Joseph P. Hurley and Pope Pius XII*, New Haven 2008.

[33] See, for example, ASV, SdS, Obolo, 1936 and 1937/184/AD Washington.

[34] J. EVANS, *A History of the Riggs National Bank*, published thesis, George Washington University, 1936.

[35] AES, Stati Ecclesiastici, IV Periodo, 1922-39, 420, 327, Città del Vaticano, ASSS, letter of 21 November, 1929.

[36] *Ibidem*, SdS, Obolo, 1936, 325 – in his letter of 5 August 1936, Cardinal Dougherty mentions a figure for the 1935 Peter's Pence offering.

[37] *Ibidem*, 1938, 365, Boston.

[38] *Ibidem*, 1936, 384, Newark.

[39] *Ibidem*, 1936, 373, Brooklyn.

Springfield, MA ($25,000 in1936)[40], and then finally St. Louis ($20,950 in 1936)[41]. After that, eight dioceses – Providence, Baltimore, Portland (Maine), Hartford, Dubuque, Manchester MA, Scranton and Los Angeles-San Diego (the dioceses split in 1937) – managed in excess of $10,000. All this confirms what might have been expected, that, with the exception of Dubuque, St. Louis and Los Angeles, the biggest «hitters» in the US Peter's Pence league were all to be found in the rich north-east.

Yet, if the figures in these files are analysed on a *pro capita* basis, we do have some surprises. On that basis, if the totals for the four years are averaged out, the top twelve dioceses in terms of contributions per head of Catholic population were Dubuque (8.3 cents), Spokane (7.7 cents), Portland, Maine (7 cents), Santa Fe (6.6 cents), Nashville (6.4 cents), Wilmington and Louisville (5.7 cents), La Crosse (5.1 cents), Charleston (4.7 cents), St. Louis (4.6 cents), Newark (4.5 cents) and Grand Island (4.4 cents), something of a reversal of positions in relation to the raw totals. It is not clear how this can be explained: did the bishops and clergy of the poorer dioceses work harder to extract money from the faithful? Certainly, there is some evidence that bishops who made the bigger contributors «rounded out» their Peter's Pence collections with money from other sources: the figures for Providence are the same for 1937 and 1938, as are those for Manchester in the same years and San Francisco in 1936 and 1937.

While the bishops' letters, and the replies from the Secretariat of State, provide ample and incontrovertible evidence of the gravity of the effects of the Great Depression in American dioceses between 1935 and 1938, they also suggest, in a rather impressionistic way admittedly, that some improvement was taking place in the economic situation over the four-year period. If an improving economic situation meant an increase in giving then out of the thirty-six dioceses for which there are figures for more than one year, twenty-three registered an increase in the size of the Peter's Pence offering over the period and only nine a decrease: in four cases the amount of money collected remained the same.

One of the *Obolo* files provides an interesting insight into a phenomenon little researched so far, the growing numbers of US Catholic lay people who were being awarded papal honours, and especially titles of nobility, between the two world wars. Charles Seldes, journalist on the «Chicago Herald Tribune», claimed that in the mid-1930s over one hundred Americans were to be found in the ranks of the papal court, mostly

---

[40] *Ibidem*, 1936, 472, Springfield.
[41] *Ibidem*, 1936, St. Louis.

with the title of «chamberlain» or «gentleman to his Holiness»[42]. We know
that Nicholas Brady, a very generous New York millionaire Catholic was
made a papal duke, Martin Maloney was made a papal marquis, and Da-
niel Murphy, Reginald Henshaw, and George MacDonald, all generous
contributors to Catholic causes, some of them in Rome and the Vatican,
were made papal counts, all in the 1920s[43]. Among the names to figure in
the last official list of the members of the papal nobility published by the
Holy See was Rose Fitzgerald Kennedy, the mother of the president, who
was created a papal countess in her own right in 1951. All this was part of
the broader phenomenon of the «internationalization» of the papal court,
both ecclesiastical and lay, which had begun under Pius IX (1846-78)[44].
Bishops all over the world increasingly nominated meritorious Catholics
to papal honorary titles and positions, especially those who had made a
major contribution in the field of charity[45].

In June 1937, Mgr. Floersch, Bishop of Louisville (KY), nominated
Mrs. Catharine O'Dougherty for the personal title of papal countess on the
grounds of the very substantial generosity of her dead husband towards
the Church and various charitable causes[46]. The Apostolic Delegate apolo-
gised to Pacelli for pressing the cause of Mrs O'Dougherty, even though
he admitted that he had not followed the normal procedures in such cases
and Floersch covered his embarrassment by making a donation of $1,000
to a fund for the restoration of St. Peter's Basilica, of which Cardinal Pacelli was the Archpriest[47].

Floersch probably did not need to feel concerned about the irregularity
of his procedure for obtaining Countess O'Dougherty's title. According
to Charles Gallagher:

---

[42] G. SELDES, *The Vatican-Yesterday, Today and Tomorrow*, London 1934, 34.

[43] In addition, Brady frequently acted as an intermediary between the Vatican and American financial institutions prior to the advent of Nogara as Vatican investment manager, as in 1928 when he tried to negotiate an arrangement whereby American banks
would have loaned the Italian Government the money necessary for the financial side
of the Lateran Pacts. See J.F. POLLARD, *Money...*, 139-40.

[44] *Ibidem*, 47-9.

[45] C. SELDES, *The Vatican-Yesterday...*, 218.

[46] ASV, SdS, 1937, 480, Louisville; see also, the official brevet in SdS, Brevi Apostolici,
1937, Pius XI, Junius Pars Ubraque: Catharina O'Doherty. It is interesting to note that
she is the only person in this volume to receive a title of papal nobility – the others, all
male, get a papal knighthood or a *commenditizia*.

[47] *Ibidem*, SdS, Obolo, 1937, 480, Louisville.

«An American Catholic financial elite was emerging along the East Coat and in the industrial belt of the United States. Since it was usually the local Bishop who approached wealthy Catholics in support for the Pope, the appointment to these sees meant instant power back in Rome»[48].

If this was so, then Floersch had amply demonstrated his financial muscle in the Vatican.

2. Vatican Finances in the Mid-1930s

The Peter's Pence collections made among American Catholics were more important than ever to the Vatican in the mid-1930s. As the balance sheets of the ABSS for 1932 and 1933 show, the costs of the Roman curia, the central government of the Church, particularly those associated with its diplomatic corps, had been rising steadily since the beginning of Pius XI's reign[49]. While Pius XI was not exactly a 'spend thrift', he was engaged in ambitious building programmes in the Vatican; in Rome for the various national colleges and in Italy to provide clergy houses throughout the 1930s[50]. In addition, the records of the papal audiences with Cardinal Pacelli and Mgr. Tardini demonstrate that the demands on Pius XI's purse from supplicants throughout the Catholic world were forever on the increase[51]. On the other hand, as a result of the Great Depression, not only was the return on the Vatican's investments falling, Peter's Pence collections world-wide were down: in the case of Germany there was the added problem that the strict exchange control regulations introduced by the Nazis in 1933 made it difficult for the Vatican to access the contributions of German Catholics[52]. The advent of the Second Spanish Republic, with its anti-clerical legislation in 1931 and then the outbreak of the Civil War in 1936 also diminished the ability of Spanish Catholics to contribute to the finances of the papacy.

---

[48] C. GALLAGHER, SJ, *Secret Vatican Diplomacy...*, 111.

[49] AES, Stati Ecclesiastici, IV Periodo, 1922-39, P.O. 510, 517-9, Città del Vaticano, Amm. Beni della S. Sede, bilancio consuntivo 1932, 1933.

[50] *Ibidem*, 518, Pontificio Consiglio Tecnico, 1936, annual report for 1935.

[51] See for example, *ibidem*, 430 (1931-1939), 348, 1933, Taccuini del S. Emo. Cardinale Pacelli, segretario di Stato di Sua Santità, udienza del 24 marzo and 4 aprile, and C.F. CASULA, *Domenico Tardini (1888-1961). L'azione della santa Sede nella crisi fra le due guerre*, Rome 1988, 355-356.

[52] *Ibidem*, 420, 327, Città del Vaticano, 1929-1939, Vaticano, memorandum of Mgr. Tardini regarding Reichsmarks «blocked» in the nunciatures of Berlin and Munich.

3. The Vatican and American Catholicism in the Mid-1930s

Already by the early 1920s, the Vatican had been forced to take serious account of the American Church. In 1922, following the arrival of Cardinal O'Connell and at the conclave after his election, Pius XI changed the rules of the conclave to allow American electors sufficient time to reach it before the doors were closed[53]. In 1924 he created two American Cardinals and in 1926 the first international Eucharistic Congress was held in Chicago, a tribute to the spiritual vigour of American Catholicism, but also a recognition of the financial muscle of Cardinal Mundelein, the first «bricks and mortar» Bishop by far. In the following decade, American priests also began to play a significant role in the Vatican. As Dr. Patulli Trythall explains elsewhere in this volume, the Jesuit father, Edmund Walsh, achieved considerable influence in the Vatican following his appointment as the head of the papal relief mission in Russia in February 1922, an appointment which was itself a result of the generous financial support for the relief work of American Catholics[54]. Also in the 1920s, Mgr. Hurley, as already mentioned, became an influential member of the staff of the Secretariat of State, working alongside Mgr. Montini, the future Pope Paul VI[55]. Fr. Vincent McCormick, SJ, became Rector of the prestigious Gregorian University in 1936 and Archbishop John Collins became the first American to reach the rank of papal nuncio in 1937. After the Second World War, three American prelates, bishops Hurley, Muench and O'Hara occupied the key nunciatures of Yugoslavia, Germany and Romania respectively.

Nevertheless, Americans were still regarded with a certain amount of suspicion in the Vatican. Both Cardinal O'Connell and his auxiliary Bishop Spellman had encountered prejudice when they worked in Rome before and shortly after the First World War[56]. The situation had not changed significantly by the mid-1930s. While Tardini in his memoirs mentions Cardinals who paid court to moneyed Americans, clerical and lay alike, he also suggests that the dollar power of some American bishops

---

[53] See the *motu proprio Cum Proxime*, of March 1, 1922, in U. BELLOCCHI, *Tutte le Encicliche e Principali documenti Pontifici*, vol. IX: *Pio XI (1922-1929)*, Vatican 2000, 15-16.

[54] See *supra*, 25-85.

[55] His former boss, Edward (later Cardinal) Mooney had been appointed Apostolic Delegate in India in 1926.

[56] See J. COONEY, *The American Pope*, New York 1983, 52.

aroused disdain in Vatican circles[57]. As will be seen, Tardini himself had a healthy respect of the money-raising capacities of American prelates.

In 1934, the Pope paid a remarkable compliment to the American Church in his encyclical *Vigilanti Cura*, citing the League of Decency, as a model to be followed by the world's Catholics in their efforts to control the moral impact of the motion picture industry[58]. Two years later Cardinal Pacelli made an allegedly «private» visit to America, carefully choreographed by his friend Bishop Francis Spellman, which included a whistle-stop tour of 12 out of the 16 Catholic ecclesiastical provinces. The visit was possibly intended as part of a programme of events – including Pacelli's visits to Lourdes, the Budapest and Buenos Aires Eucharistic congresses – to «show off» Pius XI's alleged «dauphin» to the Catholic world. It was also an attempt to establish a closer relationship with President Roosevelt who was increasingly seen in the Vatican as a hope for peace at a time when war clouds were beginning to gather in Europe, part of a broader papal diplomatic offensive to get closer to the Western democracies. But it was much more besides. It was, in the years before the papal «pilgrim journeys» to meet Catholics around the world of Paul VI, John Paul II and Benedict XVI, a very serious effort on the part of the Holy See to manifest its recognition and blessing to American Catholics, to demonstrate that American Catholicism had come of age. Much of this had to do with money, American money, the large sums that continued to flow across the Atlantic from American Catholics, despite the Great Depression.

4. Epilogue: The Cardinal Spellman Story

In his biography of Mgr. Hurley, Bishop of St. Augustine Florida, Charles Gallagher makes a trenchant point about Vatican-Catholic American financial relations in the 1930s:

> «The Peter's Pence collection was a significant tool in the scheme of any Bishop's ecclesiastical mobility. During the 1930s, the final act of any Bishop visiting Rome was to hand a financial donation to the Pope. For American

---

[57] C.F. CASULA, *Tardini...*, 315-316.

[58] J.F. POLLARD, *Electronic Popes: the popes and radio, cinema and television from Pius XI to John XXIII*, in *The Popes from Italian Prince to Universal Pastor*, ed. by T. WORCESTER, SJ, Cambridge 2010.

bishops, papal allegiance can be measured by every shifting decimal point on the check, and by every glad rising of the papal eyebrow»[59].

While it has not been possible to ascertain how far this principle applied to bishops in other countries, it really does seem to have been in force in America. This is confirmed by an incident which is recounted in the diary of Mgr. Tardini for the period in the autumn of 1938, when his boss, Cardinal Pacelli, was absent from the Vatican. According to Tardini, in a long audience with Pius XI on October 4, 1938, he discussed with him the filling of the vacancy in the archbishopric of New York (following the death of Cardinal Hayes) and, in particular, the arrival of a telegram from the Apostolic Delegate in Washington which mentioned the suitability for the post of Mgr. John McNicholas, OP, Archbishop of Cincinnati.

The Pope said that Cicognani's reply had really pleased him, because he too thought that McNicholas was the best candidate, but that he suspected that Cardinal Pacelli had something against McNicholas[60]. Tardini replied that Cardinal Pacelli greatly respected Mgr. McNicholas but that the archdiocese of Cincinnati was overburdened with debts, to which the Pope responded that while he respected Mgr. Spellman, «He has never given me the impression of being a great man... Mgr. McNicholas (on the other hand) is highly thought of and is a good man»[61]. At this point, Tardini returned to the financial argument:

«That is very true, but (the archbishopric of) New York involves the administration of substantial temporal goods and His Eminence (Cardinal Pacelli) knows very well that Spellman, in addition to his other qualities, has that of being a good financial administrator. He found in his parish a High School burdened with debts: he paid everything off in a very short time and now the school is going strong[62].
The Pope replied: What does that signify? He has paid off the debts. It means that he found someone who gave him the money!
Tardini: Very true: but this is a great gift, especially in America, where the Church lives from offerings»[63].

---

[59] C. GALLAGHER, *Secret Vatican Diplomacy...*, 111.

[60] AES, IV Periodo, 1922-1939, Diario di S. Ecc. Mons. Tardini dal 27 settembre al 29 ottobre, 4-X-1938.

[61] *Ibidem.*

[62] *Ibidem.*

[63] *Ibidem.*

Spellman, of course, got the job, thanks in very large part to his friend-ship with Pacelli who was elected Pius XI's successor a few months after this conversation. But his financial acumen played a big part in the ap-pointment as well. And he did not disappoint Pacelli and Tardini in their expectations of him in his subsequent financial administration of the New York archdiocese and his munificence towards the Vatican[64].

---

[64] See J. COONEY, *The American Pope...*, and R.I. GANNON, SJ, *The Cardinal Spellman Story*, New York 1963.

LUCIA POZZI

The Problem of Birth Control in the United States under the Papacy of Pius XI

Since the beginning of the Twenties, birth control has represented a huge concern for the Catholic hierarchy. In 1930, Pope Pius XI solemnly condemned contraception. Yet by the time *Humanae vitae* was published, it was common to think of the so-called Rhythm Method – or the Knaus-Ogino Method – as the Catholic form of contraception. However, some documents in the Archive of the Holy Office show that in the Thirties, the diffusion of the Rhythm Method in the United States provoked much uneasiness both amongst the American clergy and the Vatican. American sexual mores worried the Vatican in general. As these papers reveal, Cardinals of the Holy Office did not finally approve the publicity of a «natural» method for regulating pregnancy. They took a stand against it, though this method did not violate the letter of the doctrine against contraception. From the perspective of the Vatican, giving official approval to the Rhythm Method would have meant that the Catholic Church had accepted the *idea* of birth control.

1. The Catholic Church and the American Birth Control Movement

Although almost every American denomination was hostile to contraception until the end of the Thirties, Americans have always identified religious opposition to birth control with the Catholic Church[1]. This idea is mainly due to the influence of Margaret Sanger, the leader of the move-

---

[1] L. WOODCOCK TENTLER, *Catholics and Contraception. An American History*, Ithaca and London 2004. K.A. TOBIN, *The Changing American City: Chicago Catholics as Outsiders in the Birth-Control Movement, 1915-1935*, in «US Catholic Historian», 15 (1997)/2. From the same author, *The American Religious Debate over Birth Control, 1907-1937*, Jefferson, NC, and London 2001 and *International Birth Control Politics: the Evolution of a Catholic Contraceptive Debate in Latin America*, in «Journal for Study of Religions and Ideologies», (2002)/2, 66-80.

ment struggling for free access to contraception, the so-called Birth Control Movement[2].

On November 13, 1921, Sanger was arrested before the last session of the inaugural meeting of the Birth Control League in New York. Someone had alerted the police to the meeting: reportedly the Archbishop of New York, Patrick Hayes. The policemen claimed they were operating on the demand of the influential prelate, although the Catholic Church was never formally linked to the event. After this incident, which mobilized a coalition of prominent people and activists for civil liberties in support of Sanger, Hayes wrote a very severe pastoral letter against the «woman rebel»[3] and the Birth Control Movement. In the letter he asserted: «To take life after its inception is a horrible crime; but to prevent human life that the Creator is about to bring into being is satanic». Sanger and Hayes publicly attacked each other several times after this dispute. Afterwards, Sanger always put herself – and the Birth Control Movement – in open opposition to the Roman Church, although Catholic women kept crowding her birth control clinic in Brownsville. A few weeks after the New York City Town Hall incident, Sanger wrote: «There is no objection to the Catholic Church inculcating its doctrines to its own people, but when it attempts to make these ideas legislative acts and enforce its opinion and code of morals upon the Protestant members of this country, then I do consider its attempt an interference with the principles of this democracy, and I have a right to protest»[4]. A skillful politician, she appealed to other denominations, while accusing the Catholic hierarchy of keeping women in a condition of subordination and ignorance. Sanger was convinced of the necessity of family planning, based on a scientific understanding of reproduction, so that women could choose voluntarily motherhood. It was Sanger who brought the «indecent» subject of birth control out into the open.

---

[2] M. SANGER, *An Autobiography*, New York 1938. L. GORDON, *Woman's Body, Woman's Right. A Social History of Birth Control in America*, New York 1990. E. CHESLER, *Woman of Valor: Margaret Sanger and the Birth Control Movement in America*, New York 2007. See also the project of the New York University on Margaret Sanger http://www.nyu.edu/projects/sanger/. On the ambiguities of the Birth Control Movement see the controversial study of M. CONNELLY, *Fatal Misconception: The Struggle to Control World Population*, Cambridge, MA, and London 2008 and A. TONE, *Controlling Reproduction: an American History*, Wilmington 1997.

[3] *«The Woman Rebel»*, was the title of the magazine that Margaret Sanger founded in 1914 to challenge laws restricting the distribution of information on birth control.

[4] M. SANGER, *Mrs. Sanger replies to Archbishop Hayes*, in «The New York Times», on December 20, 1921.

Because the recent clashes between the American Birth Control Movement and the local hierarcy drew the Vatican's attention overseas, during the 1920s and 1930s the church equated Margaret Sanger and America, land of «Protestants, materialists without morals», with the Birth Control Movement as a whole.

In 1925 during the Holy Consistorial Congregation, Cardinals discussed the report of the Apostolic Delegate to the United States, Pietro Fumasoni Biondi. Fumasoni Biondi was worried about the sexual mores of American Catholics, especially the Irish, due to their proximity to Protestants who had lost a «sense of family». In his report, he chiefly reported on the «plague» of birth control in America. In his view, this social «disease» was rooted in individual selfishness, especially of women who wanted to live free from familial responsibilities, «enjoying life in freedom», and «to be maintained» by their husbands. In short, Fumasoni Biondi considered the diffusion of contraception as intertwined with a subversion of gender roles and growing secularism[5]. Above all he was concerned about the indulgence some Catholic priests showed toward married people.

Thus, it is understandable that the Holy See took a special interest in the debates over birth control that were occurring in America. According to Canon Law, the Holy Office has the duty of preserving the dignity of Confession and examining whether standards are in compliance with official doctrine[6]. For these reasons, the Holy Office was the suitable setting for analyzing this kind of subject, namely the matter of sexuality. So in June, 1925, the Consistorial Congregation sent the Fumasoni Biondi's report to the Assessor of the Holy Office, Carlo Perosi, asking him for advice. Should the Holy Office take action against the problem? And, if so, how? Perosi forwarded the request to the Jesuit Pietro Vidal, who expressed his *votum*, i.e. a written judgment, about «the problem of the birth control in the USA»[7]. In the meantime, in 1926, some additional information about Margaret Sanger and the American Birth Control Movement reached the Vatican Secretary of State.

On January 5, 1927 the secretary of the Holy Office, Cardinal Raffaele Merry del Val, demanded further and detailed information from Fuma-

---

[5] In this case, Fumasoni Biondi was probably also referring directly to Margaret Sanger's periodical.

[6] N. DEL RE, *La curia romana. Lineamenti storico-giuridici*, Roma 1970, p. 96.

[7] Archivio della Congregazione per la Dottrina della Fede, Sant'Uffizio, Rerum Variarum, 1936, 2 (407/1934). The same information is specularly located also in the Vatican Secret Archive, «Prevalence of Contraceptive Practices among Catholics of the United States», Archivio Delegazione Stati Uniti Sezione II, pos. 345a.

soni Biondi. The Apostolic Delegate replied that the spread of the disease
of neo-Malthusian theories infecting Catholics required «an immediate
and effective remedy». For that reason Fumasoni Biondi communicated
to him that he had entrusted Rev. John Cooper (1881-1949) to carry out
a survey on birth control uses among Catholics in order to understand the
extent of the phenomenon[8]. Cooper was a Catholic priest, anthropologist,
sociologist, and member of the American Eugenics Society Committee on
Cooperation with Clergymen[9]. Because of his link with the American Eugenics Society, Cooper was probably the most informed churchman about
the type of people most likely to use contraception. At the end of March
1927 Fumasoni Biondi sent to Merry Del Val Cooper's work along with
the pastoral letter of the Bishop of San Francisco, Edward Joseph Hanna
(1860-1944), about the sanctity of marriage. During the next few years,
the Holy Office proceeded to analyze the American Birth Control Movement by employing Cooper's statistics.

2. The Rhythm Method: the Interaction between Medicine and Mo-
ral Theology

The existence of an «agenesic» or an infertile period in women's cycles
was known about since the mid-nineteenth century. Three physiologists
discovered the physiology of female ovulation between 1842 and 1845[10].
One of them, the zoologist Félix Archimede Pouchet (1800-1872), discovered the spontaneous character of human ovulation, which undermined
the Galenic theory. Galeno considered the female orgasm necessary to

---

[8] Fumasoni Biondi presented John Cooper's book on birth control to the Holy Office,
one of the earliest Catholic pamphlet published against contraception, with the title
«Birth Control» (National Catholic Welfare Conference 1923). In 1916 Cooper had
already drafted a Sunday sermon on the so-called «race suicide».

[9] The American Eugenics Society was founded in 1923. Most members were against
birth control, even though they lobbied for the coercive sterilization of the «feeble-
minded». They also shared the «race-suicide» critique, typical of the end of 19th Century, based on the idea that the growing independence of women is a threat to society.
Until the publication of the encyclical *Casti connubii* – which condemned eugenic
intruding applications – eugenic theories attracted many clergymen as well.

[10] See C. LANGLOIS, *La crime d'Onan, Le discours catholique sur la limitation des nais-
sances*, Paris 2005, 312 and following. See also R. JÜTTE, *Lust ohne Last, Geschichte
der Empfängnisverhütung*, München 2003, 228; J.T. NOONAN, *Contraception. A History of its Treatment by the Catholic Theologians and Canonists*, Cambridge, MA,
1965, 439.

conception – as reported also by the moral theologian Tomás Sánchez, *De sancto matrimonii sacramento disputationum tomi tres*[11]. In contrast, the acceptance in moral theology of the theory of spontaneous ovulation remarkably affected ideas about female sexuality rendering female pleasure unnecessary and making it possible to identify a periodic infertility in the menstrual cycle.

If moral theology teaches one to observe the laws of nature, the new findings on the physiology of women required and, at the same time, authorized new adaptations to the doctrine. In this domain, the Holy Office needed to expand its knowledge for the purposes of conforming the moral doctrine to new theories and practices.

In 1853, the Amiens Bishop, Louis-Antoine de Salinis (1798-1861), obtained the Sacred Penitentiary's approval for the possibility of using the «agenesic» period for planning births, with this argument: «they [the spouses] do nothing by which conception is prevented». The sentence contained *in nuce* the next fundamental distinction between natural and artificial birth control. In 1873 a theologian from Leuven, August Joseph Lecomte (1824-1881), who had some knowledge of biology, published a book for a wider public on the contraceptive use of periodic infertility in women[12]. In his book, endorsed by the Archbishop of Malines and Bruges, called: *De l'ovulation spontanée de l'espèce humaine dans ses rapports avec la théologie morale*, Lecomte aimed to combine scientific knowledge and Catholic ethics[13]. In 1880 the Sacred Penitentiary, the Vatican tribunal which judges the forgiveness of sins, answered Lecomte by writing that «spouses, who use marriage in this way, are not to be upset and confessors could suggest the practice cautiously to restrain Onan's detestable crime»[14]. In the same years, a German physician, Carl Franz Nicholaus Capellmann, wrote several treatises on reproductive physiology, based on observations of the phases of the female cycle. He also synthesized medical knowledge and moral theology[15].

---

[11] T. SANCHEZ, *Disputationes*, II.3, lib. 9, disp. 19, n. 9, p. 228, quoted by F. ALFIERI, *Nella camera degli sposi, Tomás Sánchez, il matrimonio, la sessualità, (secoli XVI-XVII)*, Bologna 2010, 244.

[12] Neo-Malthusians defined it the «safe period» and they recommended it as well to the working class.

[13] On this topic see C. LANGLOIS, *Le crime d'Onan...*, 313-314.

[14] *Ibidem*, 334.

[15] C. CAPELLMANN, *Pastoral-Medicin*, Aachen 1877; from the same, *Fakultative Sterilität ohne Verletzung der Sittengesetze*, Aachen 1882. See J.T. NOONAN, *Contraception...*,

Even though it was taught in most seminaries from the mid-nineteenth century onward, the theory of the «safe period» still relied on some medical inaccuracies. So often the system did not function correctly for the purpose of spacing births. At the end of the Twenties, two researchers, Hermann Knaus and Kyusako Ogino, extended studies about periodic infertility. They discovered, independently from each other, that ovulation occurs between the twelfth and the sixteenth day before the putative menstrual period and they determined that the ovule survives only about a day. In the West, Knaus divulged these scientific findings around 1929[16]. But the chief popularizer of this discovery was Johannes Nicolaus Josephus Smulders[17]. Therefore in Europe the «Ogino-Knaus» method started circulating prevalently in German and Dutch.

The history of the Rhythm Method in the US began some time later in 1932. Leo Latz, a Chicago physician at Loyola Medical School in Chicago, published a booklet titled *The Rhythm of Sterility and Fertility in Women*[18]. For planning births, his book recommended that women limit marital intercourses to a defined period of their cycle, presumably infertile. Soon after, the pamphlet *The Sterile Period in Family Life* followed the first edition. The same Latz, Valère Coucke (a Belgian moral theologian) and another American physician, James J. Walsh coauthored it. Some time before, a Jesuit had reportedly requested Latz to investigate the recent research on the women's fertility. And a Jesuit, Joseph Reiner, who was once the Dean of Loyola University, wrote a glowing introduction to the book[19]. Above all the book boasted having the approval of Cardinal George Mundelein (1872-1939) of Chicago for the first edition and Cardinal Patrick Hayes of New York for the second one.

In 1934, a Catholic priest, Father John O'Brien printed a book on the same topic, the use of periodic infertility in women as a «natural» means

---

442. The first book, *Pastoral-Medicin*, had attracted the attention of the Holy Office, which analyzed the content.

[16] H. Knaus, *Die periodische Fruchtbarkeit und Unfruchtbarkeit des Weibes: Der Weg zur natürlichen Geburtenregelung*, Wien 1934.

[17] J.N.J. Smulders, *Periodische Enthaltung in der Ehe: Methode Ogino-Knaus*, Regensburg 1931, cit. in J.T. Noonan, *Contraception...*, 443.

[18] The title of Leo Latz' book gave periodic continence its new American name. On the history of Rhythm Method in the US, see L. Woodcock Tentler, *Catholics and Contraception...*, 106 and following.

[19] He had written the introduction of the book «The Rhythm». See L. Woodcock Tentler, *Catholics and Contraception...*, 106. K.A. Tobin, *The Changing American City: Chicago Catholics as Outsiders in the Birth-Control Movement, 1915-1935*, in «US Catholic Historian», vol. 15 (1997)/2, 84.

for planning parenthood, called *Legitimate Birth Control*. The title itself engendered ambiguity, because it seemed to say that birth control was – not in means but in principle – something licit. In addition, O'Brien's book had the *imprimatur* of the Bishop of Fort Wayne, John Francis Noll (1875-1956), at least at first.

These books addressed Catholic believers with the purpose of diffusing the Rhythm Method as an authorised birth control practice. They sold so many copies (around 75,000) that in the public imagination the Rhythm Method – far before the 1951 speech of Pius XII to the midwifes – was connected with Catholics beginning in the mid-Thirties. The books presented the theory as reliable to people, who, during the years following «Black Tuesday» 1929 really and desperately needed to limit their number of children. Therefore most American confessors greeted the books warmly. To these worried priests, the arrival of the Method seemed providential. They could suggest a «legitimate» alternative to simple abstinence for couples, who could not afford another pregnancy for financial or health reasons. Moreover, in recommending the Rhythm Method, priests could claim having the endorsement of bishops.

For critics, the books aroused suspicion. O'Brien had radically suggested not only a natural method for family planning, but also reflected a positive and wider view of sexuality in marriage. He asserted that the physical, psychological and also moral benefits of a satisfying conjugal sexuality represented a fundamental good, designed by God. Even Margaret Sanger interpreted this new American Catholic literature as an about-face of the Catholic Church's stance on the matter. In what might have been particularly frustrating for the Catholic hierarchy, Sanger stated that O'Brien supported birth control[20]. Sanger was correct about O'Brien, at least in principle.

Certainly, the American Catholic clergy was listening sincerely to the afflictions and the needs of common people. American priests considered the binding prescription of the Sacred Penitentiary of 1880, which recommended caution in communicating information about the Rhythm Method, inadequate for the times. In O'Brien's opinion, a passage of the pontifical document *Casti connubii,* underlining the aspects of mutual help and molding in marriage, authorised a wider interpretation of conjugality. As O'Brien implied, in this wider conception of conjugal love, sexuality occupied a more notable role, beyond sheer procreation. In the section «The Church and Birth Control», he wrote[21]:

---

[20] See L. WOODCOCK TENTLER, *Catholics and Contraception...*, 114.
[21] J. O'BRIEN, *Legitimate Birth Control*, Huntigton 1934, 27-29.

«Now what is the real doctrine of the Church on the vexing problem? Is it true that she condemns all forms of family limitation other than that of total abstinence? Such is the widespread impression. Even some Catholics seem to share it. But it is certainly more rigorous than the teaching of Pope Pius XI in his encyclical on Christian Marriage, issued on December 31, 1931. Newspapers throughout our country and the world carried scattered paragraphs from it. Most of them played up his condemnation of the deliberate frustration of the conjugal act in an artificial manner as a violation of a natural law. But few carried the following important paragraph».

The quoted paragraph of the encyclical mentions other goals of marriage besides conception: «This outward expression of love in the home demands not only mutual help but must go further; must have as its primary purpose that man and wife help each other day by day in forming and perfecting themselves in the interior life, so that through their partnership in life they may advance ever more and more in virtue [...]». And also: «This mutual molding of husband and wife, this determined effort to perfect each other, can in a very real sense, as Roman Catechism teaches, be said to be the chief reason and purpose of matrimony, provided matrimony be looked at not in the restricted sense as instituted for the proper conception and education of the child, but more widely as the blending of life as a whole and the mutual interchange and sharing thereof»[22].

Expressions, like «mutual interchange» or «mutual molding», gave to marriage a wider meaning and prelude the «unitive significance» of the conjugal act, recognized in the encyclical *Humanae vitae* thirty years later. Despite these lines in the encyclical, many inside the Church criticized the idea that knowing about reproductive physiology led believers to a substantial moral autonomy. In other terms, the circulation of the Rhythm Method among Catholics had actually raised a greater problem inside the clergy: the possibility for believers to deliberately separate sexuality and procreation. This potential autonomy of the couple made the Catholic hierarchy concerned about its loss of moral authority. Furthermore, critics feared that this position on a «natural» means of birth control could be read as a «Catholic form of contraception» and could generate a «contraceptive mentality» among Catholics. In fact, some Catholic priests interpreted this change as a general adoption of a «materialistic» view of marriage, where pleasure and self-determination played a more significant role than sacrifice. They also thought that a natural control over fertility could stimulate

---

[22] *Encyclical* Casti connubii, *Enchiridion delle Encicliche*, Bologna 1995, 604-605, 469-470. Available on the website www.vatican.va, under Pius XI.

adultery and fornication. However, a few priests, on the basis of an anti-sexual bias, considered the method intrinsically sinful and for this reason less virtuous than total abstention.

In fact, within American Catholic clergy a vocal minority, especially some Jesuits, argued against the diffusion of the theory, despite also the subtitle of O'Brien's book claiming it to be «According to Nature's Law»[23]. For example, «America», a Jesuit review, issued a critical editorial of Wilfrid Parsons against the publicity of the Rhythm Method[24]. Latz was abruptly fired from his position as a faculty member at Loyola University, not coincidentally a Jesuit institution, even though this decision was officially justified as an ordinary downsizing of the staff[25].

Despite the more drastic critics, some justified a discussion of the Rhythm Method on the basis of the high availability of other contraceptive means, a condition which modified entirely the prescription of 1880 of the Sacred Penitentiary. In the United States, contraceptive devices had been accessible under different names since 1873, because of the federal Comstock Act laws[26]. Father Augustine Ryan thought rightly that the spread of contraceptives had radically changed American Catholics birth control practices. He was among the first to have written on birth control early in 1916. He was also the head of the Social Action Department of the National Catholic Welfare Council, so he had a specific competence in economical and social issues[27].

---

[23] So L. Woodcock Tentler, *Catholics and Contraception...*, 115.

[24] W. Parsons, *The great Birth-Control Plot*, in «America», February 6, 1932, 427-429.

[25] See L. Woodcock Tentler, *Catholics and Contraception...*, 115.

[26] So was called the comprehensive federal statute entitled «An Act for the Suppression of Trade in and Circulation of Obscene Literature and Articles of Immoral Use,» approved thanks to the efforts of a young Protestant moral reformer, Anthony Comstock (1844-1915), who «had succeeded in listing contraceptive information among obscene materials to be prohibited from the mail». See K.A. Tobin, *The Changing American City: Chicago Catholics as Outsiders in the Birth Control Movement, 1915-1935*, in «US Catholic Historian», vol. 15: *Catholics in a Non-Catholic World*, (1997)/2, 67-85. J.T. Noonan, *Contraception...*, 412-413. A. Tone, *Black Market Birth Control, Contraceptive Entrepreneurship and Criminality in the Gilded Age*, in «The Journal of American History», 87 (2000)/2.

[27] The National Catholic Welfare Conference was a national conference formed by bishops and affiliated organisations of laymen and -women, lobbying mainly for keeping abortion and contraception illegal and for promoting family welfare. See J.T. Noonan, *Contraception...*, 430. L. Woodcock Tentler, *Catholic and Contraception*, 40, M. Connelly, *Fatal Misconception...*, 48. J.A. Ryan, *Family Limitation*, New York 1916. He was «a prolific writer on social ethics and prominently seated in Washington at the Catholic University» according to Tentler, in *Catholics and Contraception...*,

3. The Holy Office and the Diffusion of the Rhythm Method in the US

Considering the numerous factors involved in the debate over birth control, at the beginning of the twentieth century the United States represented an ongoing challenge for the Vatican.

The American Birth Control Movement strived to promote the free access to contraception. Among her many arguments in favor, Sanger had always claimed that contraception could positively affect the social and economic order. In her books, especially *The Pivot of Civilization*, Sanger asserted that family limitation was tightly connected with the «public good». Exactly the opposite of what Catholic moralists traditionally argued: in their opinion contraception threatened the human species[28]. Meanwhile, Sanger was promising, through birth control, a new mankind: healthier and wealthier. For Sanger, birth control promoted greater social responsibility, since limiting one's family size could have improved socio-economic conditions of one's offspring. In this sense, therefore, she mirrored the eugenic cause, which was popular at that time[29].

On the other hand, the American Eugenics Society had always had an ambiguous relationship with the Birth Control Movement. Some eugenicists always opposed birth control. Among them, Catholic eugenicists represented a remarkable percentage. On the contrary, others had been urging local governments to restrict reproductive rights with compulsory measures against the so-called *unfit*, promoting *negative eugenics*. In 1927 the United States Supreme Court confirmed Virginia's statute, which enabled sterilization and contraception for the «feeble-minded», the infamous

---

40. Even earlier, with an article issued on the Catholic Encyclopedia of 1907, Ryan had been pressing the Church to acknowledge the importance of the topic «birth control». See E. CHESLER, *Woman of Valor...*, 211. J.A. RYAN, *The Moral Aspects of Periodical Continence*, in «Ecclesiastical Review», 89 (1933), 29. Later in 1935 he wrote a commentary [*The Social Menace of America's Declining Birth Rate*, in *Miscellanea Vermeersch*, Roma 1935, 171-181] in the miscellany in honor of the moral theologian Arthur Vermeersch, SJ.

[28] See J.P. GURY, *Compendium Theologiae moralis*, Roma 1873, 510: «Onanismus volontarius est semper peccatum mortale [...] quia ad societatis extinctione per se tendit»; and A. VERMEERSCH, *Theologiae moralis, Tomus IV, De castitate et vitiis oppositis cum parte morali de sponsalibus et matrimonio*, Roma 1944, 3: «"Onanisticus" coniugii usus intrinsece et graviter culpandus est, cum coniuges tunc qua mere individualem, actum exerceant qui est speciei et propter speciem. Ordine autem ad speciem violenter abrupto graviter peccatur».

[29] E. CHESLER, *Woman of Valor...*, 195 and following.

Buck v. Bell decision. As a consequence of these events, the debate on birth control escalated and come to encompass many different topics.

Moreover the case of the Rhythm Method made an impact on the Catholic Church, which especially in the United States, was constantly defending its doctrine on marriage from the different positions of other denominations. During these years, Protestant America shifted toward the legalization of birth control practices. Not including the Anglican Lambeth Conference, in 1930 alone the Universalist General Convention, the American Unitarian Association, the New York East Conference of the Methodist Episcopal Church, and the Central Conference of American Rabbis gave public approval for birth control. In March 1931, Fumasoni Biondi informed the Secretary of State of the decision of the Federal Council of Churches of Christ in America, representing about 22 million Protestants[30]. The Federal Council had elaborated, by mutual consent, a document on birth control, resulting from the studies of a Committee on Marriage and the Home[31]. They asserted that, since birth control was already popular and was progressively becoming a widespread procedure «in preventive and curative medicine», churches had the duty to give moral guidance on the topic. So the statement from the Federal Council expressed the conditions, which made the use of contraception moral. Above all, the Federal Council claimed one concept in bitter contrast with Catholic doctrine. «The moral problem of birth control has to do with these two functions of sex. They arise in connection with spacing children, [...] on the one hand; and, on the other, they arise in considering the rightfulness of intercourse in itself without the purpose of children, and consequently the rightfulness of the use of contraceptive»[32]. By making such a strenuous defense in prohibiting contraception, the Catholic hierarchy wanted to distinguish its position on the theological ground[33]. But beyond doctrinal concerns, they also had practical motives. In the pluralistic context of America, the Catholic Church could have lost numbers of adherents, if it had approved birth

---

[30] AES, POS. 456 P.O. Fasc. 443, p. 18. Federal Council of the Churches of Christ in America, Annual Report, 1930 New York.

[31] Margaret Sanger raised funds anonymously for this Committee. See E. CHESLER, *Woman of Valor...*, 319. See also the chapter «Lambeth and Its Aftermath», in K.A. TOBIN, *The American Religious Debate over Birth Control...*, 161 and following.

[32] AES, POS. 456 P.O. Fasc. 443, p. 117.

[33] J.F. NOLL, *The Catholic Church vs. the Federal Council of Churches of Christ in America*, Huntington 1931.

control. Its legitimation would have reduced the proportion of Catholics in relation to other religious groups.

This difficult situation brought about by the diffusion of the Rhythm Method in the United States provoked much anxiety in the Vatican.

Charles Park was the rector of the little parish of St. Joan of Arc in Hershey, a city with a few thousand inhabitants, which had grown around the Hershey's Company, a chocolate factory, in south-eastern Pennsylvania. At the beginning of 1933 he informed the Holy Office that a Catholic newspaper, «The Sunday Visitor», was publishing and advertising a weekly brochure called: *Legitimate Birth Control*. In his letter, he criticized the Catholic newspaper for the shortsightedness of advertising the booklet, since, like many other birth control detractors, he believed that the circulation of such a pamphlet was a threat to moral behavior. He wrote: «In the USA our greatest difficulty is fighting this principle of materialism, which holds that whatever interferes with the comfort and material prosperity of parents is sufficient reason for frustrating conception»[34]. Therefore Park's main concern was: how would Catholic believers use this knowledge about periodic fertility in women? He supposed that illiterates and «spiritually blind» people would not be able to understand the difference between natural and artificial means of birth control, using confusion as a pretext to legitimate sinful practices. He suggested to the Holy Office: «this brochure should be suppressed quietly»[35].

Wilfred T. Craugh was a priest of the Episcopal Curia of the city of Rochester in Minnesota[36]. In February 1934, under the condition of anonymity, he reported to the Holy Office about O'Brien's book, which caused «much debate and much upset». Craugh was afraid of the «terrible consequences» of indiscreet divulgation of the theory among the married and not married. He thought that the circulation of the Rhythm Method might produce many abuses, especially in the United States, where the «plague» of (artificial) birth control (using the same expression as Fumasoni Biondi) was already widespread, even among Catholics. He did not pose any question to the Holy Office about the Rhythm Method in itself, but about

---

[34] Archivio della Congregazione per la Dottrina della Fede, Rerum Variarum, 1936, 2 (407/1934).

[35] *Ibidem*.

[36] Afterwards he became the rector of St. Bernard School of Theology and Ministry. The theologian Charles E. Curran remembers him for not agreeing with the periodic meetings of the seminary students, who got regularly together for a drink. See C.E. CURRAN, *Loyal Dissent. Memoir of a Catholic Theologian*, Washington 2006, 20, 24.

the publicity of the book in newspapers (Catholic and non-Catholic). He considered this advertising inappropriate and scandalous.

In March 1934, inside the Holy Office, the assembly, Congresso Particolare, asked Father Lorenzo C.S.[37] for a *votum*. During the last few years, the Secretary of the Holy Office had changed, as well as the Apostolic Delegate of the United States. Donato Sbarretti had taken over as secretary after the death of Merry Del Val. From 1933, Pius XI had appointed Amleto Giovanni Cicognani as the Apostolic Delegate for the United States. In the meantime, Fumasoni Biondi had became Prefect of the Congregation of the De Propaganda Fide and Counsellor of the Congregation for the Oriental Churches. Most likely he suggested Mgr. Luigi Bondini[38] for this *votum*, because they were both counsellors there. At the time inside the Roman Curia, few people understood the English language – for example Father Lorenzo did not, as the documents reveal. So the Holy Office entrusted Mgr. Bondini as an advisor with the task of carrying out research on the subject and expressing a judgement on the topic.

In his analysis, he translated and summarised the content of American newspapers, examined the diffusion of the theory, explained the matter and considered reasons in favour or against the diffusion of the Rhythm Method[39]. The core question was: how did the prescription of 1880 match with the public debate now led by Catholics in the US?

What follows, is taken from his analysis.

As Bondini translated, on January 30, 1934 «The United Press» wrote that a team of physicians, Chicago's Cosmas and Damian Associates, the Rt. Rev. Msgr. John W. Barrett (director of Catholic Hospitals in Chicago) and the doctors of the University of Loyola had examined the new theory of birth control, which «could affect remarkably the life of Catholics». After these studies, clergy and physicians convened in Chicago to speak about the Rhythm Method. In this context Rev. Joseph Reiner had public-

---

[37] Fr. Lorenzo di San Basilio was a Carmelitan.

[38] Fr. Luigi Bondini OfM conv. (1872-1937). In 1916 was elected rector of Collegio Serafico di S. Francesco – per le missioni estere dei Minori Conventuali. In 1918 he became «Assistente generale» of Frati Minori Conventuali and by 1921 also «Segretario e Assistente generale». From 1920 he was counselor for the Sacra Congregazione del Concilio. After the election of Pope Pius XI, he was designated «Socio e Assistente generale». By 1928 he was counsellor for the Sacra Congregazione per la Chiesa orientale as well. Until 1929 he was Ministro Provinciale d'Oriente in the city of Istanbul. In 1929, he was elected Archbishop of Perge until his death in 1937.

[39] Archivio della Congregazione per la Dottrina della Fede, Rerum Variarum, 1936, 2 (407/1934).

ly asserted that the Rhythm Method, as natural means of birth control, did
not contrast with the moral doctrine of the Church. In principle, according
to Reiner, only interfering with natural physiology would be sinful. Moreover, Reiner justified couples limiting births for financial reasons. Firm in
his conviction, the former Dean of Loyola University referred to Hayes'
endorsement of Latz's book for which Reiner had written the foreword.
Bondini reported that during the meeting Barrett, foreseeing the potential
Vatican reaction, recommended caution to the audience, since no official
approval of this method had yet to come from the Vatican. Barrett reminded his audience that the Catholic Church traditionally needed a long time
to make any decisions. Again from «The United Press», Bondini reported
that A.G. Miller, M.D. had proved 87 successful cases in a hundred and
fifty women applying the Rhythm Method.

Bondini also reported the content of the «Pittsburgh Catholic Newspa-
per» from February 9, 1933, which outlined some positions about the theory and quoted a significant quotation of Reiner's introduction to the book
The Rhythm. Bondini related that on February 5 Margaret Sanger offered
Catholic physicians access to her clinics so that they could investigate the
Rhythm Method more deeply. The newspaper also revealed a positive account from an anonymous Catholic priest, who considered the book *The
Rhythm* as simply teaching a technique of birth control not contrary to
natural law. Moreover the «Pittsburgh Catholic Newspaper» described the
opinion of Father Parson, who believed that the bishops had endorsed the
books, because nothing in them conflicted with morals and faith. But Parson did aknowledge that the *imprimatur* was not an official recognition of
the Church. Nevertheless, in Parson's view, the Rhythm Method was not
a birth control practice, but a plain knowledge about reproductive physiology compatible with natural law. The «Pittsburgh Catholic Newspaper»
also reported Rita McGoldrick's opinion about the Rhythm Method; she
was then president of the National Council of Catholic Women and a
mother of nine children[40]. She thought that the Rhythm Method was appropriate for Catholics, since it did not violate moral law. But she did hope
that Catholic physicians would reject Sanger's provocative offer.

From the documents taken into account in his analysis, Bondini deduced that information about the Rhythm Method had circulated widely.
Meetings, public debates on the topic, and press clippings testified that
a large number of Catholics knew about the method. Bondini was aware

---

[40] L.W. Tentler, *Catholics and Contraception...*, 127.

that very often members of the clergy had publicly endorsed the theory. He referred especially to the two editions of Latz's book.

In his analysis, Bondini condensed the new theory of Ogino and Knaus. As the researchers had defined, the «fertile window» in women did not last more than eight days a cycle. This finding described the cyclicality of female fertility more accurately and usefully than Capellmann. According to this method, avoiding sexual intercourse during this period would limit the number of offspring a woman conceived. So this method of birth control did not violate the papal decree. It was based in abstinence. As Bondini rightly reminded, the Sacred Penitentiary had already allowed this practice. But again the problem persisted: how to reconcile the caution suggested to the confessors with the diffusion of this knowledge that already occurred through newspapers and public meetings?

Bondini switched his argument to the reasons in favor of its diffusion. He recounted the introduction from O'Brien's book by Mgr. Noll, Archbishop of Fort Wayne. Noll asserted that genuine Catholics must consider children as something intrinsically positive and they must also desire numerous offspring. But Noll did not want to ignore the needs of Catholic spouses. In Noll's view, as Bondini reported, couples insisted on limiting births for licit reasons: health, social and economic problems. In Noll's opinion, if it were possible to achieve the aim of spacing births without sinning, then Catholics believers should be allowed to know *how*. Noll obviously meant the Rhythm Method. For Noll the method was not worthy of praise, but neither was it sinful: it was the lesser of two evils. Noll stressed that the application of the method should be of course not the superficial evasion of parental responsibilities, but the wise regulation of the number of one's children.

Bondini also summarized O'Brien's reasons for writing the book. First of all, he spoke of thousands of letters from people in trouble. On the one hand, they did not want to sin, but on the other hand, they could not afford another child. O'Brien could not distance himself from the sufferings of so many people. He argued moreover that the potential abuse of the method was not a sufficient reason for not diffusing the Rhythm Method. Protection against misuse of the strategy consisted not in hiding the truth, but in teaching a reasonable, respectful use. Another reason for diffusing the theory was the wide accessibility of contraceptives. O'Brien asked: was it not wiser to provide married people with a method according to moral law, instead of leaving them alone with many wicked alternatives? Bondini noted another of O'Brien's consideration. From O'Brien's perspective, since the Church had never been obscurantist, as its detractors to the contrary asserted, so he believed that it was right to share both natural and supernatural truths. Above all, O'Brien considered the Rhythm Method an improvement along the lines of the encyclical *Casti connubii*. In support of his argument, O'Brien also quoted the «The Clergy Review» and Hayes' *imprimatur* to the book *The Rhythm*. O'Brien's final argument is significant. Why did O'Brien choose to diffuse the method through the press? Because he, as a priest of the Church, was interested in the well-being of believers. O'Brien added that critics of the diffusion of the Rhythm Method aimed for an unreal ideal. O'Brien considered them like «Don Quixote fighting windmills».

Finally the universal accessibility to this kind of information lead Bondini to a cautious option. His analysis ended with a tepidly negative conclusion: prohibition of the diffusion of the Method through the press. He supported his stance with three chief considerations: the sacredness of the topic, the potential confusion derived from its knowledge, and again the necessity of observance to the rule of the Sacred Penitentiary of 1880.

Outside the Holy Office, there were critics also in Europe especially on this point, i.e. the conformity of the Rhythm Method to *Casti connubii*. Some influential Belgian Jesuits, like Ignatius Salsmans, did not agree with the enthusiastic «Oginoism». It is true, Pius XI said: «Nor are those considered as acting against nature who in the married state use their right in the proper manner although on account of natural reasons either of time or of certain defects, new life cannot be brought forth»[41]. But in Salsmans' opinion, with the expression «natural reasons» Pius XI did not intend periodic infecundity in women, but permanent sterility due to illness or menopause[42]. So in Salman's view, the doctrine did not authorize nor explicitly suggest the use of the Rhythm Method. The even more authoritative, Father Arthur Vermeersch exposed his critiques on the use of infecund days for planning births in the periodical from Gregorian University. He did not consider licit any motive for controlling births. He only deplored that the philosophy of the «empty cradle» stemmed directly from the Church[43].

In addition to these doctrinal concerns, the problem with the diffusion of the Rhythm Method was something new both in Europe and in the United States. Defenders of the orthodoxy had been dealing with a rapidly

---

[41] *Enchiridion...*, 604-605, 469-470. Available on the websitewww.vatican.va.

[42] I. SALSMANS, *Sterilitas facultativa licita?*, in «Ephemerides theologicae lovanienses», 11 (1934), 563-564.

[43] A. VERMEERSCH, *De prudenti ratione indicandi sterilitatem physiologicam*, in «Periodica de re morali, canonica, liturgica», 22 (1934), 246-247, cit. in J.T. NOONAN, *Contraception...*, 444.

changing society, where mass media had been achieving more and more power[44]. The Church as well had also taken advantage of the pervasiveness of mass media. For example, Hudson Hawley, an Associated Press Staff writer, stressed the importance of using modern mass-communication rightly to diffuse *Casti connubii*. He said[45]: «For the first time in Vatican history modern language texts of the forthcoming encyclical will be issued simultaneously with the original Latin text». In fact, the encyclical was the first radiotelegraphic message in Church history addressed worldwide.

On Saturday, February 17, 1934, the Assembly of the Congresso Particolare examined Bondini's *votum* and the documents quoted and translated in his analysis. Among the opinions of the assembly an anonymous hand-written note pointed out some significant concern. The author wrote that if America were like Italy where birth control was not spoken about, at least publicly, surely exposing such theories would be «less inopportune and maybe less scandalous». The anonymous went on: «However *we are in America*». He listed the problems: «All the newspapers discuss the topic, there are associations formed with the aim of diffusing Malthusianism and birth control anyway», and he summarised the problem with the overseas mentality: «The great majority is Protestant, and materialist or at least utilitarian». He ascribed to Protestants vague and false ideas, so that among them some ministers were even encouraging birth control. In his view, American Catholics lived in a corrupt environment in a time that he recognised as economically very difficult. In this context, he was not surprised that «many false ideas» pervaded the minds of Catholics and that not a few of them behaved in the same way as their Protestant fellow citizens by using illegitimate means of birth control. He could imagine that bishops, well-knowing this dangerous situation, tried to dissuade their spiritual children from following «the depraved stream of the Protestant masses»[46].

After a few months, in November 1934, the National Catholic Welfare Council openly condemned the publishing of information on the Rhythm Method[47]. This statement induced the majority of the American

---

[44] Reported in the Catholic periodical «La Civiltà Cattolica», 2 (1931).

[45] Rome, January 4, 1931 Associated Press.

[46] Archivio della Congregazione per la Dottrina della Fede, Sant'Uffizio, Rerum Variarum, 1936, 2 (407/1934).

[47] Minutes, meeting of the Administrative Board, National Catholic Welfare Conference, 13 Nov. 1934. Archive of the Catholic University of America, Minute of the Admin-

bishops to take a conservative course. Nevertheless the books of Latz and O'Brien continued to be sold and suggest by some priests to congregants. Sale for these books – as it can be imagined – were successful.

On February 24, 1935, Cicognani, the Apostolic Delegate, wrote to the Secretary of the Holy Office, Donato Sbarretti. He reported on the decision of the National Catholic Welfare Council to restrain the propaganda about the Rhythm Method. After its introduction in the United States – he observed – it had became common to hear of the Knaus-Ogino Method as the Catholic form of birth control. For Cicognani this kind of propaganda, even endorsed by eminent members of the clergy, seemed to be not only a prudent suggestion, but almost a public «recommendation». The problem was in the mind of the delegate: these events could bring about misunderstandings of Catholic morality and a «lowering» of the Christian ideals of the Sacrament of Matrimony. Along with this, he attached a circular letter written by the Archbishop of San Francisco, Edward Joseph Hanna. As Chairman of the Administrative committee of the National Catholic Welfare Council, he communicated the will of the members of the committee, who «thought it their duty to bring this matter to the attention of the bishops». The letter reported that open discussions on the subject «disregarded the caution imposed by the Holy See»[48].

On Saturday, March 16, 1935 the Holy Office put the «Rhythm Method» question on hold, technically: «dilata». On March 16, 1936, after having collected data and analyzed the subject, the Feria II eventually took a stance against publicity of the Rhythm Method[49]. As the records show, nine of the members (Assessore Alfredo Ottaviani, Commissario Giovanni Lottini, Consultori Giuseppe Palica, Celso Costantini, Ernesto Ruffini, Pietro Vidal SJ, Timoteo Schaefer, a member of Capuchins, Alfonso Gasperini, a Domenican, and Giuseppe Latini, as «Promotore di Giustizia») elaborated and voted on an instruction, based on their common position.

---

istrative Board, NCWC, 29 April 1930-17 Nov. 1939, p. 284. Quoted by L. WOODCOCK TENTLER, *American and Contraception...*, 301.

[48] «Illis conjugibus, caute tamen, insinuare quos alia ratione a detestabili onanismi crimine abducere frustra tentaverit». S. Poen. 6 June 1880. Archivio della Congregazione per la Dottrina della Fede, Sant'Uffizio, Rerum Variarum, 1936, 2 (407/1934).

[49] The plenary assembly of the Congregation, which included all the Cardinals of the Holy Office, regularly took place twice a week: on Thursday (Feria V) in the presence of the pontifex and on Wednesday (Feria IV), presided by the dean Cardinal (*Cardinalis antiquior*). The so-called Feria II was a further assembly for officials and counselors only, usually held on Monday, without Cardinals. On the specific functioning of the assemblies in the Holy Office, see the doctoral dissertation of F. BERETTA, *Galilée devant le Tribunal de l'Inquisition. Una relecture des sources*, Fribourg 1998.

According to their document, the Apostolic Delegate should communicate the Holy Office's disapproval of the diffusion of the Rhythm Method especially through mass media. Diffusion should be restricted to circles of physicians or to the teaching of pastoral medicine, since, as the fragment attests, the Catholic Church was also recognizing a form of birth control, albeit «in harmony with the natural law». The officials were afraid of a «materialistic» view of life, which could derive from using any kind of birth control. So to avoid misunderstanding about the Rhythm Method, the assembly forbade absolutely the expression «birth control». Two of the members, Consultori Luigi Santoro and Lorenzo di San Basilio added that bishops should prohibit publications on the topic, especially written by clergy. They thought that these pamphlets gave the impression that the Church had accepted the idea of birth control. So with this judgement, the Holy Office finally confirmed the fears of its critics.

On March 25, 1936, on the basis of this discussion, the assembly Feria IV communicated the content of the judgement to Cicognani. The day after, during the Feria V, Pope Pius XI also confirmed the decision of the Cardinals. Confessors should not encourage, but recommend the Rhythm Method only as a remedy against worse sins. This information should necessarily be accompanied with the moral teaching of the Church on marriage.

After a few weeks, on May 26, 1936, the Apostolic Delegate Amleto Giovanni Cicognani wrote to the Holy Office that he had addressed a letter with the «providential and opportune instructions» of the Holy See to every ordinary[50].

«Eminenza Rev.ma,
sono quanto mai grato all'Eminenza Vostra Rev.ma per le Istruzioni opportune e provvidenziali, che si è degnata impartirmi col venerato officio n. 407/34 del 26 aprile p.p., a proposito delle teorie diffuse sul controllo delle nascite. Mi sono recato a premura di dare immediata attuazione a tali Istruzioni, ed ho già inviato ai singoli Ordinari la Circolare confidenziale e come cosa mia di Delegato Apostolico».

The letter he sent, was enlosed:

---

[50] On the basis of National Catholic Welfare Conference papers, Tentler had thought it addressed to an anonymous prelate. Archivio della Congregazione per la Dottrina della Fede» (ACDF), SO, Rerum Variarum, 1936, 2 (407/1934).

«May 23, 1936
Confidential
Your Excellency,
Since December 22, 1934, when the Administrative Committee of the National Catholic Welfare Conference addressed a letter to the members of the
Hierarchy, there has been much discussion, both orally and in writing, by the
laity as well as by the clergy, regarding a natural method of birth control, commonly known as the Rhythm Theory.
It is deemed advisable, therefore, to emphasize the prudence which must char-
acterize any discussion of this subject by Catholics, and especially by the
priests, who must ever bear in mind the caution expressed in the well-known
reply given by the Sacred Penitentiary on June, 1880, which states: "posse
confessarium sententiam de qua agitur (caute tamen) insinuare".
Those then who would treat this matter in writing must be extremely careful
not to give the impression that the way to the limitation of births is left entirely
open; indeed it is their first duty to emphasize the teaching of the Church relative to the primary end of marriage, which is the procreation and education of
children, and to stress all those spiritual considerations which avail to eliminate conclusions derived from purely material criteria.
Consequently, the theory in question is not to be taught "sic et simpliciter",
but only tolerated as an extreme remedy and a means to withhold the faithful
from sin.
I shall appreciate it if your Excellency will communicate the contents of this
letter at the first opportune occasion to your secular priests and also to the
religious who exercise the sacred ministry or teach in the diocese. In addition,
Your Excellency will kindly see that no Catholic periodical or newspaper,
published in the diocese, advertises the theory in question, or discusses it otherwise than directed above.
This letter is not to be published; and I am certain that the Reverend Fathers,
to whom its contents are to be communicated, will regard them as a confidential and as given for their guidance and prudent use as physicians and directors
of souls. [...]».

As it can be seen, Cicognani suggested that every Catholic, especially
priests, should be extremely careful in writing about the subject and should
instead emphasise the doctrine of the Church on marriage. As established
in 1880, confessors could only suggest the Rhythm Method «caute» inside
the confessional.

In 1936 the Holy Office agreed to solicit prudence about the diffusion
of the Rhythm Method. It did not violate the natural law. However, the
Holy Office considered it only an extreme remedy, because its knowledge
could have given «the impression that the way to the limitation of births
is left entirely open»[51]. According to the Holy Office, the idea of birth
control could have produced a «materialistic» mentality in Christian married couples.

---

[51] Archivio della Congregazione per la Dottrina della Fede, Sant'Uffizio, Rerum Variarum, 1936, 2 (407/1934).

Two decades after its introduction in the United States and after the instruction of the Holy See, the Rhythm Method still created doubts among clergy and medical staff. For example, in a meeting in 1950, Italian Catholic physicians suggested limiting the use of the Method because of its unreliability[52].

Nevertheless on October 29, 1951 in a speech addressed to the Italian Catholic Society of Midwives, Pope Pius XII publicly declared that the Rhythm Method was suitable for all Catholic married couples. Fifteen years after the decision of the Holy Office, the Catholic Church had officially approved *the idea of birth control* in principle. The case of the Rhythm Method is an enlightening example of the debate over birth control inside the Church.

---

[52] J.T. NOONAN, *Contraception...*, 445.

Vatican Transnationalism

Aappo Laitinen

Early Signs of Discord: The Holy See, Britain, and the Question of Malta

Anglo-Vatican relations fell into crisis in the late 1920s and early 1930s. A local conflict between politicians and Roman Catholic clergy on the island of Malta, a predominantly Roman Catholic part of the British Empire, quickly escalated into an international diplomatic dispute. In consequence, a long and bitter quarrel over clerical involvement in politics ensued between Britain and the Holy See. The situation was made more complex by nationalistic tendencies, disputes over language – Maltese, English, and Italian were all commonly spoken in Malta – and claims of Italian (Fascist) interference on the island.

In this article, I examine the genesis of the crisis. The entanglement of religion and politics was the primary cause of the conflict, but it was exacerbated by purely personal factors, such as the evident dislike displayed by Pope Pius XI towards the head of the local government in Malta, Lord Gerald Strickland. The role played by the Vatican Secretariat of State was central to the development and eventual resolution of the crisis. This study limits itself to dealing with the initial stages of the conflict and the reaction of the Holy See to the escalation of the situation. First, an overview of Anglo-Vatican relations in the early twentieth century is presented. It is followed by a survey of the religious and political situation in Malta in the early 1920s. Next, I analyse the report of Father Alfonso Orlich, sent to the Maltese islands by Pius XI in 1928, in order to reveal the complexity of religiopolitical issues in Malta. Finally, I examine the events that triggered the collision between the ecclesiastical hierarchy and the local government in Malta. Correspondence between the Holy See, the Maltese bishops, and Cardinal Francis Bourne in London reveals how difficult it was for the Church to cope with the peculiar amalgam of religion and politics in Malta.

1. Anglo-Vatican Relations in the Early Twentieth Century

Relations between the Holy See and Britain had been gradually improving during the early twentieth century, despite the lack of a permanent British representative to the Vatican. This was attested to by the frequent courtesies exchanged between the English and papal courts[1]. The position of Rome as a vantage point gained new importance when the First World War broke out in 1914. Both the Entente Powers and the Central Powers were eager to list Italy among their allies, and Rome became a centre of intrigue, as both sides attempted to prompt Italy's intervention in the war. The Central Powers were well-represented in the Vatican, and their envoys enjoyed good relations with the ecclesiastical hierarchy. In contrast, Belgium was the only Allied nation in a position to influence the papal court. The British Foreign Office was increasingly worried by German and Austrian propaganda and the lack of Allied representatives in the Vatican. The election and coronation of Benedict XV as the new Pope in 1914 presented a fitting opportunity to improve diplomatic relations between Her Majesty's Government and the Vatican[2]. After three and a half centuries without a fully accredited representative to the Vatican, in December 1914 the British Government appointed Sir Henry Howard as British Envoy Extraordinary and Minister Plenipotentiary to the Holy See[3].

Howard was succeeded by Count John de Salis in 1916. Described as a shrewd, witty man with a «convenient diplomatic deafness», he served as the British Minister during Pope Benedict XV's peace proposals of 1917 and the last stages of the war[4]. The British Mission was conceived as a war-time measure. However, when open hostilities ended on November 11, 1918, the Foreign Office in London was not ready to bring down the curtain on the Mission to the Holy See. From its standpoint, there

---

[1] *The British Mission to the Vatican*, in «The American Journal of International Law», 9 (1915)/1, 206-208.

[2] O. CHADWICK, *Britain and the Vatican during the Second World War*, Cambridge 1986, 2; T. MOLONEY, *Westminster, Whitehall and the Vatican. The Role of Cardinal Hinsley, 1935-43*, London 1985, 13; T.E. HACHEY, *Anglo-Vatican Relations, 1914-1939: Confidential Annual Reports of the British Ministers to the Holy See*, Boston 1972, VIII, XV-XVI; W.A. RENZI, *The Entente and the Vatican during the Period of Italian Neutrality, August 1914-May 1915*, in «The Historical Journal», 13 (1970)/3, 492-493.

[3] T.E. HACHEY, *Anglo-Vatican Relations...*, XVII.

[4] A. RANDALL, *Vatican Assignment*, London 1957, 12. Like his predecessor, de Salis was a Roman Catholic. Owen Chadwick does not share Randall's positive view of de Salis and remarks that de Salis' reports to the Foreign Office «show signs of illiteracy». See O. CHADWICK, *Britain and the Vatican...*, 2.

were still numerous issues that required cooperation with the Vatican. The most pressing of these was the trouble in Ireland. Other mutual concerns and conflicts soon arose between the British and the Vatican, for example those in Malta and Quebec[5].

However, maintaining diplomatic relations after the First World War was fraught with difficulty. First, there was a traditional anti-Catholic element in British society, which was apparent from frequently raised questions in the House of Commons concerning the need for a representative to the Vatican. More straightforward opposition to Anglo-Vatican relations was delivered through the press and through petitions of protest to the Foreign Office, largely by ultra-Protestant groups such as the National Union of Protestants. Secondly, while the Vatican was eager to maintain diplomatic relations, it displayed a certain wariness towards Britain, a Protestant power. Suspicions of Protestant propaganda in areas under British rule were not uncommon even in the Vatican Secretariat of State.

In any case, the parties' mutual interests clearly overrode any reservedness that existed between them. The political and social situation in post-war Europe was chaotic. The First World War had encompassed almost the whole continent, as well as parts of the Near East and Africa, and had cost millions of lives. The task of reconstruction was daunting. As one of the Allies, Britain played a major role in the peace settlement and in shaping the new political order in the post-war world. However, while the British Empire had emerged from the war victorious and was geographically at its zenith in 1920, political and, above all, economic power was shifting from Europe to the United States. Nevertheless, Britain held the balance of power in Europe and used its diplomatic weight to further peaceful change in international politics[6]. In this connection, the Vatican was seen as a valuable partner. The Holy See, for its part, pinned its hopes

---

[5] O. CHADWICK, *Britain and the Vatican...*, 2; T.E. HACHEY, *Anglo-Vatican Relations...*, VIII; A. RANDALL, *Vatican Assignment*, 14-15. It was estimated at the time that there were 14 million Roman Catholic subjects living in the United Kingdom and its dominions.

[6] For a revisionist analysis of post-war British and American efforts to forge a stable Euro-Atlantic peace order, see P.O. COHRS, *The Unfinished Peace after World War I. America, Britain and the Stabilisation of Europe, 1919-1932*, Cambridge 2006. Britain's role in the financial and economical reconstruction after World War I is discussed by A. ORDE in *British Policy and European Reconstruction after the First World War*, Cambridge 1990.

on the British Government for restoring order to Europe and supporting the peace proposals put forward by the Pope[7].

When giving instructions to Odo Russell, who succeeded De Salis in 1923, the British Foreign Secretary Lord Curzon stressed the significance of the British mission to the Holy See as an observation post. The Vatican was an important part of the Foreign Office's overseas network for gathering information. Curzon also revealed that the temporary nature of the mission was to be changed and a permanent Legation was to be established by virtue of a cabinet decision. The importance of having an envoy among the twenty-five other nations represented at the Holy See outweighed any inconvenience which might be caused by the protests of ultra-Protestant groups in Britain[8].

The visit of King George V and Queen Mary to the Vatican in the spring of 1923 further testified to the improvement in Anglo-Vatican relations. In the Vatican, the royal couple held discussions with Pope Pius XI and other prominent figures such as the Cardinal Secretary of State, Pietro Gasparri. Although the visit was of a ceremonial nature, with very little discussion of actual politics, relations between the United Kingdom and the Holy See received a considerable boost as a consequence. Russell described the visit as a «complete success»[9]. The royal visit underlined, on a ceremonial level, the parallel interests of Britain and the Holy See in the re-establishment of peace and social stability. However, as the 1920s rolled on, this mutual understanding began to show signs of cracking, not least because of events on the far-flung island of Malta.

2. Religion and Politics Intertwine in Malta

Malta appeared on the agenda of Anglo-Vatican discussions from the mid-1920s onwards. As with other Catholic regions of the Empire, the British took up questions with the Holy See concerning local Church-State entanglements when necessary. In 1926, the British Legation to the Vatican handled a number of issues regarding Maltese Catholics, the most important of which dealt with preventing the spread of Italian influence and lan-

---

[7] For example, the British Government was the first major power to acknowledge Pope Pius XI's endeavours for peace in 1923. T.E. HACHEY, *Anglo-Vatican Relations...*, 42.

[8] *Ibidem*.

[9] *Ibidem*, 42-44. The royal visit was the first official one since King Canute in 1027.

guage within the local Church[10]. Here it was the Foreign Office that took the initiative to discuss Maltese affairs, rather than the Secretariat of State of the Holy See. Within the Imperial Government, the Colonial Office responsible for the governance of Malta was keen to avoid any problems with the Roman Catholic Church. Religious peace was considered an essential imperial interest, needed to maintain social stability and uphold the security of the British military base in Malta. The Foreign Office, on the other hand, was not as interested in Malta and had no reservations in pressing the Holy See when problems related to religious affairs occurred[11].

Even though Maltese affairs were not on the agenda of official diplomatic discussions before the mid-1920s, it had become apparent to the Holy See some years earlier that religious questions were at the forefront of the local political debate, and consequently the Vatican had kept a close watch on the situation. An entanglement on the island had already attracted the attention of the Vatican in 1921, when Archbishop Mauro Caruana, the Bishop of Malta, had protested against an article in the periodical «Il-Progress». The periodical, owned by the local politician Sir Gerald Strickland, had promised a prize for the reader who came up with the best reason for the removal of the elderly Bishop of Gozo[12], Mgr. Ioannes Maria Camilleri. Another reward was offered to anyone who could discover or reveal any immorality in the lives of the parish priests on Gozo[13]. The reason for attacking the Bishop and the Gozitan clergy lay in the defeat of Strickland's Constitutional Party in the 1921 election at the hands of the pro-Italian parties, which were fervently supported by the local priests. The Constitutional Party was markedly pro-British and was mainly supported by the middle class and the British Colonial authorities[14]. Despite Strickland's efforts to emphasise his own Catholic faith, he was portrayed by his opponents as anti-clerical and an enemy of the Church. Strickland's

---

[10] *Ibidem*, 102.

[11] D. FENECH, *Responsibility and Power in Inter-War Malta. Book One: Endemic Democracy (1919-1930)*, San Gwann 2005, 344-345.

[12] Gozo, a small island of the Maltese archipelago, constituted one of the two dioceses of Malta.

[13] *Exposition of the Malta Question with Documents (February 1929-June 1930)*, Vatican 1930, 15.

[14] D. FENECH, *Responsibility and Power...*, 109-110, 283; A. KOSTER, *Prelates and Politicians in Malta: Changing Power-Balances between Church and State in a Mediterranean Island Fortress (1800-1976)*, Assen 1984, 80-81, 85.

attacks against the clergy on Gozo also strained his relationship with the ecclesiastical authorities[15].

Although Strickland's behaviour in 1921 was objectionable to the Church, it was nothing in comparison with the uproar Strickland caused in 1924 when he openly criticized Pope Pius XI, by claiming in a newspaper article that «if enough money were forthcoming, the Pope would make a horse a Papal Marquis». Continuing his criticism of the giving of titles by the Holy See, Strickland defined the Vatican as a «business concern»[16]. Not surprisingly, the statements were received with shock by the Catholic Church. The Maltese bishops condemned Strickland's behaviour with strong words. As a result, Strickland quickly recanted and declared his loyalty to the Church[17]. It seems evident that Pius XI's antagonism towards Strickland, so clearly apparent during the following years, had its roots in these attacks against the Church and his own person.

Strickland's regular disputes with the clergy reflected the complex and highly charged political situation in Malta. Democratic elections were a new innovation on the island. The constitution of 1921 had expanded the electoral base considerably and created an arena for democratic decision-making in the institution of the Legislative Assembly. Open electioneering and political campaigns were therefore a new phenomenon in Maltese society. The political field was divided between somewhat conservative pro-Italian and more liberal pro-British factions, with the less influential Labour Party eventually siding with the latter. As the Catholic Church was part of the establishment, and a major factor in Maltese society, it was inevitably drawn into political controversies. Since members of the clergy were actively involved in these debates and took part in elections, many issues were consequently reduced to pro or anti-clerical rhetoric[18].

This political antagonism was evident in the elections of 1924, in which the pro-Italian Nationalist Party again prevailed over Strickland's opposition, albeit narrowly. Archbishop Caruana managed to limit the use of religion as a political weapon by means of a pastoral letter forbidding priests in his diocese from publicly taking political sides[19]. Despite his party's defeat, Strickland himself secured a seat in the Legislative As-

---

[15] *Ibidem*, 89-90.
[16] *Exposition of the Malta Question...*, 15-16; A. RHODES, *The Vatican in the Age of Dictators 1922-1945*, London 1973, 57.
[17] AES, *Inghilterra*, IV periodo, P.O. 178, Fasc. 16, Caruana to Gasparri, February 22, 1924; Gasparri to Caruana, 2 March 1924; A. KOSTER, *Prelates and Politicians...*, 90.
[18] A. KOSTER, *Prelates and Politicians...*, 79-80.
[19] D. FENECH, *Responsibility and Power...*, 143.

sembly. Some months later, Strickland was also elected to the House of Commons as the Conservative Member of Parliament for Lancaster. He was thus able to emphasize his political importance in the higher echelons of the British Empire when preparing for the next Maltese elections in 1927. This claim was not without resonance, for the Colonial Office and the Foreign Office were bound to take him more seriously now that he was a Member of Parliament[20].

The ecclesiastical authorities, both in Malta and in the Vatican, braced themselves for another stormy campaign, as electioneering gathered pace in Malta during the spring of 1927. As the elections approached, it seemed likely that religion would again play a central role in the political debate. Strickland's Constitutional Party had joined forces with the Labour Party, thus forming a coalition against the Nationalists. The Compact parties, as the coalition was called, accused the Nationalists of being disloyal to the interests of Malta and the British Empire. They portrayed the Italianity of the Nationalists as more than just a cultural position, even stating that the Italian language was used as an instrument of class domination. The Nationalists, for their part, accused the Compact parties of plotting against the Catholic faith. The old anti-clerical argument was complemented by the threat of Protestantism and Freemasonry. The Nationalists claimed that their pro-British opponents were in fact trying to erode Malta's Catholic heritage. Despite the fact that Strickland was a Catholic and a regular churchgoer, he was also half-English and had been educated in England. The Nationalists insinuated that because Strickland was closely connected with English society in Malta, he might even be a freemason himself[21].

The local ecclesiastical hierarchy tried to keep religion out of the political debate. Archbishop Caruana repeated his instructions of 1924 by telling his clergy to keep their distance from the political agitation. He discouraged priests from running as candidates, although he did not ban them from so doing altogether. The newly elected Bishop of Gozo, Michael Gonzi[22], on the other hand forbade the clergy of his diocese from taking part in the elections. As electoral campaigning reached its climax the bishops appealed for an end to the un-Christian fighting. Both bishops

---

[20] A. KOSTER, *Prelates and Politicians...*, 90.

[21] D. FENECH, *Responsibility and Power...*, 282-284.

[22] A native of Gozo, Gonzi had a working class background. He had been ordained in 1908 and served subsequently as chaplain to the British forces in Malta during World War I. Gonzi had been elected a member of the Maltese Senate in the election of 1921, representing the Malta Labour Party. In 1924, Gonzi was appointed Bishop of Gozo. See A. KOSTER, *Prelates and Politicians...*, 82.

were careful not to take sides themselves and refused to be drawn into the political debate. However, in spite of the instructions of the bishops, the overwhelming majority of the clergy supported the Partito Nazionale, and three priests were enlisted as candidates[23].

The August 1927 elections were a close-run affair. The Compact parties managed to obtain eighteen seats, while the Nationalists had to make do with thirteen. The last seat went to an independent candidate, who soon after joined the Nationalist Party. Thus, the Compact parties held the majority in the Legislative Assembly and Strickland was invited by the Governor to form the Government. Concurrent with the elections to the Legislative Assembly, the Maltese also elected the members of the Senate. The Compact parties obtained three members and the Nationalists four. In addition, the Senate included ten corporate or special members, who did not technically belong to any party. However, in practice, they had party allegiancies. As a result, seven of the Senators supported the Compact parties. As a further eight Senators were supporters of the Nationalist Party, the balance of power in the Senate was held by two representatives nominated by the Archbishop. This meant that political power in Malta was divided and the political machinery prone to conflict[24].

Although the representatives of the Imperial Government in Malta maintained their impartiality regarding the elections, they were none too happy with the involvement of priests in politics. Lieutenant-Governor Thomas Best lamented the fact that religion had become a major electoral issue, and hoped that the Vatican would prohibit priests from taking any part in politics in the future. However, in keeping with its careful policy concerning the Catholic Church in Malta, the Colonial Office did not wish to take this up at an official diplomatic level, and they hoped that the Foreign Office would concur[25]. However, this was to no avail, for the British Minister at the Holy See was instructed to discuss the issue with his Vatican counterpart[26].

---

[23] D. FENECH, *Responsibility and Power...*, 284-285.

[24] *Ibidem*, 287-288.

[25] *Ibidem*, 208-286.

[26] AES, *Inghilterra*, IV periodo, P.O. 182a, Fasc. 19, note by the Secreteriat of State November 25, 1927, f. 25.

3. The Vatican Dispatches Father Orlich to Malta in January 1928

Concerned by developments in Malta, the Holy See felt the need to gather more thorough and impartial information on the religious and political situation on the island. In order to find out the extent to which information emanating from Malta was accurate, the Vatican decided to send its own representative to the island. The Holy See chose Father Alfonso Orlich, Minister-General of the Order of Friars Minor Conventuals, for this private mission. Due to his position as the head of an important religious Order, Orlich was well-connected and enjoyed the confidence of both the Cardinal Secretary of State and the Pope himself. His visit to Malta was kept secret and was only known to the highest ecclesiastical authorities. Orlich's orders were to make observations *in situ* and to report directly to the Pope in an absolutely confidential manner[27]. Dispatching an apostolic visitor to gather information for the Holy See was a common practice. What was unusual was the lengths the Vatican went to in order to keep Orlich's mission secret. The decision to send as important a man as Orlich to report on the situation in Malta attests to the seriousness the Holy See attached to the state of affairs there. Taking into account the repercussions any serious conflict between the Church and the Maltese Government might have on its relations with Britain, the Holy See made sure that it was well-informed of developments on the island.

Orlich arrived in Malta in January 1928. The bulk of Orlich's investigative work took place in Valletta, the capital of Malta, but he also approached certain parish priests in the countryside. In addition, Orlich visited the nearby island of Gozo, where he held long discussions with Mgr. Michael Gonzi, the local bishop. Although Orlich's visit to Malta was kept secret from the general public and the Maltese and Imperial governments, he met over fifty people during his sojourn on the island. Apart from the two bishops and the local clergy, Orlich arranged interviews with the superiors of various religious orders, university professors and numerous professionals. He complemented his investigation by analysing the local newspapers, both English and Italian. In his report to the Pope, Orlich lamented the fact that he had not always been able to conduct his research to the full because of the need to remain incognito. Nevertheless,

---

[27] AES, *Inghilterra*, IV periodo, P.O. 182a, Fasc. 19, Orlich's report March 1, 1928; *Correspondence with the Holy See relative to Maltese Affairs, January 1929 to May 1930*, London 1930, 34.

Orlich believed that his investigation had been thorough and that his report painted an accurate picture of the situation on the island[28].

According to Orlich, the political situation in Malta was very tense. After the elections, tempers had been running high among the island's intellectuals and among the middle and working classes. The daily newspapers reflected this charged atmosphere, frequently publishing reciprocal insults. The opposition Nationalist Party, now merged together with the Italian Party, was trying to conserve Latin and Italian culture on the island, whereas the Constitutional Party, supported by the Labour Party, was keen to strengthen ties with Britain and consequently to anglicize the customs and language of Malta. Owing to these tensions, almost any question could become political, Orlich wrote. He accused both sides of partisanship and of exaggerating the other's malpractices[29].

Both parties claimed to safeguard the rights of the Church and accused the other of working against it. Nevertheless, with regard to religion and the Catholic Church, Orlich thought that the Nationalist Party was clearly the more favourable option, and it was supported by an overwhelming majority of the clergy[30]. Orlich noted that the Nationalist Party equated itself with the Catholic faith and proclaimed itself to be the true supporter of the Church. However, he had not failed to notice that this image fitted in well with the party's agenda of promoting the Maltese and Italian, and Catholic, traditions. Although he had been assured, among others by Bishop Gonzi, that the Nationalist leaders were good, practising Catholics, Orlich suspected that in some cases religion was being used solely as a means to promote their political aims. He regretted the fact that in spite of the generally acceptable politics of the party, its members often worked for a political union with Italy and were enthralled by Mussolini, whose religious and civilian merits and virtues they praised and exaggerated[31]. Nonetheless, Orlich felt that the Nationalist Party stood for the good of the Catholic Church. It was often impossible to separate religious and political elements from each other, but, in the end, actions outweighed motives.

Accordingly, it was the discrepancy between Strickland's rhetoric and his actions towards the Catholic Church that had so exasperated the eccle-

---

[28] AES, *Inghilterra*, IV periodo, P.O. 182a, Fasc. 19, Orlich's report, March 1, 1928, ff. 7-8.

[29] *Ibidem*, ff. 8-9.

[30] See D. FENECH, *Responsibility and Power...*, 204; A. KOSTER, *Prelates and Politicians...*, 85.

[31] AES, *Inghilterra*, IV periodo, P.O. 182a, Fasc. 19, Orlich's report, March 1, 1928, ff. 10-11.

siastical hierarchy in Malta. The Constitutional Party claimed to defend the constitution and with it Article 56, which defined Roman Catholicism as the «True Religion» of the island. Furthermore, Strickland and his family were practising Catholics, and the same applied to most of his Ministers. However, because the vast majority of the clergy supported the Nationalists, the Constitutional Ministers adopted critical if not overtly anti-clerical attitudes. As had become clear during the previous years, Strickland himself did not shrink from even criticising the Pope, if he felt it advanced his aims[32].

While Orlich was sharp-sighted enough to see that some of the criticism levelled at Strickland by the Nationalists was unfounded, he did not mince his words in his report to the Holy See. Orlich held Strickland responsible for most of the problems in Malta. Describing him as an opportunist, Orlich painted an unflattering picture of his political career. For instance, Strickland had been a member of the Nationalist Party in his youth, before deciding to abandon his former companions in order to pursue a career in the Governor's Office. Of course, manoeuvres of this kind to gain personal advantage were hardly an unprecedented phenomenon in politics, but more incriminating were Strickland's ties with Protestants. According to Orlich, Strickland openly fraternised with people who were anti-clerical and offensive towards the Catholic clergy. Perhaps the most damning accusation against Strickland was that of his being a freemason. Although he was unable to confirm this claim, Orlich suspected that it was the case even though Strickland was a regular church-goer and frequently took part in Holy Mass[33].

Orlich also accused Strickland and the Constitutional Party of corruption in the 1927 election. He suggested that the Constitutionals had been able to secure their majority in the Parliament with the help of Strickland's wealth. From what he had seen and heard during his visit to Malta, Orlich feared that the new Government could spell trouble for the Catholic Church[34].

Orlich stressed to his superiors that these were all signs of a very serious situation. A further concern for the Church was the fact that the Constitutional Party had allied itself with the Labour Party to gain a majority in Parliament. According to Orlich, the Labour Party had been founded,

---

[32] *Ibidem*, ff. 11-12; A. RHODES, *The Vatican in the Age of Dictators...*, 56-57.

[33] AES, *Inghilterra*, IV periodo, P.O. 182a, Fasc. 19, Orlich's report, March 1, 1928, ff. 11-15.

[34] *Ibidem*, f. 16.

and was lead, by English Protestants. Moreover, it contained a revolutionary element, which «hated the clergy and openly made Communist propaganda»[35]. Many workers had joined the party and the island's trade unions in order to find work and, as a consequence had been influenced by undesirable ideas. As a result, they now distanced themselves from the clergy. The influence of the Church among the working class was in decline, Orlich lamented. The fear was that the Government, after it had emptied the State's coffers, would soon lay its hands on Church assets in order to satisfy the ever increasing demands of the *laburisti*[36].

Besides reporting on the political situation in Malta, Orlich had been assigned to investigate the religious situation on the island. First, Orlich was to clarify the influence of Protestant churches and other religious movements on the Maltese population. Second, he was commissioned to look into the state of the Catholic Church in Malta. Under special scrutiny were the actions of the Archbishop, Mgr. Mauro Caruana, and the status of the clergy[37].

In his report to the Holy See, Orlich dedicated several pages to an analysis of Protestant and Masonic propaganda in Malta. He began by stating that it was impossible to separate Protestant activity from that of the freemasons. This was due to the peculiar nature of Anglo-Saxon masonry, which did not prevent freemasons from attending Church services. Freemasons in the Maltese capital had even sought permission to enter the local church in procession dressed in their full ceremonial attire. Thus, Orlich concluded, ties between the Anglican Church and the Lodge were very close[38].

Orlich had already hinted that Strickland himself was a freemason, but irrespective of the truth of this claim, it was his view that there was an ongoing campaign to corrupt the Catholic population. According to him, this had been continuing ever since Malta had become part of the British Empire. In Orlich's opinion, it was only the methods that had changed. Propaganda that had been open and aggressive in the 19th century had since become more cunning and tenacious. The Protestant pastors did not make a fuss of themselves. They seldom spoke of religion but rather of humanity and common faith, as well as of tolerance and charity. Contacts

---

[35] «Che odiano il sacerdozio e fanno aperta propaganda comunista». AES, *Inghilterra*, IV periodo, P.O. 182a, Fasc. 19, Orlich's report, March 1, 1928, f. 12.

[36] *Ibidem*, ff. 17-18.

[37] *Ibidem*, ff. 18-24.

[38] *Ibidem*, f. 18.

between Catholics and Protestants, which had been rare in the past, had become commonplace[39].

Along with the inconspicuous activity of the local Protestant ministers, Orlich also discovered direct efforts to influence the local population. These, he suspected, were mainly orchestrated from Britain and directed towards the working classes and the rural population. According to Orlich, thousands of pamphlets and books, written in Maltese and mainly printed by the Scripture Gift Mission, arrived daily from London to be distributed on the island[40]. Orlich expressed his worry that the Protestant agenda was also promoted in the island's schools. An example of this was a guidebook recently issued for teachers containing an apologia of *Martin Luther*[41].

Orlich also cited other factors which had contributed to the spread of Protestantism in Malta. After World War I, large hospitals had been founded on Malta in order to care for the numerous wounded soldiers. Both the soldiers and the nurses and Red Cross staff were a very heterogeneous mix representing various faiths and denominations. Orlich lamented the fact that their presence on the island had facilitated inter-faith ties, without due concern for religious difference[42].

As to the effects of Protestant activity, Orlich thought that they were difficult to measure accurately. However, what he was sure of was that the propaganda campaign was intense and that it was bound to have grave and pernicious consequences. Orlich stated that it was beyond doubt that respect for the clergy had greatly fallen over recent years, especially among the working class. Church-going Catholics were affected as well. It was not uncommon to hear utterances such as «It is God we should be praying to, not the Saints» or «All processions should be prohibited», from young and old alike[43]. Although the number of Catholics actually professing apostasy was still small, many were becoming estranged from the Church[44].

---

[39] *Ibidem*, ff. 18-19.

[40] The Scripture Gift Mission was a London-based mission, founded in 1888 by printer William Walters. Its work consisted mainly of translating and distributing portions and compilations of the Bible free of charge.

[41] AES, *Inghilterra*, IV periodo, P.O. 182a, Fasc. 19, Orlich's report, March 1, 1928, ff. 19-20.

[42] *Ibidem*, f. 19.

[43] «È Dio che dobbiamo pregare, non i Santi», «Bisognerebbe proibire tutte le processioni». AES, *Inghilterra*, IV periodo, P.O. 182a, Fasc. 19, Orlich's report, 1 March 1928, f. 20.

[44] *Ibidem*, ff. 20-21.

As for the Archbishop, Orlich had the impression that Mgr. Caruana was pious and serious in nature. However, Orlich hinted that he might lack the «spiritual resources» needed to evaluate events correctly and to face them with apostolic resolve. Orlich backed up his assessment with examples of the Archbishop's recent activities[45].

In the field of politics, Orlich thought that Caruana's judgment was impaired by his English education. Caruana preferred to preach to the nuns and the soldiers, whom he often visited, in English and openly displayed his predilection for the English-speaking institutions. In Orlich's view what was worse was that the Archbishop obviously approved of Strickland. Caruana had confessed this to Orlich personally, clearly stating that he had no problems with the Constitutional leaders, while it was the Nationalists who had caused him a lot of trouble in the past. Orlich was especially annoyed that Caruana, while prohibiting the clergy from taking any part in the election, had accepted an invitation to drink tea with Strickland on the eve of the elections. This, Orlich feared, could be interpreted as an act of political support for the Constitutionalist Party[46].

Orlich found further cause for criticism in the Archbishop's dealings with the Protestants. He thought that Caruana dismissed any complaints about Protestant propaganda on the grounds that they arose from political antipathy towards Britain. In his rare speeches, Caruana lacked the courage to publicly denounce the written propaganda of the Protestants and had confined himself to addressing the issue in a couple of «very bland» circular letters. Caruana had also recommended that the clergy refrain from preaching against Protestantism. Thus, Orlich surmised that it was useless to expect any significant or effective action on this matter from the Archbishop[47].

Orlich concluded his report to the Holy See by observing the general state of the Catholic clergy in Malta. His visit had revealed serious shortcomings in the moral standards of the island's priests. Especially dangerous were close relations with the opposite sex, which were not uncommon amongst the younger clergy on the island. Some priests led worldly and dissipated lives, frequently attending public clubs and theatres. Orlich pondered whether it was the high number of priests in Malta that was one cause of the problems. As a result of their numbers, many of them languished in idleness, which in turn led to depravity. Orlich also gave

---

[45] *Ibidem*, f. 21.
[46] *Ibidem*, ff. 21-22.
[47] *Ibidem*, ff. 22-23.

another explanation for the situation. He suspected that the relative wealth of the Catholic Church had contributed to the difficulties. According to his information, the Church owned half the land and property in Malta while the other half belonged to the government and private individuals. Many of the clergy were lulled into believing that such favourable conditions were permanent, and thus they were not sufficiently prepared for change[48].

The Orlich Report painted a very bleak picture of the situation in Malta with regard to the Catholic faith. One of Orlich's tasks was to discover whether there was an on-going campaign to undermine the Roman Catholicism of the Maltese people. Indeed, Orlich suspected that the traditionally firm grip of the Roman Catholic Church on Malta was weakening, mainly because of Protestant propaganda and freemasonry. He was presumably aware of the special nature of British masonry, which differed greatly from its continental counterpart. British freemasons were usually practising Protestants, and it was not uncommon for clergymen of the Church of England to belong to Masonic lodges. However, it did nothing to allay Orlich's fears that the Catholic Church was at risk. Although Protestantism might have been slighty the lesser of the two evils, in the event it was hard to distinguish between the two. The Orlich Report therefore echoed the somewhat disproportionate fear of Protestantism and freemasonry still prevalent even in the highest echelons of the Roman Catholic Church at the time. Added to the threat of Protestant propaganda were the efforts of the Communists to promote anti-clerical thinking and activity. To make matters worse, Archbishop Caruana was ill-equipped to handle the situation.

4. The Church and the Maltese Government Collide

The Holy See had hardly had time to digest Orlich's report, before affairs in Malta took a turn for the worse. Just as Orlich had predicted, a collision between the Compact Government and the Church occurred in July 1928. What Orlich had not foreseen was the speed with which relations between Strickland and Archbishop Caruana, whom Orlich had accused of siding with the Head of Ministry, deteriorated.

The confrontation between the Church and the Government was triggered by a dispute in the Maltese Senate. The source of the problem lay

---

[48] *Ibidem*, f. 24.

in the composition of the Senate, where the Compact parties had seven Senators and the Nationalists had eight Senators, which left the balance of power to the two senators nominated by the Archbishop. It was commonly understood that the task of these clerical representatives was to voice the Church's interests in the Senate, while refraining from taking part in other political issues or controversy. Further support had been leant to this view by the detached attitude of the Archbishop during the election and by the fact that he had advised the clergy not to take part in politics. Strickland, for his part, held the view that the clerical representatives were duty bound to support the government in issues not related to the Church[49].

The two representatives of the Archbishop had co-operated with the Government in the Senate during a debate on budget proposals in March-April. However, July 11 the two priests voted with the Opposition, causing strong protests from the Government. Strickland felt that the clerical representatives had misled the Government by voting with it in a trivial matter but voting against it when the stakes were high[50]. As a result of the Priests-Senators' decision to side with the opposition, anti-clerical demonstrations were held outside the Archbishop's Palace. The protesters underlined their anger by shouting offensive, anti-clerical slogans[51]. It is likely that the demonstrations helped Caruana to adopt an openly critical attitude towards the government[52].

Soon after, Strickland had an interview with Caruana, during which he asked the Archbishop to instruct the Priest-Senators to support the Government. Strickland emphasized that the Government's draft measure was not directed against the Church. However, Caruana pointed out that he had fulfilled his duty by nominating the two representatives. He also added that he did not interfere in politics and thus could not attempt to influence their votes. Caruana described the representatives as «men of moderate views» who were free to vote with their conscience, unless the interests of the Church were at stake[53]. Caruana's position implied that he did not

---

[49] D. FENECH, *Responsibility and Power...*, 288-289, 353, 355. The clerical representatives were not elected by and from their own number but were directly nominated by the Archbishop. Fenech notes that the Maltese Constitution thus implicitly distinguished between the interests of the Church and those of individual priest-politicians.

[50] *Malta Royal Commission*, London 1932, 30; D. FENECH, *Responsibility and Power...*, 355-356.

[51] *Exposition of the Malta Question...*, 16.

[52] D. FENECH, *Responsibility and Power...*, 356-358; A. KOSTER, *Prelates and Politicians...*, 95.

[53] *Malta Royal Commission*, 30; D. FENECH, *Responsibility and Power...*, 356.

feel that the controversy over the budget framework required action from the Church.

However, even if Caruana maintained that the budget did not concern the interests of the Church, he clearly felt that the attacks against the clerical representatives in the Senate did. On July 13, the Archbishop issued a circular letter in which he condemned the attacks against the clergy and warned against class conflict. He particularly lamented the fact that such chants as «Down with Christ the King» and «Down with Religion» had been heard during the demonstrations. Caruana also specified that special services should be held in the Cathedral and the Co-Cathedral on Sunday July 22 to atone for these grave offenses against Christ and to show the world that the Maltese people were still truly Catholic[54]. It was the criticism of the two Priest-Senators that prompted Caruana to issue the pastoral letter, but there were more fundamental reasons for his action. It seems probable that Caruana was more worried about the strengthening of anti-clericalism in Malta than about the situation of the two particular clergymen.

Mgr. Mikiel Gonzi, Bishop of Gozo, was also distressed about the developments. He wrote to Caruana to express his sorrow over the events following the session in the Senate. Gonzi was especially indignant about insults directed against the Archbishop. He had also heard that it was not only Caruana and the two clerical representatives in the Senate who had been subject to public insult but also many other priests. Gonzi vowed to protest against the violent and «sacrilegious» acts with all his ecclesiastical authority and energy[55].

The conflict further escalated when leaflets printed at Progress Press, a Maltese priting house owned by Strickland, were distributed to the public. The pamphlet accused the representatives of the clergy of siding with the Nationalists in the Senate at the expense of the workers. Archbishop Caruana reacted angrily to these accusations. He wrote to Strickland claiming that the priests had always acted in the best interests of the people, which was evident from their previous efforts to provide work for the unemployed. Caruana reproached Strickland and the Constitutionalist papers for terrorizing the two ecclesiastics, who by force of circumstances held the balance of power in the Senate. He maintained that the leaflet was designed to «deceive the ignorant and to rouse their worst passions» and

---

[54] AES, *Inghilterra*, IV periodo, P.O. 182a, Fasc. 19, Circular Letter July 13, 1928, f. 38.
[55] Archivum Archiepiscopale Melitense (AAM), *Secretaria*, Corrispondenza Caruana 1928, Privati, Gonzi to Caruana July 14, 1928.

was doing immense harm throughout the island. That Strickland, who was the Head of Ministry and Head of Police and thus responsible for public order, had allowed the printing and distribution of such a «red» leaflet was beyond Caruana's comprehension[56]. The Archbishop criticized not only the policy of the Compact Government but also Strickland himself in very harsh words. The content and tone of Caruana's letter left no room for misinterpretation. Relations between the Maltese Government and the local Church were at breaking point.

The next day, the tone set by the letter was followed by the two Priest-Senators at a sitting of the Senate. They cast blame for the controversy on the Government. Mgr. Zammit lamented the fact that the people were being incited against the clergy by certain populist newspapers. The Government's representatives responded to the accusation by maintaining that the fact that the Senators were members of the clergy did not mean that they should be immune to criticism. Professor Bartolo, Minister for Education, also protested against Archbishop Caruana's circular letter, claiming that it contained inaccuracies. A long and vehement discussion over the treatment of the clergy ensued.

On July 19 Strickland replied to the Archbishop in a verbose letter in which he denied most of Caruana's accusations. Regarding the clerical representatives, Strickland stated that «their past piety does not guarantee present or future political impeccability». Moreover, he considered the priests' decision not to vote for the Annual Appropriation Bill more «red» than the leaflet, as it could throw the administration into chaos and stop the payment of all salaries not reserved by law. Strickland went on to declare that:

> «As to the "colour" of the leaflet it is mild in comparison to attacks elsewhere against the Constitutionals, against Religion, and against morality which appear constantly and have not been described as "red" or been otherwise publicly censured by Your Grace»[57].

According to Strickland, these attacks were the work of the Nationalists, who mixed religion with politics and had terrorised the Priest-Senators into voting against the Budget estimates. Strickland also made it clear that it was in Caruana's power to re-establish and strengthen «the harmonious and cordial relations» which had existed between the Archbishop

---

[56] AES, *Inghilterra*, IV periodo, P.O. 182a, Fasc. 19, Caruana to Strickland July 17, 1928, f. 27.

[57] *Ibidem*, ff. 27-33.

and the Government prior to the confrontation[58]. Despite Strickland's appeal for the resumption of normal relations between his government and the Church, the reply was unlikely to have been interpreted as conciliatory. Strickland's criticism extended not only to the two senators but also to Archbishop Caruana himself. Consequently, instead of easing tensions, Strickland's letter had the opposite effect, and ensured that the conflict escalated even further.

This became clear some days later when Strickland asked Caruana's permission to present their exchange of letters to Parliament, as their correspondence had been the subject of a discussion in the Legislative Assembly[59]. Caruana's reply was curt. He forbade the publishing of his letter and added that he was deeply grieved by the tone of Strickland letter of July 19, which was «not worthy of a Catholic»[60]. Strickland acquiesced over the issue of publishing the letters, but he could not resist the temptation of adding that as a Catholic his conscience was «quite at rest» over the political situation. Moreover, as a Catholic, he felt it his duty to retort that:

> «The sins against this Country and against elementary morality, and departures from truth and duty, rest with the advisers of Your Grace and will rest with Your Grace if you are not willing or able to remove your bad advisers. [...] The Catholic Religion is, and must continue to be, possible to those who are educated, and do not want to make money out of it»[61].

Here Strickland's choice of words was even harsher than in his previous letter. He implied that Caruana, prompted by his advisors, was actually working against the good of the people and even against the Catholic faith.

The war of words carried over into deeds when the clerical representatives abstained from attending the sittings of the Senate. On August 1, they wrote to the President of the Senate to explain that due to the campaign against them they would not attend Senate sittings as long as the situation continued. Unsurprisingly, the Government accused the Priest-Senators of shirking their responsibility and fleeing at a crucial time. While refus-

---

[58] AES, *Inghilterra*, IV periodo, P.O. 182a, Fasc. 19, Strickland to Caruana July 19, 1928, ff. 32-35.

[59] *Ibidem*, f. 40.

[60] AES, *Inghilterra*, IV periodo, P.O. 182a, Fasc. 19, Caruana to Strickland July 24, 1928, f. 42.

[61] AES, *Inghilterra*, IV periodo, P.O. 182a, Fasc. 19, Strickland to Caruana July 24, 1928, f. 41.

ing to name names, Strickland also suspected that certain priests intended to be politically hostile towards his party in the next election. This he construed as a declaration of war. However, Strickland declared himself unworried by the politicisation of the clergy because Malta did not have female suffrage. Strickland's reference to the influence of the clergy over the women was sure to give additional offence to the Church[62].

Archbishop Caruana's next move was to issue a pastoral letter on August 15, in which he condemned the promotion of class hatred and disrespect for the clergy. These were outward signs of the real danger, which was loss of faith. Caruana stressed that this danger was neither imagined nor a product of paranoia. It was something that had been gradually developing but had only recently become visible. Caruana saw signs of this worrying development in the loosening of morality, in socialist and Protestant propaganda, as well as in indifference towards the Church[63]. The pastoral letter revealed the fundamental worry of the Archbishop, namely dwindling commitment to the teachings of the Church. In the politicized atmosphere of Malta, it was easy to interpret Caruana's actions as primarily part of the on-going political power struggle. To some extent this was certainly true, as the Church had much to lose if the Government had its way. However, the underlying anxiety of the Archbishop was of a spiritual and religious nature.

Caruana lamented the fact that the Church was suspected of pursuing its own self-interest and keeping the people in ignorance so that they could better serve the Church. He also proclaimed that the recent attacks against him and the clergy were attacks against the Catholic Church, despite protestations that they were political in nature[64]. Caruana refuted Strickland's insinuation that the Church wished to benefit financially from its members. The wording of the pastoral letter made it clear that Caruana did not see the situation primarily as a political crisis issue but, rather, as a worrying display of anti-clericalism. He interpreted the recent troubles as further evidence that the Roman Catholic faith, with which the Church was synonymous, was under threat.

Finally, Caruana announced the establishment of a diocesan organization to produce and disseminate «good» literature to «counteract the evil effects of bad periodicals». The organization was responsible for a new weekly newspaper, «Lehen is-Sewwa» («The Voice of Truth»), written in

---

[62] *Malta Royal Commission*, 31-32; A. KOSTER, *Prelates and Politicians...*, 96.
[63] *Exposition of the Malta Question...*, 63-64.
[64] *Ibidem*, 63-65.

the Maltese language. Caruana stated that the principal scope of the news-paper was the defense of religion and that it would remain above party politics. Caruana also warned that he would be forced to condemn and forbid the reading of papers that continued a campaign against the Church and the clergy as well as those that aroused class hatred on the pretext of defending a particular political party[65]. The setting up of a diocesan news-paper was an attempt to counter the influence of political publications. Caruana's claim that it would stay clear of party politics was more or less rhetoric, as the very idea of publishing a weekly paper was to participate in day-to-day discussion, which was inherently political. The on-going conflict with the government was the decisive factor in the foundation of «Lehen is-Sewwa», but the decision was undoubtedly bolstered by the Archbishop's fear of socialism and the lessening of the influence of the Church on the lives of the Maltese people.

It had become clear to the Maltese bishops that they could not control the situation alone. Caruana and Gonzi both proceeded to seek help from a high quarter, Caruana by contacting Cardinal Francis Bourne, the Arch-bishop of Westminster, and Gonzi by seeking instructions from the Vati-can. Caruana's course of action was natural in the sense that he had been educated in Britain and was already familiar with Bourne. The decision to consult the Cardinal was undoubtedly an attempt to influence the Imperial Government through the leading Catholic figure in England.

Caruana informed Bourne that Mgr. Paolo Galea, a Canon of his Ca-thedral Chapter, was visiting London, and asked Bourne to give him an audience so that Galea could explain the crisis between the Church and the Government in Malta. In addition, Galea would be able to shed light on the «peculiar Catholicism» of Lord Strickland. Caruana made no other di-rect requests than that the Cardinal receive Galea[66]. Presumably he hoped that after hearing Galea's report Bourne would be able to decide on the best course of action.

---

[65] *Exposition of the Malta Question...*, 65-66; A. KOSTER, *Prelates and Politicians...*, 96. Caruana had already established the diocesan organization on July 17, the same day he wrote to Strickland to criticize the printing of the leaflet by Progress Press. Koster holds that the decision to publish the newspaper in the vernacular was an attempt to reach the lower classes. He also suspects that Caruana's fear of Marxism may have been a motive behind the foundation of the newspaper. See A. KOSTER, *Prelates and Politicians...*, 97.

[66] AAM, *Secretaria*, Corrispondenza Caruana 1928, Privati, Caruana to Bourne August 6, 1928.

Bourne agreed to receive Galea, but after hearing his account of the situation he informed the Canon that he could do nothing as the matter was none of his business. Bourne also alluded to his busy schedule as a further reason for not becoming involved[67]. Bourne clearly had no wish to become entangled in a potentially agonising conflict which could put him in a difficult position *vis-à-vis* the British Government.

Meanwhile, Gonzi wrote to the undersecretary of State at the Holy See, Mgr. Francesco Borgongini Duca, to explain the situation in Malta. As further proof of the Maltese Government's hostile attitude towards the Church, Gonzi enclosed the leaflet attacking the clerical representatives. On behalf of Archbishop Caruana and himself, Gonzi asked for instructions on the position they should adopt towards Strickland and the Government in light of their recent «declaration of war» on the clergy[68].

The Vatican raised the idea of asking Cardinal Bourne to intervene on behalf of the Church, unaware that Archbishop Caruana had already done the same. Gonzi, who had travelled to Rome, was counseled to contact Bourne upon his return to Malta. Archbishop Caruana was far from pleased when Gonzi shared these instructions with him. Caruana felt that contacting Bourne again would seem impertinent, as the Cardinal had already declined to address the Imperial authorities on their behalf. However, Gonzi succeeded in persuading Caruana to permit him to draft a new letter to the Cardinal. Then, much to Gonzi's exasperation, Caruana changed his mind again and refused to sign the letter without further instructions from the Holy See. Caruana did not wish to act without Borgongini Duca's permission for him to inform Bourne that he was being contacted again at the request of the Holy See. Gonzi's suggestion of merely sending a copy of the letter to Rome did not please Caruana either; it would look like they were trying «either to force his hand or to compromise him with Rome». Caruana felt that it would be better if the matter were handled directly by the Holy See[69]. Annoyed by Caruana's stalling, Gonzi wrote to Borgongini Duca to explain the Archbishop's objections. Gonzi did not attempt to

---

[67] AES, *Inghilterra*, IV periodo, P.O. 182a, Fasc. 19, Caruana to Gonzi, September 9, 1928, f. 53.

[68] AES, *Inghilterra*, IV periodo, P.O. 182a, Fasc. 19, Gonzi to Borgongini Duca, August 22, 1928, f. 44.

[69] AES, *Inghilterra*, IV periodo, P.O. 182a, Fasc. 19, Caruana to Gonzi, September 9, 1928, f. 53; Gonzi to Borgongini Duca, September 10, 1928, ff. 54-55.

hide his frustration with Caruana and made sure that any blame for the delay in contacting Bourne rested with the Archbishop[70].

The dallying of the Maltese bishops spurred the Holy See into action. The Cardinal Secretary of State agreed with Caruana that the issue should be handled directly by the Vatican. While Gonzi was engaged in correspondence with Borgongini Duca, Caruana had, in fact, written directly to the Secretary of State, informing him of developments in Malta. Caruana gave Gasparri an account of the steps that he had taken to control the situation and of the contents of his pastoral letter. Gasparri was satisfied with Caruana's actions, especially with the setting up of the diocesan press organization, which he thought was an excellent idea. However, Gasparri counselled Caruana to proceed with caution, particularly concerning the «Lehen is-Sewwa» newspaper[71]. Despite the fact that Caruana had recently been the target of heavy criticism, and had also been rebuked by Father Orlich after his visit to Malta, Gasparri appears to have supported the Archbishop. Nevertheless, although Gasparri was pleased with Caruana's handling of the situation, the Holy See was to take over responsibility for the issue through the figure of Cardinal Bourne. Gasparri telegrammed Bourne to enquire about whether he could do something to help the politico-religious crisis in Malta[72].

In his reply, Bourne told Gasparri that, in addition to Canon Galea, he had been visited by Lady Strickland, whom he described as a fervent catholic and a generous benefactor. Lady Strickland had wanted to discuss the attitude of the Maltese clergy, who according to her were overly involved in politics and thus were harming the Catholic faith. However, Bourne added confidentially that although Lord Strickland was a good Catholic, he had always regarded him as inconsiderate and a very difficult character. Bourne told Gasparri that he believed Lord Strickland to be the cause of the problems in Malta[73].

As to the involvement of the clergy in politics, in Bourne's opinion it was unwise to mix religion and politics. He had informed Galea that al-

---

[70] AES, *Inghilterra*, IV periodo, P.O. 182a, Fasc. 19, Gonzi to Borgongini Duca, September 10, 1928.

[71] AES, *Inghilterra*, IV periodo, P.O. 182a, Fasc. 19, Caruana to Gasparri, September 17, 1928, ff. 62-63; Borgongini Duca to Gonzi, September 19, 1928; Gasparri to Caruana, October 8, 1928, f. 57.

[72] AES, *Inghilterra*, IV periodo, P.O. 182a, Fasc. 19, Gasparri to Bourne, September 1928, f. 56.

[73] AES, *Inghilterra*, IV periodo, P.O. 182a, Fasc. 19, Bourne to Gasparri, September 23, 1928, f. 66.

though he did not know enough of the conditions in Malta, it was certainly the case in England, and more than likely in other countries in the British Empire, that direct, active clerical involvement in politics was contrary to the interests of the Church. Bourne's advice was that it would be prudent of the Maltese clergy to give up their seats in the Senate. However, Bourne added that he left the matter entirely to the judgement of the local Ordinary and above all to the Holy See[74]. Although Bourne suspected that the root of the problems in Malta rested with Lord Strickland, he was sensitive to any amalgamation of religion and politics and could not endorse a system wherein priests were closely involved in parliamentary politics.

Bourne's opinions were passed on by Borgongini Duca to Gonzi for comment[75]. However, Archbishop Caruana apparently remained uninformed of Bourne's views, and he was not asked to comment on them. Gonzi had been the more active of the Maltese bishops in corresponding with the Holy See, especially with undersecretary Borgongini Duca, which may explain the Holy See's decision to consult the Bishop of Gozo instead of Archbishop Caruana. It is also possible that the Secretariat of State considered Gonzi more up-to-date with the situation in Malta, especially as it had received various reports of Caruana's passivity, not least from Gonzi himself. However, the Archbishop was not put out to pasture, which was apparent from the positive appraisal of his actions by Cardinal Gasparri.

Gonzi agreed with Cardinal Bourne's view that clerical participation in politics should be restricted. Gonzi told Borgongini Duca that he had already adopted such a policy in his own diocese by forbidding priests from standing in elections. However, the situation concerning the two clerical representatives in the Maltese Senate was somewhat different. Gonzi explained to the undersecretary that according to the constitution of Malta the Archbishop had the right to nominate two members to the Senate to safeguard the interests of the Church[76]. There was a difference between priests who became involved in party politics and the nominees of the Archbishop, who were, at least in principle, non-partisan.

It was clear that the Secretariat of State of the Holy See intended to tackle the situation. Of Strickland they knew enough to hold him as the

---

[74] AES, *Inghilterra*, IV periodo, P.O. 182a, Fasc. 19, Bourne to Gasparri, September 23, 1928, f. 67.

[75] AES, *Inghilterra*, IV periodo, P.O. 182a, Fasc. 19, Borgongini Duca to Gonzi, October 4, 1928.

[76] AES, *Inghilterra*, IV periodo, P.O. 182a, Fasc. 19, Gonzi to Borgongini Duca, October 19, 1928, ff. 87-90.

principal culprit for the crisis, but the political activity of the clergy was a more intricate problem for Gasparri and his undersecretary. First, there were the Pope's reservations about the participation of priests in politics to consider. In October 1927, Gasparri had personally explained to John Du Cane, the Governor of Malta, that the Holy See neither encouraged nor even countenanced the participation of priests in Maltese politics. Secondly, at least in principle, the decision to allow priests to participate in politics rested with the local Ordinary[77]. The Holy See had no wish to dictate to the Maltese clergy if it could be avoided. The latter was an argument the Holy See was to present in subsequent discussions with the British Government.

Evidently, the Holy See was faced with a complex situation. By acting against Strickland, the Vatican was bound to step on the toes of the Imperial authorities. On the other hand, remaining passive in the face of the hostile action of the Maltese Government was not an option either. What should have remained an insignificant local squabble was quickly turning into a diplomatic farrago.

5. Conclusion

The positive development seen in Anglo-Vatican relations following the end of the the First World War took a downward turn in the late 1920s. This was mainly due to the politico-religious situation in the British colony of Malta. From the standpoint of the Holy See, the activities of Gerald Strickland, the local Head of Government, were of great concern. The Holy See feared that Strickland would undermine the position of the local church by attacking the clergy and the ecclesiastical hierarchy. Thus, anticipating trouble with Strickland, the Pope decided to act quickly and dispatched an apostolic visitor, Father Alfonso Orlich, to gather up-to-date *in situ* information.

Orlich's visit to Malta exposed a number of worrying developments for the Holy See, both political and ecclesiastical. Orlich held Strickland responsible for most of the problems in Malta. Describing him as an opportunist, Orlich accused Strickland of fraternising with Protestants and anti-clericals. There were even accusations of Strickland being a freemason, in spite of his professed Catholicism. Allegations of corruption in the 1927 elections were a further indication of Strickland's ruthlessness. Fur-

---

[77] D. FENECH, *Responsibility and Power...*, 354.

thermore, Orlich believed that the Strickland Government was planning to dispossess the local church of its wealth.

Soon after Orlich had left Malta, the situation on the island came to a head. Strickland and Archbishop Caruana accused one another of acting against the best interests of Malta and its Catholic religion. As tempers flared, the Maltese bishops sought help from the Vatican and Cardinal Bourne in London, with a view to pressurising the British central authorities into curbing Strickland's activities. Neither Bourne nor the Vatican Secretariat of State could offer any easy remedy to the problem. However, while the Vatican had no wish to enter into local politics, it was prepared to safeguard the Church's interests in Malta, by political and diplomatic means if necessary.

Thus, the conflict in Malta had inevitable ramifications for relations between the Holy See and Britain. The British were less than pleased when the Holy See subsequently raised accusations of Protestant progaganda in diplomatic discussions. Outspoken criticism of a popularly elected Head of a British colony was not well received in Whitehall either. By the end of 1929, the situation had escalated into a diplomatic tug-of-war between the Holy See and the British Government.

SUZANNE BROWN-FLEMING

Pope Pius XI, Eugenio Pacelli
and the German Catholic Hierarchy (1933-1938)

> «In Munich [,] among Catholic circles [,] [the 1936 Nazi Party
> Congress in Nuremberg] had been of great interest; it was feared
> that the church would be under attack after the attack on Judaism
> last year».
>
> *Alberto Vassallo di Torregrossa, Report No. 5005*
> *to Cardinal Pacelli, September 12, 1936*

On July 21, 1933, Bishop of the diocese of Speyer (Germany) Ludwig
Sebastian received a letter from the Special Commissar for Supreme SA
Leadership of the territory of the Palatinate. The uniformed and armed political combat troops of the Nazi Party, the SA (*Sturmabteilung* or Brown
Shirts) were the Nazi Party's main instrument for undermining democracy
and facilitating Adolf Hitler's rise to power between 1923 and 1934[1]. The
letter, brief and to the point, demanded the transfer of four priests and two
curates in the diocese. «The behavior of [these] priests», wrote Special
Commissar Röhrig, «has led to unrest in the behavior of the population,
which can under no circumstances be further tolerated». Special Commissar Röhrig accused the priests of «political rabble-rousing». «It is [...]
in your interest, and also in keeping with [National Socialist] guidelines
and lines of thought for building the state, to transfer the aforementioned
priests as quickly as possible», wrote Röhrig. He concluded the letter with
a threat: «I request that you carry out these urgent measures right away
in order to avoid unpleasant incidents»[2]. One of the six priests listed was
Father Simon Burnickel of Schweigen.

---

[1] *Nazi Deutsch/Nazi German: An English Lexicon of the Language of the Third Reich*,
ed. by R. MICHAEL and K. DOERR, Westport, CT, 2002, 391.

[2] Röhrig to Bishops Palace of Speyer, 21 July 1933. Affari Ecclesiastici Straordinari (hereafter AES), Bavaria, 1933-1936, Pos. 198, Fasc. 40. Reports of the Nunciature: Position Created with Documents from the White Files Sent to the Archive by Pope Pius
XII. RG 76.001M: Selected Records from the Vatican Archives, 1865-1939, United
States Holocaust Memorial Museum (hereafter USHMM), Washington, DC.

Nearly four months later, on November 24, Bishop Sebastian wrote an agitated letter to the papal nuncio to Bavaria, Archbishop Alberto Vassallo di Torregrossa. Bishop Sebastian wrote to report a second notice from the Special Commissar received on July 22, one day after the first notice, demanding the transfer of an additional five priests. At the root of the transfer requests was conflict over confessional schools. «In all cases applications to be transferred resulted from excesses or transgressions by lower-ranking [National Socialist] party agencies against priests dutifully defending the confessional nature of schools», wrote Bishop Sebastian. «In view of the many expulsions, arrests, and cases of severe physical abuse by National Socialists that my clergy has had to endure since the Nazi Seizure of Power (January 30, 1933), and in order to avoid creating further anxiety among our priests, it was out of the question to [retaliate] against the initiatives put forward by the Nazis [attacking] our priests», wrote the Bishop[3].

Bishop Sebastian also wrote to the nuncio about the wave of physical attacks related to the November 12 (1933) elections. Father Burnickel was beaten up and arrested at 8:45 p.m. that day[4]. In Father Burnickel's rendering of the evening, two SS men arrived at his door to ask him why he had not voted that day. Father Burnickel answered that he had been ordered by his Bishop to abstain from politics, which, though Father Burnickel did not mention it, was a stipulation of the recently signed Concordat between the Nazi State and the Holy See[5]. At that point, the two SS men physically attacked him. When Dr. Hans Stöckl of Bergzabern examined Father Burnickel four days later, he reported severe bruising, a large scratch wound, and visible swelling around the right eye. Dr. Stöckl added in his examination report that «the Catholic population in the area is very agitated»[6].

This report about the beating of a parish priest from a remote town in the diocese of Speyer, approximately nine months after the accession of Adolf Hitler to the chancellorship of Germany, and others like it, became part of a «White File» kept by Eugenio Pacelli, Secretary of State to His Holiness Pope Pius XI from 1930-1939, and, thereafter, the controversial

---

[3] Attachment to Report No. 4376 Apostolic Nunciature Bavaria. Speyer, November 24, 1933. AES, Bavaria, 1933-1936, Pos. 198, Fasc. 40. Reports of the Nunciature: Position Created with Documents from the White Files Sent to the Archive by Pope Pius XII. RG 76.001M: Selected Records from the Vatican Archives, 1865-1939, USHMM, Washington, DC.

[4] *Ibidem.*

[5] *Ibidem.*

[6] *Ibidem.*

wartime Pope. This paper constitutes a small slice of a broader project that I began in earnest last summer as an Independent Study Associate of the United States Holocaust Memorial Museum. The project is a page-by-page examination of Record Group (RG) 76, *Selected Records from the Vatican Archives*. A brief word about RG-76 is in order. In February 2003, in an unprecedented break with Vatican Secret Archives[7] policy, the Holy See opened those records pertaining to the Munich and Berlin nunciatures for the period 1922 to 1939. During these years, Eugenio Pacelli, the future Pope Pius XII (1939-1958), served as nuncio to Bavaria (1917), nuncio to Germany (1920), and Secretary of State to Pope Pius XI (1930-1939). The United States Holocaust Memorial Museum's archives now hold microfilm copies of this subset of critical new primary source material. In 2006, Pope Benedict XVI authorized that additional documentation from the Vatican Secret Archives for the 1922-1939 period be opened to scholars, who were given access in Rome as of 18 September 2006[8]. These documents suggest a new reality for scholars studying the Catholic Church and the Holocaust. To borrow from the great Holocaust historian Saul Friedländer, the 1930s saw «Catholic appeasement of Hilter's regime». Pinning their hopes on the Concordat signed in 1933, Pope Pius XI and his Secretary of State, Eugenio Pacelli, remained «wary» of confrontation with the Nazi regime, Nazi violations of the Concordat excepted. Pius XI's departure from this stance at the end of his life, characterized by the never-published encyclical *Humani Generis Unitas*, never bore fruit due to his death in 1939[9].

With so much new documentation at hand, we may now look at this picture of «Catholic appeasement» anew. I will present two sets of materials in this essay: (1) first, part of the record of the correspondence between the Apostolic Nunciature in Bavaria and the Vatican Secretariat of State in Rome, which constitute the first several hundred documents in RG-76, as a prelude to the violent clashes between the National Socia-

---

[7] ASV, the Vatican Secret Archives, located in Vatican City, is the largest repository for all of the acts promulgated by the Roman Pontiff and some congregations of the Roman Curia. The archives also contain State papers, correspondence, and other documents.

[8] The newly available materials pertain to four major categories: (1) archives of the pontifical representatives; (2) archives of the Roman Curia; (3) archive of the Secretary of State; and (4) archive of the Congregation of Extraordinary Ecclesiastical Affairs, now separated by the ASV.

[9] S. Friedländer, *Nazi Germany and the Jews 1939-1945: The Years of Extermination*, London 2007, 58.

list regime and the Catholic Church that would later become common-place; and (2) second, those documents found in the folio labeled «Persecution Against the Jews», which I have viewed in their entirety. Taken together, these two sets of materials demonstrate the historical dangers of viewing the response of the Holy See to Nazi Germany's treatment of Jews *separately from the response to Nazi treatment of Catholics*. In reality, the Holy See's decisions and responses to persecution of Catholics influenced and affected its decisions with regard to the Church's response (or lack of response) to mistreatment of Jews. I would posit that the Holy See's response to Nazi anti-Catholic and anti-Jewish policy must be studied together for the most nuanced understanding of the Holy See in these years.

One of the most widely reported instances of violent confrontation between Catholics and the Nazi regime in 1933 was the Nazi disruption of the Munich Gesellentag (Congress of the Association of Catholic Artisans) in June of that year. *Gesellenvereine*, or German Catholic societies of young artisans for the religious, moral, and professional improvement of young male artisans, existed in 16 nations and consisted of more than 10,000 members by 1933. The 1933 Gesellentag, planned for June 8-11, 1933, was to center on that year's themes: God and People; People and Profession; and Profession and Country. The Congress was «being prepared very carefully and in accordance with the authorities of the Reich, Bavaria, and the municipality of Munich and the police», wrote chargé d'affaires for the Munich nunciature, Giovanni Panico, to Eugenio Cardinal Pacelli, the Vatican's Secretary of State and the future wartime Pope, in a lengthy report dated June 19[10]. Vice Chancellor of Germany Franz von Papen, Reich Governor of Bavaria Franz Xaver Ritter von Epp, and mayor of Munich Dr. Karl Fiehler had accepted invitations to participate. Reich President Paul von Hindenburg and Reich Chancellor Adolf Hitler had offered best wishes for a successful event. More than 24,000 young artisans from North and South America, England, Czechoslovakia, Holland, Switzerland, and Hungary would join approximately 6,000 German artisans[11].

---

[10] Giovanni Panico, chargé d'affaires, Munich, to Eugenio Cardinal Pacelli, Secretary of State, Vatican City, 19 June 1933. AES Bavaria, 1933-1936, Pos. 190 Fasc. 34. Suppression by National Socialists of Catholics and Catholic Associations. RG 76.001M: Selected Records from the Vatican Archives, 1865-1939, USHMM, Washington, DC.

[11] Giovanni Panico, chargé d'affaires, Munich, to Eugenio Cardinal Pacelli, Secretary of State, Vatican City, June 19, 1933. AES Bavaria, 1933-1936, Pos. 190 Fasc. 34. Sup-

The first warning sign of trouble came at 6 p.m. on June 2, when Interior Minister and Deputy Minister-President of Bavaria Adolf Wagner prohibited the Congress. According to Panico's report to Pacelli, the reasons given by Minister Wagner were as follows: «[because] the SA[12] of the National Socialist Party would have reacted against the young artisans; because Father [Emil] Muhler[13], a strong opponent of the Nazis, had been nominated president of the [lay movement] Catholic Action[14]; [because] Father [Philipp] Haeuser[15], [a radicalized «Brown» priest] from the diocese of Augusburg, had been forbidden by the authorities to bless the monument of [National Socialist martyr Albert Leo]

pression by National Socialists of Catholics and Catholic Associations. RG 76.001M: Selected Records from the Vatican Archives, 1865-1939, USHMM, Washington, DC.

[12] See W. Petter, *Sturmabteilung*, in *Encyclopedia of the Third Reich*, ed. by C. Zentner and F. Bedürftig, Cambridge, MA, 1997, 928-932.

[13] Dr. Emil Muhler, well-known for his anti-Nazi sentiments, was the head of Catholic Action in Munich. Cardinal Faulhaber of Munich was anxious not to jeopardize negotiations for the Concordat; Dr. Muhler was asked to resign from office. On 29 November 1933, Dr. Muhler was arrested for allegedly having spread reports of atrocities taking place in Dachau concentration camp. In his memoirs, Erwin Freiherr von Aretin, a prisoner at Dachau and witness to torture and murder in that camp, recalls that Dachau inmates hoped Muhler's arrest would spur stronger criticism of the Nazis by the Church. Indeed, Cardinal Faulhaber's famous Advent sermons did follow Muhler's arrest. See G. Lewy, *The Catholic Church and Nazi Germany*, Cambridge, 2000, 101, 111.

[14] The Catholic Action (Azione Cattolica) was a Catholic lay movement that began in Italy in 1886, with a political agenda. In 1922, in response to political activity by Catholic parties following World War I, Pius XI redefined Catholic Action as a religious and social (not political) movement. After the renunciation of partisan political activity in the Lateran Treaties with Mussolini, the Catholic Action became the Church's «second-line organization for influencing secular affairs». From 1928 onward, Berlin nuncio Eugenio Pacelli called upon German laity to join together in thet movement. With the conclusion of the Concordat in 1933, the Catholic Action came under fire. Hitler left Article 31 (protection of Catholic organizations) to be negotiated and thereafter did not tolerate the Catholic Action, understood by the Nazi regime as an ideological mass movement which openly sought to «Christianize all of German life». On June 30, 1934, Nazi acts of terrorism directed at Catholic Action peaked with the assassination of Berlin Catholic Action leader Erich Klausener, who had protested Nazi harassment at Catholic Action mass meetings. See *Catholic Action*, in *Encyclopedia of the Third Reich...*, 128-129.

[15] Dr. Philipp Haeuser was one of the best-known so-called «brown priests» in Nazi Germany. See K. Spicer, *Working for the Führer: Father Dr. Philipp Haeuser and the Third Reich*, in *Antisemitism, Christian Ambivalence and the Holocaust*, Bloomington 2007, 105-120.

Schlageter[16]; [because] a member of the Nazi assault troops had been killed by a member of the [Catholic paramilitary group] Bayernwacht[17]; [because of] the failure of the [Catholic workers' association headquarters] Leohaus[18]; and also because during a celebration on May 1, some Catholic youth had been chanting the Nazi hymn but with different words, and made anti-Nazi remarks against Hitler»[19]. Mgr. Panico had clear rejoinders to each specific accusation, which he included in his report, but I will not detail them here. Mgr. Panico understood the true reason for the Wagner decree to be the desire of the National Socialist regime

---

[16] Albert Leo Schlageter (1894-1923) was a member of the Great German Worker's Party (an offshoot of the NSDAP) and was involved in acts of sabotage after the outbreak of the Ruhr Conflict over the French Occupation. Betrayed to French authorities by spies within his own ranks after a successful attack on the Düsseldorf-Duisburg railroad line, he was tried and sentence to death on May 8, 1923. The National Socialists held Schlageter up as a martyr and in 1931 placed a cross of honor 30 meters high at the sight of his execution. See *Encyclopedia of the Third Reich*, Zentner and Bedürftig, 836.

[17] The Bayernwacht was the strong arm (paramilitary) of the Bayrische Volkspartei (Bavarian People's Party). It was at one time the biggest party in Bavaria. The Bayernwacht was led by Hans Ritter von Lex and was, together with the BVP, dissolved in 1933 after the Nazi accession to power.

[18] The Leohaus, located in Munich, served as the headquarters for the Federation of South German Catholic Workers' Associations (Verband Süddeutscher Katholischer Arbeitvereine, or VSkA). Following the murder of Kurt Eisner and the violence in the Bavarian *Landtag* on February 21, 1919, the headquarters of the VSkA, the *Leohaus*, was occupied by a group of Spartakists for ten days. The spartakists, a faction of militant socialists formed by Karl Liebknecht and Rosa Luxemburg in Berlin, ransacked the premises, sold off paper and other goods for money, and seized the presses to begin their own publications. They also renamed the *Leohaus* the «*Spartakushaus*» and began to use the printing equipment to publish the *Münchener Rote Fahne* (*Munich's Red Flag*). «Forces loyal to the republic», most likely *Freikorps* (Free Militia), a group of organized anti-socialist vigilantes recruited from war veterans and the unemployed, managed to arrest many of the Spartakist leaders by February 28. See D.J. CREMER, *To Avoid a New Kulturkampf: The Catholic Workers' Associations and National Socialism in Weimar-Era Bavaria*, in «Journal of Church & State», 41 (1999)/4, 739-760. The launching of a film-making enterprise led the Leohaus into bankruptcy and disgrace in 1933. The financial director diverted funds from other association sources, including the savings fund of the Catholic Housemaid's Association, to finance film production. Scandal broke; two directors went to prison, and the new NS regime used the incident to its own purposes. See D.-M. KRENN, *Die Christliche Arbeiterbewegungs Bayern vom Ersten Weltkrieg bis 1933*, Mainz 1991.

[19] Giovanni Panico, chargé d'affaires, Munich, to Eugenio Cardinal Pacelli, Secretary of State, Vatican City, 19 June 1933. AES Bavaria, 1933-1936, Pos. 190 Fasc. 34. Suppression by National Socialists of Catholics and Catholic Associations. RG 76.001M: Selected Records from the Vatican Archives, 1865-1939, USHMM, Washington, DC.

to, in essence, rid itself of the competition. I quote at length a passage of Mgr. Panico's letter because it captures an important feature of the Catholic-Nazi conflict in 1933:

«The true reason for the prohibition of the Gesellentag was a totally different one. During the first part of May, the youth festivities had been celebrated. Thousands of young people in impressive procession roamed through the streets of the city with their flags, singing patriotic songs. They were divided into two large groups: those of the Catholic youth and those of the Hitler Youth... the one composed of Catholic youth, much more numerous in number (10,000), finished at the Königsplatz. Minister Wagner remained very impressed with the enormous manifestation of the Catholic youths... During a speech he gave at Tölz he said that [...] in a National Socialist nation, the youth belongs to the state. In another speech [Minister Wagner] said word for word: «The right to represent the German people nowadays, belongs only and alone to the movement of Adolf Hitler, and nobody else. The right to be on the streets are only for the soldiers of the revolution and nobody else. [Minister Wagner continued] Maybe the colors are what they are, and the framework that the [lay movement] Catholic Action, whoever wants to serve his God, should go to the House of God; service to God is not done marching on the streets...»[20].

After negotiation with the Congress planners, Wagner revoked his June 2 ministerial decree. The Congress opened on June 8 as planned. By Friday, June 9, violence had already erupted. According to Panico's report to Pacelli, «groups of SA tore off some signs of the Congress and some Gesellen were attacked and beaten». The victims, wrote Panico, did not reciprocate in kind, but reported to their directors, who «worried about what would happen the following day, and with good reason». June 10, wrote Panico to Pacelli, «would always be a black page in Nazi history. A real hunt on the Gesellen took place[.] Kolpingsbrüder, easily identifiable because of their yellow shirts, were especially targeted. «Their shirts were torn off [and they] were savagely beaten», he wrote. That evening at 8 p.m., Munich police informed the gathered Gesellen that the wearing of yellow shirts was prohibited. «Groups of SA who had been informed about the police order» awaited the end of the session and «assaulted [...] beat and thrashed those who wore yellow shirts, which were torn off their bodies and torn to pieces right on the street». It was, wrote Panico, «a shameful spectacle which kept repeating itself wherever the Gesellen went». At 2 a.m., the SA occupied the headquarters of the Gesellen. «At least 20» were seriously wounded, and according to some reports, one priest

---

[20] *Ibidem.*

was killed. Another, Dr. Zinser, died in the Munich Cathedral of a heart attack[21].

Panico himself informed «consuls he could trust» about the «true [...] facts», and «Thank God I was successful», he wrote to Pacelli. «Le Temps», «La Croix», the «Daily Telegraph», «The London Times», and others reported the violent attacks perpetrated by the SA against the Gesellen. In Germany, where «there was no longer freedom of the press», noted Panico, «the leadership of the Gesellenverein published the truth of the events in the «Bayerische Kurier» on June 13, and the newspaper was sequestered. Panico himself did not manage to send his long report to Pacelli until June 19. «Forgive me for the delay of this report, but it has not been my fault. Everybody is very scared to compromise themselves and it is very difficult to obtain true information or real documents. [Nor can I] expedite correspondence like in normal times», wrote Panico[22].

The violence of the SA attacks are but one reason for detailing it at length here. Also compelling was the response, swift, unequivocal, and clear, from Michael Cardinal Faulhaber, Archbishop of Munich and Freising. On June 12, Faulhaber lodged protest in writing, addressed to Reich Chancellor Adolf Hitler; Minister President of Bavaria Ludwig Siebert[23]; Bavarian State Minister of the Interior Adolf Wagner[24]; and Bavarian Chief of Police Heinrich Himmler. The most salient passages of Cardinal Faulhaber's protest letter are as follows:

> «As Bishop I lodge a strong objection that Mass could not be held on Trinity Sunday [June 11, 1933][25], which was to be the closing event of the German

---

[21] *Ibidem.*

[22] *Ibidem.*

[23] Ludwig Siebert, formerly of the BVP and then a member of the NSDAP (after 1931); successor to Dr. Heinrich Held as Prime Minister of Bavaria (1933-1942).

[24] Adolf Wagner (1890-1944), the «despot of Munich», was a German politician who joined the NSDAP in 1922. In 1929 he became Gauleiter of Munich-Upper Bavaria (Gau of Tradition after 1930). As of April 12, 1933 he became Interior Minister and Deputy Minister-President of Bavaria, and, in 1936, minister of culture and religious affairs. He was the most powerful Gauleiter of the Third Reich, officially ranking above Bavarian Minister-President Ludwig Siebert and Reich governor Ritter von Epp. He personally supervised the removal of crucifixes from schools; was a «fanatic instigator» of persecution of Jews, and «kept up a permanent feud» with Cardinal Faulhaber. He had a stroke in June 1942 and died twenty months later. See *Encyclopedia of the Third Reich*, 1013-1014.

[25] In the Roman Catholic tradition, Trinity Sunday is the first Sunday after Pentecost, which celebrates the doctrine of the three persons of God: the Father, the Son and the Holy Spirit. Pentecost, or Whitsunday, commemorates the Descent of the Holy Ghost

Gesellentag in Munich. The leaders of the Gesellentag cancelled Mass, because, after the events of the last days and nights, they did not wish to expose their members to the physical attacks of SA troops...[26]. Not a single piece of evidence of a political goal or political speech on the part of the Gesellentag can be brought forth. In its speeches and its conduct, the Gesellentag was a glaring example of acknowledgment of the National State and for working together with the State... In 1922, the Gesellentag took place in Cologne under French Occupation without disruption... and in 1933 this same Gesellenverein is greeted in Munich as a "black band" or "black dogs" and the [Gesellenverein's] Kolpings-flag was ripped, after [Adolf] Kolping founded the first congress in Cologne [as a protest] against Karl Marx in 1849. I know the Reich Chancellor's inclinations do not lie toward these happenings and the disruption of the Mass, to whom the Catholics of the Reich look up to with confidence. Cardinal Faulhaber»[27].

There are several interesting features of this letter: first, Cardinal Faulhaber mentioned immediately his strong objection to cancellation of Trinity Sunday Mass. Second, he took trouble to point out that the Church was interested in *working together* with the State: «In its speeches and its conduct, the Gesellentag was a glaring example of acknowledgement of the National State and for working together with the state», he wrote. Cardinal Faulhaber took the trouble to point to the foundation of the Gesellenverein as a protest against Karl Marx at its very birth, in other words, an ideological goal shared by both the Church and the National Socialist Movement. Finally, Cardinal Faulhaber reaffirmed his faith that Reich Chancellor Adolf Hitler would be true to his word when Hitler promised in his Reichstag speech of March 23, 1933 that the Nazi Government would «respect the agreements concluded between the [two Christian confessions in Germany] and the federal states» and attached «the greatest value to friendly relations with the Holy See»[28].

If Cardinal Faulhaber represented a German Catholic hierarchy that still retained the hope, in mid-1933, that Church and State could co-exist har-

---

upon the Apostles, fifty days after the Resurrection of Christ, on the ancient Jewish festival called the «feast of weeks» or Pentecost.

[26] See W. PETTER, *Sturmabteilung...*, 928-932.

[27] Letter from Michael Cardinal Faulhaber, Archbishop of Munich and Freising, Munich, to Reich Chancellor Adolf Hitler, Berlin, Minister President of Bavaria Ludwig Siebert, Munich, Bavarian Interior Minister Adolf Wagner, Munich, and Chief of Police Heinrich Himmler, Munich, June 12, 1933. AES, Bavaria, 1933-1936, Pos. 190, Fasc. 34, Suppression by National Socialists of Catholics and Catholic Associations. RG 76.001M: Selected Records from the Vatican Archives, 1865-1939, United States Holocaust Memorial Museum, Washington, D.C.

[28] G. LEWY, *The Catholic Church and Nazi Germany*, 35.

moniously, by January 1934, on issues of major relevance to Church law and practice, the German bishops were willing to throw down the gauntlet. Concerning the question of sterilization, the bishops ordered Catholics to practice civil disobedience regarding the July 1933 Nazi sterilization order[29]. That month, the German bishops released the following statement: «Regarding the question of sterilization, for the [Catholic] faithful, the principle of Christian moral law, promulgated by the highest Church authorities, is valid. In accordance with the directive of the Holy Father, we recall: it is not allowed to arrange for one's sterilization or to order the sterilization of other persons. That is the teaching of the Catholic Church. Thankfully we show every recognition of this principle»[30]. Bishop of Würzburg Matthias Ehrenfried wrote to Bavarian nuncio Vassallo di Torregrossa about Nazi orders to prevent the reading of this statement from pulpits in his diocese. «In my diocese, police watch individual churches to see whether the sentence regarding sterilization is really read», he wrote. «I send you an order from the Nazi authorities in Kitzingen, which ended up in my hands. Consequently, we are controlled within the Church too, and we are somewhat prevented from carrying forward Catholic teaching if it collides with a state measure», he continued. «Also, the daily life of our Catholic associations grows more difficult from day to day... political supervision is ordered everywhere, as if our Catholic events are against

---

[29] Forced Sterilization (*Zwangssterilisation*): the first NS program of this kind was made possible by the *Gesetz zur Verhütung erbkranken Nachwuchses* (Law for the Prevention of Children with Hereditary Diseases), enacted July 14, 1933, meaning, anyone with «congenital feeblemindedness, schizophrenia, manic depression, hereditary epilepsy, Huntington's chorea, hereditary blindness or deafness, or severe physical malformations, and, in some cases, severe alcoholism». Hereditary Health Courts decided on recommendations for forced sterilization, which physicians and heads of institutions were required by law to make. Sterilization was to be carried out within 14 days, and could include forcible measures (police delivery of a person to a clinic; no authorization for hospital release or nursing home release without prior sterilization). 1939: Ordinance for Hereditary Cultivation (*Erbpflegeverordnung*) limited sterilizations to «urgent cases». Between 1933 and 1945, between 250,000 and 300,000 persons were forcibly sterilized. See R.W., *Forced Sterilization*, in *Encyclopedia of the Third Reich...*, 276; R. MICHAEL and K. DOERR, *Nazi-Deutsch/Nazi German...*, 189.

[30] «In der Frage der Sterilisierung gelten für die Gläubigen die von der höchsten kirchlichen Autorität verkündten Grundsätze des christlichen Sittengesetzes. Gemäss den Weisungen des Heiligen Vaters erinnern wir daran: Es ist nicht erlaubt, sich selbst zur Sterilisierung zu stellen oder Antrag zu stellen auf Sterilisierung eines anderen Menschen. Das ist Lehre der katholische Kirche. Dankbar anerkennen wir jede Rücksichtnahme auf diesen Grundsatz». See H. GRUBER, *Katholische Kirche und Nationalsozialismus, 1930-1945: Ein Bericht in Quellen*, Paderborn 2006, 148-149.

the National Government. We [Catholics][31] are regarded as suspect», he concluded his letter.

It is worth noting that Pacelli received many detailed reports from the situation on the ground in Germany in the summer and fall of 1933 and continuing into 1934, all the while negotiating the Concordat between the Holy See and the Third Reich from April to September 1933. If Pacelli hoped that a Concordat would offer protection and ward off such instances of interference in Catholic life, and, periodically in 1933, violent clashes and abuse of Catholics at the hands of the Nazis, he could not have held on to this illusion for long. In his White Files, one finds vivid reports from across Germany, like that from Bishop Ehrenfried about the disruption of a community program performed by the student congregation of the Virgin Mary by Hitler Youth on January 17, 1934. «Members of the Hitler Youth intruded and divided themselves up on the gallery... they were disruptive and rude. They threw toy torpedoes and – pardon your Excellence – stink bombs», Bishop Ehrenfried wrote in a report to the nunciature[32]. Less amusing were the numerous decrees one finds in Pacelli's White Files issued by the Nazi regime circumscribing Catholic life, like the September 19, 1933 decree signed by Political Police Commander of Bavaria Reinhard Heydrich that «any activity of Catholic organizations (including workers associations) such as public and private gatherings, theater performances, field trips, athletic events, field exercises, and likewise the new creation of organizations remains... forbidden». The wearing of uniform clothing for members of confessional associations was banned. And so the long and detailed list continued[33].

Though most of the correspondence in Pacelli's White Files pertained to German Catholics, some pertained to the particular difficulties that German Jews faced in 1933. On September 9, 1933, a wireless from Rome appeared in the «New York Times», titled «Concordat Delay Denied». «The report that the ratification of the Vatican-German Concordat has been delayed by the Pope [Pius XI]'s dissatisfaction with Chancellor

---

[31] AES,Bavaria, 1933-1936, Pos. 198, Fasc.41. Reports of the Nunciature: Position Created with Documents from the White Files Sent to the Archive by Pope Pius XII. RG 76.001M: Selected Records from the Vatican Archives, 1865-1939, United States Holocaust Memorial Museum, Washington, DC.

[32] *Ibidem.*

[33] AES, Bavaria, 1933-1936, Pos. 198, Fasc. 40. Reports of the Nunciature: Position Created with Documents from the White Files Sent to the Archive by Pope Pius XII. RG 76.001M: Selected Records from the Vatican Archives, 1865-1939, USHMM, Washington, DC.

Hitler's policies, especially sterilization and anti-Judaism, is denied both by the Vatican and by German sources», read the cable. «Admittedly, the Vatican does not approve several of the Nazi policies, but this condition existed before the conclusion of the Concordat and has become no worse since... Cardinal Pacelli... is about to leave for Switzerland for a vacation. It is expected the ratification will follow soon after his return», the cable finished.[34] In RG-76 we have one of the few direct responses by Pacelli on issues relating to persecution of Jews in 1933. Concerning the «New York Times» piece, he wrote to Secretary Pizzardo[35], «I was not displeased with the indiscretion of the United [States] Press concerning the Jews; it was an opportunity that the world should know that the Holy See has been occupied with that question»[36]. I have not yet come across any evidence that details how the Holy See «ha[d] been occupied with that question» in this first year of the Nazi regime; in fairness my research in RG-76 is far from complete.

Because this section of my paper represents only the first several hundred among tens of thousands of documents, it would be irresponsible to offer any definitive conclusions at this point. Perhaps I can offer some observations. I wrote my first book about the postwar Catholic Church; the historical actors involved had the benefit of hindsight with regard to the Nazi regime and its crimes against Catholics and its genocide against

---

[34] «Concordat Delay Denied». Wireless to the «New York Times», September 10, 1933. ProQuest Historical Newspapers: «New York Times» (1851-2006), N4.

[35] Giuseppe Cardinal Pizzardo (1877-1970). Pizzardo was raised to the rank of Mgr., and appointed Secretary of the nunciature to Bavaria, on June 7, 1909. In the Congregation for Extraordinary Ecclesiastical Affairs, he was appointed: undersecretary (1920), Substitute (1921), and Secretary (1929).

[36] Letter from Eugenio Cardinal Pacelli, Secretary of State, Vatican City, to Giuseppe Pizzardo, September 21, 1933. AES, Bavaria, 1933-1936, Pos. 190, Fasc. 34, Suppression by National Socialists of Catholics and Catholic Associations. RG 76.001M: Selected Records from the Vatican Archives, 1865-1939, United States Holocaust Memorial Museum, Washington, D.C. Brechenmacher identifies Pizzardo as the addressee for this letter. See T. BRECHENMACHER, *Der Vatikan und die Juden: Geschichte einer unheiligen Beziehung vom 16. Jahrhundert bis zu Gegenwart*, München 2005, 177. Cardinal Erhle (1845-1934) is mentioned as someone recommended by her brother, Henry Bordeaux, to whom Ms. Pinet-Bordeaux could turn for information concerning Fritz Gerlich in her letter dated September 11, 1933, Pos. 190, Fasc. 34. On this letter, Brechenmacher concludes, «Auf das Wie kam es dem Pacelli an; er zögerte nicht, auch einen Zufall zu nutzen, um eine wichtige Information über die Position des Heiligen Stuhls zur Judenverfolgung zu transportieren, ohne auf der anderen Seite diplomatische Verwicklungen mit dem deutschen Reich im Vorfeld der Konkordatsratifikation zu provozieren».

European Jews. This first foray into primary source documentation from the Nazi period is sobering. Documentation pertaining to the first year of Nazi rule in RG-76 offers a picture of Catholic life under siege, and of Catholic leaders grappling for the most effective response. Clearly, in 1933, Catholic leaders from Secretary of State Pacelli to the nuncio in Munich, Alberto Vassallo di Torregrossa, to the German bishops, hoped to find some form of compromise with the Nazi regime. One also observes that when no such compromise could be found, clearly worded, unequivocal condemnation from the German bishops, such as in the case of sterilization, was considered and exercised as a response. «[Sterilization] is not allowed... That is the teaching of the Catholic Church», the German bishops admonished their faithful. This kind of statement is very different in nature from that found in the «New York Times» wire from Rome, the source for which is unclear, concerning the pending Concordat: «admittedly, the Vatican does not approve several of the Nazi policies, but this condition existed before the conclusion of the Concordat and has become no worse since», stated that September 1933 wire. Only a continued, patient examination of RG-76, document by document, will allow scholars to recreate a nuanced account of Catholic response to Nazi persecution of their co-religionists – crucial context for the study of Catholic individual and collective decision-making when face-to-face with the legal disenfranchisement, expropriation, incarceration, deportation, and ultimately murder of Jewish neighbors in those fraught years.

The second section of this essay concerns the folio in RG-76 labeled «Persecution Against the Jews». This folio contains 15 documents: 10 letters from private individuals, some addressed to Secretary of State Pacelli and some to Pope Pius XI and all written in August 1938[37], and 5 pieces of official correspondence. Small in number, letters from private individuals illuminate the atmosphere in Europe and the United States in the months before the November pogrom. I will focus on two official reports from

---

[37] Two letters are anonymous and not dated: one originating from Sackingen, Germany, and the other from an anonymous location. The other eight letters we can identify are from (in alphabetical order): Max Cacheuse of the Rittergut Berkach über Meiningen in Thuringia, Germany (letter dated August 14, 1938); Curt Goldberg of Trieste (letter dated August 23, 1938); Magdalena Jankowska of Berlin (no date for letter); Louis Livy of Nancy, France (letter dated November 15, 1938); the wife of Dr. med. Georg Marx, temporarily in Rome (letter dated August 16, 1938); Dr. med. Dr. phil. Erich Simons of Dijon, France (letter dated August 15, 1938); Dr. Gotthold Steinführer of Chicago (letter dated August 12, 1938); and Max Weiner of Haifa (letter dated November 4, 1938).

Vatican nuncio in Berlin, Cesare Orsenigo, to the Secretary of State in Rome, Eugenio Pacelli. They concern Reichskristallnacht and are dated November 15 and 19, 1938, respectively. A brief word about Cesare Orsenigo, author of the two reports, is in order. An Italian national who was Pacelli's successor as nuncio to Germany in 1930, 56 years of age when he was appointed to Berlin, Archbishop Orsenigo has thus far not fared well in the historiography for the 1933-1945 period. His contemporary, George Shuster, described Orsenigo as «frankly, jubilant» about Hitler's election to the chancellorship on January 30, 1933[38]. Michael Phayer's important book, *The Catholic Church and the Holocaust*, describes Orsenigo as «a pro-German, pro-Nazi, anti-Semitic fascist».[39] This is why the tone of these reports, not hostile, and at times sympathetic to beleaguered Jewry, was an unexpected find. Let us begin with Orsenigo's first report about the so-called Reichskristallnacht pogrom, dated November 15, 1938. His description of the events themselves openly acknowledged the reality of anti-Semitic vandalism (as he titled the report), and, the Nazi and German popular role therein:

> «The destructions have been initiated, as if by a single order... The blind popular revenge followed one identical method everywhere: in the night, all display windows were shattered and the synagogues were set on fire; the day after, shops that did not have any defense were looted. Doing this, [the looters] destroyed all the goods, even the most expensive ones. Only towards the afternoon of the 10th, when the masses, having vented their wildest feelings, and not being restrained by any policeman, did Minister Goebbels give the order to stop, characterizing what happened as venting by "the German people...". All of this easily leaves the impression that the order or permission to act came from a higher authority... The hour is to follow of ministerial laws and dispositions in order to isolate Jews more and more, prohibiting them every commerce, every [ability to frequent] the public schools, every partaking in places of public diversion (theaters, cinemas, concerts, cultural meetings), with a fine totaling one billion [Reichsmarks] to be paid [by Jews themselves]»[40].

---

[38] G.N. SHUSTER, *Like a Mighty Army: Hitler Versus Established Religion* (1935), 188, cited in G. LEWY, *The Catholic Church and Nazi Germany*, ²2000, 27.

[39] M. PHAYER, *The Catholic Church and the Holocaust, 1930-1965*, 2000, 27, 44.

[40] Letter from Apostolic Delegate to Germany Cesare Orsenigo, Berlin, to Secretary of State Eugenio Cardinal Pacelli, November 15, 1938. Section for Extraordinary Affairs, Germany, 1938, POS. 742, Fasc. 356, 1938, Reichskristallnacht, RG 76, USHMM. This letter was first made available to scholars in *Actes et Documents du Saint Siège Relatifs à La Seconde Guerre Mondiale*, ed. by P. BLET, R.A. GRAHAM, A. MARTINI and B. SCHNEIDER, vol. VI: *Le Saint Siège et Les Victimes de la Guerre, Mars 1939-Décembre 1940*, Roma 1972, appendix 4, 536-537.

In the remainder of the report, Orsenigo noted the strong temptation of German Jewry to commit suicide in the wake of these terrible events, noted the positive if limited efforts by the embassies of Columbia, England, and Holland to document these events and protect the assets of Jewish nationals, and openly criticized Poland, writing, «it was... Poland that provoked the violent action of Germany» by refusing to extend the expired passports of Polish Jews from Germany, prompting Germany to «suddenly sen[d] back to Poland tens of thousands of Jews, and among these and also the parents the young exasperated boy [Polish Jewish student Herszel Grynszpan], that then assassinated the German ambassador[41] in Paris [Ernst vom Rath]»[42]. In reading the report as a whole, Orsenigo appears critical of the pogrom, critical of the Nazi State, and critical of the German population.

The second report, dated November 19, 1938, concerned impending legislation declaring «null and void all marriages already conducted» between «Aryans» and Jews, including those marriages in which the Jewish spouse had converted to Catholicism after the marriage[43]. Not surprisingly, Orsenigo objected to the legislation, due to its disregard for Canon Law, but more surprisingly, he added critical commentary about the increasingly radical nature of the Nazi State, noting that «serenity and competence» were «more and more lacking in high places of command» and that there existed a «state of mood that [Orsenigo thought] greased the anti-Semitic events[, a state of mood that] reveals always more and more turbulence and agitation, and is increasingly less able to be controlled», he wrote. He lamented, too, that Hitler, whom he referred to as the so-called «Supreme Legislator», was perceived as being above the law.[44]

We know that Secretary of State Pacelli received both of Orsenigo's reports of November 15 and 19, and, hence, received direct and detailed information about the pogrom. While no documentation of Pacelli's response to the two Orsenigo reports has yet been discovered, we do have

---

[41] Ernst vom Rath was actually third secretary at the German embassy in Paris at the time of his assassination.

[42] *Ibidem.*

[43] Letter from Apostolic Delegate to Germany Cesare Orsenigo, Berlin, to Secretary of State Eugenio Cardinal Pacelli, November 19, 1938, Section for Extraordinary Affairs, Germany, 1938, POS. 742, Fasc. 356, 1938, Reichskristallnacht, RG 76, USHMM. This letter was first made available to scholars in *Actes et Documents du Saint Siège Relatifs à la Seconde Guerre Mondiale*, vol. VI: *Le Saint Siège et les Victimes de la Guerre...*, 538.

[44] *Ibidem.*

available Pacelli's response to a request from Cardinal Arthur Hinsley, Roman Catholic Archbishop of Westminster, that Pope Pius XI make a statement about the pogrom. The story was this: in late November, Cardinal Hinsley sent to Pacelli a request from Lord Rothschild, whom Hinsley described as «the most famous and highly esteemed amongst Jews in England»[45]. On November 26, 1938, Cardinal Hinsley wrote to Pacelli the following:

> «On 9 December there will be a public gathering in London in order to ask [for] aid and attendance to all those who suffer from persecution [for reasons of] religion or race... If [in] principle [it] were possible to have an authentic word of the Holy Father being declared that in Christ discrimination of race does not exist and that the great human family must be joined in peace [by] means of respect of the personality of the individual, such message would [be] sure [to] have in England and America, [and] nevertheless through the entire world, the [effect of] leading to good will towards the [Catholic] Religion and the Holy See»[46].

Pacelli's notes in response to this letter, dated December 3, 1938, are published in the ADSS series. They read as follows:

> «If the [matter] were of substantially private character, it would be easier. On the other hand, it is necessary to remove the appearance of fearing that which does not need to be feared. Cardinal Hinsley could speak [if] saying he is surely interpreting the thought of the Sovereign Pontiff saying that the [matter] not only finds the Pope in a moment of much worry for his health, but also overwhelmed by the amount of matters before him. It is therefore not possible for [the Holy Father] to [respond] personally. He [Cardinal Hinsley] can say that he is interpreting the thoughts of the Holy Father which view all aid to those who are unhappy and unjustly (dishonorably) suffering with a humane and Christian eye»[47].

---

[45] *Actes et Documents du Saint Siège Relatifs à La Seconde Guerre Mondiale*, vol. VI: *Le Saint Siège et Les Victimes de la Guerre...*, 12-13.

[46] *Ibidem*, 539, footnote 1.

[47] *Ibidem*. The original Italian reads as follows: «Se la cosa fosse di carattere sostanzialmente privato, sarebbe più facile. D'altra parte, occorre togliere l'apparenza di aver paura di ciò che non si deve temere. Si potrebbe incaricare Cardinal Hinsley a parlare dicendosi sicuro di interpretare il pensiero del Sommo Pontefice, dicendo che la cosa coglie in Papa in un momento di tanta preoccupazione non soltanto per la Sua salute, ma anche per la quantità di cose. Non ha visto perciò la possibilità di occuparsi personalmente della cosa. Egli, Cardinale di S.R.C., può dire di interpretare il pensiero che vede con occhio umano e cristiano ogni assistenza a quanti infelici e ingiustamente (indegnamente) sofferenti». I thank Professor Anthony Cardoza of Loyola University of Chicago for his verification of my translation.

This response was telegraphed to Cardinal Hinsley on December 3[48]. On December 9, illustrious figures that included Cardinal Hinsley; William Cosmo Gordon Lang, Archbishop of Canterbury; Lord Rothschild; Clement R. Attlee, leader of the Opposition in the House of Commons; Sir Alan Anderson, Conservative MP; and General Evangeline Booth, representative of the Salvation Army, gathered at the invitation of Sir Frank Bowater, Lord Mayor of London, at the Mansion House[49]. A resolution «offering whole-hearted support» for the Lord Baldwin Fund for Refugees was «unanimously adopted»[50]. The Baldwin refugee fund for victims of religious and racial persecution, first announced by former prime minister, Lord Stanley Baldwin, 1st Earl of Baldwin, during a radio address on the evening of December 8, 1938, was expressly meant to provide financial aid to Jews and so-called «non-Aryan Christians»[51]. A brief article in the «New York Times», entitled, it is interesting to note, *Pope Backs Britons on Aid to Refugees*, appeared on December 10. According to the article, «one of Pope Pius [XI]'s rare messages to an interdisciplinary body was read at a meeting representing all faiths and political parties, called by the Lord Mayor of London, at the Mansion House today to support the Earl Baldwin Fund for the victims of religious and racial persecution».[52]

---

[48] *Actes et documents du Saint Siège relatifs à la Seconde Guerre Mondiale*, vol. VI: *Le Saint Siège et les victimes de la Guerre...*, 539, footnote 3.

[49] The Mansion House is the official residence of the Lord Mayor of the city of London.

[50] See *Help for the Refugees Ready Response to Appeal – Children's Gifts – Mansion House Meeting*, in «The London Times», December 10, 1938, 12.

[51] *The Refugees – Appeal By Lord Baldwin – Case for German Cooperation – New Fund Opened*, in «The London Times», 9 December 1938, 16. «Tonight, I plead for the victims who turn to England for help, the first time in their long and troubled history that they have asked us in this way for financial aid... Nothing has been more remarkable among the Jews than the way in which the wealthy look after their poorer neighbors... The number of these so-called non-Aryan Christians, who, according to German law, are regarded as Jews, certainly exceeds 100,000; in addition there are some half a million professing Jews, and no words can describe the pitiable plight of these 600,000 human souls. What can be done to help?». Earl Baldwin's appeal raised approximately 500,000 pounds. About half the proceeds were allocated to Jewish organizations and spent on helping child refugees. L. LONDON, *Whitehall and the Jews, 1933-1938: British Immigration Policy, Jewish Refugees and the Holocaust*, Cambridge 2000, 122. See also A.J. SHERMAN, *Island Refuge: Britain and Refugees from the Third Reich, 1933-1939*, London 1973, 184-185.

[52] «The New York Times», December 10, 1938; ProQuest Historical Newspapers: «The New York Times» (1851-2003), 6.

It was Lord Rothschild who read the Vatican telegram to the assembled. Before reading the telegram, Lord Rothschild remarked that «Cardinal Hinsley had written to Rome on his behalf», and that «everyone respected the Pope for his courage and unswerving adherence to the principles which the whole civilized world knew must be maintained if civilization was to persist»[53]. The Vatican telegram, as reproduced in «The London Times», read as follows:

> «The Holy Father Pius XI's thoughts and feelings will be correctly interpreted by declaring that he looks with humane and Christian approval on every effort to show charity and to give effective assistance to all those who are innocent victims in these sad times of distress. [Signed] Cardinal Pacelli, Secretary of State to His Holiness».[54]

Cardinal Hinsley's presence at the Mansion House meeting was significant. Significant also was the fact that Pacelli's message was read at a high-level public meeting with the specific purpose of support for Jews – Lord Baldwin's evening radio appeal of December 8, and subsequent reports in «The London Times», were quite clear as to the need for funds for approximately 500,000 Jews and 100,000 «non-Aryan Christians»[55]. Yet, here we have a clear example, with clear evidence, that Pacelli, despite being informed about the horrendous details of the pogrom in Germany, was not encouraging of a public statement by the Holy See condemning Nazi Germany specifically, or the November pogrom specifically, or singling out suffering Jews specifically by name – even when asked to do so by a prince of his own church. He was comfortable only with a statement broad enough to apply to all «innocent victims».

Earl Baldwin's December 8 call to active aid, Archbishop Orsenigo's empathetic reports about Reichskristallnacht – though empathy did not mean action for Orsenigo – and Cardinal Hinsley's willingness to intercede for Lord Rothschild and encourage the Bishop of Rome to make a public statement about the pogrom suggests that sympathy for Jews existed in important quarters. The Vatican Secretariat of State's official response suggests also that Pacelli had the capability to personally dictate the Holy See's official institutional response in the months before Pius XI's death

---

[53] *Plight of the Refugees – Mansion House Meeting – Lord Rothschild's Appeal*, in «The London Times», December 10, 1938, 14.

[54] *Ibidem.*

[55] *The Refugees – Appeal By Lord Baldwin – Case for German Cooperation – New Fund Opened*, in «The London Times», December 9, 1938, 16.

on February 10, 1939. In early December 1938, at least, Pacelli was not willing to aggressively and specifically condemn the November 9-10 Nazi pogrom against Jews. Pacelli *was* willing to authorize (on behalf of the Pope) a reminder of the Church's broad commandment and mission to aid the suffering and the persecuted. In these troubled times, such a response was not enough.

JOHN A. DAVIS

Vatican Transnationalism:
Discussant's Comments

The interesting papers that we have heard in this panel and in part published in this volume throw a great deal of light – much of it either new or approached from new documentary sources – on Vatican policies and politics in Poland, Malta, Brazil and Germany in a period that runs from the aftermath of World War I to the aftermath of the death of Pius XI. They serve to give a broader comparative perspective on the Italy-US focus of the conference and they raise important issues relating more specifically to the Vatican's international politics in this period and the policies pursued in individual countries. Clearly France, Spain, Belgium, Argentina and Mexico would need to be considered before any broader generalizations can be attempted, but the four cases that have been presented come by different way to remarkably similar conclusions.

Taking the papers in their chronological order, Neal Pease offered a masterly and detailed reconstruction of the ways in which the Vatican sought through the mission of Nunzio Ratti to piece together a viable policy in Poland and Eastern Europe more generally immediately after the First World War. Anticipating themes that recur in the subsequent papers, Professor Pease offers a careful reconstruction of the enormous difficulties that faced the Vatican in its attempts to persuade one of the most Catholic nations in Europe – albeit one that was only newly independent – to follow its advice and guidance. The problem of how to use local allies without becoming their prisoner is one that runs through relations between the Vatican and the secular powers and is as old as the papacy. But Neal Pease's paper usefully reminds us that Poland's overwhelmingly Catholic vocation did mean that the Polish episcopate was pliant to Vatican pressures: indeed, the reverse was often true.

The paper, which will become available to scholars very soon (and already edited in the Watson Institute website), offers the useful reminder that the Vatican never accepted the terms of the Peace Treaties, which were seen in Rome as an Anglo-Saxon imposition. Even though these positions were adopted before the accession of Pius XI, they reveal stances that remained important for understanding Vatican policies within Europe and in its relations with the US. The Italian thinker and Communist leader Antonio Gramsci, for example, believed that the Vatican's critique of the Peace Treaties went hand in hand with a vision of a new Catholic Europe that harked back to the empire of Charlemagne in in which Poland and the Catholic communities of the eastern successor states would have a major role to play. But Professor Peace shows that this needs to be treated with caution and in Poland much of Nunzio Ratti's energies were devoted to curbing Polish territorial enthusiasms. The relative failure of the Vatican's efforts to influence the policies of the Polish Republic provides a first illustration of the limits of Vatican diplomacy, a theme that recurs in the papers on Malta and Germany.

Also important for our understanding of Pius XI is the revision of the myths that had grown up around his experiences in Warsaw and his admiration for Jozef Pilsudski – in particular the claim that Cardinal Ratti's liking for Pilsudski anticipated Pope Pius XI's admiration for Mussolini. Professor Pease's is right, I think, to distinguish carefully between Pilsudski and Mussolini, but there are perhaps closer similarities between Pilsudsky and other authoritarian interwar national leaders – Dollfus, Horthy, Franco, Salazar in Europe, Getulio Vargas in Brazil – to whom Pius XI's Vatican consistently gravitated in the decades that followed. I am a little puzzled by the comparison between Pilsudski and Giuseppe Garibaldi – Garibaldi was a figure who was and remains anathema to the Italian Church, one that is demonized down to the present and could never be seen as a model for a secular defender of the faith.

From the Catholic heartland of Poland to the Catholic periphery of Malta, Aapo Laitinen's paper illustrates the value that peripheral vision has for the historian. Perhaps unexpectedly, this overwhelmingly Catholic colony of the British empire offers another insight into the limits of Vatican diplomacy. Although the anti-Catholic rhetoric of the leader of the pro-British Constitutional Party, Sir Gerald Strickland, became a matter of great concern to the Vatican, effective intervention proved difficult and ineffective. In this case, the obstacles were both different from Poland and similar. These took the form, on one hand, of the divisions within the Maltese Catholic community, within the episcopate and the clergy, and, on the other, the constraints arising from the international diplomatic issues at stake: in particular the concern not to jeopardize the Vatican's recently improving relations with Great Britain.

Dr. Laititen reconstructs the issues at stake well and sets them in their wider context, but that context could be developed further. The issues posed by the resurgence of pro-Italian feeling in Malta coincide with attempts in the mid to late 1920s by both the Italian Fascists and the Vatican to strengthen contacts with the numerous Italian communities that were settled in different parts of the Mediterranean – especially North Africa and the Greek islands. Recent studies on Rhodes and Tripoli, for example, illustrate how Mussolini's regime called on the churches – including the leaders of the Italian Jewish communities – to play an active role in this process and mobilize pro-Italian feelings and demonstrations.

It would be interesting to know more about what the Italian authorities were up to in Malta at this time and how much information is to be found in the Vatican archives on communications with the Italian government over the Maltese question and on the activities of Italian nationalist organizations in British Malta. But what Dr. Laititen calls the «early signs of discord» between the Vatican and Britain raise other interesting questions that point to later developments. From the work of Owen Chadwick and others, for example, we know that once the Second World War began Anglo-Vatican relations would follow a very different path. From the time that Churchill came to power, the belief that after the fall of Mussolini the Papacy was the only institution that could oversee the reconstruction of Italy played a fundamental role in shaping British policy towards Fascist Italy. Given Malta's critical position and critical role in 1941 when the Allies were threatened with defeat in North Africa and the Middle East, it would be interesting to know if the conflicts over nationality politics on the island in the 1920s had an after-life in the late 1930s and 1940s.

In an unpublished paper, presented at the cconference, Carlo Felice Casula's presents his comments on Getulio Vargas and Brazil's Second Republic as a research project in progress, and with his paper we return to the Americas following in the footsteps of the seemingly ubiquitous Cardinal Pacelli. The Vatican's support for Vargas is well known, although the emphasis on the abandonment of the anticlerical features of the First Republic is certainly worth noting. For a fuller explanation of the development of relations between the Vatican and Rio de Janeiro, however, more needs to be known about relations between the Vatican Nunzio and the Brazilian episcopate and clergy, the Catholic Church's relations with the different social and ethnic groups in Brazilian society, and the constraints within which the Vatican sought to influence the actions of the Vargas government, with what successes and what failures.

Suzanne Brown-Fleming's paper offers a valuable model in this respect and takes up one of the central themes of this conference: the degree to which newly available Vatican have brought earlier interpretations into question. Focusing on the debates over Pius XI's reactions to events in Germany in the aftermath of the Nazi seizure of power, she explains why documents now available in the Vatican archive have caused her to modify her own earlier interpretation of Pius XI's reactions of Catholics in Germany after the rise of Hitler. In a section of his paper in another session of the conference, Frank Coppa addresses the same issue and discusses the literature on Nazi attacks on Catholic organizations and priests in Bavaria from as early as the spring of 1933. To this Suzanne Brown-Fleming now brings the additional information from the Vatican sources that make possible a fuller reconstruction not only of the Vatican's responses, but also of the critical role of intermediary played from the start by Cardinal Pacelli.

The evidence provided here both with regard to the Vatican's reactions to the violence against Catholics in 1933 and the later attacks on the Jews seems weighty, but is perhaps best held over for the discussions on that theme scheduled for tomorrow. Set in the context of the papers presented in this panel, however, the reasons that Suzanne Brown-Fleming advances to explain the Vatican's failure to intervene more clearly in defense of the religious groups targeted by Nazi policies would seem to be consistent with its very mixed successes in influencing the policies of regimes and governments that were more friendly and even more vulnerable. The limits of Vatican interventions reflected the complexity of local political situations, and the often inseparable connections between national and international political and diplomatic considerations. Those difficulties are evident in all three of the European cases examined here – and also in the case of Italy. But those problems were also compounded by the divisions that existed both within the national clergies and within the Vatican itself: symbolized perhaps most fully in the antithesis that emerges from Suzanne Brown-Fleming emphasis on the contrasts and tensions between Pius XI and his Secretary of State. But that is another issue that will be addressed more directly in many of the papers that follow.

Pius XI and the Racial Laws

Robert A. Ventresca

Irreconcilable Differences?
Pius XI, Eugenio Pacelli, and Italian Fascism
from the Ethiopian Crisis to the Racial Laws

This paper draws upon *two* under-utilized *Vatican Secret Archives* collections from the papacy of Pius XI (1922-1939): the fourteen volumes of files pertaining to the Ethiopian campaign of 1935-1936, and the so-called «Pacelli diaries», the (mostly) hand-written notes recorded by then-Cardinal Secretary of State Eugenio Pacelli (Pius XII) of his regular meetings with Pius XI and with the diplomatic corps to the Holy See. Taken together this documentation offers important new insights into the *modus operandi* of papal diplomacy – and especially of Eugenio Pacelli, its leading figure – in the Vatican's dealings with Mussolini's Italy in the latter half of the 1930s.

This paper thus considers the extent to which Italian Fascism's imperial and racist turn in the mid-1930s – expressed principally in the Fascist invasion of Ethiopia and then in domestic racial laws – tested the logic and the limits of the imperfect but mutually convenient accommodation achieved between the Vatican and the Mussolini regime after the *conciliazione* (1929). The inexorable radicalization of Mussolini's domestic and foreign policy agenda exposed some of the fundamental *doctrinal* incompatibilities between Catholic political and social thought on the one hand, and Fascist ideology on the other. Yet, Pius XI, encouraged by his Secretary of State, continued to favor diplomatic engagement with the Fascist regime as the means to precise ends. This included a strategy to preserve the Church's distinct spheres of autonomy within the Fascist State, while continuing to cultivate diplomatic influence with the Mussolini Government so as to help steer Italian domestic and foreign policy away from closer alignment with Nazi Germany. In this respect, Italo-Vatican relations in the latter 1930s mirrored the pattern of *conflict* and *compromise* which John Pollard observed of the early years after the 1929 agreements. In the end, the Vatican's contradictory relationship with Mussolini's Italy produced mixed, often disappointing results from the perspective of the Vatican's own objectives and interests. This speaks to real limits of papal influence on Mussolini's regime, and of Pius XI's difficulty in finding an effective *political* vehicle with which to counter the increasingly radical, aggressive and racist dimensions of Italian Fascism.

1. The Lateran Accords: Reconciliation, Accommodation and Conflict

Pius IX's unrequited dream of a small corner of the world where the Pope was master was finally realized by his successor, Pius XI, some sixty years after Italian Unification had stripped the papacy of the last vestige of territorial power. The 1929 *Conciliazione* or reconciliation, usually referred to as the Lateran Pacts, formally guaranteed the Holy See «absolute and visible independence and an indisputable sovereignty». The agreements even included explicit affirmation that Roman Catholicism was the «only State religion» in Italy and expanded religious instruction in all of Italy's ostensibly public schools. In return, Mussolini extracted from the Holy See a formal promise to remain «outside the temporal rivalries between other States», while reserving the Church's solemn right «to use its moral and spiritual powers»[1]. What this meant in practice was not entirely clear at the time, as subsequent conflicts between the Vatican and the Mussolini Government over the nature and structure of Catholic lay organizations revealed[2]. At the very least, though, Mussolini could be assured that the Pope, whoever he was, would tread carefully in his public dealings with the Fascist State, especially in the area of international affairs.

Scarcely had the ink on the Lateran Pacts dried when the Vatican and Mussolini's Government began to clash over the practical application of the formal agreement. The disagreement was especially intense, even fierce, over the question of youth: the regime sought to expand the Fascist party's reach over Italian youth which necessarily meant challenging the autonomy and influence of popular Catholic organizations[3]. Tensions reached a highpoint in 1931 when Mussolini ordered the immediate disso-

---

[1]   Full text of the Lateran Pacts of 1929 and related documents can be found in J.F. POL-LARD, *The Vatican and Italian Fascism, 1929-1932*, Cambridge 1985, Appendices I, II and III, 195-216.

[2]   Pollard makes the convincing argument that, despite widespread expectations, the period that followed the signing of the 1929 pacts actually witnessed «more conflict between the Vatican and the Fascists than in the preceding seven-year period that had begun with the March on Rome». See J.F. POLLARD, *The Vatican and Italian Fascism...*, 2-3.

[3]   *Ibidem*; see especially Chapter 6 for the best concise summary of the so-called «crisis» of 1931.

lution of Catholic youth organizations, prompting Pius XI to respond with a biting encyclical *Non abbiamo bisogno* (June 1931) criticizing Mussolini's regime for its treatment of Catholic organizations, and denouncing Fascism for promoting «out and out pagan worship of the State»[4].

Having spent most of his time the preceding decade in Germany, it seemed at first that Pius XI's newly appointed Secretary of State, Eugenio Pacelli, was out of his depth when it came to dealing with the Italians. The historian John Pollard reasons that Pacelli was actually in a «weak position» with respect to «subordinates» in the Secretariat, especially in the Vatican's handling of its problems with Mussolini's regime at the start of the 1930s. Senior members of his staff had been dealing with Mussolini's Government for years, and so it was natural that they would take the lead on the Vatican's Italy files while Pacelli was still settling in to his new post[5]. It was hard to avoid the impression that for all his accomplishments in Germany, the new Cardinal Secretary of State was being eclipsed both by an energetic and combative Pope Pius XI, and by subordinates like Giuseppe Pizzardo who pursued an openly confrontational line with the Mussolini regime through to the crisis of 1931. The British Ambassador to the Italian Government wrote to the Foreign Office regretting Gasparri's departure, calling it a «great misfortune». Pius XI, the ambassador opined, «is too impulsive, too undiplomatic» in his dealings with the Mussolini Government, and Pacelli was proving «unable to moderate» the Pope's «actions and utterances». It was widely known that Pacelli preferred a more conciliatory approach to dealing with the Italians; indeed, the Italian Foreign Ministry knew as much and saw in Pacelli some hope for a resolution to the impasse between the Pope and the Duce. The Italian Ambassador in Berlin Count Aldrovandi wrote to the Italian Foreign Ministry saying that Pacelli's nomination as Cardinal Secretary of State would help to improve Italian-Vatican relations. Aldrovandi wrote glowingly of Pacelli's considerable accomplishments as nuncio in Germany and of his good working relationship with the Italian embassy. According to the Italian Ambassador, Pacelli on more than one occasion had expressed his «admiration» for Mussolini and his Government. There was no doubt about Pacelli's many attributes – his intelligence and industriousness for

---

[4] This quote is from J.F. POLLARD, *The Vatican and Italian Fascism...*, 158, but the entire encyclical in English is readily available in A. FREEMANTLE, *The Papal Encyclicals*, New York 1956, pp. 243-249, or on the site vatican.va.

[5] Notable among them were Giuseppe Pizzardo, Ottaviani and Borgoncini-Duca. See P. CHENAUX, *Pie XII diplomate et pasteur*, Paris 2003, 168-170.

instance, evidenced in his «noteworthy successes» in Germany in the face of serious obstacles. Nor could there be any doubt about the sincerity of Pacelli's deep spirituality; there was, the Italian official said, something mystical about the Secretary of State whose very expression seemed oriented toward the transcendent, as if he had already moved beyond concern for «mortal things»[6].

As much as they admired him, Italian diplomats like their British counterparts sensed that Pacelli lacked the gravitas to mitigate the headstrong approach of Pius XI and other hardliners. The British chargé d'affaires at the Vatican, G. Ogilvie Forbes wrote to the Foreign Office in his report for 1930 that throughout the year, Pius XI had exhibited «great energy, personally controlling the conduct of affairs even of lesser importance, so much so that his Secretary of State [Pacelli] was in practice reduced to the position of a clerk»[7]. The French Cardinal Alfred Baudrillart was under the impression that Pacelli was a fairly marginal player in the papal court, despite his formal title. Baudrillart wrote in his diary that Pacelli was «rather sickly and not very influential», and he identified two men – Pizzardo and Ottaviani – as Pius XI's closest and most trusted confidants. Baudrillart even hinted at some evidence of the new Secretary of State's poor judgment which had hurt Pacelli's standing with the Pope. Writing in April 1931, Baudrillart alluded to «a painful affair» when word reached Pius XI that an Italian Cardinal had blessed a fascist banner. An angry and embarrassed Pope is reported to have asked Pacelli, «Did you know about this?» Pacelli is reported to have responded sheepishly, «Yes». The Pope then asked whether Pacelli had approved the gesture. Pacelli once again said, «Yes», adding, «I told you Holy Father, that I would be incapable of carrying out the functions of the Secretary of State»[8].

It is doubtful the incident ever occurred, at least not as it was recounted by the French Cardinal. Still, Baudrillart's story speaks to the perception in certain circles at the time that Eugenio Pacelli was not firmly in command of his new job. It was no secret that Pacelli himself had hoped fervently to be passed over for the position claiming, perhaps with some false mod-

---

[6] Italian Ambassador to Berlin, Aldrovandi to Minister of Foreign Affairs Grandi, Berlin, December 10, 1929, in *Documenti Diplomatici Italiani* (DDI) *Settima Serie*, 1922-1935, vol. VIII, 245-246.

[7] J.F. POLLARD, *The Vatican and Italian Fascism...*, 156; see DDI, 7, V. X (1931), De Vecchi interview with Pacelli; for G. Ogilvie Forbes' report, see *Anglo-Vatican Relations, 1914-1939: Confidential Annual Reports of the British Ministers to the Holy See*, ed. by T.E. HACHEY, Boston, MA, 1972, 196.

[8] *Carnets du Alfred Baudrillart*, 714; 818-819.

esty, that he had neither the temperament, nor the skills, nor the inclination to be Secretary of State. Some scholars have opined that Eugenio Pacelli was selected by Pius XI precisely because he was considerably younger and with much less experience than Cardinal Gasparri, and so could be relied upon to «do his master's bidding»[9]. The more plausible explanation for Pacelli's promotion was that Pius XI saw him as the man most qualified for the job, possessing an unparalleled combination of intellectual ability, work ethic and, after a decade in Germany, practical diplomatic experience on some of the Vatican's most challenging files.

Pacelli found his footing and gravitas soon enough. It was easy to underestimate his abilities, or to mistake his reserved nature for weakness and insecurity. In reality, Eugenio Pacelli had a clear-minded understanding of his new found role and of the proper mission of papal diplomacy in the modern age. Nor would his pride and sense of duty allow him to play a marginal role to anyone but the Pope. The personal notes he kept of his daily meetings with the Pope and with the diplomatic corps reveal that Pacelli was very much engaged from the start in the day-to-day operations of the Vatican's diplomatic service. Pacelli's daily meetings with the Pope usually were lengthy, detailed and covered a wide range of issues in substantive detail. The Pope would express his thoughts on various matters and issue directives which Pacelli then had to translate into concrete measures and transmit to the small but far-reaching network of papal diplomats around the world. Pacelli met especially frequently with ambassadors of all the major European powers, and heard from papal diplomats from around the world. It gave the Cardinal Secretary of State a unique vantage point. In the course of an ordinary workday, Pacelli would meet with the Pope to discuss papal responses to a given matter; then it was off to meetings with various ambassadors, each of whom sought to influence the Vatican in ways that were favorable to their respective governments. The ambassadors and other diplomatic officials provided Pacelli with important insights into the domestic situation of the various countries. So it was that over the course of a few weeks or months, Pacelli was apprised of the rising political fortunes of the Hitler movement; of Italian territorial ambitions in Africa; of the deepening political, social and religious tension in Spain; and of ongoing fears about the geo-political and ideological threat Soviet Communism posed to Western European nations.

While Pacelli could appear hesitant and uncertain in his meetings with foreign diplomats, in reality he was exceedingly well prepared and

---

[9] So argues J. POLLARD, *The Vatican and Italian Fascism...*, 177.

displayed acumen both in articulating papal policy and in assessing the political and diplomatic situation of the day. That he was dutiful, obedient even in his work for the Pope was clear enough to everyone. It was said that if Pius XI had declared some small inanimate object to be an elephant, Pacelli readily would have agreed[10]. Still, Pacelli was capable of expressing opinions different from those of the Pope. This may explain why several of his interlocutors perceived Pacelli to be more amenable to accommodation, and less openly confrontational than his superior. This was especially true of Pacelli's dealings with Italian officials with whom he met most frequently; evidence of the unique relationship between the Vatican and Mussolini's Italy, which boosted Pacelli's assumption that the Holy See could exercise more direct influence over Italy than any other major power.

In his meetings with the Italian Ambassadors to the Holy See – first De Vecchi and later Pignatti – Pacelli expressed repeatedly his hopes for a genuine détente in Italy's relations with the Vatican[11]. It is not that Pacelli was under any illusion about the true nature of Mussolini's attitude to the Church. As he noted in his personal notes, «[a]mong the Fascists there are some good Catholics; but Mussolini is not one of them». In a similar vein, when the Italian Ambassador met with Pacelli in April 1931 to say that Fascism was the «antithesis of Bolshevism», Pacelli was not shy about retorting that there were, in fact, some fundamental similarities between the two systems[12]. In his dealings with the Italians, in fact, Pacelli's clear desire to maintain good diplomatic relations did not cloud his judgment or fool him into thinking that Mussolini Fascism was something other than what it was; from the start of his direct dealings with the Fascists, Pacelli exhibited his characteristic ability to marry diplomatic engagement with a clear-minded resolve to insist that the Mussolini Government respect the letter and the spirit of the 1929 agreements[13]. In effect, Pacelli was prepared to give Mussolini's Government considerable latitude in pursuing its domestic and international agendas, so long as this did not impinge upon the Church's free reign over its own affairs and Mussolini's policies

---

[10] See Cardinal Siri's recollection in the *Positio Summarium* Pars II, 597.

[11] See De Vecchi's memorandum to Mussolini dated April 18, 1931, in DDI, Settima Serie, Volume X, Document 207, 318-319.

[12] Pacelli diaries. P.O. 430b, Fasc. 356 (1930-1931), Entry April 10, 1931 now edited by S. PAGANO, Città del Vaticano 2011.

[13] See the Pacelli diaries, «Udienza del 12 Novembre 1933», AES, P.O. 430a, Fasc. 347 (1932-1933).

avoided the radical and aggressive tone exhibited increasingly by the Hitler regime.

2. The Italo-Ethiopian War

When Mussolini's Government reacted angrily to a speech Pius XI gave to a group of Italian nurses in late August 1935, in which the Pope expressed his concerns about the consequences of an eventual Italian invasion of Ethiopia and hoped for a peaceful resolution to avoid war, Pacelli distanced himself from the Pope's statement. Meeting with the Italian chargé d'affaires Giuseppe Talamo Atenolfi, Pacelli explained that the Pope had spoken publicly in this manner from a profound sense of pastoral duty, and thus addressed universal moral principles about the just causes for military action. Yet, Pacelli seemed eager to distance himself from the tone and substance of the Pope's public pronouncement. Pacelli knew that Italian officials appreciated how his office had tried to temper the Pope's public address on the matter.

Bonifacio Pignatti, the newly-appointed Italian Ambassador to the Holy See, reported to Mussolini in December 1935 that Pacelli could be counted upon to «pour water into [Pius XI's] pacifist wine»; an obvious allusion to Pacelli's resolve to impress upon the Pope the consequences to Church-State relations in Italy of a public papal statement in favor of a negotiated settlement to the Italo-Ethiopian conflict[14].

Of course, Pacelli's moderating influence cut both ways, which suggests that juxtaposing papal intransigence with Pacelli's moderation was part of a deliberate strategy to preserve both the moral authority of the papal office and the practical efficacy of papal diplomacy. For instance, to Italian threats against the Vatican newspaper for a series of articles advocating a peaceful resolution to the Ethiopian crisis, Pacelli counseled restraint and patience. In this instance at least, the Italians listened. In moderating both the papal line and the Fascist response, Pacelli's style of diplomatic engagement worked, at least in the short term; even if it simply was to paper over obvious ideological divisions between Church and regime which were to grow wider and deeper in the latter 1930s[15].

---

[14] See DDI, Volume II (1 Settembre-31 December 1935), Pignatti-Mussolini, December 14, 1935, Doc. 854, 836-837.

[15] See Pacelli diaries, Entry August 30, 1935, Pacelli-Talamo, in P.O. 430b, Fasc. 362 (1935).

In his effort to be constructive in dealing with the Mussolini Government over the Ethiopian crisis, Pacelli hoped to win for papal diplomacy a significant public relations coup, namely, credit for having worked diplomatically behind the scenes towards a much-desired mediated settlement. Pacelli told the Italians that the Pope hoped the Mussolini Government would accept the concessions being offered by the British and French so that the Holy Father might announce a peaceful resolution to the conflict at an upcoming Consistory. For its part, Mussolini's Government cautioned Pacelli and the Vatican against any public papal statement that might be seen to hurt Italian interests in the current crisis. Pacelli assured them that no such statement was being planned. The papal representative to the Italian Government, Father Tacchi Venturi, met with Mussolini personally in mid-December to assure the Duce that the Pope would resist saying anything at all in the upcoming Consistory about the Italo-Ethiopian conflict. Although the Vatican continued to lobby Mussolini to concede to some form of papal commentary on the conflict, it was unwilling to press very hard on the matter for fear of jeopardizing its formal diplomatic arrangements with the Italian State[16].

Not for the first or last time, the price to be paid for diplomatic engagement with Mussolini's Italy was to mute the Church's public voice on the morality of Mussolini's imperialist misadventures; the effect was to confine to secret diplomatic channels the Vatican's deep anxiety about the Ethiopian crisis, and to keep hidden from public view the Vatican's persistent efforts to lobby the major powers towards a quick and durable peace settlement[17]. So it was that the Italian Ambassador could write to Mussolini that in his public addresses, the Pope «spoke like a good Italian». In other instances Pignatti wrote to tell Mussolini that the Vatican was trying to achieve a «just» settlement that would favor Italy, and that papal nuncios in various countries were working effectively to promote the Italian cause among Catholics in those countries. Pignatti may have been overstating things for effect, knowing perhaps that Mussolini did not look kindly on bearers of bad news. At any rate, the full extent of the Vatican's anxiety over Mussolini's territorial ambitions did not receive

---

[16] For Pacelli's account of meetings with Pignatti in December 1935, see the Pacelli diaries, AES, IV Periodo, POS. 430b, Fasc. 362 (1935), Entry December 6, 1935 [n. 146]; cf. AES Italia, IV, 967, Conflitto Italo-Etiopico, Vol. II, Colloquio del P. Tacchi Venturi col Duce, December 14, 1935, ff. 256-260.

[17] See the lengthy notes compiled by Domenico Tardini in the fall-winter of 1935, in AES Italia 967, Conflitto Italo-Etiopico, Vol. 1 bis.

the kind of public airing Mussolini's critics were hoping to hear from the Vicar of Christ[18].

Behind the scenes, Pacelli and his staff worked hard to maximize their presumed influence over Mussolini's Government, while keeping open the lines of communication with the other powers by means of frequent and meaningful face-to-face meetings with British and French officials. Writing to the French Ambassador from his holiday retreat in Switzerland at the start of October 1935, Pacelli, who was unaware at the time that the Italians had already begun their military campaign in Ethiopia, noted that every effort ought to be made to resolve the conflict peacefully, lest it spiral out of control provoking «greater and more serious complications»[19]. For papal diplomacy to be effective at all, it was imperative that Cardinal Pacelli facilitate good working relationships with France and Britain whose responses to Mussolini's increasingly aggressive foreign policy plans put them on a collision course with Fascist Italy. Pacelli worked especially closely with the French Ambassador François Charles-Roux; it was an amiable and effective working relationship that was solidified through frequent meetings at the Vatican and through the Cardinal's highly publicized trips to France in the latter 1930s. Charles-Roux saw in Pacelli an astute observer and quintessential diplomat. Although the French Ambassador was at times frustrated by Pacelli's vague allusions to unspecified Vatican initiatives vis-à-vis the Mussolini Government, Charles-Roux was confident that Pacelli and the Holy See genuinely saw the Fascist invasion as ill-advised and dangerous, making all the more unlikely one of Pacelli's diplomatic hopes: a rapprochement between Italy and France. This reflected a longstanding Vatican interest in the emergence of what historian Emma Fattorini calls a «bloc of Catholic states» to maintain peace and stability on the European continent[20].

The frequency of Charles-Roux's visits to Pacelli at the Vatican did not escape the watchful and suspicious eye of Italian officials. At the height of the international crisis spawned by the Italian invasion of Ethiopia in the

---

[18] See DDI, Vol. II (1 settembre-31 December 1935), Pignatti to Mussolini, Doc. 335, October 13, 1935, pp. 310312; Document 645, November 15, 1935, p. 623; Doc. 664, November 19, 1935, p. 639; Doc. 827, December 10, 1935, pp. 810-811. For evidence that the British were puzzled by the absence of a public papal condemnation of Italian aggression, see FO 371/19227; FO 371/19135.

[19] Quoted by F. CHARLES-ROUX, *Huit ans au Vatican...*, 143. The letter was dated October 2, 1935.

[20] See F. CHARLES-ROUX's memoirs of his time at the Vatican, *Huit ans au Vatican...*, 138-143; 156; 229-233; cf. E. FATTORINI, *Pio XI, Hitler e Mussolini*, Torino 2007, 71.

autumn of 1935, Charles-Roux's meetings with Pacelli convinced Italian diplomats that the Vatican was working in tandem with the French Government towards a mediated settlement of the crisis[21]. The Italians grew even more suspicious about Pacelli's role in the opening months of 1936, when Pacelli and members of his staff started asking some blunt questions about Italy's capacity to continue fighting in Ethiopia. Ambassador Pignatti assumed Pacelli and his advisors were working on information from an unnamed source close to the Mussolini Government. In fact, Pacelli and his staff had it on reliable information from an «interlocutor» of the Vatican's financial expert Bernardino Nogara that Italy's finances were strained almost beyond capacity, which in turn exposed the Mussolini Government to serious internal political threats. Nogara reported to the Pope that Mussolini's calm public face masked the Duce's «state of physical depression, or rather, fatalism»[22].

Such reports stiffened Pacelli's resolve to push the Mussolini Government towards a negotiated settlement. Italian representatives bristled at Pacelli's intensified efforts in the early spring of 1936 to mediate between Italy and the other Western powers, but Pacelli persisted fearing that growing international reaction to Italian aggression in Ethiopia would further isolate Italy and, worst of all, strain Italy's relations with France and Britain to a breaking point[23]. The Vatican feared the consequences of a rupture in Italy's relations with both France and Britain, worrying that such a development would only push Mussolini's Italy towards a closer alliance with Hitler's Germany, with dire consequences for Italy and for all of Europe. Pacelli's distrust of the Hitler Government, caused by years of persistent violations of the *Reichskonkordat* and intensified attacks on German Catholicism, deepened with the German remilitarization of the Rhineland in March 1936. Unmoved by Hitler's assurances of peaceful intentions in the wake of remilitarization, but convinced also that the French did not want to go to war with Germany over this and other violations of the Versailles settlement, Pacelli redoubled his efforts to use papal di-

---

[21] See Pignatti to Mussolini, January 17, 1936 in DDI, Volume III [1 gennaio-9 maggio 1936], Doc. 71, 93-95.

[22] AES Italia, 967, Conflitto Italo-Etiopico, Vol. II, «Nota del Sig. Bernardino Nogara con una visione pessimistica della situazione italiana», January 8, 1936, ff. 364-367. See also in the same, «Udienza del 2 gennaio 1936», in which Pacelli recounts meeting with Tacchi Venturi with instructions to approach Mussolini urging a calm, restrained and reasonable public and private response to the other powers, especially England.

[23] DDI, Volume III (1 gennaio-9 maggio 1936), Doc. 71, Pignatti to Mussolini, January 17, 1936, 93-95.

plomacy as the cornerstone of a strategy to counter German ambitions by means of an Italian détente with the other major powers. As Pacelli told Ambassador Charles-Roux, an «irreconcilable break» between Italy and Britain had to be avoided at all costs, lest there be «more serious consequences». While concerned about British intransigence vis-à-vis the lifting of sanctions against Italy, Pacelli understood how news that Mussolini's armies were using chemical weapons in Ethiopia, including poison gas, angered public opinion in England and made a quick resolution to the crisis that much more difficult[24].

The Vatican may have hoped above all for a quick resolution to the conflict, but the Italians were in no such rush; they certainly had no sincere inclination towards the Vatican's push for negotiated settlements and compromise. Rather, Mussolini's Government was intent on using its unique relationship with the Vatican to, in the words of the historian Nicolas Virtue, «avoid isolation and modify world opinion». Rather than bending to the will of the Vatican, the Italians deliberately tried to skew the Vatican's cherished neutrality into mollifying anger and opposition to the Fascist imperial adventures, to the point of urging the Holy See's capillary diplomacy to help convey to public opinion around the world the Fascist side of the story as it were. As Virtue argues in a forthcoming study of Fascist Italy's relationship with the Vatican during the Ethiopian crisis, while the Vatican's chief diplomats were well aware of Italian intentions, and although they resolved to avoid becoming a propaganda tool for Fascist foreign policy, the muted criticism of the Mussolini regime resulted in an ineffective even «confusing policy» which served the Fascist regime's purpose just fine[25]. Irreconcilable differences between the Vatican and Fascist Italy on the morality or political wisdom of the Ethiopian invasion thus were masked by the public show of neutrality and the persistent attempts at mediation.

---

[24] See DDI, Volume III (1 gennaio-maggio 1936), Doc. 158, February 1, 1936, p. 197; Document 570, April 3, 1936, 631-633; Doc. 751, April 24, 1936, 798-799. For the corresponding Vatican files, see Pacelli diaries, P.O. 430b, f. 363, Entry April 11, 1936 and April 12, 1936, Pacelli and Charles-Roux, n. 32 and n. 33.

[25] See N.G. VIRTUE, *A Way out of Isolation: Fascist Italy's Relationship with the Vatican during the Ethiopian Crisis*, doctoral candidate, Department of History, The University of Western Ontario. *Collision of Empires: Italy's Invasion of Abyssinia and its International Impact*, ed. by G. BRUCE STRANG, forthcoming.

3. «Spiritually We Are All Semites»: The Vatican and Fascist Racial Laws, 1936-1938

As Emma Fattorini observes, the Pacelli diaries are as revealing for their omissions and silences as they are for what they reveal about decision-making in the court of Pius XI in the years leading up to the Second World War. Notable in this regard is the absence in Pacelli's notes of any reference to Hitler's meteoric rise to power by 1933, or the start of his systematic anti-Jewish campaign within months of seizing power. Nor is there any record of the discussions which must have taken place between Pius XI, Pacelli and other members of the Secretariat in the summer and autumn of 1938 when Mussolini's Government began to mimic its German counterpart by adopting, seemingly without reason or warning, a virulently racialist anti-Jewish stance. For years, of course, the Duce had insisted that Italy had no «Jewish problem» as such, and never could given that Italian Jews were so relatively few in number and because they were so well integrated into Italian society. For years, Mussolini had derided the obsessive anti-Semitism of the Nazis and even afforded sanctuary to several thousand German Jews fleeing early Nazi anti-Jewish measures. It was well known that Mussolini counted many Jews among his personal friends, and was prepared to intervene directly on behalf of so-called «foreign» Jews seeking refuge from German anti-Semitism and to flee from Europe altogether. As Galeazzo Ciano recorded in his diary as late as 1937, there simply was no reason to worry that the Italians would import the German variety of anti-Semitism. «The problem», he said, «just doesn't exist here. The Jews are few and, but for some exceptions, good... I repeat, the Jewish problem just doesn't exist here»[26].

Yet, as ever, Mussolini's most consistent quality was inconsistency and so by the latter half of the 1930s, in the period just after the invasion of Ethiopia, there were signs that Italian Fascism was about to make yet another one of its abrupt swings; this time, it was to embrace the overtly racialist and racist tones which hitherto fore had been the preserve of German and other European fascists. By the middle of July 1941, the regime approved publication in the major Italian newspapers of the *Manifesto of the Racial Scientists*, which was signed by pro-Fascist professors and purported to lend scientific credibility to the theory of an Italian version of the «Aryan» race, to the exclusion of Jews. In addition to positing an implausible pseudo-scientific theory of Italian racial purity, the *Manifesto*

---

[26] R.J.B. BOSWORTH, *Mussolini*, Bloomsbury, 334; Ciano quoted on 336.

addressed directly the threat raised by mixed marriages, thus foreshadow-
ing talk of legal restrictions on Jewish-Gentile relations in Italy[27]. That
Pius XI and the Vatican opposed such pseudo-scientific racial theories on
principle and their practical translation into policy was obvious enough;
the doctrinal rejection of these ideas was articulated in explicit and forceful ways in the 1937 *Mit Brennender Sorge*, for example, and in other public pronouncements and publications through 1937 and 1938. Notable in
this regard was the little known letter addressed to the rectors of Catholic
universities in April 1938 from the Vatican's Congregation of Seminaries
and Universities. Although it did not say anything specifically about anti-
Semitism or anti-Jewish measures, the letter nevertheless captured the essence of the Church's principled opposition to racial doctrine, including
the outright rejection of any attempt to infuse the legal order or to organize
the public realm according to racial conceptions, and of the notion that
racial identity ought to trump religious belief or affiliation[28].

The Mussolini regime, like Hitler's, understood precisely what the Pope
intended with these public repudiations of racial doctrine. By the summer
of 1938, in fact, members of Mussolini's inner circle were complaining
bitterly to the Vatican about Pius XI's anti-racist stance, which was taken
to be openly antagonistic towards the regime's evolving policy. Ciano
warned the papal representative to Italy, Borgongini Duca, to advise the
Pope to consider carefully his public statements on racial questions since
Mussolini saw it was «fundamental» to the Fascist quest for Empire. Pius
XI did not desist, of course, nor was he one to be intimidated by such
strong-arm diplomatic tactics. If anything, his resolve to combat the increasingly radical nature of Fascist racism grew firmer, and more focused,
especially when the Vatican learned that the Mussolini Government might
try to prohibit marriages between Italians and so-called non-Italians, even
those who were baptized Catholics. As it had maintained in its dealings
with the Hitler regime, the Vatican sternly invoked its treaty with the Italian State and reminded the Mussolini Government that such a legal prohibition would constitute a violation of the terms of this agreement. As
Cardinal Pacelli explained to the Italian Ambassador Pignatti, marriage
questions were the sole and exclusive sacred purview of the Church, not

---

[27] See M. SARFATTI, *Mussolini contro gli ebrei: Cronaca dell'elaborazione delle leggi
del 1938*, Milan 1994; and M. SARFATTI, *Gli ebrei nell'Italia fascista: Vicende, identità,
persecuzione*, Turin 2000.

[28] The letter can be found in «Cronaca contemporanea» in «La Civiltà Cattolica», 89
(1938)/3, quad. 2113, July 2, 1938, 83-84.

the state. Any violation of this principle would constitute a grave violation of the terms of the 1929 agreements[29].

The Fascists ignored the Vatican's warning. Between September and November 1938, Mussolini's Government began its concerted campaign to legislate the social and civil marginalization of Jews in Italy. Pope Pius XI's initial response came in an unofficial capacity, in the form of that memorable statement addressed to a group of Belgian pilgrims at St. Peter's on September 6: «Listen carefully», the Pope said, «Abraham is defined as our patriarch, our ancestor... anti -Semitism is a hateful movement with which we Christians must have nothing to do... Through Christ and in Christ we are the spiritual descendants of Abraham... anti-Semitism is unacceptable. Spiritually, we are all Semites»[30]. As evocative and as impassioned as this statement was, it was one issue in particular – the marriage clauses of Italian racial laws – which provoked the sustained ire of the Vatican and the spirited response of the Pope and his diplomatic staff. As Susan Zuccotti observes, the Vatican's reaction to the Mussolini regime's attempt to regulate marriage between Jews and non-Jews was evidence that the Pope and his men «were capable of vigorous protest in defense of their most cherished principles... These actions reveal deep concern, anxiety, and even anguish»[31].

Yet, for all of its spirited objections, voiced publicly and privately, the Vatican failed to persuade the Fascist regime to concede on the marriage provisions of the racial laws. Not even a proper diplomatic protest note issued in mid-November 1938 had the desired effect. It is true that the Church defied the legislation and continued to perform marriages according to its own edicts; Jewish converts to Catholicism were, for the Church, *bona fide* Catholics and so marriages between Catholics and Jewish converts continued. As Zuccotti points out, these marriages had no legal standing in Italy[32]. Not for the first or last time, the Vatican's doctrinal response had reached the practical limits of its political will and influence.

---

[29] Cf. S. Zuccotti, *Under His Very Windows. The Vatican and the Holocaust in Italy*, New haven 2002, 35-37.

[30] *Ibidem*, 45.

[31] *Ibidem*, 51.

[32] *Ibidem*, 52.

4. A Study in Contrasts? Pius XI, Eugenio Pacelli and the Limits of Papal Diplomacy

In the last weeks of his life, an ailing but ever-combative Pius XI resolved to make one last, definitive stand against the increasingly racialist and aggressive policies adopted by the Mussolini Government after 1938. The Pope hoped to live long enough to see the commemoration of the 10th anniversary of the Lateran Accords, the 1929 agreements between the Holy See and the Mussolini Government. Pius XI had planned to convoke a meeting of Italian bishops for the occasion, and to use the gathering to offer a pointed critique of the current state of Church-State relations in Italy, and even Germany. With his physical and intellectual capacities reduced, the Pope relied more than ever on his trusted Secretary of State. Though Pacelli worried about the Pope's drift towards more explicit public criticism of the fascist regimes, he nevertheless dutifully helped to compose the speech, making just a few minor revisions but without altering the substance of the dying Pope's forceful message[33].

The speech that was drafted as Pius XI lay dying was strongly worded; its tone biting, even sarcastic. And it was pungent in its criticism of so-called «pseudo-Catholics» – a clear allusion to professing Catholics in public life with Fascist sympathies – who took pleasure in accentuating differences among the bishops, and all the more with seeming differences between a Bishop and the Pope. It was also a poke at the ever-more acerbic Fascist press that manipulated papal statements, to the point of putting words into the Pope's mouth, while going so far as to deny the very real persecutions the Church was facing in Germany[34]. There is little doubt that Mussolini's Government, or the wider public would have grasped the substance of this papal critique loudly and clearly; if, that is, the address had ever been delivered. As it happened, the Pope did not live to deliver the speech, scheduled for February 11, the day after he died[35].

It was no secret that although he had helped to draft the speech, Cardinal Pacelli was uncomfortable with the modality and the tone of the Vatican's response to Fascist policies, whether they pertained to ongoing tensions over the status of Catholic Action, or to Fascist racial laws that

---

[33] Cf. here E. FATTORINI, *Pio XI, Hitler e Mussolini...*, 213-214.

[34] The text is reproduced in *ibidem*, 240-244. Significantly, the full text of the address was not published until 1956, under John XXIII, who had it published in the *Acta Apostolicae Sedis*, February 1959; see AAS, 51 (1959), 131-139.

[35] See A. TORNIELLI, *Pio XII*, Milano 2011, 292-293.

contravened fundamental Church teachings by presuming to regulate marriage between so-called «Aryans» and «non-Aryans». Pacelli realized of
course that the Pope was close to death, and thus felt that the Vatican's
relations with the Mussolini regime were in a kind of holding pattern.
Pacelli was resolved to steer papal diplomacy away from a frontal collision with the Mussolini regime.

Within hours of the Pope's death, Pacelli already was sending out peace
feelers to Italian officials. When the Italian Foreign Minister Ciano arrived
at the Vatican just hours after the Pope died to convey his government's
condolences, he was greeted by Cardinal Pacelli who accompanied Ciano
into the Sistine Chapel to pay his last respects to the deceased Pope.

According to Ciano's diary, Pacelli used the occasion to speak of
Church-State relations in «conciliatory and hopeful terms»[36]. Pacelli's
tone pleased Ciano who was growing increasingly worried that tension
between the Vatican and the Mussolini Government was driving diplomatic relations to a breaking point. Most worrying of all was the fact that
Mussolini himself seemed to care less and less about what the Vatican
said and did. As Ciano noted in his diary, news of the Pope's death on
February 10 scarcely made an impression on Mussolini; the Duce was
altogether «indifferent», Ciano wrote. The day before Pius XI died, Ciano
had confided to his diary that when word reached Mussolini of the Pope's
grave condition, the *Duce* responded simply by «shrugging his shoulders
in absolute indifference». Mussolini's reaction indicated a definite change
in his attitude towards the Vatican. «Strange», Ciano wrote, «for some
time now, Mussolini demonstrates a growing detachment from matters
involving the Church. At one time, things were different»[37].

Ciano and Pacelli both realized that Church-State relations were at a
decisive crossroads, accentuated by anticipation of the pending conclave
and escalating tension in European affairs. Although Mussolini may have
professed a certain indifference towards Vatican affairs, in reality he and
members of his government were keenly interested in the question of who
would succeed the sometimes irascible Pius XI, and in what direction the
new Pope would take the Vatican in its relationship with the Italian Government. Evidence of this interest comes from the Italian reaction to rumors that circulated soon after Pius XI died – Ciano said they came from
American sources – which suggested that the late Pope had left behind a
written statement or testament of some kind. Mussolini was very keen to

---

[36] Ciano diaries, 1939, 251.
[37] *Ibidem*, 250.

confirm the story one way or another, and even keener to see a copy of the document if one existed. Given their level of interest in the story, Italian officials must have suspected that the document in question related to the critical speech Pius XI had planned to deliver to mark the anniversary of the 1929 *conciliazione*[38].

If the rumored document really was the speech Pius XI had prepared on his deathbed, the Italians need not have worried. Cardinal Pacelli had already moved decisively to make sure that the speech was suppressed. In fact, after the Pope died, Pacelli ordered an immediate stop to the publication of the text of the address, which was all but ready for wide distribution to the Italian bishops. One of Pacelli's trusted advisors, Domenico Tardini, recalled that within hours of Pius XI's death, Pacelli demanded that any and all material related to the preparation of the Pope's address be remanded to Pacelli's office; any copies or templates of the speech that were with the publishers were to be destroyed immediately[39].

What are we to make of Pacelli's role in suppressing what would have been a truly historic and potentially consequential speech by a dying pontiff; even more if the speech had been published and disseminated posthumously? Emma Fattorini reasons that Pacelli's handling of the matter reveals just how deeply the future Pius XII disagreed with his predecessor's move towards an open confrontation if not an avowed diplomatic rupture with the fascist states. As we have seen, an ailing Pius XI grew more resolved and combative in the last months of his life, to the point of authorizing the preparation of a papal statement to condemn Nazi racialism and anti-Semitism, in addition to the speech planned for early February to criticize the Mussolini Government. In both instances, Eugenio Pacelli played the determinative role in steering a course away from an open confrontation or overt diplomatic rupture. It was Pacelli, after all, who made sure that Pius XI's speech to the Italian bishops was suppressed after the Pope died; tellingly, it was only published in 1959, several months after Pacelli's death. In a similar vein, soon after becoming Pope, Pacelli made the decisive decision not to pursue publication of a papal statement condemning in explicit terms Nazi racial thought and anti-Semitism in particular; the so-called «hidden encyclical» of Pius XI[40].

---

[38] *Ibidem*, 251-252.

[39] All of this is recounted in fascinating detail in a memo drafted by Tardini and conserved in the AES, Pos. 576, fasc. 607; as discussed in detail by E. FATTORINI, *Pio XI, Hitler e Mussolini...*, 214.

[40] G. PASSELECQ and B. SUCHECKY, *The Hidden Encyclical of Pius XI*, New York 1997.

In a sense, already before becoming Pope, Eugenio Pacelli had set papal diplomacy on a course that was destined to win both the praise and the scorn of contemporaries, and of posterity; praise by those who saw in the future Pius XII a mixture of principled moral leadership and doctrinal clarity, mixed with diplomatic prudence; scorn by those who saw in his nonconfrontational approach timidity, moral failure, as well as colossal political and diplomatic miscalculations that emboldened the fascist dictators who were bent on waging aggressive war while working to complete radical social and racial revolutions, at home and abroad.

Italian Fascism's imperial and racist turn in the mid-1930s – expressed principally in the Fascist invasion of Ethiopia and then in domestic racial laws – tested the logic and the limits of the imperfect but mutually convenient accommodation achieved between the Vatican and the Mussolini regime after the 1929 agreements. The inexorable radicalization of Mussolini's domestic and foreign policy agenda exposed some of the fundamental *doctrinal* incompatibilities between Catholic political and social thought on the one hand, and Fascist ideology on the other. Yet, at Pacelli's insistence, papal diplomacy under Pius XI never abandoned the path of diplomatic engagement with the Fascist regime as the means to precise ends. This included a strategy to preserve the Church's distinct spheres of autonomy within the Fascist State, while continuing to cultivate diplomatic influence with the Mussolini Government so as to help steer Italian domestic and foreign policy away from closer alignment with Nazi Germany. In this respect, Italian-Vatican relations in the latter 1930s mirrored the pattern of *conflict* and *compromise* which John Pollard observed of the early years after the 1929 agreements. In the end, though, the Vatican's contradictory relationship with Mussolini's Italy produced mixed, often disappointing results from the perspective of the Vatican's own objectives and interests. This speaks to the practical limits of papal influence on Mussolini's regime, and of the Vatican's inability and in some cases unwillingness to find an effective *political* instrument with which to combat the radical and racist dimensions of Italian Fascism on the eve of the Second World War.

ROBERT A. MARYKS

The Jesuit Pietro Tacchi Venturi and Mussolini's Racial Laws

The Fascist newspaper of Cremona, «Il Regime Fascista», reported on October 4, 1938 that even though the Italian Fascists inherited from the Jesuits their approach to the Jewish question, «Father Tacchi Venturi, who oscillated between the Vatican and his [Superior] General, must have asked his colleagues [at «La Civiltà Cattolica»] to pour much Jewish water into the fascist wine».

The priest in question was a renowned Italian historian of the early Society of Jesus, writer, and diplomat, the Jesuit Pietro Tacchi Venturi (1861-1956). True, he functioned as a liaison between the Vatican Secretariat of State and the popes themselves (Pius XI and Pius XII), and the Superior General of his religious order, Włodzimierz Ledóchowski (1866-1942). But more importantly, Tacchi Venturi had served as the exclusive (especially after March 1940) contact person between the Mussolini Government and the Vatican in what concerned the Jewish question during the period from the promulgation of the racial (anti-Semitic) laws in 1938 to the fall of Mussolini in 1943. Testimony to this is a large personal archive of Tacchi Venturi that contains thousands of documents related to his role as the key figure in Church-State relations during the entire period of the Fascist regime, 1922-43, among them documents related to more than 800 cases of individuals affected by the racial laws.

This article aims to provide a biographical sketch of the intriguing and controversial figure of Tacchi Venturi. Far from being exhaustive, my article is based on heretofore unknown archival material, and is meant to give the reader a better understanding of the reasons why this Jesuit became such a controversial and notorious figure to his contemporaries and

---

* For more detailed discussion of this topic, see my newly published book, *Pouring Jewish Water into Fascist Wine. Untold Stories of (Catholic) Jews from the Archive of Mussolini's Jesuit Pietro Tacchi Venturi*, Leiden 2011.

to historians of Italian Fascism, as well as to shed light on why the documents regarding the racial laws ended up in his archive.

Pietro Tacchi Venturi was born to Antonio Tacchi Venturi and Orsola Ceselli in San Severino Marche on August 12, 1861 – «the memorable year in the history of Italy for the proclamation of the reign of Vittorio Emanuele II», as the Jesuit wrote in the beginning of his memoir that he composed many decades later. His highlighting of this synchrony is significant, for it determined Tacchi Venturi's negative interpretation of the role the Risorgimento played in its relation to the papacy, an interpretation that he inherited from his father; it also determined his profound antipathy toward «the spirit of laicism» that, in his view, characterized the post-1870 regime. Indeed, Tacchi Venturi described his father as «a full-blooded Guelph», or a convinced supporter of the authority of the Pope against the lay ruler. The Jesuit remembered years later that as child he used to play at home with the heavy rifle that his father still kept from the time of the flight of the Garibaldi troops from Rome in 1849. Unhappy with the occupation of Rome by the Piedmontese and their new Government, Antonio Tacchi Venturi preferred to serve to the Vatican as a lawyer of the Sacra Rota, or the supreme ecclesiastical and secular court of the Catholic Church, and to later refuse a position in the state justice system, even though it meant that he had to sell a portion of his land in order to keep feeding his large family.

As the last of fifteen children, Pietro's father had been born after the death of his own father, Antonio Tacchi of Bergamo[1], who had married Angela Ragni of Ancona. After the premature death of Antonio Tacchi, his young widow married a professor of anatomy, Luigi Venturi, from her own hometown, but the couple remained childless. Luigi Venturi's role in raising his wife's children was recognized by the addition of his name to that of their real father, Tacchi. Thus the father of the Jesuit – who had been given his dead father's name Antonio – registered the double name of Tacchi Venturi when he married the Jesuit's mother, Orsola Ceselli (d. 4/30/1887). She was the daughter of Gioacchino Ceselli and Silvia Valenti, both originally from Rome. The former belonged to a rich family of merchants, «highly esteemed for their honesty and religiosity»[2].

Pietro Tacchi Venturi had five older siblings – Silvia (1851-1932), Luigi (1833-1923), Mariano (1854-1937), Gioacchino (died as an infant),

---

[1] See also Fondo Tacchi Venturi [henceforth FTV], Archivum Romanum Societatis Iesu (the Roman Archive of the Society of Jesus) [henceforth ARSI] 1012, doc. 579.

[2] FTV, 46, *Autobiografia*, 3.

Giovanni Battista (1858-1930) – and two younger siblings: Beatrice (1864-1937) and Maria (1868-1930). In his unpublished autobiography, he liked to highlight the fact that his baptismal name, Pietro, had been given to him because of his father's «devotion to the Prince of the Apostles and as a sign of his immutable fidelity to the successors of the Saint in the Roman pontificate»[3].

For the Tacchi Venturis, this devotion to the Pope meant at the same time their stubborn scepticism toward the Liberal Government that «took Rome from the Pope» in 1870. Decades later Pietro Tacchi Venturi reflected his family's political views stating in his autobiography that «the devoted Catholic families of the City [of Rome], eager to educate their children according to their traditions of sincere faith and unaltered devotion to the Roman pontiff», were deeply worried about the new Government's sheer anticlerical policy, «which – influenced by the Masonic sects – aimed to subvert all pious customs of the Christian nation»[4].

Because of his father's translocation to San Severino in the Marche region, Tacchi Venturi continued his education in the gymnasium of the town and then in the lyceum in the region's capital, Macerata, the birthplace of the famous Jesuit missionary, Matteo Ricci (d. 1610). Tacchi Venturi would later publish Matteo Ricci's works on China and in 1910 would promote a celebration of the 300th anniversary of Ricci's death[5]. Subsequently, Tacchi Venturi moved back to Rome, where he attended the Roman Seminary 1876-78, with the purpose of enhancing his skills in literary studies.

From the period of his school education in Rome, Tacchi Venturi remembered three books that, unlike Edmondo De Amicis' irreligious *Cuore* (1886), formed in him «the love for [the Catholic] religion and for the Fatherland»: *Giannetto* by Luigi Alessandro Parravicini (published in 1837), and *Giannettino* (1876) and *Pinocchio* (1880) by Carlo Collodi. The reading of these enjoyable books had been offered to the future Jesuit by his master, Pacifico Falusca, who also taught him how to hawk robins

---

[3] *Autob.*, 3.
[4] *Autob.*, 9. See also an unsigned (probably by Tacchi Venturi himself) and undated (probably from 1929) document about the alleged role of «Judaeo-Masonic plutocracy» in Italy that is found in Tacchi Venturi's archive (FTV 430a). See, for example, A. VISANI, *The Jewish Enemy: Fascism, the Vatican, and Anti-Semitism on the Seventieth Anniversary of the 1938 Race Laws*, in «Journal of Modern Italian Studies», 14 (2009)/2, 173-175.
[5] See M. RICCI and P. TACCHI VENTURI, *Opere storiche del P. Matteo Ricci, SJ*, Macerata 1911, reprinted in 1913.

with an owl – a passion so strong in the adolescent that his family judged he would not be able to renounce it when he decided to join the Society of Jesus[6].

With his mother crying hard at the Termini Railway Station in Rome[7], the 18-year-old Pietro departed November 10, 1878 for the Jesuit novitiate, located in the decaying castle of Aux Alleux in western France[8]. There he discerned during the Ignatian spiritual exercises his «response to God's calling to leave the world and consecrate himself for life and death to His service»[9]. Due to what Tacchi Venturi called the influence of Masonry on the anti-Jesuit measures of the French Government of Jules F.C. Ferry (1832-93) in the 1880s, he and his confreres had to abandon France. Pietro was transferred to Naples to complete his novice formation with the pronunciation of his first religious vows. Consequently, he studied rhetoric first in Naples and then in Castel Gandolfo near Rome, where Prince Alessandro (1800-86) had donated his Villa Torlonia to the Jesuits[10].

Two years later (1882), Tacchi Venturi was sent to the Jesuit community of Rome and then of Naples (1883) in order to complete his *maturità*, or high school exams, which he had missed before joining the Society. Having passed the exams at the Liceo Vittorio Emanuele in Naples, the young Jesuit returned to Rome to continue for two years (1883-85) his training in philosophy at the Pontifical Gregorian University. Subsequently, the Superior Provincial Ghetti sent Tacchi Venturi for the so-called regency, a two-year internship, during which he was assigned the care of noble boys in the Jesuit boarding school located in the 16th-century Villa Mondragone in the region of Castelli Romani. His duty of supervising these disciplined students gave him enough time to write his very first book – the biographical memories of a Jesuit who had been instrumental in Tacchi Venturi's decision to enter the Jesuits, *Memorie biografiche del P. Camillo Mearini* (Città di Castello, 1886). Toward the end of this experience, which was marked by an illness, the young Jesuit was transferred to Rome with the new task of pursuing studies in literature[11]. He therefore enrolled at the Royal University of Rome (La Sapienza), where in 1891 he earned his Master of Arts degree with a thesis on an unpublished Greek

---

[6] *Autob.*, 7.
[7] *Autob.*, 14.
[8] *Autob.*, 17-18.
[9] *Autob.*, 19-23.
[10] *Autob.*, 34-37.
[11] *Autob.*, 41-45.

eulogy of St Gregory of Nazianzus (c. 325-89) by John Geometra (10th Century)[12].

Thirty-year-old Pietro could now finally begin his final stage of preparation toward his priesthood – theology, which he studied once again at the Jesuit Gregorian University until 1895. One year later the young priest received his first major mission from the superior General: to write a history of the Jesuits in Italy. Tacchi Venturi would continue to work on this project intermittently until his 90s. For the next 15 years he travelled extensively through Europe to hunt archival and library materials to be used as sources for his new publication. The first part of the first volume of *La Storia della Compagnia, La Storia religiosa in Italia durante la prima età della Compagnia di Gesù* was published in 1910, when the Jesuit was 49. The second part of the second volume would be published in 1951, when Tacchi Venturi was 90, before becoming nearly blind. He would die five years later[13].

With the beginning of the Great War, Tacchi Venturi's activity as a writer was interrupted, when General Superior Franz Xavier Wernz (b. 1842), shortly before his death in 1914, appointed him Secretary General of the Society. This office, which he held until 1921, became particularly crucial when the new Superior General Włodzimierz Ledóchowski (1866-1943) – because of his Polish origins and Austrian citizenship – was not allowed to stay in Rome and thus moved away to Switzerland, leaving much of the Order's daily government affairs in the hands of Tacchi Venturi. This is when the aristocratic Jesuit – well connected to many prominent Roman families – began weaving his wide and dense web of contacts with the Vatican and the governmental officials of the Eternal City.

The Jesuit's role as Vatican's «fiduciary» – as Tacchi Venturi presented himself to Benito Mussolini – in dealings with Palazzo Venezia began in 1922. In that year, Pope Pius XI, the former librarian of the Ambrosiana in Milan who became acquainted with Tacchi Venturi there in 1899[14], re-

---

[12] *Autob.*, 9. See also P. TACCHI VENTURI, «*De Ioanne Geometra eiusque in S. Gregorium Nazianzenum inedita laudatione*, in «Studi e Documenti di Storia e Diritto», 14 (1893), 133-162.

[13] See also P. TACCHI VENTURI, *Saint Ignace de Loyola dans l'art aux XVIIme et XVIIIme siècles*, Rome 1929; and P. TACCHI VENTURI, *La prima casa di S. Ignazio di Loyola in Roma: o le sue cappellette al Gesù*, Rome 1951.

[14] See P. TACCHI VENTURI, *La promozione del P. Pietro Boetto al Cardinalato*, 1, in FTV 46, folder *I miei ricordi (1861-1891-1931)*; E. TISSERANT, *Pius XI as Librarian*, in «The Library Quarterly», 9 (1939)/4, 389-403; and G. CASTELLI, *Storia segreta di Roma Città aperta*, prefazione di E. Boggiano Pico, Rome 1959, 244-245.

quested that Tacchi Venturi negotiate together with the newly appointed
Minister of External Affairs, Mussolini, the purchase of the precious Chigi Library for the Vatican, which the Italian State had owned since 1916[15].
Instead of selling it, Mussolini decided to donate the library to the Pope,
thus symbolically initiating the process of the *Conciliazione*, or reconciliation, which led to the Lateran Pacts of 1929, giving juridical status to the
Vatican, making Catholicism the official religion of the Italian State, and
consequently ending the so-called «Roman question» that had begun with
the «occupation of the Papal States by the Piedmont troops» in 1861, the
year of Tacchi Venturi's birth. As he later put it, the donation of the Chigi
Library «was the beginning of my acquaintance and dialogue I had with
the Duce from December 1922 until the first months of 1943»[16].

In 1956 «The New York Times» wrote in Tacchi Venturi's obituary
that the Jesuit had «engineered the Lateran Pacts»[17]. Indeed, the Jesuit's
role in the reconciliation between the Vatican and the Italian State is abun-
dantly documented, yet unstudied. Tacchi Venturi's archive contains an
ample file of correspondence between the governmental officials (especially between the Head of Mussolini's cabinet, Amedeo Giannini), and
the Jesuit[18], and the notes Tacchi Venturi made of his audiences with Mussolini himself[19], which reveal the Jesuit's zealous and constant engagement
in Church-State affairs leading to the Lateran Pacts and its subsequent
preservation[20]. In his vision of Italian society as traditionally Catholic,
Tacchi Venturi sought not only the reconciliation of Church-State animosity that had resulted from the role the liberal and anti-clerical Risor-

---

[15] See FTV 1, folder 1; 2, folder 55; 16, folder 1146; 17, folder 1212; and 46, folder *I miei
ricordi (1861-1891-1931)*, folder *P. Tacchi Venturi 1915-1931* («Dati biografici», 4-5),
and *La Biblioteca Chigi al Vaticano*. See also M. SCADUTO, *P. Pietro Tacchi Venturi*,
in «Archivum Historicum Societatis Iesu [AHSI]», 25 (1956), 760; and A. GIANNINI,
Padre Tacchi in funzione diplomatica, in «Doctor Communis», 9 (1956), 229-230.

[16] See FTV 46, folder *P. Tacchi Venturi 1915-1931* («Dati biografici», 5).

[17] *Priest who aided in creation of Vatican City dies*, in «The New York Times», March
19, 1956. See also S. CORTESI, *Italy to Indemnify Church, Rome Hears*, in «The New
York Times», February 11, 1928, 4; P. BLET ET AL., *Actes et documents...*, vol. 1, 13; A.
GIANNINI, *Padre Tacchi in funzione diplomatica...*, 232-235; and F. MARGIOTTA BROGLIO,
Italia e Santa Sede dalla grande guerra alla conciliazione; aspetti politici e giuridici,
Bari 1966, especially 110-11, 151-170.

[18] See his memories on Tacchi Venturi's role in A. GIANNINI, *Padre Tacchi in funzione
diplomatica...*, 227-236.

[19] See *P. Tacchi Venturi. Udienze con Mussolini 1926-1939*, in FTV 46.

[20] See FTV 1, folder 11; 4, folders 257 and 269; 1018, docs 88-290; and 46, folder *I miei
ricordi (1861-1891-1931)*.

gimento had played in the limitation of papal temporal power but also the conciliation of Fascist ideology with Catholicism, which for him would guarantee society's moral order. It is not surprising, therefore, to see Tacchi Venturi eagerly collaborate with the Fascist Government in a number of affairs related to keeping Catholic culture and morality dominant, if not exclusive, in Italian society. Tacchi Venturi's archive contains numerous dossiers concerning his correspondence with the Fascist Government on an astonishingly broad range of issues, including the following: actions against «Masonic and Protestant propaganda»; the war with Ethiopia; Catholic assistance in the Italian colonies of Ethiopia and Albania; the «Muslim threat» in Albania; diplomatic relations with the Bolshevik Government of Russia; legislation of the Fascist Youth Organizations; exemptions from the military service for clerics; appointments of bishops and mayors; military promotions; petitions for grace, tax exemptions, jobs, visas, passports, citizenship, nobility titles, and readmission to the Fascist Party; the «Italianization» of the former Austrian region of *Alto Adige*; the attempted assassinations of Mussolini; Austrian prisoners of Hitler; the Fascist character of *Azione Cattolica*; the censorship of films to be shown in the theatres and of pictures to be published in fashion magazines; the case of Alcide de Gasperi; so-called «houses of tolerance» or brothels; the prohibition of balls; the discussion over the Fascist Youth Organization's uniform to be worn at First Communion and Confirmation ceremonies; the type of swimming outfit to be worn on public beaches; nude public statues; banks; the marble of Carrara; the presence of Catholic chaplains in various sectors of civil life; teaching religion in the public schools; remaking, acquiring, and selling churches, convents, and other Catholic institutions; the abuse of ringing bells by political parties; the diplomatic plate for the Vatican Secretary of State's car; the distribution of the Gospel among soldiers; the status of Catholicism in Sweden; anti-religious stamps, and so on and so forth[21]. Tacchi Venturi saw this commitment as an expression of faithfulness and love, with which he «sincerely served Mussolini as a poor priest of Christ»[22]. The Duce recognized the Jesuit's merits by awarding him in 1931 the highest civil decoration, the Knight Grand Cross of the Order of SS Maurice and Lazarus[23].

---

[21] See also an interesting document, probably by Tacchi Venturi himself, on how a certain kind of «Catholic discipline», corporal punishment included, would be beneficial for the raising of the young man in «new Fascist Italy».

[22] See Tacchi Venturi's letter to Mussolini from November 4, 1938 in FTV 2159.

[23] See FTV 1534.

Some journalists speculated that Mussolini made many concessions to the Vatican under the sway of Tacchi Venturi as his confessor and advisor. After all, in 1923 he baptized Mussolini's three children and blessed his marriage with Rachele Guidi in December 1925[24]. In 1928 the Jesuit received a letter from Munich informing him that a German paper had published an article which claimed that the Jesuit confessor of Mussolini exercised a role similar to Rasputin's at the imperial court of Russia[25]. After Tacchi Venturi's death in 1956, a number of newspapers published articles whose titles underscored the Jesuit's role as the Duce's confessor[26]. In his personal writings, however, the Jesuit maintained that he «did not play the role assigned to Pier delle Vigne (ca. 1190-1249) in the reign of Federico II»[27], meaning that Tacchi Venturi did not have the keys to Mussolini's heart[28]. Whatever the truth is about their spiritual relationship, which is worthy of a separate monograph, Tacchi Venturi, who was 22 years older, did care about Mussolini's eternal salvation. In a letter written a few weeks before his death to his spiritual daughter, a former Carmelite nun and a noble woman, the Jesuit revealed that he was consoled by reading the last letter of «poor Mussolini», which «opens to a hope for God's mercy – we should remember that He wants all people to be saved»[29].

---

[24] See P.V. Cannistraro and B.R. Sullivan, *Il Duce's Other Woman*, New York 1992, 343, 517.

[25] See FTV 1009, doc. 356-356a.

[26] See, for example, «La Cronaca di Roma» (March 20, 1956), 4; «Gazzetta Sera» (March 20, 1956), 3; «Il Paese» (March 19, 1956), 1.

[27] See P. Tacchi Venturi, *La promozione del P. Pietro Boetto al Cardinalato*, 5, in FTV 46, folder *I miei ricordi (1861-1891-1931)*.

[28] In Dante's *Inferno*, Vigne described his relationship to Emperor Federico II to that of Dante and Virgil with the following words: «I am he that held both keys of Frederick's heart,/ To lock and to unlock; and well I knew/ To turn them with so exquisite an art» (translation by Sayers, lines 58-60).

[29] FTV 1023, doc. 593. Tacchi Venturi alludes probably to Mussolini's letter to his mistress Claretta Petacci, in which he begged her for forgiveness for all the evil he had done to her. See, for example, B. Haugen, *Benito Mussolini: Fascist Italian dictator*, Minneapolis 2007, 94.

FIG. 1. *Postcard with the sculpture «Juda's Betrayal». Tacchi Venturi received this postcard from an anonymous sender after the Lateran Pacts had been signed in 1929. The caption beneath the photograph of the Roman statue «Judas's Betrayal» was changed into «the Jesuit's Betrayal». On the other side of the postcard, the sender (proverbial Pasquino) wrote a rhymed verse: «Fin che campa Tacchi Venturi/ Speriam la cosa duri/ Ma se more il sor Benito/ Anche S. Ignazio è bello e ito» [Until Tacchi Venturi is alive/ We hope the affair will last/ But when Sir Benito dies/ Also St. Ignatius is gone forever].*

Instead, Tacchi Venturi's relationship with the lover of Mussolini, the Jewish journalist Margherita Grassini Sarfatti (1883-1961), was surely of a more spiritual character[30]. The Jesuit's archive contains a few letters that the Duce's famous lover and biographer wrote to Tacchi Venturi[31]. Some letters from 1927 deal with the preparation for the baptism of Sarfatti's daughter Fiammetta[32], and another one dates from February 1956, one month before the Jesuit's death. This letter is signed «Most devoted in Christ, Margherita Sarfatti». A Jesuit who had a reserved access to Tacchi Venturi's archive wrote a note on this letter: «Lover of Mussolini. A

---

[30] See *Enciclopedia Italiana* 30, 870-71.

[31] See M.G. SARFATTI, *Dvx: 32 illustrazioni fuori testo e 5 autografi*, Milan 1926. The biography was translated into many languages. See, for example, M.G. SARFATTI, *The life of Benito Mussolini..*, with a preface by Benito Mussolini, transl. by Frederic Whyte, New York 1925; M.G. SARFATTI and F. MEYER-BALTE, *Mussolini: Lebensgeschichte*, Leipzig 1926; and M.G. SARFATTI, *Mussolini: Autor. Overs. fra Italiensk ved Regitze Winge*, Copenhagen 1928.

[32] FTV 1009, docs 18, 19, 20. See also FTV 1013, doc. 86. For the correspondence between Amedeo Sarfatti and Tacchi Venturi, see FTV 1013, docs 234 and 257.

Jew converted and baptized by T[acchi] V[enturi], as were, too, her son [Amedeo] and daughter [Fiammetta]»[33]. Indeed, in her letter to Nicholas Murray Butler following the promulgation of the racial laws, Sarfatti wrote:

«You know what happened to us! I am a Catholic, & so are both my children, both married to Catholics, & fathers & mothers of Catholic children. But I myself as well as my husband, are of Jewish descent, therefore both my children & myself are considered Jews, that most heinous (so it seems to be) sin of today, being searched in us, in such a measure, that my son's glorious death, as a hero, at 17 years of age in the War, & my husband's & mine own & my other son's fascist & Italian faith & works during all our lives, account to nothing»[34].

Because of his intimate relationship with her, the Jesuit was able to obtain from Sarfatti some private information regarding Mussolini, as Tacchi Venturi himself revealed describing the Church-State crisis of 1931, an event described by him as «the reconciliation of the Conciliation»[35]. Had not Sarfatti been able to avoid – by escaping to South America – the racial persecution that her own lover inflicted on the Jews, her application for «discrimination» would have most likely been supported by Tacchi Venturi. It is possible, though, that the Jesuit helped her obtain a foreign visa through the Vatican, as he did for the Jewish professors Carlo Della Seta and Gino Arias, as Bishop Fortunato confirmed in his letter from Buenos Aires on February 7, 1939[36]. Hopefully, full access to the ecclesiastical archives for the period of Pius XII's pontificate will help verify these conjectures.

Whatever the extent of Tacchi Venturi's influence on the Duce was, Italian public opinion saw him as the man behind the scenes of the Concordat agreement. Not surprisingly, it has been suggested that Tacchi Venturi's political engagement was the motive for his attempted assassination with a paper knife on February 27, 1928[37], which both «The New York Times» and «Time Magazine» reported:

---

[33] FTV 1017, doc. 315. See also CANNISTRARO, *Il Duce's Other Woman...*, 533, 538.

[34] *Ibidem*, 521-522.

[35] See P. TACCHI VENTURI, *L'accordo del 2 settembre 1931 o la riconciliazione della Conciliazione*, and *La promozione del P. Pietro Boetto al Cardinalato*, in FTV 46.

[36] FTV 1015, doc. 10.

[37] Tacchi Venturi's archive contains 879 documents, mostly condolences letters, related to this attempted assassination. See FTV 1009, doc. 201, 204-06, 212-13, 231, and the entire folder 1010. On the alleged responsibility of Masonry for this attempted assas-

«To the House of the Jesuits at Rome there had come and yanked the ancient bell pull a decently dressed youth who announced himself as Signor De Angelis. He must, he said, he must make an important confession to good Father Tacchi-Venturi. The porter, rubbing sleepy eyes, told the youth that his desired confessor was immersed in study, could not be disturbed. Next day Signor De Angelis returned, yanked the bell still more violently, and prevailed upon the porter to usher him into the Jesuit's study.

Father Tacchi-Venturi, upon raising his eyes from his papers, saw a pale, demented face and a hand which grasped a slender, dagger-like paper knife. Quickly, the assassin sprang. More quickly, the Jesuit dodged. As a result the knife barely lacerated the neck skin of Father Tacchi-Venturi. Meanwhile the sleepy porter had valorously collared Signor De Angelis.

The incident closed when Father Tacchi-Venturi's neck was neatly bound up at the Santo Spirito Hospital. Later, seated in an armchair, he received a visit of condolence from Pietro Cardinal Gasparri, suave Papal Secretary of State»[38].

The memory of the event must have been important to the 67-year-old Jesuit; he preserved in his archive many condolence letters that after the accident arrived in great number from people of all ranks, Pope Pius XI included.

Beyond his unofficial diplomatic engagement that combined the functions played by both the papal nuncio and the Italian ambassador to the Vatican, Tacchi Venturi was also an author of many articles in Treccani's monumental *Enciclopedia Italiana*[39] and a writer for «La Civiltà Cattolica», in which he published more than 100 articles, most of them on various topics in early modern religious history[40]. This bi-weekly periodical was censored by the Vatican Secretariat of State and was considered an official expression of the Vatican's views[41]. As David I. Kertzer has persuasively shown, «[*La*] *Civiltà Cattolica*'s anti-Jewish campaign, coming when it

---

sination, see F. MARGIOTTA BROGLIO, *Italia e Santa Sede dalla Grande Guerra alla Conciliazione...*, 524-27.

[38] See «Time», March 12, 1928, *Italy: Jesuit Stabbed*. See also *Stabs Jesuit Agent in Vatican Issue*, in «The New York Times», February 29, 1928, 5.

[39] See FTV 1012, doc. 493; 1013, doc. 111; 1014, docs 446 and 516; 1015, docs 96 and 103; 1015, docs 148, 149, and 151; 1017, doc. 368; and 1018, doc. 82. See also L. ARMENANTE, «Inventario analitico delle carte [del] P. Tacchi Venturi relative all'Enciclopedia Italiana conservate in Archivum Romanum Societatis Jesu», in FTV 49a; G. TURI, *Il mecenate, il filosofo e il gesuita. L'«Enciclopedia italiana», specchio della nazione*, Bologna 2002, passim; and A. GUASCO, *Chiesa Cattolica e totalitarismo*, in A. GUASCO and R. PERIN, *Pius XI: Keywords: International Conference Milan 2009*, Berlin 2010, 97.

[40] See M. SCADUTO, *P. Pietro Tacchi Venturi...*, 757.

[41] See R. TARADEL and B. RAGGI, *La segregazione amichevole: «La Civiltà cattolica» e la questione ebraica 1850-1945*, Rome 2000, especially 4-9 and 124-56.

did, proved crucial to the rise of modern anti-Semitism»[42]. Indeed, already in the early years (1865-68) of the pontificate of Pius IX, who helped found the periodical in 1850 with money he borrowed from bankers of the Jewish Rothschild family in Naples[43], the Jesuits had published 36 fiercely anti-Semitic articles[44]. In Kertzer's well-argued view, the Church – and especially the Jesuit periodical – «lay the groundwork for the Fascist racial laws»[45]. As a matter of fact, in 1884 «La Civiltà Cattolica» printed an article on the case of Alfred Dreyfus, written by the Jesuit Antonio Ballerini, which asserted:

> «The only proper remedy and more effective than any other, as we have been constantly showing for years and years, would be a fundamental and uniform law in the individual states, which likens the Jews to foreigners and treats them as guests and not as citizens. This law would be required because of the the characteristic of the Jew, in every place increasingly cosmopolitan, for only the Jews are always outsiders to any other race except for the simple case of being born on its soil»[46].

In 1937 one of Ballerini's confreres had suggested in another article «an amicable segregation» between Catholics and Jews, and Father Mario Barbera described the anti-Semitic laws passed in Hungary in 1938 as exemplary[47]. Not surprisingly, Mussolini admitted that he was inspired by the anti-Semitic tradition of the Jesuits[48], as did the Nazis, who negotiated the Concordat with nuncio Eugenio Pacelli in 1933[49].

The Fascist newspaper of Cremona, «Il Regime Fascista», founded and published by «Italy's official Jew-baiter»[50] Roberto Farinacci, published

---

[42] D.I. KERTZER, *The Popes against the Jews. The Vatican's Role in the Rise of modern Anti-Semitism*, New York 2001, 285.

[43] See R. TARADEL and B. RAGGI, *La segregazione amichevole...*, 4. On the importance of dating the Jesuit periodical's anti-Semitism and how it was at the origins of the French and European Catholic campaign against Jews, *ibidem*, 27-28.

[44] See D.I. KERTZER, *The Popes against the Jews*, 135-136.

[45] *Ibidem*, 285. See also R. DI SEGNI, *Prefazione*, in TARADEL and RAGGI, *La segregazione amichevole...*, XII-XIII.

[46] See «La Civiltà Cattolica», 6 (1884), 644.

[47] See «La Civiltà Cattolica», 2 (1937), 418, and 3 (1938), 146-53; and TARADEL and RAGGI, *La segregazione amichevole*, 129-34, and 145-146.

[48] See E. FATTORINI, *Saggio introduttivo*, to G. SALE, *Le leggi razziali in Italia e il Vaticano*, Milano 2009, 19.

[49] See V. LAPOMARDA, *Holocausto Judío y los Jesuitas*, in *Diccionario Histórico de la Compañía de Jesús* [henceforth DHCJ] 2, p. 1946.

[50] See S. WAAGENAAR, *The Pope's Jews*, LaSalle, Ill., 1974, 316. On anti-Semitism and Italian Fascism, see also SARFATTI, *The Jews in Mussolini's Italy...*, 42-78.

on October 4, 1938 an article entitled «Adaptation That Surprises». In it, the Fascist newspaper expressed its astonishment at the sudden change in the Catholic Church's policy towards the Jews. Even though «the papal encyclicals, the canons of councils, and the bishops' pastoral letters demonstrate, without exception, that the Church persecuted the Jews sometimes cruelly and mercilessly», now the Vatican claims that it should have a philo-Semitic spirit and that «the men on earth are all brothers [...] who belong just to one race of mankind»[51]. This new opportunistic approach, which came off as anti-Fascism – certainly inspired by the Jesuit Tacchi Venturi who, oscillating between the Vatican and his [Superior] General, must have asked his colleagues [at «La Civiltà Cattolica»] to *pour much Jewish water into Fascist wine*»[52] – appeared to contradict article's thesis that «the Jesuits were undoubtedly our precursors in the Jewish question»[53].

Indeed, the article described the relationship between Italian Fascism and the Jesuits as a perfect love, which was «suddenly overshadowed by a cloud». To the earlier Jesuits the Jew had been «a plague of mankind», as «Il Regime Fascista» has shown in its analysis of a Jesuit study on «the Jewish question» that was published in «La Civiltà Cattolica» back in 1890. Its vision of «the spectacle of the Jewish invasion and bullying» was so appealing, wrote Farinacci, that this study was entirely reproduced in Mazzetti's book, *La questione ebraica in un secolo di cultura italiana* [*The Jewish Question in a Century of Italian Culture*][54]. This portrayal of the Jew, which inspired the Fascist racial laws but which the Jesuits now seemed to de-emphasise, remained true for the author of the article, who continued to regard the ethical-religious doctrine of the Talmud as an expression of the «depraved madness of the Jewish race». The Jewish promise «to dominate the world in less than a century», which «La Civiltà

---

[51] This is an allusion to the speech Pope Pius XI delivered in September 1938 to a group of Belgian pilgrims. For an interview with Farinacci about the papal speech, see G. SALE, *Le leggi razziali...*, 212-13. On an analysis of the speech, see D.I. KERTZER, *The Popes against the Jews...*, 279-80; H. WOLF, *Pope and Devil: The Vatican's archives and the Third Reich*, Cambridge, Mass., 2010, 206-12; and A. STILLE, *The Double Bind of Italian Jews: Acceptance and Assimilation,* in ZIMMERMAN, *Jews in Italy...*, 29.

[52] FTV 1014, doc. 664. The italics are mine.

[53] For Farinacci's view of the roots of anti-Semitism in Catholicism, and especially in Jesuits, see F.J. COPPA, *The papacy, the Jews, and the Holocaust*, Washington 2006, 144, 171-77; and KERTZER, *The Popes against the Jews...*, 283 and 286. On the conflict between Farinacci and «La Civiltà Cattolica», see SALE, *Le leggi razziali...*, 94-95.

[54] See R. MAZZETTI, *La questione ebraica in un secolo di cultura italiana*, Modena 1938.

Cattolica» claimed to reveal in 1922, could now be fulfilled because of the infiltration of rich Jews within the ecclesiastical ranks, even at the highest levels. The Jesuits are implicitly responsible for allowing the infiltration, concludes the article[55].

Farinacci's unhidden animosity towards the Jesuit Tacchi Venturi – apparently caused by the latter's zealous intercession for Italian Jews after the promulgation of the racial laws – appeared again on the pages of the same newspaper just a few months later. In a well-written article filled with appealing sarcasm, entitled *A Singular Man*, Farinacci attacked Tacchi Venturi with the following words:

> «We want to talk about Father Tacchi Venturi. He is a phenomenon, he is a super-phenomenon. For him the day is made of sixty hours. He handles everything for everyone, and all. A lawyer, an engineer, a historian, an accountant, a businessman, and with extra time, he also cares about religion and his religious order.
>
> Now you see him in the antechamber of a minister, now on the stairs of the military departments, now at his desk to write left and right in favour of his recommended. His age, which is a bit advanced[56], does not prevent him from taking off from time to time, running from one city to another to deal with criminal investigations or civil suits, and other affairs.
>
> Now his fame in Italy no longer has borders. Everyone runs to him: the candidate for the Senate, for the National Council, for the most prominent lay canonries. And how many detainees have had his protection? To say nothing of the Jews who try to receive "discrimination" against or want to show their merits: all found in him the perfect defender. We believe that in the Ministry

---

[55] Compare the contrasting view on Tacchi Venturi's activity expressed by Eugenio Boggiano-Pico in his preface to Castelli's book (see CASTELLI, *Storia segreta di Roma Città aperta*), XXXII: «[Tacchi Venturi] ci pare emergere già e sempre più alta, nella Storia della Chiesa ed in quella d'Italia [...] soprattutto la sua azione di apostolo e di diplomatico sagace e vero Nunzio Pontificio in partibus fino al Trattato del Laterano di cui fu massimo artefice e negoziatore [...]. Egli romano, non poteva essere assente, nello spirito di San Paolo, agli avamposti segreti della difesa e dell'incolumità di Roma Cristiana, come nella difesa degli indifesi, dei deboli e perseguitati israeliti, nel turbine dell'ultima guerra mondiale [...]. Asceta, umile e santo come nei tempi aurei del Cristianesimo, la Chiesa, un giorno ne eleverà il nome agli altari, benedetto da tutti. I miracoli sono già accertati nel cuore e nell'anima di migliaia di beneficati di ogni regione d'Italia, risorti alla speranza ed alla fede nella sua parola, nella purezza del suo apostolato, all'esempio di amare il prossimo, dopo Dio, più di se stessi, in ogni giorno ed in ogni ora della sua vita quasi centenaria, di meditazione, di povertà e di azione altamente sociale, ignorata tuttora nella più vasta cerchia delle masse e dell'opinione pubblica. L'Italia lo riconoscerà tra i più degni, insigni italiani dell'epoca nostra».

[56] He was 77 at that time.

of Interior Affairs not a few Jews[57] have a word of introduction and recommendation signed by this too dynamic Father. For which profane affairs the Reverend Father justifies himself by saying that he needs a lot of money for his temple[58].

And someone will ask the purpose of our free "ad". Nothing less than licit. We want Father Tacchi Venturi to get as many customers as possible with only one hope: that one day ministers and non-ministers will get fed up with him and tell him once and for all to care a bit more about religion. Also because many people complain that his interfering for the benefit of one person causes damage to another and because the sound and honest clergy does not like this mixture of sacred and profane in the same religious man, who seems too fervent a fixer.

We speak without hatred, with good intentions».

Using the image of diluting wine with water from the previous article, Farinacci's newspaper portrayed Tacchi Venturi's role in the Catholic Church as softening its traditional alliance with Italian Fascism against the Jews[59] and even accused the Jesuit periodical «La Civiltà Cattolica» of becoming Judaeo-phile. Whether Tacchi Venturi liked the image or not, which he may have interpreted as the symbol of the Eucharistic union of wine and water that are mixed by priests, the relationship between Tacchi Venturi and the institutions he represented and Jews, as well as that between Jews and Italian Fascism, was certainly much more complex and demands a serious and unbiased historical reconsideration. Contrary to the account of the contemporary Italian Jesuit historian of the period, Giacomo Martina – now at the zenith of his life in the Jesuit infirmary of Rome – who evasively and deceitfully portrayed the Jesuit diplomat as «the coin out of circulation» after the Duce's promulgation of the racial laws in the autumn of 1938[60], Tacchi Venturi himself admitted that he «did deal with

---

[57] Tacchi Venturi's archive contains at least 800 cases of victims of the racial laws to which he attended.

[58] Tacchi Venturi was a long-term (1918-40) rector of *Il Gesù* in Rome, the first Jesuit church, located next to Palazzo Venezia, Mussolini's residence. He used to call it «my dearest Farnese temple». Indeed, he procured money for various renovations of this church, which had been funded with the help of Cardinal Alessandro Farnese, a major early Jesuit patron. Venturi also negotiated the purchase of the adjacent *Casa Professa* at a favourable price from the Italian Government.

[59] For the shared views on Jews of «La Civiltà Cattolica» and «Il Regime fascista», see D.I. KERTZER, *The Popes against the Jews...*, 278-79.

[60] G. MARTINA, *Storia della Storiografia Ecclesiastica nell'Otto e Novecento (Parte Prima)*, Rome 1990, 204: «Il gesuita ebbe ancora contatti col governo durante la preparazione delle leggi contro gli ebrei (1938), e presentò al governo alcune lettere del papa. Ma ormai egli era considerato "moneta fuori corso". Non gli restava che tornare agli

many negotiations assigned to him by Pius XI, Pius XII, or the Vatican Secretariat of State between 1922 and 1943»[61].

Among those assignments was the Jesuit's activity on behalf of Jews affected by the racial laws. Little is written about that. Most scholars have acknowledged that Tacchi Venturi did play some role in dealing with «the Jewish question»[62], but usually they limit themselves to trumpeting his reluctance to the total abrogation of the racial laws during his negotiations in the summer of 1943 with Mussolini's successor, General Pietro Badoglio (1871-1956)[63].

Apparently, current scholarship on the relationship between Tacchi Venturi, and Jesuits in general, and the Italian racial laws is based on incomplete evidence for three reasons. First, only since 2006 has Pope Benedict XVI made the documents for the period of Pius XI's pontificate housed in the Vatican Secret Archives fully available[64]. Second, only a few historians have been allowed to consult the material of the archives of the «La Civiltà Cattolica» concerning the racial laws[65]. Third, apparently no scholar who published on the subject was fully aware of the content of Tacchi Venturi's private archives, even though already in 2000 the Inter-

---

studi». See also Martina's biographical article on Tacchi Venturi in DHCJ 4, 3684-86, where he indicates the primary sources contained in ARSI with no precision, failing also to mention Tacchi Venturi's activities on behalf of Jews, unlike Lapomarda's article in the same dictionary, entitled «Holocausto Judío y los jesuitas» [The Jewish Holocaust and the Jesuits], 1947.

[61] See FTV 46, «L'accordo del 2 Settembre 1931 o la riconciliazione della Conciliazione», 1 (avvertenza). See also a proof of Tacchi Venturi's engagement in Church-State affairs in Appendix Two. See also A. Guasco, *Chiesa Cattolica e totalitarismo...*, 100.

[62] See, for example, Blet et al., *Actes et documents*, especially vol. 6, 17-18, 22-23, 56-60, 70-71, 80, 89-90, 120, 122, 128, 208, 281, 316-17, 323, 366-67, 371-72, 427, 521-22, 533-35; vol. 8, 123, 132-33, 180-81, 199-200, 274, 318-19; 386-87; 407, 416-17, 483-84, 560-61, 662-63, 699; G. Sale, *I primi provvedimenti antiebraici e la Dichiarazione del Gran Consiglio del Fascismo*, in «La Civiltà Cattolica», 3798 (2008), 461-74; E. Fattorini, *Saggio introduttivo...*,. 30; and G. Sale, *Le leggi razziali...*, passim, especially 79-80, 89-90, 95, 118, 143, 187-88, and 237.

[63] See Taradel and Raggi, *La segregazione amichevole*, 146-51; D.I. Kertzer, *The Popes against the Jews...*, 289 and 327; A. Moravia and A. Elkann, *Life of Moravia*, South Raoyalton 2000, 157; and S. Zuccotti, *Under His Very Windows...*, 56 and 139.

[64] See H. Wolf, *Pope and Devil...*, 16-17.

[65] See G. Sale, *Le leggi razziali...* A few other scholars accessed these archives to examine other material, among them José David Lebovitch Dahl. See his *A case of disagreement among the Jesuits of «La Civiltà Cattolica» over anti-Jewish propaganda around 1882*, in «Rivista di storia del cristianesimo», 7 (2010)/1, 181-202.

national Catholic-Jewish Historical Commission expressed a desire that they be made accessible to researchers[66].

Tacchi Venturi's rich archive includes ten kinds of documents:

1. Original typed letters from the Vatican Secretariat of State to P. Tacchi Venturi, usually from Cardinal Luigi Maglione (1877-1944), who succeeded Cardinal Pacelli (later Pius XII);

2. Drafts of letters by Tacchi Venturi to the Vatican Secretariat of State, usually to Cardinal Maglione (they are written by Tacchi Venturi's secretary but always with many emendations by Tacchi Venturi himself);

3. Original letters from the Catholic hierarchs, priests, and Jesuits, as well as other prominent personalities to Tacchi Venturi, asking him to intercede for the Jews who had asked them for help;

4. Original letters (typed or handwritten) by Jews to Tacchi Venturi;

5. Drafts of letters by Tacchi Venturi to his Jewish correspondents;

6. Documentation (originals or copies) supporting the Jewish cases sent to Tacchi Venturi either directly or via the Vatican, Catholic hierarchs, priests, and Jesuits (personal and official letters, family histories and genealogies, legal certificates, notes, and a few photographs);

7. Drafts of letters by Tacchi Venturi to high-ranking Italian governmental officials, most of them to Guido Guidi Buffarini and Antonio Le Pera of the Fascist Ministry of the Internal Affairs;

8. Original governmental responses to Tacchi Venturi's intercessions on the behalf of Jews;

9. Typed or handwritten notes by Tacchi Venturi on the cases he attended; and

10. Documents related to various initiatives concerning Jews, in which Tacchi Venturi had been involved (among them the documents related to the Vatican's view on the persecution of Jews in Italy; papers on an initiative to transfer 10.000 Viennese Jews to Lebanon after Hitler's Anschluß of Austria[67]; Tacchi Venturi's proposed law concerning the change of names for converted Jews and his attempt to amend the 1938 racial laws to the advantage of the mixed families; an assistance to the Jews in Slovenia, Albania, and Croatia; the Vatican's attempt to stop the Italian

---

[66] See the Commission's *The Vatican and the Holocaust: A Preliminary Report* (http://www.bc.edu/research/cjl/meta-elements/texts/cjrelations/news/icjhc_preliminary_report.htm).

[67] On March 15, 1938, Tacchi Venturi wrote Mussolini a letter, asking him to take care of «three Austrian personalities» (see ARSI, *Diary 1938*, March 15). Their fate was probably related to Hitler's Anschluß of Austria (see also *Diary 1938*, May 26).

Government from sending Jews, at least those converted to Catholicism, to the concentration camps; etc.).

Tacchi Venturi preserved and filed these precious documents with the obsessive spirit of an archivist, which he in fact was[68]. They reveal information about his devoted engagement in the Vatican's opposition towards some aspects of the anti-Semitic legislation and his continued, almost daily, intercession with the Italian authorities on behalf of Jews affected by such laws, especially – but not exclusively – for the so-called «non-Aryan Catholics», or Catholics from «the progeny of Jacob», or Catholics «through circumcision», as Tacchi Venturi called them in the report on his personal meeting with Mussolini in March 1939[69].

The ideological explanation for Tacchi Venturi's approach to Mussolini's racial laws can be found in a memorial he prepared and submitted to the Fascist Government on behalf of the Vatican in September 1938:

«The Hon. Head of Government has solemnly declared in Trieste that the Jews of Italian nationality who have earned indisputable military or civil merits toward Italy and the [Fascist] Regime will find understanding and justice. His proposal, worthy of the applause of all honest man, has consoled the heart of His Holiness, but has failed to make him totally serene. Along with the Israelites who in the last two wars, the Great War and the most recent with Ethiopia, have earned merits toward Italy, and thus deserved, according to equity, appropriate recognition of their military and civil merits, there are no small number of those who, even at the cost of heroic sacrifice for obeying the voice of their conscience enlightened by God, became detached from the Synagogue, when they asked and received baptism. Now the Church, which before incorporating them willed that each of them abhor Jewish perfidy and reject Jewish superstition, cannot forget these children of hers, many of whom come genuinely to the Christian faith and observe its laws more exemplarily than so many of the Aryan race who have received it from their fathers.
Moreover, these Christians of Jewish race have suffered many harsh persecutions from their relatives who consider them faithless and deniers of their own blood.
Therefore, the common Father of the Faithful and Head of the Church, obliged in conscience to consider all those who profess the faith and the law of Christ, whatever the blood flowing through their veins, cannot not care about the fate of those faithful who have come to the light of Catholic truth from Judaism, nor can he avoid to intercede to secure recognition of singular merit that they had by not closing their eyes to the light, confessing the true Messiah and Son of God Jesus of Nazareth, whom their ancestors condemned to death on the cross.

---

[68] See M. SCADUTO, *P. Pietro Tacchi Venturi...*, 759-60.
[69] See P. BLET ET AL., *Actes et documents...*, vol. 6, 58.

Much credit should be properly acknowledged by Who [i.e. Mussolini] with a laudable sense of justice has to take account of the possible military and civil merits of the Israelites, which are certainly less important than the great merit of having renounced the blindness and obstinacy in error, without which a Jew could not become an outspoken Christian.

For these reasons the Holy Father hopes that the next fair rules for the "discrimination" of Jews in the Italian State do not include the baptized Jews, who through baptism became living members of the Catholic Church no less than any other true Aryan.

This is a decision that every Christian state should adopt, especially Italy, which in the 1st article of the Statute of the Kingdom, confirmed by Art. 1 of the Concordat with the Holy See, which recognized only one religion of the State: the Catholic, Apostolic, and Roman religion.

Consequently His Holiness hopes:

1. That the Jews of Italian nationality and of the Catholic religion be not included in the provisions to be applied to non-baptized Jews;

2. That foreign Jews, but baptized, have the right to reside in Italy like any other honest foreign individual of Aryan lineage; and

3. That the officially recognized private schools [*istituti scolastici parificati*], differently from state or accredited ones [*governativi* and *pareggiati*], be free to allow to enroll teachers and students of the Jewish race who have become Christians»[70].

Tacchi Venturi was active in assisting «these unfortunate sons of the Patriarch Abraham» also after the German occupation of the Peninsula, putting pressure on the Secretariat of State to intervene with the German Ambassador, especially in providing information about Jews deported from Rome after the infamous round-up of 16 October 1943[71]. The letter Tacchi Venturi wrote to Cardinal Maglione in October 1943 reveals, however, a different tone than the one in the memorial quoted above:

«Many applications of Jews – which in these last five years were entrusted to me by the Holy See to discuss with the governmental authorities – have made my poor name too notorious among them. Consequently, very frequent are requests that I have been receiving in order to intercede for them with the paternal infinite love of the Holy Father.

In these days, due to the iniquitous, barbaric treatment used by the Germans against these unfortunate people, the demands have been extraordinarily increased in number and intensity.

In particular I am being asked to assure that the Holy See makes an urgent demand to at least know where so many Jews – and also Christians, men and women, young and old, teenagers and children – who were deported last week

---

[70] FTV 2153.
[71] See P. BLET ET AL., *Actes et documents...*, vol. 9, 536-37. See also *ibidem*, 35-36, 57, 122, 126-127, 164, 183, 195, 254-256, 321, 366, 458-462, 525-529, 536-537, 606-607, 610-611.

from the Military College in Lungara in such a barbarous way, almost like beasts to be slaughtered, ended up.
A step of this kind made by the Holy See, even though without unfortunately obtaining the desired result, would certainly increase the veneration and gratitude towards the August Person of the Holy Father, always the revenger of dishonoured rights»[72].

Arguably, Tacchi Venturi was among those Fascist Italian intellectuals who supported *Il Manifesto della Razza* published back in July 1938, which claimed that there is «one pure Italian race», which is Aryan, and that «the Jews do not belong to the Italian race»[73]. It has to be observed, however, that Pius XI and even «La Civiltà Cattolica» overtly criticized the biological racism of the *Manifesto*[74]. The Vatican reminded Mussolini through Tacchi Venturi that «it is the Jews who gave Christ and Christianity to the world»[75]. Tacchi Venturi's alleged support of it, therefore, sounds rather implausible. Indeed, the Jesuit's dedication to protect the persecuted Jews, whether converted or not[76], which emerges from the documentation presented in this volume, suggests that he did not share the ideas of Fascist biological racism, even though he did share the blatant and popular anti-Judaism of both the Fascist regime and the Catholic Church of the time.

Reading this vastly unknown material, one is impelled to ask what motivated Tacchi Venturi to engage so tirelessly on behalf of the persecuted Jews. A plausible answer to this question can be found in the lecture he delivered on March 27, 1940 in the Borromini Hall in Rome to members of the Institute of the Roman Studies, which commemorated the 400th anniversary of the founding of the Society of Jesus in 1540. The paper, entitled «St Ignatius Loyola, the Apostle of Rome», was subsequently pub-

---

[72] P. BLET ET AL., *Actes et documents*, vol. 9, 458. See also A. RICCARDI, *L'inverno più lungo: 1943-44: Pio XII, gli ebrei e i nazisti a Roma*, Rome 2008, 112-113.

[73] See F. CUOMO, *I dieci: chi erano gli scienziati italiani che firmarono il Manifesto della razza*, Milan 2005, 206.

[74] See the letter of undersecretary Giovanni Battista Montini (future Paul VI) to Tacchi Venturi in FTV 1014, doc. 634; and R. TARADEL and B. RAGGI, *La segregazione amichevole...*, 112-115.

[75] See R. PERIN, *Pregiudizio antiebraico e antiprotestante*, in GUASCO and PERIN, *Pius XI: keywords...*, 158-159.

[76] The Jesuit Lapomarda stated in his article on the Holocaust and the Jesuits that Tacchi Venturi «distinguished himself in the protection of Jews converted to Catholicism, against the civil legislation» (see DHCJ 2, 1947).

lished in the association's official periodical in August of the same year[77]. In it, Tacchi Venturi introduced the audience to the topic by alluding to the Fascist racial laws: «I am about to say something that for some will seem unbelievable, but it is true, very true, and because it is contrary to certain very recent thoughts, it might perhaps have the taste of a strong citrus: Ignatius of Loyola felt a peculiar predilection for the Jews»[78].

To prove his argument, which echoes the writings of early converso Jesuits, the Jesuit historian quoted two accounts of Ignatius's propensity for the Israelites that are contained in the first official biography of the Jesuit founder written by his disciple, Pedro de Ribadeneyra (d. 1611), who himself was of Jewish ancestry, although Tacchi Venturi was most likely unaware of that[79]. These accounts portray Loyola as a «spiritual Semite» – to borrow the expression from a major historian of early modern Spain, Henry Kamen[80] – who justified his philo-Semitism by his desire to be of Jewish origin so that he could become a relative of Christ and his Mother.

In Tacchi Venturi's view, those who had this kind of approach to the Jewish people could not avoid doing what would be most acceptable to Christ, namely, to work toward their conversion to Christianity[81]. To make the Jews more eager to convert, it was important not only to converse with them kindly – as portrayed in the 17th-century illustrated biography of Loyola[82] – but also to remove obstacles to their conversions by the appropriate state legislation. The Jesuit historian found an example to imitate in the approach of Pope Paul III with regard to the Roman Jews. Under the sway of Ignatius of Loyola, in 1542 the pontiff promulgated the bull *Cupientes Iudaeos*, which – among other benefits – gave Jewish converts the right to keep their property. This new law stood in contrast to the long-established papal legal tradition of the Middle Ages which – in Tacchi Venturi's view – was «contrary to the venerable traditions of the nascent Church»[83].

---

[77] See P. TACCHI VENTURI, *S. Ignazio Loiola Apostolo di Roma*, in «Roma. Rivista di studi e di vita romana», 18 (1940), 245-264.

[78] *Ibidem*, 250.

[79] See R.A. MARYKS, *The Jesuit Order as a Synagogue of Jews: Jesuits of Jewish ancestry and purity-of-blood laws in the early Society of Jesus*, Leiden 2010, 42-45.

[80] See H. KAMEN, *The Spanish Inquisition*, New York 1965, 12.

[81] See P. TACCHI VENTURI, *S. Ignazio Loiola Apostolo di Roma...*, 250.

[82] *Ibidem*, 251. See also R.A. MARYKS, *The Jesuit Order as a Synagogue of Jews...*, 60-61.

[83] See P. TACCHI VENTURI, *S. Ignazio Loiola Apostolo di Roma...*, 252.

Like Ignatius and the first Jesuits, especially those of Jewish ancestry such as Juan Alfonso de Polanco or Antonio Possevino[84], who were engaged in converting the Roman Jews, so also was Tacchi Venturi engaged in converting the Jews[85]. In the Jesuit's archive there is at least one certificate (but many more must exist in the archives of the House of Catechumens) issued after the racial laws, which proves that in 1936 at the Jesuit *Il Gesù* Church, Tacchi Venturi baptized a Jewish man by the name of Enrico Angioli, the son of Alfredo Angioli and Emma Levi[86]. In 1941 Tacchi Venturi blessed the matrimony between two famous Italian novelists of Jewish lineage: Alberto Moravia (alias Alberto Pincherle), whose father was Jewish, and Elsa Morante, whose mother was Jewish. Tacchi Venturi also baptized the daughter of the Jewish Professor Renato Pollitzer[87].

It is not to be expected that either Loyola's or Tacchi Venuri's sympathy towards Jews obliterated their negative judgment about Judaism as a religion having been superseded by Christianity. Even though separated by a span of 400 years, both Loyola and Tacchi Venturi moved within the same Catholic ecclesiological and soteriological vision of Catholic society, in which the Church would have a super-natural mission, as Tacchi Venturi wrote to Mussolini in October 1938. Thus they were primarily motivated by the eschatological concept of salvation of the faithful, which could be exclusively achieved through the sacraments, especially baptism and matrimony, whose lawful custodian was the Catholic Church alone – *Extra Ecclesiam nulla salus* [There is no salvation outside the Church][88].

In spite of his unquestionable support for those Jesuits of Jewish ancestry by whom he was surrounded in the administration of the Order, Ignatius fully supported the anti-Jewish legislation of Paul III's successor, Pope Paul IV. Indeed, Loyola had many copies of Carrafa's most discriminatory bull, *Cum nimis absurdum* (1555), shipped to Jesuit houses, and he ordered that it be observed. Among the many economic and religious restrictions for Jews in the Papal States, the Pope's document established the first Roman ghetto and forced Jews to wear a distinctive yellow hat

---

[84] See R.A. MARYKS, *The Jesuit Order as a Synagogue of Jews..., passim.*

[85] See, for example, Tacchi Venturi's notes in ARSI, *Diary 1938* (January 15, February 12, June 30, September 28).

[86] See FTV 2335.

[87] See FTV 1014, doc. 655. He taught at the Pediatric Clinic of the University of Rome and, together with GIUSEPPE TALLARICO, authored *Lo sviluppo e la crescenza degli individui*, Turin 1932.

[88] See this kind of explanation in regard to the Vatican policy toward Hitler and Mussolini in H. WOLF, *Pope and Devil...*, 1-3.

(males) or kerchief (females), for, as the Pope put it, «it is completely senseless and inappropriate to be in a situation where Christian piety allows the Jews (whose guilt – all of their own doing – has condemned them to eternal slavery) access to our society and even to live among us»[89].

Not surprisingly, Tacchi Venturi – who of course did not include the example of Paul IV's anti-Jewish legislation in his 1940 speech – dubbed the Jews as «infidels» in his lecture[90] and in his personal letter to Mussolini from October 4, 1938, while expressing his concern for baptized children of Jews who had converted to Catholicism, he emphasized that

> «these little kids whose parents took them away from the Synagogue and began their Christian formation under the care of the Catholic Church now [after the introduction of the racial laws that prohibited Jewish children from attending non-Jewish schools] would be thrown in the arms of the Synagogue to be educated Jewish. [...] In the face of this danger the Catholic Church cannot remain indifferent, nor cease calling for its elimination, even though in the veins of these new children of hers runs the Semitic rather than Aryan blood»[91].

Another personal letter that Tacchi Venturi wrote to Mussolini the night before the Duce was to decide about the full implementation of the racial laws – which coincided with the *Kristallnacht* in Nazi Germany – reveals more details about the Jesuit's interpretation of the Fascist anti-Semitic legislation:

> «Excellency, I am writing these lines late at the night. The thought that tomorrow, Thursday, with the draft of the first chapter of the law for the protection of the Italian race will inflict a serious *vulnus* [wound] upon the Concordat, a *vulnus* which will be sadly fruitful of fatal consequences for the Church and the State, forbids me to sleep. Everything could be avoided, if You, not deflecting from that spirit of compromise, of which you gave ample evidence in the long process of the Lateran Pacts, would deign to amend Article 7 in the matter that is proposed in the last draft. Direct your mind to grace. The amendment that I propose safeguards the principle of the law and makes only one exception. And how many cases will ever need to make use of it? Bear in mind the small number of Italian citizens of Jewish race, the aversion that almost all the Israelites have toward entering into marriage with Christians, and Christians with the Israelites, though converted. I'm not afraid to say that we might have fewer than 100 such marriages between spouses of different races, but both professing the Catholic religion. A drop of water in the sea,

---

[89] See R.A. MARYKS, *The Jesuit Order as a Synagogue of Jews...*, 63.

[90] See P. TACCHI VENTURI, *S. Ignazio Loiola Apostolo di Roma...*, 253.

[91] FTV 2153. See also FTV 2309 and 2591, and *Diary 1938,* October 4.

and for that drop we would shatter a solemn pact sanctioned by the venerable Majesty of the Head of the universal Church.

Please, Your Excellency, reflect a moment on the immeasurable severity of a break with the Church in this tense moment in history. He who begs You and implores You is someone who enjoys repeating that he never betrayed You in the past and will never be capable of betrayal in the future. He who tells You that tonight he feels running in his bones a cold shiver, imagining not only what and how many will be damaged, but also the awful ruins that will result from contravening the wishes and prayers of the Vicar of Christ. Forgive me, but let not these heartfelt prayers be sent in vain»[92].

Anti-Judaism and anti-Semitism, if this distinction is adequate, were closely intertwined for the majority of Tacchi Venturi's contemporaries, such as the superior general of the Jesuits, Ledóchowski[93], Father Rosa of «La Civiltà

---

[92] See the draft of this letter in FTV 2159 and the edition of the original found in the Vatican Archive in G. SALE, *Le leggi razziali...*, 255-256: «Eccellenza, Le scrivo queste linee ad alta notte. Il pensiero che domani giovedì con lo schema del capo primo della legge per la tutela della razza italiana si verrà ad infliggere un grave *vulnus* al Concordato, *vulnus* che sarà tristemente fecondo di funestissime conseguenze per la Chiesa e per lo Stato, non mi lascia prendere sonno. E sì che tutto ciò si potrebbe evitarsi, quando Voi, non deflettendo da quello spirito di condiscendenza del quale deste numerose prove nella lunga elaborazione dei patti lateranensi, Vi vorreste degnare di modificare l'art. 7 nella materia che si propone nell'ultimo schema. Ponete mente di grazia. L'emendazione che Vi propongo mette in salvo il principio della legge; vi fa soltanto un'eccezione. E quanti mai saranno i casi nei quali converrà farla? Se tengasi presente il piccolo numero dei cittadini italiani di razza ebrea, l'avversione che quasi tutti gli israeliti hanno di contrarre nozze con i cristiani, e i cristiani con gli israeliti, benché convertiti, non temo asserire che si avrebbe tra noi meno di cento di siffatti matrimoni tra coniugi di razza diversa, ma professanti entrambi la religione cattolica. Una goccia di acqua in mezzo al mare; e per una tale goccia vorremmo s'infranga un solenne patto sancito con la veneranda Maestà del Capo della Chiesa universale? Vogliate, Eccellenza, riflettere un momento sulla gravità immensurabile di una rottura con la Chiesa in questo ansioso momento storico; Ve ne prega e scongiura chi gode ripeterVi che non mai Vi tradì in passato, né sa sentirsi capace di tradirvi in futuro; chi così questa notte parlandoVi sente corrergli per le ossa un gelido brivido rammentando di quante e quali sono non solo i danni, ma tremende ruine fu sempre apportatore il contrastare ai desideri, alle preghiere del Vicario di Cristo. Scusatemi, ma non fate cadere in vano le accorate suppliche».

[93] A study of the life, including the alleged anti-Semitism, of this Polish superior general of the Jesuits is still to be written. On the Catholic Church in Poland and anti-Semitism, see R.E. MODRAS, *The Catholic church and antisemitism: Poland, 1933-1939*, Switzerland 1994.

Cattolica»[94], or Pope Pacelli[95]. But, although one could accuse Loyola or Tacchi Venturi of anti-Judaism – contextually understandable or not – one cannot simplistically dismiss either man as an anti-Semitic power-broker unless one defines anti-Judaism as theological anti-Semitism, to be distinguished from biological anti-Semitism[96]. As a close ally of Mussolini and an architect and relentless defender of the reconciliation between the Catholic Church and the Fascist State, which privileged Catholicism and discriminated religious minorities, especially Jews, Tacchi Venturi did not denounce Mussolini's anti-Semitic legislation *tout court* as unjust. Based on the principle of equity and the legal agreement expressed in the Concordat, respectively, he called for the exemption from the racial laws of those Jews who had civil or military merits and especially of those who were baptized, for he believed that converted Jews would become even better Catholics. When Tacchi Venturi's official and personal diplomatic efforts with the Fascist regime to prevent the promulgation of those parts of the racial laws that impacted the Catholic Jews proved fruitless, he devoted most of his time to interceding for the Jews who were affected by such legislation, regardless of their religious association. Tacchi Venturi certainly did not have the prophetic voice of, say, the German Lutheran pastor Dietrich Bonhoeffer (1906-45) to denounce the totalitarian regime for the persecution of Jews and the Church for the negligence of its «unconditional obligation to the victims of any ordering of society, even if they do not belong to the Christian community»[97]. Nevertheless, it should be recognized that the Fascist Jesuit represented a shift – albeit too-slow – in the Catholic Church's approaches to its centuries-long tradition of the policy of purity of blood, of which the Jesuits were the foremost promoters. The Society of Jesus quietly abrogated its law against candidates of Jewish ancestry in 1946, but the whole Church officially recognized the groundlessness of the racial discrimination only in the groundbreaking declaration *Nostra Aetate* of the Second Vatican Council in 1965, which was drafted by the Jesuit Cardinal Augustin Bea. It stated, referring to the New Testament, that «One is the community of all

---

[94] See FTV 1019, 423: «Led[óchowski] P. Wl. SJ, Roma 4.9.1931, A T[acchi] V[enturi] Acc. Ric. Lettera del 31.8. e 2.9. Dobbiamo ancora molto pregare. Lo scrivente si è meravigliato del posto attribuito da TV all'Accordo concluso. Lo scrivente spera che si riuscirà a mettere le cose a posto per la Civ. Catt. – Lo scrivente è contento che TV sia riuscito ad impedire [...] un infelice articolo del P. Rosa».

[95] H. WOLF, *Pope and Devil...*, 79-80.

[96] See, for example, O. BLASCHKE, *Offenders or Victims?: German Jews and the Causes of Modern Catholic Antisemitism*, Lincoln 2009, 1-10.

[97] See E. METAXAS, *Bonhoeffer: Pastor, Martyr, Prophet, Spy: a Righteous Gentile Vs. the Third Reich*, Nashville 2010, 151-155.

peoples, one their origin, for God made *the whole human race* to live over the face of the earth». It is impossible to correctly assess the evolution of this historical process without having full access to the ecclesiastical archives for the period of Pius XII's pontificate. For now, we must rely on the documents from the period prior to Pius XI's death on February 10, 1939, to which scholars have been granted access since 2006.

DAVID I. KERTZER AND ALESSANDRO VISANI

The United States, the Holy See
and Italy's Racial Laws

The imposition of the anti-Semitic «racial laws» in the fall of 1938 has
been taken by many historians to represent a major shift both internally
and externally in the popularity of the Italian Fascist regime. Before that
time, in this view, Mussolini's regime enjoyed great domestic popularity
and considerable support among Catholics abroad. With the announcement of the racial laws, these same historians argue, Italians and others
who were formerly sympathetic – including the Church itself – began to
withdraw their support from the regime. Special attention has been paid
to the impact that the racial laws had on the relationship between the Fascist regime and the Catholic Church and especially on the role played by
Pope Pius XI. We plan on other occasions to deal more directly with the
question of the role played by the Pope and the Vatican with respect to the
Italian racial laws. In this paper we focus instead on the way in which the
Pope's stance on the racial laws was viewed and followed at the time by
the United States Government.

Mussolini's ascension to power was enabled in part by the Vatican's
decision that he would better protect the Church's interests than the Italian
Popular Party of Don Luigi Sturzo, which had previously enjoyed Church
support. Thus, even before the Lateran Accords were signed in 1929,
many Italian-American Catholic clergy were enthusiastic about Mussolini and what he represented for Italy. Given the location of our conference it is perhaps appropriate to cite, by way of example, Rev. Antonio
Bove, pastor of Providence, Rhode Island's church for Italian immigrants,
who wrote a letter in 1926 to Rome requesting a signed photograph of the
Duce[1]. American Catholic support for the Italian Fascist regime was im-

---

* *The following abbreviations are used in the footnotes in identifying archival sources
cited in the text: ACS: Archivio Centrale dello Stato (Rome); MCPG: Ministero della Cultura Popolare, Gabinetto; MCPR: Ministero della Cultura Popolare, Reports;
ASMAE: Archivio Storico, Ministero degli Affari Esteri (Rome); APSS Affari Politici,
1931-45, Santa Sede; AISS: Ambasciata Italiana presso la Santa Sede; API: Affari Po-*

measurably increased by the signing of the Lateran Accords. Emblematic were the public festivities that took place at the new year in 1930 in New Orleans, the brainchild of the Italian consul to the city, and organized by ecclesiastical authorities together with a committee of notable Catholic citizens. In his report to Italy's ambassador in Washington, the consul described the demonstration as «the most powerful held in New Orleans since the time of the Armistice». The Archbishop led the procession, followed by the Catholic clergy of the diocese, along with the mayor, the Italian consul, and representatives of all of the local Italian-American societies. It ended in the cathedral, which was draped in Italian flags and packed with the faithful, where the Archbishop recited the Te Deum. In his benediction, the consul reports, the Archbishop «estolse il carattere provvidenziale dell'era compiuta dai "due più grandi uomini" dell'epoca presente, Pio XI e S.E. Benito Mussolini che chiamò un vero patriota ed un intelligente e coraggioso capo (leader) del suo popolo»[2].

American Catholic enthusiasm for Mussolini suffered a temporary setback during the government's conflict with Italian Catholic Action in 1931, but the conflict itself showed the impact that the Lateran Accords had had. The Italian consul to Chicago, in reporting in June of that year to the Italian ambassador in Washington, informed him that «Il dissidio Italo-Vaticano è scoppiato come una bomba a ciel sereno e ha portato in tutti indistintamente una impressione penosa e dolorosa». He continued: «V.E. ben sapeva che l'accordo italo-Vaticano aveva contemporaneamente esaltato in modo straordinario i due più grandi valori che possiede l'Italia. Il prestigio del Governo Fascista si era immensamente accresciuto... I discorsi che ho sentito e che ho anche varie volte segnalato a V.E. da parte dei vescovi, Cavalieri di Colombo, ecc. erano veri inni a S.E Mussolini e al Regime Fascista»[3]. The impact of the brief dispute was not by any means limited to Italian-Americans, as a despondent Italian consul in Baltimore reported: «Il Clero e la popolazione irlandese è come dovevasi

---

litici, 1931-45, Italia; ASV: Archivio Segreto Vaticano (Vatican City); AESI: Affari Ecclesiastici Straordinari, Italia; NARA: National Archives and Records Administration (College Park, Maryland, USA); M: RG59 State Department records, central decimal files (1910-1949), Italy.

[1] API 1287RI 97-26.

[2] AISS 19, January 4, 1930, Italian Consul in New Orleans, to Italian ambassador in Washington, subsequently transmitted to Cesare De Vecchi, Italian ambassador to the Holy See.

[3] AISS, b. 7, f. 1, sf 2, Italian consul in Chicago to Italian Ambassador, Washington, June 11, 1931.

provvedere, decisamente contraria a noi ed in favore del Vaticano ed essi sostengono che il prestigio dell'Italia guadagnato in seguito al Concordato, è ora completamente perduto...»[4].

The dispute between the Holy See and Mussolini over Catholic Action was quickly settled and enthusiasm for the regime among the Catholic clergy in the United States, in harmony with their clerical colleagues in Italy, soon resumed full force. The Fascist secret police reported regularly on this, as in a July 1934 report from a «noto informatore vaticano» who quoted Cardinal Dougherty in a conversation with a colleague in Rome, praising «l'Ordine e la compostezza fascista di Roma» contrasting this with «la immoralità animalesca dell'America». The Vatican's ability to get the Fascist State to impose many of the moral restrictions it advocated on the Italian population was clearly drawing some favorable attention in American clerical circles[5].

The Fascist regime was especially eager to enlist the support of the American Catholic clergy during the Italian conquest of Ethiopia in 1935-36 when Mussolini was facing worldwide condemnation and the sanctions imposed by the League of Nations. On November 23, 1935, Count Bonifacio Pignatti, the Italian ambassador to the Holy See, reported on «lunghe conversazioni in Segreteria di Stato» in which he received confirmation that «la Santa Sede lavora intensamente per la pace "secondo giustizia" con spiccato favore per le tesi italiane che essa rappresenta sotto un supremo aspetto di equità». This effort took advantage of the capillary reach of the Church, according to the Italian ambassador: «I punti di vista italiani vengono pertanto illustrati non soltanto alle Nunziature, ma, quel che più conta, direttamente ai Vescovi, e alle personalità influenti degli ambienti cattolici di tutto il mondo. La Santa Sede rileva già un risultato apprezzabile di tale sua attività». Officials at the Vatican Secretary of State office showed the Italian ambassador letters from North American bishops and priests that lamented the lack of a sufficiently vigorous Italian publicity campaign in the United States[6]. This telegram led the Ministry for Press and Propaganda to send a memorandum to the undersecretary of State a few days later proposing that a plan be formulated to take better advantage of the Catholic clergy in the United States in the regime's Ethiopian

---

[4] AISS, b. 19, f. 5, Italian consul in Baltimore to Amb. Ge. De Martino, Washington, July 7, 1931.

[5] MCPG, b. 158, July, 1934.

[6] MCPR b. 21, November 23, 1935, Questione Etiopica-Santa Sede-Situazione in Belgio e negli Stati Uniti.

propaganda campaign. The memo, noting with pleasure «l'opera particolarmente utile ed efficace svolta ai nostri fini dal noto Padre Coughlin»
stressed that the US was likely to play a crucial role in determining the
outcome of the conflict[7].

Curiously, given Pius XI's growing displeasure with Mussolini over
his alliance with Hitler, the Duce was reported to prefer that Pius XI's successor be a non-Italian, perhaps an American. Hence in January 1937 the
Italian ambassador to Paris, Vittorio Cerruti, reported to the Italian foreign
minister the latest rumors heard in diplomatic and elite social circles in
the French capital. «[S]i diffonde rapidamente la voce» the ambassador
wrote «che il Duce vedrebbe con molto favore che il futuro Papa fosse uno
straniero, per marcare in modo palese nella prima elezione dopo la conciliazione che la Chiesa cattolica è veramente universale. Si aggiunge anzi
fino a precisare il nome del Cardinale americano Dougherty, arcivescovo
di Filadelfia, come quello su cui dovrebbe convergere i voti dei Cardinali
italiani nel futuro Conclave»[8].

The impact of the racial laws on the American Church hierarchy's attitudes toward the Fascist regime may be captured by the rather dramatic
case of Cardinal George Mundelein, Archbishop of Chicago. On May 8,
1937, the Italian foreign ministry sent a telegram to its ambassadors in
Berlin, Paris, London, and Warsaw to report on a recent forty minute conversation that the Italian consul to Chicago had had with Cardinal Mundelein. «Il Cardinale si è mostrato molto gentile nei suoi riguardi ed ha
manifestato la sua ammirazione per il Duce e per il Fascismo asserendo
che l'Italia è oggi un paese su cui la Chiesa può veramente contare». It is
notable that these remarks by a Chicago Archbishop were regarded as sufficiently significant to merit a telegram to these ambassadors, reflecting
the importance that the Italian Government saw in the support provided to
the Fascist Government by leading Churchmen in the US[9].

Yet, just ten days after receiving this telegram, the Italian ambassador
to Berlin would be outraged by reports of comments made that day by the
same Cardinal Mundelein. Indeed, Mundelein's description of Adolf Hitler as a mere «Austrian paper hanger» and a rather mediocre one at that,

---

[7] MCPR b. 21, Ministero per la Stampa e la Propaganda, Direzione Generale per il Ser-
    vizio della Stampa Estera, Roma, November 28, 1935, «Appunto per S.E. il Sottogre-
    tario di Stato».
[8] APSS, b. 36, Cerruti al Ministero degli Affari Esteri, 6 gennaio 1937.
[9] APSS, b. 35, Ministero degli Affari Esteri, Relazione Regia Ambasciata presso la S.
    Sede e per conoscenza RR. Ambasciate Berlino, Varsavia, Parigi, Londra, May 8,
    1937.

led to outrage by the Nazi Government and pleas to the Vatican from its nuncio in Berlin to formally censure the Chicago Archbishop. This episode highlights the importance of distinguishing between the American clergy's views of Mussolini and their views of Hitler, a distinction all too often lost. Certainly following the Pope's denunciation of Nazi persecution of the Church in his March 1937 encyclical *Mit brenneder Sorge*, and following constant reports of Nazi actions against the Church in Germany, American Catholics were increasingly hostile to Hitler and his regime.

The Pope was certainly aware of this anti-Nazi sentiment in the US, an issue that received increased Vatican attention as plans were being made for Hitler's visit to Rome, to take place in the spring of 1938. In January of that year, as these plans were first being discussed, Count Pignatti reported to the Italian Minister of Foreign Affairs «che l'assistente della Compagnia di Gesù per la provincia nord-americana, ha dichiarato che se, nonostante l'ultimo discorso del Pontefice contro le Autorità del Reich, il Sig. Hitler fosse ricevuto in Vaticano, i cattolici americani insorgerebbero in massa»[10]. As it turns out, Pius XI in the end did not receive Hitler during his visit, and indeed the Pope's early departure from Rome to Castel Gandolfo so that he was not present in Rome during Hitler's visit, was greeted with favor by America's Catholics[11].

The anti-Semitic campaign, which was kicked off in Italy with the publication of the *Manifesto of Racial Scientists* in July, 1938, drew the immediate and intense attention of the US State Department. The following months, during which the racial laws were promulgated, saw a huge volume of correspondence on this topic between the American embassy in Rome and the State Department in Washington. From July until September, a considerable part of this correspondence concerned the impact of the racial laws on the Pope's attitude toward the Fascist regime[12].

On July 20 the second secretary of the US embassy in Rome sent a confidential memo to the US Secretary of State reporting on the new anti-Semitic campaign, including reports that theaters in Rome were being told

---

[10] AISS b. 87, f. 2, sf. 6, «Ambasciatore italiano presso la Santa Sede al Ministero degli Affari Esteri, January 21, 1938».

[11] The story of the Holy See's negotiations over a possible visit from Hitler is one we will tell on a separate occasion. Despite the warning from American Catholics, Pius XI did consider going through with the visit under certain circumstances.

[12] There is now a large and growing literature on the *Manifesto of Racial Scientists*. See G. ISRAEL, *Il fascismo e la razza*, Bologna 2010, 178-201; A. GILLETTE, *The Origins of the «Manifesto of Racial Scientists»*, in «Journal of Modern Italian Studies», 6 (2001), 305-323; T. DELL'ERA, *Il Manifesto della Razza*, Torino 2008.

not to present Jewish characters «unless such characters are portrayed as subjects of ridicule», and bookstore owners were being told to stop selling books written by non-Italian Jews and not to exhibit any books written by Italian Jews in their windows. The embassy official then reported at length on the Pope's negative reaction to the racial campaign:

> «It is of interest to note that Jewry in general appears to have finally received some indication of support from the Vatican. On July 15, the day morning papers carried the racial pronouncement [i.e., the Manifesto of Racial Scientists]... the Pope received in audience at Castel Gandolfo the "Sisters of Our Lady of the Last Supper" on the occasion of some of them proceeding to Abyssinia for missionary work. At that time, His Holiness referred to an "actual apostasy" which had come to his attention that day and strongly underlined the universality of the Catholic faith which by its very nature precluded Nationalistic exclusiveness... the Holy Father said that the exaggerated and misunderstood Nationalism which was causing such agitation was a direct negation of the foregoing apostolic injunction [Go ye therefore and teach all nations]. He then went on to warn against "this course of exaggerated nationalism which hinders the saving of souls, which raises barriers between people and people, which is contrary not only to the law of God but to Faith itself and to the Creed which is said and sung in all churches throughout the world". Continuing, the Pope stated that in the phrase "I believe in the Catholic Church", "Catholic" means "universal". Finally the Pope added that he had never thought on any subject with such certainty, decision and exactness of terms as he had upon the foregoing...».

Again on July 18, His Holiness, when addressing a group of newly married couples, stated that perils were not only to be feared from Bolshevism but from something worse. What the «something worse» referred to was left open to the imagination, but many suspect that it was intended to refer to Nazi religious persecution in general[13].

On July 26, the Italian ambassador to Washington, Fulvio de Suvich, paid a call on US Secretary of State Cordell Hull, to inform him that he was returning to Italy for several weeks. «He seemed to have nothing on his mind», Hull reported, «except to endeavor earnestly to explain away the reports that his government is undertaking to expel the Jews from Italy on account of their Race. He was very insistent that despite confused and misleading reports, his government itself is not a party to any such movement. I referred in reply to the temporary conditions in Germany,

---

[13] NARA, M 1423, July 20, 1938, Confidential memo from Samuel Reber, Second Secretary of (US) Embassy (Rome), to Secretary of State (cc: embassies in London and Berlin) «Growth of Anti-Semitism in Italy».

which I said were of course utterly abhorred by almost everybody in this country...»[14]. Suvich paid a courtesy call on the undersecretary of State the same day, and their conversation also focused on the incipient anti-Semitic campaign in Italy. Again Suvich sought to downplay these reports, yet at the same time claimed that his government had not kept him well informed of its plans in this area. In the undersecretary's words:

> «He said that so far as he himself was concerned "many of his closest friends in Trieste were Jews", that in the war of 1915 he himself was a volunteer and fought at the side of Italian Jews who had given their lives for Italy and he felt that some of the finest and most useful citizens that Italy possessed were Jews. I remarked that at the present time when the whole world was suffering from the effects of an inhumane policy of persecution against the Jews on the part of certain other countries, it was very natural that such countries as the United States where we regarded a great majority of American Jews as among our finest and most patriotic citizens that an indication on the part of Italy that she was going to adopt a similar policy of persecution naturally profoundly shocked American public opinion. I reminded the Ambassador of the conversation I had had with him some weeks ago in which he had said that the Jewish question would never be a problem in Italy inasmuch as the Italian Jews didn't number more than forty to fifty thousand in the entire country and that he could not conceive of any possible advantage that Italy would gain in aligning herself with the nations that were undertaking this inhuman policy of persecution and discrimination... He said he would see Mussolini immediately upon his arrival in Italy and that he hoped he would find that Mussolini had no intention of going so far as recent newspaper articles would seem to indicate»[15].

That the US Government focused a significant amount of its attention on the Pope's reaction to the anti-Semitic campaign in Italy in these first months is reflected in the fact that just four days after the US Secretary of State met with the Italian ambassador, he received a telegram from William Phillips, US ambassador in Rome, focusing on a recent speech by the Pope:

> «Today's "Osservatore Romano" carries in full a speech made by the Pope last Thursday afternoon at Castel Gandolfo upon the occasion of receiving the alumni of the Pontifical College of Propaganda for the Faith. This speech which has been completely ignored by the Roman press in general is through inference a strong denunciation of the present racial program of the Govern-

---

[14] NARA M 1423, July 26, 1938, Dept. of State, Memorandum of Conversation, Secretary of State Hull and the Italian Ambassador, Signor Fulvio de Suvich.

[15] NARA M 1423, July 26, 1938, Dept. of State, Memorandum of Conversation, the Italian Ambassador, Signor Fulvio de Suvich, the undersecretary.

ment. Taking as point of departure present difficulties existing between the Catholic Action and the Fascist Party, the Pope said that the question of race as well as nationalism in a separatist sense was being discussed far too much these days. Catholicism was universal, not racial, nationalist or separatist and this was the principle that should inspire the Catholic Action... the Pope emphasized that the human race was one universal human family. It was unfortunate that Italy now found it necessary to imitate Germany... Although at no time during the discourse was the Jewish question specifically referred to, little doubt exists in press and diplomatic circles here that besides its warning to leave the Catholic Action alone it was intended to express the Vatican's deep disapproval of the present racial discrimination being adopted by the regime»[16].

On August 12, in addition to reporting the prominent display on Roman newsstands of the new government-backed anti-Semitic biweekly, «La Difesa della Razza», a senior staff member of the American embassy in Rome informed the US Secretary of State that the «Italian public on the whole does not seem to greet the new [anti-Semitic] policy with any marked enthusiasm although it betrays no moral indignation». However, he added, «the Vatican shows no signs of modifying its attitude of disapproval toward the present racial movement»[17].

While the US Government was eager to be able to portray the Catholic Church in general and the Pope in particular as implacably opposing the Italian anti-Semitic campaign, partly as a way of trying to distance Catholics from the Italian regime and its growing alliance with Nazi Germany, it soon became apparent that the papal – and Vatican – opposition to the racial laws was limited in scope. A first indication of this comes in the message sent on August 19 by Ambassador Phillips to the US Secretary of State. After describing the recent rising anti-Semitic campaign in the Italian press, he noted that this «had the interesting result of further provoking the Vatican to come to the defense of the Jews». It will be remembered, the ambassador wrote, that «it was the original criticism of the racial program by the Vatican in a speech primarily designed to defend the Catholic Action that seems to have brought about the present strained relations between the Government and the Vatican». Yet he added that in an Au-

---

[16] NARA M 1423, July 30, 1938, Telegram, Phillips to Secretary of State. Underlining the great attention paid to the Pope's speech by the American embassy, Phillips had telegraphed the Secretary of State the previous day with news of the Pope's remarks (NARA M 1423, July 29, 1938, Telegram, Phillips to Secretary of State, «Growth of Anti-Semitic Movement in Italy»).

[17] NARA M 1423 R12, August 12, 1938, Edward Reed, Counselor of Embassy letter to Secretary of State, «Continued Progress of Anti-Semitic Movement in Italy».

gust 14 article, «L'Osservatore Romano» reviewed «the general Jewish question in a purely objective fashion and not by any sense putting up a wholesale defense of the Jews». The Vatican organ, he reported, «while describing the attitude of the Papacy toward Jewry over the centuries and pointing out that certain restrictive measures from time to time had proved necessary against it», asserted that the popes had shown compassion in dealing with the Jews. But the ambiguity of the Vatican's message was seized upon, Phillips wrote, by the Italian press, which on August 16 was filled with articles quoting only one paragraph from the «Osservatore Romano» piece, which, the ambassador thought, had «entirely distorted the Vatican's attitude toward Jewry». The paragraph of the Vatican daily quoted in the Italian press read as follows:

> «But – to put things straight – this does not mean that the Jews might abuse the hospitality of Christian countries. Along with protective measures there were decrees of restriction and persecution in their regard. The civil ruler was in agreement with the Church in this, since "both of them", according to Delassus, "had an interest in preventing the nations from being invaded by the Jewish element, thus risking the loss of their direction of society". While the Christians were forbidden to force the Jews to embrace the Catholic religion, to disturb their synagogues, their Sabbaths, and their feast days, Jews, on the other hand, were forbidden to hold any public office, civil or military, and this debarment was extended to the sons of converted Jews. These precautions related to professional activities, teaching and even trade»[18].

It is worth noting the date of this report, for only two weeks later the Fascist Government would announce the first anti-Semitic laws, which would put into practice exactly the past Church policies cited by «Osservatore Romano» on August 14[19].

The embassy continued to pay great attention to the remarks made by Pius XI to various visiting groups, unscripted talks in which he castigated «exaggerated nationalism» and theories of racial division. On August 16, Edward Reed, Counselor of the American embassy in Rome, reported to the Secretary of State that what many observers were predicting would be the relatively «moderate» character of the Fascist anti-Semitic campaign

---

[18] NARA M 1423 R12, August 19, 1938, Ambassador William Phillips to Secretary of State, «Progress of Racial Movement in Italy».

[19] The similarity between the racial laws introduced by the Fascist Government in 1938 and the restrictions on Jews promulgated by the popes in the Papal States has been noted by many scholars. See D.I. KERTZER, *The Popes against the Jews*, New York 2001.

(compared with Germany) «may be attributable to the Vatican's stand in favor of the Jews, which still shows no sign of abating». He went on to report on remarks made by the Pope on August 21: «Beware» said Pius XI «of other dangers, but above all, beware of exaggerated nationalism... God made the nations. Hence there is a place for a just, moderate, and temperate nationalism... But beware of exaggerated nationalism as of a real curse»[20].

The American Government was encouraged by these informal condemnations, but was eager to see the Pope offer a more formal and more public denunciation of the racial laws. The American ambassador, apparently worried that his pleas were not getting through to the Pope, decided to enlist the aid of Mgr. Joseph Hurley, who in 1930 had become the first American to hold a position in the Vatican Secretariat of State. The ambassador contacted Hurley and on the evening of September 2 Hurley met the ambassador at the American embassy. The next day Hurley prepared a three page report on his meeting for the Vatican Secretariat of State. The American ambassador, he wrote, «expressed his deep regret and horror at the recent measures taken by the Italian Government regarding the Jews. He is certain – Hurley continued – that these measures will have a deplorable effect on American public opinion». «I wonder» – the American ambassador added – «if the Vatican is contemplating further declarations in this regard». Indeed, at the end of the meeting Phillips held out the hope that should the Pope accede to this request, along with a second request to discourage Italy from going to war, this might permit supporters of closer US ties with the Holy See «to disarm the Protestant opposition» and so move Congress to authorize official diplomatic relations with the Vatican[21].

As members of the Catholic Church hierarchy in the US were growing disillusioned with Mussolini, one old ally offered to come to the Duce's aid. On September 6, just days after the announcement of the first racial laws which ejected all Jewish children and Jewish teachers from the schools and universities throughout Italy, Father Charles Coughlin wrote directly to Mussolini: «So much misunderstanding has been created by the unfriendly press in America relative to your statements» he wrote «that I am inclined to invite Your Excellency to write an article for our national magazine in which you can clarify your attitude toward the Jews». Coughlin went on to inform the Italian dictator that his magazine,

---

[20] NARA M 1423 R12, August 26, 1938, Edward Reed, Counselor of Embassy, letter to Secretary of State, «Progress of Racial Movement in Italy».

[21] AESI 1054/731, ff. 8-10. Note, September 3, 1938.

«Social Justice», had a million readers. Alongside Mussolini's article, wrote Coughlin, the magazine would publish an editorial in support of the Duce's position[22].

In fact, when the first of the racial laws were promulgated in early September, the American embassy was taken by surprise by their draconian nature, having been repeatedly assured that whatever measures were taken would be mild. «The severity of the decrees came as a surprise to the majority of Italians and foreign observers in Rome» the American embassy reported to the Secretary of State on September 9, adding that they were all «at a loss to account for the reasons»[23].

As it turned out, the brief period of frequent papal denunciations of Italy's new move toward imitating Nazi Germany's racial ideology had come to an end. On September 16, Ambassador Phillips reported that «With the exception of a mild statement issued by the Pope on September 6 and a criticism in the "L'Osservatore Romano" regarding the vulgarity of the new publication "La difesa della razza", the Vatican during the past week has maintained a silence regarding the recent measures taken against Italian Jews». Phillips also first references in this message the explanation that the Vatican would increasingly use as it fended off international requests for further papal denunciation of the anti-Semitic campaign. «It was explained to the Embassy by a highly placed Vatican source» wrote Phillips «that this does not mean that the Vatican approves these measures; it considers that for the time being no useful purpose would be served by outspoken opposition»[24].

---

[22] MCPR b. 3, n. 23, September 6, 1938.

[23] NARA M 1423 R12, September 9, 1938, Edward Reed, Counselor of Embassy letter to Secretary of State, «Anti-Semitism in Italy». There is now a large literature on the Italian racial laws, including: R. VIVARELLI, *Le leggi razziali nella storia del fascismo italiano*, in «Rivista storica italiana», 121 (1989), 738-772; A. CAVAGLIO and G.P. ROMAGNANI, *Le interdizioni del Duce: le leggi razziali in Italia*, 2nd ed., Torino 2002; *Leggi del 1938 e cultura del razzismo*, ed. by M. BEER, A. FOA and I. IANNUZZI, Roma 2010; V. DI PORTO, *Le leggi della vergogna: Norme contro gli ebrei in Italia e Germania*, Firenze 2000; AA.VV. *La legislazione antiebraica in Italia e in Europa*, Roma 1989.

[24] NARA M 1423 R12, September 16, 1938, William Phillips letter to Secretary of State, «Anti-Semitism in Italy». There is a growing literature and debate on the nature and extent of Vatican opposition to the Italian racial laws. See among others: B. BOCCHINI CAMAIANI, *Chiesa cattolica italiana e leggi razziali*, in «Qualestoria», 17 (1989)/1, 43-66; E. FATTORINI, *La Chiesa e le leggi razziali*; see M. BEER, A. FOA and I. IANNUZZI, 159-174; G. MICCOLI, *Santa sede e chiesa italiana di fronte alle leggi antiebraiche del 1938*, in «Studi Storici», 29 (1988)/4, 821-902; A. VISANI, *The Jewish Enemy. Fascism, the Vatican, and anti-Semitism on the seventieth anniversary of the 1938 race laws*, in «Journal of Modern Italian Studies», 14 (2009)/2, 168-183; G. SALE, *Le leggi razziali*

In fact, much of the subsequent Vatican press devoted to the racial laws would be defensive in posture, denying that the Pope was criticizing Mussolini for his anti-Semitic campaign. Hence on October 7, Ambassador Phillips reported that «the only recent comment contained in the Vatican organ with respect to the Jewish problem was published on September 25 to the effect that certain newspapers believed that the speech made at Trieste by the Head of the Italian Government, particularly the phrase "Their (of the Jews) sudden and unexpected friends who are defending them from too many pulpits" [...] contained an open allusion to the Holy Father. The comment continued that although this interpretation had been widely diffused, it could with assurance be affirmed that it did not correspond to the truth»[25]. As the fall wore on, behind the scenes the Pope was furious at Mussolini for proposing to introduce into the racial laws a ban on marriage between those born Catholic and Catholics who had been born Jews (i.e., Catholics converted from Judaism). Tremendous Vatican effort went into trying to prevent this proposal from becoming law. Opposition stemmed both from the fact that the policy went against Church teachings regarding the value of baptism and from the fact that it violated the article in the Concordat that ceded to the Church the ability to determine what constituted a valid marriage. In a November 12 telegram, the US embassy in Rome informed the US Secretary of State about this development:

«The Embassy has been confidentially informed that the Vatican considers the matrimonial restrictions to be in violation of the Lateran Concordat which recognized all marriages performed in accordance with Canon Law. Before publication of the decree the Vatican made a strong protest to the Italian Government in the hope that the decisions of the Grand Council might be modified before enactment into law. The Secretary of State of the Vatican is disturbed by the failure of the Government to respond to the protest and is inclined to take a serious view of this breach in the Concordat. For the present, however, no further action by the Vatican is contemplated»[26].

As the Pope's public criticisms of the new Italian racial policies would end, perhaps due in part to his increasing infirmity and the opposition of members of his inner circle, including his Secretary of State Eugenio Pacelli, to taking any action that would lead to a break in relations with

in Italia e il Vaticano, Milano 2009; V. DE CESARIS, Vaticano, fascismo e questione razziale, Milano 2010.

[25] NARA M 1423 R12, October 7, 1938, William Phillips letter to Secretary of State, «Racial Measures in Italy».

[26] NARA M 1423 R12, November 12, 1938, Telegram from Reed to Secretary of State.

either the Italian or the German governments, the American diplomats in Rome no longer looked to the Vatican with particular interest in dealing with Italy's anti-Semitic campaign. However, Pius XI's earlier public criticisms of both the persecution of the Church in Germany and of the growing alliance between Mussolini and Hitler did have an impact on American Catholic attitudes toward the Italian Fascist regime.

In this regard, a long report by the Italian embassy in Washington (written by chargé d'affaires Giusepe Cosmelli), sent to the Minister of Foreign Affairs in Rome on October 20, 1938, chronicles the major change in enthusiasm for the Fascist regime that had taken place over the previous months[27]. Hostility toward Nazi Germany, seen as a persecutor of the Church, served as the major context for the growing disillusionment of what had up to then been a broadly supportive Catholic clergy and Catholic population for the Italian Fascist regime. «As is known» the Italian Washington embassy reported «the American Catholics – beginning with the Church upper hierarchy with Cardinal Mundelein of Chicago foremost among these – have from the very beginning reacted with hostility and with growing anger to the officially anti-Catholic and in part anti-Christian attitude of the Nazi authorities». It was in this context that the imposition of the racial laws was being received particularly badly by the American Church hierarchy and portions of the American Catholic population. «The [German] question is of interest to us because the recent polemics between the Regime and the Papacy, regarding Catholic Action on the one hand and the racial question on the other, have led to the rise here of further worries for the future of the Church in Italy, identifying Fascism with Nazism in the not too discerning eyes of the general public... who would view them together as the not overly loved so-called authoritarian regimes».

«The papal words, the racial question, our political ties with Berlin, the absence of any Italian reaction to the alleged Nazi persecutions of Catholics in Germany and in Austria, have undermined the previously existing sympathies for us and brought about an ever greater opposition to the regimes referred to as dictatorial without the distinctions made until very recently distinguishing Italy from Germany and Russia». The Pope, the embassy concluded, had made things worse recently, for just the previous week, on October 12, on the occasion of the Golden Jubilee of the Catholic University of America, he had sent a personal message which in the end

---

[27] APSS, b. 39, f. 1, rapporto della R. Ambasciata in Washington al R. Ministero degli Affari Esteri, 20 ottobre 1938, «Stati Uniti e Cattolicesimo» transmitted November 9, 1938 to various embassies and offices.

seemed to be «una esaltazione del sistema politico liberale americano». From the Pope who had long seemed more comfortable with authoritarian regimes this was indeed bad news for the Italian Fascist Government.

Conclusions

Recent historical work has put a dent in the myth of the *italiani, brava gente*, including one of its major pillars, the notion that the imposition of the anti-Semitic laws in 1938 marked a major turning point in popular Italian support for the Fascist regime. Yet as we have shown here the imposition of the Italian racial laws did have a significant impact on Church support for the Fascist regime in the United States.

The chilling effect that the racial laws had on American Church hierarchy support for Mussolini had less to do with any concern for the persecution of Italy's Jews – although that was certainly something that offended many in the US Church hierarchy – than a reaction to the increasing identification of Mussolini with Hitler. Both the US Government and the US Church hierarchy interpreted the sudden appearance of the anti-Semitic laws as a strong indication by Mussolini that he was going to cast his lot in with the Nazi regime. In this context, Pius XI's denunciations of the new racist campaign in Italy were interpreted as an attack on Mussolini's apparent adoption of the pagan ideology of race superiority embraced by Nazi Germany.

At the broader level of Italian-American attitudes (as opposed to those of the Church hierarchy in the US) the impact that the racial laws had on support for Fascism and Mussolini cannot be simply stated. Popular reaction, and clerical reaction at the local level, were influenced by the Church's longstanding demonization of the Jews, by the longtime identification with and pride many (but certainly not all) in the Italian American community had with the Fasicst regime, and by the variegated nature of Italian Americans' interactions with Jews in the United States. This theme is beyond the scope of this paper, but a recent series of studies by Stefano Luconi has demonstrated that the significant pro-Fascist segment of the Italian-American community was not for the most part initially put off by the Italian racial laws but, indeed, important segments sought to defend them, and so defend the reputation of the Fascist regime[28].

---

[28] S. LUCONI, *The response of Italian Americans to Fascist anti-Semitism*, in «Patterns of Prejudice», 35 (2001)/3, 3-23; *Il Grido della Stirpe and Mussolini's 1938 racial legisla-*

As the Italian anti-Semitic campaign was getting launched in the summer and early fall of 1938, the US Government nourished the hope that a public denunciation by the Pope might undermine popular identification of the Church with the Italian Fascist regime. However, what looked quite promising to the US state department officials in these early days soon became a disappointment as what papal statements there were along these lines dried up, and it became clear that the only provision of the racial laws that the Vatican would oppose was the article dealing with the marriage of Catholics who had once been Jews. When, a few months later, Pius XI died and his Secretary of State Eugenio Pacelli succeeded him as Pius XII, the US Government would not have any reason to expect that a Pope would publicly denounce the racial laws.

tion, in «Shofar», 22 (2004)/4, 67-79; *Fascist antisemitism and Jewish-Italian relations in the United States*, in «American Jewish Archives Journal», 56 (2004), 151-177.

FRANK J. COPPA

The «Crusade» of Pius XI against Anti-Semitism and the «Silence» of Pius XII

Over half a century following the death of Pius XII (1939-58), controversy continues to swirl about his policies and his relationship to his predecessor Achille Ratti, Pius XI (1922-1939). In June 1939, the French Ambassador to the Holy See, François Charles-Roux, lamented the «impartial position» assumed by «papa Pacelli», towards the fascist regimes, deeming it an unfortunate departure from the course of his predecessor. Others, however, perceived little difference between the two, who were seen to collaborate for decades, with Pacelli serving Pius XI as nuncio to Germany (1922-1929), and then as the Secretary of State (1930-1939). Despite contemporary reports of their differences, most of the secondary literature has presented them and continues to describe them as close collaborators in their response to Fascism.

Although I initially accepted their conclusion, I had some doubts[1]. These were nourished by the complaints of my maternal uncle and his *fuori usciti* friends, who regretted that Pius XII (Pope 1939-1958) had abandoned the confrontational course of Pius XI (Pope 1922-1939) against Fascist Italy and Nazi Germany. They also blamed Pacelli for blocking the encyclical that Pius XI supposedly had planned condemning anti-Semitism. Their concerns were echoed in the lectures of Hans Rosenberg at Brooklyn College, which aroused my interest in the «final solution» before it was deemed the Holocaust. A number of his contentions were repeated by John Zeender at the Catholic University, who catalogued the differences between Pius XI and Pius XII. My conversion was completed by my «miraculous» receipt of Pius XI's «hidden encyclical» and the opening of his archive[2].

---

[1] See the article by F. COPPA, *The Vatican and the Dictators Between Diplomacy and Morality*, in *Catholics, the State and the European Radical Right*, ed. by R.J. WOLFF and J.K. HOENSCH, New York 1987, 199-223.

[2] I had almost lost hope of ever seeing the document appropriately dubbed the «hidden encyclical» when Professor Robert Hecht, of the City University, who I had never met,

Before then a small group of historians challenged the contention that Ratti and Pacelli agreed on the policy to pursue towards the anti-Semitism of the Axis powers. Carlo Falconi, contrasted *The Silence of Pius XII* with the outspoken criticism of his predecessor. Peter Kent, of the University of New Brunswick, saw important differences in the reactions of Pius XI and his successor towards anti-Semitism in his 1988 article *A Tale of Two Popes*. Emma Fattorini, in a series of works, has come to a similar conclusion[3].

In the hope of curbing the controversy, the Vatican made available hundreds of thousands of pre-World War II documents while Pacelli was nuncio in Germany, and then Secretary of State. Those of the Munich and Berlin nunciatures from 1922 to 1939 were released in 2003. In 2004 the papers of the *Affari Ecclesiastici Straordinari (Baviera)* were made available to the beginning of 1940. Also released were the documents of the Vatican's relations with the Catholic Center Party. Microfilm copies of part of this material (some 95 reels) is housed in the Holocaust Museum in Washington, D.C. In 2006 Benedict XVI (2005-) decreed that *all* the documents relative to the pontificate of Pius XI – some 30,000 files with millions of pages – be open to researchers including Pacelli's papers while nuncio in Munich and Berlin, and his correspondence with the German Bishops while Secretary of State. In 2007 Benedict made other documents available – some covering the war period. Included in the released papers was Pacelli's personal notes or «diary» on meetings he had with Pius XI each morning and the notes he made on the Pope's meetings with diplomats most afternoons from 1930 to the end of 1938. These «Records of Audiences» or *Fogli di udienza* – one volume of which has appeared in printed form – are important not only for what Pacelli noted but also for what he ignored[4].

Likewise available are the unpublished minutes of papal meetings, drafted by Mgr. Domenico Tardini in 1938. Among other things these documents note the increasing dissension between the Pope and the Secre-

---

wrote me. While completing his biography of John La Farge, he had found the galleys of this «long lost» encyclical, which had been prepared for publication in *The Catholic Mind* in 1973, but somehow never appeared. They were found by Hecht in the offices of the journal «America», and he sent me a copy.

[3] For Kent see his article *A Tale of Two Popes*, in «Journal of Contemporary History», (Oct. 1988); for E. FATTORINI, *Pio XI, Hitler e Mussolini. La solitudine di un papa*, Torino 2007.

[4] *I fogli di udienza del Cardinale Eugenio Pacelli Segretario di Stato (1930)*, ed. by S. PAGANO, M. CHAPPIN and G. COCO, Vatican City 2010.

tariat of state on the policy to pursue towards Hitler's regime. The recently available sources allow one to reassess the relationship between Ratti and Pacelli and the factors influencing their policies. They confirm Pius XI's vocal opposition to Nazi and Fascist anti-Semitism, which was recognized at the time of his death by the leaders of the French Jewish Community which promised never to forget the courage with which this Pope defended all victims of persecution, irrespective of race or religion. This commitment was echoed by Bernard Joseph of the Jewish Agency who promised that this Pope's noble campaign would «assure... him a warm place in the memories of the Jewish people»[5]. Despite these promises, Pius XI's efforts on behalf of the Jews have been largely neglected and many writers have criticized him for introducing the «impartial» and «silent» policies adopted by Pius XII.

In fact, from the opening to the close of his pontificate Pius XI proved critical of anti-Semitism, which he found contrary to the faith and inadmissible for Catholics. Throughout his papacy he conducted a crusade of sorts against what he perceived as Nazi excesses before Hitler's final solution led to the horror of the Holocaust. He did so even as anti-Judaism prevailed in many Church circles, which the Holy See often tolerated if it did not sanction[6]. In September, 1922, soon after becoming Pope, he emphasized that «Christian charity extends to all men... without distinction of race...»[7]. He continued to denounce racism, refusing to acknowledge any relationship between discrimination against the Jews on the basis of what they believed – or did not believe – and who they were. Later, when informed that in some states racism had been approved by law, the Pope would not be silenced. He responded that when politics or political figures infringed upon the realm of religion, the Pope had the right and duty to issue directives to the faithful[8]. Therefore in 1926 he did not hesitate to condemn Charles Maurras's racist Action Française[9].

Subsequently, in 1928 the Holy Office, with his approval, suppressed the Friends of Israel while issuing a clear condemnation of anti-Semi-

---

[5] Rabbi D.G. DALLIN, *The Myth of Hitler's Pope: How Pope Pius XII Rescued Jews from the Nazis*, New York 2005, 42-43.

[6] In this regard see F.J. COPPA, *The Papacy, the Jews, and the Holocaust*, Washington 2006.

[7] *Cum Tertio*, September 17, 1922, *Principles for Peace: Selections from Papal Documents from Leo XIII to Pius XII*, ed. by H.C. KOENIG, Washington 1943, 329.

[8] R.A. WEBSTER, *The Cross and the Fasces*, Stanford 1960, 96.

[9] Consistorial Allocution of December 20, 1926, *Discorsi di Pio XI*, ed. by D. BERTETTO, Turin 1959, I, 647.

tism[10]. Just as the Holy See disapproves «of all hatred between people», the order of suppression read, «it most categorically condemns the hatred against the people once... chosen by God, commonly indicated by the word anti-Semitism»[11]. Aware of the papal sentiments in the later Twenties, «La Civiltà Cattolica», which had often depicted the Jews as Deicides, moderated but did not end its anti-Judaic polemic[12].

Pius XI's opposition to racism was one of the reasons he was suspicious of National Socialism. Hitler, appreciating the influence of the Catholic Church, sent Hermann Goering to Rome in May 1931, but Pius XI did not receive him and forbade his pro German Secretary of State Pacelli from doing so. Later, in 1933 when Hitler had become Chancellor, the Catholic Vice-Chancellor, Franz von Papen, visited Rome and dangled the prospect of a Concordat before Pacelli[13]. Berlin rather than Rome, assumed the initiative and sought to bind the Church to the Reich[14]. Pacelli, who had long sought an agreement with Berlin, responded positively. He was supported by his old but still active mentor, Cardinal Gasparri, who favored conciliation and the conclusion of the Concordat[15]. Pius XI proved skeptical and reluctantly sanctioned negotiations[16].

Aware of the Pope's ambivalence in negotiating with the Nazis, Pacelli confessed that the Holy See deplored the anti-Semitism of the German Government, its violations of human rights, and its reign of terror. The Vatican signed the accord, he explained, because it appeared the sole means of preventing the destruction of the Church and its lay organizations in Germany[17]. On paper the agreement made concessions to the Holy

---

[10] *Decretum De Conosciatione Vulgo, «Amici Israel» Abolenda,* March 25, 1928, *Acta Apostolicae Sedis,* vol. XX.

[11] *Ibidem,* 103.

[12] G. MICCOLI, *Santa Sede e Chiesa Italiana di fronte alle Legge Antiebriache del 1938,* in «Studi Storici», 29 (1988)/4, 829-833; D. CARPI, *The Catholic Church and Italian Jewry under the Fascists,* in *Yad Washem Studies,* ed. by S. ESH, New York 1975, vol. IV, 46.

[13] «Cronaca Contemporanea» (April 7-20, 1933), in «La Civiltà Cattolica», 84 (1933)/2, 301; J.J. HUGHES, *The Pope's Pact with Hitler: Betrayal or Self-Defense?,* in «Journal of Church and State», 17 (1975), 64; K. SCHOLDER, *The Churches and the Third Reich. II: The Year of Disillusionment: 1934 Barmen and Rome,* Philadelphia 1988, 1.

[14] J.J. HUGHES, *The Pope's Pact with Hitler...;* K. SCHOLDER, *The Churches and the Third Reich...*

[15] Gasparri's memorandum of June 1933, AES, Germania, POS. 645, Fasc. 163.

[16] *Anglo-Vatican Relations 1914-1939: Confidential Reports of the British Minister to the Holy See,* 250.

[17] Mgr. Kirkpatrick (the Vatican) to Sir R. Vansittart, August 19, 1933, *Documents on British Foreign Policy,* n. 342, pp. 524-525; «L'Osservatore Romano», September 11-

See, for more than two-thirds of its thirty-three articles provided assurances for the Church[18]. An additional protocol guaranteed the right of the Church to collect funds in the Reich[19]. Pacelli was congratulated for his achievement by his predecessor Cardinal Gasparri[20], who belatedly forgave his protégé for taking his post.

Convinced that the Reich Concordat best assured the future of the Church in Nazi Germany, Pacelli made its preservation a prime concern and in large measure this accounts for his «impartiality» and «silence» *vis à vis* Nazi action. These sentiments were not shared by the Pope, who was scandalized by the numerous Nazi violations of the agreement, provoking Pius to unleash a series of complaints[21]. The Nazi sterilization law was published days after the conclusion of the Concordat, while Catholic clergy, charitable organizations, schools, and publications were all attacked[22]. In response, «La Civiltà Cattolica» condemned the Nazi mythology of race, while the Pontifical Society for the preservation of the faith noted that even those having a mediocre knowledge of Catholic doctrine recognized that anti-Semitism was forbidden[23].

Troubled by Nazi neo pagan policies, Pius XI rejected their contention that the Jewish question was an internal racial issue rather than a religious one[24]. He likewise dismissed Hitler's conviction that the Nazi restrictions on the Jews worked for the benefit of the Church as well as the State[25]. Pius considered such talk a frontal challenge to ecclesiastical teaching and felt a moral obligation to say so, assuring a delegation of visiting German

---

12, 1933; «Cronaca Contemporanea», September 7-26, 1933; «La Civiltà Cattolica», 84 (1933)/4, 89.

[18] Italian translation of Reich Concordat of July 1933, AES, Germania, POS. 645, Fasc. 157.

[19] Addenda to article XIII, AES, Germania, POS. 645, Fasc. 164.

[20] Gasparri to Pacelli, July 24, 1933, AES, Germania, POS. 645, Fasc. 165.

[21] *Anglo-Vatican Relations 1914-1939: Confidential Reports of the British Minister to the Holy See*, ed. by T.E. HACHEY, Boston 1972, 253-225; C.M. CIANFARRA, *The War and the Vatican*, London 1945, 96.

[22] N. MICKLEM, *National Socialism and the Roman Catholic Church*, London 1939, 95; A.J. RYDER, *Twentieth Century Germany: From Bismarck to Brandt*, New York 1973, 377.

[23] L. MARTINI, *Chiesa Cattolica ed Ebrei*, in «Il Ponte», 34 (1978), 1458-1459; I. GIORDANI, *Ebrei, protestanti e cattolici*, in «Fides», 4 (1933).

[24] *Anglo-Vatican Relations 1914-1939: Confidential Reports of the British Minister to the Holy See...*; C.M. CIANFARRA, *The War and the Vatican...*; *Documents on German Foreign Policy, (DGFP)* Series C, 793-794.

[25] AES, Germania, POS. 641-43.

students he would do all within his means to defend the faith[26]. Firmly convinced that the Vicar of Christ had to be involved in world affairs he rejected impartiality for an interventionist course. This led a series of voices to invoke his assistance against the Nazi persecution, including Edith Stein[27]. He responded by calling upon the nuncio in Germany to intervene on behalf of the Jewish victims, and it was at his prodding that the bishops of Germany proclaimed «God gave his only son for the salvation of all of mankind»[28].

Pius XI's vocal opposition to Nazi policy and anti-Semitic measures led some in the Vatican to fear for the future of the Reich Concordat. Once the anti-Jewish measures were backed by law, the nuncio in Germany, Cesare Orsenigo wrote Pacelli that the Pope had to terminate his crusade against the persecution of the Jews or face unfortunate consequences[29]. Pacelli agreed, but he dared not openly challenge the Pope lest he be fired as was his mentor. Meanwhile, others praised Pius XI for his efforts on behalf of the persecuted. In September 1933 «The Jewish Chronicle» of London applauded this Pope's stance, while so many others remained silent:

> «The Pope, having received reports of the persistence of anti-Semitic persecution in Germany, has publicly expressed his disapproval of the movement. [...] He recorded [...] that Jesus Christ, the Madonna, the apostles, the prophets and many saints were all of the Hebrew race, and that the Bible is a Hebrew creation. The Aryan races, he declared, had no claim to superiority over the Semites»[30].

The papal protests did not stop the Nazi persecution of the Jews and its attempts to uproot Christianity from its Jewish origins[31]. This offended Pius XI who complained to the German Ambassador to the Holy See, Diego von Bergen, who warned Berlin that the Pope might take drastic action[32]. In fact, Pius seriously considered breaking with the Nazi State and

---

[26] Speeches of April 4, 1934 and April 29, 1934 in *Discorsi di Pio XI*, III. 90-93, 114-115.

[27] Edith Stein to Pius XI, April 12, 1933 AES, Germania, POS. 643, 1092/33.

[28] Cesare Orsenigo to Pacelli, April 11, 1933, AES, Germania, POS. 643, Fasc. 158, nn. 6953-6594.

[29] Cesare Orsenigo to Pacelli, April 6, 1933, AES, Germania, POS. 643, Fasc. 159.

[30] «The Jewish Chronicle» of London, September 1, 1933, found in AES, Germania, POS. 643, 2574/33.

[31] *Dalla Germania. Voci dell'Episcopato*, in «L'Osservatore Romano», (June 8, 1934); Orsenigo to Giuseppe Pizzardo on the new paganism in the Reich, October 12, 1934, AES, Germania, POS. 670-73, Fasc. 233.

[32] G. LEWY, *The Catholic Church and Nazi Germany*, New York 1964, 126.

terminating the Concordat, but was persuaded by his Secretary of State from taking this step. Even before he became Pius XII, Pacelli invoked conciliation rather than confrontation with the Reich, deeming the latter course detrimental to the Catholic population of Germany. Pius XI, on the other hand, found it difficult to pursue conciliation towards regimes which flagrantly violated the precepts of the faith.

The triumph of Nazism in Germany and the elaboration of its anticlerical and anti-Semitic policies led Pius XI to reconsider his attitude towards *Anschluss* which he had earlier favored[33]. In June 1933, Rome concluded a Concordat with Austria's Dollfuss regime[34]. Pius was scandalized by the abortive Nazi coup of 1934 in Austria, and his outrage was reflected in a series of articles in the Vatican journal, proposing that National Socialism might better be dubbed national terrorism, and praising Mussolini for preserving Austrian independence[35].

In 1935, the Holy Office had compiled a syllabus of propositions on racism, national socialism, and statism to be condemned, but its publication was blocked by its secretary, Cardinal Francesco Marchetti Selvaggiani, who like Pacelli, feared the consequences of an open conflict with Nazism[36]. Pius XI, however, believed the dignity of the Holy See required him to denounce the German outrages, confident that the Church would survive the persecution[37]. Father Rosa, SJ, reflecting papal thought, acknowledged the danger of international communism, but insisted that the Nazi reaction was no less destructive of Christian values[38]. The Pope concurred with this assessment[39]. As a result by 1937-1938 Pius XI was perceived as one of the few world leaders defending human rights against Fascism and Nazism[40].

---

[33] *Principles for Peace: Selections from Papal Documents from Leo XIII to Pius XII*, 304-306.

[34] *Cronaca Contemporanea*, (June 9-22, 1933); «La Civiltà Cattolica», 84 (1933)/2, 609; *Cronaca Contemporanea*, (May 25 – June 8, 1933); speech of July 29, 1934 in *Discorsi di Pio XI*, III, 183-185.

[35] *Anglo-Vatican Relations 1914-1939: Confidential Reports of the British Minister to the Holy See*, 274-279; F. CHARLES-ROUX, *Huit ans au Vatican*, Paris 1947, 98.

[36] G. MICCOLI, *Santa Sede e Chiesa italiana...*, 859.

[37] *Ai giovani cattolici di Germania*, August 8, 1934, in *Discorsi di Pio XI*, III, 188.

[38] E. ROSA, *L'Internazionale della Barbarie nella sua lotta contro la civiltà*, in «La Civiltà Cattolica», 84 (1936)/3, 447-448.

[39] *Ai giovani cattolici tedeschi*, October 8, 1934, in *Discorsi di Pio XI*, III, 218.

[40] O. CHADWICK, *Britain and the Vatican during the Second World War*, Cambridge 1986, 16-19.

Pius XI opposed the Nazi laws which violated Christian teachings as well as basic human rights and transmitted a catalog of complaints to the German ambassador. Von Bergen reported that Pacelli was upset by the papal outburst but was not prepared to openly contradict his chief[41]. While the Pope railed against the Nazi violations of the Concordat, Pacelli contended that without it the situation of the Church would have been far worse. Thus Pacelli proved willing to hold his tongue as Gasparri had earlier suggested[42]. He did so out of fear, not love, of the regime he later described as «satanic». The Pope perceived matters differently and found it increasingly difficult to keep quiet. Why then, did Pius XI not dismiss Pacelli as he had Gasparri? Pope Achille Ratti never explained his rationale for retaining Pacelli but a number of reasons come to mind. First: Pius XI realized that a majority in the Vatican favored conciliation rather than confrontation, and his dismissal of a second pacific Secretary of State would have led to a dangerous dissension when the situation called for unity, Secondly: Pacelli did not openly challenge him as Gasparri had – even when the Pope by-passed his Secretary of State. Furthermore, Pacelli immediately, if reluctantly, followed papal orders. Finally, the Pope's health had deteriorated and might not have survived a major battle with his ministers and the curia. Pius XI preferred to direct his anger against the «totalitarian regimes».

Following the remilitarization of the Rhineland in March 1936, Pius XI confided to the French ambassador, «If you [French] had called forward 200,000 men you would have done an immense service to the entire world»[43]. Pius XI's exasperation over German developments may have contributed to his illness at the end of 1936. In mid January 1937 the sick pontiff, confined to his bed, met with Cardinals Adolf Bertram; Michael Faulhaber; and Karl Josef Schulte along with bishops Konrad von Preysing of Berlin and Klemens August Graf von Galen of Münster. This German clerical contingent met with Pacelli the day before. The Pope was determine to speak out despite the restraining influence of his Secretary of State, who agreed with Gasparri that arousing Hitler would do more harm than good – a sentiment shared by many, if not most, in the Secretariat of State. Pius, however, would not be deterred from condemning the Nazi and Fascist violations of the faith.

---

[41] *Documents on Germany Foreign Policy*, Series C, IV, n. 482; A. RHODES, *The Vatican in the Age of Dictators...*, 199.

[42] Orsenigo to Pacelli, June 26, 1934, *ibidem*, f. 148, n. 2168/34.

[43] F. CHARLES-ROUX, *Huit ans au Vatican...*, 106.

In March 1937 he issued the encyclical *Mit brennender Sorge*, which was secretly printed and distributed to the various parishes and read from Catholic pulpits throughout Germany on Palm Sunday[44]. «With deep anxiety and increasing dismay», Pius wrote, he had witnessed the «progressive oppression of the faithful»[45]. Denouncing the racism of the regime, and all social theories derived from the myth of blood and race, the Pope catalogued the articles of faith trampled upon by the Nazis. He was shocked by their attempt to revive the pagan belief in a national God or a national religion restricting the universal faith to one people or race[46]. His action earned him respect in the western capitals, but condemnation in Berlin[47]. Although Pacelli, under papal orders, played a part in drafting this encyclical, the Secretary of State still sought to prevent a break between Berlin and the Vatican[48]. He was told that Hitler was infuriated by the encyclical and deplored the Vatican's secrecy in its transmission along with its anti-Nazi message and vowed to take revenge at an appropriate time[49]. In the interim the Fuehrer had his police bring a number of Catholic priests to trial for «immoral conduct» and sexual abuses[50].

In May 1937, Cardinal George William Mundelein of Chicago made insulting references to the Fuehrer, as a poor paper-hanger, Pius refused to censure him, as some demanded, but praised him instead[51]. In the following month the «Civiltà Cattolica», which occasionally issued anti-Jewish pronouncements, proclaimed that the Church condemned all forms of anti-Semitism[52]. Like the Pope, its editors refused to recognize any relationship between clerical Anti-Judaism and the Nazi Anti-Semitism. By the end of the year, Pius deplored anti-Christian developments in Germany no less

---

[44] For English versions of *Mit brennender Sorge* of March 14, 1937 see *The Papal Encyclicals, 1958-1981*, III, 525-535 and *Principles for Peace: Selections from Papal Documents from Leo XIII to Pius XII*, 498-510. The original version will be found in *Acta Apostolicae Sedis*, 29 (1937), 145-167, followed by an Italian version, 168ff.

[45] Lettera enciclica sulla situazione della Chiesa Cattolica nel Reich Germanico, *Acta Apostolicae Sedis*, 29 (1937), 168.

[46] AAS, 29 (1937), 172.

[47] O. CHADWICK, *Britain and the Vatican during the Second World War...*, 20.

[48] A. RHODES, *The Vatican in the Age of Dictators, 1922-1945*, New York 1973, 228-229.

[49] Amleto Cicognani to Pacelli, April 24, 1937, AES, Germania, 1937-38, POS. 720, Fasc. 329, n. 40.

[50] E. FATTORINI, *Pio XI, Hitler e Mussolini. La solitudine di un papa...*, 137.

[51] DGFP, series D, I, nn, 665-669.

[52] *La questione giudaica e l'apostolato cattolico*, in «La Civiltà Cattolica», (June 23, 1937).

than those in the Soviet Union[53]. In fact, Nazism soon displaced Communism as his major concern[54]. Distressed by the prospect of a break in relations with the Reich, in 1938 Pacelli proposed going to Berlin to negotiate a settlement, but his offer was ignored both by Berlin and the Pontiff[55].

Relations between the Vatican and the Reich deteriorated during the course of 1938, as Pius condemned the ultra nationalism and anti-Semitism championed by the Hitler regime as a veritable curse[56]. Those who had the opportunity to examine the correspondence between Pacelli and the Nazi Government, reported that things were worse than either the Vatican or Berlin acknowledged. In April 1938, the Sacred Congregation of Seminaries, of which Pius XI was the Prefect, condemned the pernicious racism championed by Nazi Germany[57]. The Catholic press deemed it a virtual encyclical against racism! In July, Pius XI stressed the absolute incompatibility between this nationalism and Catholicism, charging the former violated the teachings of the faith[58]. He deplored the extension of anti-Semitism to Austria following the *Anschluss* of 1938, which saddened him as Pontiff and as an Italian[59]. Not surprisingly, Pius XI repudiated Cardinal Innitzer and the Austrian bishops who rejoiced at the union of Germany and Austria[60]. Innitzer was summoned to Rome and lectured by an angry Pope[61].

The Pope's public denunciation of racism worried Pacelli, who sought to prevent a break with the Nazi regime[62]. It was a difficult task in light of the Pope's visceral opposition to the racism of the Berlin Government, and the prospect of its adoption by Fascist Italy only increased his an-

---

[53] Allocution *Quod Iterum*, December 13, 1937, *Discorsi di Pio XI*, III, 671; Al Sacro Collegio e alla Prelatura Romana, *ibidem*, III, 679.

[54] *Anglo-Vatican Relations 1914-1939: Confidential Reports of the British Minister to the Holy See*, 370, 379.

[55] *Ibidem*, nn. 667, 678, 703, 714.

[56] *Principles for Peace: Selections from Papal Documents from Leo XIII to Pius XII*, 545.

[57] «La Civiltà Cattolica», (June 9-22, 1938).

[58] *Discorsi di Pio XI*, III, 770.

[59] F. CHARLES-ROUX, *Huit ans au Vatican...*, 52.

[60] *Anglo-Vatican Relations 1914-1939: Confidential Reports of the British Minister to the Holy See*, 387; *Tablet* (of London) March 26, 1938.

[61] F. CHARLES-ROUX, *Huit ans au Vatican...*, 122-123; N. MICKLEM, *National Socialism and the Roman Catholic Church...*, 206-207; 96,99; *Anglo-Vatican Relations 1914-1939: Confidential Reports of the British Minister to the Holy See*, 392.

[62] W.M. HARRIGAN, *Pius XII's Efforts to Effect a Detente in German-Vatican Relations, 1939*, in «The Catholic Historical Review», 49 (1963), 177.

ger[63]. Despite Pacelli's conciliatory stance, relations between the Vatican and the Reich deteriorated during the course of 1938 as the documents of the newly available files of the *ASV* confirm. In July, Pius XI stressed the absolute incompatibility between racist nationalism and universal Catholicism[64]. «No, it's not possible for we Christians to participate in anti-Semitism», the Pope told a group of visiting Belgians on September 6, 1938. «Spiritually, we are Semites»[65]. «I shall speak out, I will not be afraid», the Pope proclaimed in October. «I am impelled to do so... by my conscience»[66].

In June 1938, when Mussolini's Italy embraced anti-Semitism, Pius XI could not contain his outrage, despite the warnings of his Secretary of State of the adverse consequences that would flow from a disruption of relations with Fascist Italy and the Third Reich. Pius refused to keep quiet, letting the Duce know through intermediaries that this action made him «ashamed» of being Italian and regretted to see Italy imitate Germany's anti-Semitism[67]. Convinced that he could not rely on his Secretary of State for an unequivocal condemnation of anti-Semitism, Pius XI, in June called upon the American Jesuit John La Farge, the author of numerous books denouncing racism. Pacelli was not briefed on the scope of the meeting[68]. Skirting his conciliatory Secretariat of State, and its head, the Pope secretly commissioned the American Jesuit to draft an encyclical demonstrating the incompatibility of Catholicism and racism[69]. Pius XI thus planned to condemn the anti-Semitism of Hitler's Germany without involving his Secretary of State. He was also working on a speech cataloging Fascist abuses and errors.

Awaiting the draft of the encyclical *Humani Generis Unitas* on The Unity of the Human Race, the seriously ill Pope did not know it had been delivered and kept from him. He did know that some in the Vatican feared he would break with Fascist Italy and Nazi Germany, and invoked a more

---

[63] A. RHODES, *The Vatican in the Age of Dictators...*, p. 229; F. CHARLES-ROUX, *Huit ans au Vatican...*, 155.

[64] *Discorsi di Pio XI*, III, 770.

[65] G. PASSELECQ and B. SUCHECKY, *L'encyclique cachée de Pie XI*, Paris 1999, 180.

[66] Appunti di Tardini, October 1938, AES, Stati Ecclesiastici, POS. 560, Fasc. 592.

[67] Pacelli's minutes of Audience of September 9, 1938, *Fogli di udienza*, AES, Italia, POS. 1054, Fasc. 727.

[68] La Farge had been sent by the editor of «America» to the International Eucharistic Congress at Budapest in April, and on his way back stopped in Rome.

[69] R.A. HECHT, *An Unordinary Man: A Life of Father John La Farge, SJ*, Lanham, MD, 1996, 114-115.

diplomatic course[70]. He was also aware that this current hoped for the election of a more conciliatory successor. He did not know that behind his back some who favored conciliation rather than confrontation had signed a secret agreement with Fascist Italy on the racial issue. According to Father Angelo Martini, of the Society of Jesus, who was granted access to these Vatican documents, the «pact» of August 16, 1938 provided that in return for Fascist consideration of papal sensibilities on Catholic Action and its organizations and activities in Italy, the papacy was to leave the «Jewish Question» entirely to the regime[71]. Those who negotiated the pact knew that the Pope would never have agreed to such a bargain so their action was apparently predicated on the belief that Pius XI did not have much longer to live!

What part, if any, Pacelli played in this we do not know. We do know that following the death of Pius XI, Pacelli decided to shelve the two critiques of the fascist regimes that the Pope planned. Indeed, Domenico Tardini reports in documents recently opened in the ASV, that by a series of telephone calls on February 15, 1939, Secretary of State Pacelli ordered the Vatican printing house to destroy all evidence of the papal speech which he feared would widen the rift with Mussolini's Italy and its Nazi allies[72]. Pacelli had the draft of the «secret» encyclical against Nazi racism returned it to its authors. Both documents reflected Pius XI's confrontational course towards the fascist regimes, which Pacelli opposed. Following his mentor Gasparri, Pacelli favored a more diplomatic policy and chose not to release either. This was symptomatic of the new course he would pursue towards Fascist Italy and Nazi Germany from the first days of his pontificate[73]. His «impartiality» and «silence» replaced Pius XI's crusade against anti-Semitism!

For Pacelli «impartiality» and «silence» were interrelated, for the first allowed him to make moral judgments in a convoluted language that would not reach the masses, allowing him to preserve relations even with satanic states such as Nazi Germany. However, unlike some of his later defenders, Pius XII recognized the moral danger of this course. «The Pope at times cannot remain silent. Governments only consider political and military issues, intentionally disregarding moral and legal issues in which,

---

[70] G. MICCOLI, *Santa Sede e Chiesa Italiana...*, 881.

[71] A. MARTINI, *L'Ultima battaglia di Pio XI*, in *Studi sulla questione romana e la conciliazione*, Rome 1963, 186-87.

[72] E. FATTORINI, *Pio XI, Hitler e Mussolini...*, 214.

[73] *Ibidem*, XXVIII-XXIX.

on the other hand, the Pope is primarily interested and cannot ignore. His Holiness said regarding this point... that God would subject him to the most stringent judgment if he did not react to evil or did not do what he thought was his duty»[74]. Whether he fulfilled his duty remains a subject of debate.

---

[74] Report of Mgr. Montini on Pius XII's remarks to Dino Alfieri, the Italian Ambassador to the Holy See on May 13, 1940 in *Records and Documents of the Holy See Relating to the Second World War: The Holy See and the War in Europe, March 1939-August 1940*, ed. by P. BLET ET AL., Washington 1968, 423.

Jacques Kornberg

Pope Pius XI: Facing Racism and Atrocities

Pius XII's response to the destruction of European Jews still provokes fierce argument some sixty years later, while his predecessors have faded into the background, of interest to small circles, their policies not vehemently condemned or defended. Who today debates Pius XI's response to the use of mustard gas against civilians during the Italian conquest of Ethiopia? I have explained this fixation on Pius XII as an outcome of Vatican Council II, when he became the marker of all that was considered wrong with the Church: its Catholic triumphalism, its focus on institutional self-preservation, its detachment from the struggle for human rights, democracy, humanity's material well-being.

Some argue that Pius XII stands alone, that he brought baggage to the papacy that other popes did not, that his personality and training were ill-suited to the times. Even Domenico Cardinal Tardini, Pius XII's under-secretary of State, said as much while managing to keep his tone reverential. He compared the Pope to his predecessor: Pius XI «relished a fight», while his successor, inclined to «solitude and tranquility», preferred «to avoid rather than face the battles of life». Tardini believed Pacelli's temperament made him a natural fence-sitter: he sought to «please everyone and displease no one». Pius XI was therefore inclined to see both sides of an issue, both «favourable and unfavourable» consequences, and this made him hesitant, overcautious[1].

In keeping with this view of Pius XII, Michael Phayer has argued that Pacelli's predecessor, Pius XI, far more passionate, forceful, and outspoken, would have responded differently to the destruction of European Jewry, in keeping with the enormity of the crime? The conclusion is plain: Pius XII was deficient in ways other popes were not. His policy was more an anomaly than a papal norm, an outcome of his timid and indecisive personality, or of his training as a diplomat in the arts of negotiation and

---

[1] D. Tardini, *Memories of Pius XII*, trans. Rosemary Goldie, Westminster 1961, 73-74.

compromise. In Peter Kent's blunt assessment: «At heart, Pacelli... was an appeaser»[2].

I will argue, to the contrary that the immediate predecessor to Pius XII, Pope Pius XI acted no differently than Pius XII in the face of racism and atrocities. Though Pius XII faced systematic mass murder on a scale vastly more horrible than the Italian invasion of Ethiopia, I would argue that their responses were based on a similar understanding of their priorities as heads of the Church. Not so much Pacelli's personality, but the institutional role he and other popes saw themselves fulfilling, shaped common papal responses.

1. The Church and European Nationalism

Pius XI and Pius XII faced a common reality, which inhibited their responses to moral evil. A good illustration comes from a survey published in France in 1924. The French historian Maurice Vaussard had questioned prominent Catholics, many of them theologians, on the impact of national patriotism on the Church. From these answers, Vaussard constructed a instructive and disheartening conclusion[3].

Vaussard claimed that love of nation had come to trump Catholic loyalties, even among priests. Priests in France supported *Action française,* a movement valuing religion strictly for its service to integral nationalism; Flemish nationalist priests in Belgium supported a secular Flemish university to the disadvantage of the venerable Francophone Catholic University of Louvain. Further proof of the triumph of the «religion of the fatherland, the nation, the race» was the «extremely cold reception» accorded to encyclicals and other papal pronouncements on contemporary issues[4].

So deep had secularization (Vaussard calls it *laïciser*) sunk roots that most French Catholics saw the Holy See chiefly as a «moral authority» whose mission was to condemn nations perpetrating crimes, that is, nations other than their own or their allies. Vaussard explained: «Nationalism tended to dominate faith in the supernatural and submit it to its [nationalism's] laws». The Pope, however, upheld the supernatural, which

---

[2] M. PHAYER, *The Catholic Church and the Holocaust, 1930-1965*, Bloomington 2000, 19-233. Phayer cites other historians who have come to the same conclusion; P. KENT, *A Tale of Two Popes: Pius XII, Pius XII and the Rome-Berlin Axis*, in «Journal of Contemporary History», 23 (1988), 590-603.

[3] M. VAUSSARD, *Enquête sur le Nationalisme*, Paris 1924, II-III.

[4] *Ibidem*, 395-396.

submitted to its own laws. The nationalist, stuck in the mundane realm, dealt with «immediate and material responsibility», always ready to pin blame on the other side for aggression. But there was another kind of responsibility, supernatural or «moral metaphysical», shared by *all* belligerents, which was the Pope's reference point. There, guilt flowed from the «universal sin», of pride unchecked by humility. Most humans were enticed by this sin, and thus shared responsibility for the devastation it caused. Implied was a blanket moral judgment that found all belligerents equally guilty. The Pope was speaking on behalf of authentic Christianity, of «the oneness of the origin and destiny of man; the merit of suffering; the price of expiation; pardon for injuries; leaving vengeance to God; the decisive action of Providence». But war involved a life and death struggle for survival, brought untold suffering, intensified mutual hatred and self-righteousness, and brutalized nations. Supernatural judgment about the sin of self-love, war as expiation for sin, pardon for enemies, were, to say the least, not welcome by belligerents in wartime. This meant the Pope had to pander to nationalism to keep Catholics within the fold[5].

Vaussard had put his finger on the dilemma of the papacy. During national conflicts, the Pope had to square the circle, be both above the battle and uphold Catholic moral imperatives. Pius XI had tried this nimble approach while attempting to mediate during the Ruhr crisis of 1923, when French troops occupied the region to expropriate its coal because Germany had fallen behind in its reparation payments. But French Catholics – even those professing ultramontanism – were French nationalists first, and trimmed their religion to their patriotism. They considered the Pope's effort at mediation hostile to France. The Pope's intervention, as soft-pedalled as it was, only antagonized French Catholics, for what they wanted from him was support for the Ruhr occupation. Summing up, Vaussard quoted an English convert and priest, Robert Hugh-Benson, on the papacy: «The quaint old man... digresses on the subject of the cross, the inner life, and the forgiveness of sins exactly the same way as his predecessors have before, for two thousand years. And the world sees it as one more sign proving that Rome has not only lost its power, but all common sense as well»[6].

---

[5] *Ibidem*, 398-399, 402-403.
[6] Hugh-Benson quote in *ibidem*, 411.

2. Pius XI and Italian Atrocities in Ethiopia

In an age of aggressive nationalism, Pius XI abdicated his own vaunted
claims to moral authority in that large space where morals and politics
overlapped. The Italian invasion of Ethiopia of 1935 was unprovoked
aggression in violation of international treaties by an army employing
systematic terror against civilian populations. But in spite of Pius XI's
opposition during prior talk of the invasion, his response showed utter
prudence and reserve when it happened.

When the Italian Government began concentrating troops in its colonies of Eritrea and Italian Somaliland and preparing public opinion for a
prospective invasion and annexation of Ethiopia, Pius XI expressed his
growing concern both privately and publicly. In July 1935, Mussolini laid
down the gauntlet in a newspaper interview, with a blunt proclamation
of his intentions. Now the die was cast. That same month, Pius XI told
the French ambassador to the Vatican that the prospect of an Italian invasion was poisoning relations between Ethiopians and Italian missionaries,
who could operate freely under the Emperor Haile Selassie. Natives were
now inciting the population against whites, and missionaries were being
denounced as spies. As a result, heads of missions had asked the Pope to
speak out to dissociate the Church from Italian policy. Invasion would undermine Vatican efforts to foster a native clergy, which could only happen
if the Church showed respect for the native culture. In this the Vatican had
been succeeding: the overall number of native bishops from non-Euro-
pean countries had gone from zero to forty during Pius XI's reign; the first
Ethiopian Bishop was consecrated in 1930. From this perspective, Pius
XI called European nationalism «the scourge of missions». An invasion
would only set the Church back[7].

In addition, the Church had a strong stake in the Italian status quo,
while the outcome of war could upset it. The 1929 Lateran Accord with
Mussolini established Vatican City as a sovereign State with the Pope as
sovereign ruler, which amounted to a treaty guarantee of papal independ-

---

[7]   The Vatican position is well-documented. See G. BAER, *The Coming of the Italian-Ethio-
pian War*, Cambridge 1967, 284; D. BINCHY, *Church and State in Fascist Italy*, London
1970, 640; P. KENT, *Between Rome and London: Pius XI, the Catholic Church, and the
Abyssinian Crisis of 1935-1936*, in «The International History Review», 11 (1989), 255.
The French Ambassador was F. CHARLES-ROUX. See his *Huit ans au Vatican*, Paris 1947,
135; E. DUFFY, *Saints and Sinners: A History of the Popes*, New Haven 1997, 257; Pius
XI quoted in P. KENT, *The Pope and the Duce: The International Impact of the Lateran
Agreements*, London 1981, 62-63.

ence. An accompanying concordat made Catholicism the State religion, brought compulsory religious education to the schools, and recognized Catholic marriage following Canon Law, as equally satisfying the civil law.

But relations between Church and State had deteriorated in 1931, when the Government dissolved Catholic youth and student organizations. These were youth auxiliaries of Catholic Action, a nation-wide «lay apostolate» under clerical supervision, popular and thriving and not under Government control. Catholic Action had attracted long-simmering resentment and suspicion from Fascists who wanted to recruit youth for Fascism and were disturbed by the Church's continuing hold on them. A fierce confrontation followed: suppression and violence on the part of the Government, and a strong papal condemnation in the encyclical *Non abbiamo bisogno* which called for Catholics to be steadfast. Afterwards, the controversy petered out, for Mussolini did not want to squander Church support for the regime. The youth organizations were reinstated, though they could only engage in educational and religious activities; athletic and sporting activities were excluded. Relations with the regime remained relatively cordial until the Italian racial decrees of 1938. Invading Ethiopia threatened to upset this delicate status quo[8].

Pius XI spoke out prior to the invasion, weighing his words carefully. He first spoke publicly on July 28, 1935, choosing the feast day of St. Justin de Jacobis (1800-1860), founder of missions and schools in Abyssinia. Pius XI spoke of «clouds passing across the sky» between Italy and Abyssinia «clouds whose prospect, import, and to be more exact, mystery... will not have escaped anyone's notice». He then declared his hope for «the peace of Christ», and concluded: «We hope nothing happens that does not accord with truth, justice, and charity». The statement managed to be both guarded and just clear enough. The Government was displeased by the speech, and allowed the press to report it only in part[9].

Pius XI spoke more forcefully on August 27, 1935 in a speech to an international congress of Catholic nurses, published by the Vatican daily «L'Osservatore Romano» and widely circulated in the foreign press. Still, his words were carefully chosen, meant to deplore the recourse to war and

---

[8] For a detailed account, BINCHY, *Non abbiamo bisogno (On Catholic Action in Italy)*, 29 June 1931, 506-531.

[9] Abyssinia was a traditional name for Ethiopia though not the official name; «Documentation Catholique», 34 (1935), 323-324; F. CHARLES-ROUX, *Huit ans...*, 35 noted that the speech was not fully reported in the press.

its «ravages», but remaining neutral on the rights and wrongs of the dispute. The Ethiopian Government had placed the issue before the League of Nations, and Pius XI was hoping for negotiations that would avoid war.

Pius XI ended his speech, blessed the nurses, then impulsively called them back, a sign he had thought twice about the risks of speaking his mind. He began by stating that foreigners were speaking of «a war of conquest», in other words «an unjust war», something he «could not envisage». On the other hand, in Italy it was said to be «a just war, since it was a war of defense to ensure its colonial frontiers against continual dangers, a war become necessary for the expansion of a population growing day by day, a war undertaken to defend or ensure the material security of a country, [and] such a war justifies itself». Pius XI concluded: «If the need for expansion is a fact that one must take into account, the right of defense has its limits and must observe moderation, so that the defense not be a guilty one. Moderation meant first trying «to resolve all the difficulties by means other than war». My reading of this cautious wording is the following: the need for expansion was a fact, meaning it was not in itself a right, but expansion could also be considered defensive, and defense was a right. Therefore, if you first tried sincerely to avoid war by negotiating, the later resort to war would fall within the definition of a just war. Pius XI was not willing to go so far as to criticize Italy's imperialist agenda; he was stressing the need for conciliation with Ethiopia so as to avoid war. Conciliation, of course, meant Ethiopia would have to make concessions, for Italy had designs on the country, while Ethiopia had no designs on Italy[10].

For Pius XI, war was to be avoided at all costs, for the outcome of war was unforeseen: perhaps a strengthened Mussolini, or a Mussolini moving closer to Nazi Germany, in any case, more Fascist, more pagan, more anticlerical or alternatively a weakened Mussolini, regime collapse, and the threat of communism. In November, when the League of Nations imposed economic sanctions, there was every reason to fear that Mussolini would be pushed closer to Nazi Germany. For this reason, Pius XI would have Ethiopia appease Mussolini.

Yet, the Italian Government considered the speech – circumspect as it was – an attack on its policies. It banned copies of «L'Osservatore Romano» carrying the speech, and sent a formal protest to the Vatican, demanding that in a coming September 7 speech to war veterans, Pius XI say nothing to bring aid and comfort to Italy's enemies. Secretary of State

---

[10] «La Documentation Catholique», 34 (1935), 26-27.

Pacelli reported that the Vatican had received indignant complaints from ordinary Italians. Pius XI took notice, and in his September speech he appealed for a peaceful resolution of the dispute, but this time praised the Italian people and showed regard for their national aspirations: «We wish, with peace, that the hopes, the necessities of a great and good people, Our people, may be recognized and satisfied. Their rights may be assured and recognized but with justice and peace»[11].

On September 22 Mussolini rejected a League of Nations proposal for a compromise. Italian troops invaded on October 3. Then on December 11, the British and French foreign offices issued a joint proposal for peace, which ceded Italy sovereignty over of a large part of Ethiopia, though less than it had conquered, and an economic monopoly short of sovereignty over another part. Ethiopia was to retain sovereignty over about half the country, plus a seaport on the Red Sea with an access corridor.

The British Foreign Minister Sir Samuel Hoare and his French counterpart Pierre Laval, were willing to go far to keep Mussolini on their side, for they had formed a common front with Italy to try to keep Hitler within bounds. The effort took on added importance after Hitler announced universal conscription in violation of the Versailles treaty. Another aim of the Hoare-Laval proposals was to ward off the threat of war between Britain and Italy, which would follow on a British naval blockade and oil embargo. So instead of condemning Italian aggression and her violation of the League of Nations Covenant, the proposal recognized Italian claims to African land. In effect this meant that once legally installed in the country with the charge of aggression no longer over its head, Italy could always conquer the rest.

The Hoare-Laval proposals had short-circuited the efforts of the League, for almost all member states had approved economic sanctions against Italy, and would have gone on to approve crippling oil sanctions if the Hoare-Laval proposals had not intervened. Rewarding aggression was a slippery slope. George Baer has argued that the proposals helped sabotage the system of collective security laboriously built by the League. Small counties – Finland, the Baltic states, the Balkan states, and others – had counted upon Britain and France to enforce treaty guarantees and League sanctions against aggressors. Now they saw they would have to

---

[11] P. Kent, *Between Rome and London...*, 257-58; Pacelli reported the complaints to F. Charles-Roux, *Huit ans...*, 137; Pius XI's speech can be found in *Principles for Peace: Selections From Papal Documents*, ed. by H. Koenig, Washington 1943, 485-486. The translation is taken from «The Tablet», 166 (1935), 338.

fend for themselves in a world where shameless betrayal was common, and find protectors wherever they could. In consequence, Britain suffered a loss of prestige, while the campaign in the United States to join the League, was set back.

In the event, the Emperor Haile Selassie rejected the proposals, while Mussolini had yet to declare his position. But the British public was not ready to sabotage the League and the promise of collective security by appeasing aggressors. The British Government withdrew the compromise, and Hoare had to resign as Foreign Minister[12].

Pope Pius XI, on the other hand, had favored the Hoare-Laval proposals. He even sent his intermediary the Jesuit Father Pietro Tacchi-Venturi to Mussolini, to urge him to accept the offer and accept it quickly, before French and British public opinion turned against it. For all the Pope's denunciation of «extreme nationalism», his distress that mutual hatreds from the last war had not dissipated, and his talk of «the ever present menace of new wars», Pius XI counseled appeasement, signaling to aggressors that they could proceed with impunity[13].

The next time Pius XI spoke out on the Ethiopian war was to the College of Cardinals, at the consistory of December 16, 1935. By then, the Italians had full air superiority, and were using mustard gas on soldiers and villagers, which burned the skin, and caused a slow, agonizing death. In the meantime, the League of Nations had condemned Italy for invading a member State and had imposed economic sanctions, which had only served to rally the Italian public around Mussolini. Responding to the situation, Pius XI insisted he did not want to dwell upon current «military rivalries plunging...the whole world into a continual anxiety». He went on: «We persist in maintaining this reserve all the more, because among so much incertitude of men and events, it is to be feared that Our words, whatever they might be, would not be well understood, or might even be openly twisted of their meaning»[14].

Pius XI had every reason to complain: Italian news reports of his speeches were often paraphrases with crucial points omitted. For his August speech, press reports replaced the comma in front of the words «such a war justifies itself», with a period. This made the phrase appear to be a statement uttered by the Pope, though it was his paraphrase of Italian opinion. «L'Osservatore Romano» complained that in reports from the Fascist press office «distor-

---

[12] G. Baer, *Test Case: Italy, Ethiopia,and the League of Nations*, Stanford 1976, 121-44.

[13] *Ibidem*, 138-140; F. Charles-Roux, *Huit ans...*, 147.

[14] «La Documentation Catholique», 35 (January 4, 1935), 11-14.

tion is rife». On the anti-fascist side, both a French and a Spanish newspaper reported that Pius XI had called plans to invade Ethiopia a war of conquest, when he said no such thing. Misrepresentation was a constant problem. Pius XI's choice was either to take on risks by being blunt, or to say nothing at all. He chose the latter, pointing correctly to the dangers of misrepresentation as his reason. But his reserve was equally a response to another, deeper dilemma having to do with world Catholicism[15].

Taking the measure of English Catholic opinion, Cardinal Arthur Hinsley, primate of the Catholic Church of England and Wales pleaded with the Pope to dissociate himself from Italy's aggression. On the other hand, the Italian faithful, clergy, and episcopate, not only supported the war in homilies, addresses and declarations, but placed the Church in war service, ringing Church bells when the invasion began, offering the hymn of thanksgiving the *Te Deum,* blessing departing troops, contributing the gold and silver of Churches for the war effort. On October 28, Cardinal Ildefonso Schuster, primate of Italy, had blessed the Italian army who «at the price of its blood was opening the gates of Ethiopia to the Catholic faith and to [Catholic] Roman civilization, a civilization that abolished slavery, dispelled the shadows of barbarism, gave God to the people...». Pius XI had to face the harsh fact that the Italian clergy and the hierarchy were not in the least bit interested in his anti-war appeals. Instead, their religion was handmaiden to their nationalism[16].

Exasperated, Hinsley belittled Pius XI, calling him «a helpless old man». But it was not his age of 78 that held him back. His helplessness arose from a self-imposed dilemma: that is, his view of the Pope's role as head of the Church. Pius XI could not support British Catholics, without alienating Italian Catholics. He could not challenge the nationalist zeal of the Italian clergy, let alone the faithful, without insinuating that the papacy was a foreign interest opposed to Italy's national aspirations, and laying himself open to Fascist charges of encouraging dual loyalties. He could not appear too much of an Italian to English and other Catholics, or too

---

[15] All references in «La Documentation Catholique», 17 (September 14, 1935): *Dépêche de l'Agence Radio,* 329-30, *Distortion is rife,* 334; *French newspaper,* 337, *La Gaceta del Norte,* 343-344.

[16] Hinsley in P. KENT, *Between Rome and London...,* 258-259; Clerical pro-war enthusiasm in G. BAER, 161 and G. SALVEMINI, *The Vatican and the Ethiopian War,* in *Neither Liberty Nor Bread: The Meaning and Tragedy of Fascism,* ed. by F. KEENE, Port Washington, NY, 1940, 191-193; Schuster quoted in H. LAGARDELLE, *Mission à Rome Mussolini,* Paris 1955, 299. Lagardelle was a French Government emissary to Italy; For clerical nationalism, F. CHARLES-ROUX, *Huit ans...,* 149.

much of a non-Italian to Italian Catholics. Thus his preferred approach was behind-the–scenes diplomacy, sending emissaries to mediate between Mussolini, the French authorities, and the British. His silence after the invasion, after the discharge of mustard gas on Ethiopian villagers, and in the face of enthusiastic support for the war by the Italian Church, was read as acquiescence[17].

The Italians captured Addis Ababa on May 5, 1936 and on May 9 announced the war was over, though fighting continued for three more years. The Pope commented glowingly at the outcome: on May 12 at an international gathering of the Catholic press he pointed out that the gathering was taking place at a time «so propitious and unexpected» because God has allowed it «to coincide with the triumphal joy of a whole great and good people». Now he hoped God would bring peace, «as a prelude to... [a] true European and world peace»[18].

Prior to the invasion, Pius XI had deplored the ravages of war and insisted the resort to war could only be justified if sincere efforts at conciliation failed. But Mussolini wanted war and a military victory for his regime, and spurned efforts at conciliation. By that criterion alone the war was not a just one. In addition, Italy committed systematic atrocities in the conduct of war, murdering civilians from the air with mustard gas. These were not episodic atrocities committed in the heat of warfare, but deliberate strategy. Denis Mack Smith quotes Mussolini ordering a «systematic policy of terrorism and extermination». We can only broadly approximate the number of Ethiopians who perished. Ethiopians claimed that up to half a million of their own were killed. In his history of the war, Angelo Del Boca cites an American journalist's estimate of a quarter million deaths and injuries from mustard gas alone. These are not far from the later estimate of between 350,000 and 760,000 killed, most of them civilians, noncombatants[19].

Pius XI chose not to comment on the course of the war, neither on the government's war aims, nor its criminal methods of warfare against civilians. With victory declared, the Pope considered it necessary to share in

---

[17] *Helpless old man in Five Red Hats*, in «Time Magazine» (29 November 1935); Papal diplomacy in P. KENT, *Between Rome and London...*, 259-263; Lagardelle was certain Pius XI supported Italian colonial expansion. H. LAGARDELLE, *Mission à Rome...*, 180.

[18] «Documentation Catholique», 35 (13 June 1936): 1, 481-486.

[19] The half a million figure is in D. MACK SMITH, *Mussolini: A Biography*, New York 1982, 200-201; A. DEL BOCA, *The Ethiopian War: 1935-1941*, trans. P.D. Cummins, Chicago 1969, 82-83, 109; latest estimate, A. KRAMER, *Dynamic of Destruction: Culture and Mass Killing in the First World War*, Oxford 2007, 329.

the popular joy and compliment the Italian people on their achievement. His words were a post-factum exoneration of atrocities committed by Italian Catholics. By now we can understand why the Pope did so, how he fell under the constraints of the papal office, and how unavailing it was to expect the papacy to champion morality in that realm where morals and politics intersect. It is not hard to conclude that if Pius XI had lived longer, he too, like his successor, would have pressed Poland to make concessions to Hitler to avert war.

3. 1938: Pius XI, the Anti-Fascist Pope

Pope Pius XI's acquiescent response to Italian atrocities accorded with his view of papal priorities. However, some have claimed that Pius XI, unlike his successor, would have risen to the occasion and condemned Germany's unprecedented atrocities during World War II. That claim is chiefly based on the record of his last full year in office, 1938. Owen Chadwick has pointed out that between October 1935 and mid-1937, Pius XI was regarded in Britain as a «Fascist Pope». Not only had he equivocated on the Abyssinian war, but the threat of communism in Spain and the persecution of priests and nuns by its anticlerical government, as well as fear that the fall of Mussolini would bring communist rule, all led the Pope to support the Fascist regime. However, by the end of 1938, Chadwick makes clear that in the eyes of the British Foreign Office: «The Pope... came to be one of the world leaders in the fight against Nazism and Fascism»[20].

For Chadwick, the turning point was the papal encyclical of March 1937, *Mit brennender Sorge (With Burning Concern),* which opened a public rift between the Vatican and the German Government. The encyclical condemned the Government's persecution of the Church, and admonished Catholics to stand fast in loyalty to the faith against regime inducements and threats. Pius XI had the encyclical smuggled into Germany, to be read from Church pulpits on March 21, Palm Sunday. The encyclical was no less directed to Italy, for Mussolini had publicly referred to the «Italo-German Axis» in late 1936, and by early 1937 escalated what Dennis Mack Smith calls his «warlike rhetoric». The encyclical was in part, Pius XI's response to growing Italian-German friendship. Indeed Mussolini well understood that German policy towards the Church was antago-

---

[20] O. CHADWICK, *Britain and the Vatican during the Second World War,* Cambridge 1986, 7, 19.

nizing Italian public opinion and undermining the Italian-German tie. Pius XI was exploiting this popular antagonism to try to drive a wedge between Italy and Germany[21].

Pius XI was to raise the stakes in his campaign in mid-July 1938, when Italian Fascist scholars, under official patronage, published the *Manifesto of the Race*. The manifesto announced that the world was divided into «the great and lesser races»; that race was a biological concept; that there was a «pure» Italian race of Aryan origin, and that Jews were not of the Italian race and therefore «unassimilable»[22].

Michael Michaelis sees the *Manifesto of the Race* as a «major turning-point» in Italian policy: Mussolini was burning his bridges with the West. Denis Mack Smith has observed that Mussolini was keeping his options open, using the threat of an alliance to gain concessions from the French and the British. Nevertheless, both insist that the manifesto, which Mussolini claimed to have drafted himself, was a signal that he was inclined to close ties with Germany. Pius XI picked up the danger signal and without delay launched a campaign against an Italian-German accord. By the end of 1938 the British Minister to the Vatican, D'Arcy Osborne, reported to London that Pius XI was «in open conflict» with Germany and Italy, and that Nazi Germany and not Communism was now seen by the Vatican as «the Church's most dangerous enemy»[23].

Scarcely was the ink dry on the Manifesto, than the Pope let loose a barrage of criticism. On July 15, in an audience with the Sisters of Notre-Dame of the Cenacle, Pius XI referred to the *Manifesto of the Race* as «a true form of apostasy». He called it, «this curse that is exaggerated nationalism» which «hinders the salvation of souls... raises barriers among peoples, and is contrary... to the faith itself». On July 21, in a speech to the clerical mentors of the youth wing of Catholic Action, he branded racism «not human», and in violation of Catholic doctrine, for in the confession of faith, the creed, «Catholic means universal, not racist, nationalist, separatist». On July 28, he spoke to the students of the Pontifical Urban College of Propaganda [For Propagating the Faith]. There was only one race, he declared, the human race. Word usage proved his point: «Latins never say race». From ancient times on, Italians have used the «finer, more sym-

---

[21] The encylical in *ibidem*, 19-20; The encyclical and Italy in D. MACK SMITH, *Mussolini...*, 207-213.

[22] The full text in «Documentation Catholique», 39 (September 5, 1938): 1049-1052; For a summary, M. MICHAELIS, *Mussolini and the Jews: German-Italian Relations and the Jewish Question in Italy 1922-1945*, Oxford 1978, 152-153.

[23] MICHAELIS, *Mussolini and the Jews...*, 163-164; D. MACK SMITH, *Mussolini...*, 219-221; O. CHADWICK, *Britain and Vatican...*, 25-26.

pathetic: Italian people, Italian stock, Japhet's people [descents of Japhet, son of Noah]». (*Gens italica, italica stirps, Japaeti gens*). He goaded Mussolini: Why would Italy need «to go and imitate Germany». To this, Mussolini issued a heated public response, recalling the watchword of the Ethiopian campaign: «We will keep on forging ahead» on racial policy; he derided the view he was imitating Hitler, calling it «absurd»[24].

Michaelis calls the conflict in Italy between the Vatican and the regime «primarily a quarrel over foreign policy», that is, over the growing bond between Germany and Italy. When Germany annexed Austria in March 1938, Mussolini took no action, though four years earlier he had sent Italian troops to the Austrian frontier to signal his opposition to a Nazi takeover. In the wake of the annexation, the Danubian bloc of Catholic Hungary and Austria, led by Italy, disintegrated; all three, to one degree or another, now moved into the German orbit. Mussolini saw a German alliance with Italy as junior partner, as an opportunity to go to war to realize his imperial ambitions. But war would also strengthen the pro-German, anticlerical wing of the Fascist party[25].

Pius XI tried to derail the Italian-German connection because he knew that most Italians, including members of the Government, were on his side. He chose issues on which he could count on backing from Italians: the Italian-German alliance, racism, and, later, the State's violation of the 1929 Concordat. On these matters, in contrast to the Ethiopian war, the risk of alienating Italian Catholics from the Church, was non-existent. Pius XI's steadfast stance in 1938 was no indication he would have spoken out against German atrocities in World War II, when he would not have had German Catholics on his side.

In 1938, Pius XI had Italian Catholics on his side. Galeazzo Ciano, Mussolini's Foreign Minister and son-in law, noted that Hitler's visit to Rome on May 3, 1938 took place «in the midst of general hostility». Thus Pius XI could risk his pointed absence from Rome that day and his widely quoted comment on the swastika flags in the capital: «on the Day of the Holy Cross it was out of place and untimely to raise in Rome the sign of another cross, which is not the Cross of Christ». The Rome reporter of the French Catholic paper «La Croix» claimed the Pope's gesture overshad-

---

[24] All the July discourses are in: «Documentation Catholique» (5 September 1938), 1054-1062; Pius XI shared the common belief that the sons of Noah were progenitors of different «races», Japhet of the Europeans, Shem of Middle-easterners, Ham of Africans; Mussolini's response is on: 1062.

[25] M. MICHAELIS, *Mussolini and the Jews...*, 248.

owed Hitler's visit. So hostile were Italians to Germany, that one of Mussolini's ministers was later to call the May 1939 Italian-German military alliance «the breach between the people and the regime»[26].

Pius XI was a man of passionate and impulsive temperament, but he always knew just how far he could go without risks to the Church, or to his religious authority over Catholics. He picked his fights with great care. Peter Godman has documented another striking example of the Pope's prudence.

In October 1934, Pius XI authorized the Holy Office to study Nazi racial ideas with the aim of condemning them, either through an encyclical with the inclusion of a Syllabus of Errors, or by some other declaration. The Holy Office was the logical agency for this, for it passed on matters of faith and morals. It could pronounce on deviations from dogma or heresy, on error, on unorthodox theology, and issue warnings to shun certain ideas, or place books on the Index of forbidden literature. As a disciplinary body, the Holy Office could excommunicate or impose other sanctions on Catholics who disobeyed these rulings. The two Jesuits assigned to examine National Socialism laid out forty-seven National Socialist propositions on nationalism, racism and totalitarianism with the recommendation that they all be condemned by the Holy Office. By then it was 1935; Pius XI did not think the timing right to act on the recommendations[27].

To achieve wider agreement, the Holy Office asked three Dominicans to evaluate the recommendations. In 1936, they offered a revised list of National Socialist, Fascist and Communist propositions on racism, nationalism, communism, and totalitarianism, which the Holy Office was to

---

[26] The Day of the Holy Cross commemorated the discovery of remnants of the true cross in Emperor Constantine's time. When the papal nuncio to Italy refused to attend the official reception for Hitler, the Government masked the insult by excusing all ambassadors from attending. Pius XI's statement and «la Croix» comments in «Documentation Catholique», 39 (June 5, 1938), 685-90; Ciano quote in M. MICHAELIS, *Mussolini and the Jews...*, 146; Michaelis quote in *ibidem*, 248; Minister's quote in *ibidem*, 249; Binchy notes «resentful shame» among Italians over the racial manifesto, not out of «philosemitism», but out of contempt for Nazi «neo-barbarism». He also points to the open opposition of Italian bishops to racial ideology. D. BINCHY, *Church and State...*, 614, 625-626; Denis Smith also insists on the unpopularity of these policies, 220-222. Smith cites a contemporary view that the public would have supported the king's dismissal of Mussolini in September 1939, when Germany invaded Poland. SMITH, 470.

[27] P. GODMAN, *Hitler and the Vatican*, New York 2004, 58-70, 173-193. The Sacred Congregation of the Holy Office was so named in 1908. It succeeded The Universal Inquisition. Its name was changed again in 1965, to the Congregation for the Doctrine of the Faith.

condemn as «errors of the age». These recommendations were rejected as overly provocative[28].

Finally, instead of a Holy office decree, Pius XI issued the encyclical *Mit brennender Sorge* (in March 1937, in response to a plea from German bishops who were seeking Vatican support for their protests against regime violations of the Concordat. The encyclical addressed the German Government's determined – and ultimately successful campaign – to eliminate confessional schools, as well as changing confessional religious instruction in the state schools in favor of a racist Germanic Christianity that eliminated the Old Testament from scripture and made Christ a Nordic hero[29].

As opposed to a programmatic, authoritative head-on condemnation of racism, nationalism and totalitarianism, the encyclical concerned itself with violations of the Concordat. A passage condemned Nazi racism insofar as it sought to compete with Catholic doctrine: «Whoever exalts race, or the people, or the State... – however necessary and honorable be their function in worldly things – whoever raises these notions above their standard value and divinizes them to an idolatrous level... is far from the true faith in God». The passages that followed made clear the Pope's concern: Nazi racism went together with an effort to found a national German Church, «a national God... a national religion», as an alternative Christianity repudiating Catholic universalism. Aside from that, the encyclical mainly dwelt on the violations of the rights of the Church, along with appeals, admonitions and encouragement to Catholics to hold fast in the face of regime pressures to abandon the true faith[30].

However one evaluates the encyclical, issuing it was a courageous act. The risk came from alienating the German regime. Indeed, the regime retaliated by arresting those distributing the encyclical, but these measures were short-lived. There was no gain for the regime in further taking on German Catholics, for outside of Church issues they were patriotic and loyal to the Government. This was something the Pope recognized as well, and had no wish to confront. For this reason, he avoided a wider condemnation of Nazi policies. Instead, he argued that German Catholics were loyal and patriotic Germans, and should not be pressured into abandoning their faith. He could not have put it more clearly: «What We object to is

---

[28] *Ibidem*, 93, 105, 192-199.

[29] For the campaign against the Church, J.S. CONWAY, *The Nazi Persecution of the Churches 1933-45*, Toronto 1968, 158-187.

[30] *Mit brennender Sorge* (March 14, 1937), also on www.vatican.va.

the voluntary and systematic antagonism raised [by the regime] between national education and religious duty»[31].

Indicative of his caution was how he ultimately dealt with the triple evils of racism, nationalism, and totalitarianism. There would be no Holy Office condemnation, instead, in April 1938, he ordered the Congregation for Seminaries and Universities, a Vatican body of which he was the titular head, to issue instructions to Catholic Universities and Faculties to make use of their scholarly expertise to refute eight erroneous propositions on race and the State. The view of the Church was to be proclaimed, but with weaker authority than a Holy Office declaration on a matter of faith and morals, or an explicit condemnation of National Socialist ideas. Moreover, Catholic Universities and Seminaries would be speaking to the converted. The propositions to be refuted, can be summarized: races are immutable; there is a hierarchy of races; the «vigour» of the race and the «purity of blood» must be cultivated; the source of intellectual and moral qualities is in the blood; «religion is subject to the law of race»; the «burning love» of the race is the «supreme good»; there is only the universe [i.e., no God]; man exists solely for the State and the only rights he has are ones conceded by the State. A draft of the Holy Office declaration on racism had called for «justice and love toward all races, by no means excluding the Semitic race». This was the first time criticism of racism and treatment of the Jews were linked in a Vatican document. But the passage was omitted in the eight propositions to be refuted. For all that Pius XI became an anti-fascist, his campaign against racism was not directed to the persecution of the Jews, but to other threats: a pagan ideology undermining Catholic doctrine, and the danger of Italy falling into the German orbit, which would lure Mussolini into anticlerical combat against the Church, and into war[32].

The *Manifesto of the Race* was a prelude to the Italian anti-Jewish decrees, the first of which was announced on September 2, 1938. It barred Jewish students from public and private schools. In deference to the Church however, Catholics of the Jewish race [so-called], could attend primary and secondary schools. Four days later came Pius XI's pronouncement to Belgian pilgrims that «Christians can have no part» in an-

---

[31] *Mit brennender...*, par. 34.

[32] For this interpretation of Pius XI's caution, P. GODMAN, 158-59. A member of the Holy Office commented on the all-too-brief treatment of racism in the 1937 encyclical; The propositions in: «Documentation Catholique», 39 (May 20, 1938), 579-580. On making no connection between racial theory and antisemitism, P. GODMAN, 104.

tisemitism. There is no reason to regard Pius XI's outburst as a response to the school decree; he certainly did not link the two. Indeed, his attack on antisemitism came with a rider: «We recognize anyone's right to self-defense». At most, his statement could support opposite opinions on the anti-Jewish decree: if you disapproved of them, you found comfort in his condemnation of antisemitism; if you approved of them, you could read Pius XI as saying that self-defense against the machinations of the Jews was legitimate. Indeed, Pius XI was able to place into separate compartments the persecution of the Church by the National Socialist Government and the torment that same government was visiting upon Jewish-Germans. In his 1937 encyclical he portrayed biblical Jews as «repeatedly straying from God and turning to the world», and reminded Christians of the collective guilt of Jews, as «a people that was to crucify Him [Christ]»[33].

Indeed, the Pope later eased off on his July volley against racism and on goading Mussolini about copying Nazi Germany. Renzo De Felice has pointed out that when the *Manifesto of the Race* was issued in July, the Vatican had no idea how far Mussolini would take racist policy: would he introduce divorce, or decree the civil annulment of all marriages between Catholics of Jewish descent and born Catholics? Neither happened just yet, but this was the Vatican's chief concern: marriages between born Catholics and Catholics of Jewish origin. This response was confirmed by a report from the Italian ambassador to the Vatican to Foreign Minister Ciano, outlining the Vatican attitude to the anti-Jewish decrees: «Within the list of motives for discrimination of Jews of Italian citizenship, a great spirit of moderation was observed, as well as for the limitations imposed upon the Jews' occupations». The one exception – «the only point the Church would object to» – was a decree on marriage which «would come into direct conflict with the doctrine and the discipline of the Church». A related issue emphasized the Vatican's single-minded concern: the ambassador reported the Vatican's gratitude for the exemption for children of mixed marriages. They would not be considered of the Jewish race if they practiced a religion different from Judaism as of October 1, 1938. These children were from the few marriages between a Jew and a Catholic

---

[33] The anti-Jewish decrees in M. Michaelis, *Mussolini and the Jews...*, 236 and S. Zuc-cotti, *Under His Very Windows: The Vatican and the Holocaust in Italy*, New Haven 2000, 42; Pius XI to Belgian pilgrims, in «Documentation Catholique» (December 5, 1938), 1459-460: *Mit brennender Sorge...*, parr. 15-16.

that were sanctioned by the Church, provided they raised their children as Catholic[34].

However, the law for the defense of the Italian race of November 10 prohibited marriage between Aryans and non-Aryans so-called, in effect between Catholics of Jewish descent and other Catholics. The bill's target was clear: a Jew was defined as someone «whose parents were of the Jewish race, although he or she belongs to a different religion». Converting Jews, a continuing dream of the Church, was being subverted by the State. Moreover, the decree violated article 34 of the 1929 concordat, which granted automatic civil recognition to Church marriages. Pius XI sprang into action, addressing letters to Mussolini and to King Victor Emmanuel III asking the provision be dropped, as it was «in complete contradiction with the solemn Concordat». Protesting the integrity of the Concordat was so important that the Pope's emissary, Father Tacchi-Venturi proposed a compromise to Mussolini. In view of the small number of Jews in Italy, there would not be many of these marriages yearly, «a drop in the ocean!». They could be allowed as exceptions to the decree. The Government did not take up this adroit dodge. Pius XI's uttered his final words on the anti-Jewish decrees in his Christmas discourse: surveying the year, he spoke of the «grave preoccupations» he had endured «as head of Catholicism and guardian of morals and truth». He was referring to «the wound dealt the Concordat, precisely concerning holy marriage...». It was beyond his duty to mention the wound dealt Italian Jews, reduced to outcasts, banished from their occupations, property, and livelihoods[35].

In the end, Pius XI's response to the Italian anti-Jewish decrees was no different than Pius XII's later response to the anti-Jewish decrees in France, Hungary, Croatia and Slovakia. Both were concerned solely with measures that intruded upon the jurisdiction of the Church. On the other

---

[34] R. DE FELICE, *The Jews in Fascist Italy: A History*, trans. Robert Miller and Kim Englehart, New York 2001, 280. The full Ciano report, dated October 10, 1938, is in *ibidem*, 684-685; Ciano transmitted the report to Mussolini, reminding him that the marriage decree would violate article 34 of the Concordat, *ibidem*, 686.

[35] Definition of Jew in: M. MICHAELIS, *Mussolini and the Jews...*, 236-237; Article 34 of the Concordat read: «The Italian State wishing to restore to the institution of marriage, which is the basis of the family, the dignity it deserves considering the Catholic tradition of the nation, recognizes the civil effects of the sacrament of marriage as laid down by Canon Law». *Controversial Concordats*, ed. by F. COPPA, Washington, DC, 1999, 202. The letters to Mussolini and the King are in R. DE FELICE, *The Jews...*, 687-690. The Christmas 1938 discourse in «Documentation Catholique», 40 (January 20, 1939), 67-72. The Government gave in to the Vatican on one point: such marriages would not be labeled «concubinage», R. DE FELICE, *The Jews...*, 282-559.

hand, Pius XI said nothing about the November 1938 pogrom in Germany, when almost all Jewish synagogues-houses of God-were destroyed, thousands of Jewish businesses demolished, and almost 100 Jews murdered. Conditions for protest were not unfavorable: the civilized world was outraged, the violent pogrom was unpopular among Germans, and war had not yet broken out, so criticism would not be seen as undermining the war effort. However, Pius XI's stated concerns about racist ideology, statism, extreme nationalism, were over threats to Catholic doctrine, religious rights, associations, Catholic unity. Civic rights, universal human rights were not within his pastoral duty.

A final point: in policy toward the State, the Pope wanted things both ways. Pius XI worried about the dangers of statism, nationalism and racism to the Church. Yet he endorsed patriotism and respect for State authority: «Its right to command on the one hand and be obeyed on the other». Thes view accorded with his well-known policy of signing concordats with states. In the 1933 Concordat with Germany, bishops and clergy were obligated to «honor» the Government. The Concordat with Italy called for «respect» for the Government. The Pope could not place into question the respect and obedience the faithful owed Government. He could only aim to rally Catholics on behalf of the Church, against attacks by the State[36].

The papacy still relied on the State, where possible, to enforce the Church's privileged role in education, culture and society. For Pius XI, where this was not possible religious pluralism lurked in the background, namely the confusion and relativism of a so-called free society which left humans adrift to follow their subjective consciences. The Church still counted on its social and political eminence, its diplomatic weight, its access to the highest political echelons, its official face in State and society, for its spiritual influence. However much the Pope personally opposed the invasion of Ethiopia, the use of poison gas, racism, the policy of alliance with the State made him hold his tongue.

---

[36] State authority in the 1922 encyclical *Ubi Arcano Dei Consilio* (On the Peace of Christ in His Kingdom), also in www.vatican.va; Coppa, *Controversial Concordats...*, 197-209.

EMMA FATTORINI

The Repudiation of Totalitarianisms
by the Late Pius XI

1. Which Totalitarianism?

It is well known, although not studied in depth, that Pius XI, during the last years of his life, declared himself openly hostile toward Nazism and in many aspects even toward Fascism.

He was less willing to establish a diplomatic negotiation than his Secretary of State, Eugenio Pacelli, the vast majority of the German episcopate, and many important members of the Secretariat of State and of the Roman curia. Pius XI had enthusiastically supported the advent of Mussolini «the man whom providence has sent to us», and had welcomed with satisfaction the rise of Hitler as the only man who along with the Pope spoke clearly against Communism.

Pope Ratti, who contributed in giving the totalitarianism policy a sacred character, would later erect a barrier against them and would be their best antidote against them, being the Church the only true totalitarian institution. The advance of this unitary and absolute totalitarianism was incompatible with the only institution that could have been legitimately totalitarian: the Roman Catholic Church. The origin of the condemnation, which rises in a crescendo during the last years of Pius XI's life, can be found in a particular theological root which could not produce a real theological policy[1], but certainly ripened on a spiritual ground starting from a totalitarian idea of the Church.

What did totalitarianism really mean to Pius XI?

On the concept of totalitarianism and its ambiguous and floating nature innumerable pages have been written and many theories have been constructed, ones which have included the Communist regime as well.

---

[1] It seems a little contrived, although attractive the interpretation of F. BOUTHILLON, *La naissance de la mardité. Una théologie politique à l'âge totalitarie: Pio XI (1922-1939)*, Strasbourg 2001, 334.

The sacralization of politics, and its absolutization is a common feature of these theories. In Pius XI's thought there is no clear theorizing of totalitarianism, his vision evolves from terms like statolatry, neopaganism, exaggerated nationalism, authoritarianism, state absolutism, often used as neologisms or as true synonyms.

The Pope speaks of totalitarianism and defines it only in the spring of 1938 and his condemnation is not a flash of insipration, but the result of a long process in which external events and the Pope's inner maturation feed each other coming, finally, to a very significant conclusion: totalitarianisms, at first, had seemed to be a very reassuring models, a decade later, they appeared to be a threat to the heart of the Church and to faith. His rejection of totalitarianism arose from thinking about the Church as the true and genuine totalitarian organization, *Societas perfecta*, total identification between man's belonging to God and, therefore, man's belonging to the Church.

However, in Pius XI there is something more: the Church represents all of mankind and the totality of the human being, as only the Church has the basis of its authority and therefore of its power in trascendence. We will not focus on this topic here. We will only emphasize that transcendence and power, so intimately connected, would be the cornerstones of that perfect *complexio oppositorum* which is the Catholic Church in Carl Schmitt's political theology.

Pope Ratti urgently wanted to return to universal principles and their roots which lie in natural law, the only true principle of absolute equality. It is an interpretation of natural law which seems to propose a political theology of the Church, a theology emerging from the confrontation with twentieth-century totalitarianism. The papers of the Vatican Secret Archive demonstrate that the struggle of the Vatican with totalitarianism, made up of both convergence and conflict, ends with a deep and long-lasting modification of the Church's theological and pastoral systems.

Pius XI, in his speech delivered before a delegation of the Conféderation Française des Syndicats on September 18, 1938, in the midst of the Czechoslovak crisis, mentioned a doctrinal point that was particularly important, as it captured the true and deep nature of the conflict between the Church and totalitarianism, namely the fact that they were both totalitarian regimes.

«This is said almost everywhere: everything must belong to the State, and the consequence is the totalitarian State, as it is called: nothing without the State, everything belongs to the State [...] And in this case there would be a great usurpation, because if there is a totalitarian regime – totalitarian de jure et de facto – this is the Church, for human beings entirely belong to the Church, and must belong to it, since human beings are creatures of the good Lord. [...] And the representative of the ideas, of the thoughts and of the rights of God, is the Church. The Church really has the right and the duty to claim the whole of its power over individuals: every human being, whole and entire, belongs to the Church, because he entirely belongs to God.

His "conservative" ecclesiology, his traditional training, were combined with a Christocentric feeling from which he deduced the absolute centrality of the church that would make him immune, at least from a theoretical point of view (because in practice this would not happen), from real subservience to Fascist and Nazi totalitarianism of which he had already perceived the initial consonance. That inspiration will get him to the convinction that only the Church could really deal directly with nations, without lingering in the mediation undertaken by Catholic parties».

And still proceeding from this ecclesiology, in 1938, he would fully perceive the religious nature of totalitarian aggression, and realize that for this reason negotiating with it was no longer possible. Until 1936-37 the Vatican had condemned the neopaganist nature of Nazism from the moment of its rise and at various times especially with regard to the thoeries contained in Rosenberg's *The Myth of the Twentieth Century*. It was only with the encyclical *Mit brennender sorge* that a new theological perspective came out.

It is interesting to see how and in what sense this sentiment began to encompass Italian Fascism after 1938: this was well perceived by minister Bottai when in July 1938, referring to Pacelli's speech at the French Social Weeks, he stated that «the Church woud have gradually stood against the totalitarian state, fascist or not».

However, it was as a challenge to the Nazi regime that the aformentioned theological roots emerged: the indignation of Pope Ratti was not, of course, based on democratic-liberal human rights issues, nor on a generic and abstract appeal to evangelical principles. There is rather a sort of objective competition of the Church with that totalitarian regression of the concept of Volk, which entirely absorbed the community-person relationship in Nazi statolatry.

It would be interesting to investigate a few issues; how did the Pope arrive at this position, which ideas led him to these judgments? Which Catholic anti-Nazism theological currents may have influenced him? The letter that Edith Stein had sent to the Pope in 1933 should be mentioned; in the future saint's opinion the persecution of Jews was not just a general «human rights violation, but an attempt to eliminate humanity's historical roots: the Judeo-Christian religion. The Nazi fight is not just against the

Jews but also against Catholic Christianity, which is considered dangerous because it is well-structured into a single centralized organization: the
Catholic Church...»[2].

That is what Romano Guardini clearly understood when he noted how,
from the Thirties on, the stage was set for a new political messianism that
would meet the general expectation of salvation: Nazism as a neo-pagan
revival of the myth of the savior[3].

2. The Intransigence of a Sick Pope

During 1937 and the first months of 1938, signs of conflict between the
Holy See and Germany increasingly appear, especially those coming from
Pius XI: from the encyclical *Mit brennender Sorge* to the Pope's praising
of Cardinal George Mundelein, the Archbishop of Chicago, who had portrayed Hitler as an unreliable madman from the Christmas speech of 1937,
which was theologically dense and harsh in tone, to the hard scolding
given to the Cardinal of Vienna Theodor Innitzer, for expressing enthusiasm for the Anshluss and other many significant episodes.

Signs of the growing distance between the Vatican and Germany were
clear well before 1937, but it is during the period between the encyclical «shouted from the rooftops» to the one which never saw the light,
that important elements regarding the events and the main characters of
the rapprochement between Italy and Germany can be reconstructed. The
intransigence of the Pope would be manipulated by the Fascist regime
on many levels: they would try to use the Holy See's growing hostility
toward Germany to their advantage when the Rome-Berlin axis had not
yet been decided.

The intransigence of the last years, a topos in the history of the twentieth-century Church, has often been attributed to Pius XI's well-known authoritarian temperament, his strong character, his illness and his old age.

From a detailed examination of the last years of his life, two things
emerge: first, the image of a lucid and determined man, who was fully in
contact with himself and reality, and second, the conclusion that his un-
compromising behavior was the final result of a deep inner conversion.

From Pope Benedict XV, Ratti had inherited his great concern for the
spiritual dimension of the institution: in contrast to his predecessor, he

---

[2] AES, 1933-1945, POS. 643, Fasc. 158, 16-17.
[3] *Der Heiland*, in «Die Schildgenossen», 14 (1935), 97-116.

was unfond of international organizations, and Catholic political parties. Instead, he wanted laic Catholics to commit themselves to building a new Christianity on the basis of the Christ the King model: a political revisitation of cults such as the Sacred Heart and the Sovereignity of Christ affirmed in the encyclical *Quas primas* promulgated at the end of 1925.

A political restatement of these devotions could have, with an antimodern perspective, remedied the evils produced by secularization: these cults could have been used to win back lost Christian hegemony, but in his ecclesiology they would retain a strong spiritual and inner tension.

His sensibility is refined through meeting with Therese of Lisieux, who was a mediator in small things, and had a way of humility and abandonment: she was like a spiritual oxymoron, the «star of his pontificate» who tempers the impetuosity of his tumultuous action, otherwise omnipotent tense, frantic organizing, building, and promoting a hierocratic policy. Canonized on May 17, 1925, Pius XI would make Teresa no longer an icon of nineteenth-century yearning devotion, romantic and mawkish, but the model of a sober and mature spirituality, the patron saint of Catholic missions (with St. Francis Xavier proclaimed in 1927), able to interpret the most restless anxieties of French Catholicism that would have to face the season of the Popular Fronts.

Female influence was very important starting from his mother: from her he gets the urge to aim higher and higher, while keeping measure of reality, taking one step after another without ever looking too far ahead or too far back, but staying grounded in the present. A proceeding on a spiritual path that is reminiscent of the Alpine one, a passion for mountain climbing that Achille Ratti had never considered a heroic challenge.

From Christmas 1936 to Easter 1937 Pius XI was very sick and was confined to a long period of rest: his disease, taking away his physical strength, made him meditate at length on the virtues of the Cross, and its redemptive power. Indeed, the fact that his firm denunciation was based on an intimate contact with suffering builds a stronger base for a less political, more religious vision and the refusal of the vanity of power that marked the spirituality of the pontiff during the last years of his life.

As Luigi Salvatorelli wrote at the end of the 1930s: «A deep inner activity was happening inside the spirit of the Pope. He retraced all the work and the events of his pontificate and in silence and calm he had to make a sort of revision, something intermediate between an historical evaluation and a personal examination of conscience. And this last one was predominant, as was natural in a believer, in a Pope who now felt on the threshold of eternity»[4].

At the age of 80, on the very day of his birthday, the Pope realized he felt bad. For the first time in his life he felt weariness, he felt an aching in his lower limbs that would bring him great pain in the future. This man, accustomed to controlling and managing physical strength, felt confused and disoriented. Incredolous of his fragility, he had to deal with the pain in the same hot tempered and strong way he had managed his exuberance.

> «The experience of life – he said – no matter how great, lacks a large part if it doesn't deal with pain, and we must thank God when he gives us some pain [...]. I wish everyone, and this morning I told Cardinal Pacelli, to be happy, but I also hope to find a time in life to be able to suffer»[5].

Pacelli, even in those moments, even for the most profound and intimate things, was there as a distant as a careful observer.

3. The «Mit brennender Sorge»

The genesis, the antecedents and the various drafts of the *Mit brennender Sorge* (in the Vatican Secret Archives we can find at least four of them) still leave many issues to be clarified.

What is, for example, the relation between the encyclical and the doctrinal condemnation (of which there is evidence in the archives of the Holy Office)[6] proposed beginning in 1934 and promoted by the Nazi sympathizer Alois Hudal, rector of the College of Santa Maria dell'Anima? It seems it was a condemnation in principle, a sort of Syllabus against another modern heresy.

A doctrinal condemnation that probably would not have had the same weight and the same effectiveness as a pastoral and diplomatic condemnation, as in the case of a real encyclical. After all, the *Myth of the Twentieth Century* by Rosenberg had already been listed in the *Index* in 1933. The most interesting aspect of this planned doctrinal condemnation remains, however, the concept of heresy and a more explicit reference to the theory of the race.

---

[4] L. SALVATORELLI, *Pio XI e la sua eredità pontificale*, Torino 1939, 191-192.

[5] C. GONFALONIERI, *Pio XI visto da vicino*, Milano 1993, 209-210.

[6] On this topic see the considerations of P. CHENAUX, *Pacelli, Hudal et la question du nazisme (1933-1938)*, in «Rivista di Storia della Chiesa in Italia», 57 (2003)/1.

The *Mit brennender Sorge* was preceded by the famous meeting in Rome in January 1937, in the presence of the Pope, between the three German cardinals Adolf Bertram (Breslau), Michael von Faulhaber (Munich) and Carl Josef Schulte (Cologne) and two bishops among the most hostile to the regime: Konrad von Preysing (the Bishop of Berlin) and Clemens August von Galen (the Bishop if Muenster).

But, despite the request of Bertram, the Archbishop of Osnabrueck, Bishop Berning (who had not resigned from his position as advisor to the Prussian State, as the Vatican would have liked) was not invited, and this exclusion seems to have been made under the explicit request of the Pope. Pius XI, in the preparation of the encyclical, is therefore a protagonist: on January 17 he receives the cardinals in his bedroom, suffering but alert.

The position of Bertram and especially of Faulhaber, to whom Pacelli (and perhaps this was not a coincidence) would entrust the German version of the draft, wished to avoid conflict and would have limited it to a letter from the Pope to Hitler and the German bishops. And, as Faulhaber said, the pastoral letter of the Holy Father could not be contentious. According to the prelate of Monaco, National Socialism and the Nazi Party should absolutely not be named. It was necessary to keep the condemnation vague even if it had to refer to German relations. The first draft kept this pastoral spirit, intentionally general and generic so that it would not have provoked Hitler's anger. But in the second draft, doubled in length, the tone and the cut were already harsh, accusatory and totally explicit.

Pacelli is assigned the most significant revision, the one with an outcome that was so determined it contraddicted his prevoius concern about not wanting to use tones too harsh that would undermined the Concordat. What was the reason for this change? How much and in what way did the Pontiff's will to finally express an unequivocally firm position influence it, and, in doing so, abondon the exhausting diplomatic negotiations totally dedicated to the defense of the Concordat to assume, also in the language, the tones of a biblical condemnation that was little worried about political and diplomatic consequences?

The first part of the encyclical, which is focused on the Concordat, should be attributed to Pacelli. The second part should be attribuited to Cardinal Faulhaber and focuses on themes dear to Pope Pius XI who urged to present the condemnation of totalitarianism in «a spiritual light». But, in addition to Faulhaber, how much of Pacelli is there, and how much of the final version is attributable to the Pope or others?

Meaningful references to the Old Testament attest to a spiritual moment experienced by the Pope. After an audience given to him on March 22, the French Cardinal Alfred Baudrillart reported: «Even in the moment of his worst suffering, when this moment passed, if he could not sleep, he felt at rest and with an active brain. Then he thought about the three encyclicals he wished to write. He drafted them mentally, then he read and collected information, and at times he dictated. And it was thus that his work was prepared»[7].

Some comments on the use of biblical texts inside the encyclical seem to confirm intervention: «He who dwells in Heaven laughs at them» (Psalm 2:4), «Behold Him the nations count as small drops of a bucket» (Isaiah 40:15), «The spirit of God blows where it will» (John 3:8), «of stones He is able to raise executors of his designs» (Matt. 3:9; Luke 3:8).

The Old and New Testament quotations are so rich and meaningful. In the use of Isaiah in minimizing national pride – «nations are small drops in a basin of water» – one can see a pride of faith, a deep passion: there is the centrality of Christ, which, in this case, is not invoked to feed the various cults at the service of Church policies (an effective example is the cult of the Sovereignity of Christ, the Quas primas dated December 11, 1926, which not only had a religious value, but a real political and social aspect too).

On this occasion Christ was invoked against the haughtiness of nations as the only true anti-idolatrous antidote.

The profound sense, the essence of the encyclical is addressed to contrast the «religious» idolatrous aspects of Nazism: «Venerable brothers, you have to watch carefully when religious notions are emptied of their content and distorted to profane use...».

> «Blood... race... these false coins do not deserve to pass on the linguistic treasure of a faithful Christian [...] the Nazis are called "destroyers of the Christian West" [...] those laws that suppress or hinder the profession and practice of this faith are in contrast to natural law».

This concern became intense in regard to youth, towards the Nazi education of children, which had, already in the early 1930s, caused a true alarm for the Church. It is just on this issue, after all, that from 1933 to 1934 repeated and truly indignant appeals can be found. There were reports of the nuncio Orsenigo describing the pantheistic drift of the rela-

---

[7] *Les Carnets du Cardinal Alfred Baudrillart (20 novembre 1935-11 avril 1939)*, Paris, 437.

tionship between Hitler Youth and nature. Nudity in the woods, displays of the body, all sorts of promiscuity were condemned and associated with the communist education of youth, even fearing contagion and mutual imitation.

Then there was the theme concerning Sunday as the only space of possible existence of the Christian community. Pius XII would resume it, in his liturgical reform, as a possible refuge during the dark days of Nazism and war. God decides, he is dominating, he is the only one who protects. And the Church has to be a true reflection of him. In mid-February 1937 false rumors about the possibility of air strikes spread in Rome: the Pope refused to descend into the underground shelter saying that only St. Peter could defend him and nothing else.

The *Divini Redemptoris*, the encyclical against Communism, even if it is apparently harsher because in the text Communism has no chance of appeal nor redemption and is described as an «absolute evil» – it is a more cerebral encyclical, more doctrinal, less passionate and vibrant.

4. Reactions to the Encyclical

On April 12, the German Ambassador von Bergen sent Pacelli an extremely harsh note of protest against the encyclical denouncing the disruption of the Concordat and the ungratefulness demonstrated by the Church to National Socialism for having saved the Church from Bolshevism. Pacelli's response, a very long note dated April 30, is a masterpiece of sophisticated diplomatic arguments. The tone and style are diametrically opposed to that of Pope Ratti: does it mean a complementary division of tasks or a real distinction between greater determination and persistent acquiescence?

The clash between the Holy See and Germany, Pacelli seemed to suggest in each passage, was limited to a momentary break, it was a «disease» which only needed a «rapid, radical and certain cure»[8].

On the basis of the addresses one cannot deduce that the purpose was political and that therefore the accusation that it was «an attempt to mobilize the world against Germany is not justified [...] the religious purpose is clear, far from any political tendency». In the fourth point on Bolshevism one reads that: «The Holy See is not unaware of the great importance of

---

[8] AES, Germania, POS. 719, Fasc. 317: Risposta di Pacelli alla Nota di protesta dell'ambasciatore tedesco presso la Santa Sede, 30 aprile 1937. Next quotations to be referred to this same position.

those political fronts of defense, intrinsically healthy and vital against the danger of Bolshevism [...] It never missed any opportunity to consolidate and refine the spiritual front of defense against Bolshevism [...] but this cannot constitute a move toward tolerance, nothing is more unfounded than the false idea that the defense of Bolshevism can be based only on external and not on spiritual force... dignity and impartiality [...] require, however, the Holy Father, while condemning the madness of Bolshevism, not to close his eyes to similar mistakes that begin to take hold among other political and ideological currents».

With regards to the Concordat he denounced the repeated German violations and spoke of the untiring patience of the Holy See «that was considered excessive by many» taking advantage of the smallest possibilities of mediation. Pacelli seemed to suggest that there were still reasonable elements of the German Government, and basically denies that the spirit of *Mit Brennender Sorge* was really that of full frontal contrast. And there was instead a direct clash in the way of delivery more so then in its content. The total secrecy and the final surprise (the news reached Goebbels who was watching with Hitler a Zarah Leander movie and he didn't speak immediately to the Fuehrer in order to contain his fury), its great distribution (no priest refused to read the text in the homily), the extraordinary effect it had on the international press, all contributed to increase the furious reactions of the Nazi Regime.

The preparation for its launch had the pressing pace of a real clandestine operation. The directive of the Secretary of State dated March 10 ordered that the encyclical be brought to the attention of the faithful as soon as possible, and delivered to the churches as simultaneously as possible in order to have a surprise effect, and more effectively to reduce the effects of the predictable and brutal repression. The *Mit brennender Sorge*, which Faulhaber and Pacelli originally wanted to be a letter addressed only to the German bishops in the form of a pastoral letter of the Pope to Hitler, became the occasion for a full scale international campaign against Hitler.

The initial caution was completely turned upside down. Around the encyclical there was real sense of international solidarity which, after its publication, would remain constant until the death of the Pontiff. The *Mit brennender Sorge* was a true global campaign that retained elements of surprise, aggression, speed and international ubiquity. With the same characteristics of modernity it attempted to overthrow a position which had been primarily defensive until then. A true modern mass propaganda campaign.

5. The Pope's Anger over Mussolini's Visits to Hitler (September 1937), Hitler's Visits to Mussolini (May 1938) and Tacchi Venturi

Between 1937 and 1938 the last illusions about an international Catholic front that would bring Italy, Austria, Spain and Portugal together faded. *Anschluss* and the racial laws also put the accord with Fascism at risk and a period of uncertainty began. The crisis of the 1930s for the Church meant a «crisis of civilization» (according to the title of the Social Week in France in 1936) and could only be resolved with a «Catholic solution, returning to the Christian roots of Western civilization».

But in the conflict between Christianity and anti-Christianity, Concordats were not so effective anymore. So the Pope of «Concordat mania», – «I would make a Concordat with the devil if it benefited the Church», he used to say – went to the root of this struggle which was spiritual more than than political. But this time Germany and Italy would no longer be on the «side of Christianity» in the fight and the anti-Bolshevik common front wouldn't suffice to motivate the alliance with them. Pius XI no longer thought that the diplomatic solutions used and known up to then in the relations between states and the Holy See would be up to the challenges of that period.

During the spring of '37 signs of concern in some Catholic circles close to Fascism increased, as we can see in the discouraged attitude of even Father Tacchi-Venturi, always ready to grasp on to even the smallest signs of accord with Fascism:

> «The Jesuit has been quite reserved, but-writes the informant – according to his friends it seems he had shown much concern not only for the relations with Germany and the events in Spain, but especially for our economic conditions, which he defined worrying [...] Tacchi would have said he was very suspicious about the relationship with Germany, considering its Head of State as a "devious" and "unscrupulous" person... Tacchi was very discouraged because he once saw things in a very different way»[9].

During 1938 the relations between the Holy See and the German regime ended. It's well known that in those months the political game was being played at multiple tables in terms of different possible alliances of Fascism with the other European powers. Mussolini tried to use the ex-

---

[9] Promemoria del 24.5.1937, ACS Segr. Part. Duce, Carteggio riservato, b. 64, quoted in A. RICCARDI, *Roma, «città sacra»?*, Milano 1979, 178.

treme hostility of the Holy See against Germany in order to disparage Hitler.

On September 6, 1938, Pius XI pronounced the famous statement: «Spiritually we are all Semites»:

> «Every time I read the words "the sacrifice of our father Abraham", I cannot help but being deeply mooved... It's impossible for Christians to participate in anti-Semitism. We recognize that everyone has the right to self-defense and can undertake those necessary actions to safeguard his legitimate interests. But anti-Semitism is inadmissible. Spiritually we are all Semites».

Much has been discussed about the interpretation of the word «spiritually», whether it represented a reinforcement or a diminutive, a restriction on anti-Semitic condemnation tout-court, and if fighting the Jews falls whitin «safeguarding legitimate interests».

Speaking of Hitler's visit to Rome in May 1938, Pius XI had already described the swastika as the «enemy cross of the cross of Christ». And he refused to give up this invective even though he was told that it was the emblem of a country with which the Holy See, however, still maintained diplomatic relations.

For the Pope, «Der alte Herr», as Hitler's closest men contemptuously called him, Nazism was as anti-Christian as Bolshevism. After all he had said that it used the same methods and that it had the same content and seemed to even have taken the place of Bolschevism in his last year of life. This equation, in that period was an absolute novelty. It sounded outrageous and ungrateful for what the Nazis had done against Bolshevism, considered until then, however, as the true and main danger. The Pope's increasingly tough stance against Hitler brought criticism on him and he was accused of breaking the anti-Bolshevik front.

Indeed the extremist fringes even accused him of complicity with Bolshevism. This would be the strong point of the «political culture» that would inspire the struggle against the German Church after the *Mit brennender Sorge*[10].

The different expectations of the Curia about the possibility that Mussolini might influence the Fuehrer and persuade him to see reason crumbled around the coming of Hitler to Rome and were widely assigned once again to Tacchi Venturi.

---

[10] AES, Germania, POS. 720, Fasc. 330. See the report dated February 13, 1938: contro la calunnia, diffusa in Germania, di una collaborazione segreta Vaticano-Mosca.

After «Kristallnacht» Mussolini told Ciano that if something similar were to happen to German Catholics, the Axis would not have held. During the period between the *Anschluss* and the Munich Agreement the religious question had become a tool for probing, detecting, and essentially for accelerating the alliance on the part of the Germans and the Italians. And so there were both false declarations of good will and an accentuation of threats. It was difficult to find a unified solution to the problem: even from Germany there seemed to emerge totally inconsistent signs of a détente that would immediately be followed by very strong attacks. Even the men closest to Hitler showed signs of rapprochement, even if they completely lacked credibility.

On March 19, Count Magistrati, the Italian chargé d'affaires in Berlin, referred to a conversation with Marshal Goering: «Goering recognizes the importance of the religious question, especially at this moment. Hitler also hopes for religious pacification, and he looks ahead, not back», so he would be inclined to accord general amnesty. For the Vatican the moment is at hand for a «great and definitive chance» to achieve an agreement with the Reich, but for this the Vatican should appear satisfied with the *Anschluss* and convince even the Austrian Catholics to be happy about it. Goering praised Cardinal Innitzer' second «appeal».

The Marshal pointed out that the trials against religious people had been suspended for months, following Hitler's orders. And no further hostilities would be planned in the future. Goering excluded the possibility of a visit by Hitler to the Pope, though he recalled with a certain fondness the audience granted him by the Holy Father in 1933. On that occasion, however, he had the impression that the Pope did not see a big difference between National Socialism and Communism»[11].

Pacelli, despite recognizing the clearly exploitative character of these openings was unwilling, once again, to give up an exhausted diplomatic relationship and again proposed the basis for possible negotiations.

A report by the nuncio in Italy Borgongini Duca on a conversation he had with Ciano on April 30 cast light on some of those questions:

«Minister Ciano did not convey his thoughts to me, but I got the impression that he too was not enthusiastic about German policy and strongly deplored the persecution of the Church. As he has then asked what were the impressions in the Vatican for Goering's declarations to Count Magistrati, I replied that those statements could not have made any impression at all, because they were immediately contradicted by the attitude taken by Hitler. He added that

---

[11] *Ibidem.*

Goering is more conciliatory than Hitler, who hardly changes course: but, expressing his personal opinion, Count Ciano approved the moderate attitude taken by he Church of not adopting extreme sanctions (excommunication, breaking off diplomatic relations and the like).

He may have said these words to me in order to make me have some reaction, but I told him that the Holy See did not want to eliminate the last hope of negotiation, and added nothing more.

I seemed to detect in the words of Count Ciano a cooling of Mussolini's attidude towards Germany and perhaps even that he would not disapprove of those extreme sanctions»[12].

The possibiliy of taking extreme sanctions against Hitler, such as excommunication, was being discussed among Mussolini's closest men, though not very concretely. The religious question and the irrepressible intransigence of the Pope, constituted, to some Fascist hierarchs, almost a desperate attempt to contain the German ally.

6. Differences between Pius XI and Eugenio Pacelli

Between 1937 and 1939 different position toward the totalitarian regimes became evident: the future Pius XII was increasingly determined to pursue a diplomatic mediation with the Nazi regime – and he would continue to after he was elected Pope, – whereas Pope Ratti was inclined to break relations with National Socialism.

Pius XI would not, however, always confide in his indispensable Secretary of State, who was choosen as the only one truly worthy of his succession during the dark years that would have soon come. As for the profound differences of positions and temperament between Pius XI and Eugenio Pacelli in the last years of his pontificate I have discussed this in my book «Pius XI, Hitler and Mussolini»[13]. In this paper, I would like to point out that those differences were evident from the very beginning, when, during 1931, after moving to Berlin, the new Secretary of State had to face difficult situations early on.

Difficulties of which we find important traces in Eugenio Pacelli's notes taken every evening after his morning meeting with the Pope. Written on small sheets from August 10, 1930 up to December 3, 1938, these

---

[12] AES, Germania, POS. 720, Fasc. 329.

[13] Now translated in English and titled: *Hitler, Mussolini and the Vatican, Pope Pius XI and the speech that was never made*, 2011.

«audience notes» tell us a lot about the two personalities, as different as they were mutually attracted[14].

The differences within this odd couple began soon after Pacelli's arrival in Rome. 1931 was the year that put the new Secretary of State to the test: he found himself in charge of managing the conflict with fascism after the Lateran Treaty of 1929. In this case Pacelli would be much more cautious than the Pope. From the second half of April 1931 in a crescendo until the summer, the tensions with Mussolini on the nature of Catholic Action organizations (too competitive with the regime over education and training of youth) got worse. In the audience of July 12, 1931, perhaps for the first time we can find that «leit motiv» that would return throughout the whole pontificate: the Pope speaks too much and too explicitly, he is not diplomatic enough. After the encyclical *Non abbiamo bisogno* in defense of Catholic Action and against Mussolini, Secretary of State Pacelli described a furious Ratti whom he tried to moderate:

> «Mussolini will give a reasonable speech, as the Holy Father hopes and wishes, otherwise the Holy Father will be forced to protest about it, and while he now stated his intention not to condemn the Party and the regime as such, the future may require the Holy Office to examine this question: on the righteousness of being a member of the fascist party,the answer must be: negative [...] The Church has an obligation to seize morality [...]. He sees the serious consequences of that decision, but cannot allow that whithin his silence consciences fall asleep. I asked His Holiness to look at the fact that, in my humble opinion, he had already extensively discussed and explained the Catholic doctrine in the last encyclical»[15].

In the note about the audience of April 12, 1931, regarding Borgongini Duca's report on his conversation with ambassador De Vecchi, one reads about De Gasperi:

> «When it comes to the love of God and the salvation of his diocese's souls, he can only act as a Bishop. Leave the moral and religious primacy of the fascist government aside, we would have too many things to say [...] the Holy Father himself knows well, not to be easily influenced, what has to be treated with a pastoral actitude and what has to be dealt with through diplomatic channels»[16].

---

[14] *I «Fogli di udienza» del Cardinale Eugenio Pacelli Segretario di Stato, I (1930)*, a cura di S. PAGANO, M. CHAPPIN, G. COCO, Città del Vaticano 2010.

[15] AES, Germania, POS. 720, Fasc. 329.

[16] *Ibidem.*

Here we find Pius XI's peculiar tone and his fundamental distinction in facing totalitarianisms: the distinction between a pastoral approach and a diplomatic one. Even the pages offer many hints on the different tones used by Pius XI and Pacelli in this matter.

1931 is really a difficult year for Pacelli who is besieged by enemies of the curia allied with his predecessor Gasparri who very reluctantly cede him his place. Not yet in full harmony with the Pope, the Secretary of State seems on the verge of being swept away by the struggle with Mussolini. The audience of May 29, 1931 was very tense: Pius XI was enraged at the famous article published on «Il Popolo di Roma» in which the discontent of some members of the Curia who were more pro-Fascist than the official line of the Church was expressed. The Pope ordered Tardini to «take a taxi in order to reach the Cardinals Granite, Boggiani, Gasparri and Cerretti to tell them to move in to attack» and that they would have to deny as soon as possible the rumors of a split in the Curia, that could even have provoked the resignation of the Secretary of State. In the letter of June 24 from Pope Pius XI to Schuster, we read: «You had done well when you broke the silence: you certainly understood that the Holy Father had never missed the opportunity to do the same. [...] the Pope is proposing a big [...] breaking of the silence». Here, I think the first sentence is by Pacelli while the second is tipical of Pius XI.

We should not view the differences between Eugenio Pacelli and Achille Ratti in a negative light, two personalities that were very different but which shared a similar destiny. They have such different characters, family backgrounds, almost opposite spiritual dimensions. They are irresistibly attracted to each other, and perhaps precisely because of their differences, according to the rule that opposites attract. Ratti would probably never have let himself launch his harsh attacks if had he not know the faithful and diligent Pacelli would be there to smooth over the edges off and patch up diplomatic wounds, and vice versa. It was not only their need of each other, it was also a profound esteem that tied them, but what prevailed was certainly the mutual need for each other. Pacelli was the perfect Secretary of State, perfect in a way that that role would have been his forever, so that we might somehow say that he would have become his own Secretary of State when he became Pope Pius XII. And a simple analisys of the relationship between the cautious and diplomatic Pacelli and the impetuous Pope could reawaken the endless controversies on Pius XII's «silence». But it would be misleading.

We must be wary, in fact, of superficial contrapositions, a juxtaposition that arises from a judgmental attitude in history and essentially a projection of a later historical and ecclesial consciousness, acquired immediately after the Second World War and then in the culture that followed the Second Vatican Council. It is only in this period, in fact, that the relationship of the Church with the world as mother of all human beings and not only an entity concerned with protecting her own children is acquired and fully interiorized.

7. Conclusion

The documents of the pontificate of Pius XI, in my opinion, could significantly change studies on the relationship between the Church and totalitarianism, adding nuances sometimes substantially different to the knowledge of catholicity during the crisis of the 1930s. They could certainly help to understand various, different positions at the highest levels of the Vatican. Also due to the closure of sources, the research was impoverished for a long time, allowing for the simplified reading of a Church subordinate to Fascism.

Pope Pius XI died on February 10, 1939, but his death does not seem like the end of a pontificate: his death seems more like a beginning, as if his legacy were there, waiting to be accepted and to be built. Yet his death was expected by all, many had also hoped for it, so that in the Roman Curia circles there was a sense of relief at the death of this Pope, who in the last years of his life, had become more and more obtrusive, an awkward presence[17].

In 1941 Domenico Tardini gathered together all the documents relative to the final weeks of the Pontiff's life, including the records of the audiences with Pacelli. Those were the days during which the Pope, ever more exhausted by illness, prayed to God and asked the physicians to help him live until the tenth anniversary of the Lateran Pact, a very important celebration that would have fallen during a period of acute conflict with Mussolini. The alliance with Germany had been forged, and one of its bitter fruits were the racial laws about which Mussolini was not willing to make concessions, not even the request to reconsider the part relative to mixed marriages celebrated between Christians and converted Jews.

---

[17] Luigi Salvatorelli underlines that his relationships with different States were inspired by a discrete behaviour, and by a major distance from their internal affairs and was there an aloofness of the taken up by the Holy See and Catholicism from politics. The same caused his indifference about PPI e for the condemnation of Action française.

The accords with Catholic Action intensified. Those were the days of a strenuous and decisive battle for the dying Pope, who, during his final nights, wrote the speech that he intended to deliver to the bishops convened for the celebrations. That speech that promised to be a harsh one, worried Mussolini. There was a tense air, all those around him were worried, Pacelli advised Pius XI three times not to proceed with his plan. Yet the Pontiff completed the text for his speech and died directly afterward. Pacelli immediately destroyed the text: «Not even a line must survive». A very eloquent act that symbolically announced a new climate, less in conflict with Fascism and, from there to the conclave, also with the Nazis. A new pontificate began, and the legacy of the late Achille Ratti was halted.

MARA DISSEGNA

Anti-Semitism in Universities and Schools in Romania and Hungary (1920-1938)

This study originated from a curiosity to combine two «stories» which are in themselves very different from one another but, at the same time, offer snapshots of the same historical period. The two sources taken into consideration here are the American Jewish Yearbook (AJY) and the documents of the Secret Vatican Archive. The historical period under analysis extends through the first forty years of the twentieth Century but with a different extension: the volumes of AJY analysed here run from 1899 to 1945, while the Vatican documents are collocated between 1920 and 1938. If we consider the range of this work as well as the situation of Hungary and Romania, the temporal period goes from the Treaty of Trianon to the beginning of 1938 (the limit, as I write, for consultation of Vatican documentation). This essay is a sort of «historical laboratory». My intention was to study the process of the promulgation of anti-Jewish laws in the educational system of these southeastern European countries, in particular within their university systems. With regard to this point, the AJY and the Vatican documentation represent two different lenses through which one can observe this microcosm. The first lens will be the Vatican, which after the Treaty of Trianon begins to have diplomatic relations with these two countries. For this purpose, the first nuncio, and their staff, are nominated for these countries and, in this situation, are privileged observers for our purposes. The drafting of the AJY will serve as my second lens, presenting a longer, more distant view provided by different conformation channels.

Some observations are necessary before presenting and analyzing these different sources. First of all, the nature of the sources: the American source is edited while the second is an archival source. When considering the *author* of the text, the Yearbook is signed by a group of people who work at drafting the review while the Vatican documents are written by a single person, the nuncio or another individual of the Vatican hierarchy. In any case, the latter is a person from within the inner circle of both the diplomatic world and the Catholic Church.

The environment of the authors is very different: in the first case, we are dealing with the world of the press and the publishing industry, in the second the world of the Church and diplomacy. It is necessary, then, to observe the motivations that form the basis of this writing. The creation of the AJY was linked to the development of the Jewish-American community and almost represents a degree of self-consciousness and acquaintance with its potential with regard to American society and international Judaism. The different texts cover general questions about the Jewish world in all aspects of daily life, American and worldwide, without particular geographical or temporal borders. In every volume of the AJY there is a « review of the year», where it is possible to read a summary of all the events of the year that have to do with the Jewish world. In the case of the ASV, the documents are built through and for the diplomatic channels of the Vatican. They are edited by individuals holding diplomatic offices who live immersed in their (self-described) environments. They are almost like aliens that observe and describe what happens around them. They try to enter into the mechanism of power plays and, if it necessary, to influence events according to a logic that is partly inherent to these realities and partly improvised. Unlike the drafting of the AJY, the Vatican writer describes a contemporary world, either personally or through his staff of people, who are religious or Catholic believers.The American editorial staff has indirect knowledge of events because all the writers live in the United States and have no direct contact with the realities that they describe. As such they represent a sort of sounding board for the perception that American Judaism has about worldwide events. While AJY and their writers are ascribable within a defined and declared context, for the diplomatic documents the perception, and of course the description, of the environment around is strongly influenced by the observer and the writer. This implies that it would be necessary to have a deeper knowledge of the process of creation of a single nuncio and about the educational process through which the Vatican creates its diplomatic network. Knowledge of the building process of these nuncios would perhaps be useful in order to understand the individual personalities of these people as well as their capacity to observe and understand their surrounding environment. At the same time, it would be very important to understand the mechanisms underlying the political choices relative to the destination of every nuncio and the rotation of personnel among different positions[1].

---

[1] P. LEVILLAIN, s.v. *Nonciature*, in P. LEVILLAIN, *Dictionnaire historique de la Papauté*, Paris 1994, s.v.

Other reflections can be made about the spatial and temporal elements of these writings. The Vatican documents were written in the time and in the place of the events, with the potential pressure of the situation, and were sent shortly thereafter to Rome. The AJY had a longer editorial process with a fixed end-time that coincided with its annual publication. With regard to the message and circulation of this information, the AJY was edited (it would be interesting to know its diffusion and influence), sold and read, before and after events, by people of totally different backgrounds, while the Vatican documents were written with a clear idea of who was the receiver, how the message had to be written and very often with the hope of a response within a short time. The writer of these papers was almost positive that they would not be distributed. This situation was connected with the sense of responsibility of the writer: for the AJY it was primarily deontological, for the nuncio it was not. He is the most external gear of a complex mechanism, and can create negative effects on subsequent events in the same environment through his behavior.

The two countries chosen as examples, represent very different realities born from the treaties at the end of WWI and, in the case in question, from the Treaty of Trianon; they maintain an opposite point of view with respect to this treaty. Thus, we have two different realities representing two different economic, social and political development systems with strong past influences from the historical context before WWI[2]. These two countries belong to different international spheres. This is reflected in the way they participate in international life. From their founding until WWII, Romania and Hungary had to deal with one of the most important problems of the first half of the twentieth Century: the relationship between the State and the national minorities living within its borders. With regard to this question we can consider the relationship with local Judaism, which presents very different characteristics in the two countries. This led to the development of anti-Jewish behavior, which had some characteristics typical of other countries, but was also defined by the particular national situation. As in the rest of Europe, initially movements, and then parties, on the extreme right developed with original elements serving as answers to complex local situations, and not only in terms of political loyalty to the Nazi-German system[3]. In this contest the position of the Vatican is very different and, as a result, the influence of the Catholic Church on the

---

[2] I.T. Berend and G. Ranki, *Lo sviluppo economico nell'Europa centro-orientale nel XIX e XX secolo*, Bologna 1974.

[3] R. Hilberg, *Die Vernichtung der europäischen Juden*, Frankfurt a.M. 1999[9], 794.

internal and international policies in Romania and Hungary is complicated to analyze.

The first volume of the AJY[4], was published in 1900 by the Jewish Publication Society of Philadelphia (JPS), which was founded on June 3, 1888[5]. At the end of the 19th century, the leaders of the JPS began to see the United States as the future centre of Judaism in the world. For this reason the leaders thought to begin an «educational» process within the American Jewish community. The aims of this internal process were as follows: to provide the community with a form of self-consciousness and acquaint them with its potential; at the same time, it was an external process, mainly directed to European Jewish communities and in particular those in Germany. This annual publication, which is still around today, is the result of two different traditions of yearbooks. The first is represented by the almanac, whose calendar is maintained in the AJY. This calendar is the only part written in Hebrew and indicates the Jewish festivities and some information about sunrise and sunset in relationship to different geographical areas. The German *Jahrbuch* represents the second tradition. From this model the AJY derived the idea of a publication with different academic articles about the American-Jewish world. The American editors drew inspiration from the structure of *The Jewish Year Book*, which had been edited in Great Britain since 1896 by Joseph Jacobs[6]. The aim of Jacobs was to provide facts that the community needed to know about itself so that it might plan its future intelligently. In other words, the yearbook was a basis for Jewish home education and for the self-protection of the community. Only a year after the publication of the first number of this English yearbook, the *American Hebrew*, one of the most important Jewish journals in the United States, asked the JPS to complete such a review for the American Jewish community. A few years later, this product, the AJY, became the worldwide point of view of the international Jewish communities.

The structure of the yearbook is always a matter of discussion during its preparation. Should it be a *Sammlung* of annual reports or a sort of update of fields that are thematically pre-determined. The trend is a hybrid solution: the first part of the AJY is a «Sammlung» of different

---

[4] For the history of AJY see J.D. SARNA, *The Twentieth Century Through American Jewish Eyes: A History of the American Jewish Yearbook, 1899-1999*, in *American Jewish Yearbook* [AJY] (2000), 3-146.

[5] A.A. NEUMAN, *Cyrus Adler. A Biographical Sketch*, in AJY, 42 (5701 / 1940-1941), 48.

[6] M. SULZVERGERN, *Joseph Jacobs*, in AJY, 18, (5677 / 1916-1917), 68-75.

articles, while the second part is an update on the American and international Jewish situation. More interesting for this paper is the report of the events from the month of September (the beginning of the Jewish year) to the following September, divided by countries. For the historian multiple elements of this source are important and, among others, the aim of this report is to provide future historians with some material on his/her time period. So although the report of the events is organised in a chronological order by country for some years, in most cases it is simply a text.

«Everything must have a beginning, and the beginning is necessarily imperfect»[7]. With these words the first issue of the AJY opened in September 1899. In this first volume one finds news about anti-Jewish measures in the educational system in Lueger's Vienna where there was a separation of educational paths in the school and a form of anti-Semitism at the university. One can find a similar situation in Romania where the government adopted a plan to marginalize the Jews: only 3,000 of 36,000 Jews are admitted to the public schools and this behaviour remains consistent through the course of the following year[8]. The situation of the Jews in Romania[9] is the central theme of the third volume of the AJY. There, the government, ever since 1860, had invited Jews to attend public schools so that in 1882 the Jewish students represented 15% of the total students and, in 1891, 39%. As of 1896, this trend changed because the government began to issue laws against the presence of Jews in the educational sector[10]. In the following volume, the fourth, the writer provides new elements of the difficult situation in Romania: Jewish teachers, in order to continue their activities, have to present an authorization from the local authority but of course this meant the end of their career. To complain against this situation and in general against the treatment of Jews in Romania, the

---

[7] AJY, 1, (5660/1899-1900), IX.

[8] AJY, 2, (5661/1900-1901), 24.

[9] For the history of the Romanian Jewish comunity see C. IANCU, *Les Juifs en Roumanie 1866-1919. De l'exclusion à l'émancipation*, Aix-en-Provence 1978.

[10] June 6, 1896: «Instruction in the primary grades shall be free for Rumanian only; aliens are to pay a tuition fee, and even so, they are to be received only if there are places available»; March 23, 1898: «Jews are excluded from high schools»; April 9, 1893/March 31, 1899: «Jews are banned from all professional and agricultural schools (they are admitted in commercial and art schools where the number of foreign students can't be more than the 1/5 of the total). Jewish schools are proihbited from teaching on Sunday or during Christian festivities. There is the requirement to open the schools on Saturday and during Jewish festivities. Covering one heads during lessons is prohibited»; AJY, 3 (5662/1901-1902), 75-76.

United States government sent, through the Greek Foreign minister, an official letter citing non-compliance with the Berlin Treaty[11].

The educational situation in these East European countries is described in the ninth volume. In Romanian universities, Jewish students, in general, are seen as an economic danger. The country, which was primarily agricultural, was undergoing a heavy economic crisis and the political leaders use the nationalization of the agricultural sector as an instrument to pacify the masses but in practice what occurs is an appropriation of land from Jewish landowners. The riots (beginning in March) which consequently developed are mostly against the agricultural situation and not specifically against Jews. On December 23, in Craiova, there is an attack against a meeting of Zionists and the day after some students assail the Jewish shops without any intervention of the local authorities. During the following days, there were numerous acts of violence against Jews by young Romanian people without consequences for the Romanian attackers. The general situation for Jews is described as very bad. The government repeats that all people are equal before the law but in the practice this principle is not uphold. The consequently high level of emigration reveals the need to reach international agreements in order to organise these movements of people across borders. The writer reports, in 1908, about some clashes between Jewish and Christian students in Vienna with hundreds wounded. In the same year, in August, the mayor of Jassy (Romania) prohibited the Jews from repairing their own schools due to the lack of resources and the school authorities of Botoschani forced students to buy their school books from local bookshops[12]. The description of the Jewish situation becomes increasingly problematic. In July 1909, in Jassy, Christian students become hostile toward Jewish students and at the end of 1909 the government proposes two laws against liberal professions: all Jewish physicians with a foreign degree would need an authorisation

---

[11] «This Government cannot be a tacit party to such an international wrong. It is constrained to protest against the treatment to which the Jews of Romania are subjected, not alone because Italia has unimpeachable ground to remonstrate against the resultant injury to itself, but in the name of humanity. The United States may not authoritatively appeal to the stipulations of the Treaty of Berlin, to which it was not and cannot become a signatory, but it does earnestly appeal to the principles consigned therein because they are the principles of international law and eternal justice, advocating the broad toleration which the solemn compact enjoins and standing ready to lend its moral support to the fulfilment there of by its co-signatories, for the act of Romania itself has effectively joined the United States to them as an interested party in this regard»; AJY, 4 (5663/1902-1903), 38-41.

[12] AJY, 11 (5670/1909-1910), 103-140.

from the Interior Minister to work. On February 18, 1910, M. Panu, a journalist of the «Septamana», reports anti-Semitic riots in Jassy, encouraged by the local university professors Jorga and Cuza. As an example of this atmosphere, the Romanian minister for public education and religion sends a memorandum to school inspectors on April 1, reminding them that they are required to admit students who would become rabbis to examinations[13]. On November 11, 1910, the Romanian Minister of Education proposed a law, according to which only a limited number of young people can be admitted to the Romanian universities and high schools. A few days after that, on November 25, Leon Kellner, of the University of Czernowitz, presents an appeal on the behalf of the Jewish students of Bukovina as a protest against the growing anti-Semitic trend in this province[14]. On January 19, 1912, the «Adeverul» writes about the Jewish question in relation to the process of constitutional revision and argues for the necessity of equal rights for Jews and non-Jews. As an example of this point of view, Paul Bojor, professor at the Jassy University, a day later refuses a reward from the Ministry of Education because the same reward in the past has been assigned to professor A.C. Cuza, a known anti-Semite[15]. During the month of August of the same year, the Romanian war minister abolishes the right for medicine students to stay at the university until the age of twenty-eight and postpone military service. In December, in Berlin, a delegation of Jewish students decides to establish an organization of East European Jewish university students. The Romanian situation sees no improvement and, in February 1913, the students of Bucharest University adopt a resolution opposing the equality of the Jewish students of the new Romanian territories and in May there are many clashes between Jewish and non-Jewish students. The situation is so serious that the academic authorities are obliged to take a position against the violence[16]. In July 1913 the Hungarian Low Chamber approves a law that establishes the possibility for shops to close for the Sabbath but stay open on Sunday. At the same time, in the neighbouring country, there are new conflicts between Jewish and German students at the University of Czernowitz which require the intervention of the police. During the following year, in February 1914, professor Cuza in Jassy initiates a propaganda campaign with the aim of creating a pogrom. In the same month, on the 20th, France adopts a law

---

[13] AJY, 12 (5671/1910-1911), 99-218.
[14] AJY, 13 (5672/1911-1912), 129-204.
[15] AJY, 14 (5673/1912-1913), 116-195.
[16] AJY, 15 (5674/1913-1914), 129-204.

that keeps foreign physicians without a French degree in medicine from competing for a post. In Romania, the national-liberals report a proposal for a law that would limit the presence of Jews that are not Romanian citizens in the public administration and schools. In this last sector, the government introduces new schoolbooks with anti-Jewish content[17]. On July 3, 1914, Romanian soldiers and a group of students assail Jews in Botoshani, and other citizens try to defend them. After some days, on July 17 the Hungarian prince Esterhazy grants the local Jewish community a part of the territory for building a new school[18]. At this point an international catastrophe explodes: the First World War. The attention of the editorial staff is, at this time, totally concentrated on the war aspects and only in a few cases is news about the educational sector provided. An example is what happened in Bucharest, on June 1, 1915, where A.P. Cuza, professor at the local university, dismisses the manager for a student-home because he admitted a Jewish girl. The girl was expelled and the other students, that tolerated the girl in the home, were reprimanded[19].

With the return to a formal situation of peace, the AJY's editorial staff again consider the daily conditions for Jews in the different countries and therefore the educational sector as well. On June 14, 1918 the Jewish students from Galicia are expelled from the medicine faculty of Vienna with the excuse of a lack of accommodations. In the autumn, on November 15, the deputy of Czernowitz, Benno Straucher, portrays the difficult situation for the Austro-Hungarian Jews in a report before the Reichsrat. He presents many questions but the most important are the recognition of a Jewish nationality and the right to educate children according to Jewish tradition. A month later in Romania, a new flow of protests against Jews develops and many of those involved are active professors at the University of Bucharest. In this case, on December 27, the Gymnasium of Braila, in Romania, blocks the admission of Jewish students and other schools follow this example. «Local born» Jews petition the Ministry of Education to no avail. In April 1919 the National Jewish Council of Bukowina sends a petition to the Prime Minister with many requests for the Jewish educational system. The following month all the schools in Bessarabia are closed with the justification that the lessons are in Hebrew and not in Romanian[20]. On August 9, the press association in Budapest reports that two

---

[17] AJY, 16 (5675/1914-1915), 128-204.
[18] AJY, 17 (5676/1915-1916), 199 ss.
[19] AJY, 18 (5677/1916-1917), 80 ss.
[20] AJY, 21 (5680/1919-1920), 169-170.

hundred students are terrorising the city and assailing ex-communist military members and Jews. After a few days, on the 22nd, new violence breaks out at the university of Budapest, where fifteen students were attacked and others were insulted. The police stops all violence and anti-Jewish riots. Nevertheless, the protest of the students against the Jews continues and the Jewish professors refuse to teach until Jewish students are banned from the university. At the same time, the Chief Rabbi, Dr. Hevesy, writes a memorandum to the English mission in Hungary to denounce the situation of the Jewish community, particularly the Jewish students after the end of the Bela Kuhn government. In some areas of the Hungarian countries, «white terror» officers incite the population against Jews. For these reasons, the Rabbi asks the protection of the English. In October, the Minister of Culture decides, following the wishes of the Christian-socialist students, to close the university so that Jewish students are unable to present themselves for exams. The premier expresses his satisfaction over the creation of a department of Jewish affairs in the Ministry of Education. In January 1920, at the University of Budapest, Christian students, who oppose the right for Jewish students to take exams, assail thirty students. At the same time and always in Budapest, the expulsion and internment of Galician Jews begins and the first train leaves the city with almost seven hundred people. Given these conditions, on February 6, the Jews of the Hungarian capital collect four million croons to open a Jewish university. The hospital of Budapest opens its doors to the many Jewish medicine students expelled from the university. Only on March 8 does the university of Budapest definitively close its doors to Jewish students. During the following months the situation begins to be very difficult for Jewish professors and lectors as well. Due to continuing boycotting from Christian students, the rector of the university asks to the Jewish professors and lectors to protract their absence period. Many of these present their resignations. According to the journal «Vilag» the number of Jewish students enrolled at the university of Budapest is extremely low, meaning that many young Jews had decided to attend foreign universities. Another journal, «Pesti Naplo», reports that Hungary finances the study abroad with a negative impact on its national financial situation[21]. On September 7, 1920, the Hungarian minister of Education proposes that parliament reduce the number of Jewish students admitted to Hungarian universities and the national council votes – 57 against 3 – for the restriction of admissions on the 27th of the same month. Almost one month later, on October 16, Jewish students are

---

[21] AJY, 22 (5681/1920-1921), 131-133.

attacked by some colleagues despite the appeal of the academic authorities. In Austria, as well as in France in almost the same period, on October 30, the University of Vienna decides to issue medical degrees only to foreign students who renounce to work as physicians in Austria. In Hungary, 18,000 Jewish students at the University of Budapest apply for admission to the Department of Medicine but, of all these, only 214 are accepted and 140 are young Jews which converted to Christianity before admission. Protests come from the protestant church against this new position of the Hungarian government against the Jews in the schools and universities. Riots against Jews go on at the university, on the streets and in the cafés of Budapest. On November 19 the Hungarian Minister of Education declares that he is strongly against allowing Jews to enter the university or the high school. On the occasion of the ratification of the treaty of peace, on December 3, new anti-Jewish riots explode in many Hungarian towns. At the same time, the Romanian government implements new regulations on the non-Romanian schools: the lessons have to be in the Romanian language; Romanian language, literature, history and geography have to be taught by Romanian teachers and the admitted students have to pass an exam in Romanian by Romanian teachers. At the end of December, new anti-Jewish riots develop at the University of Budapest. Beginning March 11, 1921, Jewish students are banned from art schools so the Jewish academy opens a new section for painting and sculpture[22].

In the following volumes, the review of the year analyses many individual aspects of Jewish life, and is not as a simple chronology. The editorial staff notes that, in many countries, the use of Hebrew as a teaching language is not tolerated, even in private Jewish schools. In any case, the experience of war, on the other hand, has been an incentive for the creation of educational institutions for the Yiddish language, institutions for technical training, and other high schools such as those of Berlin, the Institute for Jewish Economic Research and the Polish Jewish People's University «Tarbuth». All of which are part of the important issue of the rights of ethnic and national minorities, in particular in East European countries. The following section of this volume considers the theme of «anti-Semitism» in many sectors of daily life. For the educational part, many descriptions are provided. In this sector, Romania, has guaranteed financial support for the Jewish schools only at the end of the year causing great difficulties for these institutions. During the 1920s the feeling of anti-Semitism has begun to circulate within intellectual circles and in many European universi-

---

[22] AJY, 23 (5682, 1921-1922), 112-115.

ties so that the authorities are required to intervene. Within the field and practice of medicine the differentiation between Jewish students and Jewish physicians and gentile students/physicians begins to be increasingly frequent. Discrimination also begins to be introduced in the new generation through the organization of school life. In Hungary, the Minister of Education expels two professors from the local university and around the end of 1921 the educational commission of the government advises the parliament to dismiss Jewish teachers from schools with a majority of Christian students. According to this trend, many professors of the technical schools are transferred without an indication of the new school or without a subject to teach. This situation is common in Romania, particularly for Czernowitz and other towns of Bukowina, where many teachers are expelled. The measures are taken not only in relation to the teaching staff but also the students. The Hungarian educational law reintroduces the old Tsarist discrimination law according to which only a fixed percentage of Jewish students has access to high schools. In a short time this information becomes public worldwide and the League of Nations refuses the admission of Hungary to its international organization unless it withdrawls[23]. In the following volume the editorial staff reports the admission of Hungary (to the League) on September 4, 1922. On this occasion Count Banffy assures that minorities will be considered equally and the educational law of 1920, in particular the numerus clausus (n.c.), will be interpreted in the most liberal way. The commissioner of the League writes in her report that this admission has, as its aim, the safeguarding of the rights of minorities, in particular in Hungary, and the Hungarian government communicates that the number of applications of Jews is greater than the percentage of the Jewish population in Hungary. The League sends a special commission to observe the modalities of the application of the law of 1920 (n.c.). On September 30, 1922 this commission asks the Hungarian government to supply more information so that they can form an opinion.

In the report on the period from 1922-1923, the editors of the AJY carefully comment on the situation of Jews and observe how religious issues influence educational ones. In some cases, children are exempted from school or simple writing during the Sabbath. But in this period another question is connected with Jewish life: the demand for Jewish cadavers for educational programs in the medicine departments in some countries, amongst others Romania. The anti-Semitic students know there is strong opposition from Orthodox Judaism, so they strongly request it to the authorities. Again in

---

[23] AJY, 24 (5683/1922-1923), 43.

the sector of education, the writer observes the serious financial situation of the educational system in Eastern Europe. There are some international associations that try to help but that is not sufficient. The question of whether Yiddish is used in schools is important. The Romanian education Minister decides that Romanian is the only teaching language admitted in the schools of Bessarabia and the Yiddish schools, despite public liberal opposition, have to be closed. In Hungary Prime minister Bethlen declares that the government will continue with a Christian policy but won't admit anti-Jewish excesses. On the first days of school, the students of the technical high school of Budapest try to hinder Jewish students form attending lessons. The Christian students argue that after the introduction of the n.c., the same number of Jews are employed in Hungarian factories. The explanation of this situation is that the non-admitted students have been financed by the state to study abroad but after their degree they return to their homeland and work in high-level positions of the Hungarian financila sector. So, the application of the n.c. has no effects. The government answers with the closure of the school but the protest movement expands its power to other schools and universities. The students ask, after the limitation of the n.c. of 1920, for a limitation in the recognition of foreign degrees. This question was discussed in parliament and the final vote (83 against 38) on January 23, 1923 maintained the regulation of the Jewish presence in Hungarian universities. In Romania there is also a development of riots in the universities. On December 9, 1922, a delegation of Jewish students presents the Romanian king with a request for a direct intervention against the anti-Jewish violence in the universities. At the same time this problem is presented in parliament. The government prohibits all mass meetings and appoints some inspectors for the schools and universities to maintain order. All this is insufficient and the riots result in the closure of the universities; they are re-opened on January 22, 1923. In this case the government promises that the Jewish students won't be subject to violence but the first riots develop in a very short time in Jassy. The government decides to close the Department of Medicine of the University of Jassy and, on March 15, 1923, opens all universities and asks the Jewish students not to attend the lessons in the department of Medicine because there is a lack of cadavers for educational use. At the end of March new riots develop in Bucharest and the intervention of the police is necessary[24].

With regard to the situation in Romania, the editors report an official protest from the Zionist organisation of Transylvania: the Jewish students are not exempt from writing during the Sabbath and other Jewish festivities.

---

[24] AJY, 25 (5684/1923-1924), 23-25.

In Bessarabia there are actions against the inspectors because they oblige the Jewish private schools to close on Sundays and work on Saturdays. The Romanian Minister of Education permits Jewish children to attend the Heradim at the age of seven but they must then attend the public schools where the Romanian language is mandatory. In the universities the situation become worse everyday and the violence of Christian medical students against Jewish colleagues continues. The decree of the educational system and the obligation for minorities to study Romanian history, language and geography, provokes a great fuss within the provinces. At the same time, the League of Nations discusses the legitimacy of the n.c. in Hungary and there is a proposal to open, without pre-exams, the doors of the university to all students who come from a country that is a member of the League. The question of tlanguage in Romanian schools becomes a great problem because Jews are a religious and not an ethnic minority so the Jewish schools are required to use the Romanian language. The idea that underlies these measures is a form of «nationalisation» of the new provinces. With regard to the use of the mother tongue for minorities, a new decree in Hungary declares that in public schools it can be used if there is a request from at least forty students. In Romania, following the request to the King from the Jewish delegation of students, the King and later the metropolitan Primate denounced the anti-Jewish movement in the country in the summer of 1923.

With regard to the general situation in the universities, implementation of the n.c. admission permissions is considered in many of these countries but the only country which formally applies this norm is Hungary, where the liberals had tried many times to repeal it. In Romania, the king declares that is impossible to limit admissions to university for Jewish students, as requested by some students of Jassy and Cluy. So on February 14 some students enter the department of medicine in Bucharest and carry their Jewish colleagues out of the rooms. In Transylvania, in Cluj, the situation is so dire that the government in March 1924 decides to close the medical institute. Nevertheless there is a Romanian opposition to these measures: the congress of academics in Jassy expresses its opposition to the n.c. during 1923 but not everybody agrees with them and professor Cuza, ex-rector of the university of Jassy and leader of the Romanian anti-Semites, is an example. Deputy Simionescu speaks before Parliament about the anti-Semitic movements arguing that «the students are a tool in the hands of anti-Semites who desires to become Romanian Mussolinis»[25]. The riots

---

[25] AJY, 26 (5685/1925-1926), 98.

of the anti-Semitic students pro n.c. continue in many Romanian cities (Bucharest, Czernowitz, Cluj the most important)[26].

In the next volumes (1924-1925) the Romanian minister of education issues a decree that permits Jewish children to observe the Sabbath in the schools where a Jewish majority is present. With regard to the issue of the use of Jewish cadavers in laboratories of medicine departments, a solution is not found and the question remains open both in Romania and Hungary. In 1924 the Hungarian minister of education, Klevelsberg, declares that a department of medicine is not allowed to ban Jewish students with the justification that the Jewish community does not find enough cadavers for the educational activities of the department. During this year the Romanian Minister for Education declares before parliament that no minority schools can be maintained for Jews because they have only one language and so attending the public Romanian schools is the only solution. After this declaration, the Jewish community presents a written protest against the suppression of their Jewish educational system for children. In Hungary, Cardinal Csernoch openly expresses his opposition to the anti-Semitic excesses and explicitly condemns any support of these movements by the Christian Church. For the cardinal, this is all impossible because it means considering Jews not only Christian but not human too. The Romanian Ambassador to the United States reiterates the will of his government to stop and eliminate the different forms of excesses against the Jewish community. But in reality the activity of different anti-Semitic organizations continues. In Romania some students have been organised in «educational groups» with the aim of spread anti-Semitic ideas in the country. During this year anti-Semitism in the university is always present with the opposition of the liberal forces, in particular during the spring of 1924 at the universities of Czernowitz, Bucharest, Jassy, Cluj and Oradea Mare (to list the most important). In December, during the anniversary of the student movement, new riots against Jewish students and professors develop in Romanian universities to the extent that the issue arrives in Parliament, where the minister for the education is accused of encouraging riots. On February 12 the anti-Semitic students declare a strike at the University of Bucharest without success[27]. The editors provide a description of the event that can be very useful as an example. During the riots in Jassy the Head of Police arrests some students, one of whom assails the policeman and accuses him of illegal arrest. On October 26, 1924, there is a trial for these students. When the council come sout of

---

[26] *Ibidem*, 21-24.
[27] AYJ, 27 (5686/1925-1926), 85.

court, Zelea Codreanu, one of the witness for the prosecution, shoots to the Head of Police and injuries two other policemen. Codreanu and other four students are arrested and as a consequence a demonstration develops with slogans such as «death to the Jews!» or «this is the end for those opposing the movement!». Many other manifestations take place in other universities in support of this anti-Semitic movement. The government does not take any position on them. The academic senate discusses the situation in plenum and professor Cuza explains that the events would be justified by necessity. On response other professors ask for the resignation of Cuza and the assembly approves a document requesting the official resignation of Cuza. The Romanian government denies the request from the students of a n.c. and seeks other ways to limit the admission of Jewish students to the university. The School of Medicine of the University of Bucharest for the next academic year refuses the admission of 250 Jewish students out of 450 applicants. Stating that there is a lack of funds for laboratories. In the same vein, at the beginning of 1925, the Minister of Education proposes a new law in parliament. This law introduces a new admission exam on Romanian literature, history and geography which is opposed by Hungarian and German minorities. After that a memorandum of the minister to the school inspectors suggests giving preference to the Christian students for the admission. In Hungary the National Assembly refuses to withdraw the Education Law of 1920, typically known as the Law of n.c. Following the position of the League of the Nations, the Joint Foreign Committee directly appealed this law to the International Permanent Court of Justice. Another incident occurred in Oedenburg, at the Hungarian geological school, where the students refused to sit down in the same class with two admitted Jewish students. The strike expands to other universities where students call for expulsion of these two students. This fact reaches the National Assembly where the Minister of Education decides in favor of legal action against the professors who caused this riot. In Romania there are some riots, in particular in Targumeres, where the students force a young housekeeper to publicly denounce her Jewish employers for attempted ritual murder. As a consequence, panic explodes and riots against the Jewish community take place the day after, on May 22, 1924. Other riots take place during the Romanian trial against John Motza and the five students who tried to murder one Jewish editor, Rosenthal, (for whose murder they will only receive a financial penalty) and a banker, Aristide Blank. To combat the numerous anti-Semitic riots, the Romanian government establishes martial law in the universities during the first part of 1924. Meanwhile a secret anti-Semitic student fascist group, which is planning the murder of many Jews, is discovered in the Danube Kingdom. At the same time some professors of the universities of Bucharest and Czernowitz are arrested with charges of cooperating with the anti-Semitic student riots. Finally professor Cuza presents his resigation[28].

The Romanian government sets the day for the admission exams to Romanian universities on the day of the Jewish New Year. The Jewish community tries to protest without success. The question of allowing Jewish childre abstain from writing during the Sabbath remains open. In 1925, the senator and rabbi Zirelsohn denounces that the memorandum of the Minister of the Education to Parliament, stating that the provision is not respected in practice and that many children are forced to write during the Sabbath. With regard to the issue of Jewish cadavers for the laboratories of medicine departments, the Romanian senate approves a law stating that the number Jewish students admitted to the department of medicine will be approved in proportion to the number of cadavers that the Jewish community can provide. This of course represents a violation of the right to education for Jewish people. For children, who attend private Jewish schools, there is the problem that their diplomas from these schools are not regarded as equivalent to those of public schools. The Romanian Minister of Foreign Affairs, Mr. Duca, declares, in Geneva, that Romanian anti-Semitism is a product of some university circles and that the government is doing its best to fight the problem. A report issued from Budapest speaks of an attempt to organize an international anti-Semitic conference. On October 3, 1925 a secret meeting takes palce between three Hungarian leaders (among them the deputy Eckhardt), nine foreign and some Romanians (professor Cuza aas well). The content of this meeting was published casuing serious problems for the National Assembly. During the meeting, Mr. Cuza declares that the anti-Jewish measure should be tested in Romania and then, if successful, exported to all of Europe.

The question around the n.c. in Hungary reaches the International Permanent Court of Justice because it was feared that the Hungarian n.c. might become a model for other countries. Legal advice is asked and the Brazilian delegate, Mello Franco, on December 12, 1925 presents this advice before the Council of the League. For Mello the n.c. represents a legitimate temporary measure that is linked to the situation. If the situation were to change, the measure would have no more reason to exist and would be repealed. According to this argument, Mello suggests not taking any measures against Hungary and waiting for new conditions to arise in

---

[28] *Ibidem.*

the country and for the Hungarian government to withdraw the law. The Hungarian Minister of Education, count Klebelsberg, does not defend the n.c. as a legal principle but totally supports the point of view of Mello. In Romania, in 1925, there are some riots against the Jews in Bucharest and other cities and according to professor Aulanrd in Paris, a n.c. does not officialy exist in Romania but the violence against Jewish students gives the impression that in practice it exists. With regard to the trial against the students of Jassy and the murder of the policeman, Codreanu is arrested. The anti-Semitic students asked for his liberation and the government delays in punishing him. The trial is transferred from Jassy to Focshani and then to Turn-Severin where Codreanu pleads not-guilty[29].

During the year 1920, the Hungarian government decides a census of the population, including the Jewish population but the results are published only during that year. According to this census, Jews represent 5.9% of the population but they mostly live in the cities. 45% of all the Hungarian Jews live in Budapest[30]. For the university system, there are two different universities: Budapest, Debrecem and, before World War I, Szeged and Pecs. The latter is known as a «refugee university» and is shortly re-incorporated within the new borders of Hungary. From census data, it is interesting to note that the enforcement of the n.c. effectively decimated the number of Jewish students admitted to university. By analysing the distribution of preferences between the different departments one can see that, in the first place, medicine, law, and the polytechnic department show up often even if admission to the department of medicine has been diminished by the n.c. while in the sector of professional education the Jewish presence is strong for the agricultural, industrial and trade sectors. The n.c. doesn't touch this type of school. It is interesting to note the range of illiteracy among the population and in the Jewish community. In the sector of higher education, Jewish presence goes from 36.4% to 13.4% after the n.c. The impact of the legal advice presented before the Council of the League of Nations causes numerous protests from the Jewish Hungarian community. During the summer of 1926 the government decides that the quota of admitted Jewish students for each year would not be calculated on the basis of the number of the Jewish students present in the universities, but rather the government would reserve a fixed amount of places for students of declared Jewish faith; for the year 1927 this number is 190.

---

[29] AJY, 28 (5687/1926-1927), 23-25.
[30] Statistical data are regularly published by the yearbook.

In 1926, a commission is established in Czernowitz to examine the high school students with regard to their continuing education at university and of 257 students, 218 are rejected. The majority of these are Ukranian, German and Jewish students (of 68 Jewish students, 51 are rejected). As consequences, riots explode and the police intervene and arrest 5 students. One of these is Davis Falik, a jew who was murdered during the trial. The murderer, as in the case of Codranu and Morarescu, was judged by another court; he was absolved and in the end seen as a hero. In December 1927, a conference organised by Cuza takes place in Jassy with 5000 anti-Semitic students, after which many riots break out in various cities. In Kishinev the bishop invites anti-Semitic students, who are in Jassy for the conference, to walk around the streets, defended by the police; they bring about damage and violence on the population and the city. Reactions to these events come within the country and abroad. New riots occur at the time of the reopening of the universities with demands for the official use of the n.c. in Romania too[31].

In the summer of 1927 Bethlen, the Hungarian Prime Minister, declares that the government will withdraw the n.c. law. Heavy protests develop in November in the universities from the anti-Semitic groups, in particular, before the discussion in parliament over the government proposal of the new law. The new system is not a n.c. system but a quota system built on categories. The first quota is for children of governmental officials, the second for children of veterans or soldiers, the third for farmer or small artisans' children, the fourth for the children of industry men and the fifth for the children of tradesmen. So Jews that habitually come from the industrial and trade sectors have great difficulty attending the university. In this way, the government formally respects its promise to the League of Nations and at the same time maintains, in practice, a form of n.c. In Romania, after June 1927, there are numerous anti-Jewish riots after the creation of the Student Christian League following the suggestion of professor Cuza. With the election of the new government all this violence is stopped. Nevertheless, in December, a meeting of Christian students in Oradea Mare in Transylvania results in anti-Hungarian and anti-Jewish violence, there and elsewhere; as a result, and after long discussions in parliament, the government decides in May 1928 to disband this association and at the same time takes a series of measures in the educational sector: re-open the Jewish schools, which were previously closed by the

---

[31] AJY, 29 (5688/1927-1928), 21-23.

Averescu government, and withdraw the exemption for Jewish children to write during the Sabbath.

In the review the editors report that numerous Hungarian Jewish-students are expelled from the student-home. This is an example of the difficult general situation that results in the emigration of many students which are required to go abroad to study.

In Romania, the position of the government against anti-Jewish violence is weak. In November the minister of education in parliament defends the idea of the introduction of the n.c. for the university. As a resulte strong riots develop in the universities of Cluj, Timisoara, Maresti, Bucharest and in particular in Jassy, following the rejection of the n.c. by the academic authorities. All this has a heavy influence on the entire society[32].

The relationship between Romania and France with regard to the university sector is very interesting, especially in this period. In 1853, prince Barbu Stirbey decided to reorganise the national healthcare and educational healthcare system in Romania with the support of France. For this purpose, this Western country opens the doors of its Department of Medicine in Paris, than through France, to all Romanian young people, which are studying medicine. The number of Romanian students in France before WWI is not much higher after the war due to the increase of anti-Semitism during the Danube monarchy; this presence increases and the number of Romanian students increasingly coincides with the number of Jewish Romanian students. In this period the scarcity of employment and the increase in the presence of foreign students often results in anti-Semitic episodes as well. The situation in France is so bad that the Jewish immigration commission in France publicly suggests to foreign Jews not come there. In June 1931 it is officially communicated that, in the future, Romanian students in French Departments of Medicine would not receive, at the end of their studies as in the past, the certification necessary to work in France. Instead, they would have to pass the medical exam given to any foreigner who come to France to practice medicine[33]. This is of course a political measure against the Romanian students and in particular the Jewish Romanian students. Romanian medical students are the only for-

---

[32] AJY, 32 (5691/1930-1931), 57-58.

[33] See too D. EVLETH, *The «Romanian Privilege» in French Medicine and Anti-Semitism*, in «Social History of Medicine», XI, 2, 213-232, G. VITALE, *La svastica e l'arcangelo. Nazionalismo e antisemitismo in Romania tra le due guerre mondiali*, Rimini 2000, 46 e H. NAHUM, *La Médecine Française et les Juifs 1930-1945*, Paris 2006, 56-71; Archive of Centre de documentation juive contemporaine of Paris.

eign students that, for the purposes of the diplomatic relationship between the two countries, are exempted from the admission exam to departments of medicine (this was known as «Romanian privilege»). For this reason many of them study in France and, particularly the Jews, don't go back to Romania after their degree primarily because of the anti-Semitic problems in their home country.

The situation in the universities in Hungary continues to be dire. In November some newspapers ask for the implementation of the war law against violence in the universities. The minister of the education speaks of an «alarming» number of Jewish students in the university. The Jews, after the census, represent 6% of the population but in the university they make up between 10 and 55% of the students admitted across the different departments. To illustrate the severity of the situation, I present the following incident. In March 1929 a Jewish student paid an official of the university to be admitted to the department. The official asked for Catholic baptism certificate for the boy, who knew nothing of all this. Two years later, the student discovered everything and asks the court to invalid the baptism[34].

On August 15, 1933 one of the staff members of the Romanian Minister of Education denies that a n.c. will be introduced in the Romanian universities. Admission to the university will be regulated by the laboratories. The opening date of the new academic year, the Department of Medicine of Budapest University only admits 6 out of 60 Jewish applicants. The total number of admitted non-Jews is 155. On November 9, King Carol, during a visit to the university dormitories in Jassy before the re-opening of the local university, declares his disapproval of the position of the anti-Semitic students. After a few days, on November 15, the students of the university of Debrecem, which is closed for anti-Semitic demonstrations, organize a strike and one week later 130 of these students are arrested. On November 21, some student organisations in Budapest threaten to strike the government unless some of their requests are respected. Firstly they ask for a n.c. for Jewish students, and secondly a limit on the concession of working licences for Jews that had studied abroad; thirdly they request strong control over Jewish immigration into Hungary and lastly a limitation on licences given to Jewish artisans. In Bucharest, during an interview with the deputy Michal Landau, Jon Inculetz, Minister of Interior of Duca's government, declares that the Romanian government would not tolerate new manifestations of anti-Semitism. The day after the Hungar-

---

[34] AJY, 33 (5692/1931-1932), 23-24.

ian minister for education publishes statistics stating that Jewish students constitute 9.5% of the the student population of the university. He then refuses requests from the anti-Semitic group for more restrictions against Jewish students. After some days, due to the numerous anti-Jewish riots, the government closes Budapest University. In Romania, the Iron Guard is the cause of some riots and the Romanian government takes a strong position against it. At the end of November, the anti-Semitic students issue an ultimatum that forces the government to re-open the closed universities. On December 11, the Hungarian Minister of Education reveals the existence of a secret agreement between the government and anti-Jewish student organizations, stating that the government would limit the number of Jewish students admitted at universities so the organizations won't organise new riots. Nevertheless the riots go on and, as a result, the government decides, on December 13, to close the polytechnic institute and the universities. In January 1934, the riots against the Jewish students continue and some rectors ask for help from the government. For the following five months the difficulties for the Jewish students are constant[35]. News from France reports hostilities against foreigners where, on January 31 1935, a strike begins in the technical schools of Paris and then spreads to the Department of Medicine. The hostility is not against the students who study in Paris but against those who decide to remain after their degree. Of these people the Jews from Eastern European countries represent the majority; they are forced to emigrate due the introduction of the n.c. in their countries. In Hungary there are reports that Rudolpf Ruppert, the Catholic deputy, comes under heavy criticism for requesting the repeal of the n.c. law of 1920. In April new riots develop in the University of Bucharest. The university remains closed for 6 days, and after that a meeting of the rectors decides to give the government authorisation to maintain order in these institutions. As of May 1, 1935 students in Romanian universities have to declare their ethnic origin in order to correctly apply for the quota system[36].

On November 21, 1935 the anti-Jewish students organise a demonstration at the University of Budapest and 32 of them are imprisoned. Emericana, the Catholic University Union, protests against these manifestations and prohibits his members from participating. In February 1936, a group of democratic and progressive individuals creates the Democratic Student Front with the aim of defending the University of Bucharest against new

---

[35] AJY, 36 (5695/1934-1935), 121-123.
[36] AJY, 37 (5696/1935-1936), *passim*.

riots. In the same month the Central Jewish Council in Romania is instituted with Filderman as president. The Council expresses protests the idea of a racial regime and strongly criticises the fact that, after the introduction of *numerus valachicus*, five Jewish students admitted to the Department of Medicine of Bucharest were unable to enter their classroom. So the council presents an appeal to the Romanian people: «We appeal to your conscience in these difficult times in which we are being treated with more injustice than ever before. We appeal to the sense of justice and the tradition of harmonious collaboration of all the inhabitants of the country. We appeal to your intelligence to repudiate the falsehoods spread about us and to your intelligence to repudiate the falsehoods spread about us and to denounce those who are attempting to sow discord among our people. Let us live in brotherly cooperation and let us work together for the common welfare of our country, so that we can serve the interests of Romania and protect the security of her frontiers»[37]. By means of this appeal the council tries to shed light on the fact that the anti-Semitic movement in the country is not only a student phenomena but is also the expression of a structured political organization that has great influence on the government and which can, through illegitimate means, be a danger for democracy in the country. On April 30, the court of Galatz orders the arrest of Codreanu, leader of the extreme right and of the Iron Guard, as well as of Ion Stelescu, a member of the movement, who had been in charge of organising riots during the last elections; however, on May 11 the same court withdrew the charges. During the month of June, anti-Jewish student riots continue in Bucharest and in other cities in Romania[38].

In November 1936 some anti-Semitic Hungarian students present a memorandum to the Prime minister. They ask that admission to the university follow racial criteria in order to attain a sort of cultural segregation of the Jews. They then ask for a prohibition of and an extension of the n.c. for the trade sector. The Jewish students present a report about the presence of Jews in the universities and note that this number decreases every year. On December 6, 1936, the Third Annual Conference of the Association of the Hungarian-American Jews takes place. The members have protested against the Hungarian educational system and in particular against the n.c. In February 1937 the police take action at a manifestation at the University of Pecs which began in protest of three Jewish students

---

[37] AJY, 38 (5687/1936-1937), 293.
[38] AJY, 39 (5698/1937-1938).

who had received a degree in medicine. As a result, the Minister of Education closes the University of Pecs[39].

The following year is described by the writer as the worst for the condition of the international Jewish community since the end of World War I. The «national socialism plague» and «international brigandage» enters countries such as Poland, Romania, Hungary, where difficulties for the Jewish people existed but not at the same level as NS Germany.

In March, the Hungarian Minister of Education declares that Jews can't be assimilated into the Hungarian race and Daranyi says that the Jewish question in Hungary has to be solved with a decrease of Jewish influence on Hungarian industrial, financial and cultural life. In May, the social democratic leader Karl Peyer declares that the Hungarian high school is «nazified»; that teachers encourage anti-Jewish hate. The riots in the universities are part of daily-life. On September 12, at the time of the meeting of the Romanian teachers in Czernowitz, the assembly asks that all Jewish teachers be dismissed from public schools and restricted to Jewish schools (where a Romanian professor teaches Romanian language, history and geography). As of January 4, 1938, Romanian Jewish physicians are automatically dismissed according to a memorandum of the Ministry of Health and replaced with Christian physicians. The ministry decides that all foreign degrees in medicine, obtained after 1919, are to be re-evaluated.

Before considering the point of view of the Vatican on these issues, it is important to define the position of its representatives in these countries. In the case of Hungary, the relationship with the Vatican was not formally defined by a concordat. Instead, the two powers follwed a treaty that Pius IX had established with Franz Joseph in 1855[40]. With regard to this point, the Primate of Hungary, Seredi, was very skeptical about signing such an agreement between Hungary and the Vatican of Pius XI[41].

Romania was the country that had inherited the Eastern Orthodox Church and, since the Middle ages, had been the homeland of orthodox faith in Southeastern Europe. A concordat with this country represented

---

[39] AJY, 40 (5699/1938-1939).
[40] A. MERCATI, *Raccolta di concordati su materie ecclesiastiche tra la Santa Sede e le autorità civili*, I, Città del Vaticano 1954², vol. I, 821-829.
[41] A. CSIZMADIA, *Rechtliche Beziehungen von Staat und Kirche in Ungarn vor 1944*, Budapest 1971, 19.

the first time the Vatican formed a treaty with a country with a non-Catholic majority[42].

The treaties at the end of WWI modify the borders of southeastern Europe and new states enter into the international communities of countries. Like other states, the Vatican also opens new diplomatic seats in the form of nunciatures, sending influential individuals to establish these diplomatic channels.

In the nunciature of Budapest[43] one can find individuals such as Lorenzo Schioppa and Cesare Orsenigo while in Bucharest[44] there was Francesco Marmaggi, Angelo Dolci and Andrea Cassulo. In Romania, the indications for the opening of this nunciature are interesting to understand the behaviour of the nuncio[45]. The most important goal is the drafting of a concordat with the Kingdom. In this country, the orthodox church is the state church and its hierarch is a member of the parliament, according to the Romanian constitution. So the scope of the concordat would be to give a relevant place to the Catholic Church in the local political arena. In the specifications for Dolci[46], the nuncio in Bucharest after Marmaggi, the most important question that is raised is the balance of power between the Orthodox hierarchy and the general communal life of different Christian groups[47]. In all these documents there is no mention of the Jewish question.

The first Vatican document[48] about the Jewish question bears the date of January 19, 1928. This is a report of the nuncio to Gasparri about an article that appeared in the journal «Adeverul» following the advice of an American commission for minorities which travelled for almost three months around southeastern Europe. The report of the commission is very critical about Romania. The nuncio underlines the situation of the Catholic minority but the report speaks very critically of the Jewish people and

---

[42] M. VADAN, *Le relazioni diplomatiche tra la Santa Sede e la Romania (1920-1948)*, Città del Vaticano 2001; M. DISSEGNA, *Il Concordato tra la Santa Sede e il Regno di Romania: un'introduzione*, in *Pio XI: le parole chiave. Atti del convegno internazionale*, a cura di A. GUASCO, R. PERIN, Milano 9-10 giugno 2009, Münster 2010, 361-381.

[43] G. DE MARCHI, *Le nunziature apostoliche dal 1800 al 1956,* Città del Vaticano 1957 (2006²), 255.

[44] *Ibidem*, 225-226;

[45] ACO (Archivio della Congregazione per le Chiese orientali), Prot. 3245/28, Romeni (ex Rappresentanze della S. Sede), Affari generali, f. 4.

[46] ACO, Prot. 3245/28 I, Romeni (ex Rappresentanze della S. Sede), Affari generali, f. 1.

[47] ACO, Prot. 3245/28 I, Romeni (ex Rappresentanze della S. Sede), Affari generali, ff. 6-8.

[48] AES, Romania, Pos. 45 P.O. (Continuazione), Fasc. 40, 1923-1936, prot. 4845.

about the university situation as well[49]. No responses from the State Secretary has been found amongst the consulted materials. The Jewish question comes back to the attention of the nuncio Cassulo in July 1937 when he writes to Pacelli describing travels around some Romanian provinces and the Jewish situation is described; there is no mention there of the university situation[50]. But only on December 27, 1937 does Cassullo write a report that is entirely about the Jewish Romanian community. This is motivated by the government's position which is increasingly more anti-Jewish.

«Il problema ebraico è molto grave e complesso in Romania. Venuti gli ebrei, specialmente dopo la grande guerra, in queste regioni, hanno, direi, sconfinato dalla Polonia, dalle altre parti, e si sono stabiliti in grande numero nel Maramures ed io stesso ho potuto vederli numerosissimi a Sighet, proprio sul confine, e in quegli altri centri ed anche nei villaggi, misti ai cattolici, agli ortodossi etc. Conservano ancora il loro carattere, i loro costumi e vivono per lo più a sé, trafficando in ogni maniera. Una parte poi, notevolissima di ebrei l'abitano in Bessarabia. Quella Provincia, unita al grande regno rumeno soltanto da una ventina d'anni, ha delle città che sono proprio piene di ebrei, fra le quali Chisinau, Otin. Anche a Iasi, Oradea Mare, Satu Mare etc. Sono, come ho già detto, un po' dappertutto, ma specialmente nei grandi centri industriale e commerciali. Il minor numero è tra i tedeschi, perché l'elemento tedesco sa attendere da sé agli affari commerciali e non lascia quindi che l'elemento ebreo si stabilisca e si mescoli con lui. Coll'elemento ungherese si confà maggiormente perché molti ungheresi sono anch'essi ebrei e fra essi alcuni sono molto influenti e doviziosi. Coi Rumeni l'elemento giudaico si è specialmente

---

[49] «*Il non voler fare delle leggi scolastiche eque per le minoranze* è un grave errore da parte di una Nazione che desidera trasformare gli elementi minoritari in cittadini leali. I tentativi di romanizzare i gruppi minoritari colla forza e di distruggere le loro scuole confessionali, avranno come effetto sicuro, che all'estero molti, che altrimenti sarebbero stati amici della Romania, perderanno ogni fiducia in questo paese. *Politica scolastica.* Perciò crediamo che se la Romania vuole porsi in una posizione favorevole dinnanzi agli occhi del mondo, deve permettere alle minoranze di avere le scuole a cui sono abituate: deve lasciare ad esse un'autonomia ragionevole; *riconoscere loro il diritto che si imparino le lingue delle rispettive razze, così come la lingua romena.* Il Controllo dev'essere ridotto in modo da non impedire il lavoro di coteste scuole, limitandosi ad assicurare un insegnamento privo di irredentismo. È necessario che le scuole minoritarie ottengano stabilità anche per il futuro, e siano liberate dal timore costante di poter essere chiuse. *La campagna anti-semita.* La Commissione ha constatato nella sua visita, che una mostruosa campagna di intimidazione e brutalità, è condotta contro i cittadini ebrei, e che ne è causa un insieme di superba intolleranza e di odio ignorante. A questo riguardo è assai deplorevole che la Chiesa di Stato abbia sanzionato la «Lega della difesa cristiana» (antisemita) e l'«Unione degli studenti cristiani» (antisemita), il cui programma e le cui pubblicazioni sono una vergogna per la civiltà, ed una macchia nera per il buon nome della Romania», *ibidem.*

[50] AES, Romania, POS. 108 P.O., Fasc. 115, 1936-1938, prot. 1271/37.

consolidato perché il popolo rumeno è di preferenza agricolo e quello che è nelle città e nei centri non è portato al commercio. Non è attivo e si dà piuttosto alla vita comoda, mentre le famiglie ebree sono industriose e sanno cavare il guadagno anche dal piccolo commercio. Quando il Governo ha lasciato che gli ebrei entrassero in si gran numero, ora sono circa un milione, in Rumenia, non si è reso conto, direi, del malessere e della reazione che si sarebbero poi verificati. Ora, autorità e popolazione tentano reagire perché vedono che una gran parte degli affari e del commercio gli è sfuggita di mano, ma non è facile portare alla grave disuguaglianza un efficace rimedio. Di qui, le proteste, i tentativi di boicottaggio che per ora non possono ottenere l'effetto desiderato. L'"Universul", giornale forse il più importante ha aperto la campagna e il Patriarca, il Prof. Iorga, ha scritto articoli veementi per arrestare l'influenza giudaica, e anche il Governo, benché non ufficialmente, fa conoscere la sua avversione all'elemento ebreo, tanto più che i comunisti che sono in Rumenia e gli agitatori sono per lo più soggetti che vengono al di fuori e appartengono alla stirpe giudaica. Non si può prevedere, per ora, quello che la reazione otterrà, perché si è lasciato troppo fare in passato. È certo però che l'antipatia è grande e molti viva e non poche famiglie sono state costrette a cambiare anche nome per non avere noie e attendere in pace al loro commercio. Noto ancora che, le famiglie ebree non intaccate dalle idee sovversive, antireligiose, mandano senza difficoltà i loro figli a ricevere l'educazione presso le suore nostre e presso i religiosi. Nelle scuole dei Freres, qui a Bucarest, e nei Pensionati delle Suore di Notre Dame de Sion, Bucarest, Galati, Iasi, molte alunne sono ebree»[51].

The figure of professor Iorga can't be left out. The nuncio comments of him: «Si dice nell'esposto inviatomi che il Prof. Iorga è una delle figure esponenti che combattono l'elemento giudaico in Romania. É vero, ma è pur vero che in un passato non lontano egli proteggeva gli ebrei, o almeno non era loro contrario. Il Sen. Iorga, già Presidente del Consiglio dei Ministri, è un personaggio eminente per le sue doti e specialmente per la sua erudizione storica. Più che un capo politico, è un letterato, conosciuto molto anche all'estero, specialmente a Roma, è un amico dell'Italia, e a Parigi ove tiene spesso conferenze interessantissime»[52].

The Jewish question is an issue which is increasingly important for the agenda of the government and on January 1, 1938 the nuncio writes about the new government of Cuza and Goga and describes its actions as an «atteggiamento deciso» (determined attitude) against the Jews in accordance with the «aspirazioni dei giovani studenti» (aspirations of the young stu-

---

[51] AES, Romania, POS. 108 P.O., Fasc. 116, 1936-1938, prot. 1802/37.
[52] *Ibidem.*

dents)[53]. The following reports[54] about the situation of the Jews are more interested in the situation of the converted Jews and for the first time, on January 19, 1938, Pacelli answers: «La Santa Sede segue infatti con viva attenzione tutto ciò che riguarda la vita della Romania ed è desiderosa di [continuare non solo a] conservare [ma a sviluppare sempre più]col Governo attuale le relazioni amichevoli già strette con i Governo che lo hanno preceduto»[55]. On February 14, 1938 Cassulo answers Pacelli and asks for more information about the possibility of the Cuza-Goga government maintaining power for a long period.

«Purtroppo il dubbio allora manifestato aveva qualche fondamento. I nuovi uomini chiamati dalla fiducia del Re al Governo, erano, è vero, molto bene intenzionati e, basandosi sul principio nazionale cristiano, si erano accinti a portare radicali riforme, a togliere gravi abusi, a risanare l'ambiente, ma l'atteggiamento troppo brusco relativo agli ebrei che avevano invaso, dopo la guerra, il paese, non sempre per via legale, impadronendosi delle industri importanti e meno importanti, delle professioni civili, l'avere inaugurato una politica che si allontanava dal passato, pur rimanendo fedele agli impegni assunti, pur cercando altre amicizie con tendenze opposte a quelle già acquisite, sono le cause che hanno scosso gravemente gli animi sia nell'interno del paese che all'estero. E il Governo pressato da ogni parte a dare dichiarazioni a dovuto quasi ogni giorno concedere interviste ai corrispondenti esteri dei principali giornali onde calmare le masse e spiegare quali erano le sue intenzioni. Per quanto queste dichiarazioni fatte con la migliore intenzione, facessero vedere quale era realmente il programma del nuovo Governo, in fondo nazionalista, la Romania ai Romeni, la stampa estera, spinta forse anche dall'elemento ebraico che si vedeva mettere in grave imbarazzo dalle nuove misure di epurazione, non cessava di agitare l'opinione pubblica. Anche in Rumania, il nuovo Governo, non avendo una base larga e sicura, non si sentiva appoggiato e gli altri partiti, ben più forti e sostenuti da masse importanti, si sono naturalmente, quasi in massa schierati contro il ministero che si affrettò ad indire contro il parere degli altri, le nuove elezioni onde procurarsi il favore del popolo»[56].

With regard to the situation in Hungary, the first documents about the Jewish question are two reports that the nuncio Orsenigo writes to Gasparri about the n.c. The first is dated October 15, 1926 and begins with reports on the next trip to Italy the minister who has proposed this measure wil make.

---

[53] AES, Romania, POS. 114 P.O., Fasc. 119, 1937-1938, prot. 1812/38.
[54] *Ibidem*, prot. 1883/38.
[55] *Ibidem*, prot. 181/38.
[56] *Ibidem*, prot. 2031/38.

«Verso metà novembre verrà a Roma per tenervi una conferenza, invitato dal Governo Italiano, il Ministro dei culti e dell'Istruzione, il cattolico (regalista) conte Klebelsberg; [...] Molto ferocemente fu invece attaccato il Ministro dai giudei per una certa sua disposizione scolastica, che accorda ai giudei solo un limitato numero di posti nelle scuole universitarie; e la legge sul Numerus clausus, che costringe non pochi studenti giudei ad arrestarsi alle porte dell'università. È una disposizione affatto antisemita, che noi popoli latini difficilmente possiamo concepire. Il Ministro cerca volentieri di raccogliere alte approvazioni alle sue misure disciplinari e amministrative»[57].

One year later, on October 28, 1927, Orsenigo provides information about anti-Jewish riots with classic anti-semitic arguments.

«Eminenza Reverendissima, Poiché penso che anche ai giornali esteri arriverà l'eco dell'antisemitismo, che agita in questo momento l'Ungheria, credo mio dovere inviare a Vostra Eminenza Reverendissima alcune notizie di fato e alcune considerazioni, che ritengo utile aver presenti, qualora anche i giornali cattolici credessero di interloquire; ciò che ora del resto non è consigliabile. In conseguenza alla famosa rivoluzione comunista del 1918 e 19, capitanata, come si sa, dai giudei, è rimasto fra i cristiani di Ungheria una specie di terrore antisemita, che se non è giustificabile a stretto rigore di carità cristiana, è però psicologicamente spiegabile. Siccome i Giudei qui appartengono in gran parte alle classi ricche e colte, finiscono ad occupare i migliori posti professionali, con un sopravvento che non corrisponde affatto alla loro percentuale demografica. Per arginare questo fenomeno, dal quale i cristiani pronosticano le peggiori conseguenze, fu votata nel 1920, auspice un Ministro cattolico, una legge detta del "Numerus clausus", la quale accorda agli studenti semiti solo un determinato numero di posti nelle università ungheresi, cioè solo il 6% dei posti disponibili, in conformità alla loro percentuale demografica: i Giudei infatti sono qui 474.000 ossia 5,9% della popolazione ungherese. Contro questa legge i semiti ungheresi hanno lottato ripetutamente per mezzo dei loro poderosi giornali, ma sempre invano: ora pare abbiano trovato modo di far pressione sul Governo per mezzo di qualche potente nazione straniera; pressione a cui il Governo non ha creduto di poter opporre un reciso rifiuto, in vista forse di quanto egli attende dalle potenze straniere; così che recentemente, per bocca del Presidente del Consiglio, dichiarò formalmente che il Numerus clausus sarà mitigato. – Contro questa [sic] promessa governativa si è scatenata subito una serie di proteste e di dimostrazioni studentesche in tutte le Università del Regno, e nelle varie sezioni del partito politico antisemita (cioè cristiani e cristiani cattolici). Per essere completo devo aggiungere che è difficile sapere se il Governo è del tutto estraneo a queste proteste e dimostrazioni... antigovernative: sono questi i misteri della politica, che si possono intuire, ma non documentare. I cattolici specialmente hanno preso vivissima parte a queste dimostrazioni antisemite, limitate finora a comizi incruenti e a ordini del giorno focosi. – I giornali cristiano-cattolici vi consacrano articoli

---

[57] AES, Ungheria, POS. 29 P.O., Fasc. 30, 1925-1930, IV Periodo, prot. 324, f. 98.

di fondo e larga cronaca, dichiarandosi recisamente contrari a qualsiasi miti-
gazione del "numerus clausus". Il partito politico dei cristiani sociali (che conta 22 deputati fra cattolici e protestanti) ha votato all'unanimità un ordine del
giorno in senso antisemita, e il Ministro Mons. Vass presente si è incaricato di
portarlo a cognizione del Governo. – La massa dei fedeli si mantiene tranquil-
la e quasi estranea; sebbene tutti sappiano che anche il clero, compreso l'Episcopato, sia tutto a favore della conservazione del "numerus clausus". Come
Vostra Eminenza vede, non si tratta di antisemitismo religioso, ma piuttosto di
una lotta "professionale" dei cattolici e protestanti uniti contro la superiorità
intellettuale di una minoranza, che è considerata responsabile dell'esperimen-
to sovietista in Ungheria nel 1918. Ritengo che tutto finirà tranquillamente,
perché il Governo dichiarerà di trovarsi impotente ad effettuare quanto aveva
promesso a proposito di questa legge antisemita»[58].

Gasparri received this report on November 9 but no comments have
been found about it[59]. The following reports about the Jewish situation
are more focused on the general situation of the community and they give
no news about university movements. The preoccupation of the church is
mostly over baptised Jews[60]. The description of the reaction of the Hungarian people to the new anti-Jewish decrees is interesting:

«In generale furono accolti bene, perché qui il movimento antisemita trova
una profonda corrispondenza nella mentalità attuale degli Ungheresi. Anche
gli ebrei convertiti qui sono molto in sospetto e si considerano come elementi
difficilmente amalgamabili con la razza ungherese. Ecco perché anche i nuovi
progetti di legge non considerano più come ebrei coloro che solo si converti-
rono al cristianesimo prima del 1° agosto 1919 ed i loro figli (cioè prima della
vittoria sopra il comunismo): gli altri convertitisi dopo, in ordine di applicazione di queste leggi, sono considerati come ebrei: evidentemente è un senso
di diffidenza che di loro si ha, quasi si tratti di pseudo conversioni, ed in tale
apprezzamento convegno anche molti cattolici»[61].

Rotta continues with his reports by speaking about Emericana, the association of Catholic university students, and writes that «l'Emericana
non ritiene incondizionatamente ungheresi l'ebreo battezzato ed i suoi
discendenti»[62]. The report describes the situation in general:

«La stampa liberale e democratica, in maggioranza dominata dagli ebrei, ha
fatto il viso d'armi a tali progetti, che trova non conformi allo spirito della

---

[58] AES, Ungheria, POS. 29 P.O., Fasc. 31, 1925-1930, IV Periodo , prot. 1054, f. 16-17.
[59] *Ibidem*, f. 18.
[60] AES, Ungheria, POS. 77 P.O., Fasc. 57, 1938-1940, IV Periodo, prot. 1168/38, ff. 6-9.
[61] *Ibidem*.
[62] *Ibidem*.

Costituzione ungherese ed allo stesso spirito cristiano e che sono anche un atto d'ingratitudine verso l'elemento ebraico, al quale si deve lo sviluppo ed il fiorire dell'industria e del commercio in Ungheria: detta stampa riconosce pure, per quanto a malincuore, che le circostanze rendono d'attualità il problema ebraico, ma ne reclamano una soluzione che dovrebbe essere più umana. La stampa di destra invece si mostra soddisfattissima ed incoraggia Daranyi a portare presto in porto le leggi relative e ad applicarle con energia».

And then:

«Potrebbe sembrare che dopo tutto gli ebrei non avrebbero motivo di lagnarsi per il trattamento che loro verrà fatto dalla legge, perché vi si parla della proporzione del 20%, mentre gli ebrei sono solo circa il 5% della popolazione. Bisogna però osservare che in certe branche dell'industria, del commercio, delle finanze, come in certe professioni come l'avvocatura, la medicina ecc. gli ebrei vi sono rappresentati in proporzioni molto più elevate, il 50 e 60%; posseggono poi anche stabili e fondi, comperati specialmente nel tempo difficile del dopoguerra, in misura sproporzionata al loro numero. Ciò spiega come il quoziente 20% mentre sembra insufficiente agli ebrei è d'altra parte considerato come fin troppo largo dagli altri: il Governo ha dovuto adottare una misura di mezzo per nono compromettere con salti troppo bruschi l'economia generale. Per amore della verità però bisogna dire che nell'esercito e negli impieghi pubblici la quota degli ebrei è molto bassa, al di sotto del 5%»[63].

On May 8 Pacelli answers:

«Mi sono soffermato sulla *questione ebraica* ed ho letto quanto Ella diligentemente espone in proposito, tanto più che qualche eco ne è giunta qui indipendentemente dal di Lei Rapporto. In modo particolare il giudizio *troppo generale* che si vorrebbe dare sull'insincerità delle conversioni dal giudaismo al cristianesimo avvenute dopo il 1919 sembra strano e arbitrario e in contrasto con [quello spirito di liberalità di cui ha dato tante prove cotesto Governo in questi ultimi tempi] *lo spirito di generosità del popolo ungherese*. È da augurarsi che, pur tutelando i giusti interessi della Nazione magiara, cotesto Governo non scenda a misure di eccessiva severità contro gli ebrei, e che i cattolici ungheresi facciano in questa circostanza opera di sana moderazione»[64].

There are many appeals[65] and, with Maglione as Secretary of State, this flow of requests continues without influencing the political life of the country[66].

---

[63] *Ibidem.*
[64] *Ibidem*, prot. 1476/38, f. 10.
[65] AES, Ungheria, POS. 77 P.O., Fasc. 57, 1938-1940, IV Periodo, ff. 39-42.
[66] *Ibidem*, prot. 2159/39, f. 45.

The main focus of this text is to provide observations on anti-Jewish student movements in these two countries. It represents a peculiar area in the study of anti-Semitism because, in comparison with other experiences of anti-Semitism, the importance of student movements and the educational sector is, in these countries and in particular in Romania, higher. At the same time the university sector partially internationalizes these movements.

The situation in the two countries should not be considered too similar. At the beginning of the 20th century, Romanian Jews lived in a state of very heavy crisis which became worst every year. The idea of a mono-thematic volume of the AJY about the Romanian case is significant. The report of the American Commission for the minorities is another signal of the urgent state of this situation. Some of the most important figures of the Romanian anti-Semitism come from the university sector, such as Codreanu, one of the most important leaders of the student anti-Semitic movement and later of the Iron Guard, as well as Iorga, the intellectual leader of fascism in Romania. The situation in Hungary is different. First of all, the past of this country is influenced by the experience of the Haps-burg Empire (Catholic) and the treaty of Trianon with the whole issue of lost territories (for Romania it is the opposite, the country gains new territories and at the same time is faced with the question of minorities). Hungary lives through the experience of the «Red Terror» with Bela Kuhn and that contributes to anti-Jewish feelings. The promulgation of a *numerus clausus* in 1920 needs to be understood within the general context of the general situation of this country.

The nuncios that open new apostolic delegations in these countries arrive to find difficult situations and, from some perspectives, issues that are new not only for the diplomat, but for the international community. This implies that the issue of the protection of national minorities in the countries of Southeastern Europe is particular strong. In this environment, the Jewish community can't find a clear position. Often it is seen as a national minority and in other cases as the subject of traditional anti-semitic feelings. Only during the second half of the 1930s, the question of baptized Jews begins to be seen as a question that requires the intervention of the nuncios and of the Vatican. This behaviour is in line with the findings of the research on this theme[67]. The Secretary of State, initially Pacelli and later Maglione, begins to more carefully note the drafting of anti-Jewish

---

[67] Vedi G. Miccoli, *I dilemmi e i silenzi di Pio XII. Vaticano, Seconda guerra mondiale e Shoah*, Milano 2007; R. Moro, *La Chiesa e lo sterminio degli ebrei*, Bologna 2002.

laws in many countries and the attack against converted Jews requires an intervention through diplomatic channels, i.e. the nuncios. This is only a hypothesis for these countries since the study of this area is not as reliable as in traditional western countries. With regard to the issue of anti-Semitism in the university and for the case of Hungary, the nuncio in Budapest, Orsenigo, provides information about anti-Jewish measures not in 1920, when the n.c. have been promulgated, but in 1926. In this case, no answers can be given for this period of silence. It would be interesting, for exemple, to compare the position of the nuncio Orsenigo on the Jewish situation during his mission in Budapest and that of his counterpart in Berlin.

The questions anti-Semitism in the university sector is open and particular interesting due to the influences between the different fascist movements and countries. Education is the basis for ta country's economic structure. Controlling access to education is thus a way of safeguarding against inequalities in society.

MICHAEL R. MARRUS

Pius XI and the Racial Laws:
Discussant's Comments

With the racial laws – both of Nazi Germany and Fascist Italy, we can imagine our conference Geiger counter going from «tick... tick... tick... tick... tick» to «tick/tick/tick/tick». In other words, we are entering potentially dangerous, radioactive territory, crowded with polemicists with axes and even heavy equipment to grind. My thanks to all three speakers for having not only avoided these hazards, but also for contributing so admirably to our discussion of highly charged issues. Which of course doesn't mean that they all agree with each other or that I agree with everything that everyone said. I begin these comments by asking the indulgence of my colleagues as I present three guidelines that might help to deal with this hyperactive and difficult environment.

First, to the extent possible, I think our assessments of Pius XI and his associates should be guided by the idioms, preoccupations and world views of the time and people we are studying, rather than those of the present day. This may sound obvious, even presumptuous on my part, but I do think that such perspectives are not always kept in mind, to the detriment of historical analyses. To be blunt: Achille Ratti and Eugenio Pacelli are not candidates for a B'nai B'rith human rights award, and should not be measured or understood by that standard. Rather, they need to be seen as part of a pre-Vatican II Catholic Church that cleaved to a highly supercessionist theology and a preference for authoritarianism and a reverence for its own institutional structures that were part and parcel of their age, their culture and their religious heritage. This means that their views on all kinds of issues – whether the war against Abyssinia, weapons of mass destruction of the day (that is, poison gas), fascist regimes and, need I add, Jews need to be understood in that context. Among other things this also means that we need to exercise caution when applying labels that have come to reflect our own, purportedly superior vantage point: we know how things turned out, and for the most part we prefer our own perspective to theirs.

That is why I am just a bit discomfited by Peter Kent's assessment, cited by Jacques Kornberg, that «At heart, Pacelli... was an appeaser». Perhaps, if appeasing means failing to embrace the later Ratti's militancy when faced with the blandishments of the fascist dictators; but no, if it means adopting a Chamberlain-like policy, based on tired calculations of what would satisfy Hitler and the advisability of turning the other cheek in the face of major threats such as the Anschluss with Austria or threats against Czechoslovakia, for example. As you see, I am leery of labels that reflect our *own* frustration with these clerical actors who turn out to have made what *we* now know to have been the «wrong» calculations.

My second guideline has to do with Catholic pluralism. As we try to penetrate this distant culture we also need to keep in mind that the Vatican's leadership corps of the day was much more pluralistic than often presented – doubtless not as diverse and disputatious as in our own day, but nevertheless full of men of differing views, which deserve to be explored if we want fully to understand what made this ancient institution tick, what choices various participants made, and how they responded to the crises of the day. In this regard, I tip my hat to one of our participants, Giuliana Chamedes, whose fine paper on the mid-1930s debates within the Holy Office traces not only competing factions on the subject of the Hitler and Stalinist regimes, but also outlines a current of Catholic anti-totalitarianism that found an affinity with notions of human rights – and for which, I want especially to note, was one affiliated with my own institution, the University of Toronto. I am referring to the Pontifical Institute of Medieval Studies, founded by Etienne Gilson and where one of the leading lights, up to the German invasion of France, was Jacques Maritain.

Finally, my third guideline, a word about the Holocaust. As we look at the involvement of Achille Ratti and Eugenio Pacelli with the racial laws – a subject of obvious major interest for this volume – let us not be so overwhelmed with present-day debates about the history of the destruction of European Jewry that we impute to either or both preoccupations with Jews or genocide that have been fashioned in a post-Holocaust world, rather than in the era in which they lived. There is considerable danger of distortion, I believe, in imposing our priorities and concerns over those that animated churchmen of the time.

Rather than looking at each of the three papers in turn, I would like to raise three different themes, touched upon to one degree or another by Professors Frank Coppa, Emma Fattorini, and Jacques Kornberg. My three are: first, the issue of moral choice – what has been termed, in one paper, as «ris[ing] to the occasion»; second, the relationship between Ratti and Pacelli, and third, the relationship of Jewish and racial matters in the Vatican's confrontations with Hitler and Mussolini.

Jacques Kornberg, it seems to me, is most explicit of our three presenters in declaring that both Pius XI and Pius XII failed to conduct themselves according to their own declared moral standard. «Both Pius XI and XII [were] inhibited [in] their response to moral evil». Both «abdicated their own vaunted claims to moral authority in the large space where morals and politics overlapped». This is effectively what Father John Morley wrote in 1980 about wartime Vatican diplomacy, saying that «the Vatican betrayed the ideals it set for itself». The assumption here is that there was an appropriate response to «moral evil», referred to elsewhere as a capacity to «rise to the occasion» – such rising being a thoroughgoing condemnation of «Germany's unprecedented atrocities during World War II». These men did not rise. They did not issue what Guenther Lewy once called «a flaming protest» against concrete wrongs.

Ever since encountering this charge years ago in Lewy's work, I have felt that it strikes the wrong note for historical understanding. The weight of this historical assessment is what did *not* happen and what our two popes did *not* believe, rather than an exploration of the contours of their world view. In the end, we explain what they thought and did from the standpoint of our own standards and our own moral commitments. Kornberg puts this forcefully with his charge that the Church sought a «privileged» place in society, rather than «religious pluralism, the confusion and relativism of a so-called free society which let humans loose to follow their subjective consciences». While I respect this approach, I simply do not agree with it as a guide to historical inquiry. My problem with it is that these churchmen came from a culture and a society quite different from our own. There was no «alternative», for them, of «religious pluralism», or «the confusion and relativism» of a society «which let humans loose to follow their subjective consciences». Such ideas would never have occurred to them, and it is a mistake to consider them an «alternative». Neither Ratti nor Pacelli shared our society's sense of individual liberty or our notions of a diverse society; and, even more important, people differed at the time about just what was the moral thing to do. We need to spend more time with their views, rather than explaining why popes failed to live up to our own. I think we go wrong when we set our standard as an analytic point of departure; our job, I believe, is to look as deeply as we can into those of another time and place.

As I wrote myself on this subject with regard to Pius XII: «Pacelli exemplified a profound commitment to the spiritual and pastoral mission of the Holy See... his goal was to limit the global conflict where possible and above all to protect the influence and standing of the Church as an independent voice... As Leonidas Hill reminds us, "the theology of the Church [of the day] lays far less emphasis on saving lives than on saving souls through the consolations of religion". Seeing the institutional Church as a supreme value in its own right, those in charge of its fortunes tended unhesitatingly to put these ahead of the victims of Nazism» – and also of Fascism, I might add. They did not see reason to apologize for their conduct or see themselves in contradiction to the ideals they set themselves. Nor did they consider their real-world preferences, compromises and trade-offs as anything other than the discharge of the Church's responsibility as «the guardian of morals and truth» – the God-given role of the Catholic Church in a gravely imperfect world.

This brings me to the second theme of my comment – the relationship between Ratti and Pacelli, and how we should understand the relationship between Pope and Cardinal Secretary of State, particularly in the two years or so before Ratti's death in February 1939. As I have already noted, in his focus on the Vatican's responses to atrocities Jacques Kornberg sees little difference between the two beyond, perhaps, superficial matters of style and temperament. Ratti «picked his fights with great care», and, like Pacelli, avoided risks in his pronouncements. Essentially, Pius XI «acted no differently than Pius XII in the face of genocide and atrocity» and Pius XI's response to the Italian anti-Jewish decrees was no different than Pius XII's response to the anti-Jewish decrees in France, Hungary, Croatia and Slovakia».

By the way, and just by way of speculation, I wonder whether Professor Neal Pease believes that, had he lived, *il Papa Polacco* (that is, Pius XI) would have «pressed Poland to make concessions to Hitler to avert war» as Kornberg contends. What I *can* tell this audience is that Father Peter Gumpel, the indefatigable *relator* of the cause of Pius XII on the matter of his proposed beatification, argued essentially this when Father Gerald Fogarty and I, together with a few other colleagues, heard him out on the Vatican on the subject some years ago.

Returning to our comparison, Professor Frank Coppa sees Pacelli the diplomat as sharply at odds with the mercurial and far-seeing Ratti, with the former exercising a restraining influence on the latter, at least until the issuing of *Mit brennender Sorge*, in March 1937. Thereafter, says Coppa, Pacelli worked behind the scenes to prevent a break between the Holy See and Nazi Germany. Coppa suggests that Pacelli feared to confront his superior directly on the issue of the persecution of the Jews, «lest he be fired as was his mentor», Cardinal Pietro Gasparri. Coppa admits that we do not know whether Pacelli helped delay the delivery of the draft encyclical, *Humani Generis Unitas*, to the ailing Ratti at the end of 1938 and whether the Secretary of State participated in the quest for a more conciliatory policy behind the scenes as the Pope neared the end of his life. Coppa does note that, a few days after the Pope's death on February 10, Pacelli ordered the destruction of Ratti's draft confrontationist speech roundly denouncing the fascist dictators. As I understand, apologists for Pius XII have declared that Pacelli, as *camerlengo*, was simply discharging his duties under canon law – to which Hubert Wolf has replied that, while this may indeed have been his duty during the transition to a new Pope, he certainly was at liberty to resurrect his predecessor's drafts and projects after becoming Pope himself. And of course, he never did.

I do wonder how Coppa would account for the evidence suggesting that Ratti – the «steely and imperious» Ratti, as Neal Pease refers to him – had such strong affection for his Secretary of State, and even his preference for Pacelli to succeed him as Pope.

Placing some emphasis on the Pope's progressive illness and his emotional and spiritual development, Emma Fattorini supports the claim of «clear differences» between Ratti and his Secretary of State, and concurs with the idea that the latter was inclined, toward the end of his life, to break off relations between the Vatican and the Nazi State. As I understand, Fattorini's emphasis is on Ratti's religious impulse, thwarting Pacelli's more practical preferences for diplomacy and conciliation. However in assessing the two, she also speaks of their «sostanziale complicità» and even «sostanziale sinergia». I confess I need help here. Does she mean a conscious working together? And a deliberate synergy? Or is this just the way things worked out?

Finally, I turn to the oft-debated question of the Jews. How important was the Jewish issue in the Vatican's dealing with Nazi Germany and Fascist Italy in the lead up to the Second World War? To me at least, the answer to this question depends in part on what one means by «Jewish issue». Frank Coppa is right, I believe, in underscoring the distinction between «antisemitism» and «anti-Judaism», making it plain that it was Ratti's understanding of the former, and not the latter, that so stuck in his craw when dealing with the fascist dictators. And I agree with Jacques Kornberg that «the notion of a common humanity was [fundamental] to Catholic doctrine».

Two of our papers refer to the draft encyclical *Humani Generis Unitas*, commissioned and nurtured by Ratti and rightly seen as a planned high water mark in his inclination to confrontation on the subject of antisemitism and his increasing disposition to confront Nazism, heedless of the diplomatic consequences. But as much as we are inclined to resonate with Ratti's insistence that «antisemitism is inadmissible» or that «spiritually we are Semites», I think we must also recall how this document retained so much of the Vatican's traditional disparagement of Jews as Jews, and how the clarion call that might have closed his papacy sounds what can't help to be, for us, a sour note.

To be sure, the draft insisted, there *was* a Jewish question, but this was a *religious*, and not a racial, national or territorial question. Explaining, the text then rehearsed a traditional Catholic view of the Jews: having been chosen by God to prepare the way for the coming of Christ, the Jews rejected Jesus, violently repudiated him, and, in collusion with others, put to death. Ever after, «this unhappy people [...] doomed, as it were, to perpetually wander over the face of the earth, were nonetheless never allowed to perish, but have been preserved through the ages into our own time». Having obstinately rejected Christ, the Jews showed a constant enmity toward Christianity and as a result there was a continuous tension between Jews and Christians.

Ardently hoping for their conversion, the draft continued, the Church had been attentive to the dangers that contact with the Jews could expose the souls of its followers – a concern that was certainly as urgent now as in the past. «As long as the unbelief of the Jewish people persists, as long as there is active hostility to the Christian religion, just so long must the Church use every effort to see that the effects of this unbelief and hostility are not to redound to the ruin of the faith and morals of her own members». To defend the faithful, therefore, the Church supported «energetic measures to protect both the faith and morals of her members and society itself against the corrupting influence of error...». Antisemitism, however, was the wrong way to go. Rather than eliminating the characteristics of the oppressed group, such measures only accentuated them. Those who were unjustly persecuted often became persecutors themselves, and their hatred of Christianity intensified.

What was to be done, therefore? The American priest John Lafarge and his German associate Gustav Gundlach, responsible for the draft, wanted Ratti to express a view that, particularly in view of the great diversity of circumstances in which Jews lived in various countries, policies concerning them were best left «to the powers concerned». Defensive moves, for that was what such anti-Jewish policies were, should eschew solutions that had to do with violence, force, or brutal means of coercion, and pre-

fer «measures dictated by a healthy spiritualism». There was one requirement, however: «no solution is the true solution if it contradicts the very
demanding laws of justice and charity».

Justice and charity – these words came often from the Vatican during
the fateful years of the Second World War. I read them years ago in the
September 1941 report that the French ambassador to the Holy See, Léon
Bérard, wrote to Marshal Philippe Pétain, communicating what the diplomat believed to be the Vatican's exoneration of the Vichy regime for
its anti-Jewish laws. Explaining the Vatican's opinion, Bérard noted that
the Holy See seemed unconcerned with French policies in this regard.
Nevertheless, the Church was fundamentally opposed to racist theories,
being committed to «the unity of mankind». Given that the Jews were not
merely a religious community but a people with «ethnic particularities»,
there was every reason to «limit their activity in society and ... restrict
their influence». But then came the cautionary note: whatever policies
against the Jews were adopted, these had to be applied with «justice and
charity». And so far as could be judged from this report, Vichy was thereby absolved. To be sure, the Vatican had its own conception of justice
and charity, and as historians of the papacies of both Pius XI and Pius XII
know, or should know, these concepts are not necessarily what we believe
these mean today.

Index of Names

Index of Names

Authors

SUZANNE BROWN-FLEMING, U.S. Holocaust Memorial Museum
LUCIA CECI, Università di Roma, Tor Vergata
FRANK J. COPPA, St. John's University, New York
GIULIA D'ALESSIO, Università di Roma, Sapienza
JOHN A. DAVIS, University of Connecticut
MARA DISSEGNA, Università di Modena e Reggio Emilia – John XXIII Foundation for Religious Studies, Bologna
EMMA FATTORINI, Università di Roma, Sapienza
GERALD P. FOGARTY, University of Virginia
CHARLES R. GALLAGHER, S.J., Boston College
DAVID I. KERTZER, Brown University, Providence
JACQUES KORNBERG, University of Toronto
AAPPO LAITINEN, University of Helsinki
MICHAEL MARRUS, University of Toronto
ROBERT A. MARYKS, Lehman College (CUNY)
ALBERTO MELLONI, Università di Modena e Reggio Emilia - John XXIII Foundation for Religious Studies, Bologna
MARISA PATULLI TRYTHALL, Università di Roma, Sapienza
JOHN F. POLLARD, Trinity Hall, Cambridge
LUCIA POZZI, John XXIII Foundation for Religious Studies, Bologna
ROMANO PRODI, former President of the European Commission
Mons. ROBERT TRISCO, The Catholic University of America, Washington, DC
ROBERT A. VENTRESCA, University of Western Ontario
ALESSANDRO VISANI, Università di Roma, Sapienza

Christianity and History
Series of the John XXIII Foundation for Religious Studies in Bologna
edited by Prof. Dr. Alberto Melloni (Fondazione per le scienze religiose Giovanni XXIII, Bologna)

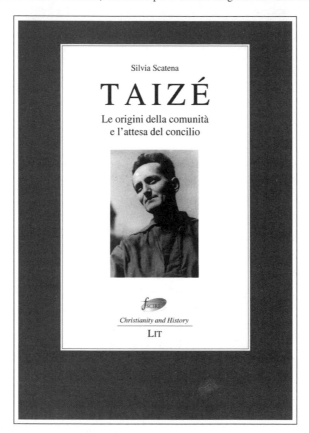

Silvia Scatena
Taizé
Le origini della comunità e l'attesa del concilio
An important chapter in the history of ecumenism of the last century, the "parable" of Taizé still lacks
a rigorous historical reconstruction. Based on a significant amount of unpublished sources, this volume
offers two initial results of a multi-year research project on the history of the Taizé community, from its
beginnings, in the years of World War II, until the construction of the many informal networks of friendship intertwined for more than twenty years amongst Christians divided by the Iron Curtain. A first study
focuses, in particular, on the years of training of Roger Schutz in Lausanne, as well as the birth of a first
confrérie and his arrival in Burgundy in the summer of 1940. A second study, on the other hand, describes
in detail the dynamism of the ecumenical community in the years marked by the announcement and in
expectation of the Second Vatican Council.
Bd. 10, 2011, 144 S., 19,90 €, br., ISBN 978-3-643-90127-9

LIT Verlag Berlin – Münster – Wien – Zürich – London
Auslieferung Deutschland / Österreich / Schweiz: siehe Impressumsseite

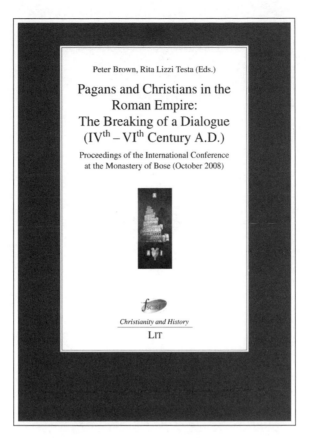

Peter Brown; Rita Lizzi Testa (Eds.)
Pagans and Christians in the Roman Empire: The Breaking of a Dialogue
(IVth-VIth Century A.D.). Proceedings of the International Conference at the Monastery of
Bose (October 2008)
Scholars of the last generation devoted much attention to Late Antiquity: to its institutions, economy, social relationships, culture. Nevertheless, it was thanks to Arnaldo Momigliano that not inferior consideration has been given to religion as an important factor of transformation and development. Fifty years after the publication of his *The conflict between Paganism and Christianity* (Oxford in 1963), a group of scholars wanted to reflect on the relationships between Pagans and Christians, in order to measure how much his legacy has been developed by the contemporary research.
Bd. 9, 2011, 648 S., 79,90 €, br., ISBN 978-3-643-90069-2

LIT Verlag Berlin – Münster – Wien – Zürich – London
Auslieferung Deutschland / Österreich / Schweiz: siehe Impressumsseite

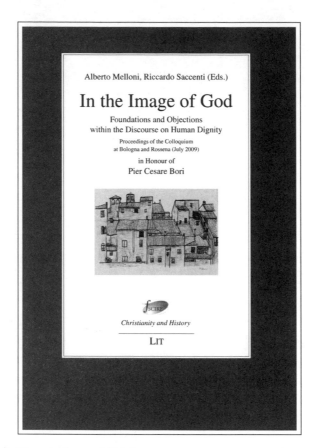

Alberto Melloni, Riccardo Saccenti (Eds.)

In the Image of God

Foundations and Objections
within the Discourse on Human Dignity

Proceedings of the Colloquium
at Bologna and Rossena (July 2009)

in Honour of
Pier Cesare Bori

Christianity and History

LIT

Alberto Melloni; Riccardo Saccenti (Eds.)
In the Image of God
Foundations and Objections within the Discourse on Human Dignity. Proceedings of the Colloquium Bologna and Rossena (July 2009) – in Honour of Pier Cesare Bori on his 70th Birthday

In the last years, starting from the study of the foundations of human rights, Pier Cesare Bori has focused his research on the exegesis of *Genesis* 1, 26-28, according to which man is created in the image of God. In the Christian framework the *imago Dei* has led to different interpretations: a charismatic and eschatological, an ontological and a functional one. To solve the contradictions between these different exegesis of *imago Dei* Bori has suggested to consider a larger context, looking not only at the Christian tradition, but also at the other monotheisms, cultures and religions. The proceedings here presented are the result of this attempt to develop new approaches to the study of the topic of *imago Dei*. It has been undertaken by an international group of scholars from different research fields (history, theology, hermeneutics, philosophy, exegesis) during a few days of scientific exchange and dialogue.

Bd. 8, 2010, 424 S., 39,90 €, br., ISBN 978-3-643-10456-4

LIT Verlag Berlin – Münster – Wien – Zürich – London

Auslieferung Deutschland / Österreich / Schweiz: siehe Impressumsseite